THE ROCKIES

THE

ROCKIES

by
David Lavender

University of Nebraska Press
Lincoln and London

First Bison Book printing: 1981
Most recent printing indicated by first digit below:
    2   3   4   5   6   7   8   9   10

Library of Congress Cataloging in Publication Data
Lavender, David Sievert, 1910–
  The Rockies.

  Reprint. Originally published: 1st ed. New York: Harper & Row, 1968 (The Regions of America series)
  Bibliography: p.
  Includes index.
  1. Rocky Mountains regions—History. I. Title. II. Series: Regions of America series.
F721.L3 1981   978   81–3427
ISBN 0–8032–2857–0   AACR2
ISBN 0–8032–7906–X (pbk.)

Published by arrangement with the author
Maps by Harry Scott

CONTENTS

PROLOGUE: THE SHAPING OF CHAOS   1

I   NOTHING BUT SKY   15

II   EACH HIS OWN WILD DREAMS TO TRY   24

III   "HONOUR TO OUR NATIONAL ENTERPRIZE"   40

IV   THE WAR THE INDIANS WON   57

V   THE SKIN GAME   72

VI   BRIEF CANDLE   87

VII   THE BARRIER LAND   101

VIII   THE MOUNTAIN WARS   114

IX   THE UNREASONABLE GOLD RUSH   129

X   THERE IT IS, HELP YOURSELF   139

XI   STILL BIGGER BONANZAS   156

XII   THE LOAVES AND THE FISHES   174

XIII   CASH IN AND GET OUT   186

XIV   THOSE WHO STAYED   207

XV   BOOSTERS AND BOOMERS   224

XVI   SILVER THREADS   242

XVII   RAILROAD WRANGLES   258

XVIII   THE RUSSET HILLS OF BUTTE   274

XIX   THEY MISSED MILLIONS   288

XX   AMONG THESE DARK SATANIC MILLS   299

XXI   BENEFICIAL USE REDEFINED   323

EPILOGUE: THE NEW STAMPEDE   348

WITH THANKS—   367

BIBLIOGRAPHY   371

INDEX   389

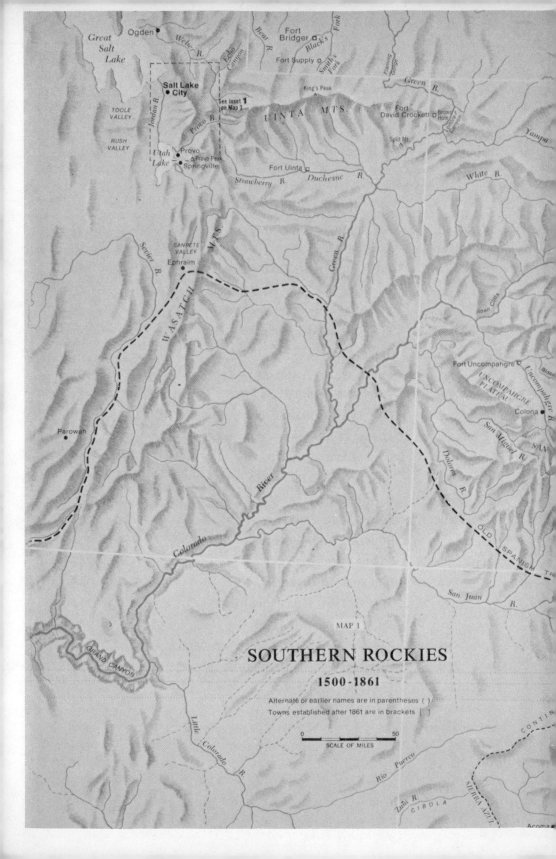

Great
Salt
Lake

Ogden •

Weber R.

Bear R.

Fort
Bridger □

Black's Fork

Smith's Fork

Fort Supply □

Flaming
Gorge

Green R.

TOOLE
VALLEY

Jordan R.

**Salt Lake
City**

See inset
on Map 3

Echo Canyon

King's Peak

U I N T A   M T S .

Fort
David Crockett □

Brown's
Hole

Lodore
Canyon

Yampa R.

RUSH
VALLEY

Provo R.

Provo •

Split Mt.

White R.

Utah
Lake

△ Provo Peak
• Springville

Fort Uinta □

Strawberry R.

Duchesne R.

Green R.

SANPETE
VALLEY

Ephraim •

W A S A T C H   M T S .

Sevier R.

Roan Cliffs

UNCOMPAHGRE
PLATEAU

Fort Uncompahgre □

Uncompahgre R.

Colona •

San Miguel R.

SAN

Parowan •

River

Dolores R.

OLD

SPANISH TR

Colorado

San Juan
R.

GRAND CANYON

MAP 1

SOUTHERN ROCKIES

1500-1861

Alternate or earlier names are in parentheses ( )

Towns established after 1861 are in brackets [ ]

0   50

SCALE OF MILES

*Little
Colorado
R.*

Rio Puerco

CONTIN

Zuni R.

CIBOLA

SIERRA AZUL

Acoma

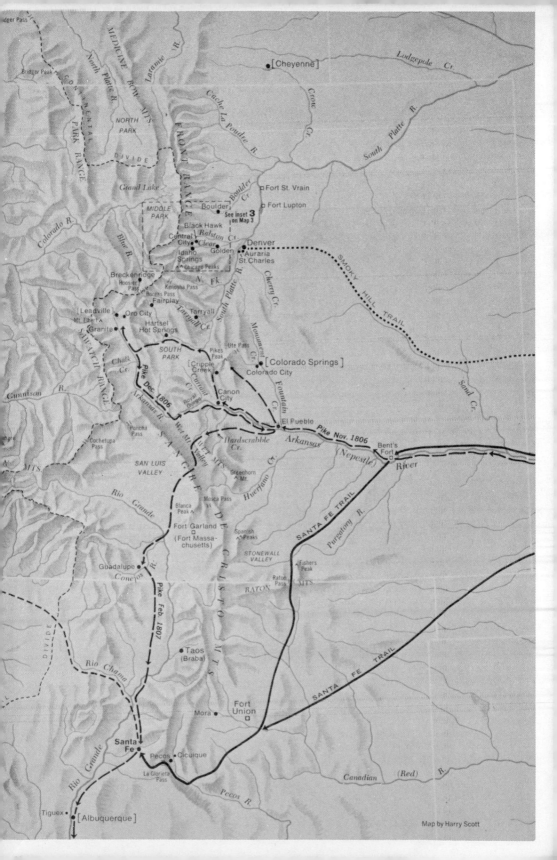

Map by Harry Scott

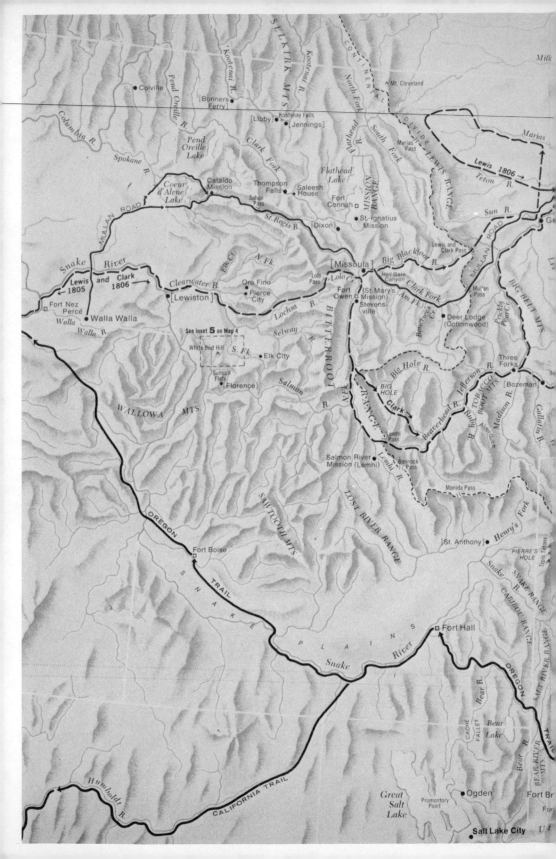

MAP 2

NORTHERN ROCKIES

1500-1861

Alternate or earlier names are in parentheses ( )
Towns established after 1861 are in brackets [ ]

0   50   100
SCALE OF MILES.

BEAR PAW
MTS.

Fort
Union

Fort
Benton

← Lewis and Clark 1805

Missouri   River

alls

LE MTS.

Yellowstone   R.

□ Fort Cass
Fort Raymond

← Clark 1806 →

Powder   R.

Granite Peak
△

Lamarie

BIG   HORN

Little Bighorn R.

Shoshone Canyon   ● [Cody]

Shell Canyon Cloud
Peak

Shoshone R.
(Stinking Water)

ABSAROKA   MTS.

Bighorn   R.

MTS.

BLACK

HILLS

CKSON
OLE

[Dubois] ●

OWL   CREEK   MTS.

Union
Pass

Wind   R.

Gannett Peak △
Fremont Peak △

[Lander]

North   Platte   R.

Popo Agie
Cr.

RATTLESNAKE   HILLS

WIND RIVER MTS.

Sweetwater   R.

Independence
Rock

LARAMIE

OREGON

CONTINENTAL

(Sandskeeduse R.)

GREEN MTS.

□ Fort Laramie

● South Pass

R.

Laramie

TRAIL

Green

GREAT DIVIDE BASIN

LARAMIE
PLAINS

LARAMIE
HILLS

R.

MEDICINE BOW MTS.

Black's Fork

Bridger Pass

North   Platte   R.

DIVIDE

Smith's
Fork

ly

Bridger Peak

Cheyenne

Lodgepole   Cr.

A   MTS.

Crow
Cr.

Map by
Harry Scott

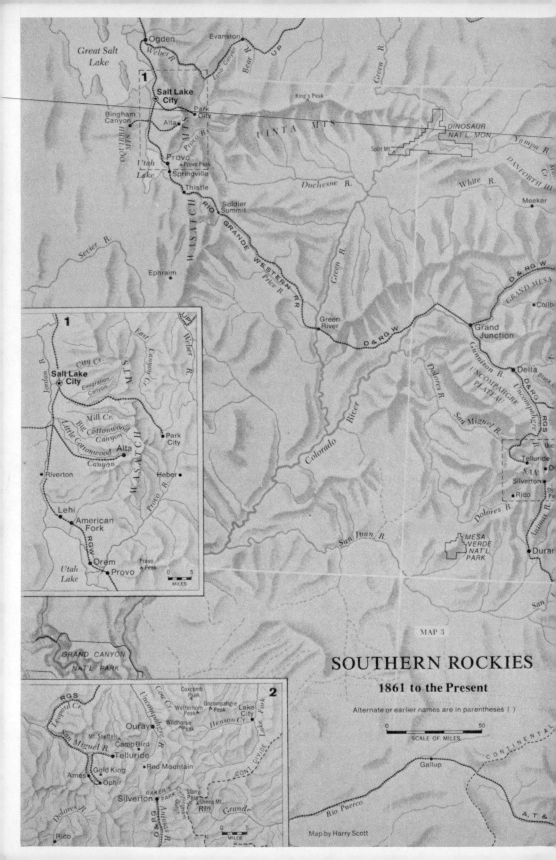

MAP 3

SOUTHERN ROCKIES

1861 to the Present

Alternate or earlier names are in parentheses ( )

0   50
SCALE OF MILES

Map by Harry Scott

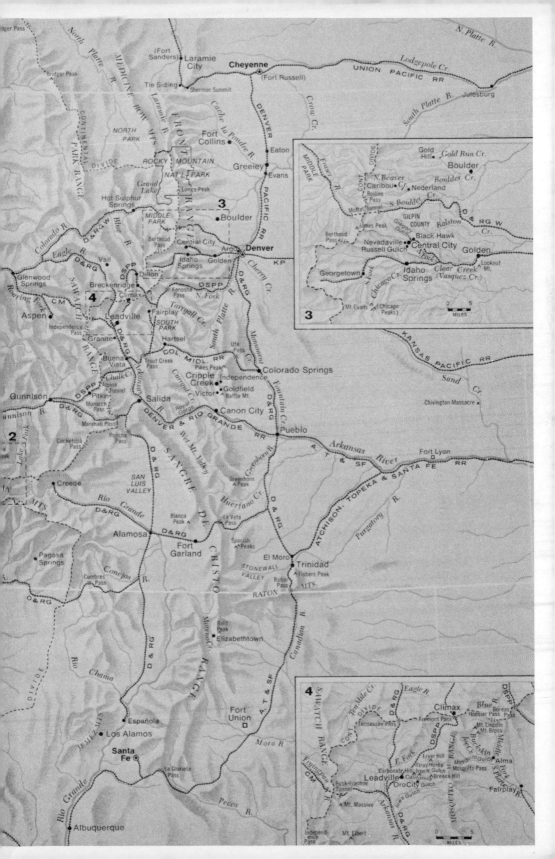

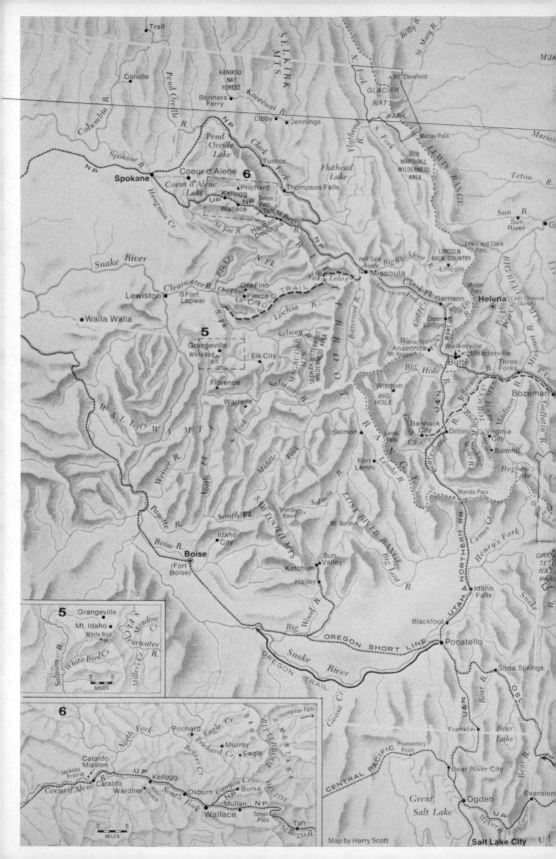

Map by Harry Scott

MAP 4

NORTHERN ROCKIES

1861 to the present

Alternate or earlier names are in parentheses ( )

0   50   100

SCALE OF MILES

To Mildred *and* Leith,
in memory of those high places

PROLOGUE: THE SHAPING OF CHAOS

But I was going to say when Truth broke in
With all her matter-of-fact . . .

ROBERT FROST in "Birches"

THE little camp of Telluride, 8,800 feet high in the San Juan
Mountains of southwestern Colorado—the mining clusters of the Rockies
were never called "villages," and were called "towns" only on formal
occasions—was a very isolated and a very special place in which to grow
up. Theodora Kroeber, who later moved to California and there wrote that
enthralling account of *Ishi in Two Worlds,* a tale of the last wild Indian in
North America, remembered it this way:

> In that thin, dry air life moved at a pace of almost terrible intensity. There
> were no neutral moments—the galloping brevity of spring and summer, the
> long months of winter with the threat of tragedy always hanging near. Colors
> were high—the reds in the soil, the fall gold of the aspens, the indescribable
> sky. Riding in summer and tobogganing in winter were fast and dangerous;
> the heights of the mountains and the depths of the canyons were beyond the
> norm. One went about totally sensitized. No wonder recovery for the elders
> was a trip to the Coast, and for a youngster, introversion. Get on your horse
> and ride and ride. . . . God was a pagan god, in the air, over the mountains,
> in the waterfalls. But how can I give the feeling-tone of my childhood in that
> high Alpine valley, which simply is one of the most beautiful spots in the
> world?

My own memories of Telluride keep returning to the celebrations that
were held each Fourth of July. By that time of year the camp needed to
whoop. Winter had stretched endlessly. In spite of long periods of brilliant
sunshine, the elevation was such that snowdrifts lingered. Mechanized
plows for removing them did not exist. After each storm the merchants on
Colorado Avenue, the main thoroughfare, shoveled the snow off the plank
sidewalks onto the edge of the street. By March the ridge was taller than a
child's head, and shoppers moved about their business in a kind of canyon,
store fronts on one side and that grimy ridge on the other.

For relief, skaters repaired, so long as snow permitted, to a section of the nearby marshes, flooded each fall for just that purpose. An even more popular sport was tobogganing down the steep side streets. Skiing was utilitarian. The Scandinavian miners, who made up a large percentage of the laboring force, sometimes came down from the workings on homemade boards much longer than those in use today, their bindings only a leather strap across the boot toes. A more spectacular descent was to sit on a miner's broad scoop shovel, hold the short handle up between your legs, and flash down a course packed by a recent avalanche.

Socializing was another, and highly ritualized, antidote to winter. Each wife who lived in the tony part of town above Colorado Avenue held an afternoon "at home" once a month on her own unvarying date—the second Friday, say, or the last Tuesday. There were regular cotillions and infrequent theater parties, the latter eagerly held whenever the narrow-gauge train brought in a bedraggled traveling troupe. Both events were studiously formal—white ties, long gowns, shoulder-length gloves. For a really lavish do, hostesses imported dream desserts from Baur's, a famous confectioner in Denver, carefully preserved for the trip in blocks of ice. And still the winter dragged and dragged.

Contrary to what the song says, there is very little springtime in the Rockies. It is a dull, soggy, fitful time, melting icicles one hour and blowing snow the next. But the drifts do shrink, water pours down the hillsides, the bare branches of the quaking aspens mist with green. The sun rises earlier and ascends straight overhead. The ground dries, crimson paintbrush and blue-and-white columbines fleck the meadows. Suddenly—more suddenly each year than you are prepared for—July arrives.

The Fourth was the whole town's day. Gold pieces (paper money was a distrusted curiosity) bulged in the pockets of the miners and of the cowboys from the mesas farther down the river. The clothing stores were their first stop on reaching town. On the eve of celebrations these stayed open until midnight. A single clerk could wait on three or four men at once. He'd gauge the build of a customer by eye, pull a six-dollar black clay worsted suit off a pile according to size, say, "This looks about right," and sell it for $25—no try-on, no alteration. Shoes, white shirt, and stiff collar went the same way. The store threw in a black tie and a pair of suspenders free. A clerk I knew, Ed Pierce, boasted that he often sold, by himself, on a single Fourth of July eve, merchandise worth $2,000. Each miner rolled his part of the transaction into an uncovered bundle, thrust it under his arm, and went to one of the barbershops for a bath, haircut, shampoo, shave, and facial. He was ready then for the dance halls.

The next day, as I remember it through a boy's eyes, was magnificent beyond telling. A parade launched the morning—brass bands, marching miners and millmen from the labor unions, fire engines buried in crepe paper, fraternal orders in gaudy uniforms, the sheriff's posse, princesses on wagons piled high with evergreens and festooned by flowers. Dogs and firecrackers. Everywhere the unabashed ripple of muscle. Rock-drilling teams struggled to punch, within a specified time, the deepest hole into a ten-ton block of granite set on a platform in the middle of Colorado Avenue; two men per team, bare-chested, grunting prodigiously, one swinging a massive sledge, the other on his knees holding the drill steel while the packed mass of spectators cheered their favorites and bet fantastic sums. Foot racers in spangled tights. Tug-of-war teams, heaving on either end of a rope. Hose teams trying to blast each other off their feet with fierce heads of water that had dropped from the peaktops.

In the afternoon there were horse races and a baseball game at the park below town. You went down with picnic baskets, tingling so from expectancy that you could hardly stand it. The special quality seemed a part of the very air. Literally. About halfway through the day you realized what it was—the profound stillness beneath the gaiety. The distant *brump-brump-brump* of the stamp mills above town, where the ore was ground to a powder for the extraction of the metals—that dim insistent rhythm as pervading and vital and unnoticed as the pumping of your heart—today the mills were closed and the sound was gone. And you let out another whoop, louder than ever, shouting back the silence.

The truth had broken in: the prime determinant of Rocky Mountain history has been the high country's nonferrous metal mines, principally gold, silver, copper, and lead. This limitation is true in spite of the fact that the history of the Rockies is older than the history of the rest of the country. Coronado's Spaniards first encountered the southern spurs of New Mexico's Sangre de Cristo Mountains in 1540. For centuries after that France and Spain fumbled toward the rumored peaks in an intricate game of empire. The young United States very early sent its explorers into and across the Rockies. Beaver hunters coursed every stream. Government surveyors and emigrants bound for the Pacific coast threaded the easiest passes. Yet, save for the somnolent Spanish villages in New Mexico, these things brought no permanent settlement. That step awaited the discovery of the mines, shallow placer diggings first and then, during three subsequent decades, the opening of deep lode mines whose exploitation demanded more money and better technological facilities than individual prospectors could provide.

Primitive towns burgeoned into industrial complexes. Railroads arrived overnight. Lumber camps sprang up as near to the workings as might be in order to provide mine timbers and the endless piles of ties required by the new railroads. Hay ranches were opened to feed the work animals; livestock and vegetable growers fed the men. To keep the crops growing, irrigating water was diverted along ditches that grew swiftly into a network of huge canals fed by massive reservoirs. Adolescent labor unions, hungry for a bigger share of the underground riches, fought some of their bloodiest clashes with capital in remote places like Telluride, Cripple Creek on the back side of Pikes Peak, in Leadville, in Wallace, Idaho, in Butte, Montana.

In time, of course, many of the ore bodies were exhausted—though a few huge ones still remain. Railroads and, later on, mammoth slat-sided trucks began moving livestock to other markets than mining towns. Water was whisked under entire mountain ranges to add new dimensions to cities engaged in pursuits unrelated to mineral extraction. But the vital years were the mineral years, when a tiny splash in a remote canyon could create ripples that reached around the world. George Pullman, for instance, is said to have patterned his famous railroad sleeping cars after the double-decked bunks he saw in the narrow little miners' cabins near Central City, Colorado. Or take the case of L. L. Nunn of Telluride, an odd-looking little man whose work with electric power helped alter not only mining economics but industrial procedures everywhere.

Nunn was 5 feet 1 inch tall and weighed 115 pounds. He had abnormally long arms, pale-blue eyes, a retreating hairline, a wide forehead, and a sharp, receding chin. He kept a picture of Napoleon on his wall and often declared, "The character of Napoleon I understand better than do any of his biographers."

In 1881, aged twenty-eight, Nunn drifted into Telluride. His first home was a tent, his first job shingling a roof. Because he had studied a little law in Germany after graduating from Cleveland Academy in Ohio and later had done some desultory reading in a Boston law office, prospective litigants came to him for advice. In the evenings, when his shingling was done, he brushed up enough to be admitted to the Colorado bar and, inevitably, began specializing in mining matters.

One of the mines with which he was associated was the Gold King. It contained quantities of good ore, but like most of the properties in the district it was foundering under exorbitant costs, partly because no railroad had yet penetrated that part of the San Juan Mountains. The property lay above timberline southwest of town, and coal packed to it by donkey train for generating steam to run its machinery cost $2,500 a month, in 1890 prices. Nunn decided that this was the point at which to start salvage operations.

What about electricity? By that time Telluride had begun experimenting with a little direct-current generating plant whose output was used for lighting street corners and a few saloons. (Householders were afraid of the stuff.) So far no one in the area had transported electricity for turning machines across any appreciable distance, but Nunn, who never suffered from lack of confidence, saw no reason why it could not be done. He sent his younger brother Paul, a high school science teacher, to Pittsburgh, Pennsylvania, to talk to George Westinghouse about motors. In the meantime the little Napoleon hired surveyors to run a line from a fork of the river below town up a cliff-studded mountainside and across a storm-swept timberline flat to the Gold King, 2.6 miles away.

The project should have proved impossible. Wire for carrying direct-current electricity increases in size with distance; after 2.6 miles, costs for so much copper and for massive towers to support it would have been exorbitant. Alternating current, however, can flash long distances across lightweight wires, and it so happened that Paul Nunn talked to Westinghouse shortly after the inventor and George Stanley had managed to light a village or two in the East with alternating current. No one had yet produced a successful alternating-current motor—machinery was still being turned by direct current—but Westinghouse had one on the boards. The Nunns' proposal gave him an opportunity to put his new theories to the test. He built them a primitive single-phase generator that they installed in a log cabin beside the river and a synchronized motor that they installed in the mine. The cost of operating the machinery at the Gold King promptly tumbled from $2,500 a month to $500, and an entirely new era of mining began.

In the fall of 1891, while Nunn was still proving that a gold mine could be run by electricity generated at a distance, a tight little narrow-gauge railroad, the Rio Grande Southern, at last reached Telluride. En route, it ran out a siding to the log-cabin power plant and dignified the place with the name Ames. Ames became a local sensation. Every Sunday afternoon during good weather people rode by train and carriage from Telluride to see the generator start up after its Saturday night–Sabbath morning shutdown. Vicious arcs jumped six feet long when the switches were thrown. A deep-throated hum filled the tiny room, and after the display was over, some popeyed miner always asked how long it took the alternating current to rush up the hill to the Gold King, give the armature a twist, and return. By dark, maybe? When told, the questioners were invariably indignant: 186,000 miles a second? Whose leg are you trying to pull, mister? Farmers from the low country were equally suspicious. So imperious a substance obviously was draining vital essences from the water and their crops would suffer during the next irrigation.

Professional knowledge was, relatively speaking, not much better. Trained electrical engineers did not exist. Nunn, no scientist himself, had to develop on the spot the men he needed. He assembled a library in the shack at Ames and persuaded promising young collegians to work for him for board, room, $30 a month, and practical training in a promising new field. They had to do everything—cook their own meals, patch flumes, repair motors, shovel snow, string wire, and above all, improvise ways to meet emergencies that no man had ever faced before.

Locally the trainees were called Pinheads. They, too, bred legends. In September, 1909, a telephone rang at Ames and a frantic voice told the

Pinhead who answered to run for his life; the dam at Trout Lake, a storage reservoir up a side canyon, had broken and a mass of water bristling with timbers was bearing down upon the plant. Instead of running, the Pinheads took out their slide rules, calculated the volume of the water and the dimensions of the canyon. They then made a mark on a pole at the height they thought the flood would reach. Deciding they were safe, they climbed onto the roof and waited. Sure enough, the waters reached within three inches of the mark and then subsided.

Maybe so. But if the facts of the yarn aren't strictly true, the spirit is. That was the kind of resourcefulness Nunn wanted to develop. When he left Telluride to become one of the leading entrepreneurs of the infant power industry, a career which culminated at the vast Ontario works at Niagara Falls, he carried with him certain novel educational ideas which he had first put into practice at Ames. These grew into two unique institutions to which he devoted much of his energy and money during his later life: Deep Springs, a self-help college preparatory school for boys in the isolated White Mountains near the California-Nevada border, and the famed Telluride Association for advanced work at Cornell University, Ithaca, New York.

And so, if mining seems to bulk large in the pages that follow, it is because its effects also bulked large from one end of the Rockies to the other, and on beyond.

An even more vital mountain sound than the *brump* of the stamp mills above Telluride, and just as unnoticed, was the everlasting rush of water. Though the town's elevation is high above sea level, it is low in the mountains, in the bottom of a profound, cliff-girt trough. One reaches the camp by climbing past torrential cascades. At the camp's northern side Cornet Falls plume over red ledges. Eastward the trough closes, a giant horseshoe of gray-brown cliffs topped by conical peaks 13,000 feet in altitude, streaked with snow until late summer and collared with bright alpine grass. Streamlets sparkle down the V's between the peaks. At the very head of the valley, lifting the eye 3,000 feet above the level of the town, is the silver pinpoint of Ingram Falls. Farther to the right are misty Bridal Veil Falls, 365 feet high, the longest unbroken water drop in the Rockies, I have always believed, although I have never really checked.

Water courses like these created most of the mountain towns. Creeks had always been pathways, of course; explorers followed them and early-day mountain men scoured them for beaver. But the full economic impact came later, after prospectors, discovering specks of gold in gravel beds, launched the first gold rushes. When deep veins were opened subsequently, the ore had to be milled; that is, enough of the waste rock surrounding the metal had to be removed so that the concentrate which remained would be light enough to be hauled by train to smelters for reduction. Water was essential to the milling—and to the trains, too, which followed the streams to reach the new camps.

We absorbed all this with our breathing. Busy little narrow-gauge freight locomotives, each wrapped in a swirling ball of its own smoke, snorted through town with carloads of equipment for the complex of mills that lined the valley above. Some of the material stayed there. The rest went by mule or wagon or, in the case of the major companies, by aerial tram buckets swaying on lofty cableways to the mines (and a few mills also) perched at timberline or higher. Ore came down by the same means, was ground to dust and the waste spewed into the streams. I do not recall any outcry against the practice. It was livelihood. The residents learned not to see the ugliness, and only in recent times have state-wide antipollution laws forced the mines that still operate to take steps—rather inadequate ones, be it said—to keep their appalling sludge out of the creeks.

Seasonal rhythms were a part of the vast drama of water—the melting away of winter, the grudging freeze-up in the fall. In time my stepfather left off running mule trains up to the mines and began raising cattle, wintering the animals down in the dry red desert and summering them in mountain pastures west of Telluride. We learned then to estimate the snow packs on the high ridges. Ample runoff meant ample irrigating water for the hay-fields and hence plenty of feed for the following winter. Yet an excessive pack would delay our reaching the meadows.

We drifted the herds slowly, keeping pace with the sprouting of the grass. As elevation increased, so did the annual average of precipitation. We could recognize the difference by the different bands of trees. Gnarled junipers and piñon pine blanketed the semiarid plateaus. Above them in the gravelly foothills were stately, yellow-barked ponderosa pines. Higher, where the bunch grass was tall and mariposa lilies nodded on their slender stems, came magnificent stands of aspen.

Groves of quakies, as the cowboys call the shimmering aspen trees, grow in many places throughout the Rockies. In Colorado they are perhaps the most characteristic vegetation of the mountains, giant rolling forests, their slim white boles, spotted with black, soaring to a canopy of leaves that the slightest wind sets to rustling and twinkling. In summer a sea-green luminosity filters through them; in autumn, after frost has burnished mile upon dazzling mile of them, it becomes an all-pervading golden haze.

Mingling with the aspen and then climbing the slopes far above them are the tight-packed lodgepole pines, the slim alpine firs, the red-barked Engelmann's spruce. And on still higher, above the last stunted, twisted timberline warriors, come fields of tundra, spangled with tiny flowers and verdant with tough grass, that cattle seldom reach but that provide pasturage, during a few brief summer weeks, for hundreds of thousands of sheep.

Water in its various forms—ice, snow, liquid, cloud vapor, and volcanic steam—shaped with incredible slowness the varied hills where these forests have taken root. According to one hypothesis, the uplift was set into motion two billion years ago, more or less, by the weight of the oceans gathering to the west. Slowly the semiliquid foundations of the land bulged upward like bubbles in porridge, under a relatively plastic crust formed by sea-dropped layers of sediment—shales, sandstones, limestones. The tremendous heat accompanying the activity metamorphosed the sediments it touched into schists, slate, gneiss, or marble according to their original natures. Molten magma, welling up into the hearts of the straining domes, solidified into granite.

There was time for revisions. Streams of ice and water, gale-like winds, and the expansions and contractions resulting from temperature changes eventually eroded the uplift to a peneplain, a broad, elevated plateau marked here and there by mounds later named monadnocks. Eons drifted by; the sea encroached again and deposited more sediments. More uplifts occurred, more strata bent upwards, more erosion attacked the highlands. Here and there volcanoes burst through the thin crust and laid down tablelands of lava and ash.

The lifting rock fractured and cracked. Sometimes, at fault lines, part of a rising mass sheered away and pushed independently upward, its cloven front forming a cliff thousands of feet high. The east face of the Tetons, soaring 7,000 feet above the Snake River in Wyoming and deeply weathered now, and the west face of the Wasatch Range above Salt Lake City are the most familar Rocky Mountain remnants of such fault blocks.

The slow upthrust reached its greatest altitude in what is now Colorado, where fifty-odd peaks reach an altitude of 14,000 or more feet above sea level. These peaks, however, neither look nor feel higher than those of Glacier Park, Montana, whose loftiest point, Mount Cleveland, touches a mere 10,448 feet. The equalizing factor is latitude. Montana lies far enough north that its mountains are cooler, on an annual average, than those of Colorado. Timberline in Glacier Park, as tourists shivering atop Logan Pass well realize, is very little more than 7,000 feet. On the protected slopes of Uncompahgre Peak, 14,301 feet high in southwestern Colorado, tree line approaches 12,000 feet.

Although the cool ranges of northern Montana receive only a little more precipitation each year than do the Sangre de Cristo Mountains of New Mexico, the moisture, especially in the snow packs, lingers longer and does not dissipate so readily into the air by evaporation. As a result the Montana Rockies contain more lakes, larger streams, and wider forests of evergreens than do the mountains of New Mexico, Utah, or Colorado. In traveling the Rockies one needs to bear these facts in mind as counters to the fancy figures about altitude of which Coloradoans are so proud.

The last ice sheet to thrust south from the pole did not actually touch the American Rockies. Nevertheless, the chill that spread throughout the area was such that snow piled high on the ridges and then compacted into glaciers that scoured relentlessly as gravity dragged the ice down the slopes. Its gouging created deep, steep-walled cirques at timberline and above. Sometimes these cirques lie close together, separated only by thin aretes whose upper ends pull together in sky-scratching horn peaks, beloved by photographers. Still more scenery resulted from glacial moraines that trapped hundreds of cold, lovely lakes in the upper valleys—round-bottomed valleys gouged so deep that streams entering them from the side often form breath-taking waterfalls scores of feet high.

Most mountain shaping takes place too slowly to be perceptible to either human view or human memory. Occasionally, however, a landslip will cut loose which, though insignificant to the mountain pattern in general, serves to remind human beings in the neighborhood that in this world of change the eternal hills change too.

About 4:30 in the afternoon of June 23, 1925, a cowboy named Huff, driving a small herd of cattle along Wyoming's Gros Ventre Valley near Jackson Hole, saw a piece of rain-soaked hillside a mile and a half long begin to slide toward him. With feelings that have never been adequately described, Huff managed to outrun the avalanche, though six of his cattle were overwhelmed. The debris that settled into the valley weighed an estimated 50 million tons. It created a blockade 225 feet high and impounded a lake five miles long. There was no spillway, of course, and seepage through the loose mass proved inadequate to maintain a safe water level. Overflow in May, 1927, cut a channel across the dam top. Suddenly the unstable barrier collapsed. Telephone warnings flashed ahead of the wall of water held fatalities to six persons, but most of the hamlet of Kelley and part of Wilson disappeared, as did several bridges and dozens of farmsteads.

Montana's Hegben slide was more cataclysmic. Just before midnight on August 17, 1959, a major earthquake shook the western part of Yellowstone National Park, scaring approximately 20,000 tourists half out of their wits. Actual disaster was reserved for the Madison Valley, just west of the park. A mountainside there cracked apart and spilled 80 million tons of earth into the canyon. Cyclonic gusts booming ahead of the slide whisked automobiles off a nearby campground like foil plates. Boulders crashed like artillery salvos. Three hundred dazed survivors, some dreadfully injured, told of incredible escapes and daring rescues. Twenty-eight people are known to have perished. This barrier is not likely to collapse. The top has been carefully channeled and the lake behind it is rapidly developing into one of Montana's richest tourist attractions.

And we still have not spoken of the bewildering complexity of Rocky Mountain geography, though that too is a truth that breaks in early on any dweller in the high camps. Telluride, for instance, looks on flat maps to be close to other deep-cupped San Juan mining towns—Ouray and Silverton and, a little farther on, Lake City. But in order to visit those neighbors one either had to go high up or far around. The first effort involved riding horseback across trails 13,000 feet high, a scenic adventure but slow.[1] Automobiles had to circle, threading abysmal canyons and burrowing through forests to find more negotiable passes. A visitor's sense of direction often grew so scrambled during the process that on climbing from his car only twenty or so airline miles from where he had boarded it he could not aim his finger even approximately toward his starting point.

Traveling to Denver—we called such trips "going outside"—was an Occasion and involved a train ride of twenty-four hours. (Automobiles coursing paved roads now cover the distance in a third of that time.) On arrival, my stepfather attended to mysterious errands known as business; Mother bought clothes; my brother and I were subjected to the orthodontist and, later, to school. We were soon eager for home and that, I suppose, is the reason I recall the rides back to Telluride so much more vividly than those away.

The first part was uneventful. Shortly after dark we climbed into a green-curtained Pullman car and slept our way south past Pikes Peak and west through the stupendous Royal Gorge of the Arkansas River. At dawn, at a place called Salida, we descended to an indescribable, glutinous breakfast in the dingy restaurant of the ocher-colored depot. Then, shivering as much from anticipation as from the early-morning chill, we scrambled into the dwarfed narrow-gauge coaches for the lift across the Continental Divide.

Narrow-gauge railroads, which once touched nearly every part of the Rockies, were peculiarly suited to the hurry-up days of mining. Their lightweight rails were set only 3 feet apart in contrast to the standard-gauge separation of 4 feet 8½ inches. Grading these narrow roadbeds around tight curves and leaping chasms on relatively flimsy trestles could be done quickly. Even better, it was cheap, as was the shrunken rolling stock.

Two locomotives, roaring and jerking and belching ravels of smoke but seldom rising above a creep, hauled our handful of baggage and passenger cars from Salida up the zigzags leading to the top of Marshall Pass, 10,846 feet above sea level. Sometimes when there were girls to show off to, an older boy would leap from the iron platform of the rear coach, dart off to the side, swoop up a wild flower in a fistful of grass, and bring it back in panting pride.

Deplorable doggerel and worse jokes were endlessly repeated:

> *It doubles in, it doubles out,*
> *Leaving the traveler still in doubt*
> *Whether the engine on the track*
> *Is going on or coming back.*

---

[1] Nowadays during the few open weeks of summer it is possible to make the crossing in four-wheel-drive vehicles, excursions that are growing increasingly popular among hardy tourists.

Or this: Lady to conductor, "Can't the train go any faster? I'm about to have a baby." Conductor, "You shouldn't have gotten on in such a condition." Lady, "I wasn't in this condition when I got on."

And yet we really were learning. All the way to the top of the Divide—which at the last minute was rendered invisible by a dark wooden snowshed mephitic with coal fumes—and all the way down we gazed far out into complexity; irregular clusters of gray-flanked peaks, curving valleys, canyon-seamed ridges melting away into the blue haze created by exhalations from the dark spruce forests. Reaching one of those valleys, the wide Gunnison, we rolled smokily past hayfields, past cattle and sheep grazing in the sagebrush, past distant buttes rimmed with basalt and feathered with clumps of aspen trees. Wherever there were gaps in the hills we could see, shimmering in the distance, still more chains of peaks.

We dived into the upper reaches of the Black Canyon of the Gunnison, awesome once and splendid with trout, but inundated now by a reservoir. We climbed out over the oak-brush hills of Cerro Summit and reached the desolate clay desert of the Uncompahgre Valley, a Ute Indian name first recorded by Escalante's Spaniards when they were traversing the area in the year of our revolution, 1776. Green patches appeared, product of water brought from the lower Black Canyon through a massive irrigation tunnel. Bending south, we labored up the gray Uncompahgre River toward the glittering San Juans, a sea of pinnacles split into subranges by giant gorges —the Uncompahgre Mountains, the San Miguels, and out of sight to the south, the serrated Needles.

West now, past the ramparts of Mount Sneffels and down the spirals of Leopard Creek into San Miguel Canyon, lovely with its leaning evergreens and terraces of red sandstone. The wheel flanges shrilled between the steep walls, the roar of the rapids twined up in a ball of noise with the labored petulance of the engine. Twilight deepened. The lamps came on, pale yellow. Shadows leaned—left and back and right and back—as the coaches creaked around the curves. In fall or winter a spot of hot metal glowed red in the stove at the end of the aisle and the stale air grew—brassy, is the only word I can think of, and everyone sank deeper into his red plush seat, head lolling, not resting, just numb. And then, after we had crawled up the last hill below Telluride and onto the willow flats, the door opened and the click of the rail joints deepened. Leaning in, the conductor bawled out over the racket his invariable wit, "To Hell You Ride!" and we were home.

No child who traveled back and forth to a place like Telluride—or Aspen or Jackson Hole or Missoula—would ever assume, as I have since discovered many people do assume, that the Rocky Mountains and the Continental Divide are synonymous terms for a single long chain of hills. The misconception arises, I suppose, from the precise line of dots with which the Divide is indicated on uncritical maps and which make it seem as dominant and as singular as the ridge of a house. It is singular, to be sure, a great splitter of waters and the only natural pathway in the United States by which a person can walk, in theory at least, from Canada to Mexico without wetting his feet in some stream or another. It is not isolated, however, and it is not always dominant. Though its ultimate course is, roughly, from north to south, it wanders along as erratically as a ribbon dropped by a careless girl. It is accompanied by a multitude of parallel ranges, some of which (the Big Horn Mountains of Wyoming, the Wasatch Range of Utah) are more than a hundred miles away from it. In southern Wyoming it sinks so limply into a gray sage desert that it is perceptible only to sophisticated instruments. In New Mexico it abdicates its sway entirely; its streams become meager, its forests scraggly, its ridges devoid of majesty. The commanding mountains of New Mexico are an offshoot far to the east, the Sangre de Cristo, Blood of Christ, so called from the alpenglow that flushes them at sunset.

The shifting course of the Divide and the variety of its satellites have created a chaotic geography and pockets of climate at variance with the normal rules of thumb. Rivers born in one of the interior chains must, on meeting an outer range, either circle it, wrench a violent way through, or both. The Wind River of Wyoming, famous in fur trade annals, makes so pronounced a bend near today's Riverton that it emerges with an entirely new name, the Big Horn. Farther to the west the Snake River, blocked from a direct route to the Columbia by the swells that culminate in the Salmon River Mountains, has to describe a huge arc across the entirety of southern Idaho before it can finally force a way outside through mile-deep Hell's Canyon. A host of other streams—the upper Missouri in Montana, the North Platte in Wyoming, the Green where it bumps up against the Uinta Range in northwestern Utah, the Arkansas and Dolores in Colorado —these and many others fluctuate almost as uncertainly before finally settling to a course.

Ragged canyons and tidy valleys are not the only dividing lines between the ranges. From Montana south into New Mexico there is a series of broad flats called variously parks, basins, and sometimes holes. In their own way these huge cups are as dramatic as the peaks. Novelist D. H. Lawrence flatly declared that the Taos Valley in New Mexico is backed by the most beautiful skyline he had seen anywhere in the world—not nation, world. Part of the charm that led Lawrence to such hyperbole arises from the feeling of release which the openings bring to the viewer. Much mountain scenery is austere, violent, constricting. Then suddenly the land spreads out. There are not even many trees, save for the distant girdle of forest that runs around the middle of the fat hills in the distance—two timberlines in effect, upper and lower. Streams coil quietly through meadows rather than dash headlong among boulders. Cattle and sheep graze as pastorally as in Iowa. There is no feeling of Iowa, however. Always on the horizon loom the snow-streaked peaks of another range: the abrupt Mission Mountains east of Flathead Valley in Montana; the Tetons soaring out of the upper reaches of Jackson Hole; Idaho's Sawtooth Range scratching the sky west of gentle Stanley Basin; the smoother mounds, high and cold, that rim Colorado's almost oceanlike North, Middle, and South parks, and sweeping San Luis Valley.

Because of the mountains that border them on the west, the larger parks and valleys are not as moist as one might expect from their elevation. They lie in rain shadows. When warm air drifting east across the desert strikes the western ranges of the Rockies, it lifts and cools. Water vapor condenses into clouds—on summer afternoons one can literally watch the billowing cumuli take shape out of nothing—and moisture falls. Then, the crossing completed, the air settles into the basins and valleys, warms again, and seldom will yield more water until meeting another uplift. Thus the between-range valleys and parks of the Rockies are arid, but most are either so high that evaporation is slow or so narrowed by rain-breeding ranges on their eastern sides that true desert conditions do not appear. In openings that are relatively low and wide, however, real parching develops —in the tumbled red deserts bordering the Colorado River west of the Wasatch Plateau; in Wyoming's Big Horn Basin, where Buffalo Bill Cody spent his fortune trying to develop irrigation; along the eastern skirts of Colorado's San Luis Valley, where Sahara-like dunes of fine white sand are piled so high that they have been apotheosized as a national monument.

In a similar manner temperatures also escape the dominance of elevation. Generally speaking, the plains east of the mountains are colder than the high country. When the first of the major Rocky Mountain ski resorts, Sun Valley, Idaho, was advertising its carefully coined name, it attracted a good deal of surprised attention in the East by flooding publicity channels with pictures of tanned male skiers stripped to the waist amid the snowbanks. Miners, of course, had learned long before that it is possible to be more comfortable in sheltered basins at timberline or above than in valleys that lie three-quarters of a mile lower and look kinder. They are not. The cold that settles into unprotected basins like Middle Park in Colorado is as palpable as a stone. Winds are bladed. At times the roads across the different parks are completely obscured by ground blizzards, although the sky overhead is an unstained blue. A wry joke in the upper Green River Valley of Wyoming says that the snow there never melts; it just blows around until it wears out. And yet no cold snap lasts unendurably. Warm dry winds—so noticeable in Wyoming, Montana, and Canada that they have gained a special name, chinooks—roll over the mountaintops, lift temperatures, suck up the snow, and smooth the humps out of the backs of the grateful cattle. Though Montanans are less inclined to mention the matter, chinooks occasionally occur also in summer and then are blisteringly hot, a development that creates pained surprise among the unprepared tourists.

A myth has grown up that the high country also influences the basic nature of the people who dwell in it—men to match the mountains, so to speak. The notion has certain superficials to recommend it. Altitude, dryness, and long successions of sunny days do produce an invigorating climate. Tremendous vistas, ever changing under each day's varying slant of light, do fascinate even those who are used to the scene. And so a mystique sets in, unsettling even people who should know better. "Great things are done when men and mountains meet," declared poet William Blake; "This is not done by jostling in the street"—a generality which, cast as a historical hypothesis, might be hard to document, as might Arthur Chapman's more saccharine verse: "Out where the handclasp's a little stronger, out where the smile dwells a little longer, that's where the West begins." All of which reminds me of rounding a clump of trees not far from Telluride and coming across a cowboy who had just performed by himself the considerable physical feat of roping a wild range cow, throwing her, and tying her four feet together. He had then whittled out a club and was passionately beating off her horns. She had tried to hook his horse, he said, there under the shadow of the Lone Cone, one of the loveliest peaks in the land, and he was teaching her a lesson.

Scenery does choke people up on occasion. A stroll beside a Montana lake or a vigorous climb to the top of the Grand Teton can be cleansing to the spirit. Eventually the paramount value of the mountains may prove to be neither their metals nor their water but the refuge that their last wild places offer a population increasingly harried by itself.

And yet, for those who would write about the Rockies in terms of the human spirit, this sense of remoteness from petty human problems is their ultimate deception—as if the height of a peak or the depth of a canyon somehow bears relevance either to human grace or to human cussedness. No. Mountain conditions may change patterns of living but not the natures of the men who produce the patterns.

That, fundamentally, is what this book is about: patterns of living that developed within the mountainous sections of Idaho, Montana, Wyoming, Colorado, central Utah, and northern New Mexico. It is not concerned, except incidentally, with the adjoining high plains and the deserts. Most of the shaping which it will follow came during the hundred years subsequent to the widespread discoveries of gold that began in 1859. The first threads, however, go back much further, to Francisco Vásquez de Coronado and his men, groping out of Mexico toward the fabled Seven Cities of Cíbola. And so that is where we start.

I

NOTHING BUT SKY

IN THE summer of 1540 Indian runners following trails already ancient left the hot Rio Grande Valley in what is now the north-central part of New Mexico and climbed urgently eastward along a little defile, through scrub oak and piñon, to a low break in the mesa top. Though not particularly impressive—its altitude was scarcely 7,500 feet—the gap had long been one of the major gateways of what became the American West. Indian peddlers frequented it; hunters eager for the buffalo of the eastern plains used it; furtive war parties slipped cautiously back and forth. When white men later found the pass, they called it La Glorieta, meaning a secluded, parklike nook. The name persists today.

The messengers of 1540 dropped down the eastern side of La Glorieta Pass into a broad valley, formed by the meager Pecos River as it breaks southward out of the southern spurs of the Sangre de Cristo Mountains. Reaching the valley bottom, they turned north. Soon they saw fields of stunted maize, squash, melons. Rising nearby were two dwelling complexes, vast human antheaps, already known by hearsay to Coronado's Spaniards as Cicúique but in later years more generally called the Pecos, after the bordering stream.

Each of the two buildings was four stories high. Each story was set irregularly back from the one beneath, so that three terraces ran around each unit. Since for defensive reasons ingress was by ladder to the roofs and then down through holes into the interiors, the outer walls showed blank, tawny faces. There was, however, communication between the inner chambers.

One of the Pecos units held 585 rooms; the other 517. The cubicles were small, about 8 feet by 10, for horses did not exist in the New World and the Pueblo Indians had to transport roof beams from the mountains on their own backs. The number of oblong stones and heavy wall bricks that the Pecos Indians molded out of clay and dried grass and passed from hand to hand up the shaky, nailless ladders staggers the imagination. The

Pueblos, incidentally, were a small race, the men averaging about 5 feet in height, the women 4.

Most of the cells they built on the ground level were used for storage. On the three floors above more than two thousand people lived, divided approximately in half between each of the two complexes. Their planners had developed ingenious flues for ventilation and for the escape of smoke. Even so, the air must have been stale.

There is no way to resurrect the means by which the messengers passed on their news to the inhabitants of Pecos. There may have been a grand assembly of the populace in an inner plaza. Or the chiefs and high priests may have hurried the runners into one of the several ceremonial chambers around which the cultural life of every Pueblo village centered—the kivas, sometimes square and sometimes circular, generally underground but occasionally above—and there have listened in private to the most extraordinary story ever to reach the edges of the mountains.

The runners had come from the west, from the Zuñi Valley near the present border between New Mexico and Arizona, where six Pueblo villages scattered for fifteen miles along the valley formed a loosely knit entity called Cíbola.[1] The westernmost pueblo was named Háwikuh and was the scene of the astounding events that had put the messengers in motion. Being human, they no doubt exaggerated their news in the telling. Almost certainly they misinterpreted much that they had seen or had been told. But even when stripped to the bare bones of fact the yarn almost passed comprehension.

The year before, in May, 1539, as Europeans measured time, a tall black man "with chili lips," followed by a large retinue of Indians, had reached Háwikuh afoot from the southwest. His name was Esteban or Estevancio or something outlandish like that. Walking with Esteban as a sort of companion-servant was an Indian lad from Mexico with the name Bartolomé. The retinue of Indians that accompanied the pair evidently believed Esteban, or Estevancio, was a medicine man or ruler of some sort. They worshiped him, and the homage had made him arrogant. He adorned himself with ribbons, feathers, and little bells, and he shook a gourd rattle when he delivered pronouncements. He spoke of other people, lighter skinned than he, coming behind him with a powerful symbol shaped like a cross. Those who followed him apparently desired some mysterious thing which they thought the villagers of Háwikuh possessed—just as Esteban wanted Háwikuh maidens delivered up to him for his pleasure.

Frightened and angered by the indefinite threat, the people of Háwikuh

[1] Coronado at first spelled the name Cévola and persistently referred to seven cities, perhaps because his imagination had been fixed on the Seven Cities of Spanish legend, New World civilizations supposedly founded by seven Portuguese bishops after their flight across the ocean from conquering Mohammedans.

killed Esteban and most of his retinue, save three who escaped. But they spared the Indian lad, Bartolomé, and kept him with them.

Bartolomé spoke Aztec. Several Aztec words had filtered into Cíbola along the primitive trade routes. On his part, Bartolomé probably had picked up Pueblo words from Indians he had met while journeying north with Esteban. Communication was established in time, and presumably the boy won consideration from his captors by telling them stories of what was happening in the south.

Years earlier, he related, Esteban had been shipwrecked far to the southeast with a small group led by a man named Cabeza de Vaca. While wandering painfully toward Mexico, the miserable handful had heard rumors of the Pueblo villages north of them—of vast herds of humpbacked cattle, of cotton cloth woven on looms, of cities rising story on story, of gleaming emeralds. To their wondering ears all those things were proof of an advanced civilization.

There was truth behind the yarns. The Pueblos did weave cloth and they did live in multistoried buildings. The cattle were wild buffalo, however, and the emeralds were bits of turquoise which the Pueblos strung into necklaces and set into their doorposts to ward off evil. But then Bartolomé told the Indians of another thing they could not relate to any material they knew of—a yellowish substance, hard like stone yet easy to shape without breaking. The light-skinned people called the stuff *oro* and lusted for it more fiercely than Esteban had lusted for women.

There were other frightening greeds, Bartolomé said. A chief named Guzmán not long before had led his soldiers from Mexico City into the north and had seized every wild Indian he could find, turning them into slaves. Resistance was hard. The Spaniards rode astride terrible monsters whose square, stained teeth were big enough to masticate human flesh. The riders pointed magic rods that roared and belched smoke and killed across great distances. Obviously their god was very powerful, and when the Spaniards insisted that the Indians pay reverence to it, most of them wisely obeyed.

And, yes, the Spaniards would probably seek to avenge Esteban's slaying.

The people of Háwikuh grew afraid. They were brave, however. When scouts brought word in the summer of 1540 that the Spaniards actually were approaching on the backs of their dreadful monsters, a war party sallied out and attacked an advanced detachment of the enemy while it was encamped for the night in a narrow pass. The effort failed and the invaders pressed relentlessly on. The Pueblos drew a magic line of cornmeal on the ground and forbade the Spaniards to cross. In the ensuing battle the enemy killed several Indians. Still the Pueblos did not run away. They sent their women, children, and old men to hiding places in the cliffs. Then they went with bows and arrows and heaps of stones to the terraces of the village and prepared for a final stand.

For a few inspiriting minutes they succeeded. Their hail of stones and arrows hurt the monsters and the Spaniards fell back. The respite was short. Dismounting, the invaders stalked ahead on foot. Flint arrow points made little impression on the hard, smooth helmets and breastplates. The enemy crossbows drove iron-tipped arrows deeper than the Pueblos had imagined an arrow could penetrate. The harquebuses they aimed at the rooftops looked awkward but roared fearfully and hurt terribly.

The Indians concentrated their missiles on the leader, a tall young man (thirty that year) whose armor glowed golden in the sunlight and whose headpiece was brave with plumes. At the foot of the walls he dropped under the shower of stones as though dead. The Pueblos shrieked in triumph, but other men stood over the fallen leader to protect him from further blows and the rest drove on. At last the defenders lost heart and with signs begged for peace.

The conquerors, gaunt and half-starved after their long march from Mexico, seemed disgusted with their prize, as though they had expected much more. Left to themselves, they might have used cruelty to assuage their disappointment. Their captain prevented. Recovering quickly from his stunning, he treated the villagers kindly, though he did say, through signs and stumbling interpreters, that they must become Christians and swear allegiance to the king of Spain—whatever that meant. His name was Francisco Vásquez de Coronado. He visited the neighboring pueblos and asked many questions about the country's soil and climate, intimating that other Spaniards might wish to settle among the Indians.

When he discovered the lad Bartolomé, communication moved ahead much faster. By way of gentle warning, Coronado directed the boy to tell the people of Cíbola that they had seen only a tiny part of Spanish power. Coronado's main force of more than two hundred soldiers and several hundred Indian and Negro camptenders, laborers, and herders was on the road behind him, driving great flocks of sheep and cattle. Tame animals good to eat: how amazing! The Pueblos repeated their protestations of good will, and Coronado felt free to scatter his advanced guard for exploring.

Hearing of other clusters of villages in the distance, his eyes brightened, as though he hoped the new cities would hold the riches that Cíbola lacked. He sent out a patrol to visit the nearest group, the Moqui (today called Hopi) pueblos, which lay northwest of Zuñi Valley; and he suggested that the men of Háwikuh themselves dispatch runners to the more distant villages in the east, asking that ambassadors visit him.

And so the messengers jogged on foot nearly two hundred miles across La Glorieta Pass to the village of Cicúique beside the Pecos River.

There must have been earnest consultations in the kivas. Finally it was agreed that a small delegation should visit these strange, bold newcomers, a step that no other of the eastern villages seems to have dared take.

Leader of the Pecos delegation was the cacique himself, a sort of combined high priest and governor who, by Pueblo custom, held office for life. Second in command of the travelers was a handsome young man, tall for a Pueblo; he sported long black mustaches, unusual on an Indian. Coronado mistook the title of the first man for a name, and the chroniclers thereafter wrote of him as Cacique, as one might say Bishop or possibly King. Coronado called the younger man Bigotes. To Anglo-Saxon ears *bigotes* sounds like a name. It isn't. It means "mustache," and we will more nearly approximate the Spaniards' attitude if we refer to the young warrior as Whiskers.

Bishop and Whiskers extolled their own pueblo and those along the Rio Grande so highly that Coronado was intrigued. Although he had just dispatched another captain, García López de Cárdenas, northwest to check out unbelievable tales of the yet-unnamed Grand Canyon of the Colorado River, he decided to thin his forces still more by having twenty-four-year-old Hernando de Alvarado examine the eastern area with twenty men. More than hope and curiosity lay behind the calculated risk. There was not enough food, clothing, and forage in Cíbola to provide for the main army that was approaching. Alvarado might locate more provident winter quarters. And of course a chance always existed that he might stumble across gold or emeralds.

Guided by Whiskers and Bishop, this first band of Rocky Mountain pioneers left Cíbola on August 29, 1540. Very soon (so Juan de Jaramillo reported in his journal of the trip) they noticed that the streams no longer flowed toward the Southern Sea, as the Spanish then called the Pacific, but toward the Gulf of Mexico. For the first time white men had crossed the Continental Divide north of Mexico. What is more, they recognized what they saw, although in the vicinity of Zuñi there was little about the slight uplift to suggest its significance.

Some miles beyond the Divide they visited the village of Ácoma, perched spectacularly on a rock-girt white mesa 357 feet high. After another week of travel they struck the Rio Grande a little north of present Albuquerque. They investigated the dozen or so pueblos that made up the "kingdom" of Tiguex, as they called it, and then marched on north to Taos. Alvarado named the place Braba and reported that it was well worth seeing. He meant the three-tiered village and not the handsome skyline behind it which four centuries later would so impress D. H. Lawrence. Alvarado was used to mountains. He had seen Popocatepetl, towering nearly 18,000 feet high southeast of Mexico City; and besides, scenery wasn't his concern. Ignoring the Sangre de Cristo Mountains except to say that the sierra made Braba's climate cold, he directed his men to lash two large timbers together in the shape of a cross and erect it in front of the pueblo, as they had done at other villages. Through either Whiskers or Bishop he informed the curious watchers that the object was to be venerated. The Indians complied enthusiastically. Holding yucca fibers in their teeth, they climbed onto each other's shoulders and tied feathers and wild roses (so the narrative says, though the season was mid-September) to the cross's arms.

Taos was as far north as the explorers went. Nothing lay beyond, the Indians said—only harsh mountains and wild Indians who had no settled towns. Accordingly the explorers returned to Tiguex, the cluster of pueblos they had first encountered on the Rio Grande. From Tiguex Alvarado sent Coronado an enthusiastic report.

Here was the place to winter. There was ample forage for the horses and cattle, ample supplies of dried vegetables for the soldiers. The Indians, fearful of drought, maintained three-year surpluses of corn and beans and squash in their storage rooms. They were a peaceful people, devoted to their fields and homes. They made baskets and were good potters. In warm spots near the river they grew cotton that they wove into clothing. Buffalo skins furnished sturdier work garments. Dogs seemed to be their only domestic animals, but they did raise fine, plump turkeys which they valued more for their feathers, used in religious ceremonies and for making warm feather robes, than for eating.

The climate was very dry but the Pueblos overcame the drawback to an extent by diverting irrigation water from the sluggish Rio Grande and, farther to the north, from the little tributaries that danced down the side canyons of the Sangre de Cristo Mountains. Just how completely they had mastered irrigation—a skill well known to the desert peoples around the eastern Mediterranean—is impossible to determine from what Alvarado said. Certainly the Rio Grande Indians were well ahead of the Moquis of northeastern Arizona. Those Indians caught rainwater in cisterns—they had very few living trickles in their country—and the women carried it in jars on their heads to the fields. The Rio Grande Indians were more advanced than that. On the other hand, their engineering was far inferior to that of the prehistoric people who once dwelt along the Gila River of southwestern Arizona and who are credited with irrigating more than 200,000 acres by means of canals as much as 10 miles long, 7 feet deep, and 30 feet wide at the surface.

Some of the small New Mexican ditches simply caught floodwaters after a rare storm. Even the somewhat bigger ditches that tapped running streams seem to have been inadequate, for the villagers regularly tried to entice rain from the unpredictable gods with elaborate dances. Still, according to one modern estimate, 30,000 people scattered along the Rio Grande Valley managed to draw sustenance from 25,000 irrigated acres.

Food and clothing! On receipt of Alvarado's recommendation, Coronado started his entire army in sections toward the Rio Grande. To their thin southern blood the high-altitude cold of late fall seemed almost unendurable. Without compunction an advanced agent provided shelter for their shivering bones by requisitioning Alcanfor, the southernmost of the Tiguex pueblos, and ordering the inhabitants to leave. And then, just as the Spaniards were settling in, they received another message from Alvarado that brought the deeper warmth of hope surging back.

Alvarado had continued with Whiskers and Bishop across La Glorieta Pass to Pecos. While making arrangements in Pecos to visit the buffalo country to the east, he had found an Indian from the plains, a captive of the Pueblos, whom he called The Turk "because he looked like one." Impressing El Turco as a guide, the explorers moved away from the foothills into the flatlands of northeastern New Mexico, where they saw such a multitude of shaggy, heavy-chested bison "that I do not know what to compare them with unless it be the fish of the sea." Stirring though the hunts were, El Turco created a greater sensation by remarking casually to Alvarado that in his home country of Quivira, far to the northeast, there was—and it is impossible to say exactly how he had learned of the Spanish madness—there was gold.

Could he prove it? Certainly. He owned a golden bracelet which Bigotes and Cacique had taken from him and had kept.

Informed of the charges, Whiskers and Bishop insisted that they had never before heard of such an object. Their earnestness was of no avail. The excited Spaniards chose to regard the two Pueblos, helpful over so long a time, as liars rather than consider that the Turk might be serving up chimeras in order to get away from Pecos back to his homeland. They applied a little torture. When it produced no results, they took the two men and the Turk in chains to Coronado. He attempted to persuade the stubborn pair by setting dogs on them. No success—but never mind the evidence. Bracelet or no, the invaders would follow El Turco to Quivira as soon as spring made travel possible.

The inhabitants of Tiguex, already infuriated over the way the people of Alcanfor had been turned out of doors to provide shelter for the army, were further outraged by the episode of the dogs. Resentment increased when one of Coronado's chief officers raped a young wife of Arcenal, a village five miles upriver from Alcanfor, in her own home. When foragers next passed among the towns making harsh requisitions for food and clothing, the fury boiled over.

Rebels, as the Spaniards would soon term them, concentrated in Arcenal and in Moho, a similar pueblo a few miles to the north. Afoot one cold night in December they raided the Spaniards' horse herd and drove as many of the animals as they could manage back to Arcenal. There they killed twenty-five or thirty of the monsters with bows and arrows and cut off the tails for trophies.

Swiftly López de Cárdenas, discoverer of the Grand Canyon, led out a retaliatory force. The Indians crowded on the rooftops jeered down his offer to negotiate. After a fierce battle, during which fifty of his men were wounded by the primitive weapons, Cárdenas occupied the terrace of the two-story village. The Indians, sheltered in their maze of rooms, still refused to negotiate. Grimly Cárdenas had his soldiers batter holes through the outer walls and built smudge fires in such a fashion that drafts would carry the smoke through the interconnecting chambers. Choking and weeping, the Indians ran outside. Some were killed as they appeared, some were captured and burned at the stake. The invaders, greatly outnumbered in an unknown land, far from hope of succor, were determined to teach the natives respect.

The ferocity, however, served to stiffen the resistance at the nearby pueblo at Moho. Coronado himself directed that attack. Although the first wave of Spaniards, equipped with scaling ladders, managed to gain the terrace through a barrage of stones and poisoned arrows, the defenders rallied and drove them back. Five or six Spaniards died, more than sixty were wounded. Unable to afford such casualties, Coronado broke off the engagement and turned to a siege, drawing a tight cordon around the spring on which the town depended for water.

Kept alive by moisture from two light snowfalls, the Indians tried desperately with crude wooden tools to dig a wide-mouthed well. They had no way to shore up the sandy walls. The banks collapsed and smothered thirty diggers. The town gave up that effort then and settled to a hopeless wait.

Suffering terribly from the cold, the shelterless Spaniards launched several halfhearted attacks that gained nothing. Thirst proved more effective. To spare the women and children, the Pueblos surrendered a hundred of them, though many others refused to leave the doomed town. Two more weeks dragged by. Just before dawn one day late in March, 1541, the Indians rushed outside and tried to flee across the icy Rio Grande. Mounted Spaniards rode them down, killing many, capturing more. Only a few escaped into the snowy mountains.

Late in April Coronado's triumphant force moved with its thousands of head of livestock through La Glorieta Pass to find the Quivira. It was one of the most famous marches in American history and, as every schoolboy knows, it discovered no gold—"nothing," reported one discouraged chronicler, "but cattle and sky."

After a fruitless eastward march as far as the panhandle of today's Texas, Coronado sent the bulk of his disheartened army back to Tiguex and pressed on north with only thirty cavalrymen and six infantrymen. Somewhere in what became central Kansas he admitted that he had been tricked. After ordering El Turco strangled for his falsehoods, he turned back to another hard winter beside the Rio Grande. In April, 1542, suffering acute depression because of failure and a severe injury he had received when his saddle cinch broke during a horse race, he led his wrangling explorers back to Mexico and disgrace.

He had found knowledge. From his own long marches and from the reports of an expedition he had sent west almost to the Gulf of California, he knew that North America was no small bulb perched atop Mexico, as some theoretical geographers of the time were saying. There was no hope of supporting an inland expedition by means of supply ships skirting the nearby ocean shores. If a water passage to the Orient existed through the New World, it must lie much farther north than anyone believed. Furthermore, the enormous northern reaches of the New World were formidable to cross, carved by mile-deep canyons, rumpled by huge mountains, spanned by illimitable plains. "A cold and sterile land," he and his men reported out of their disappointment, although they had lived for two years on grass-fattened livestock and on vegetables easily grown in irrigated fields.

Why bother studying such a hopeless country? The maps and factual information resulting from Coronado's expedition disappeared into the archives. Rumor replaced reality. Although awareness of the Rio Grande and of the Colorado River seeped outside, nothing about the Continental Divide did. As a consequence cartographers, who had little more than their own imaginations to work from, combined the streams and showed a single river flowing from New Mexico into the Gulf of California. Quivira migrated westward toward the Pacific coast. Cíbola floated unanchored through the white spaces of *Terra Incognita*. The upper extremities of North America remained small—on paper—and were topped by a water passage known as the Strait of Anian. The Rocky Mountains, the most impressive reality of the new land, shrank so completely out of memory that scarcely an impression of even their southernmost toes rippled the fine flat maps of the theoretical geographers. Two and a half more centuries of intermittent wrestlings with ignorance would have to pass before even a faint notion of the mountains' actual extent began to emerge again from the mists.

II

EACH HIS OWN WILD DREAMS TO TRY

IN 1579 redheaded Francis Drake of England raided the ports of Valparaiso and Callao de Lima on the west coast of South America, then looted a treasure galleon bound from the Philippine Islands to Panama. Six years later, in 1585, Thomas Cavendish raided and burned another Manila galleon off the coast of California. To explain these astounding appearances, the hitherto secure Spaniards ignored the obvious route through the Strait of Magellan and jumped instead at that intriguing invention of imaginative mapmakers: the Strait of Anian, the reputed waterway around the top of North America. Had the English freebooters found it?

Dread of Anian increased in 1588 when England destroyed the Grand Armada and gained control of the seas. If the Pacific slope of the New World was to be protected, the defenses would have to be based on land. Straightway orders were issued for the colonizing of California, so that galleons from the Philippines would have a haven en route to Panama, and for establishing presidios in New Mexico from which the Strait of Anian could be blockaded.

In Mexico interest in the northern lands was reviving for more immediate reasons. During the 1540's, very shortly after Coronado's return, prospectors working up through the heart of Mexico's high, dry central plateau had found rich deposits of gold, silver, and mercury in the province of Zacatecas. Other fortune hunters, pressing still farther north, soon found more silver in what is now the state of Durango. Why suppose this was the end? A folk saying took shape—*Más allá,* there is more beyond.

In southern Chihuahua Indian traders accompanying the miners found Rio Conchos, which flows northeast to join the Rio Grande several miles upstream from today's Big Bend National Park, Texas. The valley of the Conchos furnished a natural route for commerce, and from northern Indians who had wandered in to barter with the local villagers the white traders picked up fresh rumors of city-dwelling Pueblos. Their curiosity piqued, the frontiersmen dusted off Pedro de Casteñada's old book about the Coronado expedition and studied it afresh. Soon a conviction grew that blame for the early failure rested on Coronado, not on the land. If he had searched harder . . . *Más allá!*

Stirred by the hope, four small parties risked the unknown during the decade of the 1580's. All suffered losses to the Indians. None was truly profitable. But one, commanded by Antonio de Espéjo during 1582–83, was suggestive: it obtained by trade with the Moqui Indians 4,000 cotton blankets and in the vicinity of modern Prescott, Arizona, it unearthed veins of what Espéjo took to be gold-silver ore. Commerce, and minerals, and a world of semicivilized Indians to convert to Christianity! When the crown decided early in the 1590's to colonize New Mexico as a step toward closing the Strait of Anian to English raiders, several men, Espéjo included, bid for the right to lead the expedition.

To save drains on her treasury, Spain customarily farmed out colonial projects to private individuals, each eager (to borrow a quotation from Herbert E. Bolton, famed historian of the Spanish borderlands) "his own wild dreams to try." There might be profit from a monopoly on mines and trade. There was the prestige of a governorship and the probable elevation of one's family to the ranks of the aristocracy. Helping the church reach the heathen natives held out promise of heavenly bliss. And although expenses and risks were great, a man could generally ease the burden by selling concessions, so to speak, to lesser entrepreneurs who, for the sake of their own wild dreams, were willing to invest time and money in the project.

Competition for the New Mexican plum was keen. After months of hesitation, intrigue, and countermanded orders, it finally went to Juan de Oñate, then about forty-seven years old. Oñate had money and position. His father had made the equivalent of a million or more dollars in the silver mines of Zacatecas. Juan himself had been a distinguished Indian fighter and mine operator, but he lived high—his wife was a descendant of both the Emperor Montezuma and the great conqueror Cortez—and his patrimony had shrunk. The New Mexico adventure promised to restore his fortune and to add luster to the family name.

It took him nearly three years and tens of thousands of pesos of borrowed money to fight through government red tape and assemble an expedition of 130 farming families, 270 single men, many of them Indian and Negro slaves, and 11 Franciscan friars. Drovers, most of them working afoot, herded 7,000 head of cattle. Baggage traveled on strings of pack mules and in 83 ox-drawn carts, most of them no more than four feet square and squealing on two solid wooden wheels sawed from the rough trunks of cottonwood trees. When the awkward train started north in January, 1598, it stretched out nearly four miles.

Instead of following the Conchos River, as the expeditions of the 1580's had done, Oñate's scouts pioneered a hard, dry route almost straight north to El Paso. Thereafter he stayed as close as the terrain allowed to the Rio Grande, known also as Rio Bravo or, from its direction, Rio del Norte, River of the North. In July he and his advance guard reached the Rio Chama, future gateway to the San Juan Mountains of southwestern Colorado and the Great Basin of Utah.

Near the confluence of the Chama with the Rio Grande were the twin pueblos of Yuque and Yunque. Oñate persuaded the inhabitants of Yunque to turn their terraced dwelling over to his colonists and to move in with their neighbors. He then prevailed on 1,500 Indian laborers to excavate an irrigation ditch from the river to the nearby fields—the first ditch north of Mexico to be devoted to the sustenance of Caucasians. When the main body of colonists arrived in August with their seeds and livestock, the fields were almost ready for farming.

Other Indians were impressed to help erect a church, adapting its architecture to the materials at hand. It was narrow, for there were no long timbers suitable for roof beams. The thick walls, like those of the nearby pueblo villages, were built of adobe bricks. In time thin sheets of translucent mica were brought in for covering the window openings. The dark interior was brightened by whitewashing the walls and then painting gay red, blue, and yellow religious scenes on the light background.

To keep his people alive through the winter Oñate, like Coronado, was forced to requisition food and clothing from the resentful Indians. Resistance boiled up. In December, 1598, the three thousand or so people of Ácoma allowed a party under Juan de Zaldívar to climb 357 feet to their city atop the white rock. Then they attacked. The only foreigners to escape were the men who had stayed below with the horses, and three who fought a way back down the dizzy trail, and four who lived through an incredible leap over the towering cliffs.

In revenge Juan's brother, twenty-five-year-old Vincente de Zaldívar, led seventy armored men, equipped with two crude brass cannons, against the mesa fortress. While the bulk of his men pretended a frontal assault, Zaldívar and eleven others scaled a neighboring pinnacle, bridged a narrow chasm to the main rock, and set the city afire. Flame, harquebuses, lances, swords, and the two cannons killed an estimated thousand Indians of all ages and both sexes. The town was razed and the survivors were ordered to re-establish themselves on the plains below. Of the seventy steel-clad attackers only two had been slain. Against men who possessed only stones and reed arrows, armor was an almost impregnable defense.

Hoping to find both gold and the Strait of Anian, Oñate, like Coronado, marched northeast to Quivira. Somewhere on the plains Indians attacked and he fell back. Later, seeking ports to which supply ships might come, he marched west, as one of Coronado's captains had done, to the Colorado River, but that route obviously was impossibly rough for merchandise caravans. The only direction in which he did not explore was north into the high Rockies, where gold and silver did in truth lie.

Even if his prospectors had found mineral there, they probably could not have overcome the transportation, labor, and Indian problems involved in mining it—just as they failed to exploit successfully the veins Espéjo reputedly had discovered in remote Arizona. Nor did diligent search reveal anything closer to the Rio Grande.

Discontent gathered. Neither supplies nor reinforcements arrived from Mexico. In that dry, brisk climate traditional methods of crop cultivation produced only skimpy harvests. Many colonists deserted. The rest, unable to feed or clothe themselves, laid heavier and heavier hands on the Indians. The friars, meeting sullenness among prospective converts, blamed Oñate's administration. Factions appeared. In 1607, probably as a bluff to force support out of the viceroy, beleaguered Oñate sent in his resignation. To his surprise it was accepted. Juan de Oñate, colonizer of New Mexico, was forced, like Coronado, the province's discoverer, to return south bankrupt and in disgrace.

Far westward, meanwhile, the naval expeditions exploring the California coast collapsed and further colonial efforts in that direction were shelved for another six decades. Except for the crown's desire to further God's great glory, New Mexico might have suffered similar abandonment. By their own count Franciscan fathers along the Rio Grande had converted 2,000 souls. Ten or fifteen times that number still awaited salvation. To Catholic Spain such work was far too important to be dismissed. The colony was ordered maintained, and in 1609 Pedro de Peralta was sent north in Oñate's place.

Either late that year or early the next Peralta established a new capital on a tributary of the Rio Grande a few miles southeast of Oñate's old headquarters. He called his capital La Villa Real de la Santa Fé de San Francisco—Santa Fe for short. The name, Holy Faith of St. Francis, accurately reflected the colony's new status. New Mexico was a mission station. The primary function of the civil and military administrations was to support and protect the Franciscans at their work—and, as an incidence to this, to maintain Spanish claims in North America against the Virginia Company of England, which had established Jamestown in 1607 and Samuel de Champlain of France, who had raised the fleur-de-lis at Quebec in 1608. For all that anyone in Madrid or Mexico City knew, the distance from either Jamestown or Quebec to Santa Fe was dangerously short. It was well, therefore, to have a settlement in the west as evidence of prior occupancy and also as a screen to keep foreign interlopers away from the rich silver mines of Mexico proper.

Life in the languishing outpost was intolerably dull. Once every *three* years a supply train of thirty-two carts accompanied by a few soldiers and

colonists came creaking in from Mexico City. Its main cargo consisted of
religious objects for the missions, armament for the presidios, and only a
scattering of jealously desired symbols of status for the laity—choice
furniture, rich table settings, ornate clothing, and the like. The return
caravan went south with buffalo hides, piñon nuts, sheep for feeding the
miners of northern Mexico, and Indian slaves for working underground,
the last a dismal commerce whose actual extent, because it was ostensibly
illegal, can never be accurately gauged.

Most of these slaves were war prisoners of the Utes and Apaches, passed
on to the Spaniards in exchange for guns and horses. Whenever trade
proved insufficient to satisfy the Indians, they used the newly acquired
mounts and weapons to plunder the outlying Spanish ranches. Raids and
commerce spread swiftly. Captive human beings appeared in New Mexico
from great distances. Bartered horses, stolen horses and lost horses, multi-
plying rapidly in the favorable environment, were soon familiar to native
tribes throughout the American West. The Navajos, a subtribe of the
Apaches, and the Moquis (Hopis) also developed a taste for sheep and
built up large herds from progenitors acquired mainly through theft,
meanwhile learning to weave blankets from wool as once they had woven
them from cotton.

The Franciscan fathers objected strenuously to the slave trade, and also
to the enforced labor which the civil administrators imposed for short
periods each year on the Pueblo Indians as a corrupt form of taxation. The
protests achieved little. New Mexico was a remote place. Many of the
administrators who came there did so in hope of petty gain through
malfeasance, and free Indian labor was one way to pad profits. Furthermore, they resented criticism from churchmen whose own practices were
not above reproach, for the padres often exploited their converts, forcing
them to till fields, do housework, and weave cotton *mantas* for sale—for
the good of the church, to be sure, and not for personal gain. For the good
of the Church also, the friars sometimes laid fierce whips across the backs
of converts who dared return to the ancient gods. Medicine men who
opened the closed kivas were hanged for being in league with the devil.

Civil authorities, smarting from the criticism of the friars, were vitriolic
in denunciation of those practices. Recriminatory feuds burned hot, and all
too often affairs in New Mexico were paralyzed by the contention.

The Pueblos meanwhile were slowly acquiring horses and guns. Thus
fortified, they lost some of their fear of the armored Spaniards. Firebrands
began whispering of revolt.

Leader of the resistance was Popé, a medicine man of San Juan pueblo
near the mouth of the Chama River. Early in the 1670's, Popé and forty-
seven other village priests were arrested for witchcraft and sorcery—that
is, for following the old tribal forms of worship. Three were hanged, each
in a different pueblo, as object lessons. The others were flogged, jailed, and

eventually released. Burning with hatred, Popé retired to remote Taos, where he could escape close surveillance. There, working slowly and carefully, he laid plans to drive the invaders completely from New Mexico.

August 13, 1680, was set as the date for the uprising. As the critical time approached, Popé's messengers carried knotted leather thongs to the different pueblos. A ceremonial untying of the knots signified the town's commitment.

To ensure secrecy no woman was told of the final details. When Popé's son-in-law was suspected of treachery, the old medicine man himself slew the youth. In spite of the precautions, disquieting rumors reached Governor Antonio de Otermín in Santa Fe. He began fortifying the central part of the capital—the governor's long, low palace on the north side of the plaza; the military quarters to the west; the church to the east. The walled corrals were enlarged.

Before preparations were completed, neophytes at two different pueblos whispered warnings to their padres, who hurried to Otermín. The governor in turn dispatched couriers with orders for the settlers in the southern part of the province to retire to El Paso, and for those in the north to assemble in Santa Fe—the only two fortified towns in New Mexico, for most of the 2,500 settlers lived on ranches scattered throughout the Rio Grande Valley and the nearby tributaries.

Realizing that he had been anticipated, Popé advanced the date of the uprising to August 10. He was not quite quick enough. A thousand or more settlers reached Santa Fe. Another four hundred or so did not and were massacred along the sun-smitten trails. Of the thirty-two friars in northern New Mexico, twenty-one died, some after suffering brutal indignities.

On rallying the fugitives Governor Otermín found only 155 of them capable of bearing arms. He formed them into militia companies and passed out such weapons as his armory possessed, an antiquated hodge-podge. To counterbalance the limited material resources, the fighters possessed the courage of desperation. When Indian emissaries arrogantly offered to let the Spaniards live if they would leave the country, the governor defied them. Some five hundred Indians thereupon attacked, setting fire to the outlying houses and cutting the ditch which brought the besieged their only water. A charge from the palace enabled the defenders to restore the ditch, but the respite was brief. Twenty-five hundred Indian reinforcements arrived from the north, seized the church at the east end of the plaza, and put it to the torch.

On August 20, after days of thirst and terror, Otermín mounted a hundred of his best men for a last frantic counterattack. The charge killed 300 Indians, captured 47—after interrogation the prisoners were lined up in the plaza and shot—and cleared the town. The Spanish lost five killed and several wounded, among them the governor, slashed across the face and in the breast.

The settlers took stock. They could repair the ditch, but the city was in rubble, food almost gone. Deciding that further resistance was pointless, Otermín ordered a retreat. His earlier victory was not without fruit. As the settlers streamed south carrying their possessions on their own backs—the surviving horses were needed for military baggage and for the soldiers who guarded the bedraggled column—the Indians watched grimly from a safe distance, reluctant after the slaughter in Sante Fe to risk an attack.

On the first day of the uprising, so legend says, a dying priest at one of the missions at the foot of the great mountains had knelt beside his desecrated cross and prayed for a sign that would reveal the future. Immediately a deep red glow suffused the gray peaks—Sangre de Cristo, Blood of Christ. The Church would return. In this wise, the tale finishes, the great southern spur of the Rockies received its name.

The prophesied reconquest was long delayed. During the next decade sharp little attacks reached as far as present Albuquerque, but the commanders lacked the will and the supplies to hold onto what they took. The Indians meanwhile were joyfully extirpating everything Spanish. They washed away Christian baptisms with Indian soap made from yucca roots, befouled sacred objects, reopened the forbidden kivas. The people of Ácoma rebuilt their city on top of the white mesa. For reasons that today are not fully clear, many villagers abandoned their pueblos and either amalgamated with other groups or erected new towns on fresh sites. Bickering broke out among them. Popé, reigning in Santa Fe as a more tyrannical despot than the governor he had ejected, became the focus of new hatreds.

He died in 1690. Shortly thereafter a new Spanish governor was appointed for New Mexico, Diego de Vargas, a tall man, dark and implacable. Not content, as some of his predecessors had been, to bear the title of governor without something to govern, Vargas bombarded his apathetic superiors with appeals for support suitable to the task. The friars backed him, and he added more inducement by repeating legends of Sierra Azul, the Blue Mountain, located off toward the land of the Moquis, home of a marvelous quicksilver spring that dripped pure mercury into a pool hidden deep inside a mysterious cave.

In 1692 he was able to begin. With an "army" of 210 men, more than half of them Indian auxiliaries, he brushed aside the defiant Pueblos of the lower Rio Grande and marched north through withering summer heat to Santa Fe. When he cut the water supply and aimed two cannons at the town, the occupants agreed to negotiate. Swift marches through other key sections of the province brought further protestations of peace. He returned then to Mexico for his colonists. When he led them, shivering with December cold, to Santa Fe, the Indians renounced their promises and refused to vacate the town. Vargas broke down the gates and drove them out. Resistance in other towns fared no better. When eight northern pueblos tried a

Popé-style coordinated revolt in 1696, Vargas reacted so swiftly that he caught them off balance. By year's end opposition was completely crushed.

Eastward in the Mississippi Valley, which La Salle claimed for France in 1682, equally significant events were transpiring. Colonies took root in Illinois and Louisiana. As soon as the bases were established, official expeditions began searching the plains for routes to the Pacific, which was deemed to lie close by, and for trails to Santa Fe. In 1719 Claude du Tisné penetrated as far as central Kansas and Bénard de la Harpe coursed part of Oklahoma. Five years later Etienne de Bourgomont pushed into eastern Colorado.

Unofficial parties of France's indefatigable, generally illiterate New World Indian traders may well have reached as far as the mountains. Juan de Ulibarri, marching northeast from Santa Fe in 1706 in pursuit of runaway Pueblo Indians, noted French goods among the Apaches, who in those days occupied northeastern New Mexico and southeastern Colorado. Alarmed by the discovery, Ulibarri suggested countering the encroachment with a Spanish colony located near the foot of the Rockies in the valley of the Nepestle River (today's Arkansas), which he described as "the best and broadest valley discovered in New Spain."

In 1720 Pedro de Villasur was finally sent out onto the plains with 120 soldiers and Indian auxiliaries to investigate persistent rumors of increased French trading activity and to locate possible sites for the colony Ulibarri had proposed. Chasing chimeras, Villasur ventured too far. Somewhere along the Platte River in what is now Nebraska he was surprised by Pawnee Indians equipped with a few French muskets. They killed the Spanish captain and 53 of his men. In Santa Fe the frightened survivors reported that the attack had been directed by Frenchmen. Possibly. Or perhaps the defeated were trying to save face.

Plans for a colony in "the best and broadest valley" were abandoned, but only partly because of Villasur's defeat. A more immediate reason was the sudden emergence of a terrifying new tribe of Indians, the Comanches. They were a squat, bandy-legged people, an offshoot of the Shoshoni of Wyoming, and until they acquired horses they had been too insignificant to leave any impression on early records. Mounted, they became scourges. To obtain control of the buffalo range of the southern plains they fell mercilessly on the Apaches, slowly forcing the Jicarilla band into the mountains along the Colorado-New Mexico border. Other bands of the far-flung Apaches were harried south into Texas, still others into the unoccupied lands of southwestern New Mexico and southeastern Arizona.

A principal factor in the Comanches' success during the first years of their emergence was their ability to keep firearms from reaching their enemy. They would not let French traders onto the high plains and they waged relentless war against tribes allied with the French, tribes who might otherwise have acted as intermediaries in the prairie commerce. Meantime they themselves obtained fresh supplies of horses and guns through their allies in the east, the Wichita tribe. They traded sometimes with the Pueblo Indians and with the adjacent Spanish settlements along the foothills of the Sangre de Cristo—or else raided them whenever war seemed profitable. They enslaved many Spanish prisoners, whom, on occasion, they brazenly ransomed off within sight of Spanish officials at the annual Taos summer trade fair.

Spanish policy toward them wavered. The *Comancheros,* as traders who dealt with them were called, did not want to lose the commerce of so rich and powerful a nation. Civil officials wanted them to continue as obstacles to the French. Military men feared them. As a result Comanche raids were never seriously punished. Unscathed, they grew arrogant, boasting in time that they allowed the Spanish and Mexican people to live in Texas and New Mexico only to raise horses for them.

Far north of the contentious tribes of the plains one of Canada's great pioneer fur traders was meanwhile trying to turn his own wild dream into reality. He was Pierre Gaultier de Varennes, Sieur de la Vérendrye, and his goal, as he kept paddling farther and farther up the singing beaver streams, was to find a canoe route to the Western Sea. In the fall of 1738, aged fifty-three and as dark-skinned as an Indian from his years in the wilderness, he and his grown sons pushed with their *voyageurs* up the Assiniboine River as far as the south-central part of Manitoba. Indian gossip, much of it told in sign language and inaccurately translated, led the French to believe that south of them was a great river that flowed through New Mexico to the Gulf of California. Guesswork maps of the time did show a combined Rio Grande-Colorado following such a course, and Vérendrye may have supposed he was hearing of the headwaters of the supposititious stream. Accompanied by two of his boys, several *voyageurs,* and a disorderly band of Indians, he made a hard winter trip to the villages of the agricultural Mandan Indians in present North Dakota—to check and also to develop trade relations.

The river was the Missouri. At the point where the Vérendryes encountered it, somewhat above today's Bismarck, it had left its eastern course and had begun a long sweep toward the south. The Mandans said that white men lived near its mouth—and indeed they did, in the French settlements of Illinois. Vérendrye, however, hoped stubbornly that he was hearing of Santa Fe.

Intermittently during the next years, whenever the arduous work of trading allowed, he and his sons kept probing for more information. Although they soon straightened out the Missouri, they remained convinced that not far to the west, beyond a ridge of mountains, they would find the ocean. During the summer and fall of 1742, partly for their father's sake, two of the sons, traveling from tribe to tribe, made an agonizing effort to learn. On New Year's Day, 1743, they glimpsed snowy peaks on the horizon. Just beyond—but the savages they were with took fright at rumors of an enemy war party and stampeded back east. The dejected young men had no choice but to follow.

It is not possible to say which range the Vérendryes saw. It may have been the Black Hills of western South Dakota. Perhaps it was the Big Horns of central Wyoming. If the latter speculation is correct, then those two Frenchmen were the first whites to glimpse a section of the northern Rockies. They were never able to try again. In 1744 the family lost its trading privileges to the area, and their successor had no desire, in spite of urgings by the government, to waste money and energy on any such wild dream as unprofitable discovery.

About the time the Vérendryes first reached the Mandan villages in the north, the Comanches to the south began evincing a more friendly attitude toward French traders from Illinois. Taking advantage of the softening, another family group, the brothers Peter and Paul Mallet, in 1739, hired six men and started with a barge load of merchandise up the Missouri River, hoping it would lead them to Santa Fe—this at the same time that the Vérendryes were wondering whether they could reach the same destination by going *down* the river!

The Mallets' misconception arose, like the Vérendryes', from errors perpetrated by the mapmakers of the time. One mistake placed Santa Fe farther north than it actually was. Another, confusing the Platte and the Missouri, showed a single river flowing due east along the Platte's course. An inevitable corollary followed: Santa Fe was close to the headwaters of the Missouri.

After the Mallets had struggled against the current almost as far as the present border of South Dakota they realized something was amiss. The river led persistently northwest—north of even the mapmakers' Santa Fe. They questioned Indians, who pointed southwest. After trading part of their merchandise for a string of pack horses, they angled off across the treeless plains, grumbling, as many after them would do, that they could find no fuel for fires other than dry round cakes of buffalo dung. In trying to cross one flood-swollen stream, they lost seven loaded horses. With the skimpy remnants of their goods, the traveling storekeepers forged ahead to the Arkansas and turned west.

On July 5 they reached, somewhere in eastern Colorado, a village of Comanche Indians, who not only welcomed them but even lent the white men a captive Arikara who knew the way to New Mexico. A day or two later the eager party glimpsed the dim blue lift of what they called the Spanish mountains, dominated to the southwest by two magnificent cones still known as the Spanish Peaks—or, as the pantheistic Indians said, Huajatolla, Breasts of the World. They were the first white men definitely known to have reached the Rockies by crossing the plains. Although the

Front Range ran as far north as their wondering eyes could see, there is no record that suggests that either the Mallets or their contemporaries ever supposed a possible connection between the Spanish Mountains and the snowy peaks that the brothers Vérendrye were destined to glimpse three years later.

The Mallets spent the winter in New Mexico. On their return to the Louisiana frontier they created a sensation, for the Plains tribes had formally laid down their arms and the way to Santa Fe was open. Four of the Mallet group were delegated to guide a party of treaty makers to New Mexico and establish commercial relations. Quarrels and an inability to procure horses halted the group at the edge of the plains. Other, unsanctioned, parties won through. Some were composed of unlicensed traders; some were deserters from military outposts. Their general mode of operation was to find a village of Comanches, hunt with them for a while, and then tag along when the Indians rode to the annual summer fair at Taos to trade buffalo hides and captive slaves for knives, horses, and gunpowder.

Spanish merchants from Chihuahua, who had paid for their trading licenses, objected to the intrusion. Spanish officials in Mexico City, ever suspicious of outsiders, fidgeted uncertainly, especially after reports reached them of increased French activity in Texas. In 1752 the viceroy slammed the door. Unhappy victims of the sudden order were Jean Chapuis and Luis Feuilli, who had just arrived in Santa Fe with elaborate plans for systematizing the prairie commerce. In spite of their protest that trade had been unrestricted for more than a decade, their goods were confiscated and they themselves were sent in chains to Mexico and eventually to Spain.

In 1763 the French ceased being a threat. As a result of complex political and military maneuvering in Europe, their nation was swept out of North America. England acquired what became Canada. Spain received Louisiana, a name that in those days spread across the entire western drainage of the Mississippi Valley, and now she owned everything between the Father of Waters and the Pacific, save for the unknown lands of the far northwest.

It was a fantastic area, cloaked by miasmas of ignorance, and Spain was not quite sure how best to protect it. The English were aggressive. Eager to exploit the new land, English fur men were pushing west from the Great Lakes and south from Hudson Bay. As the jittery dons studied their inaccurate maps it occurred to them that a hostile army landing surreptitiously on the shores of Hudson Bay could march undetected to New Mexico, snap up Santa Fe, and sweep ahead to the silver mines of Mexico. Equally frightening, on paper, were the Russians, newly established in Alaska and inching southward. Unchecked, they too might roll on to the same destination.

During the next decades the Spaniards devised a series of ill-coordinated countermoves. Mariners were sent up the Pacific coast toward Alaska with instructions to make frequent landfalls, claiming everything in sight. California was ordered settled. Overland routes from Canada were to be blocked by posts strung along the Missouri. Santa Fe, the one city near the center of this proposed activity, was to become a communications hub. From her presidio, trails were to be opened to Texas, to St. Louis on the Mississippi, to California, and to the busy ports of mine-rich Sonora. Some theoreticians even argued that New Mexico was the logical place from which to supply the proposed settlements in California.

One major obstacle in the way of implementing this enormous concept was Spain's own self-created ignorance, a Frankenstein sprung from her refusal to collate the meager bits of geographic information possessed by her own frontiersmen. No one seemed to recall what Cárdenas had learned about the Grand Canyon, what Oñate had experienced in marching to the Gulf of California, what the Mallets had told about the plains separating New Mexico from the Missouri River. Policy makers underestimated not only distances but the possibility of major interruptions by the canyons, deserts, and mountains. Yet in spite of the handicaps, some extraordinary results were achieved.

Sailors enfeebled by scurvy established shadowy claims to the Northwest coast. Soldiers and friars groped into California. Paramount among the military men was taciturn, hard-bitten Juan Bautista de Anza, Indian fighter and frontiersman of Sonora. In 1774 Anza worked out an overland road from northwestern Mexico to Monterey, and a year later proved its practicality by conducting 240 colonists across it, more than half of them children. Having located the settlers at Monterey, Anza continued north and selected sites for two missions and a presidio beside San Francisco Bay.

In the spring of 1775, while Anza was readying his colonists, orders were sent to young Fray Silvestre Vélez de Escalante, stationed then at Zuñi in western New Mexico, to make a preliminary survey of possible routes between Santa Fe and Anza's new settlements. Obediently Escalante rode 46 leagues west to Oraibe, a Moqui village of eight hundred families located atop an almost impregnable, tawny mesa. Ever since Popé's revolt in 1680, during which they had killed three missionaries, the Moquis had clung to their heathen ways. Fearful of allowing an opening of any sort to Spain's persistent Catholics, the caciques of Oraibe told Escalante that he could go no farther.

They did him no harm, however, and let him take a census of the district—7,494 souls, he reported later and added that for their own good they ought to be conquered. During his survey he met an Indian from the Grand Canyon country who said that if Escalante did manage to pass the Moqui villages he would still be faced with "one hundred leagues of impassable road . . . most of it pebble and flint, and water and pasture is [sic] scarce." He would have a better chance of reaching California if he struck north from Santa Fe in order to skirt both the inhospitable Moquis and the unfriendly land.

The shift was authorized. Escalante's senior, Fray Francisco Atanasio Dominguez, was placed in nominal charge of the expedition, but Escalante was both its journal keeper and its true leader. Bernardo de Miera y Pacheco, an experienced militia captain, one-time mayor of Santa Fe, and a self-trained cartographer, was sent along to make maps—in itself a novel attitude on the part of Spanish officialdom. Two men who had accompanied an exploring expedition into southwestern Colorado ten years earlier served as guides for the small group—it numbered twelve men—during the first stages of the journey.

In July, 1776, driving cattle along for food, the Dominguez-Escalante party moved up the Chama River into the foothills of the San Juan Mountains. They swung west past towering Mesa Verde, then bent north again. The cattle were troublesome at times and the guides frequently grew confused, at one point losing the party in the harsh dry canyons tributary to the Dolores River. After breaking out of that cul-de-sac they crawled over one plateau after another, zigzagging erratically in obedience to the terrain but maintaining throughout today's western Colorado a remarkably consistent northward trend.

When they reached the Colorado River Escalante recognized it as part of the same stream that had carved the Grand Canyon far to the southwest.[1] According to the Indians, it headed in a large lake deep in the mountains—today's Grand Lake in the southwestern part of Rocky Mountain National Park. Huge mountains, the Indians added. The explorers could believe that. Eastward at the head of every major valley they had crossed, particularly the Uncompahgre, they had glimpsed magnificent panoramas of snowy peaks. When Miera came to draw his map, he wrote beside that long line of mountains an astute geographical notation:

> This mountain range is the backbone of North America and the rivers which rise from it on the east flow into the North Sea or Gulf of Mexico, and those of the opposite side into that of the South. It is very cold, and for the most of the year is covered with snow.

From the Colorado the party moved on north to the White River and followed that stream into Utah. They crossed the Green, which they did not recognize as part of the Colorado River system, and continued west along the southern foothills of the Uinta Mountains. A pass through the Wasatches led them into the broad Utah Valley, near Utah Lake. From the swarms of Indians who visited them there they heard of Great Salt Lake, a

---

[1] Because of the stream's bordering red cliffs and red water, the mountain Utes were already calling it by a name that in their language meant Colorado, or Red.

scant 50 miles to the north but did not visit it. Like Spain herself, they were running out of energy. Wherever Monterey was, it obviously was farther off than they had anticipated. Ghastly deserts lay ahead; December was at hand; the cold hurt. It seemed more important to hurry missionaries to the Utes than to struggle longer with a trail that had already proved too rough and roundabout to be practical. After continuing a little farther southwest, quarreling among themselves about the future, they abandoned the effort and returned home through southern Utah. There was no follow-up. The Utes received no missionaries, and the opening of a trail between New Mexico and California had to wait for another half century. But there was a map of the area.

Before their reports were in, Juan Bautista de Anza, founder of San Francisco, was appointed governor of New Mexico. The situation there was chaotic. Apaches driven south by the Comanches were fighting desperately to establish themselves in Texas and on westward through southern New Mexico into the Gila Valley of Arizona. Between the years 1748 and 1772, according to one report, they killed throughout the area 4,000 people and destroyed a million pesos' worth of property; in 1771–72 alone they stole 7,000 horses and mules. They paralyzed travel. So long as they and the Comanches roamed unchecked, it would be impossible to connect Santa Fe with Missouri, Texas, or Sonora.

After fruitless years of fighting both tribes indiscriminately, the policy makers came up with a grand scheme. Why not make allies of the Comanches, who liked Mexican trade, and use them for imposing a Spanish peace on the Apaches? The new governor, Juan Bautista de Anza, was charged with executing the plan.

He spent his first several months in office collecting accurate statistics about his province—Miera drew the first reasonable maps of New Mexico for him—and trying to persuade the scattered ranchers to move into central communities that could be fortified. To the Comanches he spoke in soft tones at first, sending emissaries to propose a conference with Cuerno Verde, Greenhorn, the haughty chief of the bands that occupied southern Colorado—"a scourge," Anza described him in one letter, "who has exterminated many pueblos, killing hundreds and making as many prisoners whom he afterwards sacrificed in cold blood." When Cuerno Verde rebuffed the overtures, Anza decided that only a thorough trouncing would make the Indians listen.

In mid-August, 1779, he assembled the strongest force that New Mexico could provide, 100 regulars and 500 ragged militia, Indians and settlers together, wretchedly mounted and badly armed. Before that time forays against the Comanches had crossed the Sangre de Cristo Mountains east of Taos and had moved north over Raton Pass to the Arkansas River. Hoping to catch Cuerno Verde by surprise, Anza took a different route, marching directly north through Colorado's San Luis Valley. Along the way he too studied geography. Like Miera, he recognized the Continental Divide for what it was and correctly guessed that the great red river on its western slope, of which the Indians and his guides told him, was the upper part of the same stream he had crossed four years before on his way from Sonora to Monterey. Like Miera, he too drew usable maps. At long last the geography of the Southern Rockies was beginning to take shape.

To keep the Comanches from seeing him Anza traveled much of the way at night; and although the high-altitude weather was cold, he forbade the lighting of fires that might reveal the column. In what is now called South Park his hungry men fell eagerly on a herd of buffalo and slew fifty of the shaggy beasts in ten minutes. The meat cut into thin slices and partly dried, he ordered it loaded on packhorses and worked out a difficult way across the rough southern shoulders of Pikes Peak. From a canyon bivouac he sent scouts onto "three eminences" to watch the plains. Dust revealed a Comanche "rancheria" (an Indian camp) of 120 tents. A slashing attack on August 31 killed 18 men, captured 64 women and children. The victors also seized 500 horses and enough booty to load a hundred pack animals.

Learning from the vanquished where Cuerno Verde was, Anza marched south to meet him. The chief, learning simultaneously from fugitives of Anza's whereabouts, marched north with an outnumbered force for the showdown. Anza ambushed the Indians in a gully at the foot of the pine-clad mountains that rise dramatically out of the plains southwest of today's Pueblo, Colorado. There were two fights, one in the evening, the other when the sun was just breaking wanly through the clouds after a cold, rainy night. Charging recklessly, Cuerno Verde and a handful of his followers found themselves cut away from the main body of Indians. Dismounting, they killed their horses to form a barricade of the bodies and made, Anza wrote in grudging admiration, "a defense as brave as it was glorious" before being slain. As a memento of that stand, the tallest of the peaks overlooking the battlefield still bears the chief's name—Greenhorn Mountain, 12,334 feet high.

International upheavals kept Anza from following up the victory. Spain declared war on England in order to help the revolting American colonies and withdrew necessary troops and funds from the frontier. Even so, vigorous Anza found plenty to do. In 1780 he was able to impose peace on the Moquis, decimated cruelly by drought and smallpox. In spite of the Apaches, he found a route from Santa Fe to Sonora. He lured the Navajos onto the side of the Spanish and set them against the Gila Apaches.

When the American Revolution ended, he and the governor of Texas were able to resume their campaigns against the Comanche. Finally, in 1786, the once-obstreperous tribe sued for peace. They were so thoroughly beaten, for the time being, that Anza was even able to persuade one Colorado band, the Jupes, to try agriculture. In order to help them start, he sent out thirty workers to build nineteen adobe houses for them just east of today's city of Pueblo, within clear sight of Greenhorn Mountain. The experiment was short-lived, however. Within months the restless Comanches had abandoned the village and had returned to their horses.

The Comanches helped cow the Apaches. The plains quiet at last, Pedro (Pierre) Vial, a French adventurer employed by the Spanish, succeeded, 1787–88, in blazing a trail from San Antonio, Texas, to Santa Fe. Next Vial was ordered to St. Louis. On May 21, 1792, he started east from Santa Fe with only two companions. Indians robbed the trio near the Great Bend of the Arkansas River in southern Kansas and made them prisoners. They were ransomed by a Spanish-licensed French trader from Missouri, and finally reached their destination on October 6.

While in St. Louis Vial must have heard that rough, illiterate Jacques d'Eglise, another French trader licensed by the Spanish, had just come back from pushing higher up the Missouri than any other white man had ever gone: from its mouth to the Mandan villages, which the Vérendryes had found half a century earlier. English traders, d'Eglise reported, were in regular contact with the Mandans. The seeming nearness of their old enemies to Santa Fe startled Spanish colonial officers into a riposte. They authorized the formation of a company which, in return for exclusive trading privileges, was to string posts which the military could use across the western part of the continent. To increase initiative the government also offered a prize of 2,000 pesos, later raised to 3,000, to whoever first reached the Pacific by land.

D'Eglise was not admitted to La Compagnie pour la Découverte de Nations du haut de Missouri, which was formed as a result of his report. But he did receive financial backing from Jacques Clamorgan, one of the directors of the company, and on the strength of that he went stubbornly upstream to trade again with the Indians and to win the prize money.

Harassed by hostile savages, by the continuing need to stop and trade, and by the slack morale that pervaded most Spanish ventures during those days of growing moribundity, neither the company nor d'Eglise came close to the Rockies, let alone the Pacific. Besides, time was running out. Napoleon wrenched Louisiana away from feeble Charles IV of Spain. Then, breaking his promise not to alienate the huge territory, the French emperor sold it to the United States, a vigorous young nation already much more eager to learn what lay on its distant frontiers than aging Spain ever had been.

III

"HONOUR TO OUR NATIONAL ENTERPRIZE"

BETWEEN CANADA at the 49th parallel and New Spain's undefined northern limits, the border of Louisiana Territory was the Continental Divide.[1] But did the United States necessarily end there? No, argued some American diplomats, pointing to Robert Gray's discovery of the mouth of the Columbia River in May, 1792.

The contention was disputed. After leaving the river Gray had encountered a British naval expedition exploring the Northwest coast under command of Captain George Vancouver and had told the Britons of his discovery. A few months later one of Vancouver's men, Lieutenant William Broughton, took his small ship *Chatham* across the foaming Columbia bar. The river was low, and to Broughton its appearance did not match Gray's description of what he had seen during floodtime. Had the Yankee really pushed from the estuary into the river proper? To make sure of his own claims, Broughton sailed a hundred miles up the broad stream, naming landmarks as he went, among them Oregon's spectacular Mount Hood. A little east of where Portland now stands he landed and on October 30, 1792, under the light of a full moon, went through the ritual of claiming possession for Great Britain.

Spain too had claims, based on landfalls made by her mariners during the 1770's as part of her counter to the Russian occupation of Alaska. In 1789 she attempted to reaffirm these rights by seizing the ships of English sea-otter traders in Nootka Sound, Vancouver Island. Insisting that free trade meant freedom to trade or settle in any unoccupied part of the world, Great Britain thundered threats of war. Spain backed down and made restitution to the traders. Obviously the United States could claim similar freedoms for herself, and so neither Gray's nor Broughton's adventures really proved anything in particular, unless and until one country or the other decided to found settlements in the unoccupied land.

[1] The border of Louisiana with Texas, New Mexico, and upper California was disputed until resolved by treaty in 1819.

Settlement entailed lines of communication. Sea routes from the eastern United States around Cape Horn were both time-consuming and dangerous. Partly out of natural curiosity and partly because of an instinctive understanding of American expansionism, Thomas Jefferson decided, on becoming President, to press ahead with his long-standing desire to find a commercially feasible land route across the continent. Before he had the least notion that France might sell all of Louisiana (and while Spanish officials were still administering the province) he began preparations for a major expedition to be headed by his young friend, Captain Meriwether Lewis of the United States Army. Lewis himself added Lieutenant William Clark as a co-commander equal in everything but rank—and even rank would have been equal save for contrary action by the War Department.

Some of Lewis' instructions reflected Jefferson's interest in natural science. The party was to gather as much information as circumstances allowed about plants, animals, fossils, soils, geology, and so on. It was to study Indian life. Equally important, however, were the more utilitarian concerns that developed after this country's unexpected purchase of the territory. What furs lay within the area? Might additional pelts be lured out of British hands and down the Missouri to the United States or via the Columbia to the Orient? Above all, was the character of the land and the disposition of the Indians such that a year-around commerce could be developed between the Atlantic and the Pacific?

Although Jefferson himself maintained an official calm concerning prospects, some of his correspondents felt no such restraint. A famous French naturalist, Count Bernard de Lacépède, on May 13, 1803, wrote the President an ecstatic letter whose contents Jefferson promptly passed on to Meriwether Lewis:

> If your nation could establish an easy communication by river, canal, and *short* portages, between New York, for example, and the town that would be built at the mouth of the Columbia, what a route that would be for the trade from Europe, from Asia, and from America! . . . What greater means to civilization than these new communication routes!

Civilization on the Columbia! To be sure, there might be natural obstacles. In 1791–92 a Hudson's Bay Company trader named Peter Fidler, pressing up the South Saskatchewan, had bumped into a high, bleak range that he called the Stony Mountains, and had followed it south for some distance without discovering a break. A year later Alexander Mackenzie of the rival North West [Fur] Company of Montreal had reached the Pacific well north of the Saskatchewan, and he too had encountered formidable mountains. Both items of information were available to Meriwether Lewis and William Clark: Fidler's data through Aaron Arrowsmith's newest maps, published in London, which showed the Stony Mountains as a single chain lying no great distance inland from the

Pacific; and Mackenzie's through the explorer's own book, issued in 1801—a book which advocated Britain's occupying the Columbia ahead of the Americans on the plea that its navigable waters, the only ones opening into the interior, were necessary for the development of the British fur trade.

No one could say how far south the northern range extended or even in which direction it ultimately led. (Bernard de Lacépède speculated wildly, in the letter already quoted, that Mount Hood on the lower Columbia was an extension of Fidler's Stony Mountains!) Surely the explorers could either skirt the obstacle or find an easy passage through it. After all, did not the Mohawk River of upper New York State open a gentle way through the Appalachian Range?

Lewis and Clark's toiling men carried the image of a single small range with them up the Missouri into central North Dakota. At Fort Mandan, the camp they built in Mandan Indian country for spending the winter of 1804–5, the two leaders sought additional information from every native they could reach, especially the war-loving, far-ranging Minnetarees.

As the primitive maps took shape, drawn in sand with sticks or on buffalo hides with charcoal, the whites began reluctantly to revise their estimates. They were faced not by one range of mountains but by at least three parallel chains, probably more. The situation was not hopeless, however. The Minnetarees said, as nearly as their talk could be deciphered, that the Missouri, bending far south, broke a way through at least the outer barriers. Furthermore, a tribe of Indians living deep within the mountains owned many horses they regularly rode on hunting trips to the buffalo plains. Probably the western Indians would sell enough of the animals for portaging the goods over the ultimate divide to navigable water on the Pacific slope.

The Minnetarees' sign-language designation for the mountain tribe was a weaving motion of the speaker's hand. Lewis and Clark, like many others before them, translated the gesture to mean Snakes. Probably, though, it referred to the way the western Indians wove their huts out of grass and pliant willows. The tribe's own name for itself was Shoshoni.

The Minnetarees fought the Shoshoni whenever possible. A few years earlier, during a raid on a hunting camp pitched where the Missouri divides into three equal branches, they had captured a young girl. Later her owner had lost her in a gambling game to a lecherous old French trader out of Canada, Toussaint Charbonneau, who lived in one of the neighboring Mandan villages. The girl, whose name was Sacajawea, was sixteen or seventeen years old and pregnant.

The captains promptly hired Charbonneau in order to obtain the services of his young wife. True, Sacajawea's baby would be a burden. But the presence of a woman carrying an infant would help convince her shy tribespeople that the whites came in peace. Then, after contact was made, she could interpret while the expedition bartered for the horses it must have in order to cross the mountains. There is no indication that either Lewis or Clark seriously considered that Sacajawea might serve as a guide—and she didn't, a point frequently but futilely made. The myth of so winsome a child-bride, chin up, pointing resolutely ahead to the future is too sugar-coated ever to perish.

On April 7, 1805, thirty-three people set out from Fort Mandan for the west. Twenty-eight were members of the Army of the United States—the two leaders, three sergeants, and twenty-three volunteer privates. Clark had a slave with him, a huge, handsome Negro named York. There were two official interpreters on the roll, George Drouillard, an expert in sign talk who doubled as hunter, and lazy Charbonneau. Not listed, because she drew no pay for her work, was Sacajawea, carrying her two-month-old son in a cradle on her back.

The party fought the Missouri's imperious current for almost two months before the snow-topped mountains slowly took shape in front of them. Although slight breaks appeared in the rampart, the captains ignored them, for the Minnetarees had advised them to follow the river to its source. (Actually, the Indians seem to have spoken also of direct trails through the mountains, but in the process of interpretation the point had been lost. Anyway, where were the necessary horses?) Accordingly, the men weren't disturbed when the Missouri's direction shifted from west to southwest. The exhausting 18-mile portage around thunderous Great Falls was more alarming, for it devoured twenty-four priceless summer days— grim warning of how difficult the mountains themselves might be without horses. Then the river turned due south and they struggled into the jaws of a deep canyon between the Big Belt Mountains and the front range of the Rockies—black granite below, a yellowish-brown rock above. Water filled the channel from side to side. "From the singular appearance of this place," wrote Lewis on July 19, "I call it the *gates of the rocky mountains.*"

Widening somewhat, the canyon grew drab and suffocatingly hot. Setting poles slipped jarringly on the pebbles of the river bottom. When the men had to disembark and drag the canoes ahead with tow ropes, they found that their moccasins furnished no protection against stone bruises and cactus spines. William Clark, hurrying ahead with a few men to try to locate horses, pulled seventeen thorns out of his feet one night by the light of the campfire.

After a miserable week, the constricting walls opened "suddonly to extensive and beatifull plains and meadows which appear to be surrounded in every direction with distant and lofty mountains." Here the river forked into three branches which the explorers named, clockwise from southeast to southwest, Gallatin, Madison, Jefferson. They chose to follow the Jefferson as having the most water and pointing most nearly in the direction they wished.

Hills pinched briefly in on the stream and then fell away again to form a typical, treeless, high-country valley. The sun blazed across the distant snowy peaks. Mosquitoes and eye gnats swarmed voraciously. The swift, shallow stream was split by islands and gravel bars, choked with beaver dams, its banks matted with willow brush. It was not navigable. They dragged the canoes up it nevertheless. What other way was there to transport equipment for thirty-three people and the trade goods that might mean life itself among the Indians?

The coiling stream forked again. They chose the shrunken channel called Beaverhead. Obviously they would not be able to move the canoes much farther. Where were the Shoshoni? They had to have horses. They had to have directions.

A hunting party had already spotted the whites from a distance. Fearing Blackfeet, the Indians set fire to the drying grass as a warning to the rest of their band and fled back across the mountains. Because of the smoke the captains surmised part of what had happened. Was the size of their group responsible for the shyness of the natives? In desperation Lewis decided to push ahead with only three men.

The first lone rider they saw fled from them, but two days later, on August 13, in a narrow, twisting ravine on the Columbia side of what is now called Lemhi Pass, they managed to lay hold of "an Elderly woman and a girl of about 12 years old." Lewis calmed their terror by giving them beads and pewter looking glasses, and by painting "their tawny cheeks with some vermillion which with this nation is emblematic of peace." Through this astounded pair he eventually made contact with a village of half-starved Shoshoni led by a chief called Cameahwait.

They were a wretched people. "I really did not untill now think," Lewis wrote after being with them a few days, "that human nature ever presented itself in a shape so nearly allyed to the brute creation." Contrast intensified the poignancy of the Shoshoni's situation. In the days before horses they had held their own against the Minnetarees and Blackfeet, ranging the plains on foot far north into Canada. After obtaining Spanish horses through trade with the Utes and Comanches they had become, for a brief time, invincible. Then the Blackfeet had obtained guns from English traders. The Shoshoni had been driven in terror far into the mountains, where hunting was poor. When the salmon appeared each summer in the headwater streams west of the Divide they lived on fish. Otherwise they had to venture timorously after buffalo, enduring dreadful losses whenever the Indians of the plains happened to catch them.

Lewis, who could communicate with Chief Cameahwait only through his own amateurish and Drouillard's professional sign language, of course did not learn all this background. But he saw plainly enough what their primitive weapons reduced them to. A climax of sorts came when Drouillard, having shot a deer, began butchering it to divide among them. Unable to control themselves, the famished savages fell on what the white man was throwing away—raw, uncleaned liver, kidneys, intestines, devouring them "most ravenously . . . blood running from the corners of their mouths. . . . One . . . had provided himself with about nine feet of the small guts one end of which he was chewing on while with his hands he was squezzing the contents out at the other."

Such hardships would not prevail, Cameahwait told Lewis, "his ferce eyes and lank jaw grown meager for want of food . . . if we had guns[.] we could then live in the country of the buffalo and eat as our enimies do and not be compelled to hide ourselves in these mountains and live on roots and berries as the bear do."

The heartfelt remark let Meriwether Lewis, commercial ambassador for the United States of America, make his sales pitch. After his party had returned home, he would make sure that other "whitemen would come to them with an abundance of guns and every other article necessary to their defence and comfort . . . in exchange for the skins of beaver Otter and Ermin." He added that he and his fellow chief, William Clark, had already persuaded the Minnetarees to promise not to wage war against the Shoshoni (a promise never kept), and he said that he would try to reach similar understandings with their other enemies. "They expressed great pleasure."

None of these things could come to pass, however, unless the expedition kept moving. With such eloquence as he could muster Lewis tried to persuade the Indians to accompany him back east across the Divide with enough horses to carry the goods on to the next navigable water. They grew shy, suspecting trickery, and the best he could do was win a promise from them to come look at the merchandise he had to offer and then make up their minds about selling the necessary animals. Even then the trip was punctuated with continual alarms. He kept them going timorously eastward by promising rewards, sneering at their courage, telling them that a woman of their own tribe was with his people. In the end the lure that prevailed was a chance mention by one of his soldiers that there was "a man with us who was black and had short curling hair, this had excited their curiossity very much. and they seemed quite as anxious to see this monster as they wer the merchandize which we had to barter for their horses."

Along the way he learned from talking to Cameahwait that, although he had crossed the Continental Divide, range after range of mountains still lay ahead, their streams far too rough to be navigated. The only way to go was to follow the difficult trails used by the Pierce-nose (Nez Percé) Indians when riding to the buffalo plains.

This was dismaying news. The long, roundabout horse trail would necessitate more stock for riding and packing than the Shoshoni, eager to be off on another hunt, were willing to sell, even after viewing the merchandise in the stranded canoes. But perhaps the Indians underestimated the abilities of trained rivermen. Clark and some of the party went ahead to check the supposedly impassable canyons. A few more men went with Charbonneau and Sacajawea (amazingly Cameahwait had turned out to be her brother) back to the Indian camp to get a dozen or so horses for the portage across the Divide. Meanwhile Lewis and the rest of the men buried the supplies they would pick up on their return journey, lashed the rest into bundles for the portage, and made pack saddles. They also dressed several beaver skins the soldiers had taken time to trap, in spite of bone-deep weariness, while toiling through the Jefferson's hitherto untouched cornucopia of furs.

Clark sent back word that the howling canyon of the Salmon River, into which the Lemhi ran, was fully as unmanageable as the Indians had reported. With considerable difficulty Lewis managed to purchase seventeen more horses to add to the twelve which the Indians had eventually brought over the Divide for the portage. The total did not amount to even one animal per person, but he had no time to argue any longer. September was at hand and ice was forming on the water each morning. If snow caught the whites in the mountains, any number of horses might prove too few.

They strung out behind an old Indian called Toby, who claimed to know something about the Nez Percé trails across what is now the panhandle country of northern Idaho. Toby bungled things more than they ever realized. Through either ignorance or carelessness he missed the southernmost of the Nez Percé trails, which would have spared them several days' travel; and in the North Fork of the Salmon, which leads to Bitterroot Valley, he strayed from the main route and plunged them into such a maze of down timber, steep hillsides, rocks, and brush that in one day they made only five miles, "with the greatest dificuelty risque &c."

After traversing the Bitterroot to within a few miles of today's Missoula, they met a camp of friendly Flathead Indians and from them learned what they already suspected: direct trails led almost due west from Great Falls to the point where they then were; the laborious semicircle along the Missouri and Jefferson had added scores of unnecessary miles to their ordeal. Actual exploration of these shorter routes would have to await their return, however. Time was short, the ocean far away. After buying more horses from the Flatheads, they followed Toby up Lolo Creek and over still another divide to the heavily timbered headwaters of the Lochsa River, one of the principal forks of the Clearwater.[2]

The Lochsa's canyon, like the Salmon's, was impassable. The party soon left it and struggled up the steep, timbered slopes on the north side until

[2] Lolo and Lochsa are names that appeared after Lewis and Clark's time.

they reached the top of the bordering ridge. Standing there even today one can guess how appalled they must have been at the view that spread in front of them—a labyrinth of rolling ridges and shadowed canyons stretching without apparent limits. The giant hilltop they had climbed coiled bewilderingly, sagged into deep saddles, rose to great round knobs, sent off laterals so huge that a stranger could not distinguish the main ridge from dead ends.

There was a trail of sorts along the hill's spine, but it was unimproved and hard to relocate after dizzy detours around thickets and mats of tumbled trees. Early wet snowfalls soaked the riders through and made the dim path still harder to find. Horses fell. Game was short; each night the men went hungry to bed and awoke ravenous with only emergency rations to sustain them. They had started the crossing weary from their ordeal with the canoes along the Jefferson. Soon the greater ordeal of the ridges exhausted them totally, and for the first time on the long trip morale threatened to crumble.

Clark, riding desperately ahead, came down out of the high mountains to a village of Nez Percé Indians, bought pack loads of dry salmon and camas roots, and sent them back to those behind. The gorged joyfully—then were cramped and dizzied by some ptomaine-like sickness. Weak though it left them, they were able to build canoes. Entrusting the horses to the Indians, they launched themselves toward the Pacific.

When they returned in the spring the animals were still there. After a restless wait for the snow to melt and the grass to start growing, the home-hungry explorers again bulled across Lolo Pass. On July 1 they emerged into the Bitterroot Valley, killed a deer, and feasted.

There the party split. Clark returned with the bulk of the group, including Sacajawea, by an easy trail through the Big Hole Valley to the head of the Jefferson. After retrieving the material cached there, he descended to Three Forks, turned up the Gallatin, and then crossed today's Bozeman Pass to the Yellowstone, which he explored to its junction with the Missouri. Lewis meanwhile went east up the section of Clark Fork later called Hell Gate because Blackfeet raiders slipped through its dark canyon on their way to raid the mountain tribes. Leaving Clark Fork, he jogged along what is now the Big Blackfoot River, crossed the Divide at misnamed Lewis and Clark Pass (Clark never saw the gap) and cut north to Sun River, which led him to Great Falls.

He knew the short way across the country now—but it was far too long and difficult to be commercially feasible for bulky goods. Only one assignment remained, to learn whether Saskatchewan furs could be brought down a northern tributary of the Missouri into the United States.

They couldn't be—the Marias River, which he and three other men explored, did not lead far enough north. As the quartet were returning in disappointment toward the Missouri they encountered eight warriors of the

Piegan tribe of Blackfeet. Though intensely suspicious of each other, the two groups camped together that night. While they sat around the fire, Lewis in all innocence told the Blackfeet that he had been bringing peace to the western tribes, promising them trade. Earnestly he added his wish that the Piegans too would trade with the whites and the other Indian tribes in amity.

The mountain Shoshoni, Flatheads, and Nez Percé, yearning desperately for cloth and knives and guns, had listened ecstatically to that kind of talk. The Blackfeet, who could obtain guns from the British, did not. Arms for the enemy! What, then, became of their mastery of the high plains and intermountain vales? No, the western tribes should not have guns! And besides, the horses and weapons of the outnumbered white men looked like tempting booty.

Pressed by Lewis, the eight Piegans muttered that peace was a fine thought, but what of the relatives they had lost recently to the enemy? Undisturbed by their lack of enthusiasm and forgetting, evidently, the warnings the Nez Percés and Flatheads had given him concerning Blackfoot treachery, Lewis at 11:30 turned the watch over to one of his men and fell "into a profound sleep."

In the first dim light of dawn the Piegans struck—clumsily. The whites recovered from the surprise, fought back, and killed two. The survivors fled pellmell, leaving their horses behind, to carry word to their tribesmen not just of a humiliation that needed revenge but also of traders who next summer would be seeking their foes.

And so the great crossing left several of Jefferson's hopes unrealized— universal Indian peace, a fur route to the Saskatchewan, a commercial waterway to the Pacific. Its accomplishments were extraordinary, nevertheless. The explorers had found the richest beaver country within the nation's borders. They pointed out that these furs could be transported on Indian horses to the Columbia and transshiped to the Orient at far less cost and effort than British furs could be sent to the same destination through either Montreal or Hudson Bay. Of course, if the British controlled the Columbia, *they* could use it as an outlet for *their* western furs—the unspoken implication being that perhaps the British shouldn't be allowed to have the Columbia.

Most important, the expedition brought to the young nation a great sense of pride and the first bits of true understanding about the northern reaches of the continent. Dr. Samuel Mitchill, one of the men who had helped Lewis gather information before the launching of the expedition, expressed the feeling of his contemporaries when he wrote that the trip was "a rare performance. It does honour to our national enterprize."

Much still remained, however. Because their route of necessity had led as nearly east and west as they could travel, Lewis and Clark had had no opportunity to investigate what lay north or south, and when they tried to use guesswork and Indian sign talk for filling the gaps they erred egregiously. Their preconceived idea that neither long distances nor rough mountains separated the upper Missouri drainage from New Mexico was confirmed, in their minds, when they noticed Spanish horses, Spanish bridle bits, and even two Spanish coins among the Shoshoni and Nez Percés. On seeing the Willamette, which floods north along the western slopes of the Cascade Mountains in central Oregon, they surmised that it too must rise somewhere in the central Rockies in the "short" gap between the Missouri and Santa Fe.

During the early years of the nineteenth century, when the United States and Spain were pushing each other toward the brink of war, Spanish officials were alarmed by thoughts of the same sort of compression. On learning that a detachment of the United States Army was actually marching up the Missouri under an officer whose name was rendered either Captain Merry or Merry Weather, the Marqués de Caso Calvo wrote an urgent warning from New Orleans to the commander of the Internal Provinces at Chihuahua, Nemesio Salcedo. The invaders, Caso Calvo said, almost surely would cross the boundary into New Mexico. As soon as they did they must be arrested in order to prevent their establishing posts on the Pacific and bringing about the "ruin and destruction of the Provincias Internas."

The instructions reached Salcedo too late in the spring of 1804 for him to do anything about Meriwether Lewis. Besides, he was worried over intruders much closer to home—St. Louis Frenchmen who had started west as soon as they could make arrangements for the trip after learning that the United States had acquired Louisiana Territory. Among them were Jeannot Metoyer, Joseph Gervais, and their leader, Baptiste LeLande, who had been outfitted for the trip by William Morrison, a merchant of Kaskaskia, Illinois. There was also a certain Laurent Durocher, about whom little is known. And finally, traveling perhaps with a separate group, there was Jacques d'Eglise, who had been the first white man to ascend the Missouri from St. Louis to the Mandan villages in North Dakota and who afterwards had tried unsuccessfully to continue to the Pacific.

In 1805 Apaches brought in three more—Dionosio Lacroix, Andrés Terien, and (odd name in that grouping) James Purcell. Purcell, a Kentuckian, was the first American known to have crossed the plains to the central Rockies. He did it unintentionally. After an adventurous but unprofitable time hunting around the headwaters of the Osage River in northwestern Arkansas, he had fallen in with a trader bound up the Missouri and had signed on for the Mandan villages. He was an independent soul, however, and soon wanted to strike west on his own, assisted by Lacroix and Terien. The trader agreed, staked them to traps and ammunition, and sent them on their way. Set upon by a war party of Sioux, they fled up the South Platte River into mountain-cupped South Park. There, according to Purcell's own telling, he discovered gold. Quite possibly he did. At least gold was there; more than half a century later quantities of it would be taken from the streams of South Park during Colorado's first gold rush.

While in South Park the trio were captured by Kiowas. Escaping, they reached Apaches, who took them to Santa Fe. Neither they nor the French who had arrived earlier were jailed, but they were not allowed to leave the province and had to earn their own living. Purcell, after recovering from his body-wrenching experiences, set himself up as a carpenter. Jacques d'Eglise's career is unknown, except its ending: in 1806 he was murdered by two Mexicans who later were shot and then hanged beside the public highway for their crime.

Baptiste LeLande, who had been equipped by William Morrison, and Laurent Durocher journeyed to Chihuahua to appeal for their freedom. It was not granted. Returning to Santa Fe, they were put in charge of Pedro Vial, the first man to open a trail to St. Louis from Santa Fe. With Purcell's companions, Lacroix and Terien, they were sent onto the plains to turn the Pawnees against any Americans who tried to come that way. Apparently the French were chosen for the mission because they knew the Pawnees, but they did not prove helpful. They whispered to the Indians that the Americans were really a more generous people than the niggardly Spanish. They did little harm, however. An unidentified war party attacked them; although they won the battle, it left them short of ammunition, so that Vial called off the trip and returned to Santa Fe.

While the Spanish were still exercised over these private adventures they learned, early in 1806, that another detachment of United States soldiers, this one commanded by a Lieutenant Zebulon Pike, was preparing to march directly west toward Red River just across the mountains from Taos. Rich, dapper Facundo Melgares was ordered to stop the threat. With uncharacteristic dispatch he marched forth in the summer of 1806 at the head of 600 soldiers equipped with 2,075 horses carrying supplies for six months. (Pike had twenty-three men.) Soon half the Spanish force were sent back because of lame mounts and mutinous dispositions. With the rest Melgares angled north across Kansas, sweeping up every trader he could find, although this was United States territory. Reaching a Pawnee village near the Nebraska line, he discovered that he had been too prompt; his quarry had not yet appeared. His undisciplined men were too restive for him to hold them longer. Giving the Pawnees some Spanish flags and medals and urging them to stop any interloping Americans, he marched his grumbling soldiers south to the Arkansas River and west along it toward home.

Pike, who had been holding peace councils with various tribes, reached the Pawnee village about a month later, in late September. When the Pawnees told him to go home, he coolly defied them and followed Melgares' course south to the shallow Arkansas. There he sent five of his party downstream with dispatches. The other eighteen turned resolutely west, deliberately following the trail of several hundred armed troops who, they fully realized, would gladly make captives of them all.

Pike probably wanted to be captured. For a century and a half an aura of mystery has clung to his expedition and perhaps always will. What was he after? Jefferson had made no plans for an examination of Louisiana's disputed border with New Mexico, although he did approve of Pike's expedition after learning of it.

The exploration had been initiated by General James Wilkinson, who in 1806 was functioning both as the commanding general of the Army of the United States and as governor of Louisiana Territory. Wilkinson (it is now known) was also in the pay of Spain. He seems to have been involved, to some indeterminate extent, in Aaron Burr's nebulous scheming about the Southwest. Since no one knows what Burr intended, no one can be sure about Wilkinson's role, if he had a role. If there was a conspiracy involving New Mexico, then perhaps the plotters wanted statistics that would help a filibustering expedition attack the province. It is equally possible, however, that Wilkinson dispatched Pike on an honorable spying mission to gather information that would be useful if the army was called on to fight Spain along the distant frontier.

Pike's official instructions told him to be scrupulous about boundaries. In 1806 the United States was insisting that the upper Red River was the dividing line between Louisiana and New Mexico. So that Pike could tell where the Red lay, he was given a Spanish-derived map that purported to show the sources of the stream in the Sangre de Cristo Mountains east of Taos. The original of that map had been prepared three years before in Mexico City by a famous scientist, Alexander von Humboldt. In drawing it, Humboldt had relied on information derived from Bernardo de Miera y Pacheco, the cartographer who had gone into Utah with Escalante and who later had drawn maps of New Mexico for Anza. On his maps Miera clearly labeled the river rising east of Taos as the Red, which was its local name. Today it is called the Canadian.

The Canadian runs into the Arkansas. As long ago as 1740 the Mallets had learned as much. (The Canadian River may even have received its name from the French-Canadian Mallets.) In Miera's time, however, no one in Mexico remembered the Mallets. Hearing the name Red, most people surmised that it was the upper part of the same Red that runs into the Mississippi below Natchez. That Red, however, heads in the Texas panhandle, far east of the mountains.

Humboldt had paused in Washington on his way back to Germany and had let officials there see his yet unpublished map. Somehow Burr got hold of a tracing. He passed this on to Wilkinson. Wilkinson gave a copy to Pike, with instructions that Pike should try to discover the sources of the

Red. Since the map indicated that the Rockies consisted of more than a single range of hills, Pike quite naturally concluded that the Red, which he knew to be a large river at its mouth, might rise inside the front range. As Donald Jackson, a close student of the expedition, points out, this map-based misconception probably explains many of Pike's otherwise incomprehensible actions in the southern Rockies.

What secret instructions Pike may have received (if any) are unknown. But once he had found the Red he could easily find Santa Fe, or so his map suggested. If he chose not to cross the line, then his surgeon, John Hamilton Robinson, could. Young Dr. Robinson, a nephew of Alexander Hamilton, was a last-minute addition to the party, a volunteer who carried with him authorization from William Morrison to collect money owed Morrison by Baptiste LeLande for trading goods furnished in 1804. This power of attorney from Morrison might enable Robinson to justify an appearance in Santa Fe. Either he (or Pike, if circumstances warranted) could then go about gleaning information, to be put to whatever use Wilkinson intended.

Although Zebulon Pike had taken a hard trip to the headwaters of the Mississippi the year before, he was not well fitted for his new assignment. In 1806 he was twenty-seven years old—five years younger than Meriwether Lewis, nine years younger than Clark. He lacked Lewis' scientific training and Clark's easy adaptability to wilderness conditions. His men were not nearly as capable as Lewis and Clark's. The soldiers who went up the Missouri were all volunteers; unsatisfactory personnel were weeded out during the early stages of the trip and sent back down the river. Since Pike's journey was classed as a military reconnaissance rather than an official exploration, he accepted, to an extent, whatever men were assigned him. "Damned rascals," he had called some of them on the Mississippi the year before, and their quality had not improved.

He did have certain attributes to compensate for his shortcomings. He was intensely ambitious to succeed—he was jealous of Lewis and Clark— and he had an abundance of bulldog determination. Although October was at hand and ice was running in the Arkansas; although he and his men were equipped with only light summer uniforms, he never hesitated about striking for what he knew from the map were high mountains. If he did not expect to reach Santa Fe before winter was over, then he must have been either very brave—or very foolhardy.

Early in the afternoon of November 15, Pike, who was in advance of his men with Dr. Robinson, distinguished off to his right a mountain which appeared like "a small blue cloud. . . . When our small party arrived on the hill they with one accord gave three cheers to the *Mexican mountains.*" He called the dim summit—it was about 120 miles away across the cold brown plains—simply "Highest Peak" or, at times "Grand Peak." Decades later it was officially named Pikes Peak.

On November 23, after a humiliating brush with Pawnees who pilfered a number of useful tools from the small group, Pike reached a point where sandy Fountain Creek joined the Arkansas after winding southward parallel to the Front Range of the Rockies. To the northwest the highest peak loomed tantalizingly, apparently only a day's hike away. What a magnificent lookout its summit would afford! Leaving most of the men behind in a small log breastwork, Pike, Dr. Robinson, and two privates set off in their light clothing to make the ascent. Height, distance, and the roughness of the intervening foothills deceived them. After three and a half cold days, including a snowstorm, they gave up and turned back to the breastwork, prepared to push diligently on to the sources of the Red.

Near present Canon City, where the gigantic Royal Gorge of the Arkansas burst through the Front Range, Pike halted in perplexity. The river seemed to split into three branches, much as the Missouri had divided in front of Lewis and Clark at Three Forks. Which was the proper way?

He sent out reconnoitering parties. The scouts who followed the main river into the narrow canyon, its tawny granite walls a sheer half mile high, reported the way impractical for horses, which indeed it was. They said also that the stream dwindled to a mere brook. From the vantage point of today's armchairs this seems an inexplicable observation, unless the frozen river somehow looked much smaller than it actually was—or unless the men were trying to dissuade their stubborn commander from entering so terrible a chasm.

The same scouts also reported that the Spanish trail led up a nearby dry valley to the northwest. This was another strange observation. Although Pike had missed the fact, Melgares and his dragoons had turned southwest some distance downstream, and the trail Pike had been following through intermittent snowfalls must have been made by Indians. Now he was being told that the Spanish trace turned northwest, away from Santa Fe, unless his map was wildly wrong. Very odd . . . but on the assumption that Melgares was still ahead, Pike determined to follow.

Passing behind his Highest Peak, within a few miles of future Cripple Creek, he reached another frozen river. This one flowed northeast, "the occasion of much surprise, as we were taught to expect to have met with branches of the Red river, which should run south east. Quere. Must it not be the headwaters of the Platte?"

It was. How, then, did he reach the Red? With growing uneasiness the party turned up the South Platte, its hungry, sore-backed horses so enfeebled that every other day or so the men had to abandon one or more animals. Eventually they worked west out of South Park into a broad north-south valley bordered on the west by lofty white summits. The Red surely! Now to find its sources! With two men Pike marched an indeterminate distance north—probably not quite as far as present-day Leadville— climbed a snowy point, and saw what he took to be the stream's headwaters. On his maps and in an official report, but *not* in his daily journal, he indicated that he had also seen, from some point or another in the area, the beginnings of the "Pierre Jaun"—the Yellowstone. What led him to this misconception no one can say. For in reality the Yellowstone rises hundreds of miles away in the northwest corner of Wyoming.

He rejoined the main group. After a cold, hungry Christmas Day, he led the ill-clad men down the Red, as they supposed the stream to be. Soon they ran into the upper end of the Royal Gorge. After dividing into eight small groups and struggling terribly to get out of the canyon and over the bordering hills—"many of our horses much wounded in falling on the rocks"—they emerged onto the plains, totally dismayed. Their supposed Red was the Arkansas; their long agony had brought them right back to the point at which they had left the river.

The hard-used horses could cross no more ranges. Retreating to the junction of Fountain Creek and the Arkansas, Pike had the men erect "a small place for defense and deposit." There he stored his baggage and left the horses, appointing two unhappy men to watch the property until relieved. Loading 70-pound packs on their backs, the remaining sixteen slogged west and then southwest, across the northern part of the Wet Mountains, through Wet Mountain Valley, between two soaring peaks of the upper Sangre de Cristos, past cold dunes of sand almost as white as snow, and down onto the floor of the broad San Luis Valley. They froze their feet. They grew famished but always managed, with heart-wrenching suspense, to kill game at the last minute. One man collapsed, then two more. All had to be left in crudely prepared shelters, fortified by chunks of raw meat, to await rescue.

They found another river. The Red! They crossed it into what they presumed to be Spanish territory and stumbled up a western branch, the Conejos, to the nearest timber, a grove of bare-branched cottonwoods. There they built a stout little fort surrounded by a moat of water. It commanded a pleasing prospect: wide meadows covered with "innumerable herds of deer . . . great and lofty mountains . . . luxuriant vale . . . terrestrial paradise."

Pike sent rescuers after the abandoned men—eventually all were accounted for—and then, presumably after consulting the Humboldt map, decided that Dr. John Robinson, armed with Morrison's claim on Baptiste LeLande, should strike out alone for Santa Fe. Robinson began his trip February 7, 1807. Completely alone, he started up the Conejos toward the San Juan Mountains to the west, which is exactly the way anyone depending on the Humboldt map and presuming himself to be on the Red would have gone in an effort to reach the nearest settlement. Fortunately for himself, the solitary adventurer encountered two Indians armed with bow and arrow. Somehow he managed to communicate with them. They put him straight—the Americans were on the Rio Grande, not the Red—and after looking over such trinkets as he possessed, agreed to take him to the nearest town.

From that town, word of his and the other Americans' presence was hurried to Santa Fe. Troops were ordered to march to the Conejos and apprehend the intruders. Pike surrendered gracefully and rode to Santa Fe with his captors, his eyes busy all the while. The suspicious governor impounded his papers but dared not hold an officer of the United States Army as the private traders who had arrived earlier were being held. Escorted by several very agreeable military peers, among them the one who had been looking for him earlier, Facundo Melgares, Pike was sent the long way home—south to Chihuahua and then in a great looping curve through the desert to Texas and eventually to Natchitoches near the Louisiana border.

Although he reached the East more than a year after Lewis and Clark, he managed, because of Lewis' early death and Clark's many distractions, to publish his reports ahead of theirs. He had little to say about beaver, perhaps because winter conditions kept him from noticing what signs there were. What he did dwell on was the high prices which ordinary cloth and hardware brought in New Mexico, a foreshadowing of the economic forces which led in time to the famous Santa Fe trade.

The map he offered with his two-volume book was a bald plagiarism of Humboldt's work, somewhat refined by Pike's delineation of the upper Arkansas, Platte, and Rio Grande. Assuming that the tributaries of the Colorado River, which Humboldt showed flowing southwest from the Continental Divide, were navigable—an observation confirmed to him by "Spanish gentlemen of Intelligence"—he tried to steal a march on Lewis and Clark by saying that *he,* Zebulon Pike, had discovered the "best communication between the Atlantic and Pacific oceans." During the spring runoff small boats could push up the Arkansas into the mountains. A land carriage of two hundred miles, no more difficult than the "public high ways over the Alleghany mountains" would bring freight to the pleasant bosom of the western river. The Grand Canyon, in short, though grimly familiar to Cárdenas in 1540 and to Escalante in the spring of 1777, had been quite forgotten by the Spanish gentlemen of intelligence if, indeed, they had ever made any such statements to Pike at all.

Equally egregious was Pike's declaration that he had found the "grand central reservoir of snows and fountains" that gave birth to most of the major rivers of the mountain west—the Yellowstone, Platte, Colorado, Arkansas, Rio Grande. "I have no hesitation in asserting, that I can take a position in the mountains from whence I can visit the source of any of those rivers in a day." This tidy gathering in of waters seemed to William Clark to confirm his own views about the tightly constricted nature of the central Rockies. From Pike's plagiarism of Humboldt's reworking of Miera y Pacheco, Clark also picked up the notion of a San Buenaventura River flowing from roughly the same area into San Francisco Bay. Additionally, as we have already noted, he extended Oregon's Willamette (he called it the Multnomah) toward the same convenient central reservoir. Thus, though his own great map of the west was magnificently done in many ways and although he modified it each time he talked with some trapper, still the central Rockies remained a mystery, a neat, unreal hub for a grand wheel of misunderstood rivers. Not until the amazing mountain men of the fur trade decades had finished their exploitive, often bloody rambles through nearly every one of the high valleys would the actualities of the country finally fall together into a meaningful pattern.

IV

THE WAR THE INDIANS WON

IN THE cold fall of 1800, stocky, black-haired David Thompson and five half-breed *engagés* of Canada's North West Company led three loaded pack horses into a Piegan village beside the Bow River, somewhere between today's Calgary and the gray, slab-sided peaks of Banff National Park. A buzz of excitement attended the arrival—the first trade goods of the year. The rituals of greeting completed—a passing around of a long-stemmed, stone-bowled pipe decorated with horsehair and feathers, a savory feast, a distribution of a few gift packets of vermilion and tobacco, a swallow or two of rum for the chiefs—the bales of merchandise were opened for display, either in a borrowed leather tepee or in a crude, low-roofed log cabin hastily erected by the *engagés* for the purpose.

There were beads from Italy, blankets and calico from the textile mills of central England, highly distilled rum from the West Indies, tobacco from Virginia, steel traps, iron hatchet blades and silver ornaments made by artisans in Montreal, short-barreled muskets whose lock plates were decorated by the North West Company's curling brass serpent. The assortments had been gathered and baled in Montreal, then carried in 40-foot birchbark canoes up the Ottawa River and through the upper Great Lakes to the company's rendezvous at Grand Portage near the western tip of Lake Superior. There, in July, Thompson and his men had picked up a portion of the wares and had labored with other brigades through lakes and swamps and foaming rapids, through swarms of mosquitoes and crashing thunderstorms, across the dangerous waves of dirty-colored Lake Winnipeg, up the strong North Saskatchewan, paddles driving without rest until the dim peaks at last prickled the flat horizon of the plains, up to the wooden gates of Rocky Mountain House, built one year before, in 1799. October now—and still no rest. Again the bales were divided. Five of Thompson's *engagés* boosted nine or ten bundles onto the three pack horses and off the little cavalcade jogged almost a hundred miles due south, their route forming a long V with the huge peaks that slid obliquely at them from the northwest.

The Piegans came to the display carrying their glossiest pelts. Their dark eyes glittered. They looked and fingered and took their time dickering. Unless they themselves rode to Rocky Mountain House with more furs later in the winter, this scant half ton of goods was the year's supply; an awl instead of painted bone for sewing leather, a brass kettle instead of a tight basket for boiling meat, coarse black grains of powder, shiny bars of lead that could be melted and molded into musket balls for hunting.

They wanted no other tribe to share the bounty, unless they themselves passed the goods on for whatever profit was involved. In spite of their jealousy, however, some one of them told either Thompson or his half-bloods that a handful of Kutenai Indians from beyond the mountains were camped twenty-two miles farther west, out of sight in the trees at the foot of the peaks.

The informants probably spoke with contempt. Like the Shoshoni farther south, the Kutenais had once lived on the rich buffalo plains just east of the Rockies but had been driven by armed Blackfeet back among the crags beside the winding rivers of extreme northern Idaho and south-eastern British Columbia. Though they were a small tribe, they possessed a wealth of horses. The animals, spread northward from New Mexico by Utes and Comanches, flourished on the rolling hills of eastern Washington and in the park-like valleys of the western Rockies. Stray animals collected in large herds. The Shoshoni, Flatheads, Nez Percés, and Kutenais learned to capture them; they even mastered the technique of gelding poor males and keeping the strongest and swiftest for selective breeding. By the close of the eighteenth century the tribes of the northern Rockies owned better horses, perhaps even more horses, than did the Blackfeet of the plains.

The Kutenais swapped some of their better animals to the Blackfeet for a little cloth, some iron, a few guns. They wanted more. In 1795 and on other occasions thereafter they offered the Piegans many horses if only the Indians of the plains would let them ride across Blackfoot land to one of the trading posts on the tributaries of the Saskatchewan. The Piegans steadfastly refused.

Learning of the band hidden in the trees, Thompson determined to reach them. His motives were varied. Unsophisticated Indians were profitable customers. In addition, he wanted to learn about the other side of the mountains. Alexander Mackenzie's great crossing seven years before, in 1793, had not revealed navigable rivers on the Pacific slope of the Canadian Rockies. But perhaps easy passes existed farther south which would enable North West Company traders to pick up their goods from ocean-supplied depots located somewhere along the Columbia and so eliminate the hard, expensive, cross-continent canoe trip from Montreal. Moreover, Thompson was a geographer and surveyor as well as a trader.

Though his zest at times grew tepid, he liked as a general thing to gather knowledge for its own sake. Obviously the Kutenais, who had just crossed the mountains, could point out paths that might lead to much of the knowledge that both he and his company desired.

His goods disposed of in the Piegan camp, he pretended to start back to Rocky Mountain House. As soon as he was sure he was not being followed, he veered west and overtook the Kutenais. There were twenty-six men and seven women, and they owned 110 beaver pelts. Thompson shepherded them to Rocky Mountain House, let them gaze on its wonders, and opened trade. When the Indians started home rejoicing, he sent two French-Canadian half-breeds along to help them slip past the Piegans and to scout out the resources of the transmontane region.

Because of a ferocious trade war in the East with a rival concern called the XY Company, the adventure did not result in the immediate founding of a post among the eager Kutenais. Almost surely, however, there was activity within the mountains. Because western Indians did not understand trapping, the North West Company often sent Iroquois and Abnaki Indians from the East to train them and to trap as energetically themselves as the local inhabitants would allow. These ill-supervised tutors ranged farther than surviving records show. They married at convenience in the nomadic villages, learned smatterings of many languages, and accumulated more geographic data than they were able to coordinate into clear patterns. But they could guide from one point to another—and did in 1806 when the North West Company was at last jarred into making another attempt to breach the Rockies.

The motive for the effort was Lewis and Clark. In 1804, while the American explorers were wintering at the Mandan villages in North Dakota, the Nor'Westers settled their troubles with the XY Company. Profit-hungry after the expensive trade war, the directors of the Canadian firm were eager to cement relations with the western tribes before the Yankees could. Early in 1805, accordingly, they ordered François Laroque to carry a North West Company sales pitch along behind Lewis and Clark to the Rockies (Laroque reached only as far as the northern tip of the Big Horns) and in 1806 instructed Thompson, by that time a full partner in the company, to do the same sort of thing on the western side of the mountains.

While Thompson was returning from Lake Superior to Rocky Mountain House with these orders, his brother-in-law, John McDonald of Garth, helped prepare the way by ordering half-breed Jacques Raphael Finlay, known as Jaco, to cut a usable pack trail across the Divide in present-day Banff Park. During the winter Thompson prepared to follow. He had to work secretly, for by that time the Hudson's Bay Company had built a competing post close to Rocky Mountain House, and he did not want either his white rivals or the Piegans to guess his intentions.

Helped by shaggy, redheaded, 6-foot 4-inch Finan McDonald (no blood connection with John McDonald), the explorer and his *engagés* surreptitiously sledded his equipment upstream to a cache inside the snow-covered mountains. As soon as the ice broke in the spring Finan and five men slipped ahead as far as they could go in a canoe. Thompson followed on horseback with three men, ten loaded horses, his twenty-two-year-old half-breed wife, and their three children. To its relief the vulnerable party did not see a single Piegan. Later Thompson learned that the tribe had swarmed south to the Missouri to block the traders who, Meriwether Lewis had told a party of them on that almost fatal night near the Marias River, would soon be coming upstream to open trade with every western tribe.

The main stream on the far side of the narrow, high-peaked Divide flowed north. Thompson did not recognize it then as the Columbia—the river later makes a hairpin curve around the Selkirk Mountains on its delayed swing south—and in any event his first concern was not to find the ocean but the Kutenais. Building canoes, the party labored upstream through heavily timbered bottomlands to the two lakes, Windermere and Columbia, from which the torrent springs. On a rocky, high-banked point a little downstream from Windermere, the men built a warehouse and some huts in which to live. Thompson named the post Kootanae House.

Before the establishment was finished, two Kutenai Indians brought him a list of written trade restrictions purportedly emanating from an American military expedition camped somewhere on a southern tributary of the Columbia. The Kutenais added other details. There were forty-two Americans in the group and they were a trade threat. As soon as the Nez Percés and Flatheads in the area had learned of Thompson's approach, they had started north to trade with him. A war party of Blackfeet hit them hard and the mountain Indians gave up the trip, veering away to deal instead with the Americans who had just arrived from the Missouri.

Thompson was too busy hunting food to reply to the peremptory American letter. Deer had left the nearby valley for the high country, and the spawning salmon were not fit to eat. Fortunately wild horses abounded in the grassy openings. His hunters shot some, and then he got the idea of trying to capture a few for riding. With a few well-mounted men he charged one herd in "a wild steeple-chase, down hills up others," harried them for four hours, and went home, leaving the wild ones trembling with fright. The next day the men charged them again "with a hunting halloa." The wild ones had no heart left: "Strange to say," Thompson marveled, "a horse with a good rider will always overtake a horse without a rider." He left the captives tied overnight, returned with stout work horses, yoked the animals together, forced bits into the mouths of the wild ones, and soon had them broken.

He outmaneuvered the Piegans almost as adroitly. As soon as the Indians realized where he was, they tried to frighten him away. By that time, however, the fort was too strong to be attacked directly. Nor did a halfhearted siege avail. The whites had ample stores of dry horse meat on hand and were able to get water by lowering kettles over the riverbank during the night. The Piegans next tried to alarm the besieged with tales of big war parties on the march. Thompson retorted that the mountain Indians were gathering in great numbers to help him. In the end the Piegans accepted enough gifts to save face and withdrew.

The day before Christmas the Kutenai messengers reappeared with another letter from the American "military" party. After chiding Thompson for not acknowledging the first set of instructions, the writers warned him that he was on American soil, complained that British traders were arming hostile Blackfeet, and all but ordered him away. Thompson replied, also in writing, that Broughton's explorations of the lower Columbia gave Great Britain first claim to the river and sent the messengers back to his rivals.

To this day no one knows the identity of those forty-two Americans. During their homeward journey in 1806 Lewis and Clark had met at least eleven fur-trading groups pressing up the Missouri as fast as their limited resources and the sullen temper of the river Indians would allow. The explorers' remarks in passing about the fur paradise of the Rockies evidently inspired one or more of these parties to push on up the river to reap the treasure before rivals could appear. Because the hunters did not have proper licenses for the distant country, they probably were secretive about goals and this may help explain why no records survive.

On reaching the Mandan villages of North Dakota, with whom Canadian traders maintained regular contact, the ambitious trappers apparently let the cat out of the bag. Some Nor'Wester thereupon bragged that they were too late, that members of his own firm were already preparing to cross the Divide from Rocky Mountain House—or at least the letter that Thompson received later on stated that information about his whereabouts had been picked up at the Mandan villages. The threat did not deter the Americans. On they hurried, so promptly that the Blackfeet who intended to close the river missed their passage. After crossing the Divide and learning from excited Indian talk that Thompson had also reached the western slope, they tried to frighten the Canadian away, as we have seen, by pretending a military status they did not possess.

When Thompson did not leave, they let the matter drop. Their hands, like his, were full. The Blackfeet located them, attacked, and (according to their second letter to Thompson) wounded one of their men. After that there is only silence.

Thompson, meanwhile, went diligently on with his trading. In April, 1808, he defied the Americans by leading a small canoe party directly south toward them. From sapphire Lake Columbia, deep-cupped among the spectacular mountains, he portaged across a flat meadow to the

Kootenay River, whose southward surge carried his craft swiftly into what is now northwestern Montana.

At present Jennings the river begins a wild horseshoe curve to join the Columbia, first swinging west to Libby, Montana, and then northwest through upper Idaho. Much of the first part of the curve, from Jennings past roaring Kootenay Falls, is deeply canyoned. Thompson's group had a rough time along the stretch, partly because they were weak from hunger. Earlier in the spring they had been so short of provisions at Kootanae House that they had had to eat the post's dogs and consequently had not been able to bring much food with them. They found little game in the growling canyon to fill the void. Gnawed by hunger pangs, they worked out a dangerous portage high along the steep cliffs above the rapids, treading on sharp black stones that cut their moccasins and tortured their feet.

Back and forth they stumbled, carrying their trade goods on their backs, to quiet water below the falls and then bringing up their fragile birchbark canoe, "which was with difficulty preserved from breaking against the rocks." They shot a lean "tiger"—probably a mountain lion—but it was not enough. They plucked black moss from the firs, its strands six inches long and as fine as hair, and baked it Indian-fashion into a kind of bread. Chancing upon the putrefying carcass of a deer, they devoured it avidly, "although we could hardly bear the smell." The tainted meat made them sick. Unable to sleep, they rose at the first glimmer of dawn and paddled another 50 miles downstream to the flats near present-day Bonners Ferry, Idaho. There they found the village of Kutenai Indians for whom they had been looking.

The previous winter Thompson had sent messengers to the Kutenais, urging them to produce pelts to trade for the goods he would bring. Piegans following the messengers had scuffled with the Kutenais; and although one of the raiders was killed, the others had made off with thirty-five horses. Nervousness induced by the episode had kept the Kutenais from hunting diligently, and to top the disappointment, floodwaters from melting snow crippled the rest of the venture. Flatheads and Pend d'Oreille Indians from farther south could not cross the swollen streams to reach Thompson "and thus all my fine hopes are ruined." If there happened to be American fur men in the vicinity to benefit from his frustration, Thompson does not record the fact.

Unable to push his canoe upstream against the flooded Kootenay, he bought horses for transporting his meager 300 pounds of fur and persuaded a few reluctant Indians to guide the party overland back to Kootanae House. It was another miserable journey: rough, soggy trails, dense windfalls, churning streams. In one of the rivers he lost sixty pounds of fur. He added the remainder to the bundles Finan McDonald had gathered near Kootanae House, crossed the Rockies, and paddled 1,500 miles east and south to his company's busy transfer depot at Rainy Lake

House, near today's International Falls, Minnesota. After resting two days at Rainy Lake, meanwhile loading fresh supplies into his canoes, he retraced his route against the current, toiled over the Divide, and turned up the Columbia to his post—a notable summer journey even for a Nor'-Wester.

Again he wintered (1808–9) at Kootanae House. Meantime Finan McDonald and a new clerk, James McMillan, who had accompanied Thompson from the East, built a temporary post near present Libby, Montana. Jaco Finlay and a few half-breeds pushed on south to Clark Fork River. In the spring they reassembled at Kootanae House with their furs and their reports. After assessing results and remembering his own experiences of the previous year, Thompson decided that the fur potentials of the Kutenai country were not worth developing. Farther south, however, in the mountains around Clark Fork from Pend Oreille Lake upward into today's western Montana, prospects were better. Should he not transfer activities there even though competitors from the United States might still be operating in the vicinity?

Although he again made the long summer journey to Rainy Lake, he had no time to send his question from there to the council of partners at Lake Superior and receive an official answer. Quite possibly, however, he did learn relevant information from the mail that was handed him by one of the canoe men who brought his supplies. The year before, John Jacob Astor of New York had incorporated the American Fur Company. In September, 1808, Astor had visited Montreal and had offered to buy the North West Company's trading interests around the Great Lakes and on the still-undeveloped Columbia. The Canadians had rejected the overture. The possibility now loomed that the Nor'Westers would have to wage a trade war with Astor to control the navigable streams flowing from the Rockies to the Pacific.

If Thompson received such information—and no evidence exists that he did—he must have wondered whether it would be wisest for him to press on into Montana or explore the Columbia and lower Clark Fork in order to learn what possibilities they offered as trade routes. In hindsight it would seem that the Columbia was the important point.[1] On reaching the eastern foot of the mountains, however, Thompson received a surprise that gave his Montana plans a new urgency. He encountered Joseph Howse of the rival Hudson's Bay Company, who had just returned from following Thompson's tracks into the mountains to learn what the Nor'Westers were up to beyond the Divide.

[1] The company may have been counting on Simon Fraser to work out a feasible route to the ocean. In the summer of 1808 Fraser explored the river in British Columbia that now bears his name. He soon discovered that its canyons were far too rugged ever to be used as highways to the mountains and that the Columbia offered the only opening. It is not likely that the council heard this news in time to notify Thompson, however.

The meeting alarmed Thompson. He had been a partner in the North West Company since 1804, and he knew the store his hard-fisted associates set by the profits which they divided annually among themselves with little provision for the future. Under the circumstances he may well have thought that his most pressing task was not to explore the Columbia (where he supposed Simon Fraser was) but to consolidate his mountain trade ahead of both Joseph Howse and the Americans already pressing in on him.

Whatever his reasoning, he did hurry south to the mouth of Clark Fork River. On a handsome bit of ground that sloped gently toward the eastern shore of Idaho's Pend Oreille Lake, his men whittled out ax handles, fitted them to the blades they had brought along, and built a house of upright logs, French-Canadian style, roofing it with small logs, grass, and mud—a drippy, uncomfortable expedient, as they discovered the next spring when melting snow leaked through.

While the post was building Thompson explored. The lower Clark Fork was not navigable. He turned upstream and by November, 1809, he knew where he wanted to locate next—some 60 miles up the Clark Fork on a meadow a short distance above a foaming cataract today called Thompson Falls. There, where he had an unobstructed view along the lovely U-shaped valley, its sides of dense evergreens punctuated by tawny cliffs, he built a post he named Saleesh House.

He liked the Salish, or Flathead, Indians. They were clean and handsome; their ethical standards corresponded to his own. "[They] set a high value on the chastity of their women," he reported; "adultery is punished by death to both parties." The necessities of trade could bend moral standards, however. During the winter a delegation of Indians called on Thompson to demand the life of a *voyageur* who had seduced the daughter of the chief called the Orator. To protect the trader Thompson said he would not bring the Indians any more guns unless they gave him another man, in effect a slave, to replace the worker they intended to execute. While they chewed this over, he added to the Orator, ". . . you are noted for being a good gelder of Horses; if this man ever again enters your Tent, geld him, but let him live." Amused, the Indians agreed—and kept the armament flowing.

The Flatheads were wild to obtain weapons. During the winter they brought Thompson enough beaver pelts to buy twenty or so guns and several hundred iron arrowheads capable of piercing the tough bullhide shields of their enemy. Exulting in their new power, they actually began to hope, for the first time in years, that they would meet Blackfeet the next time they went on a hunting trip to the plains. Moreover, they wanted some of Thompson's men to join their excursion—but more of that later.

All this while, from the summer of 1807 through 1809, American trapping parties were operating no great distance away. One was the group that had tried rather clumsily to frighten Thompson off by letter. Another, almost as shrouded in mystery as the first, was a party headed by Charles Courtin, a recently naturalized French-Canadian out of Michilimackinac Island.[2] At least Courtin's end is known. In February, 1810, Thompson, who was wintering at Saleesh House, learned from a party of Flatheads that Blackfeet Indians had killed Courtin and some of his crew 60 miles or so farther southeast, in the open parks near today's buffalo reserve at Dixon, Montana, beside the Flathead River, a main tributary of Clark Fork.

Somehow—the steps are by no means clear—a hunting camp of Flathead Indians wandered into the vicinity, laid hold on the survivors of Courtin's party, and divided up the furs. One of the whites, it seems, managed to reach Thompson and ask for help. Thompson hurried to the Flathead camp, paid the Indians "for Services rendered to the property of the deceased" and for burying him. He gave Courtin's *engagés* the wages due them and in exchange evidently acquired the bulk of Courtin's furs for the North West Company. Swelled by the acquisition, his spring returns overflowed the warehouse at Thompson Falls. He had to move into a tent so that he could store the excess in his dwelling house.

In commenting later on Courtin's death, Thompson wrote that all the early "Traders and Hunters from the United States" had been attacked and killed by Piegans in the treeless valleys of the Montana Rockies, "until none remained"—a three-word requiem to the first American efforts to exploit the western slope of the Rocky Mountains. Coronado's straining for riches was no more futile; Spain's initial incursion at least left records.

Other Americans working farther east did survive—in part. These were the hunters of the Missouri Fur Company, founded in 1807 by Manuel Lisa, a Spanish trader of St. Louis, and by Pierre Menard and William Morrison of Kaskaskia, Illinois. Included in the Missouri Fur Company's roster were four veterans of the Lewis and Clark expedition: John Colter, George Drouillard, John Potts, and Peter Wiser.

John Colter was even more obsessively restless than the other three. As the expedition had been floating homeward down the Missouri in 1806, it had met two Illinois trappers, Joseph Dickson and Forest Hancock, bound upstream. Obtaining a discharge from his captains, Colter faced around and led the trappers toward the mountains he had so recently quit. He chose to follow the Yellowstone branch of the river. Having just descended it with Clark, he knew that it offered the quickest approach to the spurs of the Rockies. He may also have wanted to avoid the main Missouri for fear of meeting Blackfeet out to avenge the two warriors Lewis had slain earlier in the summer.

[2] Possibly, but not probably, the first group of Americans and Courtin's party were one and the same. For recent speculations about the identities of both mysterious groups, see Alvin M. Josephy, Jr., *The Nez Percé Indians and the Opening of the Northwest* (New Haven, 1965), pp. 656–660; and William Goetzmann, *Exploration and Empire* (New York, 1966), pp. 45–46.

Presumably the trio wintered on one of the tributaries that rise south of the Yellowstone in the Absaroka Mountains. Some terrible incompatibility soon tore the new partnership asunder. Years later Joseph Dickson told Peter Cartwright, a famous itinerant preacher of Illinois, that after a heated quarrel Colter and Hancock abandoned him in the wilderness. Alone in deep snow the derelict vowed to become a Christian if spared. His prayers were amply answered. Trapping entirely by himself during the spring thaw, he caught, so the tale runs, between fifteen and twenty packs of beaver. Although the figure is somewhat elastic, one can conclude that he must have harvested about a thousand pelts—say ten a day, which means that he owned a generous supply of traps whose setting required cold, arduous work. Without help, unless Indians chanced by to lend a hand, he skinned each animal, stretched and grained each pelt, and packed them into bales. These he loaded aboard two dugout canoes lashed side by side. Still alone, he started home with a fortune of close to $5,000, a handsome sum in those days when boatmen worked for $120 a year.

This was religious testimony, told for a purpose, and was perhaps exaggerated. Still, there is no question that when spring came the three men were traveling separately. Early in June, 1807, Colter, bobbing down the Missouri in a homemade dugout, met Lisa's Missouri Fur Company men toiling upstream with their keelboats. He joined them and again turned toward the mountains. On June 14 Joseph Dickson landed at the mud huts of the Arikara Indian villages located near today's South Dakota–North Dakota boundary, some 800 river miles above Lisa's laboring boats. On June 22, while Dickson was still at the Arikara villages, Forest Hancock appeared from farther upstream. Both arrivals were duly noted by Charles Courtin, who was there at the time and knew both men. Courtin says that Dickson had furs in his canoe (singular) but he makes no mention of Dickson's almost unavoidable meeting with Hancock, one of the pair who had so heartlessly deserted him. Nor is there any description of a meeting with Colter, for by the time Lisa's party reached the villages Courtin was well on his way toward the Rockies, where he eventually would be slain. What is tantalizing about the omissions are not the details of the quarrel, however—probably it was the result of ordinary cabin fever—but the failure to explain how three men, the first of their race to see that gigantic wilderness, each managed to survive its rigors entirely alone.

Colter's subsequent adventures are equally phenomenal. Lisa's slow-moving party did not reach the junction of the Yellowstone and Big Horn rivers in south-central Montana until early in November. While the rest of the men were chopping down cottonwood trees to build a stockade, Colter put a 30-pound pack on his back and set out to tell whatever Indians he could find that another party of American traders had reached the edges of their country. He was aware of Meriwether Lewis' promise of trade to the Shoshoni and Flatheads. He knew how easy it was to cross Bozeman Pass from the Yellowstone to the Three Forks country and work up the Jefferson's broad valleys until he met one or the other of the mountain tribes. They would remember him and welcome him, surely an inducement. Yet, instead of following the familiar trails, he struck southwest into the Big Horn Basin near today's Cody, Wyoming.

Why? Did one of the other veterans of the Lewis and Clark expedition—Drouillard or Potts or Wiser—take the easy way? Did Colter prefer new ground because Courtin was ahead of him, skimming off the cream of the Flathead country? Had he met Crow Indians during his wanderings the winter before and did he seek them out in the belief that their acquaintanceship with manufactured goods would make them more likely customers than the mountain tribes?

Whatever the reasons, he seems to have worked out a way, on foot, from the stinking hot springs around Cody (they gave the region its brief-lived name of Colter's Hell) into a favorite Crow wintering ground, the upper valley of the Wind River above Dubois, Wyoming. Crows may have led him still farther west over the Continental Divide into Jackson Hole. Possibly he continued on west beside the leaping Trois Tetons for a look at the Idaho slopes before returning to Jackson Hole and hiking north past Yellowstone Lake to a main trail used by Bannock Indians of Idaho in reaching the buffalo plains. Following this trail eastward, Colter regained Lisa's Big Horn post, Fort Raymond, early in the spring of 1808. It was a lonesome, thousand-mile winter walk, one of the most extraordinary hikes ever taken in the Rockies. Unhappily the only record of it is an uncertain line that William Clark later drew onto the inaccurate map of the West that he kept in his office in St. Louis.

Another line on Clark's map represents the tour George Drouillard made in the spring of 1808 southward to the Big Horn Mountains. Drouillard was looking not only for Indian villages but for Spanish settlements as well, for according to Clark's calculations, Santa Fe was relatively near. Nothing is known of that trip either, except that Drouillard found no Spaniards.

Colter's next lonesome foray, taken after only a few days' rest at the fort, led him into the familiar Three Forks country. There he met a hunting party of about 500 Flatheads seeking buffalo. As he was starting with them toward Fort Raymond to introduce them to the wonders of trade, a strong force of Blackfeet struck. The din of the conflict attracted several hundred Crows, who joined the battle with noisy relish. What focused the hatred of the outnumbered Blackfeet, however, was the sight of a white man with their enemies. Wounded in the leg, Colter crawled into a bush and from its thin shelter pumped out balls as fast as he could load and prime his rifle. Finally the Blackfeet withdrew. Casualties on both sides were high according to the wide-eyed recollections of Thomas James who the next year saw "skulls and bones . . . in vast numbers" littering the battlefield.

When Colter recklessly returned to the Jefferson area with John Potts later that year, the Blackfeet caught them. Exultantly they killed Potts and then decided to amuse themselves by stripping Colter naked and ordering him to race for his life barefooted across the stony, cactus-spiked ground, under a burning sun. He outdistanced all his pursuers but one, whom he killed. After eluding the rest by hiding all night in the icy Madison River under a mat of driftwood, he trudged without food or clothing 300 miles back to the fort.

That same fall (1808) a quartet of Missouri Fur Company trappers under Casé Fortin were forced to cache twenty packs of pelts near Three Forks and flee for their lives across the Divide to refuge among the Flatheads—another adventure about which no details are known. Meantime Lisa and Drouillard had made a hurried summer trip to St. Louis. By reorganizing the company Lisa obtained additional financing and strong reinforcements. He was eager to push his exploitation of the mountains. Blackfeet? He brushed the objection aside. A big, quarrelsome party went to Three Forks under Colter's guidance so early in the spring of 1809 that some of the men suffered agonizing snow blindness. After erecting a crude fort, they scattered to trap. Blackfeet hit twice, killing three men and making off with irreplaceable equipment. Among the dead was George Drouillard, "his head cut off," wrote Thomas James, who saw the corpse, "his entrails torn out, and his body hacked to pieces."

Colter had had enough. He and James and others went home. The twenty or so who remained under command of one of Lisa's new partners, young Andrew Henry of the Missouri lead mines, were attacked once again by ten times their number of Blackfeet. Though they killed twenty-two Indians at a loss of only one man, they were afraid afterwards to scatter out in the loose formation that successful trapping demanded. Looking for safer ground, they retreated up the Madison River along a trail pioneered the year before by Peter Wiser and crossed an easy pass to what today is known as Henry's Fork of the Snake. Near present St. Anthony, Idaho, they built a few huts and settled down to a wretched winter. Because of heavy snow and almost unceasing spring rains, game was scarce and trapping arduous. Crow Indians stole their horses. Hungry and disgusted, the group scattered. Some headed toward Santa Fe; nothing reveals whether they succeeded. Others, including Andrew Henry, turned east toward the Missouri. Staggered by the piling disasters and by supply and price problems arising from American embargoes against British merchandise essential to the fur trade, Lisa abandoned the post at the Big Horn and tried to consolidate his remaining strength in safer regions near the Mandan villages farther down the Missouri.

As John Hoback, Edward Robinson, and Jacob Rezner of Henry's fragmented group were rowing down the muddy river toward St. Louis they met sixty-five people moving upstream under the leadership of a twenty-eight-year-old St. Louis merchant named Wilson Price Hunt. The untried party was bound for the Columbia as part of Astor's bold plan to capture the fur trade of all western North America. After warning Hunt of the Blackfeet, Hoback, Robinson, and Rezner offered to show the party a shorter way to what they said was a navigable branch of the Columbia, Henry's Fork of the Snake.

Using horses purchased from Arikara and Crow Indians, the party, many of them sick, dragged across the hot plains, over the Big Horn Mountains, into the Wind River Valley. From there they wormed across the Continental Divide at Union Pass. On the headwaters of the Green they paused to kill buffalo and jerk the meat, and promised a band of shy Snake Indians they met that they would soon return to trade knives, cloth, and beads for beaver pelts. Along the rest of the chill way to Henry's deserted cabins, Hunt here and there dropped off small trapping parties, among them Hoback, Robinson, and Rezner, to start furs flowing toward a collecting post called Astoria, being simultaneously founded at the mouth of the Columbia by a party that had sailed around Cape Horn.

Nothing went right. Although Henry's Fork was navigable, as Henry's men had promised, the main Snake was not. Shattered by the canyons through which the river roars in southern Idaho, Hunt's overland Astorians broke apart and by different routes floundered west, lucky to reach Astoria alive. Collecting furs by means of boats on the Snake was obviously impossible. Meantime Indians robbed all the trappers who had been left behind in the mountains and killed some. Although Robert Stuart, returning overland from Astoria to St. Louis with a small party of hunters and malcontents, did find a feasible horse trail through South Pass and down Sweetwater Creek to the North Platte, international politics and then war kept the Americans from developing the route.

The Blackfeet did their best to close the other routes. In 1810 a band of Piegans caught a group of Flatheads in Marias Pass, just south of today's Glacier National Park. They attacked joyfully and ran into a stunning surprise. This was the hunting party that David Thompson had just armed with twenty guns and several hundred iron arrow points. With the Flatheads were three of Thompson's white traders: massive Finan McDonald, crisp little Michel Bourdon, and a clerk called Baptiste Buche.

As soon as the Flatheads heard the Piegan war yells, they forted up behind their baggage. With their guns they easily blunted three horseback charges. Infuriated, the attackers dismounted and tried to lure the defenders into the open by darting forward on foot, taunting the Flatheads and protecting themselves the while by "springing from the ground as high as they could, then close to the ground, now to the right and to the left," as hard to hit with the old-style muskets, Buche said, as geese on the wing. Alexander Henry, the North West trader at Rocky Mountain House beside the North Saskatchewan, heard later that sixteen Piegans died. Thirteen or so were wounded. (The Flatheads lost seven killed, nine hurt.) Their ammunition expended, the attackers finally retreated. It was their first major defeat by mountain Indians in a generation or more.

The Piegans knew where those devastating guns had come from. Hurrying to the North Saskatchewan, they stationed four tepees of warriors beside the crossing at the first ridge of mountains. The rest besieged Rocky Mountain House, not to do harm there lest they lose their own sources of trade, but to make sure no more supplies went across the pass. Their lust for drink betrayed them. Alexander Henry befuddled them with rum and then helped David Thompson, who had been hiding in the woods, work out a new route much farther north, up the Athabasca River through present Jasper National Park, past the Columbia Ice Fields, down under the towering peaks to the western river—a prodigious crossing in the dead of the Canadian winter (1810–11).

The snow along the Columbia was nearly waist-deep and soggy. After bucking it for five days, Thompson gave up and built huts in which to wait for spring. He sent some of his men back over Athabasca Pass for supplies. Most of the rest deserted and followed the messengers. Short-handed, Thompson decided he could not continue down the Columbia to Astor's new post, as he had been instructed to do during his annual summer visit to Rainy Lake, but would have to go first to Saleesh House in Montana for additional men.

Haste did not seem important. He had been told at Rainy Lake that the North West Company had purchased an interest in Astor's Pacific Fur Company and that there would be no competition west of the mountains. Actually the arrangement had fallen through, but he had no way of knowing that. In mid-April, 1811, he and the two men left with him wallowed upstream through slush and flood. When they reached Saleesh House near Thompson Falls they found that Finan McDonald and his crew had deserted the post in fear of Piegan vengeance.[3]

Thinking that Hunt's overland party might come down Clark Fork from the Missouri and expect to find him at Saleesh House, Thompson scribbled a message for them with charcoal on a board, saying that the war with the Piegans had forced him out of the country. Then off to the mouth of the Columbia he went, arriving at Astoria and then turning upstream again into Montana months before Hunt's emaciated men began straggling in from their ordeal in the canyons of the Snake.

Trading parties of the Astorians—competitors and not partners as he had at first supposed—followed him into the western foothills of the Rockies. It was a short-lived effort. Fearful that the War of 1812 would

[3] It was not an idle fear. During the winter of 1810–11 Joseph Howse of the rival Hudson's Bay Company wintered with seventeen men near Flathead Lake a little southwest of present Glacier National Park. Although Howse came out in the spring with thirty-six packs of fur, a good harvest, he reported to his superiors that even those returns were not enough to counterbalance the peril from Blackfeet.

result in the appearance of British naval vessels, Astor's partners at the mouth of the Columbia sold out for what they could get to the Nor'Westers and left the country. At first the acquisition did the purchasers little good. They were deep in their own private war with the Hudson's Bay Company by then and little energy remained to exploit the mountains against the formidable opposition of the Blackfeet.

The worldwide economic and military cataclysms that functioned as unseen allies meant nothing to the Indians. As they saw it, they had defeated two great nations. They had closed the Saskatchewan. They had kept the Hudson's Bay Company out of western Montana. They had driven Lisa's Americans back down the Missouri. In August, 1812, they fought again with the Flatheads and this time they won. Deprived of fresh supplies of ammunition by wartime interruptions to commerce, the mountain tribes grew shy again. The Piegans strutted unchallenged. The northern buffalo plains and the high passes that opened onto the hunting grounds were still their private domain.

V  THE SKIN GAME

WOULD-BE traders and trappers who followed Zebulon Pike's route into the southern Rockies found New Mexico's governing hierarchy less crudely violent but scarcely more hospitable than the Blackfeet. Jacques Clamorgan of St. Louis, a sometime partner of Manuel Lisa, who risked the plains with a few pack horses in 1807; McLanahan's small party of 1809–10; and an 1812 group headed by James Baird, Samuel Chambers, and Robert McKnight were arrested, deprived of merchandise, and jailed for varying terms. In spite of the hostility, however, the magic name Santa Fe continued to ring with a golden sound along the cash-starved frontier.

No one listened more eagerly than Manuel Lisa. He told every hunting party he sent south from the upper Missouri River to stay alert for trails to New Mexico. He was exhilarated therefore when Jean Baptiste Champlain, one of his best brigade leaders, appeared in the summer of 1811 with word that he had penetrated as far as the headwaters of the South Platte within the Colorado Rockies and had encountered Arapahoe Indians who each year were visited by pack trains from Santa Fe. Though Lisa by now realized that New Mexico lay farther away than he at first had supposed, he promptly equipped Champlain with goods designed for the Santa Fe trade and sent him south again.

The experiment was another disaster. While trapping at indeterminate points in the Colorado Rockies, Champlain's group heard through the Indian grapevine that the tribes of the northern plains were growing increasingly hostile toward Americans. Should the trappers risk being cut off from their base by staying away? Eight thought not. Joining a band of Crows, they eventually regained another of Lisa's parties. Four other men decided it would be safer to ride to Taos and throw themselves on the mercy of the Spanish. Champlain and five more stayed in Colorado, drifting forlornly back and forth along the Front Range in hope that Lisa would get a messenger to them with instructions. (Lisa did try—too late.)

Indians picked off three of Champlain's companions. In despair, the starving survivors sought the protection of a village of sullen Arapahoes. In time one of the whites, a free trapper named Ezekiel Williams, decided he'd had enough. Entrusting his furs to Champlain for eventual accounting, he headed alone for his home at Boone's Lick, Missouri—and made it, too, in spite of being held captive for two months by Kansas Indians.

In Missouri, where he made contact with Lisa, Williams learned that the War of 1812 was under way and that Indians inflamed by British traders had driven the Missouri Fur Company off the upper river. Furthermore, Lisa added glumly, he had learned from the messengers whom he had sent in search of Champlain's party, that Champlain and his sole remaining companion had been killed.

What of the furs? A possibility of learning presented itself in the spring of 1814 in the form of one Joseph Philibert, who had decided that, since the northern fur areas were closed by the conflict, he would test the unknown mountains farther south. Williams hired two helpers and went along.

Amazingly, Williams retrieved his cached pelts and after hair-raising difficulties brought them home. Philibert's men were less successful. Intentionally or not, they strayed onto territory claimed by Spain and were jailed in Santa Fe. Philibert had to surrender his trade goods to the officials in New Mexico to pay the expenses of the captivity. On being released in February, 1815, the trappers moved north into Colorado and reaped well enough that they decided to stay one more year. In order to replenish their supplies and obtain horses for transporting their catch Philibert rode to Missouri. He promised the men that he would be back in time for a fall hunt and appointed as a rendezvous the junction of Huerfano Creek with the Arkansas River, 17 miles east of today's Pueblo.

He failed the appointment, for he was delayed in Missouri. When he at last started west on September 10, 1815, it was in company with a well-equipped party commanded by Auguste P. Chouteau and Jules De Mun, members of two of St. Louis's most potent mercantile families.[1] Philibert decided against bucking such a group in the field. As they jogged up the Arkansas, he sold his goods and horses and the contracts of his men to his potential competitors.

No one was waiting at the Huerfano. Indians explained the defection. When Philibert had failed to appear on schedule, his men had bethought themselves of the coming winter and had retreated to Taos, evidently hoping to pay for shelter with whatever furs they had collected. De Mun followed their cold trail up Huerfano Creek to one of the easy passes that

[1] One mildly historic member of the Chouteau-De Mun party was Toussaint Charbonneau, who had gone with Lewis and Clark to the Pacific and whose wife Sacajawea had died three years earlier at Lisa's Fort Manuel, 12 miles up the Missouri River from the Arikara Indian villages.

open from its headwaters through the rugged Sangre de Cristo Range. He
then angled across San Luis Valley to the Rio Grande, and followed the
stream south toward Taos. Along the way he noticed enticing beaver signs,
and when he learned that Philibert's errant men had not been molested in
Taos, he was emboldened to ride on to Santa Fe and ask the governor for
permission to trap the New Mexican streams.

The governor passed the buck to Chihuahua. A long wait began. During
it De Mun returned 800 miles to Missouri for fresh supplies. Chouteau
trapped as far, perhaps, as Colorado's high North Park. When the Americans ventured back toward the border to learn the fate of their request a
new governor ordered them out of Spanish territory. They did not comply
fast enough to suit him. In May, 1817, New Mexican troopers seized
about half the party as it was digging up its cached furs on what the victims
insisted was American soil. (Actually, the boundary was not established
until 1819; but if the line had existed in 1817 Chouteau and De Mun
would have been within their rights.) After being imprisoned in Santa Fe
under unsavory conditions for forty-four days, the Americans were haled
before the governor and his council, violently berated, and turned loose
with a single scrawny riding horse each for returning to Missouri. The rest
of their property was confiscated, a loss of approximately $30,000.[2]

Discouraged by such experiences and by the economic depression that
gripped the frontier after the war, fur men stayed away from the mountains. The government made only feeble efforts to help. In 1819 the Adams-
Onís treaty established the Arkansas River as the border with New Mexico
and thus placed the Front Range of the Rockies clearly in American hands
—if anyone wished to risk going there. Also in 1819 the War Department
started the so-called Yellowstone Expedition up the Missouri to build forts
"for . . . the protection of our northwestern frontier," declared Secretary
of War Calhoun, "and the greater extension of our fur trade."

Mismanagement and the inability of the expedition's steamboats to
breast the river brought the venture to a humiliating collapse near today's
Omaha. An outraged Congress denied further appropriations, and the
project dwindled to Major Stephen Long's "scientific" scouting trip with a
handful of bored riflemen and naturalists up the Platte to the Front Range
and then south to the Arkansas.

On July 13, 1820, on the site where Colorado Springs now stands, the
explorers paused while Dr. Edwin James, the party's botanist, Lieutenant
Swift, and guide Joe Bissonette, formerly of the Chouteau–De Mun party,
attempted to climb the Grand Peak that had stopped Pike fourteen years
before. After floundering upward through thick evergreens and over slippery granite, the three men bivouacked for the first night on ground so

[2] In 1819 the U.S. government assumed the claims of American citizens against
Spain. Eventually the heirs of Chouteau and De Mun recovered the sum and interest
—some $81,000.

steep that "we were under the necessity to secure ourselves from rolling into the brook by means of a pole placed against two trees." The next day they slogged past the weather-runted trees at timberline onto enormous fields of slide rock, crusted here and there by congealing patches of snow. Though a cold wind numbed them, Dr. James was enthralled: "a region of astonishing beauty . . . low but brilliantly flowering alpine plants." At four in the afternoon they climbed, thoroughly winded, onto the summit. After admiring the panorama for an hour, they raced darkness back to the timber and another hungry bivouac. It was the first recorded ascent of a major peak in the Rockies. In honor of the feat Major Long named the vast massif James Peak. Trappers insisted in calling it after Pike, however, and in the 1840's Frémont made the stubborn folk name official: Pikes Peak, the most famous single mountain within the United States.

On the Arkansas River, Long's party divided. Captain John Bell led some of the men eastward down the stream. Long and the others continued south in search of what Pike had failed to find, the headwaters of Red River. The major thought he had succeeded when he stumbled onto the Canadian, which the New Mexicans did call Red. To their discomfiture, the "discoverers" came back to the familiar old Arkansas in what today is the eastern part of Oklahoma.

Not far up the Arkansas from them stood a trading post run by a thirty-two-year-old man whom Bell and Long had reason to know well. He was Hugh Glenn, an energetic storekeeper and one-time banker from Cincinnati. He had helped provision American troops during the War of 1812 and had found the business so profitable that afterwards he had sought contracts for furnishing supplies to some of the new military posts being spotted along the western frontier. His responsibilities also embraced the ill-managed Yellowstone Expedition of which Long's exploring party was a lethargic offshoot. Signer of Glenn's $45,000 bond and his associate in the supply venture was a man considerably older than he, Jacob Fowler, aged fifty-six. The postwar depression and the failure of the Yellowstone Expedition caught them both. Bankrupt, Glenn sought the West, as desperate men so often did. Salvaging a little merchandise from the wreckage, he moved into the Indian country of eastern Oklahoma and opened a trading post. Competition from the Chouteaus was so intense that he did not fare well.

Learning from either Captain Bell or Major Long of the untouched beaver streams and goods-hungry Indians along the base of the Rockies, Glenn returned to Cincinnati and told his friend Jacob Fowler that opportunity was knocking again. By working feverishly the partners were able to start up the Arkansas next fall with a motley crew of twenty men: American frontier hunters, Negroes, French Creoles, and strayed Spaniards.

Almost at once they were overtaken by another waif of the depression, Thomas James, one-time employee of Manuel Lisa. After forsaking the

Three Forks country in 1810 for fear of Blackfeet, James had tried store-keeping in Illinois. After the war things grew bad both for him and for another storekeeper with whom he was associated, one John McKnight. McKnight's brother Robert had gone to Santa Fe in 1812 and had been arrested. Recently some of Robert's companions had been freed, but Robert himself had not reappeared. John wanted to go west with a trade party to learn why. James offered to join him. After all, Santa Fe just might offer an outlet for the unsold goods that both of them had on their shelves.

On overtaking the Glenn-Fowler group, James and McKnight proposed combining forces. The Cincinnati partners declined, probably because they had no interest in testing the temper of the New Mexicans. As they made their independent way up the river, Fowler kept a journal of their progress, an account so untrammeled in spelling and punctuation that the temptation to quote it has proved irresistible to historians ever since the diary was first published in 1898.

For instance, the entry of "13th novr 1821 tuesday." On that day the party glimpsed the Rockies for the first time and pitched camp in a buoyant mood. "While some Ware Hunting and others Cooking Some Picking grapes a gun Was fyered off and the Cry of a White Bare [that is, a grizzly] Was Raised We Ware all armed in an Instent and Each man Run His own Cors to look for the desperet anemel." The bear sprang on Lewis Dawson. After a wild melee, rescuers slew it, but not in time. Although many of the animal's teeth proved to have been broken off at the gums, Dawson was badly hurt. "It appears that His Head was in the Bares mouth at least twice—and that When the monster give the Crush that Was to mash the mans Head it being too large for the Span of His mouth the Head Sliped out only the teeth Cutting the Skin to the bone . . . Which Wounds Were Sewed up as Well as Cold by don by men In our Situation Having no Surgen or Surgical Instruments." To no avail. Dawson died at "day Brake," November 16.

A little farther up the river the trappers encountered 400 tepees of Arapahoes, Comanches, Kiowas, Cheyennes, and Shoshoni, "with a great nombr of dogs and Horses So that the Hole Cuntry to a great distance was Coverd." Although the Indians were eager to trade, they had nothing to exchange but "Horses and them We do not want." They made the whites stay around, however, for a cold, uncertain month. Then sixty Spaniards arrived to trade corn. After talking with the newcomers Glenn too caught the Santa Fe fever. With four men he rode south to ask permission to trap in New Mexico.

The Americans remaining on the Arkansas with Fowler were sure Glenn would simply attract attention to them and they would be arrested. "We Ware Soon in a Scoffel," Fowler reported dryly. By threatening to call on a friendly Arapahoe chief for help, he restored order. Moving upriver a ways, the waiters built a three-room cabin and horse pen to protect their animals from thieving Indians. Another month dragged by. On January 29, 1822, Glenn reappeared with astounding information: "the mackeson [Mexican] provence Has de Clared Independence . . . and is desirous of a traid With the people of the united States."

But the Thomas James-John McKnight party and a third group under William Becknell, who chanced to be in the vicinity at the same time, had already heard the news and had rushed for Santa Fe. After so much expectation, it seemed a poor place: small, flat-roofed adobe houses unevenly lining the dusty streets that radiated out from the plaza. Fuzzy little donkeys plodded along under mountainous loads of firewood or cornhusks that were used for fodder. There were no wagons—only two-wheeled carts with wooden axles, their frames built of gnarled branches so that they looked like oversized bird cages. Tame Indians seemed as numerous as the dusky-skinned New Mexicans. About 4,600 people lived in the isolated city.

Becknell, who arrived first, skimmed off most of the available cash. Thomas James, whose cloth was of a drabber color than the New Mexicans liked, did not fare well. (John McKnight eventually found his brother Robert, however.) There is no record of how Glenn made out with his trade goods. He did obtain permission for Fowler and the trappers to push up the Rio Grande into the San Juan Mountains, and although they found many of the creeks frozen too solidly to be worked, they returned with furs that their employer sold in St. Louis for enough to pay their wages and still net a profit, on fur alone, of $2,624.85.

This was the beginning of the famous Santa Fe trade. Becknell, the first to reach home, promptly returned with three wagons, the first wheeled vehicles to reach the edges of the mountains. Others quickly followed. Many, perhaps most, of the workers in the early caravans had scant interest in peddling dry goods and kitchen utensils. They were trappers— and suddenly they had been presented with a shorter, safer trail to the mountains than the long haul up the Missouri.

Money, organization, and numbers were necessary to force a way up that traditional route, past the sullen Arikaras, into the land of the Blackfeet. Because rewards seemed great, money appeared as the depression relaxed. After Lisa's death in 1820, his two ablest partners, Robert Jones and Michael Immell, joined with Joshua Pilcher, a St. Louis banker, to reorganize the Missouri Fur Company. In the spring of 1822 they moved upstream to reoccupy the site at the mouth of the Big Horn that Lisa had been forced to abandon a dozen years earlier. That same spring Lisa's prewar partner, Andrew Henry, started for the upper river with a heavily laden keelboat financed in conjunction with William Ashley, a brigadier general in the Missouri militia who, for the sake of his political ambitions, was eager to make a fortune in the quickest time possible. Other well-heeled companies—Berthold, Pratte and Chouteau of St. Louis and the

Columbia Fur Company of the upper Mississippi—also were eying the Missouri. The competition that loomed threatened to be as disastrous as the Blackfeet. To men backed by little more than their wits and courage, the southern Rockies looked like a safer bet.

One of the ablest of those who tested the new grounds was Etienne Provost. Very little is known of Provost, partly because he could not sign his name and hence left no records. In 1817 he had been arrested in New Mexico with A. P. Chouteau and Jules De Mun. Presumably he returned to Missouri with that unfortunate party, but what happened to him during the next few years remains a mystery. Apparently he liked New Mexico and sought out the province in 1822, as soon as he knew the border was open. He was about forty years old and fat. But he had talents. The governor of New Mexico recognized them and in the summer of 1823 sent Provost and a boon companion, one Leclerc, first name uncertain, back east to help arrange a peace with the Pawnees, so that the new commerce across the prairies would not be subjected to their interference.

In the course of the errand Provost and Leclerc visited Fort Atkinson near today's Omaha. Also at the fort (early August, 1823) were six or eight remarkable visitors from the British fur posts west of the Montana Rockies. A few of the men were white; the rest were Iroquois Indians. It is not likely that any was educated enough to entertain comprehensive views of the international fur trade. Still, it would have been possible for Provost to piece together from their talk a fair insight into what the British had been doing in the Columbia country since buying Astoria from Astor's men during the War of 1812.

At first the Nor'Westers had neglected the mountain trade along the tributaries of the Columbia. Traditionally the British considered the game in a tribe's territory to belong to that tribe and did no hunting themselves.[3] They obtained the pelts by trade—by building a post in a likely area, stocking the shelves with goods, and inviting the customers to visit them. The system did not work well in the Rockies. The mountain Indians did not understand trapping, and even after some of them had been taught they were halfhearted about the onerous work involved and felt their time was better spent in the never-ending quest for food and clothing. Faced with the indifference, the first Nor'Westers beyond the mountains sat on their hands and complained—until Donald McKenzie reappeared.

McKenzie weighed three hundred pounds and supposedly could shoot a dozen rifle balls in succession through a Spanish dollar at a hundred paces. The tale should be taken as symbolic rather than factual. Except under optimum conditions it would be hard even to see a dollar at such distances;

---

[3] American hunters did not concede the point but invaded Indian territory and took the game themselves. The point was a basic factor in causing animosity among the tribes of the high plains, most notably the Blackfeet. Although Congress passed laws against trapping on Indian grounds, American hunters ignored the edicts.

what the statement really says is that McKenzie, like Achilles, was a handy man with the tools of his trade. He had left the North West Company to go overland to Astoria with Wilson Price Hunt, and after the sale had been rehired by his former employees to revitalize the trade of the western mountains. He did it by going into the mountains with bands of trained trappers whom he supplied with long strings of pack horses rather than with the traditional canoes and barges.

His base was Fort Nez Percé at the junction of the Walla Walla River with the Columbia in southeastern Washington. Between 1818 and 1821 he worked out a route more or less along the course of the future Oregon Trail into the mountainous area where the present states of Idaho, Wyoming, and Utah converge. He did it with little help from his peers, who were jealous of his swift rise to authority and were reluctant to leave the old ways and small comforts of their fixed posts.

McKenzie's trappers were mostly "freemen." Originally they had been lowly *engagés* bound to the company for a fixed term of years at wretched salaries. Among them were Iroquois, half-breeds, French-Canadians, and a few Americans left over from Astor's collapse. Though their contracts had expired, they wanted to stay in the mountains, either because they had no homes in the East to tug them that way or because they had married Indian women and did not wish to leave their families. They roamed with the tribes, hunting negligently for a living and now and then picking up extra rations by doing odd jobs around the posts. The company bought their furs at picayune rates, sold them supplies at astronomical markups. Enslaved by hopeless debt, they lost ambition. They were explosive and quarrelsome, much more inclined to race horses or gamble with the Indians they met than to attend to their traps. When they traveled with the brigades they insisted on having their families with them. This eased housekeeping—the women pitched the tents, cooked, and helped scrape and stretch the raw pelts—but it added staggering confusion to each day's march.

McKenzie was able to manage the motley crews. He retired in 1821, however, the same year in which the Hudson's Bay Company absorbed its old rival, the North West Company, and the brigade leaders who followed him lacked his knack. Difficulties intensified when the Hudson's Bay Company shifted the mountain trappers' base of operation to Flathead Post, at the site of David Thompson's old Saleesh House beside Clark Fork River in northwestern Montana. This move brought the brigades closer to the heart of good beaver country. Quickly they worked out the great north-south highway of the northern Rockies: from Flathead Post to the site of present Missoula, thence south to the westward-bulging Continental Divide either through Deer Lodge Valley or Bitterroot Valley. On reaching the eastern slope, they ascended the Beaverhead (the upper part of the Jefferson Fork of the Missouri) to its tributaries, recrossed the circling Divide at one of several gentle passes—Lemhi, Bannock, Medicine Lodge,

Monida—and then drifted across the broad Snake Plains to the rich streams of southeastern Idaho and southwestern Wyoming. Easy trails, good hunting—but all of it within reach of the Blackfeet. Parties needed strength to be safe, yet productive trapping necessitated a scattering of forces. Hoping to increase their meager profits, the freemen insisted on roaming the creeks in small groups, and regularly suffered for their temerity.

McKenzie's first successor was one of his chief assistants, Michel Bourdon, who had first come to the northern Rockies with David Thompson. On his first trip in 1822 Michel lost two men killed and two wounded. The next year he went back with redheaded Finan McDonald. In 1810 in Marias Pass the two of them had helped the Flatheads win their first great victory over the Blackfeet, but in 1823 Michel's luck ran out. On the Lemhi River, not far from where Meriwether Lewis first encountered Cameahwait's Shoshoni, he and five men died. In a fury for revenge, Finan rallied the rest, drove the Blackfeet into a thicket, and set the brush afire. Sixty-eight Indians were either roasted to death or shot down as they tried to break free. "We Shoe them what war was," Finan wrote grimly in his report. In spite of the victory, he'd had his fill and vowed never to return until beaver grew "Gould Skins."

Danger and debt heaped together diluted loyalty. In the summer of 1822 fourteen of Michel's freemen deserted and rode across the Wyoming mountains with their furs in search of the American posts on the Missouri River. A few of the fourteen were white, most were Iroquois. Some were bachelors, a few had families. They would have been better off with the brigade. Crow Indians killed six of the men, seized all the furs, and made captives of the women and children. The surviving males somehow reached Fort Atkinson. Those with lost families appealed to the United States Indian agent at the fort for help, and in time a few of the women were returned to their husbands.

Etienne Provost and Leclerc, the Pawnee peacemakers, were at the fort at the time. Evidently they talked to the bachelors. Perhaps Provost felt that with them as guides he could outflank the competition on the Missouri and work from New Mexico into the northern Rockies from behind. Anyway, at least three of the wandering freemen showed up later in his company, edging north, and so it does not seem farfetched to assume that he signed them on for exactly this purpose at Fort Atkinson in August, 1823.

Their first stop was probably Taos. In those days the name referred not to a particular town but to the whole broad valley, flooded with radiant light and clear color, that sloped westward from the Sangre de Cristo Mountains to the deeply canyoned Rio Grande. The valley's most populous village was the one made up of two terraced Indian pueblos. Five miles from the pueblos was the Spanish town of San Fernandez de Taos, the town now called simply Taos and the one historians mean when referring to the famed trapper haven of New Mexico.

Fernandez de Taos was small (fewer than three thousand inhabitants), poor, dirty, and relaxed. Most families lived crowded into a single room. Several such rooms were built wall to wall, either in a row or around a courtyard and often were entered Indian-style through a trap door in the roof. Protestant interlopers regarded the people as priest-ridden, hypocritical, lazy, and lax in their sexual standards. The newcomers quickly added a vice of their own, stills for turning valley grain into a potent brew known as Taos Lightning, designed primarily for corrupting the mountain Indians rather than for use at home.

Trappers swiftly spread from Taos throughout the Southwest. Provost and Leclerc went north, following in general the trail used by Escalante and after him by shadowy slave buyers and horse traders about whom nothing is known. In the summer of 1824 the partners reached that desolate area of eastern Utah where the Duchesne, White, and Green rivers come together. Leclerc may have returned from there to Taos for fresh supplies. Provost meanwhile moved west up the Duchesne and Strawberry rivers and crossed a spur of the Wasatch Mountains to a sparkling stream that now bears his name, though spelled phonetically, Provo River. He threaded the Provo's somber canyon to fresh-water Utah Lake at the western foot of the steeply soaring mountains. (Today's city of Provo stands on the lake's east shore.) Turning north to a stream later named Jordan, he started toward Great Salt Lake.

He may not have glimpsed that amazing inland sea. Pretending peace, a war party of Shoshoni rode into his camp beside the Jordan and massacred seven men, including Patrick O'Connor, one of the deserters from Bourdon's Hudson's Bay brigade of 1822. The survivors fled back toward Green River. Reinforced and re-equipped somehow, they went west again in the spring of 1825, but stayed clear of the Provo and turned north instead to what became the Weber. Near the Weber's mouth on May 22, 1825, the other two deserters with Provost came full circle: they met a brigade of Hudson's Bay Company freemen being led that year by stocky, hard-fisted Peter Skene Ogden.

The next day Provost himself rode over to talk with the Briton. Before he had been in the camp very long, several belligerent Americans appeared. From them he learned what had been happening to the Missouri fur men since his visit at Fort Atkinson in 1823.

It was shocking. Early in the spring of 1823 on the upper Yellowstone River, Blackfeet had killed Robert Jones and Michael Immell, the principal partners of the reorganized Missouri Fur Company, and five of their men, and had seized their fur and equipment. A little later Arikara Indians had killed fourteen or fifteen of William Ashley's men and had wounded ten.[4] Farther upstream still other war parties chipped away at the men Andrew Henry was sending out from his new post at the mouth of the Big Horn.

After a military expedition sent out from Fort Atkinson to chastise the Arikaras had bungled the job, Ashley decided he would have to find some other route to the Rockies. At Fort Kiowa, a fur post in south-central South Dakota, he outfitted Jedediah Smith, William Sublette, Thomas Fitzpatrick, James Clyman, and half a dozen more men. This party he sent due west on horseback across the dry plains. They passed the winter of 1823–24 in the upper Wind River Valley among Crow Indians, along with several more whites who had worked south into the same area from Andrew Henry's post on the Yellowstone.

Jedediah Smith's group got off ahead of the others in February, 1824. Suffering terribly from icy blizzards, thirst, and hunger, they rediscovered South Pass, the soon-to-be famous gateway that Robert Stuart's returning Astorians had first used in 1812. On the Green River they trapped with fabulous results. While four of the men struggled with gruesome hardship to take the pelts and the latest news back to Ashley, Jedediah Smith and six others drifted west into Idaho. Eventually they encountered the Hudson's Bay Company Snake River brigade, led that year by Alexander Ross, and tagged along with it back to Flathead Post to spy out how the British managed things. When Peter Ogden replaced Ross as brigade leader and started south for the spring hunt (1825), Smith's party clung to him, too. Fresh tracks in southeastern Idaho showed that by that time Henry's men from the Yellowstone had also found their way through South Pass into the richest beaver preserve of the Rockies. Smith swung his group away from Ogden to rejoin his countrymen.

Hoping to avoid the Americans, Ogden moved south into the Wasatch Mountains and camped not far up the Weber River from the site of the city that now bears his name. Trapping was splendid but he had no chance to monopolize it. First Provost's unexpected group appeared from the south, and after it some of the Americans whose tracks he had seen earlier.

There were about twenty-five of the latter. They were accompanied by fourteen of Ogden's freemen whom the Americans had picked up at their work along the nearby streams. They rode in a marshaled column, grimly militaristic. One of the men in the lead carried an American flag, a somewhat unlikely object to have been in a trapper's possibles sack. But there it was, and the moment its staff was thrust defiantly into the ground it became not so much a symbol of patriotism as of a dark, insecure, vigilante way of thinking.

The ground where the colors rippled so boldly lay 55 or so miles south of the 42nd parallel and hence was Mexican territory as defined by the

4 Much of this Provost had already learned during his stay at Fort Atkinson.

Adams-Onís treaty of 1819. Neither the British nor the Americans had any way of knowing where the parallel ran, of course. If they considered the matter—and there is no evidence that even Provost, just arrived from Taos, did so—they probably assumed that they were north of the line, in what was called Oregon country. By a Convention of 1818, citizens of both the United States and Great Britain had equal rights to trade or settle anywhere in Oregon.

This was not the way the American fur hunters under the leadership (at that moment) of one Johnson Gardner wanted things to be. They were free trappers. In order to reduce overhead, Ashley and Henry did not pay them salaries, but instead grubstaked them with guns, powder, traps, and other essentials. In return the trappers agreed to deliver half their furs to the company. The other half was theirs to dispose of as best they could. (As time passed, different arrangements came into being, until some trappers achieved full commercial independence.) Private ownership made each hunter an embryo capitalist, eager to increase his wealth. Under licenses issued to Ashley by the United States government for trading (but not for trapping, which was illegal on Indian lands) they had made a perilous trip across the Continental Divide, expecting to reach untouched grounds. Instead, they found their traditional enemies, the British, ahead of them, reaping as many as eighty skins a day.

Although the continental stirrings of the United States had not yet been labeled Manifest Destiny, its thrusts were already at work in the American people. One of its wellsprings was insecurity. Theirs was a new nation ringed by older countries bent on containing its growth. The natural reaction was belligerence. (Witness Israel today.) When Gardner's crew encountered Ogden's freemen in the Wasatch Mountains, the vanguard of America's westering once again collided with forces that might be representative of national frustration. The Hudson's Bay Company was a century and a half old, barnacled with Old World traditionalism. Its scarlet flag was almost a duplicate of the Union Jack, with only the addition of the initials HBC in the lower right-hand corner. Upstarts unexpectedly meeting so much established power must have felt uncertain.

Their reaction was typical of all vigilantism. The accustomed bulwarks having crumbled, it was up to them to throw out their collective chests, declare their own rules, and show the enemy what was what. This Gardner proceeded to do. First he raised a supporting scaffold of patriotism. Pointing to the American flag, he told Ogden's gaping men that they were in the land of the free and were entitled to remove whatever beaver they had caught to the American camp, where they would receive higher prices for it than the Hudson's Bay Company paid. He then assured Ogden that American forces would soon occupy all Oregon.

Ogden retorted that the matter of sovereignty was up to their governments. The remark had no effect. That night and the next day twenty-nine of his debt-oppressed freemen gathered up their furs and left him. Although the exodus was taut, no one pulled the trigger that would have precipitated real disaster.

A point to notice is this. Neither Johnson Gardner nor any other man in his column acquired pelts from the episode. The freemen kept their furs until selling them later on to William Ashley at standard mountain rates. Johnson's gain lay in discomfiting the Hudson's Bay Company. He also hoped, of course, to disrupt Ogden's organization enough so that the Briton would retire, leaving the field to the Americans. But mostly Johnson's vigilantes could warm away the chill of insecurity with the thought that they had asserted the right as they saw the right, that their ways would prevail. Though aggressive self-righteousness of that sort—the Minuteman on the march—was by no means limited to the Rocky Mountains during the subsequent century, it did produce some of its most violent manifestations there. And most of it occurred, so this text will indicate, because men had outrun the familiar and, as they saw matters, had nothing but their own raised hackles to guard against the jaws of unexpected frustration.

The clash between Ogden and Gardner finished, Provost rode back east along the Strawberry River toward the Green. Along the way he had another surprise meeting, this one with William Ashley himself.

Ashley had just completed a remarkable adventure. Late the previous fall he had learned through messages from Fitzpatrick and Clyman that there were furs on the Green (his trappers called the river Seeds-kee-dee until Provost told them the Spanish name was *Verde,* after the brush that shone so brilliantly along its banks in that gray-red, blasted country) and that the men needed supplies. Ashley had to have those pelts. Discouraged afresh by the Blackfeet, Andrew Henry had once again quit the mountains, and the burden of saving their company was entirely on Ashley's shoulders. Promptly he started a caravan west into the teeth of winter. Fumbling still for the best route, he followed the South Platte onto the Colorado plains, sat out the worst of the blizzards, and then crossed the Front Range into North Park. From there he skirted Wyoming's Medicine Bow Mountains and slanted through waterless Great Divide Basin. In the spring, after losing seventeen of his horses to Crow thieves, he came down through endless sagebrush to the "Shetskedee," as he spelled it. He followed the river south toward the glittering peaks of the Uinta Mountains. Along the way he divided his men to hunt and make contact with whatever other whites they could find. Curious about the Seeds-kee-dee, he built two boats out of buffalo hide, loaded in some trade goods, and floated into the mountains to see where the river went.

They bobbed like tormented corks under the towering red precipices of Flaming Gorge, rested briefly in the future outlaw hideaway of Brown's Hole, portaged around the roaring rapids of Lodore Canyon, and plowed through Split Mountain in today's Dinosaur National Monument. In the deserts beyond they encountered two of Provost and Leclerc's hunters. The men assured Ashley that he would find neither beaver nor game farther south and added that Provost was somewhere off to the west. Unable to return to his rendezvous through the howling canyons, Ashley buried his merchandise, bought a few riding horses from the trappers and from some poverty-stricken Utes, and set out to ride around the mountain. En route he met Provost.

Provost and at least four of his hunters accompanied Ashley to the rendezvous. About 120 men were waiting there. As they flocked to the temporary booths to swap pelts for cloth, tobacco, fishhooks, knives, powder, coffee, and sugar for themselves and thread, beads, and other trinkets for the women that a few of them had already acquired, Ashley realized that if men were willing to stay isolated in the mountains year after year, big profits might lie not so much in the furs a freight caravan handled for them but in the supplies it brought each summer to a great high country trading fair. Generous markups would cover the exorbitant costs and risks. Compact goods would be best, especially alcohol. He had made a mistake in leaving it out of this year's essentials. Whiskey was what the men had really clamored for as soon as their barest needs had been filled. Next year he'd bring plenty.

As a field manager to replace Andrew Henry he selected Jedediah Smith. They prepared a list of desirable items, appointed Cache Valley on the Utah-Idaho border as the next year's gathering place, and hurried east. Eager to join the spring hunt, Jedediah tried to go straight back in winter, as Ashley had done. This was a harsher season, however. Snow bogged him down hungrily in Kansas, and he had to send an urgent appeal to Ashley for help and horses. Ashley responded with twenty-five men and in the spring of 1826 the combined parties went west together.

The trappers meantime had been working the same general area that they had merely touched the spring before—southwestern Wyoming, northeastern Utah, southern Idaho. In April a group of them had run into Ogden again. This time the Hudson's Bay Company man had been ready, and there was no Johnson Gardner along to stiffen the Americans' bluff. Ogden's freemen stayed put; in fact, a few of last year's deserters even promised to return to him. Obviously, then, the stubborn British would have to be taken into consideration in the future. So, too, would the Blackfeet, who had attacked some of the hunters.

In spite of those threats, prospects looked good to Jedediah Smith and his friends William Sublette and David Jackson as they surveyed the riotous rendezvous. The trappers had garnered 123 packs of fur— perhaps five tons—and were feeling expansive as they threw their money away on alcohol and foofarraw. By trial and error a pattern for handling the trade had been established. The best season and route for bringing in the annual freight caravan had been worked out—in springtime up the North Platte and its tributary, Sweetwater Creek, and over South Pass. They knew how to live off the country during the rest of the year and had thoroughly mastered the not-very-complex craft of the trap. Indians, weather, and shattering accidents would always be dangerous, but at least the mountain men were beginning to learn what pitfalls they had best beware of.

Even without knowing the fine details of those things Ashley had managed, as an entrepreneur, to make his fortune. Now he was willing to sell out and turn to politics. Why not take the chance of doing even better than he had? Smith, Jackson, and Sublette plunged—Ashley agreed, for a stiff price, to bring in supplies to their new company the next year—and then busily they laid plans for the coming season. For two decades the mountains and the Indians had frustrated efforts like theirs, but now the skirmishing was over. The necessary forces had coalesced, and for the first time the Rockies were about to yield a major resource to a highly organized, totally ruthless campaign of exploitation.

VI

BRIEF CANDLE

FOR A dazzling, deceptive year or so fortune cradled the new firm of Smith, Jackson & Sublette. As a part of his bargain with them Ashley promised not to outfit competitors, and although he was briefly tempted to an apparent double cross with the powerful Bernard Pratte-Pierre Chouteau interests of St. Louis, the deal fell through. Nor did the Pratte-Chouteau firm have better luck in trying to invade the central and northern Rockies from Mexican Taos in the south.

The attempt was made in 1827 with twenty-five trappers under the leadership of Bernard Pratte's son Sylvester. From the beginning things went wrong. In Colorado's North Park young Pratte died of sickness. His second-in-command, Ceran St. Vrain, kept the brigade plodding ahead into the barren Green River Valley of southern Wyoming, but there they were immobilized by one of the most merciless winters on record, that of 1827–28. When laggard spring finally arrived, high water made trapping almost impossible and the men lacked supplies enough to wait for better conditions. Back to Taos they went with a meager 1,636 pounds of beaver.

Political conditions did not justify a second effort. Although American merchants were welcome in Santa Fe, where their cloth and hardware filled a real need, the trappers who mined the beaver streams without returning commensurate value quickly made themselves as undesirable as locusts. Sternly the government announced that henceforth licenses for trapping would go only to Mexican citizens.

A few trappers who wished to stay in New Mexico yet were unwilling to give up American citizenship entered into dummy partnerships with bona fide Mexicans. Others smuggled their goods into the mountains and their furs into the outlying hamlets. Some swore allegiance to the Catholic faith and were allowed to take out naturalization papers: Antoine Robidoux, for instance, became the leading legitimate trader of the southern Rockies as an ostensible Mexican.

Obviously any American company that supplied men who were skirting the edges of the law left itself open to harassment and possible confiscation of goods. No St. Louis firm in this early period felt that the risks were justifiable. As a result no effective competition to Smith, Jackson & Sublette appeared from the south, despite the advantages that Taos offered as an outfitting base close to the mountains.

The firm's first challenge from the east fared no better. This was led by Joshua Pilcher of the erstwhile Missouri Fur Company. After that hard-luck firm had collapsed following the Robert Jones-Michael Immell massa-cre on the Yellowstone River in 1823, Pilcher had acquired new partners and new money; and in the fall of 1827, about when Sylvester Pratte was leaving Taos, he headed up the Platte with forty-five men and a hundred pack horses. Under cover of a blizzard on mountain-girt Sweetwater Creek, Crow Indians stole their livestock. Burying their trade goods, the whites hiked glumly on into the gale-swept valley of the Green in search of game. It was a rough winter for them, too, and when spring arrived they found that their cache of merchandise had been ruined by melting snow water. That finished Pilcher, though with nine loyal (or were they foolish?) *engagés* he spent one more forlorn winter (1828–29) on the shores of Montana's Flathead Lake before admitting the inevitable.

In 1828, then, things looked good for Smith, Jackson & Sublette. Actually, a relentless squeeze was developing. Success in the beaver trade had always depended on finding new streams to exploit. But as soon as Smith, Jackson & Sublette tried to expand they discovered that they were being squeezed into the northern Rockies with no avenues of escape open.

Mexican hostility was a check against legitimate expansion into the Colorado Rockies. Westward the Hudson's Bay Company maintained a jealous vigil over the Oregon country; its Snake River brigades were ordered to trap Idaho and western Montana so bare of beaver that the opportunistic American hunters would not be tempted to inch toward the coast stream by stream. In the east, meantime, Astor's American Fur Company had absorbed its principal rivals, the Chouteau people and the Columbia Fur Company, and had begun pushing up the traditional Mis-souri River highway toward the mountains, protecting its flanks by building stout trading posts as it went. In 1828 American Fur Company agents hired Etienne Provost to trade among the Crows in the Big Horn country. Shortly thereafter the firm employed some of Pilcher's former partners— Lucien Fontenelle, Andrew Drips, and Henry Vanderburgh—to probe the edges of the Rockies with trapping brigades.

Free hunters within the mountains added to the pressure. Smarting under the high charges placed on goods at the rendezvous by Smith, Jackson & Sublette, the trappers sent a delegation to the American Fur Company's new Fort Union at the junction of the Yellowstone and Missouri rivers, urging the firm to hurry its invasion of the mountains so that competition would reduce prices.

Indians heaped more trouble onto the partners. During his exploratory trips to the Pacific coast, Jedediah Smith lost ten men to the Mojaves along the Colorado River and fifteen to the Umpquas in Oregon. Between 1827 and 1829 Blackfeet killed eleven company trappers within the Rockies. Shoshoni accounted for four more. Lives were not the only loss. In an angry report to William Clark, superintendent of Indian Affairs, Smith, Jackson & Sublette declared in a joint letter: "Horses and Mules taken by force and stolen by different tribes is 480 Value of Mercdz. taken $10000; Beaver fur 1500 lb." They accused the Hudson's Bay Company of complicity in the disasters: ". . . until British interlopers are dismissed from off our territory Americans will never be respected or acknowledged as patrons by the Indians on the west side of the Rocky Mountains. . . . We, for no other reason than because we are Americans, are tormented and annoyed by Every tribes."

Presumably the partners hoped that their complaints would stir the government into providing military aid against the Indians and diplomatic aid against the Hudson's Bay Company. The Rockies, however, were too far away and the fur trade too limited economically to justify either kind of intervention. Moreover, the government could offer no protection from the other Americans who were pouring into the region. Hoping to escape while their skins were relatively whole, Smith, Jackson & Sublette on August 1, 1830, sold out to Thomas Fitzpatrick, Milton Sublette, Jim Bridger, Henry Fraeb, and Jean Baptiste Gervais, styling themselves the Rocky Mountain Fur Company.[1]

By 1832 the mountains were, from a trapper's standpoint, densely crowded. American Fur Company brigades dogged the heels of the men of the new Rocky Mountain Fur Company wherever they went, trying to learn the dim trails to the best beaver streams. Small independent firms like Gantt & Blackwell and Alexander Sinclair strutted into the rendezvous with little besides optimism to underwrite their venture—and quickly learned that optimism alone was not enough. Companies of free trappers—Kit Carson's men out of the southern Rockies, for instance—occasionally roamed through. Bonneville's strong brigade brought the first wagons across the Continental Divide to Green River, adding their trade goods to the available supply and their traps to the streams. Two years later, in 1834, the Hudson's Bay Company began sending pack trains of merchandise to the summer fairs. Nathaniel Wyeth built Fort Hall in southeastern Idaho and thrust his men into the scramble. Financed by Ashley, William Sublette came back to the mountains with Robert Campbell, built Fort Laramie on the North Platte, and prepared to tackle not just the high-country trappers but the American Fur Company along the Missouri as well.

In spite of the handful of forts that were built here and there in the mid-

[1] The next year, 1831, Smith, Jackson & Sublette entered the Santa Fe trade. While searching for water in the sun-blistered Cimarron Valley of the Oklahoma Panhandle, Jedediah Smith was killed by Comanches.

1830's, the heart of the system, where the bulk of goods and furs changed hands, remained the rendezvous. Its location shifted each summer. The early ones assembled for the most part in the vicinity of Bear Lake, deep-set among lightly timbered, rounded hills on the Idaho-Utah border. The meeting of 1832, highlighted by a rousing battle with Gros Ventres Indians, was held in one of the loveliest spots in the mountains, Pierre's Hole (today's Teton Basin) directly west of the Teton Mountains. Two assembled east of the Divide, near the stark hills where Popo Agie Creek runs into Wind River. Most, however, were held in the wide Green River Valley of Wyoming, at one point or another along the tributaries where meadows opening into the gray sage plains provided enough forage for the thousands of horses involved.

The gatherings began and ended within a decade and a half. Those that have become notorious in our folklore were the hectic ones of the competitive years during the early and middle 1830's—a brief glow, but to the nostalgic mountaineers of the fur trade a lovely one.

At each tumultuous gathering hundreds of whites once again established a fleeting contact with the civilization they had abandoned. They picked up letters from home, newspapers, and word-of-mouth reports from workers just arrived with the freight caravans.

In vivid contrast to these faint echoes from the East were the barbaric accouterments of the assembly. The men used leather tepees for houses, campfires on the ground for cooking, animal skins for clothing. Side by side with them were hundreds of gaily bedecked Indians, offering their own stock of furs and horses and dried meat to the companies in exchange for kettles and guns; handsome moccasins, buckskin shirts, and the satisfactions of their women to the men in return for bright cloth, beads, and silver hawk bells.

A high old time, the accounts all say. Yet, except for the surroundings, it was not a particularly original form of celebration; town-arrived sailors, cowboys, lumberjacks, and prospectors have always tended toward similar entertainments. The trappers bragged, raced horses, wrestled each other, held shooting matches, gambled, and fornicated. They fought duels and soused themselves and the Indians in alcohol. During their stupors they were gouged unmercifully by the traders, first for cash and then for credit; a man deep in debt was a man whose future catch could, to the extent of his honor, be controlled. Yet to the men themselves and to later commentators this disregard of money seemed a form of independence. As Washington Irving put matters in *The Rocky Mountains,* later entitled *The Adventures of Captain Bonneville:* "For a free mountaineer to pause at a paltry consideration of dollars and cents, in the attainment of any object that might strike his fancy, would stamp him with the mark of the beast in the estimation of his comrades."

With his money a company trapper was able to buy raw alcohol (mellow liquor was bulky to pack), trinkets for his woman, and such luxuries as woolen trousers, some coffee, a pound or so of sugar, and perhaps, if the year's luck had been good, an extravagant new Hawken rifle from St. Louis. Free trappers also had to provide their own equipment, traps at $12 to $15 each and horses that might run under the stress of bidding as high as $300. But why worry? Weren't they rich? During the competitive years wages for skilled hands rose to unprecedented heights, and contracts for service were broken with impunity whenever a rival company offered better pay. For a brief while the situation was so unnatural that at the very time the price of beaver was sinking in St. Louis to $3.50 a pound, it was climbing in the mountains, a thousand expensive miles away, to $5 or more. Considerations about tomorrow lost their meaning. Today was the harvest.

One free trapper, John Robertson, writing his father from Pierre's Hole in 1832 to explain why he was not coming home (he had left nine or ten years before with some of Ashley's original men), said, "I got lazy and do not believe I could go to work." No doubt he had grown feckless by conservative standards. But he could hardly have been "lazy." The distances covered during a three-month spring or fall hunt by the competitive brigades, numbering sixty or so men each, were phenomenal—up to a thousand miles a season over rugged trails and across dangerous river fords where men frequently drowned. Nearly every evening the camp tenders had to pitch shelter, cut firewood, and tend to the livestock. Nearly every morning they had to dismantle the camp and load up a hundred or more cantankerous animals. Every day the trappers had to course the ice-cold creeks, wading out thigh-deep to set their traps in the beaver runs. Each animal that was caught had to be hauled ashore and skinned; the hides had to be carefully scraped, washed, folded, and tied into bales. Hunting buffalo, bear, deer, or elk was a daily necessity; each heavy carcass had to be butchered and packed in to the cooks.

Sickness, surprisingly rare, was treated with whimsy rather than knowledge. Jacob Fowler treated one man's sore throat by applying "a sock With ashes Round His neck—He finds Releef in about two Hours." When one of Ogden's men was "poisoned" by eating tainted beaver, the bourgeois cured him by having him drink gunpowder and pepper mixed in water. Gall from a buffalo's digestive tract was considered a good blood tonic; crude oil from a seep near today's Lander, Wyoming, was rubbed onto rheumatic joints. Patent medicines brought from St. Louis were available in first-aid kits, but quite possibly the barks, powdered roots, and decoctions learned from the Indians were equally effective. On the other hand, an Indian sweat bath followed by a plunge into cold water probably was not as beneficial as reputed.

Thirst sometimes resulted in such expedients as drinking mule's blood. Hunger once led Milton Sublette's trappers to bake locusts into black, bitter cakes. Accidents sometimes called for heroic remedies. After a grizzly bear had lacerated Jedediah Smith's scalp and had torn off his right ear, James Clyman "put in my needle stiching it through and through and over and over laying the lacerated parts together as nice as I could with my hands." David Thompson had less success with James McMillan's hands, shattered by an accidental gun discharge: after three weeks, "the fore finger of the left hand having a bad appearance & no hope of it joining with the stump I separated it." Thomas L. Smith of Ceran St. Vrain's 1827–28 brigade out of Taos became Pegleg Smith when the men of his camp amputated his bullet-shattered leg below the knee with a hunting knife and improvised saw, and stopped the bleeding by searing the artery ends with a hot iron.

Certain Indian tribes were potential sources of hurt: the Arapahoes, Comanches, Utes, Bannocks, and Shoshoni on occasion; the different bands of Blackfeet (Piegans, Bloods, Siksikas) and their neighbors, the Gros Ventres or Atsina, almost invariably. Between 1805 and 1845 the different tribes killed at least 182 trappers, a startling percentage of the relatively small total involved—a thousand or so at the most. There seems no accurate way of estimating how many men were wounded.

Ferocity marked the warfare on both sides. After Blackfeet had killed Henry Vanderburgh of the American Fur Company in one of Montana's broad valleys, they cut off his arms to keep for souvenirs, stripped the rest of his flesh from the bones, and threw the meat into the river. The whites could be just as ruthless. Near the head of Powder River in the Big Horn country one of Bonneville's brigades captured two Arikaras from a band raiding their horses. They sent word to the thieves that unless the animals were returned the hostages would be killed. The Arikaras tried to barter— a horse for a life. The trappers were adamant: all the horses. The Indians declined and abandoned their tribesmen "with lamentable howlings." The whites thereupon roasted the captives to death on a pile of blazing logs.

Although the whites would trade almost anything for beaver, they jealously retained one advantage—good rifles—and sold the Indians less accurate, short-barreled, smoothbore muskets called fusees (fusils). As a result the Indians generally avoided pitched battles and struck from ambush. When direct confrontations occurred, the whites often triumphed over what statistically would seem to be hopeless odds.

One affair recounted by Osborne Russell in his journal typifies many. In the spring of 1838 a brigade under Jim Bridger intersected the trail of a wandering village of Blackfeet in the Madison Valley of Montana. The men insisted on attacking, even though it was evident that some of the Indians were already dying of smallpox, which had been introduced to the tribe the previous fall by a Missouri River steamboat.

Although caught by surprise, the Indians managed to gain the protection of a rocky knoll. After an interval of long-range sniping had proved ineffectual, an Iroquois with the whites, heeding his "medicine," stripped himself naked except for powder horn and rifle and led a charge "under an incessant storm of bullets. . . . Although 7 or 8 times our number they retreated like rats among the ruins of an old building whilst we followed close on their heels until we drove them entirely into the plain where their horses were tied. They carried off their dead with the exception of two and threw them into the river." The next day the Blackfeet tried to ambush the brigade in revenge but were discovered and routed again. Because of the Indian custom of carrying away corpses, no one knew how many warriors died. But not a white man did, although the advantage of position rested both times with the Blackfeet.

To some men danger and the endurance of hardship were a fulfillment, as though in risking life they savored it more fully. There were milder compensations as well. Osborne Russell, who exulted in the death of Blackfeet, also wrote with deep relish of the feel of space, the sound of water across rocks, the winter fire of the aurora borealis, the charm of his favorite "Secluded Valley," the Lamar Valley of northeastern Yellowstone Park: "I almost wished I could spend the remainder of my days in a place like this where happiness and contentment seemed to reign in wild romantic splendor surrounded by majestic battlements." There were good nights: elk ribs roasting before the campfire "on sticks down which the grease ran in torrents. The repast over, the jovial tale goes round the circle . . . good jokes and witty sayings such as Swift never dreamed of."

Perhaps those are the feelings Robertson had in mind when he wrote his father that he had grown too "lazy" to go to work. Perhaps he meant he could not endure the cramping routines of a more civilized life. And yet the trappers' trade had its own rigid organization and division of labor—camp tenders, horse herders, hunters—all under the absolute sway of the "booshway" (bourgeois) sometimes called the partisan, and his chief assistant, the "little booshway," or clerk.

Independent souls resented binding themselves, as one man put it to Russell, "to an arbitrary Rocky Mountain Chieftan to be kicked over hill and dale at his pleasure." To avoid the ignominy, the free trappers who were not tied by contract to some company banded together in a loose-knit organization—and then of necessity wrote their own rigid rules and submitted to their own leader. Theoretically they could dissolve the connection whenever they desired, but go where? Save for the bright years of the mid-1830's there was only one supplier of goods and one buyer of pelts at the rendezvous—Pierre Chouteau, Jr., successor of the American Fur Company in the West. The very vehemence with which the Chouteau organization was cursed throughout the mountains suggests not true independence for the trappers so much as a grinding lack of it.

By the time the Chouteau firm had won control of the mountain trade it was scarcely worth having. Prices were down because of a new craze for making men's hats of silk rather than of beaver felt. Besides, the wild exploitation had stripped the streams. A German traveler, F. A. Wislizenus, noted that although hundreds of Indian tepees lined the Green River at the rendezvous of 1839, few of the men, either red or white, had many furs to offer. "There was little drinking of spirits and almost no gambling," sure sign of discouraging times. A year later the end came. Only a meager handful of carts creaked with their supplies across South Pass into the vast sage valley, and after them there would be no more.

What to do? Many trappers returned east. Some took up farming near the Pacific coast; in general men from the southern Rockies sought California and those from farther north Oregon. An indeterminate number of others, doubting their ability to resume stabler forms of living, stayed behind, scratching out whatever precarious existence they could, mostly in Colorado where the streams had not been so ruthlessly harvested.

These were the true free men of the mountains, unbound to anyone mainly because business firms no longer saw profits enough to justify organizing their trade. They were adrift and they liked it. George Simpson, black-sheep member of a good family, explained his feelings almost euphemistically enough to make them sound high-minded: ". . . freedom from conventionalities and a disregard of those social amenities to which I was accustomed." George Ruxton, an English traveler who lived with the mountain men in Colorado in 1847, was blunter, though he too loved the roving life. "Constantly exposed to perils of all kinds they became callous . . . and destroy human life with as little scruple and as freely as they expose their own. Of laws, human or divine, they neither know nor care to know. . . . They have many good qualities, but they are those of the animal."

The trappers hunted now in small groups, joining others of their kind as convenience suggested and traveling wherever fancy directed, generally taking their Indian wives and half-blood children with them. When they needed supplies they rode out onto the plains to one of the forts—Bent's Fort, Fort St. Vrain, Fort Lupton, Fort Laramie, Fort Cass and lesser ones—that had been built out beyond the edges of the foothills for gathering buffalo hides from the Sioux, Cheyenne, Arapahoe, and Crow Indians of the high barrens. Or else they sought one of the handful of ramshackle mountain posts that had been erected here and there in the central Rockies during the days when the organized beaver trade had been dwindling away.

The most famous of these posts, because it ended up serving emigrants on the Oregon Trail rather than fur hunters, was Fort Bridger, built in 1841–42 in the broad, meadow-dotted valley of the Black's Fork of Green River in southwestern Wyoming, almost in the shadow of the high Uintas. More obscure and far more noisome than Fort Bridger was an earlier post, Fort David Crockett. Commonly called Fort Misery, David Crockett was a

huddle of one-story log huts erected in 1837 in Brown's Hole, an unexpected opening in the deep canyons formed by the Green as it pounds
through the Uinta Mountains. Habitué of both spots was Jack Robertson,
the same Robertson who had written his father in 1832 that he was too
"lazy" to go home. Robertson had a cabin on Black's Fork. There he
collected from time to time a few knives, hatchets, fishhooks, ammunition,
and the like. When the spirit so moved him, he packed up the goods, went
to Fort Misery and swapped with the Indians for horses, with the trappers
for furs, and with travelers who chanced by, as an Oregon-bound party did
in 1839, for money. ("A white man," remarked one of the travelers,
Thomas Farnham, "has no business here.") Later Robertson, and Bridger
too, picked up worn draft oxen from emigrants on the Oregon Trail.
Robertson ran his share of the livestock along Black's Fork near his cabin;
it was, in a manner of speaking, Wyoming's first cattle ranch.

Farther south were two other supply posts maintained by Antoine
Robidoux of Santa Fe. One lay south of the Uinta Mountains in Utah and
was called, logically enough, Fort Uinta, or, in nasal Western drawl, Fort
Winty. The other, Fort Uncompahgre, was located near the junction of the
Uncompahgre and Gunnison rivers, where the town of Delta, Colorado,
now stands, the broad green hump of Grand Mesa at its back. Uncompli-
mentary descriptions of both posts have been left by Joseph Williams, an
itinerant preacher sixty-four years old who in 1841–42 rode to Oregon and
back by different trails just to see what the land was like.

Williams, who was inclined to unearth depravity everywhere, was outraged at Fort Winty by "the debauchery of the men among the Indian
women. They would buy and sell them to one another. . . . Mr. Rube-
deau [sic] has collected several of the Indian squaws and young Indians,
to take to New Mexico, and kept some of them for his own use! The
Spaniards would buy them for wives." Williams tried to preach to the
rascals at Fort Winty about their evil ways, but they would not listen. A
little later at Fort Uncompahgre he had better luck: "I felt the power of the
word. . . . I spoke plainly and pointedly to them, and felt as though I
would be clear of their blood on the day of eternity." In fairness to
Robidoux it should be noted that Rufus Sage, who was roaming the
mountains in quest of material for a book, visited Winty the same season
and was attracted by other articles of trade than human beings: mountain
sheep and deer skins, "dressed so neatly as frequently to attain a snowy
whiteness, and possess the softness of velvet." Robidoux bought these from
Ute and Shoshoni Indians for a few cents' worth of powder each and resold
them in Santa Fe for one to two dollars apiece.

East of the mountains, where Fountain Creek runs into the Arkansas
River, George Simpson, aged twenty-four, whose views on freedom are
quoted above, and two friends, Joseph Doyle and Alexander Barclay, early

in 1842 built an adobe wall around a square of ground 70 feet to the side. Tiny, single-room apartments lined three of the square's inner walls; a wagon gate broke the fourth—"a wretched species of fort," sniffed Francis Parkman, who stopped by in 1846. The builders called the place El Pueblo. Today's city of Pueblo, second largest in Colorado, stands on the site and derives its name from that rude settlement.

El Pueblo's inhabitants, many of them Mexicans, grazed cattle, hunted, raised a few chickens, some corn and pumpkins, and traded with the Indians. Their chief article of barter was whiskey brought by packtrain from Taos onto American soil, where its sale to Indians was illegal. The traffic made serious inroads on the legitimate activities of Bent's Fort 70 miles farther down the Arkansas and led one of the proprietors, Charles Bent, to ask that a United States military post be erected nearby to stop the smuggling. Such an establishment, Bent added in a letter to Senator Linn of Missouri, would also protect the Santa Fe Trail and in case of war would be "a greate advantage in preventing the Mexicans" from rousing Utes and Apaches against "our frontears."

No post was built, though feelings along the frontier were growing taut. The so-called Texas-Santa Fe "commercial" expedition against New Mexico had recently been overwhelmed and its members cruelly imprisoned by Governor Armijo. In revenge, filibusterers recruited in part from idle mountain men hanging around the forts at the base of the Colorado Rockies began harrying Mexican wagon trains on the Santa Fe Trail. One gang of twenty-three slipped nearly 200 miles across the border (the Arkansas River) and ambushed sixty Mexican cavalrymen near the hamlet of Mora in the eastern foothills of the Sangre de Cristo Mountains.

Armijo retaliated by closing New Mexico to American commerce but left one loophole: foreigners who lived on Mexican soil with their families could continue their normal trade. On learning of the edict, Simpson, Doyle, and Barclay scrambled 25 miles up the Arkansas from El Pueblo, crossed the river, and ascended Hardscrabble Creek a few miles toward the Wet Mountains. There, on Mexican soil, they built another crude fort to live in with their Shoshoni wives (some had more than one). Having thus complied with the law, they were able to get the whiskey they wanted for their Indian trade in spite of being Americans.

War broke out three years later, in 1846. Dragoons under Stephen Watts Kearny marched through Bent's Fort into New Mexico and entered Santa Fe on August 18. Not a shot was fired. Bloodshed came later, during a fierce uprising in the bitter cold of January, 1847. At Taos, Mexicans and Pueblo Indians battered into the home of Charles Bent, whom Kearny had appointed military governor of New Mexico, scalped him in front of his family, and with their grisly trophy tacked to a board roared off in search of more Americans. At various hamlets throughout northern New Mexico several men died violently. A pitched battle raged through the streets of

Mora. Raiders struck at the livestock ranches maintained in the foothills by army freighters.

The disorganized uprising had no chance to succeed. Army troops and a volunteer regiment of mountain men under Ceran St. Vrain, partner of the murdered governor, marched swiftly north from Santa Fe, brushed aside a ragtag force of insurgents, and burst into the church at the Taos Pueblo, where the diehard rebels had fortified themselves. At least 150 perished. The Americans lost 7 killed and 45 wounded.

The initiators of the revolt were tried before highly prejudiced juries. "Hang 'em!" cried one French-Canadian trapper as his group discussed its verdict. *"Sacrés enfants de grâce,* dey damn grand rascale, dey kill Monsieur Charles, dey take *son* topknot. . . . Hang 'em, hang 'em, *sa-acré-é!"* Fifteen did hang, six simultaneously by being forced to stand shoulder to shoulder, white cotton caps pulled down over their eyes, on a plank across a wagon bed under a specially erected gallows. As a silent crowd watched from the flat rooftops of Taos, the driver gave the two mules hitched to his wagon a cut with his whip, and that was that.

In 1846 a treaty with Great Britain brought the Pacific Northwest under American sovereignty; the 1848 treaty of Guadalupe Hidalgo with Mexico added the Southwest. Army forts appeared in New Mexico as the United States government set about fulfilling a promise to protect its new citizens from the Indians. Caravans of enormous freight wagons groaned with increasing frequency into Santa Fe. Long canvas-topped emigrant trains threaded South Pass on the way to Oregon and California. Supplying and servicing this new activity afforded more economic opportunity than did the remnants of the fur and Indian trades. Gradually the mountains north of New Mexico emptied of white men, save for those clustered around the posts that serviced the Oregon Trail. Other handfuls gathered around tiny Fort Connah, operated by the Hudson's Bay Company south of Flathead Lake in Montana and around a station very different from any emigrant or fur trading center—St. Mary's Catholic mission to the Flathead Indians in the beautiful Bitterroot Valley of Montana.

During the 1820's and 1830's the Flathead, Nez Percé, and Spokane Indians had picked up smatterings of Christianity from Catholic French-Canadians and Iroquois trappers who settled among them, and also from a few of their own young tribesmen who had been educated at the Anglican mission school maintained by the Hudson's Bay Company near today's Winnipeg. Eager for further instruction—the Indians at first equated religion with a "medicine" that would bring them both invulnerability and a command of such wonders as guns—the tribes sent various delegations to St. Louis to ask for teachers. The first missionaries, Protestants, went right on through the mountains to the Oregon country. Finally, in 1839, two Catholic Iroquois who had been adopted by the Flatheads caught the attention of a short, fat, red-faced Belgian-born Jesuit named Pierre Jean De

Smet. While one of the Iroquois spent the winter of 1839–40 in St. Louis in order to guide De Smet west the following spring, the other hurried back to the Bitterroot Valley to prepare the Indians.

Racked by malaria, the Jesuit father traveled with a supply caravan to the last rendezvous on Green River. There he met another Belgian who became an indispensable helper, Jean Baptiste de Velder, who had been trapping the mountains for fourteen years. In company with Bridger's brigade, De Smet, Velder, and an advanced deputation of Flatheads rode north to Pierre's Hole, just west of the Trois Tetons. Sixteen hundred Flatheads and Pend d'Oreille Indians gave the missionary an uproarious welcome: a few days earlier, after chanting prayers learned from the Iroquois, they had slain fifty Blackfeet without loss to themselves— obviously great medicine.

Singing and joking and each morning standing in circles around De Smet to learn further prayers, which half-breed Gabriel Prudhomme translated into their language for them, the nomads moved on north over the Divide to the headwaters of the Missouri. Though De Smet had first intended to inspect the Bitterroot Valley as a potential mission site, he now decided to hurry straight back to St. Louis. Enthralled by his reception and convinced of success, he wanted to spend the winter raising money and gathering a party so that he could start his work in the mountains the next year. This he did, returning to Montana in 1841 with two more priests, three lay brothers, and five teamsters, guided by ex-trapper Thomas Fitzpatrick. Their goods and the religious objects for their proposed chapel they carried in four two-wheeled carts and one small four-wheeled wagon.

They traveled with Pacific coast emigrants as far as southeastern Idaho and then struck north across the Divide into Beaverhead Valley, through Deer Lodge Valley, and down Hell Gate Canyon, a hard trip with the vehicles, whose draft oxen had to be supplemented with priests straining at the ends of ropes. After reaching the Bitterroot Valley where Missoula now stands, they turned south 25 miles and near today's Stevensville picked out the site for St. Mary's Mission. Racing winter, they erected a mud-daubed log building 25 feet wide by 33 feet long, its tiny windows covered with scraped deerskin. Surrounding the chapel and a dwelling hut was a crude log stockade. "At night," Father Mengarini recalled, "we rolled ourselves in several blankets, and then in a buffalo-robe; yet in the morning we awoke to find robe and blankets frozen into one piece. We crept out of our frozen shell and set it before the fire to thaw; and this we did daily through- out the long months of winter."

De Smet was called to other fields in 1846. Until then he traveled indefatigably, visiting many tribes and founding two more missions, both in the northern part of today's Idaho, one near Coeur d'Alene Lake and the second on Clark Fork River below Pend Oreille Lake. Each year, mean- while, a handful of reinforcements reached St. Mary's, bringing bits of equipment, packets of seed, a few head of livestock. They built a bigger chapel, set up a gristmill and a sawmill, the blades of the latter improvised from iron wagon tires, and enlarged their fields. With boards from the sawmill they erected twelve small frame buildings of various sorts. By 1846 they owned forty cattle and hogs.

At first the Indians were fascinated. Sprouting seed was a miracle with which the mountain nomads were unacquainted. Each day during the mission's first spring they came out to squat on the rail fence and watch, and were delighted when the plants began to appear. They were enthralled by the color and ritual of the church services, by the puppet shows with which they were entertained, and by the little orchestra that Father Mengarini formed with imported instruments. But as the novelty wore off they discovered many things they did not like. The fathers wanted them to devote less time to their exciting buffalo hunts and more to agricultural work, "toil being next to godliness," Father Palladino assured them, "and after piety, the best aid for fallen man." Their easy divorces and the polygamy that cared for the widows of men slain in battle were decried, as was their ancient joy of torturing captive Blackfeet. Dissolute mountain men who wintered among them added doubt by scoffing at the priests. Too, De Smet promised more things than his diocese could send and this created dissatisfaction. Another disillusionment to primitive minds was the discovery that prayer and religious medals did not necessarily make a warrior either invincible or invulnerable in battle.

A growing fear of white men increased the disenchantment. Westward, in Oregon, passing emigrant trains sowed deadly epidemics of measles. Greedy settlers seized Indian lands without recompense, and after the Whitman massacre of November, 1847, a punitive army marched ruthlessly through eastern Oregon. As word of these upheavals flashed from tribe to tribe, the mountain Indians began to regard even their priests with suspicion. Soon the fathers were shunned and could no longer count on supplies of dried buffalo meat nor on protection from raiding Blackfeet. In 1850 they gave up and for $250 sold their buildings to John Owen, a one-time army sutler who wanted to open a trading post.

Results disappointed Owen, too. His volume of trade dwindled from $1,880 in 1850 to $517 in 1853. Blackfeet harried his herds and killed one of his workers within sight of the post itself. In the summer of 1853 he decided, as others had decided throughout the mountains, that he might as well pull out.

Paradoxically, the increasing emptiness of the Rockies made them desirable to one group of people: the persecuted members of the Church of Jesus Christ of Latter-Day Saints, or Mormons as they were commonly called. Wherever they had settled within reach of non-Mormon neighbors, in the frontier regions of Ohio and Missouri, they had been brutally harried. An attempt to build a secure city, Nauvoo, in Illinois was frustrated when their leader, Joseph Smith, was lynched and his people, some 15,000 of them, were later forced, in February, 1846, to flee across the icy Mississippi to snow-chilled camps in Iowa. If their church ever was to rebuild, the Quorum of the Twelve Apostles decided, it would have to be in some isolated mountain wilderness where the Mormons could grow strong enough so that they would never again have to run from anyone.

Carefully they studied reports just published by the government of John Charles Frémont's two recent exploring expeditions into the West—of the first, which had taken him across South Pass to the upper tributaries of Green River and a romantically exhilarating climb of massive Fremont Peak in the Wind River Mountains; and, more pertinently, of the second, which in 1843–44 had taken him to Oregon and California. During the course of the latter adventure, Frémont had visited the Valley of the Great Salt Lake. Casually he remarked, in a somewhat perfunctory description of the area, "The [valley] bottoms are extensive; water excellent; timber sufficient; the soil good, and well adapted to the grains and grasses suited to such an elevated region. . . . A civilized settlement would be of great value here."

This generalized information was not very much to stake a whole people's future on but nothing better was available to guide Brigham Young and the Quorum. After anxious discussion and the perusal of all other travelers' tales they could find, the leaders decided to move their people across the Continental Divide into what came to be called Utah, there to establish the first and one of the very few planned American settlements, as distinct from Spanish, within the Rocky Mountains.

VII

THE BARRIER LAND

IN THE spring of 1846, 525 Mormon men reluctantly enlisted as the Mormon Battalion in the Army of the United States and joined the forces marching against Santa Fe and California. Thirty-five wives enrolled with them as laundresses, which was militarily acceptable in those days, and took their children along. This was a religious, not a patriotic, exercise. Most of the men drew advances against their pay and surrendered the money to the church, some $21,000, to aid their fellows toiling in confused segments across Iowa to the Missouri River.

Thirty-five hundred or so of these Saints passed the snowy months of 1846–47 in a cluster of huts called Winter Quarters, located just north of today's Omaha. Another 7,000 remained strung across Iowa, living out of their wagons or in wretched shanties. A disproportionate number were women, most of whom necessarily did the work of men. Although morale was generally high, some malcontents had defected and more would do so unless a firm future could be promised.

It was not possible to let so many people jump blindly westward. Hope demanded structuring: someone in authority had to assay a precise destination and come back to tell his followers, "This is the place. This is good." More practically, there had to be food and shelter waiting at the end of the trail, so that the first families to arrive in the fall could survive the mountain winter.

To provide these things, an advance party of 148 persons started west in seventy-two wagons as soon as the grass began to show in April, 1847. Three of the leaders—Brigham Young, his ponderous brother Lorenzo, and Heber Kimball—each had a wife along. Lorenzo Young's Harriet took with her two sons by an earlier marriage. The other 143 persons were adult males.

At Fort Laramie the group picked up several castoffs from the Mormon Battalion. The previous fall upward of a hundred ailing men and all but five of the women and children of that military detachment had been weeded out and sent north from the Santa Fe Trail to winter at the adobe trading fort of El Pueblo on the Arkansas River. Forty-three other Mormons journeying from the state of Mississippi to join the main migration had also landed at El Pueblo. In the spring a handful of these hard-tested mountain winterers, six women among them, rattled their wagons out of El Pueblo ahead of the others, coursed northward along the base of Colorado's Front Range, and by good chance encountered Brigham Young's advanced party on the North Platte.

As far as Fort Bridger the trail west had been worn deep by fur traders, missionaries, and Pacific-bound settlers—up the long valley of the Platte, through the Laramie Hills, streaked with black piñons and juniper, and across glaring flats of crusted alkali to blessed Sweetwater Creek, bordered on the north by the hard, angular Rattlesnake Hills. To the northwest there were startling views of the tall Wind River peaks, and then came treeless South Pass, so broad and level that one could not be quite sure at what point he crossed the Divide. A little beyond South Pass, the main Oregon Trail struck west across waterless wastes. A longer branch angled southwest through limitless sagebrush, crossed the Green, and led to eye-soothing cottonwoods dotting the grassy meadows along Black's Fork. Here was Bridger's stockaded fort, a haven for emigrants who had run out of supplies.

The year before, in 1846, fifty-seven California-bound wagons had tried to shorten their journey by opening a trail from Fort Bridger through the rugged Wasatch Mountains and on around the south shore of Great Salt Lake. The ordeal of the crossing had so delayed the last group of wagons, the ill-fated Donner party, that it had been disastrously trapped by snow in the Sierra Nevada. Still, wagons had managed to penetrate the formidable mountains to the southwest. Heartened by the knowledge, the advanced party of Mormons followed the faint wheel tracks over dismaying hills, where timber grew only on the steep north slopes, and down abrupt canyons choked with boulders and almost impenetrable mats of willow brush. Each stubborn obstacle increased the wayfarers' tension. The middle of July had slipped by, and they still must plant seed for the unknown number of Saints who were coming up the Platte Valley of Nebraska on their tracks.

They broke through the mountains at Emigration Canyon, shouted hosannah at the sight of the blue lake in the distance, and then turned north along the foothills. Reaching rich alluvial soil bordering what they would call City Creek, they halted. It was a desolate, wind-swept spot, absolutely treeless, midway on the long slope between the stark mountains and the southernmost tip of the sterile lake of brine. No life was visible, save for a few rabbits and wolves, many rattlesnakes, and hordes of loathsome black crickets. They had no time to be repelled, however; they must start food growing at once. Promptly they began to plant, softening the ground first by flooding it with water from the bright, cold creek. Three days later, after quick explorations in all directions, they voted, with only one dissenting voice, that here, beside their first garden, they would settle permanently.

A hundred and forty or so people from the Pueblo detachment soon appeared, and the combined forces began with a will to construct the rude beginnings of their metropolis. The Plat of the City of Zion, as the plan was called, had been conceived years before by Joseph Smith out of suggestions drawn from early New England town-settlement practices and from the socialistic utopian colonies that dotted the East from the 1820's into the 1840's. Wide streets divided a mile-square city into blocks of ten acres each. The central block was reserved for a temple. The rest were divided into lots one and a quarter acres in size, large enough for every dwelling to have its kitchen garden and barnyard. Farmers would not live on their farms, but in the town, along with artisans and merchants (as the Spanish colonists of New Mexico did) and would travel out to their fields each day, a custom calculated to avoid Indian raids on outlying houses and also to foster the tightly knit, church-oriented social culture of the people.

While surveyors laid out the city, other workers of the advanced party smoothed a wagon way to the nearest timber, seven miles distant, and cut logs for twenty-nine cabins, 16 by 14 feet. The buildings were lined up wall to wall so that their backs could form one side of a square stockade. At the suggestion of the winterers from El Pueblo the other three walls of the fort were built Mexican-style of adobe bricks. Farm workers meantime lengthened the irrigating ditch from City Creek and enlarged the original garden to a total of thirty-five acres planted to potatoes, corn, and vegetables.

As these preliminary steps neared completion, many of the men, Brigham Young among them, returned east in small parties to meet their families and to arrange for the orderly migration of still more Saints during subsequent years. For those who stayed the dry, hot benches became a still and lonely place. Then, in September and early October, the first inundation came—about 1,550 people in 556 wagons, driving herds of 2,213 oxen, 887 milk cows, 358 sheep, 124 horses, a few hogs, and 716 chickens.

Not so many people had been anticipated. Worse, the newcomers were ill-supplied. Although ordered to bring with them enough flour, sugar, salt meat, and the like to last for a year, most had fudged; when a man is contemplating an overloaded wagon, it is easy to underestimate needs and to overestimate the resources at the end of the trail. The shortages were further compounded when a surge of livestock broke into the garden and destroyed much of the late-maturing crop.

A rationing committee was formed "to buy, sell, exchange and distribute." Flour was limited to half a pound per person per day. Fortunately the winter was mild. Unhampered by snow, foragers ranged far to find edible plants and roots. One diarist tells of going out at sunrise with a grubbing hoe and a sack and walking six miles "to where the thistle roots grew. . . . I would dig until I grew weak and faint and sit down and eat a root and then begin again," until he had unearthed perhaps a bushel of roots for his family.

Work went busily on. Four hundred and fifty more cabins were hastily erected, many of adobe. An 11-mile fence was built around the city and a "Big Field" to the south. Nearly nine hundred acres in the field were planted to winter wheat. Gristmills and sawmills went hopefully up.

When the sun strengthened in the spring of 1848 voracious householders spaded and planted kitchen gardens—too soon. Late frosts nipped the sprouting greenery. And then the crickets came, a wriggling black carpet slithering over trenches and ditches, past anguished fighters flailing with sacks and branches and brooms. In despair the High Council discussed moving the gaunt people on across the terrible deserts to California. Before a decision solidified the gulls descended, wheeling flashes of white wings, and waddled along the furrows, gorging on crickets, vomiting, and gorging again. That took some of the pressure off the colonists. Partial harvests were achieved, but not enough to feed the 2,400 people who arrived in the fall of 1848. Again there were starving times throughout a snow-heaped winter as harsh as its predecessor had been mild. But there was no flagging in energy. Fields were enlarged again and planted with experience hard won from previous failures.

Again an apparent miracle intervened—the discovery of gold in California. When John Marshall made his famous strike several Mormons were nearby, discharged Battalion members and Saints who had sailed around the Horn to San Francisco. It would have been possible for those people, fortified by others hurrying from Utah, to have engrossed the best of the placer grounds before the rush from the East arrived. On the other hand, any such dispersal might have ended the church. Earnestly Brigham Young urged his suffering people to stay in Salt Lake City. The Lord, he declared, "will rebuke the frost and the sterility of the soil, and the land shall become fruitful. . . . We have the finest climate, the best water, and the purest air that can be found on earth. . . . Then, brethren, plow your land and sow wheat, plant your potatoes."

All but a handful heeded him. Though the main gold-rush trail passed through southern Idaho, well north of the Great Salt Lake, thousands of stampeders, desperate for provisions and fresh draft animals, detoured by way of the Mormon colony. The Saints, whose persistence had finally resulted in a surplus of crops, were able to sell food, animals, and services at high prices throughout both 1849 and 1850. They bought at bargain rates castoff iron bars, cloth, cookstoves, axes, chinaware, grindstones, plows, wagons, emaciated livestock, and harness—to say nothing of the discarded goods they salvaged along the main trail from South Pass as far as Nevada. And when the miners began trickling east again, many with bulging pokes of gold dust, the Mormons were waiting along the hardest stretch of their journey to supply them afresh.

This windfall of cash provided the church with funds for evacuating the faithful still waiting in Iowa and at Winter Quarters, and for aiding thousands of converts in England and the Scandinavian countries to reach the promised land. New settlements were projected as far away as western Nevada and southern California. Most, however, were tucked into the irrigable valleys that opened out of the Wasatch Mountains.

First a likely spot was located by scouts. Then a selected group of artisans and farmers was "called" by the church hierarchy to move into the region and form a town. Because of Indian dangers, the initial step often was the enclosing of a plaza for living and defense. Later the town was surveyed and dwelling sites distributed by the drawing of lots. At Sunday church services the whole town discussed the assignment of labor for community projects such as roads, bridges, fences, ditches, and sometimes flour mills and cooperative stores. Public supervisors allocated the two rarest commodities, timber and water, both of which were withheld from private ownership. The ideal was to let everyone share in a region's resources. Problems of distribution were solved with spontaneous folk ingenuity—the wild hay near Ephraim in the Sanpete Valley, for instance. Those who wanted a share of it attended a dance that lasted until midnight each July 25. Every male then dashed for the meadow. Each man, using a hand scythe, mowed a swatch around the hay he reached first, but he could have no more of the patch than he was able to cut during the subsequent daylight hours. There were some mighty sleepy men in Ephraim by sunset on July 26.

Irrigation, though familiar to the Spanish colonists of New Mexico, was strange to Anglo-Saxon people from the humid areas of Northern Europe and the Eastern United States. By painful trial and error the Mormons learned its techniques: the depths to which varying kinds of soil should be soaked for best results; the frequency with which water should be applied; the slope and contours a ditch should have for maximum efficiency. While struggling with these practical matters they also took, almost instinctively, the first tentative steps toward evolving a new jurisprudence (later codified more fully in Colorado) that would justify what they were doing.

English common law envisioned streams as highways or as sources of power for turning mill wheels. Custom decreed that water could be used by persons residing along riverbanks—riparian rights—only if it was returned to the stream in undiminished quantity. In the arid West, where crops far from riverbanks needed water to survive, this provision would not work.

Furthermore, agriculture to the Mormons was fraught with religious overtones, a renewal of self as well as a renewal and purifying of the earth. Water thus attached mystically as well as necessarily to crop land. If it could be beneficially used away from the river, then it could be legitimately diverted, no matter what loss was occasioned to the stream flow.

The Mormons also developed unique land-use patterns. In the humid East, where land was sold by the government only to actual settlers (in theory at least), pioneer farmers had scattered far and wide to suit their personal whims. In Utah, by contrast, fields were tightly clustered by the location of irrigation ditches and by the fact that farmers lived in town and did not wish to travel far to work. Limited acreage and numerous applications meant small plots. When the Big Field south of Salt Lake City was divided in September, 1848, individual holdings were restricted to five and ten acres each, the smallest being those nearest town. As was the case with dwelling and building sites within each village, church authorities imposed fairness in distribution by the casting of lots.

None of this accorded with American land laws. No official government treaty quieted Indian claims to the region; no official government survey established precise rectilinear bounds for the homesteads; no provisions were made for paying the government for the acreage. (This was in pre-homestead days, when lands were sold to settlers.) Finally, the Mormon solution ignored the standard American practice of awarding land only to people who resided on the plots they claimed.

The California miners were equally presumptuous in the ways in which they allotted mineral land to themselves. There were more miners in California than Mormons in Utah, however. Besides, extensive gold fields, like shortages of water, were something new under the American sun, whereas land was land, wasn't it? (The answer is no. Eastern land laws were as unsuited to the West as were Eastern water laws, but Congress never managed to realize this.) In any event, the government eventually bowed to the demands of the miners and the irrigators, but it refused to make exceptions in its land system in order to accommodate the Mormons. Angry clashes developed before the Saints yielded and gradually legalized their holdings by means of ghost homesteads and intricate quitclaim deeds to neighbors whom the homesteads threatened to displace.

Except to the Mormons, the Rockies were an unwelcome barrier on the way to California and Oregon. Even before the gold rush, frontier dwellers were crying out (in words like those put into italics by the *Herald* of Fort Smith, Arkansas) that it was the duty of the U.S. Army's Corps of Topographical Engineers "to *survey, mark, and* CUT OUT" a national wagon road to the West. To hard-breathing visionaries wagons were not enough. They insisted on railroads, a demand eagerly taken up by half a dozen Mississippi Valley towns, each hoping that it would fatten prosperously if it became the Eastern terminus of the line.

Seeking to further the claims of St. Louis, a handful of Missouri businessmen, led by Senator Thomas Hart Benton, urged a crossing due west through the central Rockies of today's Colorado. Too impatient to wait on the uncertain moods of Congress, they dug deep into their own pockets and commissioned Benton's flamboyant son-in-law, John Charles Frémont, to test the route's year-round potentials by examining the mountains during the winter of 1848–49.

Frémont seemed like a good choice. As a former member of the Army Corps of Topographical Engineers, he had taken three expeditions into or across the Rockies. The third adventure, which had landed him in California during the Mexican War, had also swept him into disgrace. Torn by conflicting orders during Commodore Stockton's struggle for authority with Brigadier General Stephen Kearny, Frémont had supported Stockton. Kearny triumphed. Vindictively he arrested Frémont and saw a court-martial sustain charges of mutiny, disobedience, and conduct prejudicial to good order. It was an overly severe verdict. President Polk would have reinstated Frémont, but the explorer refused to re-enter the service. Gathering together thirty-three men, many serving him devotedly without pay, he marched west into the teeth of winter, hoping that a successful railroad survey would restore his luster as a national hero.

On November 21, 1848, the party reached El Pueblo, whose wretched inhabitants were just beginning to abandon the place. The mountains ahead shone white with early snow. Though most trappers shook their heads over prospects, Frémont managed to hire as guide a man who had served him before—Old Bill Williams, sixty or more years old, shambling, cantankerous, and eccentric. Old Bill knew the mountains and the Indians, however, and at first Frémont felt lucky to have him.

At the Hardscrabble settlement, 25 miles nearer the white mountains, the men loaded every mule they had with shelled corn. Walking and leading the livestock, the adventurers surmounted the Wet Mountains and tackled the abrupt Sangre de Cristo Range at Mosca Pass, the gap which Antoine Robidoux had used in taking wagons to Fort Uncompahgre on the Gunnison—but that had been in summertime. In December, 1848, blasting winds, deep snow, and below-zero cold held the party to an agonizing creep, even after they had skirted the strange sand dunes at the foot of the pass and had pushed on to the sage flats of San Luis Valley.

In spite of appalling difficulties, Frémont regularly took the observations and made the calculations he needed for his reports. He kept his men in heart, though corn for the mules was dwindling and game for the men was rarely found. Shrouded by a frozen fog they marched up the Rio Grande toward the serrated peaks of the San Juans, one of the most chaotic sections of the Continental Divide. They could have skirted the canyon-torn area to the north or to the south, but Frémont was implacable about sticking to a direct route. Bewildered by the heavy snow, Old Bill Williams apparently forgot the exact location of the high summertime trails he had used in years past. Looking for a pass that wasn't where they had supposed it would be, the men floundered through a silent immensity of upended snow, among black trees, and out onto a barren ridge 12,000 feet high. Ahead of them rolled a heartbreaking tumble of blankness.

They staggered down the other side to a clump of trees. Storms pinned them beside eye-searing fires that slowly melted each mess group down into icy wells. The starved mules, braying their hunger to the howling nights and desperately eating each other's tails, began to die.

Frémont ordered a retreat. Foolishly he insisted on trying to retrieve the baggage, but had to abandon it near the Rio Grande. The party disintegrated. Before an advanced group of the strongest could reach a scattering of huts in northern New Mexico and send back help, eleven of the thirty-three men had perished.

Six of the survivors were so embittered at Frémont that they refused to continue with him when he went on west from Taos. Among them were Old Bill Williams and the three Kern brothers, Edward and Dick, the expedition's artists, and their older brother Ben, the doctor. The Kerns had been serving without pay because they had believed in Frémont, and their resignations left them destitute in a strange land. Hoping to retrieve their instruments, paints, and some coin that was cached with the baggage in the mountains, Benjamin Kern and Old Bill Williams rested two weeks in Taos and started back with several Mexican helpers.

Ute Indians had meantime been raiding the nearby settlements. To punish them Lieutenant James H. Whittlesey marched north from Taos with twenty-four soldiers and several civilian scouts. The detachment surprised a Ute camp a few miles south of the present Colorado border. In a confused fight in deep snow under tall yellow pines the soldiers, at a loss of two men, killed five Utes, wounded eight or more, and captured the tents, provisions, and horses of the defeated. Burning for revenge, the Utes trailed sullenly up the Rio Grande. By chance they stumbled across Ben Kern, Old Bill Williams, and the Mexicans, homeward bound with the retrieved baggage. The Indians slew the whites and seized the booty, but spared the Mexicans to take the story back to Taos. Although Edward Kern and Antoine Leroux, a trapper friend of Old Bill's, tried hard in the spring to recover the bodies, they failed.

Before word of Frémont's disaster had trickled back to Washington, Congress yielded grudgingly to frontier vociferations and appropriated a skimpy $50,000 for surveying wagon roads between the edge of settlement and the far side of the Rockies, but not to the Pacific. Part of the sum went to Lieutenant James H. Simpson of the Corps of Engineers, who during the summer of 1849 was to search out a route from Fort Smith, Arkansas, around the southern toes of the Sangre de Cristo Range to newly acquired Santa Fe, and on beyond if opportunity afforded. The rest of the money financed a smaller party under Captain Howard Stansbury, assisted by Lieutenant John Gunnison. They were to follow the heavily used Platte River-South Pass trail as far as the Hudson's Bay Company post of Fort Hall in what is now southeastern Idaho, swinging aside from the main route wherever short cuts appeared possible. That done, they were to link Fort Hall (under consideration as a military station) with Salt Lake City. Salt Lake City was then to be tied to Santa Fe by a military road that followed the Old Spanish Trail through southwestern Colorado.

Although wagon routes were the primary goal of both Stansbury and Simpson surveys, the dazzling news of gold in California raised frontier demands for a railroad to such a pitch that the explorers felt compelled to eye those possibilities as well.

Neither group completed its mission. Simpson's work was swallowed by a campaign against Navajo Indians in western New Mexico. Stansbury ignored part of his instructions. In his mind his greatest service to the mile-weary gold rushers would be a shortening of their journey. Travelers whose wagons swayed from South Pass southwest to Jim Bridger's stockade on Black's Fork, then northwest to Fort Hall, and southwest again to the Humboldt River in Nevada described an enormous, reversed letter S. Those who avoided the curves by following the Mormon Trail through Salt Lake City and on around the south shore of the lake ran into implacable deserts. The logical compromise, Stansbury decided, was a route just north of the lake, if a way suitable for wagons could be found through the dismaying canyons of the Wasatch Range.

With lanky Jim Bridger leading him first into one rock-sided, tree-filled gash and then another, Stansbury finally worked out a possible route into the mountain-backed valley, 15 miles from the lake, where the city of Ogden soon took shape. That done, he and his assistant, Lieutenant Gunnison, marked a wagon way to Fort Hall, wintered in Salt Lake City (where they got on well with the Mormons), and in the spring of 1850 completed the first thorough survey of the country around Salt Lake and Utah Lake. Deciding then that there would never be enough traffic between Salt Lake City and Santa Fe to justify a road through such inhospitable terrain, they headed back east.

To compensate for ignoring Santa Fe they sought to shorten the way from Bridger's Fort to the Platte River. Again Bridger was their guide, leading them eastward across the bleak sage deserts of southern Wyoming, along trickles of water bitter with alkali, up gentle slopes to a barren gap in the Continental Divide called Bridger Pass. "Here . . . our universal shout arose . . . and visions of home and all its joys floated through the imagination." Nor was home the only reason for whooping. They had found "a perfectly feasible, a most excellent route for wagon or railroad— easy grades, few bridges, no high, narrow, snow-filled canyons."

The optimism continued as the party worked on around the Medicine

Bow Mountains to the grassy, "undulant" Laramie Plains. Stansbury meant to finish the work by running a survey from the area of present-day Cheyenne down Lodgepole Creek to the South Platte, but a crunching fall from his horse landed him in an ambulance wagon that took the more conventional route home through Fort Laramie to the north. Even without Lodgepole he calculated that his new route would save emigrants 61 miles (three or more days in a wagon) between the eastern flank of the Rockies and Fort Bridger. Furthermore, he had seen nothing that would check a railroad.

Stansbury's survey was a more remarkable job than anyone realized at the time. Within a decade the stagecoaches of the Overland Mail would be rolling through Bridger Pass. Within two decades the Union Pacific would be following most of the same route, avoiding Bridger Pass for an easier grade a short distance north but coming down into Ogden rather than into Salt Lake City almost exactly as Stansbury first suggested. The survey's main trouble (aside from its saying nothing about the country west of the Great Salt Lake) was political: the proposed railroad would start from Iowa and that suited no one except Iowans.

Simpson meantime reported from New Mexico that a railway was physically possible there too. But he questioned the economics of so costly a project in areas devoid of population and of developed resources. "To my mind," he wrote, "the time had not yet come when this [Southwestern] or any other railroad can be built over this continent." He was right, of course, but the expansionists of his time were in no mood to heed either his explicit pessimism or the implications of Frémont's disaster. The railroad chorus swelled in all sections until finally, in 1853, in a political ploy designed to please everyone, Congress authorized four parallel surveys to determine which crossing would be "the most practicable and economical."

None of the authorized routes went up the Platte, ostensibly because Stansbury had covered the section but actually because the weight of votes did not lean that way. Two of the routes went south of the main Rockies, one of them duplicating much of Simpson's work. (The Secretary of War, who had ultimate responsibility for the surveys, was Jefferson Davis, a Southerner.) Of the remaining two, one followed Frémont's ill-fated steps into the central Rockies. The fourth, starting at St. Paul, pushed into the northern Rockies of today's Montana.

This northern survey was by far the most elaborate of the four. Its leader was Isaac I. Stevens, a slim, short, fiercely aggressive veteran of the Mexican War who had just been appointed governor of newly formed Washington Territory. Eager to populate his wilderness by enticing in a railroad, Stevens managed to obtain financing for 240 men. Part of this force he sent around the Horn by ship. It was to work east from the Columbia while Stevens himself led the main group west from St. Paul.

The east-bound detachment met John Owen as he was disconsolately riding away from Fort Owen, the successor to St. Mary's Mission in the Bitterroot Valley, and encouraged him to return to his stockade. Stevens meanwhile split his own contingent into several groups and sent them across the Continental Divide by various easy passes. The surveyors also located five far more difficult ways over the heavily timbered, long-ridged mountains that slope from the Bitterroots westward across the Idaho Panhandle. To test winter conditions, Stevens left a detachment behind near Owen's Fort in charge of Lieutenant John Mullan, a twenty-three-year-old graduate of West Point. Mullan's men explored exuberantly, even taking a wagon over the Divide at Mullan Pass in March, 1854. No trouble there, they reported, not realizing that they were benefiting from an unusually mild season.

The search for a route through the central Rockies was led not by Frémont, who wanted the assignment, but by Captain John Gunnison, who had surveyed the Salt Lake area four years earlier with Howard Stansbury. Fortified by several survivors of the Frémont disaster and blessed by a kindly summer, Gunnison followed the old trapper trail across Sangre de Cristo Pass into San Luis Valley and avoided the San Juans by swinging north over Cochetopa Pass. Beyond Cochetopa he ran into the startling half-mile-deep slit of colorful granite known today as the Black Canyon of the Gunnison River, a National Monument. In skirting that impassable gorge, Gunnison had to surmount several sage-covered hills so steep that he, like Simpson, doubted the economic possibilities of a railroad. He kept diligently on, however, crossing the thirsty deserts of east-central Utah and threading a difficult way through the Wasatch Plateau well south of Salt Lake City.

Near Sevier Lake he walked into an ambush of Pahvant Indians, blood-hungry because California-bound emigrants had wantonly killed one of their tribesmen a few days earlier. Eight surveyors died. Among them were Gunnison, Frederick Creuzefeldt (sometimes rendered Creutzfeldt), botanist for Frémont's disastrous fourth expedition, and Richard Kern, whose brother Ben had been killed by Utes in Colorado.

Frémont meanwhile had stubbornly decided to outdo Gunnison by following the same route over Cochetopa Pass in the dead of winter. Bolstered once again by private financing, he hired ten Americans, two Mexicans, and ten Delaware Indians. Compared to the winter of 1848–49 this was a gentle year. Even so, the party had to kill and devour at intervals twenty-seven of their horses to avoid starvation. In the Utah deserts an engineer named Oliver Fuller fell behind and had to be rescued by the Delawares, his feet "frozen black to the ancles." Famished though they were, the others lugged Fuller with them as they struggled across the snow-heaped southern arms of the Wasatch Plateau. Their camps were so miserable that Frémont could not look at his men's gaunt faces without suffering, he said, horrible memories of the San Juan debacle; most of the evenings he brooded alone in his tent. At the point of rescue Fuller died. The others dragged on into the new Mormon settlement of Parowan, and there the expedition fell apart.

The four government exploring parties, whose reports were published in twelve fat, entrancingly illustrated volumes, furthered railroading no more than did Frémont's private fiasco. All were deficient in the kind of meticulous engineering data a railroad builder would need and as a result their cost estimates were little more than guesses. What ultimately killed them, however, was not their inadequacy but the virulent sectionalism between North and South. No matter what the surveys said, neither side would yield the route to the other.

To the mountain Indians, who of course knew nothing about the divisions among the whites, the surveys were one more indication that their remote lands would soon be faced with absorption. Look at what had already happened. In 1851 the Indian agents of the United States government had assembled 10,000 barbarically clad nomads onto a council ground beside the North Platte River east of Fort Laramie. Most of the natives were from the high plains, but there were observers there from as far away as Utah and the eastern slope of the Montana Rockies. They watched uneasily as the tribes of the plains consented to confine themselves within arbitrary boundaries; they heard them accept the government's offer of $50,000 a year in goods in exchange for a promise that emigrants along the Platte would not be molested. The beginning of the end . . . ?

None of the $50,000 went to the Shoshoni of Wyoming or to the Bannocks of southern Idaho, although the endless tramping of the whites was equally devastating to their desert-cramped grass and trees and game. Thus it was a sour satisfaction to them, perhaps, to learn that the United States Senate broke the promise of its own negotiators and without consulting a single Indian cut the terms of the annuity agreement with the Plains tribes from fifty years to ten. The unilateral change also suggested how much faith an Indian could place in a white man's word.

Other portents unsettled the mountain tribes. They knew how swiftly and brutally the scattered bands in California were being displaced by the gold rushers. They listened to tales of the wars in southern Oregon and to reports of the growing rebelliousness among the tribes of the Columbia Plateau. With grim joy they heard of the success of the Apaches and Navajos in New Mexico, where red warriors raided the settlements with such impunity that angry citizens of Santa Fe hanged their territorial governor to the flagpole in the central plaza in protest. The United States Secretary of War grew so discouraged that he seriously proposed what has since become a dull joke: let the government buy out the inhabitants of the more vulnerable areas of New Mexico, resettle them on safer lands, and give the vacated country back to the Indians. A quixotic remark, surely— though it would not have seemed so to the Indians, if they had heard it. To them the persistent little hit-and-run victories were food for hope. Perhaps the whites could be stopped after all, at least in the mountains.

VIII

THE MOUNTAIN WARS

IN 600 B.C., according to the Book of Mormon, white men from ancient Israel reached the New World. Some of their descendants, the Lamanites, fell into evil ways and waged a thousand-year war on the defenders of the good. The Lamanites eventually won the war, but were stamped with a dark skin as a sign of their evil. From them sprang the Indians, fallen souls but capable of redemption, a calling undertaken with varying degrees of earnestness by Mormon missionaries.

In January, 1850, a band of Utes stole half a hundred head of livestock from the families who had recently settled on choice meadows below jagged Provo Peak, where the Provo River rushes into Utah Lake. Dutifully the settlers wrote Brigham Young, asking that they be allowed to forget theology for the moment and chastise the hostiles. Young agreed. Reinforced by militia from Salt Lake City, the settlers cornered the Utes in an abandoned log building, killed several, and imposed a frontier-style peace on the survivors. This done, the Mormons resumed their proselytizing, baptizing the Ute chief Walkara in March, 1850, and a year later designating him as an elder in the Mormon Church.

The conversion failed to stick. Settlers kept felling the land's few trees, diverting its water, slaying the game. When the Mormons capped these affronts in 1853 by ordering the Utes to end their century-old slave trade with New Mexico, Walkara retorted by raiding the adobe hamlet of Springville just outside Provo. Other attacks terrified the raw little towns in Sanpete Valley. An unknown number of Indians and twelve whites died (or perhaps nineteen; accounts vary) before Brigham Young and Walkara worked out a solid peace in the spring of 1854—solid in the sense that there was no more trouble with the Indians of central Utah for another decade.

Other difficulties developed farther east, however, in Green River Valley. Each summer the last derelict mountain men gathered with their native wives and half-breed children at strategic spots beside the stream.

There they built huts and picked up cash by operating rickety ferryboats for the westbound emigrants. They also traded buckskin and fresh livestock for flour and kettles and worn-out animals that they could take into the hills and fatten. Part of their fiber was woven out of the valley's feel of space and freedom, out of the lift of the Wind River peaks to the northeast, the Uintas to the south. They did not wish to leave, and thanks to a few weeks of work and barter while the emigrants were passing through, they hoped they would not have to.

The Mormons waved aside their tenuous squatter rights. When Utah Territory was created by Congress, it extended east to the crest of the Continental Divide and north almost to South Pass. Governor Brigham Young immediately asserted jurisdiction by creating Green County out of what is now southwestern Wyoming. As he had a perfect right to do for the sake of internal improvements, he dispatched a party of workers to eliminate the ferryboats by building toll bridges across the winding river during the fall of 1852 while the water was low. He also offered Jim Bridger and Bridger's partner, fat, hard-drinking Louis Vasquez, $8,000 for Fort Bridger on Black's Fork of the Green.

The "fort," which hadn't a loophole in it for muskets, consisted of eight low log buildings—dwelling apartments, a store, a carpentry shop, a blacksmithy—arranged around a hollow square. High pickets surrounded the structures and the livestock corral to the north. Vasquez, who had opened a mercantile establishment of sorts in Salt Lake City, perhaps wanted to sell. Bridger did not. Besides, he thoroughly disliked the Mormons, who took hundreds of wagons past the trading post each summer, devouring the grass and frightening the game but buying scarcely a thing. The Mormons were well aware of his feeling. Brigham Young wrote in one letter: "I believe that Old Bridger is death on us, and if he saw that 400,000 Indians were coming against us, and any man were to let us know, he would cut his throat."

The mountain men who used Bridger's Fort as their headquarters shared Jim's antipathy. Most of the trappers came from, or had connections with, the settlements of western Missouri, scene of virulent anti-Mormon demonstrations during the late 1830's. Predisposed by these old hatreds to think the worst of their new neighbors, the trappers reacted violently when the Mormon bridgebuilders threatened their ferry monopoly. Through their native wives they spread tales among the Indians that the Mormons planned to dispossess the red men of their best meadows. The Indians (Utes and Shoshoni, enemies of each other but united in dislike of settlers) put on a show of force that frightened the bridgebuilders back to Salt Lake City.

Young retorted by granting three residents of Salt Lake City a license to operate the Green River ferries. In the spring of 1853 the grantees and their men occupied the empty ferry sites without trouble, but when the vanguard of the year's emigration appeared a gang of armed trappers seized the boats and cabins and ran the Mormons off. The licensed operators thereupon entered a suit for trespass in Salt Lake City, asking $30,000 in damages.

Meantime the Walkara war had erupted in central Utah. Like most territorial governors, Young was also ex officio superintendent of Indian Affairs for his district. By virtue of that authority he revoked all licenses within Utah for bartering with the Indians "to prevent trading of guns, powder, and lead to our enemies." Jim Bridger, far removed from the scene of conflict, paid the order no heed. He probably would have said, with colorful asides, that he was being humane; his Indians had to have ammunition for the hunting on which they subsisted. To this the embattled settlers would have replied that in wartime an armed Indian did not always confine his targets to animals.

Whether the church hierarchy really feared the Walkara trouble would spread to the Green or whether they saw in Bridger's lawbreaking an opportunity to get rid of him—or both—is impossible to say. In any event, in August, 1853, a posse marched to Fort Bridger to arrest the trader. He escaped. The disgruntled posse confiscated his goods and continued northeast to retake the ferries. There was a battle. Apparently two or three mountain men died. (Surviving accounts are sparse and contradictory.) The rest fled. The posse confiscated the losers' livestock and withdrew.

In spite of the victories, the Mormons feared they could not hold the area, through which thousands of their converts passed every summer, unless they placated the Indians, over whom the trappers exerted great influence. Accordingly a mission was dispatched in November, 1853, to woo the Lamanites, even to the extent of marrying among the Shoshoni as the trappers did.

The missionaries intended to base themselves on Fort Bridger, but when they arrived on November 15, after a hard struggle with snow on the Bear River Divide, they found that Jim had outfoxed them again. During the first week in November he and a professional surveyor had measured off nearly 4,000 acres along the stream. Since this was far more land than the U.S. government allowed to pre-emptors, Bridger probably hoped to validate the claim under the Mexican laws that had prevailed when he and Vasquez had built the fort. Having completed the survey, he departed again, after telling several mountain men who were holed up in the buildings for the winter that he intended to file the plat with the General Land Office in Washington, which he did.

This information the trappers relayed to the missionaries with sour relish. Fearing legal complications if they jumped the claim now, the Saints moved on past the juniper-dotted bluffs to Smith's Fork, twelve miles away. There they built Fort Supply, designed to be a rest stop for Mormon emigrants as well as a mission station.

By the spring of 1854 nearly a hundred men were working around Fort Supply, plowing, planting, building, ditching. The energy evidently convinced Bridger's partner, Louis Vasquez, that there was no use bucking such competition. In August, 1855, he agreed to sell the fort to the Mormon Church for the $8,000 that had been offered Bridger earlier, $4,000 down and the balance in fifteen months. (The remaining $4,000 wasn't actually paid until 1858.) This gave the Mormons control of the best hay lands in the area, high sweeping valleys with the Uintas looming grandly behind—a haven of almost incalculable value for incoming converts, if the church could keep the area.

The mission fared less well. Early in 1854 a handful of workers who had picked up a smattering of the Shoshoni language visited Chief Washakie to assure him that their hearts were good and to ask for Indian girls to wed. According to the recollections of missionary James S. Brown, Washakie replied that "if any one of us found a girl that would go with him, it would be all right; but the Indians must have the same privilege among the white men." That ended that line of approach. Afterwards Brown held other talks with Washakie, giving him a copy of the Book of Mormon and flattering letters from Brigham Young, but the growing strength of the whites in the area was probably more effective than those gestures in keeping the Shoshoni calm. In any event, Brown switched to ferry operations and the mission seems to have withered away for want of urgency.

A less pragmatic Mormon mission and hence more nearly comparable to the stations which the Presbyterians located among the Cayuses and Nez Percés and those which the Catholics built for the Coeur d'Alenes and Flatheads was the Salmon River Mission of the Church of Latter-Day Saints, in east-central Idaho. Established in 1855, it commanded a fine narrow valley, well timbered to the east, on the ancient north-south Indian and trapper trail that connected the Snake River with the upper Missouri and the Bitterroot Valley. Lewis and Clark had descended to that particular branch of the Salmon River after their epochal crossing of the Continental Divide half a century before. In spite of their great adventure, the Mormon names were the ones that stuck. The twenty-seven male missionaries who built the stockaded post named it Limhi after a king in the Book of Mormon. The word, soon corrupted to Lemhi, extended quickly to nearby geographical features—Lemhi River, Lemhi Pass, and so on.

The local Bannocks, a subtribe of Shoshoni under a chief called the Le Grand Coquin, greeted the Mormons as other mountain tribes had earlier greeted the Presbyterians and Catholics—with curiosity, enthusiasm, and an eager hope that through this new medicine they could obtain the goods the white men knew how to produce. Within a year the Mormons at Lemhi could boast that they had converted and baptized a hundred savages. Otherwise luck was bad. Grasshoppers destroyed their crops in 1856 and again in 1857, and they had to send to Salt Lake City for help. Many were ready to quit, but Young revived inspiration by visiting the station early in 1857 and praising the work. Families arrived to relieve the austerity, and with the growth of normal home patterns hope lifted again. Best of all, the Bannocks, though losing their initial interest in religion, did appear to be staying peaceful, although across the mountains in northeastern Oregon and eastern Washington, vicious wars were beginning to erupt.

During the early years of settlement the Mormons relied on their own negotiators and missionaries to calm the Indians and, persuasion failing, on their own militia. By contrast, southern Colorado's first Spanish-Americans (as U.S. Mexicans came to be called) turned to the United States government.[1] In taking over the Southwest after the war this country offered the inhabitants two sweeping promises: it would review the enormous land grants made along the northern perimeter of New Mexico shortly before the conflict, confirming them in so far as the vague descriptions allowed; and it would protect the residents of the newly acquired territories from the Indians, something the Mexican government had never accomplished.

On the strength of these guarantees the owners of the grants were able, during the early 1850's, to persuade settlers to occupy chosen sites along the eastern foothills of the Sangre de Cristo Mountains in northeastern New Mexico; in the southern stretches of San Luis Valley; and at the base of Colorado's Greenhorn Peak, where long ago Anza had killed the Comanche chief Cuerno Verde. In addition, a handful of independent souls ventured into the Greenhorn-Arkansas River area on their own. A trapper named Marcelino Baca took up cattle ranching near crumbling El Pueblo, which in 1853 was reoccupied by a ragtag collection of farmers. To protect all these settlements the War Department built Fort Union in a treeless swale near Mora, northeastern New Mexico, and Fort Massachusetts on the spectacular western edge of San Luis Valley, well up the massive flank of Blanca Peak (14,363 feet).[2]

Indians raided the settlements in spite of the forts. The bloodiest of the attacks came at dawn on December 24, 1854. A band of Utes and Jicarilla Apaches drove off Marcelino Baca's livestock, killed a man or two they encountered along the trail, and splashed across icy Fountain Creek to knock on the gates of El Pueblo, crying out that they were hungry and

[1] The term "southern Colorado" in this context is an anachronism. Until Colorado Territory was formed in 1861, New Mexico extended north to the Arkansas River east of the Sangre de Cristo Range and, on the west, embraced the drainage of the Rio Grande, that is, the entire peak-girt San Luis Valley. Locations are easier to visualize, however, if current boundaries are used as points of reference.

[2] Fort Massachusetts' location was more eye-catching than strategic. It was supplanted in 1858 by Fort Garland, a few miles away. Fort Garland has been restored as a museum by the Colorado Historical Society. Fort Union is maintained as a National Monument by the federal government.

wanted to trade for corn. Inside, an all-night party was just breaking up. (It was Mexican custom to celebrate Christmas Eve on December 23.) A foolish drunk opened the gates. The Indians massacred seven or more men and kidnaped the few children and the one woman in sight. Later, after they had been defeated by a war party of Arapahoes, the Utes killed the woman because she kept weeping, and hung her scalp, its black hair streaming, to a tree branch in Wet Mountain Valley.

For some time before the raid citizens in New Mexico had been belaboring the army for its ineffectiveness. If this last massacre went unpunished, a great outcry would surely follow. With grim and unusual celerity, therefore, Colonel Thomas Fauntleroy marched a column of regulars out of Fort Union to reinforce the eighty-man garrison at Fort Massachusetts. Volunteers hurried up from New Mexico under Ceran St. Vrain, with Kit Carson as his chief of scouts. They chased the Utes out of San Luis Valley over Poncha Pass into the Arkansas Valley, killing several in a series of running skirmishes. Then, as their horses began to fail in the deep snow, the soldiers returned through bitter cold to Fort Massachusetts.

The commanding general in Santa Fe ordered them back into the field; popular sentiment in New Mexico would not be satisfied with so mild an action as that. Surprisingly, the soldiers were eager to oblige. While Ceran St. Vrain's volunteers harried the Apaches through the Raton Mountains to the east, Fauntleroy's command marched back toward Poncha Pass hunting Utes. Learning of a big village camped within the throat of the pass itself, Fauntleroy drove his men thirty-two hours with only one pause for a cold meal. They found the Indians dancing and whooping around a large fire. Under cover of darkness they boxed the camp and attacked. Their rifle flashes—"most beautiful to behold," Fauntleroy wrote in his report— almost eclipsed the light of the fire. The surprise fusillade killed forty Indians and wounded more. At their leisure the soldiers captured six bewildered children and destroyed a huge pile of equipment. Two whites were wounded, one of whom died when surgeons sawed off his maimed leg.

That quieted the Utes for a while. The little settlements in the San Luis Valley, each built around a Spanish-style plaza with an adobe church at one side, dug out their irrigating ditches (they hold the first water rights on record in Colorado), planted their fields, and grazed their scrawny sheep up into the piñon-clad foothills. A few gringos (Americans) moved in to build stores and gristmills. Notable among them was Lafayette Head, founder of the town of Guadalupe and first lieutenant governor (1876) of the state of Colorado, the benevolent political boss and long-time legislative representative of several thousand Spanish-speaking, largely illiterate colonists who formed—and to an extent still form—in the heart of the southern Rockies a pattern of settlement far more uncharacteristic of the sweep of American pioneering than even the "peculiar" Mormons, to use the Mormons' own adjective for themselves.

In the north, meantime, Governor Isaac I. Stevens of Washington Territory was bustling off toward the Rockies to implement a new notion in American Indian policy: the confining of the nomads to carefully delineated reservations. In return for ceding lands outside the reservation to the government, the Indians were to be fed and clothed after a fashion and instructed in the civilized arts.

At Walla Walla in eastern Washington, in the Bitterroot Valley of Montana, out in Blackfoot country on the plains, the busy little governor assembled, throughout the summer of 1855, huge councils of suspicious tribesmen, and during long, hot sessions of oratory gave them his pitch. Reluctantly the listeners agreed to what he suggested—or seemed to agree, although the interpreters at the councils were so incompetent that neither the red men nor the whites really understood what the other side said. One way or another, however, Stevens had his reservations recognized and his treaties signed by the chiefs. The War Department, which had been fearing a general uprising throughout the Northwest, drew a sigh of relief. Perhaps the worst was over.

It wasn't. During that same summer of 1855 gold discoveries drew a rush of miners to the region of Colville in eastern Washington. The invasion and its attendant clashes with the Indians gave the tribes of the Columbia Plateau justification for repudiating Stevens' treaties and going to war. They sought help from the mountain Indians. But though the tribes of the northern Rockies were likewise dissatisfied with the treaties Stevens had rammed down their throats, they felt no immediate pressures. The only settlements in their area were Fort Owen, where a few mountain men raised cattle and helped John Owen farm, and two Catholic missions. One white church stood on a bold eminence a few miles away from the scalloped shores of Coeur d'Alene Lake in Idaho. The other, St. Ignatius', a replacement for St. Mary's, had been founded in 1854 by the persistent Jesuits in a valley south of Flathead Lake, Montana, close to the square-faced ramparts now called the Mission Range. Able, dedicated fathers ran both places. Together with John Owen, who doubled as government Indian agent for the region, they worked diligently and successfully to preserve quiet. Since Stevens often followed the common northwest line of charging every Jesuit in range with fomenting Indian dissatisfaction, there was a certain selflessness in the fathers' tidying up behind him.

When the Army of the United States finally did march across the Continental Divide in 1857 it was not against Indians but against American citizens, the 45,000 or so Mormons of Utah Territory. The Saints had been stiff-necked in their relations with the federal government ever since the formation of the territory in 1851. Although Brigham Young had been appointed their governor, the other officials proved to be uncooperative strutters of mediocre ability, at least from a Mormon point of view. They were captious about some of the things Young had done before they arrived. They elevated themselves in their own eyes by being difficult in the matter of releasing federal funds for necessary projects. One of them, with singular ill tact, used a Pioneer Day platform to harangue a large audience about its patriotism and about the virtue of Mormon women—the last an infuriating reference to church-sanctioned polygamy.

Badgered unmercifully by the excited Saints, the first group of officials went home before their terms expired (the Mormons thereupon derided them as Runaways) and recriminations began to fly. Mormons, not Indians, were accused of being the true murderers of Gunnison's railroad surveyors. Bridger and the federal Indian agents who visited the Green River country spread wild tales about the clashes over the ferryboats. An inefficient, perhaps peculating freighter named Magraw, who lost a lucrative mail contract to a Mormon, added his share of lurid accusations.

The Mormons' own antics gave basis to widespread charges that they were openly opposed to the government. Fearful that federal land surveys would upset their own land patterns, many of them refused cooperation in every annoying way they could devise and bullied one recorder so mercilessly that he fled to California. They were particularly antagonistic toward the federal judges, most of whom were sorry hacks and one of whom brought a Washington prostitute with him to Salt Lake City and let her sit in court, passing him ribald notes as he heard cases. In an effort to circumvent the courts presided over by these men, the Mormons illegally expanded the jurisdiction of their own local probate courts. When the device failed to work as well as hoped, a mob broke into the office of the federal judge involved, secreted his official records, and threw his books and private papers into a privy, where they were burned.

Feverish reports of these doings filled the Eastern press. Mormondom was pictured as an iron-clad theocratic dictatorship, the antithesis of American democratic ideals, where church and state were rigidly separated. Nativists pointed to the large foreign immigration into Utah as another sign of un-American activity. But what really stirred public ire were tales of universal polygamy (actually only 3 percent or so of the Saints ever indulged in plural marriages), of white slavery and downtrodden womanhood. Unheard in the clamor were Mormon retorts that in Utah, where women outnumbered men, polygamy was a social benefit and not a sign of immorality; that there was far less adultery in Utah than in New England; and that the Salt Lake City newspapers, unlike those of New York City, found no need to advertise cures for venereal disease.

In May, 1857, the uproar reached such a pitch that President Buchanan, urged on by Secretary of War John B. Floyd, a Southerner, declared Utah to be in rebellion. Ever since then speculative historians have been burrowing into the pronouncement in search of hidden motives. They have found all kinds of skeletons. A favorite one runs something like this: Although John Charles Frémont had been defeated in the Republican party's first bid for the Presidency, the new group had drawn surprising strength from the plank in its platform that promised to wipe from the Western territories "those twin relics of barbarism, polygamy and slavery." A demonstration against the less explosive issue, polygamy, might steal some Republican thunder and distract attention from the slavery conflicts that were currently giving bloody Kansas its nickname.

Be all that as it may (the slavery argument as well as several others are summarized in Norman F. Furniss' study, *The Mormon Conflict*), Buchanan removed Young as governor and appointed in his place a waddling butterball of a man, Alfred Cumming. The President then ordered the United States Army to march west as a *posse comitatus* to see that Cumming was properly installed.

No official notice of these developments was sent to Utah. A Mormon mail carrier who chanced to learn in Kansas what was afoot rushed the word back, averaging a phenomenal hundred miles per day. By good chance he gained Brigham Young's side in Big Cottonwood Canyon near Salt Lake City during the annual Pioneer Day celebration, an emotional occasion when Mormons gathered to glorify past martyrdoms as well as past accomplishments. With a thrill of religious fervor the assembly in the canyon listened to Young's announcement of their country's threat against them. Persecution again, to be resisted with all their might!

They had little to work with. In 1855, a year when 4,225 emigrants poured across the plains into Utah, plagues of grasshoppers and a severe drought sorely hurt crop production. Deep snow the following winter killed half the cattle in the territory; the church herd lost 1,600 of 2,000 animals. Of the many disastrous results, one of the worst was a withering away of the Perpetual Emigrating Fund, which was used to finance converts coming from Europe.

In an effort to make-do, the church devised the famous two-wheeled handcart of Mormon mythology—a small wooden vehicle capable of transporting the baggage of four or five families if they traveled light. During 1856, 1,900 footsore European newcomers pushed and pulled these creaky contraptions from Iowa City to Salt Lake City. Winter caught the last two companies near South Pass. In spite of heroic rescue work by helpers from Utah, 202 exhausted walkers simply lay down in the wind-driven snow and died.

The horror prompted the church to work out better means for transporting not only converts but mail and freight as well. The upshot was the Brigham Young Express and Carrying Company, commonly called the YX

Company (from Young Express). Mormon-style villages were to be laid out every 50 miles or so along the emigrant trail, so that crops could be raised, animals fed, travelers sheltered. Donations in cash and goods for financing the project were solicited throughout Utah. Workers had been recruited, purchases made, several sites selected, and actual construction had begun when word arrived that the army was marching. Every single trail station was abandoned and the workers pulled back to Utah. It was a staggering loss; the Saints had been straining every resource to make the bold scheme work and its abrupt failure left them strapped.

There was no cash in the treasury. The Nauvoo Legion, a citizens' army of upward of 3,000 men, was organized to repel the invasion but lacked sufficient ammunition and rifles. No factories existed for remedying the deficiencies. In the face of these appalling difficulties Brigham Young prepared to fight—or at least went through the motions of preparing. Again one can only speculate about underlying motives. Quite probably the church hierarchy was simply running a desperate bluff, hoping that if it was able to delay the army until it was snowbound somewhere outside Utah, they could use the resultant period of quiet to start negotiations with the government.

On the credit side, the Mormons that year had raised bulging barnfuls of crops. Some ammunition and revenue were provided by calling back to Utah colonists in two prosperous settlements located beside the trails to California—one at Genoa, Nevada, near the eastern foot of the Sierra Nevada and the other at San Bernardino in Southern California. Both groups were well equipped with rifles and powder, and both raised cash by selling their holdings to non-Mormons. Three years later the fantastic gold and silver mines of Virginia City, Nevada, roared into prominence near Genoa; three decades later real estate values in Southern California soared dizzily. The retreating Mormons, in other words, lost more heavily than they realized at the time they abandoned future hopes to meet a present emergency. But the very fact that they did it at all indicates the defenders' greatest strength—a hardy, devoted people used to organization and intense, unquestioning discipline.

Another Mormon resource was the ineptness of the United States Department of War. Although strategists must have known how early the Rockies might be blanketed by the kind of winter that a year before had killed 200 handcart Mormons, the first infantry contingents, 1,200 strong, did not straggle out of Fort Leavenworth, in eastern Kansas, on the start of their thousand-mile march until July 18. (Buchanan had ordered the expedition about May 20.) They were unsupported by cavalry, which was detained by continuing troubles in Kansas. A supreme commander, Colonel Albert Sidney Johnston, was not named until September 11. The governor-designate, Alfred Cumming, and his wife, did not start west with an escort of dragoons until even later. Interim command devolved on

Colonel Edmund Alexander, an indecisive martinet who quailed under the responsibilities of his position.

In early October the advance units straggled over South Pass into the valley of the Green. Free to roam at will because of the lack of United States cavalry, Mormon raiders destroyed three wagon trains carrying 150 tons of food. They made off with 1,100 head of draft oxen. To cripple the effectiveness of the rest of the animals they burned the dry grass in the rare meadows along the Green's meandering tributaries. They did it without shooting at anybody.

Although Alexander was now desperately short of stock, he decided to try to climb across the Bear River Mountains in order to outflank the reputedly impregnable forts (he did not order a reconnaissance of them) that the Mormons had built along the main trail in Echo Canyon. Blizzards and starved oxen checked him. In dismay he plodded back toward the Green. By then 3,000 oxen had died. When Colonel Albert Sidney Johnston at that point overtook his command, he gave up all thought of reaching Salt Lake City before spring and ordered the army, swollen now to 2,500 men, into miserable winter quarters along Black's Fork, near the scorched remains of Bridger's Fort, burned by the Mormons as they retreated. Bridger, incidentally, tried to realize something out of the place, which he did not concede had been legitimately sold, by renting it and its pasture lands to the army for ten years at $600 a year—if he could establish title. He never succeeded.

Johnston's greatest need was livestock, and the closest place to buy them was New Mexico. He assigned the errand to Captain Randolph B. Marcy and ordered him to take a strong party along lest Mormon guerrillas or Mormon-inspired Indians try to interfere. On November 24, 1857, Marcy started south with 40 soldiers and 24 civilian packers, their gear aboard 66 mules. They drove a few cattle for food. One of their two guides, Tim Goodale, had his Indian wife along.

Save for a hair-raising time urging their animals down the towering Roan Cliffs, which border the Colorado River near present-day Grand Junction, Colorado, they had no notable trouble until they neared Cochetopa Pass across the Continental Divide into the San Luis Valley. As the drifts deepened, Marcy jettisoned baggage to lighten the loads of the failing mules, which had nothing to eat but pine needles. Soon the men were stripped to a blanket each, their arms and ammunition. The strongest of the mules were reserved for twelve men whose feet were frozen.

Near the top of the pass (10,032 feet) they ran into powder snow, "so dry and light," Marcy wrote later, "that the men, walking in upright position, would sink to their waists and could not move. . . . Our only alternative now, in the deepest snow was for the three or four leading men to lie down and crawl . . . each man following the tracks of the leaders, and all placing their hands and feet in the same hole." This packed the snow sufficiently for the men behind to walk, and they tramped down a path for the remaining mules.

For twelve days the party lived on the meat of starved mules. When only three animals remained serviceable, Marcy sent two men ahead with them to bring back help from Fort Massachusetts. On the eleventh day three wagons appeared. From this sudden plenty the captain rationed out a deliberately light meal. Unsatisfied, some of the men broke into the stores later that night and gorged until one of them, Sergeant William Morton, died from overeating. He was the only casualty of the trip.

Between January 21 and March 9 Marcy shuttled back and forth between Taos and Fort Union, buying and gathering 1,600 horses and mules—oxen would be too slow. Completely respectful of the mountains now, he determined to drive the herd north along the base of the Front Range to the Overland Trail and west through South Pass, a long way but (he thought) a safer one. The night before the cavalcade's departure, Lucien Maxwell, one-time mountain man, gave a dance for the men at the headquarters ranch of his huge land grant. "The women," one happy trooper wrote, "were plenty and quite pretty." At dawn the heavy-eyed herders hit the saddle and started for the war.

Their dust had scarcely settled when a wild-eyed express from Colonel Johnston came pounding into Fort Union. The Mormons were planning to attack and scatter the stock. It was a false alarm, but who knew that? Off to Marcy from Fort Union went Special Order Number 30: wait for reinforcements. This he did, going into camp under the shoulder of Pikes Peak a little north of El Pueblo. There he hired as teamster for one of his thirty-odd wagons George Simpson, one of the original builders of the decrepit fort.

On the last day of April, 1858, the reinforced party rode on across the high roll of timbered ground that runs east from the Front Range between the Arkansas and Platte valleys. Toward sunset they were engulfed, in Marcy's words, by an unexpected and "frightful winter tempest . . . a dense cloud of driving snow against which it was utterly impossible to ride or walk." The herd scattered; two men froze to death. Sixty hours later the spring sun emerged, and the dazed soldiers rode out to gather up the animals, all but a hundred of which had survived among the big pines and against the tawny bluffs.

At the spot where Denver soon would take shape, the drovers found the Platte River in flood and halted to build a raft for ferrying the wagons and baggage. Bored with the waiting, teamster George Simpson went with a frying pan to a tributary stream, Cherry Creek, named for the wild fruit along its banks. As he had seen miners do during a trip to California in 1850, he scooped up some sand and panned it out. The effort produced a few shiny flecks that he showed to Marcy, saying that they were gold. Very interesting, Marcy replied. Right then, however, the captain's main interest was to reach Johnston with the essential livestock. On the herders went, thinking no more about Simpson's discovery—at the time.

Winter had brought Brigham Young the delay he needed for starting negotiations. Luck brought him a negotiator, glossy-bearded, short-statured, hypochondriacal Thomas L. Kane. A non-Mormon with influential connections in Washington, Kane had helped the Saints before in their dealing with the government. In December, 1857, he won President Buchanan's permission to travel to Utah via Panama and Southern California and in a strictly private capacity try to preclude bloodshed by working out some sort of compromise between Young and the invaders.

Kane reached Salt Lake City in February, 1858. No record of his talks with Brigham Young survives and hence it is not possible to say what offers he carried with him through blustery weather to the army's bored, sprawling camp along Black's Fork.

Time was running out for the Mormons. They could not strengthen themselves, but Johnston's men could. In spite of the weather, cavalry and a few foot soldiers had kept drifting in from the East until the invasion force numbered 4,000. Adequate supplies were on the way. The transportation firm of Russell, Majors & Waddell, which held exclusive contracts for army freighting throughout the West, had been ordered to make ready to move 16 million pounds of materiel—a requisition that caused the company to provide, at what proved to be a ruinous expense, 4,000 teamsters, 2,600 wagons and 40,000 head of work stock. Marcy was due with 1,600 more animals for moving the freight already at Black's Fork.

Johnston was chafing to put this mass into motion against a people whom he considered to be out-and-out rebels. The leaders of the Church of Jesus Christ of Latter-Day Saints were aware of his feelings and of his resources. In spite of belligerent statements about what they would do to the army when they caught it in the Wasatch canyons, Young and the Apostles had no illusions about being able to hold out for long, once spring came. Kane, to be sure, was negotiating. But if he failed, then what?

Their answer launched one of the incredible episodes of Western history. The Mormons of northern Utah—some 30,000 men, women, and children —were ordered to abandon their homes, pack up what belongings they could carry with them, and move south to Provo. There they were to camp on the bleak flats west of town until the Church told them either to return or to flee farther south to sanctuary in whatever remote desert oases and hidden valleys they could find.

Various motives impelled the desperate order. If Johnston did prove implacable, the people really might have to seek new homes and it was well to be prepared. Johnston, however, might be forcibly softened if American citizens in the East felt enough sympathy for the uprooted people to urge moderation on Congress—and surely the sight of so miserable a flight, scarcely a decade after the abandonment of Nauvoo, was enough to stir sympathy, or so the church hierarchy hoped. Finally, and most urgently, it was necessary to avoid an irreparable battle. Yet a battle would surely come if frightened and outraged citizens began shooting from the rooftops. The remedy was to clear the towns. That drastic step the church proceeded to take, grouping the people into the units of tens, fifties, and hundreds that had brought the early pioneers safely over the plains. Only a few chosen men were to be left behind to destroy the crops and burn the houses, if this was necessary to keep Mormon property from falling into enemy hands.

Into the middle of the frantic planning clattered another emergency. Far north beside the Lemhi River the Bannock and Shoshoni Indians were growing increasingly hostile toward the Mormon missionaries there. The whites blamed B. F. Ficklin, whom Johnston had sent with ten men north into the Beaverhead and Bitterroot valleys to buy beef cattle from the mountaineers. (Montana's pioneer ranchers, ex-mountain men, wintered animals in those grassy parks and sold them by summer to emigrants on the Overland Trail.) According to Granville Stuart, who was in the Beaverhead at the time, the cattle raisers declined the prices that Ficklin had been authorized to offer. Ficklin, the Mormons charged, then tried to prevail on thirty less affluent trappers to steal the cattle belonging to the Salmon River Mission and sell the animals to him. Trader John Owen of Fort Owen reputedly upset the plan (if ever it existed) and Ficklin in final desperation turned to the Indians to do his dirty work.[3]

Whatever their motives—perhaps the Bannocks and Shoshoni resented the Mormons having traded with their enemies, the Nez Percés, or perhaps they were simply excited by the ferment across the mountains in Oregon and Washington—they did attack the Lemhi mission-settlement. After killing two men, they made off with 235 cattle and 21 horses, which seem not to have reached Ficklin. The settlers rushed an appeal to Salt Lake City for help, forged an experimental cannon out of iron barrel staves and iron wagon tires (it blew apart when they test-fired it), straightened their scythes into spears, and through their portholes watched the Indians derisively wave the scalps of their two fallen comrades. In March word came from Young that help was out of the question. They must abandon the mission and join the retreat to the south. When the missionaries told the

---

[3] Ficklin denied the charges and produced affidavits stating that he urged all the Indians he encountered on his northern swing to remain at peace. At Fort Bridger, meanwhile, Johnston rejected Chief Washakie's offer of Shoshoni allies. No firm evidence supports Mormon charges that simultaneous raids in the Toole and Rush valleys resulted from army machinations. On its part, the army accused the Mormons of trying to fire up the restive Indians as far away as New Mexico, on the plains, and in the Northwest. Evidence of such extensive activity is wanting. However, missionary James Brown in northern Utah and Jacob Hamlin in southern Utah apparently did urge the Indians in those areas to regard the Mormons rather than the 'Mericats as their friends. For a fuller discussion of the recriminations see Norman Furniss, *The Mormon Conflict* (pp. 159–163).

Indians they were pulling out for good, and were leaving many possessions behind which the red men could have, the natives let them pass unharmed.

They made scarcely a ripple in the great flow to Provo. At the height of the retreat 600 laden wagons moved each day through Salt Lake City on the way to the refugee camp beside Utah Lake. Mixed among the wagons trudged a whole people, bound they knew not where, most of them leaving their homes with loud plaints but going nevertheless in a blind faith that the church was wise. For two months they lived amidst swarms of flies in wagons, tents, huts of brush, even caves.

Kane meanwhile was getting nowhere with Johnston, a brigadier general now by brevet. The negotiator did succeed, however, in persuading Governor-designate Alfred Cumming to visit Young with him. Appalled by what he saw, Cumming became an earnest advocate of compromise. He was soon reinforced by the arrival of a two-man peace commission from Washington. Soured by events in Kansas, apprehensive of what might happen to Indian relations everywhere if the bulk of the American Army was tied up in Utah, and dismayed by the mounting cost of the Mormon expedition (eventually its charges reached $15 million, more than $100 million in today's terms), Congress had decided to look before leaping any farther. The upshot was that Young and the Apostles agreed to step aside in favor of Cumming and the other federal officials and promised not to contest the army's approach, provided that the soldiers camp in a barren valley west of Utah Lake, far from any town where a rupture might take place.

The refugees at Provo stayed where they were until they were sure the army really was not going to occupy their cities. Thus the streets of Salt Lake were totally deserted on June 26, 1858, as the troops marched through the town, listening to the eerie echo of their own footfalls. One band played the tune of a ribald song when passing Brigham Young's house, but otherwise the progress was disciplined.

When the streets all over northern Utah were empty again, the homeless trudged back, 30,000 of them, dirty, ragged, sullen with hate, carrying their babies, driving their pigs and cows. A strange war. Twenty-two months later, when Fort Sumter at Charleston, South Carolina, was fired on, they would recall (as perhaps Albert Sidney Johnston did when he resigned from the Army of the United States to join the Confederacy) that their rebellion flared and was resolved without anyone on either side discharging a gun at another human being.

IX ⌃⌃

THE UNREASONABLE GOLD RUSH

JOHN BECK, a half-blood Cherokee Indian and an ordained Baptist preacher, was tormented by yearnings for wealth that outmatched his persistence. Before his tribe's removal in 1838 to Indian Territory (now Oklahoma) from its homelands in northern Georgia, where gold had been discovered in 1828, he had learned something of placer mining from the intruding whites. This knowledge led him, in 1850, to attach himself to a California-bound party of 105 white men and Indians, several attended by their Negro slaves, and head for the coast to make his fortune.

After traveling up the Arkansas River to within sight of the Rockies, the party turned its wagons north toward the Overland Trail. A long, slow climb past the foot of humpbacked Pikes Peak brought them into the fragrant shade of pine trees cloaking the low east-west divide separating Arkansas drainage from that of the South Platte. They reached the Platte by following the sandy trickle of north-flowing Cherry Creek. After fording the river and another tributary, deep Vasquez Creek (now called Clear Creek), they camped on the evening of June 21 beside an unnamed little stream that wound pleasantly out of the austere foothills a few miles to the west.

While waiting for dinner, a man named Ralston experimentally tested a panful of sand from the creekbank and found flecks of yellow. It wasn't worth much, but it didn't have to be. If a man's diggings were not littered with boulders and solid reefs of rock, he could, with diligence, wash out a hundred pans of sand and light gravel between sunup and sundown. Since pure gold was worth $20.67 an ounce, the merest flecks would produce 5 cents a pan—approximately $5 a day, or more than triple the day wages current in the East in 1850. Moreover, panning was inefficient. Group operation of sluices and rockers would yield wages out of gravel that assayed less than 5 cents a pan, especially if mercury was obtainable for catching, through amalgamation, the fine gold that settled behind the transverse riffles in the sluice boxes.

Excited by Ralston's find, the rest of the party tried their hands in what was inevitably named Ralston Creek. John Beck's efforts were fruitful enough that he joined several others in arguing that there was no use struggling on across the mountains and deserts to California. Hadn't they a mine right here?

The majority refused to heed. What did a few flakes of gold amount to when compared with the tales that were soaring back from California? On they went, leaving fourteen wagons—three disgruntled messes—beside the creek.

Purple thunderheads gathered over the range, as they do nearly every summer afternoon. Puffs of wind stirred dancing eddies of dust; lightning forked; distant thunder growled through the immensity. The pinpoints of gold in the pans all at once shrank to insignificance. Shamefaced, the stay-behinds hitched up and followed.

Beck did not do well in California. After his return to Indian Territory he kept remembering Ralston Creek. In 1857 he and his grown son Ezekiel threw in with a small party of Cherokee buffalo hunters, and when their wanderings brought them within sight of the Rockies, Beck tried panning the creeks. Color—just enough to tantalize. Ralston Creek had been better —but again he lost his nerve. A big war party of Cheyenne Indians had recently been defeated by U.S. cavalry in what is now western Kansas and, characteristically, the vanquished were spoiling for revenge. Any strangers might look tempting to them—or at least Beck and his Cherokees feared so. Home they went.

Hoping to form a mining company big enough to defend itself, Beck next wrote letters to Indians and whites whom he had known in California and also sent announcements to frontier newspapers, some of which published his notices. The upshot was that, in the spring of 1858, 104 men followed the familiar trail up the Arkansas River and crossed the timbered divide to the South Platte. More than half the party hailed from Indian Territory. Thirty-five or so of the remainder were from Kansas and Missouri. The balance, about eleven, were Georgians.

Leaders of the Georgia contingent were the three Russell brothers, all of whom had had experience in the Georgia gold fields and in California. Levi Russell, a doctor by training, was twenty-six years old. His brother Oliver was twenty-nine. Head of the family was William Green Russell, thirty-six, tall, neat, blue-eyed. He sported a luxuriant, red-gold mustache whose tips he waxed into sharp points and a full, bushy beard that he plaited into two remarkable pigtails.

As the Beck-Russell party crossed the divide between the Arkansas and South Platte rivers they saw at the foot of a tall, yellow-gray cliff the grave of one of Captain Randolph Marcy's men who six weeks before had frozen to death during a spring blizzard while driving horses to Johnston's stranded army. They did not know at the time why the grave was there.

Although their diarist, Luke Tierney, does not mention that it caused any undercurrents of apprehension, still one can imagine that the Cherokees looked nervously about as they followed the tracks of the (to them) inexplicably huge horse herd on toward the Platte. This was the heart of enemy country; any omen was enough to start a man fretting.

Unknown to the wayfarers, eleven more wagons were sixteen days behind them, captained by John Easter, a butcher from Lawrence, Kansas. Indian connections had put this party into motion also. One of the guides for the cavalry that had whipped the Cheyennes in western Kansas in 1857 had been Fall Leaf, a burly Delaware from the reservation across the Kansas River from Lawrence. After the Cheyenne battle, Fall Leaf and several companions had drifted on west to the foot of the Rockies, just to look around. There is no telling what really happened there in the foothills. Easter remembered Fall Leaf's saying that he had noticed some hard shiny grains while lying on his stomach drinking from a creek and that he had picked them up on impulse. Another story has it that the Indians met a party of Missourians who had paused to prospect while returning east after freighting for Johnston's army. Anyway, when Fall Leaf returned to the Delaware reservation he had a bit of gold dust in the hollow quill of a feather. He showed it to John Easter one day while they were bargaining over a beef steer the Indian wanted to sell.

On the strength of that little gleam of yellow Easter recruited a party of about four dozen people. Two of the men in the group took their wives along, Robert Middleton, who also had a child, and James Holmes. James's wife, Julia Archibald Holmes, was twenty years old and by all accounts pretty. On her journey west, most of it afoot, she carried a copy of Emerson's *Essays* and wore the new "American Costume," a knee-length calico skirt under which daringly peeped the era's badge of female emancipation, a pair of bloomers. She was also an indefatigable letter writer. Because of these things Julia Holmes has been remembered, whereas Mrs. Middleton, an unemancipated pioneer who kept close to her wagon and her child, has been forgotten.

Captured by the scenery near the site of today's Colorado Springs—the upended, weirdly eroded, thin red slabs now called the Garden of the Gods, with the brooding hulk of Pikes Peak filling the background—the Lawrence party went into camp. The only one of them who knew the least thing about mining was a man who had been to California. Under his leadership various contingents prospected desultorily for more than a month. One group followed a broad Indian trail up rugged Ute Pass as far as the high grasslands of South Park. Like the others, the South Park group found nothing. The failure did not bother them particularly. They were having a wonderful summer outing, a heady release from the slavery struggles that had racked Lawrence not long before.

Shortly after their arrival three of the men climbed Pikes Peak. Stirred by their stories, Julia Holmes coaxed her husband into trying to duplicate the feat. The young couple left on August 1, planning to be gone a week. James carried 35 pounds of supplies, Julia 17. Together, their packs held six quilts, a change of clothing, one tin plate, a pail, 19 pounds of "bread" (it must have been hardtack), 1 pound of sugar, 1 pound of "hog meat," and ¾ of a pound of coffee. Plus Emerson's essays.

For three days they struggled thirstily up steep, gravelly slopes, wound among the trees, slithered into precipitous canyons, and finally, near timberline, found a cave where they could read Emerson and write letters while resting for the final assault. Julia vibrated with excitement. "Think of the huge rocks projecting out in all imaginable shapes, with the beautiful evergreens, the pines, the firs, the spruces, interspersed among them and the clear, cold mountain stream . . . rushing, tumbling, hissing down over the rough mountain sides."

On August 5 they clambered on, marveling at "tiny blue flowers most bewitchingly beautiful . . . children of the sky and snow." From the summit Julia gazed at a view that no other white woman, and perhaps no red woman, had ever seen, a breath-taking panorama westward across South Park to the Continental Divide and eastward over the plains until details melted into the blue haze of distance. It was cold, too. Crouched out of the wind, the record makers turned to their everlasting letters, "using a broad flat rock for a writing desk." Just being up there, Julia told one correspondent, "fills the mind with infinitude, and sends the soul to God." Afterwards she read Emerson aloud to James: "A ruddy drop of manly blood/The surging sea outweighs . . ." They were very young, very exhilarated. Like all lovers, they believed their experience was unique, and for a little while this one really was.

A snow flurry that turned to rain at lower elevations sped their return to the wagons. On August 10 the party broke camp, intending to winter in New Mexico. They had crossed Sangre de Cristo Pass to the high edges of San Luis Valley and were prospecting there when Mexican packers bound for Fort Garland told them that members of the Beck-Russell party had indeed discovered gold on the South Platte. Dissension thereupon split the Lawrence party. Uninterested by now in cold gold, the Holmes and Middleton families continued with a few others to Taos. Some of the remaining men swung into Fort Garland to buy supplies enough to carry them through a Colorado winter. Others goaded their ox-teams back north, hoping to file claims before the best ground was absorbed.

Anticlimax met them. Though they found several pits where people had been digging gravel from the banks of the South Platte, no miners were in sight. A few miles downstream, however, where Cherry Creek ran into the river, they came across a few Arapahoe Indians and two or three mountain traders camped with their native wives. From these people the Lawrence hopefuls learned what had happened.

Ralston Creek had not proved as lucrative as John Beck of the Cherokee party had predicted. The thin colors and the nagging fear of enemy Indians wore down his persistence once again. Within a week he and half the Cherokees had decided to flee home while still they could. The others returned to the South Platte and panned its sand without much luck. More defections occurred until only thirteen men remained, mostly Georgians held to their fading hopes by the firmness of William Green Russell.

A lift came to their spirits when they found small pockets of drift gold near what would become the southwestern edge of Denver—the diggings the Lawrence people saw. Though the yield was a mere $600 to be divided thirteen ways, it encouraged the Georgians to try harder. Realizing that the gold had probably washed down from the mountains, a few of them pushed into the Platte Canyon, toiling over boulders and deadfall. Finding nothing, they turned back. Searching for other leads, the entire party had then started north along the Front Range, panning each stream they crossed. They might or might not return; the traders at Cherry Creek had no idea.

One other item of interest emerged. While the Georgians had been digging their $600 worth of gold from the placer workings, several people had drifted by: Mexicans bound south (the Lawrence party had met some of those), mountain men going to Westport on the Missouri River with their furs, a few freighters returning from Utah. One of the freighters, named John Cantrell, had taken a sackful of the gold-bearing earth with him when he continued east.

What to do? While some of the Lawrence party shoveled earth into the abandoned sluice boxes, hoping to retrieve a few dollars, their less energetic companions laid out a town. This was standard Midwest practice. Promoters of real estate created "cities" wherever they thought population might gather. Cantrell's sack might attract settlers, or the Georgians might find other diggings in the vicinity. Anyway, what was there to lose? The idlers drove a few stakes into the brown sod and declared that Montana City now existed. But wouldn't the junction of Cherry Creek with the Platte be a more likely site? At that thought six of the magicians moved down near the Indian tepees and waved St. Charles into being on Cherry Creek's east bank.

They were ready to ride east and file their town claims when Green Russell's thirteen prospectors reappeared, driven back from the north by still another Indian scare. Not to be outdone, the Georgians too created a town. Theirs was on the west bank of Cherry Creek, opposite St. Charles. They named it Auraria (from the Latin *aurum,* or gold), a word first coined in 1832 for a town near Russell's home in the Georgia gold country. As for gold itself, they had found no more.

Discouraged by the reports, most of the Kansans pulled out for home. The Georgians were more resilient. Buoyed still by their $600, they agreed to spend the following summer trying to trace the South Platte gold to its source. For that they would need additional men and equipment. To recruit this help, Green and Oliver Russell and Valarious Young returned to Georgia.

Dr. Levi Russell and the others rode to Fort Garland to buy supplies (Levi had to pawn his gold watch to pay for the groceries) and then returned to what they supposed was Auraria's single cabin. To their amazement they saw a whole village of parked wagons, brush huts, tents, and half-built cabins of cottonwood logs. Catching his breath and calculating dizzily, Levi wrote home that on the basis of current growth he anticipated "at least one thousand persons to spend the winter with us, and WHITE MEN AT THAT."

Seldom has so unexpected an oak sprung from so modest an acorn. Eastward, in the middle of a Kansas City street, watched by a fascinated throng, a former Californian had washed out a panful of freighter Cantrell's Rocky Mountain earth. Color—perhaps 25 cents' worth! It was better than a man could do digging postholes in Kansas.

The fur trappers who had paused at the South Platte diggings on their way east to market their pelts attracted attention to themselves by spinning exaggerated yarns of corroboration. Marcy's quondam teamster, George Simpson, who also drifted back to the Missouri River that fall, said grandly that he had long known of gold deposits along the headwaters of the mountain rivers.

Even before Cantrell's appearance many people in Kansas, Nebraska, and western Missouri had heard of the two parties (Beck and Easter's) that had set forth in the spring to explore the Rockies for gold. It was an easy next step to believing that the seekers really had discovered metal. Had not the same sort of thing happened in California only ten years earlier?

The talk fell on wistful ears. The year before, a virulent depression had crippled the speculative new towns along the frontier. Laborers without work, storekeepers without customers, lawyers without clients, farmers swamped in unmarketable wheat, real estate promoters holding land they could not sell, all began wondering whether a quick trip to Pikes Peak might not repair their fortunes.[1] Only 600 miles to go—why, they could be back within months, their pockets bulging.

Merchants, hotelkeepers, mule dealers, and the proprietors of wagon shops, saloons, newspapers, and stage lines fostered the mania, for they too

---

[1] Catchily alliterative and the only Rocky Mountain landmark familiar in the Midwest, the name Pikes Peak quickly became synonymous with the entire gold-bearing Front Range.

would prosper if their towns became outfitting centers for the stampeders. *Ho for the gold fields!* Economic salvation in the Rockies!—and be sure to equip yourself on the way at Leavenworth or Kansas City or Omaha or wherever else the dispatch you happened to read came from.

Early birds who were able to scare up the necessary credit started west from the Missouri River or came south from the thronged Overland Trail as soon as the rumors began to stir. By no means all of them intended to mine. The ubiquitous gamblers moved promptly, of course, but so did less parasitic souls—David K. Wall of South Bend, Indiana, for one. Wall had been to California earlier in the decade and knew how intensely miners craved fresh vegetables. He headed west with several packets of garden seed.

Others like D. C. Oakes of Iowa hurried to Cherry Creek to see what demands most needed filling. At once Oakes perceived two possibilities. One was for a guidebook based on a clumsy start already being attempted by Luke Tierney of the Russell party. The other was for a sawmill. Back to Iowa Oakes went, Tierney's manuscript in his saddlebags, to push both ideas to profitable completion.

Town promoters were equally nimble. General William Larimer, whose Larimer City, Nebraska, had just died in the depression, bustled forth with his son and several others, jumped the St. Charles townsite, named his substitute creation Denver after Governor James W. Denver of Kansas Territory (Denver meanwhile had resigned and was not as useful an object of flattery as Larimer supposed), and by means of judicious disbursements of cash made the usurpation stick. Merchants were right behind him. Blake and Williams of Crescent City, Iowa, arrived during a snowstorm on October 29 with a load of groceries. Canny John Kinna appeared a week later with sheet iron for making stoves. Joseph Doyle, Simpson's erstwhile partner at El Pueblo, who was farming on the Huerfano River within sight of Greenhorn Peak and who already operated stores at Fort Union and Fort Garland, sent an agent north with a hastily gathered assortment of grain and tools. Dick Wootton of Taos, trapper and Indian trader, loaded two wagons with dry goods and whiskey.

Not everyone went to Cherry Creek. One large party of Nebraskans pushing their wagons up the South Platte during October kept watching the peaks with field glasses until finally half of them could resist the tug no longer. Eager to take the shortest route possible, they broke away from the others and headed due west to the thick timber and tilted red rocks where Boulder Creek bursts through the foothills. There, with eleven small cabins as a nucleus, they formed the town of Boulder, today one of the state's most charming cities. In Taos, meanwhile, Robert Middleton felt a resurgence of the excitement which earlier had led him to join the Lawrence party. In November, 1858, he returned with his wife and children and several associates to stake out a town at the mouth of Fountain Creek near the ruins of El Pueblo.[2] They named their clutch of cabins Fountain City; it was the precursor of modern Pueblo, Colorado's second largest metropolis. Short-lived El Dorado, one cabin and four tents, took form at the foot of Pikes Peak. Bemused by the activity, a few of the region's mountain men, led by Antoine Janise, declared their single cabin on the banks of the Cache la Poudre River, near today's Fort Collins, to be the town of Colona.

To support all this there was still only $600 in gold, removed by then to Georgia. Ah, but tomorrow! After reaching Denver with his wife on November 3, 1858, Colorado's first barber, self-styled Count Henri Murat, took a deep breath of the tingling air and sat down to write a friend what everyone in the area believed, or at least wanted others to believe. "When spring comes . . . the whole world will be in a blaze of astonishment at the riches that will be taken out of the earth."

Tens of thousands of people did believe it. Throughout the winter they feverishly formed mining companies and made plans for leaving as soon as the weather moderated. Of them none was busier or bolder than William Newton Byers. An Ohio farm boy of limited education, Byers had taught himself practical surveying and in 1852 had gone across South Pass to Oregon to ply his trade. Discontented, he returned through the California goldfields and Nicaragua to Omaha. He did well in Nebraska as a surveyor and real estate agent, until the panic of '57 stripped him of clientele. He might have started for Pikes Peak as soon as the first rumors of gold reached Omaha, but he was severely wounded during a street brawl while trying to help a newly arrived German immigrant beset by bullies.

Immobilized, he decided to write about going. He scribbled down his memories of plains travel and of the California gold fields. To these he added a hodgepodge of material gleaned from letters from the diggings that were beginning to appear in the frontier newspapers. He showed the heap to Nebraska's superintendent of public instruction, prevailed on him to mold it into coherent form, and then rushed the manuscript to press as an authentic guidebook. It was such a success that the convalescing Byers, who had no true facility with words, decided to publish a newspaper at Pikes Peak. He enlisted an Omaha editor and a skilled printer as his partners, and they named their still unborn paper the *Rocky Mountain News*. To save time they composed the front page in Omaha—stale news and tired features clipped from operating journals, "news" which they hoped would not seem quite so stale when it reached the lonesome mountains. They did not, however, set type for the date or the place of

---

[2] James and Julia Holmes stayed in New Mexico, where James became territorial secretary and Julia served as New Mexico correspondent for the New York *Tribune*. Unhappily, the bloom wore off the ecstasy that had taken them up Pikes Peak. They separated. Julia went to Washington, D.C., plunged into the suffragette movement, and became the first woman member of the U.S. Bureau of Education.

issue, for they could not know until they arrived in the Rockies when or where their paper would appear.[3]

In March, 1859, after locking the type for the front page into its form and loading it with press, composing stone, paper, and camping equipment into one of their two wagons, the partners started along the Platte River trail. Thirty thousand or more people were streaming along the same route. Other thousands thronged the Arkansas Valley. More, seeking the shortest possible way, toiled up the Republican River in Kansas and then struck due west across arid wastes. A wild conglomeration of ox- or mule-drawn wagons, carts, buggies, and impatient horsemen jostled for the best campgrounds. A few ingenious souls tried, unsuccessfully, to speed themselves along the way by hoisting sails onto their vehicles. Impoverished men trudged along with their possessions in wheelbarrows or in packs on their backs. Enterprising travelers financed themselves by carting chickens and driving cows, selling the eggs and milk each night.

Suffering was often acute, especially along the Republican and Smoky Hill trails in western Kansas, where water was scarce and game often failed to appear. A young man named Blue kept alive, but deranged himself mentally, by lunching on the bodies of his two starved brothers. Many injured their draft stock by starting into a wet, laggard spring before the grass was up. Very few of the travelers were properly equipped, in spite of a spate of advice in eighteen guidebooks besides Byers'. Sorely blistered feet from the long hike in poor shoes and rheumatic joints from sleeping on the cold ground were not as dramatic as the Blue misadventure, but left many an argonaut wondering why he had supposed this summer trip to the Rockies would be a joyous outing.

The oxen hauling the first newspaper played out within sight of the mountains and had to halt to recuperate. Feverish with impatience, Byers rode ahead to locate quarters. Although William Larimer's struggling Denver town company offered him several free business lots as an inducement for him to locate there, Auraria looked more prosperous. He splashed his horse across Cherry Creek, under cottonwood trees that were just beginning to leaf out, and rented the low, sloping loft of a building recently erected by Dick Wootton. It was a miserable place, lighted by a single window and approached by a rickety outside staircase. The roof leaked, as the belated printers discovered when a wet April snow fell just after they had carried their press up the stairs. They had to pitch a tent inside the loft to protect the paper, and use candles to supplement the gray light of the stormy day. But thanks in part to their ready-made front page, they had an issue off the press at 10 P.M., April 22, 1859, twenty minutes ahead of a nearby rival, who thereupon gave up the struggle.

[3] They were not even sure of the territory. In those days both Kansas and Nebraska stretched west to the Continental Divide. The boundary between them was the 40th parallel. Unorganized Arapahoe County, Kansas, embraced the Cherry Creek settlements. Infant Boulder lay, just barely, within Nebraska.

The triumph threatened to be hollow. So far as anyone knew, the only metal that had been found since the Russell strike was a discovery made in January on little Gold Run Creek, twelve precipitous miles west of Boulder. Hundreds rushed there and found the area too cramped to hold them all. As thousands more kept appearing across the plains, a panic as unreasoning as the earlier optimism swept the wretched camps. A vast exodus began. Stampeders still traveling west halted in dismay on hearing false tales of hungry mobs burning and sacking the Cherry Creek towns. According to one estimate, of the hundred thousand persons who started for the Rockies in the spring of 1859 at least half turned back.

Byers did his one-paper best to stem the retreat. He named the returnees "Gobacks" and poured vitriol on them in his columns, describing them as "howling like whipped curs—creatures who should never have been unloosed from their mother's apron strings." Like Green Russell holding the discouraged Georgians together, he appealed to logic. Was it not true that color, however faint, could be washed from nearly every foothill stream? Very well then: "When this state of things exists in a country unheaved by volcanic eruptions," he wrote on page two of the first issue (there was no room on page one), "it is almost a physical certainty that gold in lump must be found in the mountains whence the sands are washed. By next week we hope to make a beginning at least for precise information."

It was a monumental example of whistling in the dark, whistling not only for himself but also for the 50,000 other stampeders who in spite of the Gobacks kept plodding toward the mountains, ears straining for any whisper, however faint, that might reaffirm their faith.

X

THERE IT IS, HELP YOURSELF

TWO WEEKS or so after William Byers had promised his readers to search out information about the gold country, electric questions began to crackle along the dusty streets of Denver and Auraria. A pioneer of '58, Henry Allen, embryo politician and booster of the Auraria Town Company, began paying bargain rates for the unused mining equipment which hoarse Gobacks were auctioning off on the street corners. Many speculators were doing the same sort of thing. Allen, however, was different in that he offered unminted gold.

Where had that dust come from?

Pestered unmercifully, Allen at last said that he was acting as agent for George A. Jackson. Swiftly the crowd hunted Jackson out. After frantic badgering, he began to talk.

He was a Missourian, slight of frame. Transverse lines across his forehead gave him a faintly quizzical, wistful look. In 1857, on his way home from fruitless years in California, he dropped south from Fort Laramie and was loafing around the base of the Front Range with a few mountain men when the first Cherry Creek stampeders appeared. Somehow he fell in with a prospector named Tom Golden. In November, 1858, Golden found color where Clear Creek breaks out of the foothills between two drab, flat-topped, rock-rimmed mesas. The promise faded, but in the interim Golden built a cabin near the spot. (Hence today's town of Golden, home of the Colorado School of Mines.) George Jackson and a man named Jim Sanders moved in with him.

During a spell of warm weather at the close of 1858 the trio decided to hike around the hills to see what they could see. Avoiding the difficult canyon by which Clear Creek made its noisy exit from the foothills, they climbed the steep slopes to the south. On reaching high benchlands among the evergreens they spied elk and pursued the animals until they emerged at length on a bluff far above the South Fork of Clear Creek. The canyon bottom was gentler there than farther downstream, and Jackson suggested prospecting. The others were more interested in the elk, so he slid alone down the gravelly, snow-streaked slopes, followed by his two dogs, Kit and Drum. The only tools he had with him were a sheath knife, a hatchet strapped to his belt, and a large iron cup.

Although Western mythology often pictures the prospector as a company-shunning hermit, Jackson's independence was unusual. Safety, camp chores, and the labors of mining demanded cooperation. (Green Russell, an experienced hand, had started west with a hundred men; those dwindling to thirteen, he had returned to Georgia for more.) But Jackson, who was not far from his shelter, who knew the area, and who perhaps had a touch of cabin fever, took the chance.

Tendrils of white mist drew him to bubbling hot springs (Idaho Springs today). Hundreds of mountain sheep had congregated there to graze where the snow was melted from the grass. After killing one for food, Jackson moved a short distance upstream to a side creek. He found gravel at its mouth by scraping away the snow, but the mass was frozen too hard for him to chip into it with either his hatchet or his knife.

He camped under a big fir and the next morning, January 6, 1859, built a huge fire to thaw the ground. While he was dragging up dead timber for the blaze, he heard a fearful snarling and barking. His dogs were attacking a mountain lion that had tried to raid his freshly killed meat. With his hatchet Jackson waded into the melee and finally was able to break the lion's neck. "A hell of a fight," he told his diary laconically.

He let the fire smolder all night. The next morning he dug into the gravel with his sheath knife and washed the sand in his iron cup. Before the knife wore out under the punishing treatment he had recovered half an ounce of gold, strong suggestion of a real bonanza. Back at the cabin he told Tom Golden of the discovery, without locating it precisely, and they agreed to keep quiet until they could work the claim in strength.

To earn money Jackson carried a load of mail to Fort Laramie. On his return in mid-April he was approached by twenty-two Chicagoans who wanted to hire an experienced California miner as a guide. Here was a ready-made, amply financed mining company. Why not let them in on the find?

Golden protested, but the discovery was Jackson's and again they separated, this time for good. Off Jackson went with his Chicagoans. Stretches of the route were so rough that they had to take the wagons apart and carry the pieces, and when they arrived at what they named Chicago Creek, where the bar was, they had to use the wagon lumber to make sluice boxes. In one week they produced gold dust worth $1,900. Jackson took it to Cherry Creek to buy more supplies. That was the mineral that agent Henry Allen had been using.

A wild scramble developed. In the van rode Henry Allen, eager to be a principal, and William Byers, hot for news. They too took up a claim in company with several other men (it proved of little worth) and then tramped up and down Clear Creek's South Fork, under the vast cliffs, talking with everyone, pointing, estimating. His notebook crammed with material, Byers was about to start back to Cherry Creek when word swept into camp of an even greater find across the hill near Clear Creek's North Fork.

Shortly after Jackson's discovery, so the story went, another lone prospector, a shaggy semiliterate Georgian named John H. Gregory (not a member of the original Russell party) had clambered into the North Fork, and, in a tributary ravine had spotted what he called "blossom rock," quartz streaked with reddish-brown stringers that might contain gold. Before he could investigate, a blizzard drove him back through the canyon to a cluster of shacks on the plains two miles downstream from Golden's cabin. There Gregory met David K. Wall of South Bend, Indiana, and hit him for the price of a meal.

Because Wall gave him a dollar untinged by condescension, Gregory told him, after several days of thinking it over, that he believed he had something good back in the hills but needed help in making sure. Busy breaking out a truck garden and irrigating ditch, Wall was not free to pursue the possibilities, but said he had some friends from Indiana who might be interested. The upshot was the opening of Gregory Gulch and the famous Gregory Lode, heart of what became Gilpin County, Colorado, producer during the next century of some $100 million in gold and silver. Those gay days, however, were still a long way off in May, 1859.

Byers, Allen, and companions made a wild ride straight over the track-less mountain from the South Fork to check on this newest strike. On reaching Gregory Gulch they found perhaps two dozen men ahead of them. Among the miners was a roving reporter, twenty-four-year-old Henry Villard of the Cincinnati *Commercial Enquirer*. Villard was assiduously taking notes, as well he might. Gold was pouring out of a few little pits on the hillside—not placer gold, but gold from veins, or lodes, that might run to great depth. Fortunately the surface rock was soft. The discoverers were able to dig it out with picks and lug it in sacks on their backs to the streams. There they pulverized it and washed it in crude rockers and sluice boxes. It was grueling work—too grueling for Gregory. He hired a pair of improverished miners at $1.50 a day each and watched them produce nearly a thousand dollars for him in less than a week.

During Byers' five-day stay in the narrow, heavily timbered gulch, 400 men appeared. Nights were still icy, but shelter was easily provided. In a single day a group of partners could chop down one of the tall thin pines, frame the logs into a crude cribwork, roof it with boughs and earth, and then be free to swarm over the hillsides looking for leads of their own. After washing $5 in gold dust from a single panful of Gregory's pulverized blossom rock, Byers joined some others in filing another claim on a steep slope a little farther up the gulch, and then rushed with his stories back to Auraria. The Cincinnati reporter, Henry Villard, meanwhile rode over to the South Fork of Clear Creek to see what was happening there.

Oddly enough, neither newsman dwelt in his stories on what elsewhere might have been regarded as a phenomenon: the unquestioning assumption that the Clear Creek gold should be shared with later arrivals.

Think of the possibilities. Each discovery had been made by a lone man who revealed his secret to a handful of others only in order to obtain help in exploiting his find. At various critical moments during the revelations either Jackson or Gregory or his supporters might have tried, storybook fashion, to hog everything within reach before the word spread. They might, for instance, have tried to establish control over large areas of ground by filing pre-emption claims to agricultural sites of 160 acres per man, as allowed by government statute. They might have been cruder; they might have hired strong labor forces among the destitute stampeders and then have hurried to dig up as much ground as possible while holding the rest of the world at bay with armed guards.

They did none of these things. If they were secretive, it was so that they could be free to poke around until they found the best piece of ground for themselves—not the most. So far as area was concerned the land was to be shared.

This insistence on equality in the distribution of natural resources had its roots in a colonial antipathy toward speculators who attempted through wealth, family connections, or political pull to engross huge areas of wilderness land beyond the Allegheny Mountains. One of young America's first ideological battles had been the settling of that problem: potential farm lands were to be distributed in small, family-sized units, one per applicant—an area eventually decreed by Congress to be 160 acres. Furthermore (and this battle took longer to win), a man who went into the wilderness ahead of the government surveyors was entitled to select the land he wanted and hold it inviolate by "squatting" on it until surveys caught up with him and the plot could be properly recorded and purchased —for until the passage of the Homestead Act in 1862 land in the public domain was sold to applicants at a minimum price of $1.25 an acre. Although speculators continually devised ways of beating the system, the theory behind the laws remained constant; in so far as acreage was concerned, the West was to be a land of equal opportunity.

The theory of squatter rights—pre-emption of desirable land ahead of survey—went west to California with the gold rushers of 1848 and 1849. (Both George Jackson and William Gregory, it is worth remembering, had mined in California before coming to the Rockies.) Every miner, in theory, had the right to lay hold of his fair share of California's gold-bearing land, even though no government agency existed to pass title to him. But how much was fair?

Placer gold, as the miners quickly realized, was not distributed uniformly throughout mineralized earth. Generally it was concentrated erratically near bedrock, either at the channel bottom of an existing stream or, equally often, in the bed of a former channel left dry by shifts in the creek's course. A miner had to dig through five, ten, sometimes as much as sixty feet of overburden to reach what he hoped would be a rich pocket. If he missed, he wanted to be able to move over a few yards and try again.

Though quartz veins were more likely than placer bars to show continuous values, the gold in them also was distributed unpredictably. There, too, disappointed miners wanted a second chance. At that point philosophic tensions arose. How much space should a prospector be allowed so that he could run future tests if he wished—yet what limitations should be imposed to keep him from being a hog if he hit?

By intertwining Spanish custom with American theories of equality and pre-emption, the California stampeders quickly worked out practices of land acquisition that later were accepted in every American gold field, the Rockies included. After a rush had begun to some creek or vein, the men who arrived first in the vicinity met and established a "district." A district was a relatively small area, seldom more than a few miles in length, its boundaries delineated by natural landmarks. No attempt was made to extend jurisdiction to later settlements outside those boundaries; if gold was found on the far slope of the hill, the miners over there would have to manage themselves.[1]

The next problem related to the size of claims permissible in each district and was resolved by a democratic vote of the miners concerned. Although variations were frequent in early California, custom gradually imposed certain standards. In the Rockies lode claims tended to reach either 100 or 200 feet along the vein and to extend 25 feet to either side. Gulch claims for placer diggings also stretched 100 or 200 feet along the creek and were as wide as the gulch. If the ravine promised to be unusually rich, the number of claims might be doubled by designating the middle of the stream as one boundary, thus stringing two rows of claims along the rivulet.

Except in wide gulches, claims were rarely as large as an acre. (A square acre is approximately 208½ feet to the side.) On this less-than-an-acre a placer miner not only dug his prospect holes but strung out his sluice boxes for several dozen feet, piled his waste earth, built his cabin perhaps, and, where water was limited, scooped out a pond to serve as a reservoir. The man (or men) who made the district's first mineral discovery was entitled to two such claims each. All others were limited to one. In general a man was not allowed to buy more than a single claim, or fraction thereof, a

---

[1] Most districts also laid down rudimentary criminal codes, as will be noted later. Their primary purpose, however, was to establish procedures for perfecting, holding, and transferring title to real estate.

restriction that gradually relaxed with the thinning out of values and the introduction of hydraulic mining, which depended on moving large quantities of earth with hose-driven water.

Measurements sometimes followed the winding of the creek or the slope of the hill. At other times they were made as nearly on a flat plane as the workers could manage. One early locator of a hillside lode in Gregory Gulch described methods there as follows: "All three claims were measured with an aspen pole about sixteen feet long. When measuring downhill, we held the pole level and dropped a stone from the end, and from the spot where it struck the ground we would measure the next length." Once the bounds were determined the corners were marked with "stakes . . . four inches square, set two feet under the ground and four feet above." On the hewn faces of these stakes the name of the claimant and the date of the claim were inscribed. The claimant then registered his claim with the district recorder, elected by popular vote and paid for his work through the fees he was entitled to charge for each transaction. This official entered a description of the plot in his record book, locating the holding generally in respect to the discovery claim—number 3 above discovery, number 9 below, and so on. Entry completed, the ground belonged to the claimant and could be sold. There was no provision for any payment to the government, however, a lack which bothered Congress until after the Homestead Act of 1862 had established a national principle of free distribution of public resources.

To maintain his title a claimant had to work on the ground as many days each week during open weather as the district laws prescribed (it tended to be one day per week) or else show cause why not. This provision sprang from another frontier tenet: resources of land, gold, timber, water, and grass on the public domain should be used for the immediate benefit of the community and the individual and should not be hoarded for future speculation. If a prospector failed to comply, his claim reverted to the public domain and was open to new entry.[2] Disputes concerning abandonment and/or jumping were settled, if possible, by the elected judge of the district, who might appoint arbiters to assist him in arriving at the facts. Appeals from the arbiters' decision could be referred to an assembly of the residents of the district, acting as a miners' or people's court.

No outside force imposed compliance with the rules of the early districts. Congress did not pass a national mining law until 1866; and where territorial laws did exist, enforcement agencies were generally too far away to be effective. The citizenry had to handle their own affairs, a process often tarnished in practice by the reluctance of the miners to lose

[2] The requirement means, of course, that titles were provisional, and when Congress passed the first national mining laws in 1866, means were afforded for securing full patent to mineral land and once patent had been achieved the work requirement vanished.

valuable working time in attendance at the courts, by horseplay and by liquor dealers who produced their portable bars at every public gathering. None of these defects produced any change in theory, however. Beliefs in equality were so ingrained in frontier thinking that neither Jackson nor Gregory nor any other discoverer of a major gold field seems ever to have been seriously tempted by schemes for personal aggrandizement.

However laudable these midget democracies may have been in meeting mining problems, their scope was nevertheless limited. For broader difficulties broader authority was needed. But what was it to be, so far as the central Rockies were concerned? An almost hopeless hodgepodge of jurisdiction exercised nominal control over the mining districts. Kansas and Nebraska embraced the eastern slope of the Continental Divide, Utah the western. New Mexico included the drainage of the Rio Grande and, on the plains, extended north to the Arkansas River. Because the capitals of these four territories lay 400 to 700 miles from the mining area, the time and costs of travel added formidable obstacles to the problem of decentralization.

In March, 1859, before the Goback movement developed, it seemed that a huge influx of voters was on its way west to engulf the area. At once hopeful politicians began buzzing at each other: why not solve the jurisdictional problem by creating a new state, to be called Jefferson? Why not let it enter the Union as California had, directly, without limping along for an indeterminate period as an immature territory?

As soon as William Byers had his press running he became, along with Henry Allen, one of the plan's most active proponents. A state-making convention was called to meet in Denver on June 6, 1859, and both men were busy with arrangements when word arrived of the gold discoveries on Clear Creek. After their swift trip into the mountains to investigate, the pair returned more sanguine than ever. While Allen attended to the political fires, Byers rushed his paper to bed and then went straight back to Gregory Gulch, this time to urge that the miners pause in their activity long enough to elect delegates to the coming convention.

During his short absence affairs in the gulch had grown frenzied. Wearied of watching his hired hands make money for him, Gregory had sold his claim for $21,000, to be paid for from the proceeds of the ground itself. Tales of the transaction stepped up the inflow of people from Cherry Creek to an estimated 500 a day. A string of self-styled cities sprawled from Black Hawk (at the junction of Gregory Gulch with the North Fork) on up through Mountain City to Nevada City (later Nevadaville), almost five miles away. When Byers discovered that the cluster of tents and cabins near his own claim in the middle stretch of the gulch had not yet been named, he remedied the defect by calling the place Central City. In time it became the area's dominant town.

On June 1 William Green Russell arrived with 170 men recruited in

Georgia and Kansas. He was dismayed, and not just because he was envious that someone else had beaten him to the mountain gold he had hoped to find for himself. The area was too crowded. Although the district had voted to limit claims to 100 feet each, this allowed only 53 placer holdings per mile; if every man in Russell's group took a separate claim, they would need three miles of ravine just for themselves.

Some newcomers were already growling that a meeting should be called to discuss reducing the size of future claims to 25 feet. Russell's reaction was more vigorous. He led his party four miles across the mountains to another ravine, soon called Russell Gulch. There he and his men found placer diggings as rich as Jackson's discovery on the South Fork of Clear Creek. Almost instantly a new rush developed to that area.

In the midst of this confusion Byers had difficulty persuading delegates to accompany him to Cherry Creek for the state convention. Ten men, including John Gregory, came from Gregory Gulch but none appeared from Clear Creek or from Russell Gulch. All told, of the fifty delegates that had been elected in twenty-three "precincts," only thirty-two, representing thirteen precincts, assembled on June 6 in Denver City.

Those who did attend were impatient to return to the diggings. They were also disheartened to discover how drastically immigration had fallen off because of the Goback movement, initiated before the Clear Creek discoveries. This, the nucleus of a state! They decided to mark time. Assembling hurriedly the next morning, June 7, at eight o'clock, they appointed a handful of interim committees and voted to adjourn until the first Monday of August, to reconsider their ambitions then.

Byers refused to be deflated. The gold rush was sound and immigration would resume, he predicted in an editorial to be printed in his weekly edition of June 11, when "the people in the States have been disabused of the erroneous ideas into which they have fallen. . . . That we will have a sufficient population and be admitted as a sovereign state before the adjournment of the next session of Congress we have scarce a doubt. . . . All hail the future State of Jefferson!"

He had reason to be hopeful. On the evening of June 6, the very day the convention assembled, there arrived in Auraria, on a private fact-finding trip, the editor of the New York *Tribune,* round-faced, albino-pale Horace Greeley himself. With Greeley was another correspondent, young (26) Albert D. Richardson of the Boston *Journal,* who had chanced to board the same stagecoach in Kansas. Here indeed were resounding voices to help disabuse the East!

Greeley's stagecoach had upset on its way west, and the forty-eight-year-old editor was so bruised he could hardly hobble. No matter. While Byers stayed at home to write his convention stories for the *News,* several local boosters swept Greeley and Richardson into a wagon, added ubiquitous

Henry Villard of the Cincinnati *Commercial Enquirer,* and jolted them to the edge of the mountains. There they were transferred to mules for the rugged trail into Gregory Gulch. When the cavalcade reached its first night's campground, so Greeley admitted later, "I had to be lifted tenderly from my saddle and laid on a blanket," but he arose resolutely at dawn the next morning for the rest of the trip.

The reporters' arrival in the gulch on June 8 coincided with a miners' meeting called to discuss a set of new rules for the district. Four thousand or more men—plus five white females and seven Indian women—had by that time crowded into the narrow ravine. They had pressed up its stubby tributaries and had overflowed into neighboring gullies. As they advanced, gold showings dwindled. Panicking suddenly, the crowd turned back on itself and found that no more ground remained open near the producing claims. Equality? Now was the time to show the meaning of the word!

Two thousand or more men tramped to the meeting place. Pleased that they had attracted attention from the outside, they called for speeches from the visiting dignitaries. While listening, they sat on stumps, boulders, or the earth itself, under the flickering light of pine torches. It was a grand spectacle, Villard wrote later—"unique and picturesque costumes . . . the cheers of the crowd . . . the frequent discharge of firearms and the distant songs of those encamped in the upper part of the valley." After Richardson had amused the throng with humorous anecdotes, sobersided Horace Greeley harangued it with his pet topics: the rewards of agriculture and thrift, the evils of drink and gambling, and his certainty, shared by most of his listeners, that a transcontinental railroad would soon be searching for a pass through the mountains on its way to the Pacific. He then retired to the tent that served that part of the gulch as a hotel and the miners settled down to business.

Without dissent they whooped through a criminal code based on a realistic awareness that jails were unlikely to be built for some time. "Any person guilty of murder upon conviction thereof shall be hanged by the neck until he is dead." In addition to stiff fines, grand larceny was punishable by not less than fifteen and not more than three hundred "stripes on the bare back as a jury of six may direct," followed by banishment from the gulch. And so on, with roaring approval—until the assembly reached the problem of claim size.

At that point the disorganized malcontents realized that the firstcomers to the district had planned well. Firstcomers presided over the meeting. Motions prepared in advance were read quickly, seconded on the instant, and rushed to passage before the opposition could collect itself. "A claim shall be construe to mean whenever applide to a Load, One Hundred feet running the length of same and fifty feet in *width.* When applide to a Gulch. One Hundred feet following its meanderings and extending from

Bank to Bank. . . ." Which was exactly the way it had been from the beginning.

The next morning Greeley, Richardson, and Villard trotted up and down the gulch, peering into sluice boxes, panning gold with their own hands, and in general adding to the information they had collected the afternoon before. These data they incorporated into a joint story. Ziegler, Spain & Company had earned $3,000 in three weeks; Defrees & Company had taken out $2,080 in twelve days and then had sold half their claim for $2,500; Casto, Kendall & Company were averaging between $50 and $150 a day. . . . To these glowing details the journalists added a warning. The trip across the plains was difficult, supplies were scarce, expenses high, winters arduous. Beyond that, there was the troublesome matter of luck— either finding no claim at all or filing on one that would never repay the labor expended.

Byers was the first man other than the authors to see the joint story. Its gloomy reservations bothered him not one bit. The statistics were what would impress readers, and he was anxious to broadcast the findings. Unhappily, the June 11 issue of the *Rocky Mountain News* was already on press, devouring the last of his newsprint, and no more paper would be available until a delayed wagon train arrived the following week. Seeking a substitute, he scoured Auraria-Denver and found in the markets enough brown wrapping paper so that he could issue the complete Greeley-Richardson-Villard report as the first extra ever printed in the Rocky Mountains. He followed this on June 18 with a scathing editorial on the Gobacks. "We hope this class are all safely at home to their Pa's and Ma's, their sweethearts or 'Nancy and the babies'. . . . Farewell . . . they have had their day and soon will be forgotten."

That paper put to bed, he hitched a fast team to a light wagon and journeyed east with some of the Indiana boys from Gregory Gulch. Content with their month's work, they were going home with approximately $4,000 in gold dust—at least $40,000 in terms of today's purchasing power. In Omaha, Byers won their permission to exhibit the gold briefly and created what he considered to be a sensation.

Satisfied, he swung the team west again. The world knew the truth now: there was gold in the Rockies.

The world would have learned, of course, without his efforts. He simply quickened things a bit. Thousands of fresh hopefuls poured into Gregory Gulch, to discover in their turn that no matter how much money Ziegler, Spain & Company might have made, no gold-bearing ground was left for them.

Other men who had arrived in time to file claims close to rich producers were beginning to learn, meanwhile, that gold deposits are unpredictable and that their plots were barren. Others failed through incompetence. Men who did produce metal were shaken to learn that, although gold was worth $20.67 an ounce when pure, the dust they mined was invariably adulterated with oxides and clinging bits of quartz and was mixed with a fine black sand that they could never manage to remove completely. Because of these impurities, and for the sake of their own profits, Denver merchants in 1860 outraged the mountain miners by setting arbitrary prices of $6 to $8 per ounce for unretorted gold, the variations arising because dust from some localities was even less desirable than that from others. Even gold "refined" in crude, homemade retorts brought as little as $12 to $15 an ounce. Very few stampeders had expected, on leaving Kansas for the mountains, to see their prospects diluted that way.

The most sobering blow was the appalling labor involved. Swinging a pick in gravel from sunup to sundown was a discouraging experience even for boys raised on frontier farms. Bedrock might lie twenty or more feet deep, and then each bucketful of earth had to be hoisted to the surface by hand windlasses or horse-powered whims, and trundled by wheelbarrow to the sluices. Shafts in loose soil had to be timbered for safety, unprofitable work and, to the neophyte, mysterious. A man was wet much of the time, either from working in the creek itself, in a damp prospect hole, or with the sluice boxes. The sun baked him by day; night winds chilled him at dark. He seldom had a chance to launder or replace his clothes; the vanguard of prospectors, who outran their services, often wore their garments until they rotted. They were lucky if their roofs did not leak and if they possessed anything so luxurious to sleep on as a canvas-ticked mattress filled with cottonwood leaves. Much of the time food was limited to pancakes, beans, bacon, and coffee, cooked when the worker was dead-tired or prepared in sodden masses on Sunday so that it would last throughout the week. If a man washed his dishes at all, it was generally by scouring them in the doorway with a handful of sand and wiping them off with a clump of grass.

Because this was not the easy money they had dreamed of, many would-be miners went home in disgust at the first hint of winter. Others shifted to more conventional jobs—it has been estimated that five hands in allied trades were required to keep one miner at work. A man who was broke could labor on someone else's claim, whipsaw lumber (which was almost as arduous as mining), keep store, forge picks, freight, build roads, or farm at the edge of the plains. Consider, for instance, burly, long-bearded Rufus Clark, notorious even in early Denver for his drinking bouts and prodigious profanity. He made his fortune growing potatoes. Or raw-boned Sam Hartsel, who for six years had earned meager wages as a cow drover in Pennsylvania, Iowa, and Kansas. After a few grim weeks of prospecting he resumed his old trade, herding gaunt oxen for freighters and for immigrants who could find neither time nor pasturage near the diggings to do the job themselves. Gradually he accumulated a few abandoned creatures of his own, fattened them, sold them to mining camp butchershops, and used the proceeds to import better stock. By-and-by he had a famous ranch in South Park, noted for its purebred cattle and fancy horses—plus a trading post, sawmill, wagon shop, and a resort hotel whose successor is still operating near Hartsel Hot Springs.

Even so dedicated a miner as Green Russell found other ways to wealth than digging. He formed the Rockies' first big-business concern, the Consolidated Ditch Company, incorporating it for $100,000 in order to bring water 12 miles to Russell Gulch. Water, indeed, was so essential to placer mining that men who could round up enough capital for hiring a gang of laborers and buying thousands of feet of flume lumber and were good enough managers to push the work through before the excitement faded, these nimble executives generally reaped far better than did the miners.

Everyone knew those things. But everyone also knew of some farm boy or cobbler no better than himself who had arrived in time to file on a claim and had struck it lucky. Not a bonanza—there were relatively few of those in early Rocky Mountain mining—but a competence, as prices ran those days: $1,500 or possibly $5,000, enough to pay off the mortgage, marry the girl, or buy a share in the smithy back home. Off across the hill, perhaps, was exactly the right ravine, blessed with ample water, where the gold lay shallow and came out pure. Why not? Hadn't such things happened in California, and even along Clear Creek in the first stages of the stampede?

More insidious motives mingled with the thinking. Henry Villard tried to define them. Although gold mining demanded "pluck, energy, perseverance, and power of endurance," it attracted, paradoxically, the very sort of men who were most likely to be discouraged by slow returns and routine labors. Gamblers, Horace Greeley would have said. . . . And yet that was not the whole story either. A miner's life, Villard noted almost ecstatically, was harsh but nevertheless marked by "an absolute freedom of mind and body; the elevating influence of the steady contemplation of . . . mystic peaks, mighty vales of rock, endless pineries, broad, waving, mountain meadows, idyllic glens and glades, roaring torrents and lisping rivulets."

If mobility brings freedom, then the mountain prospector certainly had it. Whatever his motives—pique at the present, hope for the future, love of the outdoors, a search wherein the looking was as valuable as the thing found, or mere restlessness—whatever the reason, a discontented miner needed only to drop his shovel, whether he had been using it for himself or for someone else, buy a minimum of equipment, and join the tide that at any wild rumor flowed toward the far side of the mountain, there to try his luck afresh. Tramp printers, itinerant peddlers, wandering cowboys and blacksmiths were equally unrestrained, of course. A printer could not expect virgin gold at his next stand, however. A miner could, and for that they kept on roaming into the most unlikely glens and glades. They might not find a thing. But they surely would have stories to take back to Missouri.

As early as mid-June, 1859, about the time that Byers was starting for Omaha to invigorate the faltering rush, a group of empty-handed men left inhospitable Gregory Gulch to seek open ground elsewhere. They rode south around the canyon-seamed slope of the swollen gray massif known then as the Chicago Peaks (today called Mount Evans, the most prominent hump visible from Denver), crossed the northernmost fork of the South Platte, and in the vicinity of present Kenosha Pass looked out across South Park, its vast plains dappled with cloud shadows and bordered by mountains blue-hazy with distance.

Ute Indians killed some of that first party. Avengers riding out from Gregory Gulch missed their quarry and paused beside an unnamed stream, wondering whether to prospect or ride farther. Let's all tarry, someone said. They agreed, found gold, and named their camp Tarryall. A new rush developed and soon the creek was lined with claims. History repeated. When latecomers tried to persuade the first miners to reduce the size of the holdings, they were rebuffed. Sneering at the town as Graball, the disappointed miners jogged a few miles northwest, found gold of their own, and named their camp Fairplay.

Hurry! Hurry! The firstcomers to a diggings had things all their way. Forming companies big enough to defy the Utes, eager prospectors left crowded Fairplay and Tarryall behind and raced each other into the northwest corner of South Park, where the vast slide-rock peaks of the Continental Divide lump more than 14,000 feet high, as gray as elephants. Halting near timberline at the headwaters of the South Platte, some of the gold seekers built the cold town of Montgomery. Others continued through a saddle they named Hoosier Pass (11,541 feet above sea level) and dropped down the far side to the tributaries of Blue River, one of the principal forks of the upper Colorado, in those days called Grand River. Still others reached the same river—the Blue's main camp was called Breckenridge—by climbing from Tarryall among weather-stunted evergreens and across meadows spangled with blue-and-white columbines to Boreas Pass (11,482 feet).

The various groups had scarcely discovered the gold they yearned for when the first snow of winter frightened most of them out again. The handful who did brave Breckenridge's altitude fashioned ten-foot skis from pine boards, slid over Boreas Pass to Tarryall, and teetered back to their claims with 100-pound packs on their backs. There they discovered a fact of climate that the mountain trappers had learned long ago—a fact skiers continue to encounter to their surprise: winters in the high mountains are, on the average, milder than those in the upper Midwest or in New England, a delightful sequence, between blizzards, of blue-and-crystal days when it is possible to do nearly any sort of outdoor work in comfort.

Hurry! Learning of the parties that had gone northwest from Tarryall, a few later arrivals disdained that area and thrust west from South Park into the broad valley of the Arkansas. Reaching the river, they turned north, panning as they went, until they had reached about as far as the present hamlet of Granite. They found color at what they called Kelley's Bar, close beside the ponderous summits of the Sawatch Range, highest part of the entire Rocky Mountain chain. Under winter's first snowfall the bleak land looked as chill as judgment day. Like the prospectors along the Blue, the men at Kelley's Bar took fright and fled.

News of their discovery leaked back to the established camps, and as it became evident that winter was not as rigorous as expected, little groups began edging west, hoping to be first on the new scene. Among them were five or six Georgians from Russell Gulch, led by a man who had been to California, Abraham Lee.

By the end of March thirty or forty men had reached Kelley's Bar. Others began working up the river, digging through the snow to test the gravel in the gulches they passed. Spring blizzards wet them, and after Lee's Georgians had gone a dozen miles or so they were ready to turn back. One yarn has it that Lee paused to test a final pan before giving in. A more prosaic story says that he was digging through snow to dip water for his coffee from a little side creek. Both tales agree that he let out a sudden whoop: "Boys, I've got all California in this here pan!"

Reinforced by two more miners who chanced by, Lee's Georgians spent two weeks thoroughly testing the stream, which they named California Gulch, pressing five miles back into the heavily forested hills and in places digging through twelve feet of snow to reach gravel. When they found what seemed to be the gulch's richest section, they established their district, recorded their discovery claims, and went back to Kelley's Bar to dry out and to brag.

By midsummer, 1860, a reputed 8,000 to 10,000 people were either in California Gulch or on their way to its center, Oro City. This time late-comers succeeded in shrinking claim sizes from 200 feet to the more conventional 100. Even so, the gulch's 33,000-foot length was filled solid within days and packed with feverish people living in brush huts, under wagons, and only occasionally in cabins, which took time to build. Tales of dizzy fortune flashed from mouth to mouth. The discovery claims produced $60,000 in a matter of weeks. Two partners reaped so handsomely that a saloon and gambling house was built adjacent to their holding to absorb their trade alone. The area's miners were so delighted by the arrival of the camp's first woman, Augusta Tabor, that they built a cabin free of charge for her and her husband, Horace A. W. Tabor, who twenty years later would be the bonanza king of Leadville, Colorado.

Historically, the chief significance of the proliferating discoveries in South Park, along the Blue and its tributaries, and in California Gulch was the money they put into circulation almost overnight. Unlike the cash-starved farmers of the slowly growing, barter-oriented towns of the agricultural frontier, many miners in the high country could buy outright the goods and services they wanted—and wanted fast. Their suppliers weighed the gold dust on their scales, brightened, and immediately created fresh demands of their own.

Rivalries to cut in on the currency flow led to intense competition between towns that aspired to be distribution centers. In order to top Golden's determination to become chief supplier for the Clear Creek mines, Denver and Auraria left off fighting each other across Cherry Creek and voted to form a single municipality. Farther south a group of entrepreneurs (including Robert Middleton and his wife from Lawrence, Kansas) cast one speculative glance at the Santa Fe Trail and another at the new diggings in South Park and along California Gulch. To link buyers and sellers they formed Canon City at the mouth of the Royal Gorge of the Arkansas River and built a toll road up Currant Creek to the mines. Dismayed by the unexpected threat, the merchants of Colorado City at the foot of Pikes Peak responded by gouging out a free road along the rugged Indian trail through Ute Pass.

Stimulated thus, some of the "cities" quickly began to take on metropolitan airs. Brick buildings appeared in Denver while Arapahoe Indians were still pitching their tepees under the cottonwood trees along the Platte. Faced by an earnest challenge from a hard-working competitor, William Byers changed the *Rocky Mountain News* from a weekly to a daily. Stagecoaches, the Pony Express, and, a bit later, telegraph lines extended branch facilities up the South Platte to the foothills. Such nonutilitarian institutions as churches were eagerly welcomed partly for themselves, partly out of sentiment—and partly because their appearance seemed an assurance of stability.

Actually there was no stability. Very few men who worked in the non-renewable placer mines intended to stay at the onerous labor any longer than necessary to make a stake. As a result, small-time politicians and their heelers were the only ones interested in government. When the mountain electorate was asked to choose between the proposed state of Jefferson and a federally administered territory, only 3,656 men appeared at the polls, although by then (September, 1859) the area could have mustered perhaps 20,000 eligible voters.

Fountain City, from which the proposal for statehood had first emanated, reported 1,090 votes, compared to Denver's 1,130. Of Fountain's votes, 1,089 declared for statehood, 1 for a territory—all from a population of approximately 100. In spite of the brazen fraud, the territory was approved, the majority of the voters being swayed by the argument that if a territory was created the federal government would foot most of the bills. Even this was mere hope. Congress had not yet said a word, though only Congress could decree territorial status or demark territorial boundaries. As one disgusted miner put matters in a letter home, "Politics in this country are much like the whiskey, plenty and most villainously mixed."

The mountaineers nevertheless elected a governor of Jefferson Territory and a voiceless delegate to Congress. (Two thousand fraudulent ballots were tossed out of that election.) This "provisional government," as it called itself, fared poorly. Many residents rejected it on the ground that the Indians still held title; civil authority therefore was illegal and would remain illegal until Congress entered into treaty with the tribes concerned. Other dissenters argued that jurisdiction below the 40th parallel belonged to Kansas; with lofty punctiliousness *they* held county elections of their own. When the hapless officials of Jefferson Territory sought to impose taxes, such support as they had evaporated. They were enthusiastically hanged in effigy, and hundreds of miners who until then had shrugged off the whole affair suddenly began signing resolutions that declared they never would submit to taxation. Mountain County, one of twelve established by the provisional government, went so far as to hold an election and vote itself out of existence.

Wrangling between North and South kept Congress from breaking the impasse. Not until Lincoln had been elected and the Southern states began to secede was it possible for the Republicans to push through, on February 28, 1861, an organic act creating Colorado Territory. Lincoln's appointee as governor was William Gilpin. An extraordinary Missourian, graduate of West Point, Gilpin had explored with Frémont and, as a major of volunteer troops, had fought Indians in the southern Rockies and on the Western plains during and after the War with Mexico. On reaching the mountains, Gilpin developed a notion that the Rockies were to be the center not only of the United States but of the world, with railroads radiating from Denver to the tip of South America and across Bering Strait and Siberia to Europe. According to one acquaintance, scientist Nathaniel Hill, the new governor wanted to be buried atop the Continental Divide with one eye pointing toward the Atlantic, the other toward the Pacific.

He arrived in Denver on May 27, 1861, and immediately realized that the territory was in trouble. The year before, federal census takers had found 34,277 persons in the area. Gilpin's census, held as a guide for dividing the territory into voting districts, turned up only 25,331—20,758 of them males—and this total included the Spanish-Americans in a strip of land below the Arkansas River and in the San Luis Valley, which the year before had belonged to New Mexico.

The war, of course, was the primary cause of the drop. During the opening months of the conflict emigration west almost ended. At the same time miners streamed east from Colorado to join the gathering armies on one side or the other or just to help their families brace for whatever developed.

Hoping to keep loyal Union men in the territory and fearful that Confederate designs on New Mexico (whose legislature had legalized slavery in 1859) might extend to Colorado, Gilpin began, late in August, 1861, to buy firearms and recruit militia. Although these activities were not authorized by Washington, he confidently issued $375,000 in drafts to pay for what his troops needed. To his astonishment the War Department refused to honor the drafts.

Chaos threatened Denver's economy. The distraught Gilpin hurried east to plead his case. While he was on his way a Confederate army swept out of Texas and up the Rio Grande into Santa Fe. The conquest was so easy that the Southern commander decided to drive on north, seize the Colorado gold fields, and cut the Overland Trail to California.

Marching south at forced speed through squally March weather (1862), Gilpin's volunteers joined the Union stand in La Glorieta Pass. The battle seemed to be ending in a stalemate—until a Colorado contingent under a one-time Methodist preacher, bull-sized John Chivington (6 feet 4 inches tall and nearly three hundred pounds heavy), circled through the shaggy hills to the Confederate rear and came squalling down a 1,000-foot slope onto the enemy's supply dump. He destroyed 85 wagons loaded with ammunition, clothing, and food, and methodically bayoneted to death 500 or more horses and mules. Deprived of matériel and transport, the Confederates retreated to Texas.

For Gilpin it was a fruitless victory. Although his drafts were honored eventually, he was censured for exceeding his authority and was replaced as governor by John Evans. Immigration did not pick up. Meantime the only lode mines in the territory, those around Gregory Gulch, began running into complex ores which the miners could not refine. Indian-beset, snow-chilled prospecting trips as far away as the San Juan Mountains in the southwestern part of the territory revealed no new placer diggings, and those already being worked would soon be exhausted. Stagnation loomed.

Where next?

Even as the uneasy question arose it was answered, early in the summer of 1862, by wild rumors of strikes along the Salmon River.

What river?

The Salmon, the fellow said, a big stream up north on the western slope of the Rockies. Rich strikes—richer than even the diggings of California Gulch. Hurry! Without waiting for specific directions, hundreds of men hitched up their wagons. The first to reach a new diggings always fared best, or so they were convinced. So ho for the north! Hurry, hurry!

XI

STILL BIGGER BONANZAS

THE sweets of peace? For half a century the Nez Percé Indians maintained a tradition of openhanded friendship toward the nation that had sent Lewis and Clark across their deeply canyoned homelands on the western slope of the northern Rockies. Throughout the tormented decade of 1848–1858 they stayed aloof from the intermittent warfare that broke the tribes who lived to the west of them. Many of them functioned during the campaigns as scouts, packers, and providers of supplies for the American troops. Yet in the end they were as overwhelmed by the American victories as if they had fought among the enemy. For there was gold in their country. In the face of that, tradition meant little.

Although records are elusive, it appears that a few whites had stumbled onto hints of the gold shortly after the rush to California. Among them was Elias Davidson Pierce. After a fruitless period of mining in California, Pierce had switched to Indian trading and in 1852 had drifted north to a Nez Percé village located near the two main branches of the Clearwater River, in the west-central part of the Idaho panhandle, a country of deep valleys, steep grassy hills, and scattered ponderosa pines. True prospector that he was, he dug compulsively into a gravel bar beside the sparkling North Fork. Swirling a bit of the coarse earth in his pan, he saw a tiny glint of gold—not enough in 1852 to counteract reports of new mines being opened in northern California. Off he went, chasing that shadow. Failing, he tried British Columbia. Unsuccessful still, he returned in 1858 to the village near the forks of the Clearwater.

That glint again!—but the closing spasms of the Indian wars immediately to the west kept him from pressing the search until the spring of 1860.

Meanwhile the country to the west was filling up. During the wars Fort Walla Walla had been built where the city of Walla Walla, Washington, now stands, and steamboats had begun plowing with supplies up the Columbia to the nearest landing place. The war ended, the Indian lands of the Walla Walla Valley were thrown open to settlement by whites. The dropping of barriers did not include the resounding gorges of the Clearwater and Salmon rivers, where the Nez Percés farmed a little and grazed a few cattle, as Protestant missionaries had taught them to do, hunted deer, and fished during the salmon runs. Nor did it include the long, heavily timbered ridges that twist between the gorges eastward toward the awesome Bitterroot Mountains. According to the treaty which Governor Isaac Stevens of Washington Territory had signed with the tribe in 1855, the only whites eligible to enter the region were licensed traders.

Pierce had visited the country before as a trader. When he asked in the spring of 1860 for a permit to return with a twenty-five-year-old helper named Seth Farrell, the Indian agent in Walla Walla apparently offered no objection. Arrived on the North Fork, the pair quickly found color, just as Pierce had told Farrell they would, but it was still nothing more than a tantalizing promise. As they moved restlessly from bar to bar, a few curious Indians watching them the while, it became evident that two shovels were not sufficient for searching out the truly productive spots in that enormous sweep of canyon. But would the Indians admit a company of prospectors large enough to be effective?

In an effort to win their consent Pierce assured some of the village headmen that a gold rush would be a good thing for the tribe. Unlike the farmers to the west, miners were not greedy for land—he said. They would simply take out the mineral along the edges of the streams and leave. While they were working they would buy horses and cattle from the Nez Percés and would teach the Indians how to retrieve gold from the gravel for themselves. With it they could buy anything they wished.

As evidence of his good intentions, he took a few Indians to Walla Walla with him and equipped them with mining tools. Then obstacles appeared. When he sought permission from the Indian agent to lead a company of prospectors *through* the reservation (he said falsely that he meant to prospect east of the boundary) he was rebuffed. The agent, moreover, told the Nez Percés that a gold rush would not be the benefit that Pierce had claimed.

Dismayed by the contradiction, the Indians decided to resist illegal entries. That and the agent's declaration in Walla Walla that he would use troops if necessary to protect the reservation cooled off the gold fever that had been building in the town. When Pierce left Walla Walla on August 12, 1860, to sneak back onto the forbidden ground, only ten men had nerve enough to go with him.

To elude pursuit they crossed the torrent of the Snake and zigzagged north and east through dense forests until they reached the upper stretch of the Clearwater's North Fork. Failing to find the riches Pierce had promised, they crossed the river and pushed doggedly south through the tangled mountains to the headwaters of an unnamed creek. Beside a trickle which they named Canal Gulch they made a fabulous strike. Other strikes followed in neighboring gulches, and because the dust was unusually pure, they named the main creek of the area Oro Fino. Taut with excitement, they worked the ground for two weeks and then, in mid-October, headed back to Walla Walla for enough provisions to last them throughout the winter.

From then on the Indians had no chance of excluding the ravenous whites. Throughout the winter and spring defiant miners swarmed in heavily armed parties into the mountains. After a few ineffective attempts at upholding the treaty, the agent yielded to white pressure and persuaded the more peacefully inclined Nez Percé chiefs to sign a new agreement ceding to the United States the mineral grounds *north* of the main Clearwater and of the Lolo Trail which Lewis and Clark had followed half a century before.

The whites paid no more attention to this new treaty than to the old one. Steamboats thrashing up the Snake River from the Columbia found their only good landing place to be on the south bank of the Clearwater just above its confluence with the Snake. Overnight, Lewiston sprang into being, a raucous transshipping center compounded of noisome shacks, tents, corrals, and boat docks. In the mountains, meanwhile, the twin log towns of Oro Fino and Pierce City, located two miles or so apart, became the centers of feverish activity.

As usual there was not enough ground to go around. To those who could find none that was open and to others who were disappointed in what they had found the sirens of hope once again sang the old song: something better lies out yonder.

John J. Healy is a good example. Five feet five inches tall, swarthy and blue-eyed, he had run away from his Irish home at the age of fourteen. After a spell in Nicaragua with William Walker's notorious filibustering expedition, he had landed in New York and, seventeen by then, had enlisted in the army. In August, 1860, after more than two years' service in the Utah area, he was mustered out and went to Portland. When word of gold arrived there he and a group of friends caught the first steamer of 1861 up the Columbia. They reached Oro Fino Creek while snow still covered the ground and filed their claims some distance below Pierce City. It was a hard-luck venture. Healy was badly hurt by a falling tree, and while he was laid up a spring freshet swept away the improvements his partners had been making on their claims.

At that point in came word of the adventures of fifty-two men who had started south into Nez Percé territory only days after the signing of the new treaty. Indians had frightened thirty of the party into turning back. The rest slipped past the watchers, found the southernmost of the Nez Percé trails leading to buffalo country and followed it eastward, well above and north of the Clearwater's South Fork. In time they reached Elk Valley, a grassy opening seven miles long bordered on either side by low, pine-clad hills.

Pushing through the green stringers of willow brush along meandering Elk Creek, the men dug holes to bedrock and turned up such a spangle of color that their eyes popped. While some of the party hurried to Oro Fino for supplies, the others established a mining district they called Elk City— nothing less than full-blown cities anywhere in the West in those days —and on June 14, 1861, recorded claims for the entire party. By the beginning of August 2,000 men were jammed into little Elk Valley.

When word of the strike reached Pierce City, young Healy was re- covered enough from his injury to ride again. With some of his partners and a few others he went down Oro Fino Creek to the Clearwater and turned south up the river.[1] Nez Percés blocked them too. Enraged by what seemed an unwarranted interruption of a legitimate enterprise, the whites returned to the Oro Fino area for reinforcements. Twenty-three strong, they charged howling through the Indians who, in spite of the provocation, did not resort to shooting.

Having succeeded, the whites took alarm at their own temerity. Instead of turning east toward Elk City, they sought to elude pursuit by fleeing west over the canyon rim. Finding White Bird Creek on the other slope, they descended it to the Salmon, a new river to most whites. Hopefully they prospected south along the unknown stream, following it around its right- angle turn to the east. The engorged country grew wild; years later the white water foaming through the narrow bottom would be known to boat- men as Idaho's fabled "River of No Return."

Short of food and unable to take their horses farther along the boulder- littered banks, the party decided at last to strike for Elk City. Rather than circle back through the canyon, they headed straight northeast through the trackless hills. A hard climb up Meadow Creek brought them to what became Summit Flats, a marshy piece of land in the heart of a rolling, tree- choked basin seamed by little ravines. Healy and some of his friends wanted to prospect the boggy gulches. The others disdained the unlikely spot and pushed on toward Elk City.

One of Healy's friends, accepting a careless wager, dug without much interest into a pit left by the upheaved roots of a wind-toppled tree. Heartened by the faint show of yellow he uncovered, the others scattered out, shoveling through peat moss to red gravel that yielded as much as 75 cents a pan. Though not a bonanza compared to the best claims at Oro Fino and Elk City, the discovery led them to stake claims on either August 12 or 20, 1861 (accounts vary), and then go outside for supplies.

A number of footloose prospectors followed them back. Mining proved to be laborious. Although the ground itself was wet, not enough water flowed in the little ravines to operate sluice boxes or even rockers, the latter a cradle-like apparatus into which water could be dipped while the

[1] Present Oro Fino is at the junction of Oro Fino Creek and the Clearwater. The mining camp of Oro Fino was twenty-five miles farther east in the mountains.

worker agitated the machine on its curved underpinning. The miners solved
the problem by digging shallow wells, letting them fill by seepage, and then
using and re-using the water until it was almost viscid. When it was too
filthy to serve longer, they baled the wells dry and let them refill with clear
liquid.

Results were sometimes astounding. One of the earliest arrivals, a man
named Miller, produced $25 from the first shallow hole he dug, tried
another, and earned $100 in a single afternoon. Some distance away at
Baboon Gulch (named for a shaggy Dutchman called Baboon) a certain
Weiser reputedly produced $6,600 during a single working day. One
famous single shovelful yielded $151.50. Gold poured from many claims in
such quantities that normal containers did not suffice to hold it; discarded
yeast powder boxes, pickle bottles, and oyster cans had to be pressed into
service as substitute "pokes."[2]

Although word of these sensational strikes did not reach Walla Walla
until late in the season, a thousand people rushed into the area and the raw
town of Florence sprawled alive among the evergreens at the head of
Baboon Gulch. Eager to cash in on the wild demand for supplies, packers
rounded up every available mule in eastern Washington, loaded on tools,
flour, and whiskey and started through the canyons. Hostile Indians
stopped some of the trains; early snowfalls blocked more. Sobered by the
prospects of a mountain winter without adequate supplies, most of the
prospectors thereupon fled outside.

The few who tried to tough out the winter soon regretted the decision.
The storms of 1861–62 were rigorous even for the Idaho Rockies. Supplies
moved only aboard human backs. Men in Oro Fino warded off scurvy by
walking 20 miles through swollen drifts for potatoes that they carried back
and ate soaked in vinegar. One miner in the Florence district survived on
membrane scraped from the inner side of pine bark, a last-resort food long
familiar to the mountain Indians. Another made out on plain flour and tea
steeped from fir needles. The first pack trains that tried to break through to
Florence in the spring of 1862 were halted by huge drifts 40 miles from
their goal. The packers put the food on their own backs and for 10 cents a
pound lugged it 10 miles to a place called Mountain House. Famished
miners met them there and carried it the rest of the way—for 40 cents a
pound.

Elk City survived with the help of friendly Indian farmers. Although
most of their country was either forested or split by rocky gorges, there
were, on some of the hillsides, long grassy openings that sufficed for beef

2 The ubiquitousness of the oyster in early mining camps is always mildly surprising to modern readers. For some reason oysters lent themselves better than did
most foods to the canning processes of the time, which required that tins be boiled at
least five hours to ensure safety. They emerged less stew-like and more nutritious per
ounce, factors which brought them high popularity in districts where weight was a
primary consideration.

cattle; and in some of the canyons, open hollows where vegetables could be grown. During the desperate winter, when hungry miners were offering astounding prices for anything to eat, the Indians took their produce and even their private little hoards of flour and coffee to wanderers stranded along the trails and in isolated Elk City.

Enthralled by the sudden prosperity many of the Indians lost interest in fighting and offered only nominal objections when some of the peace-party chiefs were cajoled into selling to the U.S. government nearly nine-tenths of their reservation, retaining only 785,000 acres out of an original 6,932,000. For this cession the Nez Percé tribe received, mostly in the form of "services," $325,000—less than 5 cents an acre for land that would produce, between 1860 and 1867 alone, an estimated $20 million. But that is getting ahead of the story.

Before the snow was gone in the spring of 1862 thousands of prospectors were struggling to reach the Salmon River mines, as the diggings around Florence were called. The first parties had to walk. Though they tried to protect themselves from sun glare by smearing a black mixture of powdered charcoal and bacon grease around their eyes, many went snowblind and had to be led by their friends. Later arrivals traveled by saddle train—long lines of saddle animals rented in either Walla Walla or Lewiston, often without provision for baggage. Wranglers herded the dudes along, cooked miserable meals for them at the campgrounds, dumped them unceremoniously into Florence's filthy streets, and wheeled the sore-backed horses around for another trainload.

One contemporary journalist estimates that 9,200 hopefuls landed in Florence that summer. About 3,000 of them obtained claims or parts of claims. At Miller's Creek in the same vicinity, 558 men operated 186 claims. According to historian Hubert Howe Bancroft, these 3,500 shovelers averaged a fantastic $4,000 each for the season, perhaps $40,000 each in terms of today's purchasing power. But other thousands who swirled into the area found nothing. Lacking money enough to buy a piece of ground, they either went home or pressed restlessly ahead, looking for something else.

Once again a few were lucky—and that is why stampedes kept rolling. One group crossed from Florence to the south side of the Salmon Canyon and opened the Warrens district, producer of $6 million during the next five years. Another small party pushed on south beyond the reservation, joined forces with a group from Oregon, and began prospecting in broad Boise Basin. Just as the shout of "Gold!" went up, Bannock Indians struck. They killed only one of the whites, but that was warning enough. The Bannocks, a belligerent branch of the Shoshoni, were a far more dangerous tribe than the Nez Percés and had proved it thoroughly during the 1850's by an intermittent series of gruesome raids on wagon trains traveling the Oregon Trail. Deciding not to press their luck, the prospectors buried their fallen friend in his own prospect hole and retreated in search of reinforcements.

The rush of circumstance was on their side. Emboldened by the withdrawal of federal troops from western outposts at the beginning of the Civil War, the Bannocks of Idaho, the Shoshoni of Wyoming, and the Paiutes of Nevada guaranteed trouble for themselves by burning stage stations and running off stock belonging to the Overland Mail Company. To protect communications on the eastern side of the Continental Divide, the government replaced some of the troops in Wyoming and built Fort Halleck at the edge of the Medicine Bow Mountains. California volunteers under red-headed, red-bearded Patrick Edward Connor were ordered to defend the western side.

Uneasy about the loyalty of the Mormons among whom he would be stationed (the Mormon War was still a green memory), Irish Pat Connor disguised himself as a civilian and went ahead of his troops to spy. One suspects he saw what he wanted to see. To a superior he reported tensely, "I found . . . a community of traitors, murderers, fanatics and whores. The people publicly rejoice at reverses to our arms . . . I have a difficult and dangerous task ahead of me." He refused to garrison his volunteers in the isolated fort which Albert Sidney Johnston had built after the Utah War several miles from Salt Lake City. Instead, he built a new post on a plateau overlooking the town and, according to James Knox Polk Miller, a non-Mormon youth living in Salt Lake at the time, trained a cannon on Brigham Young's house, just in case.

Connor, be it said, was equally grim about the Indians. When Mormons in the hamlet of Franklin just over the present Idaho line appealed to him in January, 1863, for help against raiding Bannocks, he marched without hesitation 140 miles to Bear River through bitter cold that froze the feet of 75 of his 350 men. The Bannocks, who had grown used to triumphing in small raids, waited overconfidently behind steep creekbanks in a tributary ravine where hot springs melted the snow from the ground but did not warm the air. On the day of the battle the temperature was 23 degrees below zero.

The fight lasted four hours. Connor estimated that he killed 224 warriors and captured 160 women and children. Mormon observers, noting corpses piled eight feet deep in one place, estimated 400 slain. The cost to Connor was 14 troopers killed and 49 wounded, seven of whom later died.

The crushing defeat kept the Bannocks quiet the following spring when miners poured into newly discovered Boise Basin. In case the trouncing wasn't enough, the army also built Fort Boise beside the Oregon Trail, 40 miles south of the basin's mining center of Idaho City. The site of the fort, where the climate was mild and the soil fertile, became a natural magnet for farmers and for merchants eying the mine-created markets to the north. By 1864 there were perhaps 20,000 people spread from Boise Basin down to Boise City (always a "city," however meager) beside the fort. It was Idaho's richest mining and mine-oriented district, and as usual there wasn't enough ground to go around. Prospectors spilled on southwest out of the Rockies into the desert mountains of the Owyhee country in extreme southwestern Idaho and made new strikes there. Fresh hope was urgently needed. Fabulous Florence in the Salmon River country was fading as rapidly as it had bloomed.

The locust-like sweep of the prospectors gave Pat Connor an idea. Surely there was gold somewhere in Utah. If the trained miners among his bored California volunteers found it by prospecting during their leave time, then perhaps a rush of "gentiles" would appear in numbers sufficient, in his words, to "wrest from the church—disloyal and traitorous to the core— the . . . control of temporal and civic affairs."

The first strike was not made by a soldier, however, but by George Ogilvie, an apostate Mormon. Ogilvie picked up a few pieces of ore while cutting logs among the scattered red pines of Bingham Canyon, a narrow ravine that sliced northward out of the barren Oquirrh Mountains into the southern part of Great Salt Lake. He took these samples to Connor's Camp Douglas and showed them to the general. One yarn has it that a group of officers, many accompanied by their wives, thereupon went to the canyon on a picnic, located a few outcrops, established the West Mountain Mining District, filed claims (the women too), and began to dig. They found no bonanzas. Neither did the soldiers who subsequently tramped over the rest of the Oquirrh Mountains and up the canyons of the Wasatch Range behind Salt Lake City.[3] The strikes they made were almost entirely of a complex silver-lead ore that could not be mined in profitable quantities until better transportation and smelting facilities had appeared in Utah. Connor tried. He trumpeted each find to the skies in a violently anti-Mormon newspaper that he founded, and then went broke pouring money into a smelter whose failure presumably caused no distress to the Mormons.

As he had during the California rush, Brigham Young used his enormous influence to keep his people from being infected by the virus. "Instead of hunting gold," he cried from the pulpit, "we ought to pray the Lord to hide it up. Gold is not wealth, wealth consists in the multiplication of the necessaries and comforts of life. Instead of hunting gold, go and raise wheat, barley, oats, get your bread and make gardens and orchards."

Stay at home they did, as they had in '49, and because they were the supply center of a vast region clamoring for food and clothing and simple tools, they and the non-Mormon merchants who lived among them in Salt Lake City almost surely profited more than if they had dropped their

---

[3] In 1864, to be sure, modest placer mines were found in Bingham Canyon; by the end of 1869 they had produced something more than $1 million, or a little better than $200,000 a year. This was not enough to attract attention from other areas. During approximately the same period, Boise Basin turned out close to $20 million. The camps of Alder Gulch, Montana, were meantime producing $30 million.

scythes for shovels. Wagon trains of flour and onions went to Fort Boise and even to Denver, in spite of competition in the Colorado market from the frontier towns of Kansas. But their big bonanza was the sudden opening of Montana.

And that brings us back, finally, to twenty-one-year-old John J. Healy, who in the summer of 1861 had ridden away from Oro Fino to help discover the sensational Salmon River mines around Florence.

During the fall Healy unearthed about 125 ounces of gold dust. Impure, it was worth about $1,500. This was far better than the army pay he had known in Utah, but compared to the finds being made by many of the men around him it must have seemed like the thinnest sort of poverty.

Hoping for better luck in the spring, he wolfed out the grim winter of 1861–62 in Florence. On May 1, while the snow was still too deep for mining, he heard rumors that a party was secretly forming to search out a quartz vein far up the Salmon River, its location reputedly known to a certain Beaver Dick. Healy consulted friends of his own and they decided to cut in on the adventure by the simple expedient of following Beaver Dick's group wherever it went. After skiing down Meadow Creek to the Salmon they dug up from its cache in the sand a rowboat they had bought sight unseen from its owners. Then they blandly attached themselves to the other gold hunters. Although the first group was enraged by the intrusion, there was nothing they could do about it, and in unfriendly sequence the two parties, totaling about twenty-four men, started up the river.

In Healy's words, they crossed and recrossed "from one side of the river to the other in search of a foothold along the high and perpendicular banks. Portage after portage was made around the most dangerous rapids, many of which could be more properly termed falls, and when the river was comparatively smooth and free from whirlpools and rocks . . . the current [was] so swift that we could make little or no headway against it." When the lead party lost one of its boats, loaded with $1,500 worth of equipment, five men turned back. The others struggled hungrily on, a few miles a day, too busy to hunt during sunny hours and too tired in the evening.

After they had covered about 60 miles they were astounded to meet two gaunt men on a raft. The pair had started from the Bitterroot Valley for Florence on horseback. Unable to push the animals through the Salmon's howling canyons, they had abandoned them and built a raft, hoping to float to their goal. All they had for food was "a dried bearskin which they were pounding with rocks and eating." With heartfelt earnestness they urged the men from Florence to turn back; it was not possible to buck a way upstream against the spring floods surging through the canyon.

When most of the Florence group persisted, the raftmen added a bit of information. Gold had been struck in the northern part of the Deer Lodge Valley about 60 miles up the Clark Fork River from the mouth of the

Bitterroot.⁴ No, the wanderers had not visited the new field. Florence sounded better—and on they bobbed.

As the canyon grew wilder, more and more of the Florence men dropped out until only Healy and three others remained, one of them deranged by the six-week agony. They gave up trying to find Beaver Dick's vein and concentrated on escaping from the gorge. Staggering at last into the open valley where Salmon, Idaho, now stands, they swung south up the Lemhi River in the unreasonin hope that they might find succor at the old Mormon mission of Fort Lemhi, 50 miles away.

By wild chance a wagon train appeared shortly after they reached the ruins. It was the vanguard of stampeders from Utah and Colorado. On hearing of the Salmon River discoveries, they had rushed off (as noted in the preceding chapter) without knowing quite where to go. Encountering a Mormon who had been at Lemhi during its missionary years, they had hired him as guide. But he had never seen the dreadful canyons below the Lemhi's junction with the main Salmon.

Told the truth by Healy, the train halted in dismay. During the confusion Healy and a friend borrowed horses, tried to reach the reputed quartz vein, and failed. What next? No matter how much gold there might be on their claims in Florence, they had no intention of bucking that chasm again. Yet they could not stay where they were.

Back to Lemhi they went. By then nearly a thousand stampeders were milling about between the old mission and the upper mouth of the gorge. All were asking the same question: what now? Some decided to abandon their wagons for packhorses and try to find a way through the mountains. Others said they had heard of a new government road, the Mullan Road, somewhere farther north; if they could reach it, perhaps they could follow it into eastern Washington and come up to Florence from the west.

Incurable prospector that he was, Healy mentioned the new diggings at Deer Lodge, which the men on the raft had spoken of. Others nodded; they had heard the same story from an old trapper called Michaud Le Clair, who ran a ferry over a fork of the Bear River nearly 150 miles to the south. Some of the Coloradoans added more evidence. A pair of ex-California prospectors named James and Granville Stuart had written their brother Thomas in the Pikes Peak country of finding gold in the Deer

⁴ The different names of the Clark Fork are a confusion even to Montanans. The stream begins at the Continental Divide near Butte as Silver Bow Creek. Where the creek turns north through Deer Lodge Valley it becomes, locally, the Deer Lodge River. Bending west, it meets Little Blackfoot River and becomes Hell Gate River. Either above Missoula, where it meets the Big Blackfoot, or below Missoula, where it meets the Bitterroot, it becomes Clark Fork. Sometimes, though, it is the Missoula River from Hell Gate to the St. Regis River. Or sometimes it is the Bitterroot as far as St. Regis, and then becomes Clark Fork. Below Pend Oreille Lake, Idaho, it is sometimes the Pend Oreille River. The U.S. board concerned with geographic names would prefer that the whole stream from the Columbia to the Divide be called Clark Fork, but the battle seems lost, at least locally.

Lodge area and had invited him to join them. Though Thomas Stuart had decided to stay in Colorado for the time being, he had shown the letter to friends. Excited, they had formed a party and started early to be ahead of the rush. Perhaps those first Coloradoans were in the new diggings already.

The listeners hesitated. Deer Lodge? What kind of name was that? And how did one get there?

Deer Lodge (the gold seekers eventually learned) was the English translation of an Indian name for a cone of earth, formed by thermal activity, that stood 30 feet high in a flat plain and was shaped like a tepee. Deer congregated there during freezing weather to drink the open water of the hot springs and to crop the grass that was free of snow. Early-day white trappers had extended the name of the cone to the surrounding valley. They liked its waving grass and the equally lush pastures of the other broad, mountain-girt plains strung along both sides of the Continental Divide. Because of marauding Blackfeet, however, only strong parties dared camp in the area; and after the beaver trade had declined the few trappers left in the mountains avoided the basins, save for occasional trips along the fading trails to visit John Owen's post in the Bitterroot Valley.

As noted earlier, some of these roving mountaineers developed a brisk summertime trade with emigrants toiling along the Oregon Trail. Their most profitable item of barter was oxen. The trappers would swap one stout work animal for two trail-worn ones, fatten the weary beasts in some grassy pocket in southern Wyoming or southeastern Idaho, and trade the animals off again the following season. Some of the traders collected nice little herds that way, but they had trouble settling down with the livestock. There were frequent quarrels with the Mormons all the way from Green River in Wyoming to Fort Hall in Idaho; as we have seen, there were even shooting scrapes at the Green River ferries. Shoshoni and Bannock Indians added more trouble with occasional raids. Thus the mountain men listened with sudden interest when they heard that Governor Stevens of Washington Territory had made a treaty of peace with the Blackfeet late in the summer of 1855. If the calm held, then perhaps those mountain valleys in what is now Montana might furnish a refuge, in spite of their distance from summer markets.

Among the first to try were young Robert Dempsey, Robert Hereford, Jake Meeks, and John Jacobs. At the close of the 1856 trading season the quartet pushed 60 head of livestock over low Monida Pass into the Beaverhead country.[5] After locating the animals near the mouth of the

5 The Jefferson Fork of the Missouri River—the fork which Lewis and Clark followed—splits into three branches near present Twin Bridges, Montana. (Twin Bridges is some 30 miles downstream, north of Dillon.) The Stinking Water, now refined to the Ruby, enters the Beaverhead from the east, just south of Twin Bridges. The looping Big Hole enters a few miles farther on from the west. The combined streams are then known as the Jefferson.

Stinking Water, the men jogged west and north and then west again over familiar trails to John Owen's post in the Bitterroot.

Along the way, beside a little creek in the northern part of Deer Lodge Valley, they saw several prospect holes. These had been dug as early as 1852 by François Finlay, nicknamed Benetsee, a Hudson's Bay Company employee from Fort Connah in the Flathead Valley. Finlay had not found a great deal of metal, but no matter. The very fact that someone had tried prospecting in the area was a tidbit of gossip for Montana's first ranchers to pass along, together with reports of the trouble-free grass, when they returned in the warm months of 1857 to their trading stations beside the emigrant trail.

Both items of talk found eager listeners. One who heeded was "Captain" Richard Grant, who, as the Hudson's Bay Company trader at Fort Hall from 1841 to 1851, had developed a violent dislike for the Mormons—and they for him. He was trading on his own now, in a loose partnership with his grown son John and he liked the sound of all that uncontested rangeland up north. In midsummer of 1857 the Grants started several hundred cattle for the Beaverhead. On arriving at the mouth of the Stinking Water the old man halted and built a three-room dwelling cabin and Indian trading post for himself and his half-blood wife.

Three other listeners were the Stuart brothers, James, aged twenty-five, Granville, aged twenty-four, and their partner Rezin Anderson, whom they called Reece. The trio had been on their way home to Iowa after five fruitless years prospecting in northern California. In southeastern Idaho, not far from the camp where Jake Meeks, Hereford, and Dempsey were trading, Granville Stuart fell desperately ill with fever. He was still wobbly when the Mormon War broke out and Mormon guerrillas closed the trail. Fearful of being arrested as spies and intrigued by the tales of Benetsee's gold, the Stuarts and Anderson decided to ride north with their new friends and look around.

When Richard Grant heard news of the Mormon War he panicked. Danite assassins, he was convinced, were already on their way north to settle old scores with him. Although he was ill and the December cold was bitter, he rounded up his cattle, hired helpers, abandoned his new cabin, and fled still farther away, to the area of present-day Missoula. There he stayed, but his son John liked the lower (northern) part of Deer Lodge Valley better and moved back to where the Little Blackfoot entered the main river. By 1859 John had enough surplus cattle so that he hired cowboys to drive 400 of them all the way to California for sale. With the proceeds he moved farther up the Clark Fork River to the site of today's town of Deer Lodge and there built a two-story house awesome with glass windows and green shutters.

After spending the winter of 1857–58 on the Beaverhead, the Stuarts and Reece Anderson visited Benetsee's prospect holes. Lacking shovels for digging and saws for cutting planks for sluice boxes, they could not do much mining. But they liked the country and the footloose life, and they spent the next few years with the Grants and Dempsey and the others drifting back and forth between Deer Lodge, Beaverhead, and the Oregon Trail. They married Indian girls, traded for their simple needs, lived well on abundant wild game and trout, and forgot Iowa.

A surprising number of others slipped into the easygoing pattern of this mountain idyll—prospectors, trappers, freighters, discharged soldiers, the usual flotsam of the nation's westering. Some clustered around Owen's post. Others gathered at Hell Gate Ronde, as they called the grassy cup a bit downstream from today's Missoula. A handful more settled with the Stuarts at the mouth of Benetsee's creek, which they named American Fork; all told, they had six cabins in their "town," plus tepees.

Growth accelerated with the coming of the Mullan Road. On realizing that no railway was likely to be built for years along the northern transcontinental route he had surveyed in 1853–54, Governor Stevens of Washington had urged Congress to stimulate emigration by providing at least a wagon way across the Rockies to his territory. As supervisor of the work he recommended one of the most energetic of his railroad surveyors, Lieutenant John Mullan, twenty-five years old in 1855.

Appropriations were authorized, but the Indian wars of the Northwest kept delaying Mullan's start until 1859. By that time the road had achieved military priority as a means of hustling troops into the Northwest. Its eastern terminus was to be the fur-trading post of Fort Benton, located 40 miles or so below the Great Falls of the Missouri River. The first troops were scheduled to arrive at Benton in the summer of 1860 aboard steamboats operated by the Chouteau fur-trading interests of St. Louis.

Mullan began his work in 1859 at Fort Walla Walla, the road's western terminus. With a hundred workers he marched north across the Snake River to Coeur d'Alene Lake. It was rolling, open country, and for much of the distance he simply bridged streams and put up mileage posts marked "MR." By "MR" he meant "Military Road," but emigrants so persistently interpreted it as "Mullan Road" that the error helped freeze his name firmly in the history of the northern Rockies.

From Lake Coeur d'Alene he chopped a difficult way eastward up narrow ravines and through dense timber. After crossing the Bitterroots at Sohon Pass, he holed up for a miserable, scurvy-ridden winter in the valley of the St. Regis. Heartened in the spring of 1860 by the arrival of additional workers, he pushed on past the Hell Gate and American Fork settlements and topped the Continental Divide at Mullan Pass, which he had first discovered in March, 1854.

When he arrived at Fort Benton on August 1, 1860, he found 300 troops already landed there from Chouteau's steamboats. Wheeling around, Mullan hurried back ahead of them, cleaning more obstacles out of the way, so that the soldiers were able to march the 624 miles to Fort Walla Walla in fifty-seven days—an average of eleven miles a day, not bad considering that all commissary and camping supplies had to travel from bivouac to bivouac by mule train.

In 1861 and again in 1862 Mullan kept polishing. He relocated weather-vulnerable stretches, strengthened bridges, excavated sidehills, blasted out rocky points, and everlastingly hacked away at the dead trees that were toppled across the trace by each winter gale. He spent $230,000. As soon as he quit, floods and wind began obliterating his work, especially in the Bitterroots and on west to Coeur d'Alene Lake. Not a wagon ever used the western half of his road. Scores of packtrains did, however, and in the east the tracks became a goal for stampeders churning up the Missouri on shallow-draft steamboats, bound for the fabled mines of Florence, word of which reached St. Louis and other Mississippi Valley towns early in 1862.

Among the passengers aboard the Chouteau steamer *Spread Eagle* were James and Julius Morley. They were not restless youths. Julius had already roamed through parts of China and the South Pacific on various jobs. James, thirty-eight years old in 1862, had been a civil engineer and surveyor for water systems and railroad construction jobs from New York to Missouri. Knowing the freedom of movement gained by adequate resources, the Morley brothers formed a mining company with four other stable Missourians and went into the adventure with far sounder financing than did most of the stampeders. But none of that, as matters developed, helped them pinpoint the spot where placer gold might lie.

At Fort Benton they paid $140 for a wagon to haul their tools, $105 per yoke for oxen, and $50 each for riding horses. Wanting advance information about the Salmon River country, they joined forces with other companies in dispatching scouts who were to visit Florence and then report to them in Deer Lodge Valley, of whose existence they had first learned on the steamboat.

Those traveling by wagon enjoyed the trip. They ate their fill of trout and ripening berries; and when they crossed the Divide at Mullan Pass on July 7 James Morley was excited enough at seeing wind-drifted snow in the gullies that, so he wrote in his diary, "I went to it, filled my canteen with it and had a roll and slide." Remembering the journey years later, China-wanderer Julius asked nostalgically in his reminiscences, "Was there in the World ever a country half so pretty as was this mountain land before civilization ruined it?"

Civilization was hard at work when they reached American Fork, where they were to wait for their scouts. In 1860 a man named Henry Thomas, whom Granville Stuart nicknamed Gold Tom, had wandered into the area and near the site of Benetsee's original prospect, where the Stuart brothers had also mined briefly in 1858, had singlehanded sunk a shaft 20 feet deep. His labors astounded Granville:

He [Gold Tom] made a primitive windlass, and hewed out and pinned together with wooden pins and bound around with a picket rope, a bucket with which he hoisted the dirt while sinking the shaft. He would slide down the rope, fill the bucket with gravel, then climb up a notched pole . . . and hoist the bucket of gravel. He encountered many boulders too large to go into the bucket. Around these he would put a rope and windlass them out. . . . He also hewed boards [with an ax] . . . and made four little sluice boxes . . . put together with wooden pegs . . . and then dug a ditch from the creek. . . . He could not make more than one dollar and fifty cents a day and often less than that sum, owing to the great disadvantages under which he worked.

Inspired afresh by Gold Tom's work, the Stuarts in 1861 had brought in some tools. After finding color on a tributary of American Fork, which they named Pioneer Creek, they had (as we have seen) written their brother Thomas in Colorado to join them. Meanwhile some of the mountaineers in their own neighborhood had caught the fever and begun to mine along the fork.

On June 24, 1862, the first Coloradoans had arrived. Finding Pioneer Creek full, they moved to a parallel ravine that they named Pikes Peak Gulch and in it located a little more color. Slowly the population increased. Forty-five people celebrated the Fourth of July along American Fork. That evening James and Granville Stuart decided that storekeeping might offer more profit than mining and made arrangements to go into partnership with Frank Woody, an embryo merchant at Hell Gate Ronde. As if to confirm the wisdom of their decision the first family arrived a week later, on July 12—B. B. Burchett, his wife, their two daughters, and a pair of towhead boys. White women! "Miss Sallie Burchett," Granville told his diary, "is sixteen years old and a very beautiful girl. Every man in camp has shaved and changed his shirt."

The sight of mining here beside the trail, where they had not expected it, shook the travelers. Some canny but anonymous promoter among the miners added a sly tug of propaganda to the temptation to linger. "This place," Granville Stuart wrote on July 14, "here before known as American fork, has been re-christened Gold Creek." Hearing the ring of the words, many of the farmers bound for Walla Walla and prospectors headed for Florence paused uncertainly. Why not find out what was here before rushing on across the mountains?

For many of them the clincher came July 22 with the reappearance of two of the scouts who had been sent ahead by the Morley brothers and their associates. The weary pair told a grim tale of wandering helplessly in the Salmon River mountains, "suffering untold hardships," Granville reported, "and almost starving to death." James Morley added in his diary the discouraging word that the pair had somehow discovered that the

Florence district was already overflowing with stampeders from Oregon and Washington.

At the same time vanguards of the hundreds who had been stranded along the Lemhi began trickling in. There would have been more except that some of the frustrated groups had lost the trail to Deer Lodge and were wandering about the Beaverhead and Big Hole basins, prospecting in desultory fashion as they traveled. Unless they found something, they too would be along soon and so it might be a good idea for those already at Gold Creek to grab what ground they could while some was still open—or so the emigrants argued among themselves.

Unimpressed by the looks of the area, a few finally went on, racing winter. Others fanned down American Fork, staking claims until every tributary was full. It was wasted effort. None of the ground paid well. Desperate, the gold hunters rushed blindly to neighboring creeks, panned frantically, found nothing, and listened with increased apprehension to each new rumor that spun through their camps. There *had* to be gold somewhere.

Eastward Henry Thomas—Gold Tom—kicked up another stir. During the early summer of 1862 he had wearied of his backbreaking shaft at American Fork and had wandered east across Mullan Pass to Prickly Pear Valley. There he had started another hole. While he was working, 125 Minnesotans appeared, escorted by Captain James Fisk and a handful of soldiers. Like their predecessors on the road that summer, they had been aiming for either the Salmon River or for Walla Walla, but when they saw the shine of yellow in one of Tom's pans, at least half of them abandoned their original goal and started scratching away beside him—to little avail, as the hopefuls in Deer Lodge Valley learned when they hurried over to check.

Simultaneously, reports began coming in from the wanderers from the Lemhi: color found July 12 by Mortimer Lott's Coloradoans near the Big Hole River west of today's hamlet of Wisdom; color found July 28 by John White and his party of Pikes Peakers on Grasshopper Creek, 12 miles from its junction with the Beaverhead. The Morleys rode a hundred miles south to check the latter spot. "A bleak, barren looking place . . . not promising," James told his diary. Nevertheless, his little company filed claims.

Maybe off yonder . . . and away they went 70 miles across the magnificent Big Hole Basin to look at the diggings there. While they were hesitating, unimpressed, rumor arrived that yields were picking up at Grasshopper Creek. Hurry scurry! They sent John Ault back to the creek's new town, Bannack City, to watch their claims while the others hurried to Gold Creek for their equipment.

When they reached Bannack City on September 8 they found that 300 men were ahead of them, turning the gravel upside down. In spite of Ault's protests, roughs had jumped the company's claims. The friends repossessed the ground "at the point of the bayonet," in James's words, and summoned a miners' meeting (B. B. Burchett of the pretty daughters was its judge). It legalized their action. On the first day that Ault mined his share of the recovered ground he earned $10; the next day he built a rocker and made $15. It was not enough. On September 27 snow fell. Shivering with the thought of January, Ault transferred his interests to James Morley and left for home. The others laid aside their shovels long enough to build a cabin, finishing it on October 19.

Contrary to Ault's fears, the winter proved mild. Late in November the Stuart brothers and their new partner, Franklin Woody of Hell Gate, rode in over snowless roads with cattle for starting a butchershop and with goods for a store, including 15 pounds of chewing tobacco that Granville sold for $15 a pound. A few wagonloads of merchandise arriving from Salt Lake City kept the prices on other commodities more nearly in line.

Storekeeping was too dull for James Stuart. He advertised for a party strong enough to help him stand off Crow Indians, in case the tribe proved hostile, and on April 10, 1863, rode off to prospect the Yellowstone country, well below the present National Park. Six men who had meant to go with him arrived late at the rendezvous point. While trying to overtake the Stuart party they were captured by Indians but released after three nerve-racking days. On their way back to Bannack, they took a short cut from the Madison Valley over the low Tobacco Root Mountains, emerging in what they eventually called Alder Gulch, a tributary of the Stinking Water (now the Ruby). There at sunset on May 26, 1863, they tapped the greatest stretch of gold-bearing gravel in the Rocky Mountains, 17 miles of it, reaching from the junction of Granite and Alder creeks to the head of the main ravine.

By the summer of 1864 Alder Gulch and its principal town, Virginia City, were overrun by 10,000 people, including the Morley and Stuart brothers, who, like John J. Healy, never had much luck mining. Neither did hundreds of others. And so, as had happened in both Colorado and Idaho, a wild spin-off took place. Among the disgruntled searchers for new fields were four partners called the Georgians. (Actually only two were from Georgia; the third hailed from California, the fourth from England.) Wandering north from Virginia City, they landed eventually in Prickly Pear Valley. Prickly Pear was where Gold Tom had been mining two years before, but Tom had not picked the right place. The Georgians finally did. In what they named Last Chance Gulch one of them, Bob Stanley, dug up nuggets, he wrote later "that made the pan ring when dropped into it—and a very refreshing sound it was." The result was Helena, producer, with its neighboring gulches, of more than $15 million, the only state capital in the nation that began as a true mining center.

Other finds quickly followed. During the years of the gold boom

Montanans turned up more than 500 producing gulches, some as far away as the isolated Little Rockies in the central part of the state. A few of the discoveries were enormously rich: in 1866, for example, four Germans shipped out of Confederate Gulch, east across the Missouri from Helena, two and a half *tons* of gold, worth, even with impurities, about a million dollars. Of those 500 gulches, however, Alder and Last Chance were the culmination, fitting climax for the first mineral rush to the Rockies. Each swirl had been more productive than its predecessor. Colorado yielded during her first decade about $27 million. From 1861 through 1867 Idaho miners unearthed $45 million. During the same period Montana produced $65 million, nearly half of it from Alder Gulch.

These were pleasant figures to contemplate, but hardly cause in themselves for a major shift of population. (California's gold fields, by way of comparison, produced $550 million during their first decade of operation.) But of course no stampeder knew at the time of his rushing into the mountains how long the gold might last. What interested him was the fact that only a small proportion of the metal came from deep lode mines. The bulk was scooped from placer bars, "poor man's diggings," whose exploitation required relatively little time and capital—instant money, so to speak, widely distributed.

What appeared to be instant settlement accompanied the giant lottery. Actually of course it was a very unsettled sort of settlement, in spite of the gaudy word "city" that nearly every ten-cabin camp spread peacock-wise at its tail, like a charm to ward off extinction. Basically, the hex was a form of both self-deceit and self-reassurance, for very few stampeders truly intended to stay in the high valleys about which they trumpeted so loudly. And yet, paradoxically, they were building better than they knew. Without really intending to do so they dragged after them, as a matter of stark necessity, systems of supply, agricultural development, and even embryo industrialism that would linger shakily on, struggling for permanence, long after the transient majority had pocketed its hopes and gone home.

XII

THE LOAVES AND THE FISHES

THE ebb and flow of people into and out of the early gold camps of the Rockies was fantastic. Each fall thousands of departing prospectors headed east from Colorado and Montana and west to the coast states from Idaho. Each spring fresh hordes replaced them. One contemporary, J. S. Campbell, who visited Alder Gulch in 1864, estimated that upward of 75,000 persons tramped through the district that same summer. The great bulk of them, he added, surged restlessly on in pursuit of new rumors, then lost heart and returned home. In 1865, according to another estimate, there were 120,000 summertime people in Montana, roaming from camp to camp.

Suppliers of goods in the scattered mountain towns obviously battened on this extreme fluidity. Yet they were its chief victims as well. How could a merchant plan? Orders for material to be shipped from California or St. Louis had to be dispatched months ahead of the date when delivery was expected. What conditions would prevail when the merchandise arrived? Would coffee and candles still be in high demand—or a drug on the market because competitors had overstocked the same items? For that matter, would customers still be around?

Dozens of camps, their names all but forgotten today, bloomed and faded within a year. Even the principal towns were subject to violent fluctuations. Florence, Idaho, dwindled within two or three years from 10,000 inhabitants to a few hundred. The discoveries at Alder Gulch reduced Bannack's population by more than half within a few weeks; the development of Helena drained thousands from Virginia City almost overnight. Obviously a grocer or hardware dealer needed caution in ordering. On the other hand, who among the early tradesmen—and they scampered after rumors as feverishly as the prospectors did—could be sure which tiny sparkle might flame into a real stampede, creating a once-in-a-lifetime opportunity?

The temptation to manipulate the future, as William Byers had sought to do in early Denver, became irresistible. To an extent, stampedes snow-balled on their own momentum; whenever a number of men started toward a district with mining tools lashed atop their pack animals, a string of others invariably followed. Often they found gold as they fanned through the hills, and so luring them in was not entirely a matter of cynical expediency.

As had been the case in Colorado, the common form of advertising for both Montanans and Idahoans was the publication of guidebooks. Even so notable a personality as Granville Stuart (in time he would be a political power in Montana, a friend of Theodore Roosevelt, and Grover Cleve-land's appointee as U.S. minister to Uruguay and Paraguay) tried his hand at a volume entitled *Montana As It Is*. Although Granville wrote the account in Virginia City, which he condescended to call "incredibly rich," his heart was in the highlands farther north and he concluded his survey of the gold fields with a characteristic though not entirely accurate brag: "It is well established that the main chain of the Rocky mountains from the head of Deer Lodge, sixty miles northeast to the head of Prickly Pear Creek contains more rich gold and silver leads than are to be found in the same extent of country in any other part of the world."

To unemployed clerks in Ohio assertions like that were not without impact—and furthermore Granville Stuart knew exactly what he was up to. In another part of *Montana As It Is* he put his tongue in his cheek and described the effect of such fancy talk on naïve prospectors: "Now the man who can sit coldly by and hear this without turning a double summersault and coming down with the seat of his breeches on a big bunch of prickly pears, and shouting, 'Scat! go away, gals! I'm *on* it, you bet your life,' is no man at all."[1] So ho for Montana!

Instead of writing books, a few vigorous souls sought to lay actual hands on potential customers. Such a one was John M. Bozeman, a tall, blond, red-faced Georgian picturesque in a buckskin suit. Gossip said that Boze-man had deserted a wife and three children on rushing to Colorado. While down on his luck in the central Rockies he chanced to pick up word of the letter which James and Granville Stuart had written to their brother Tom about the mines at Deer Lodge. Joining the small group that went north in response (though Tom Stuart lingered in Colorado), Bozeman reached American Fork on June 24, 1862.

Gold eluded him once again, but he did meet John Jacobs, the mountain man who had been one of the quartet that took the first beef cattle into the Beaverhead country. The new friends joined the rush to Bannack City, and

---

[1] Actually not many people read Stuart's book. A friend, S. T. Hauser, who had been one of the advance scouts for the Morley brothers' party, took the manu-script to New York to be printed. Most of the copies disappeared during a fire; others were destroyed by being wet on their way to the emigrant jumping-off places. The tone of the book, however, is typical and even significant, for it came from a man who knew the country far better than did most writers of guidebooks.

again Bozeman found nothing exciting. After the winter freeze had slowed work on the placer bars, the pair took to yarning in one of the stores. Why not work out a short cut around the Big Horn Mountains to the Overland Trail in the Valley of the North Platte and use the route they discovered for diverting gold seekers from Salmon River into Bannack?

They began unraveling the way as soon as snow melted in April, 1863. Jacobs took his eight-year-old half-breed daughter along, presumably because something had happened to the mother and he did not know what else to do with the child. The odd trio followed the Jefferson River toward Three Forks and then veered south up the Gallatin toward what became, inappropriately, Bozeman Pass, the ancient entry to the Yellowstone River.[2] From the Yellowstone they angled southeast around the massive northern shoulder of the Big Horn Mountains. Somewhere along the way Crow Indians stripped them of everything but the clothes they wore, gave them three miserable horses in exchange for their better ones, and ordered them out of the country. Nibbling occasionally on grasshoppers, they finally reached the North Platte at the stage station of Deer Creek (today's Glenrock, Wyoming, 20 miles or so east of Casper).

By promising gold at the end of an easy trail, they recruited a train of forty-five wagons, transporting ninety men and an unrecorded number of women and children who were willing to pay for guidance. Among the families were the Kirkpatricks, Scots who had paused a time in Wisconsin before catching the gold fever from stories in their newspapers—a father, mother, two young daughters, and sons Robert, aged sixteen, and James, fifteen, both of whom in their old age left reminiscences of the trip.

It was not as easy a journey as the promoters had promised. The July sun was punishing. Alkali water in the failing creeks north of the Platte physicked the overworked oxen so badly that they bled; "fat chunks of bacon," Robert remembered, "was the relief." The eyes of the horses grew "sunken and ghostly." The Kirkpatrick girls tried to save a favorite horse by dismounting and walking beside it, coaxing, but eventually were forced by the remorseless train to abandon the animal.

Spirits rose when they reached good grass and water among the eastern foothills of the Big Horns. But then a traveling village of Sioux and Cheyenne Indians ordered them back; the whites could not open a road through one of the last unspoiled hunting grounds. Though the Indians rode on after the parley, they said they would keep the train under surveillance.

After acrimonious discussion about whether to bull ahead or obey, the group compromised by sending riders back to the newly completed trans-

[2] William Clark had traversed the pass on his return from the Pacific in 1806; John Colter crossed it stark naked after escaping from the Blackfeet; Lisa's fur men used it repeatedly. Almost surely Jacobs showed the way to Bozeman. Nevertheless, Bozeman's is the name that stuck.

continental telegraph line along the Platte, by means of which they were to appeal to the nearest army garrison for help. These messengers failed to reappear on schedule and the debate resumed. Many years later James Kirkpatrick recalled that Bozeman and Jacobs urged the party to continue, saying they would risk the gantlet if as few as eight wagons agreed to go with them. Only four, James said, responded. Robert's memory was different: Bozeman told the nervous emigrants that it would be madness for families to take the chance; he would consent to continue only in the company of single men unburdened by wagons. Be the truth as it may, a paltry eight riders lashed their possessions onto packhorses and continued north with the two guides, traveling much of the way at night to avoid detection.

The rest of the train turned back. As they toiled south they met the messengers, who reported that soldiers, delayed by army red tape, were coming along behind them. It was too late then. The train crawled on to the main Overland Trail and crossed South Pass to Fort Bridger, where the quartermaster doled out beef, tea, coffee, sugar, flour, and rice to those who were destitute. Joining several Coloradoans, who lent fresh stock to the Kirkpatricks, they turned north through eastern Idaho. "Mother," Robert wrote with what may be classed as understatement, "was weary as she had walked a good part of the way."

Snow startled them—it was October by then—but bright days followed and at long last they topped the hill overlooking Bannack City. Mother's heart sank, Robert said: "Piles of dirt and gravel all about where mining had been done, a cluster of single storied log houses with square board fronts on some of them where business was done all without paint. The hills gray and yellow . . . the willows all brown and no other timber on the bottoms was anything but cheerful."

For his family of six the father rented a log cabin 12 feet by 14 feet with a dirt floor, a dirt roof, and a single window, which, however, boasted a pane of glass. He hauled in great wagonloads of wood for the fireplace in which the cooking was done, and built chairs by stretching green rawhide across sturdy frames and letting it dry tight. To Robert the quarters seemed fine: "warm and a palace of comfort to what we had been used to on the road." With less pleasure he remembered the pie he bought in the town bakery. Beef tallow had been used for shortening in place of unobtainable lard, and as the pie cooled the tallow congealed. "Vile" was the hungry, disappointed boy's description.

By then the fever for Virginia City was at such white heat that Bozeman and Jacobs decided to try the guide business again during the summer of 1864. They were greeted in the Platte Valley by enough eager emigrants that they divided the wagons into two trains, each man leading one. All told, upward of a thousand vehicles used their route that summer, in spite of competition from old Jim Bridger, who was currently working for the army at Fort Laramie. Bridger said that the Bozeman route was exposed to attack by Indians and that he knew a shorter, safer way through the Big Horn Basin on the west side of the Big Horn Mountains. The boast led a company of 300 Coloradoans traveling in sixty-two wagons to hire Jim as guide.

He was right, after a fashion. His route was shorter in miles; his party had no trouble with Indians. Grass was sparse, however, and the river fords were difficult. When the army decided to build forts along the main emigrant road to Montana, the Bozeman Trail was the one they picked. For a little while, and in the face of furious protests from the Indians, untold thousands of people traveled the road—as much as 90 percent of all passenger traffic to the northern mines, according to the *Montana Post* of March 23, 1867, a statistic possibly open to revision downward.

Fortunately for the reckless thousands who poured into the mountains— into Colorado and Idaho as well as into Montana—the beginnings of a supply system already existed. Army operations against the Indians in New Mexico and against the Mormons in Utah had created well-beaten roads along the Santa Fe and Overland trails and had brought into being well-organized freight companies. Thus in the spring of 1860, only a year after the rush to Colorado had begun, it was possible for 11,000 supply wagons to line out up the Platte toward Denver—to say nothing of other thousands traveling the Smoky Hill and Arkansas River trails farther south. John Owen, John Grant, the Stuart brothers, and other trapper-ranchers in Montana's broad mountain basins had already determined the best approach from Utah. Steamboats carrying Indian trade goods up the Missouri to Fort Benton and army material up the Columbia to the Walla Walla Valley were able to adapt with remarkable speed to gold-rush traffic.

St. Louis controlled the Colorado trade. Portland commanded northern Idaho but had to yield the south to aggressive Californians who cut wagon roads out of the northern part of their state across the Nevada deserts to Boise. Montana was invaded from both east and west, and at first Oregon seemed to have the advantage because of the steamboats already plying as far as Lewiston and the efficiently organized packtrains that traveled from the Lewiston docks on to Florence and Elk City.

Lloyd Magruder, remembered for his violent death rather than for his enterprise as a supplier, is a useful example. He had founded a store in Elk City shortly after the town's birth and had acquired three- or fourscore mules for supplying it. He was prepared, accordingly, when news of Bannack's booming growth reached him in the summer of 1863. Hurrying to Lewiston, he loaded sixty mules with merchandise and in August wound 300 miles along the southern Nez Percé Trail across the Bitterroots to the new camp. Learning there of the strikes at Virginia City, he pushed on another 70 miles northeast and within a week or two had disposed of his goods for approximately $25,000 in gold dust.

On his way home Magruder joined four other travelers for mutual protection; together they had more than seventy mules with them. In a snow-swept camp in the tangled mountains between the Bitterroots and Elk City—convulsed forest country known today as the Magruder Mountains —he and his companions were murdered with axes and bowie knives by outlaws they had unwittingly hired as helpers. Fearful that the mules would reveal the happening by following them out of the snowy high country, the murderers drove the animals into a canyon and slaughtered them. They fell under suspicion anyway; a persistent friend of Magruder's ran them down and they were executed—a drama that has diverted attention from Magruder's more representative role as one of the hard-driving pioneers of the mining camp supply business.

Dozens of other packers meantime went stolidly on with their laborious work of each day loading, unloading, and fighting rebellious mules along the mountain trails. In 1865 approximately 5,000 pack animals carried 750 tons of freight (300 pounds per mule) into Montana from docks along the Columbia and Snake rivers. To help speed the northernmost of these packtrains, enterprising haulers launched a steamboat, the *Mary Moody,* on Lake Pend Oreille and used it as a ferry; it could carry sixty mules and their packs per trip across the lake and up Clark Fork River to the first rapids. One imaginative freighter even tried camels along the Mullan Road. The effort failed. Although a camel could carry three or four times as much weight as a mule, its smell and ungainly appearance stampeded other livestock. The first camel train was promptly ordered out of Virginia City—an anticlimax that had befallen earlier experiments with the exotic and hence suspect animals in the Southwest, in Nevada, and even in British Columbia.

The material that could be carried on muleback was limited; and because the government did not keep the difficult western stretches of the Mullan Road in repair for wagons, ponderous material had to seek other routes. The Bozeman Trail proved unsatisfactory. One example—the moving of two steam boilers across the Platte—will indicate why. The freight wagon carrying the smaller machine had to use twenty-six yoke of oxen and fifteen drivers to overcome the sandy shallows. The larger required the monumental tugging of forty-eight yoke (ninety-six animals) belabored ahead by twenty-one bullwhackers.

Shallow-draft steamboats that could ride the spring floods as far up the Missouri as Fort Benton offered a more economical answer. In 1865, before the impact of the Helena discoveries had been felt in St. Louis, six of the twenty steamers that bucked the headlong current managed to reach as far as Benton. The next year thirty-one appeared with 6,000 tons of freight, including twenty quartz mills destined for the newly discovered lode mines near Bannack and at Summit in the head of Alder Gulch. In 1867 thirty-nine boats reached Benton with 8,016 tons and 10,000 passengers.

Moving this freight 135 miles west to Helena, the distribution point for the northern mines, required close to 30,000 horses, mules, and oxen. The first outfits to reach the mountains after the long winters reaped the highest prices, and so grim races developed through the spring mud at 16 or 20 miles a day. Robert Kirkpatrick remembered it as very picturesque. For sport in the canyons the ox drivers would swing their heavy, 15-foot whips around their heads two or three times and snap them straight in such wise that the 10-inch buckskin poppers on the end cracked like shotguns and sent echoes rolling between the rock walls until it sounded as though a battle were under way.

Against this traffic the mule trains could offer only speed. Because they were able to hurry compact material into Bannack and Virginia City ahead of the ox teams in the spring they were able to keep competing for several years. Certain amounts of light traffic from the East avoided the congestion at Fort Benton by using the Bozeman route, and quantities of foodstuffs moved in regularly from Utah.

The local produce—hay, grain, leather, blacksmith work, storage facilities, labor, and so on—involved in the widespread efforts had a profound impact on mountain economy. Because of it the principal distribution points—Denver, Helena, Lewiston, and Boise—achieved a permanence the rest of the fluid countryside lacked. Significantly, it was in these supply cities that the first banks located—not, save with rare exceptions, in the mining towns despite the large sums of loose money floating through. There in the distribution centers the local boosters strutted most vigorously ("Our future destiny becomes inevitable," crowed Libeus Barney of Denver; "our city must be the sojourn and mart of all who come and go in quest of gain, or health, or pleasure") and there civic leaders struggled energetically to bring in traditional signs of stability—churches, schools, theaters, and the rest—that would reassure outside capital.

Of the few supplies that could be produced within the mountains, wood (of which more later) and beef were the most important. As we have already noted, the first steaks came from draft oxen, but limitations in their quality and quantity soon led to demands for something better. Texans, who had driven cattle as far as California during the 1850's, were eager to answer this newest call. In 1860 hard-twisted Oliver Loving drove a herd north across today's Oklahoma to the Arkansas River and then followed the stream west to the mountains. The Civil War soon blocked that source, however, and the mining regions were forced almost in spite of themselves to develop their own beef industry. In 1861 John Iliff invested the meager profits of his Denver store in a small herd that he ranged east of the city; within little more than a decade he had 35,000 head grazing across 650,000 acres of open range in the high plains country at the foot of the mountains. Sam Hartsel, as we have seen, found more gold in the grass of South Park, Colorado, than in its gravel. In Montana the leading mountain rancher turned out to be not one of the trappers already established in the peak-girt basins, but Carston Conrad Kohrs, an impoverished emigrant from Holstein, which at the time of his birth, August 5, 1835, was a part of Denmark.

Kohrs ran away from home at the age of fifteen. He worked as a sailor, as a butcher in a New York City meat-packing plant, as a raftsman floating logs down the Mississippi. He tried his hand at mining in California and in British Columbia, then returned to Iowa to help a sister whose husband had died. Restless again in the summer of 1862, he started working his way back to California. In Salt Lake City he heard of the Salmon River excitement, turned that way, and landed among the thousand frustrated men milling around the Lemhi. He joined a party that found a short-lived placer bar in the Big Hole country. While working in the cold water he contracted acute rheumatism. According to his reminiscences, his friends killed sixty or seventy rattlesnakes and fried the oil out of the carcasses. After bathing Kohrs in the icy river, they rubbed him raw with a gunnysack, applied the snake oil, and cured him completely.

Running out of provisions and fearful of snow, the party drifted on into the town of Cottonwood, now Deer Lodge. Henry Crawford, recently elected as sheriff of Bannack, was there buying cattle for his butchershop. Learning that Kohrs had had experience in a packing plant, Crawford hired him as a helper.

It was a wild winter. Among the idlers in Bannack was a lean, agile, smooth-talking, gray-eyed man a bit under six feet tall whose name was Henry Plummer. Plummer, as Montanans eventually learned, had appeared in Nevada City, California, from New England during the 1850's and set himself up as a baker. Imprisoned for killing the husband of a woman with whom he was having an affair, he was soon paroled as a consumptive. After murdering another man in a bawdyhouse affray, he fled to Lewiston with a woman who deserted her husband and children to accompany him, only to be deserted in Lewiston in her turn.

In Idaho Plummer joined a loosely organized band of highwaymen who preyed on travelers along the trails between Walla Walla, Oro Fino, and Florence. In September, 1862, when a vigilante committee began breathing hot on his neck in Florence, he and a friend named Charlie Reeves fled through Elk City over the southern Nez Percé Trail toward Deer Lodge. Encountering James and Granville Stuart near Hell Gate, they rode with them to Gold Creek to look over the situation there. The Stuarts found them a pleasant pair.

At Gold Creek, Plummer and Charlie Reeves ran into two or three other outlaws, among them a certain Jack Cleveland, whom Plummer had known in California. According to Kohrs, who also encountered the group in Deer Lodge, these birds of a feather flocked together to pursue some miners who were carrying gold dust to Fort Benton. Somehow the victims eluded them and the disappointed robbers halted at what local residents called the "government farm" on Sun River, an Indian agency project not far from present Great Falls. There in a lovely valley bordered by grassy tablelands and threaded with cottonwoods, the agency staff was trying with scant success to teach the Blackfoot Indians how to farm.

One of the staff people at the farm was A. J. Vail. Living with Vail were his wife and her handsome sister. The latter's name is variously given as Eliza or Electra Bryan. Let's say Electra; it has a more fatal ring. Both Cleveland and Plummer fell in love with Electra, and when they turned back to pass the winter in booming Bannack, they were no longer friendly, a development of considerable import to Sheriff Henry Crawford, the Bannack butcher, and to Conrad Kohrs, his new employee.

A little before the end of 1862, Plummer manufactured a quarrel with his rival in love and shot him down in the street in front of Crawford's butchershop. Kohrs carried the fallen man inside, laid him on a cot, and with Sheriff Crawford nursed him until Cleveland died three hours later.[3] Plummer was agitated by all this, for fear that the dying Cleveland might have revealed Plummer's criminal past to the sheriff.

Before any action was taken on the killing, a new uproar distracted the town. Plummer's friend, Charlie Reeves, had recently purchased an Indian woman who found his abuse so unbearable that she ran away to the tepees that some of her tribesmen had pitched at the south end of town. Liquoring up, Reeves and two friends, William Mitchell and Augustus Moore, began shooting into the tepee they suspected of sheltering her. The wanton attack killed three Indians, including a child, and an old Frenchman named Cosette.

Astounded by the indignation that the deed aroused, the trio fled. Plummer, nervous over the Cleveland affair, went with them. It was early January, 1863, bitterly cold, and after 12 miles of riding they were so miserable that they took shelter in a clump of willows where they hoped to build a fire undetected. Pursuit overtook them and they surrendered on the promise of being granted a jury trial, their idea being that their friends would intimidate the jury into returning a favorable verdict. The scheme worked. Cowed by open threats of violence, the jury found the shooters at the tepee, Reeves, Moore, and Mitchell, guilty of manslaughter only. They were ordered banished from the camp. Within a few weeks they were back without a hand being raised in protest.

Plummer meanwhile had been granted a separate trial for the killing of Cleveland. He pleaded self-defense and was acquitted. This experience, together with his ardor for Electra Bryan, may have suggested reform. In

[3] This according to Kohrs's manuscript autobiography. Nathaniel P. Langford, who also was in the vicinity and who, like Kohrs, wrote his account many years later, says in Chapter XV of *Vigilante Days and Ways* that the shooting took place in a saloon and that Sheriff Crawford and a friend named Phleger carried Cleveland to Crawford's cabin.

any event, on January 29, 1863, he filed on a patch mining claim near Bannack. On February 22 he filed on a pre-emption claim, a doubling-up permissible because the claims were of different kinds. He remained nervous about his past, however, and the tension made him foolish. Early in March he forced a quarrel with Sheriff Crawford, who in fact had learned nothing from the dying Cleveland. Although the pistol duel resulted in Plummer's, not Crawford's, being wounded, Plummer achieved the end he wanted. Fearful of vengeance from Plummer's friends, Crawford on March 13 resigned as sheriff and left the country. By default Conrad Kohrs, twenty-eight years old at that point, became owner of the abandoned butchershop.

The unpredictable voters of Bannack now elected Plummer sheriff in Crawford's place! When the rush to Virginia City began in June the new peace officer rode along out of curiosity. He conducted himself with such propriety in the new camp that on the resignation of the area's first sheriff, J. B. Caven, remarkable for his fiddling and his beautiful eighteen-year-old wife, Plummer was elected sheriff in his place, an early-day attempt to achieve something more than purely local law enforcement.

Throughout this time of political elevation Plummer had been pressing his suit of Electra as well as volunteer mail carriers going in that direction allowed. Thus it is conceivable that he meant what he said when he told Nathaniel Langford, as Langford recalled the words, "I will show you that I can be a good man among good men." The opportunities inherent in his new position were too much for him, however. Behind the mask of his star he either formed, or let his outlaw acquaintances form, a fairly cohesive gang of highway robbers. It is possible that in those early days Plummer was a moral captive of the roughneck crew rather than the coolly efficient organizer remembered by legend. Very soon, however, he took over the running of things.

The center of the web was Bannack, where Plummer maintained his headquarters. To run affairs in Alder Gulch he appointed three hoodlums and, curiously, one honest man, D. H. Dillingham. That done, the eager lover rode off to Sun River to marry his sweetheart. The ceremony was held in the chapel of St. Peter's Mission to the Blackfeet Indians.

Before the newlyweds had returned to Bannack, accompanied by the bride's sister and brother-in-law, the A. J. Vails, the three dishonest deputies in Virginia City decided to rid themselves of honest Dillingham. In a crudely staged duel designed to make Dillingham look like the aggressor, two of them shot him down in the street in full view of several bystanders. The staging was not convincing enough. The assassins were immediately seized and tried before a disorderly people's court of several score miners. Throughout the proceedings Dillingham's body lay untended on a table in a nearby gambling saloon.

At the end of the trial the crowd shouted out a verdict of guilty and a sentence of death by hanging. The prisoners were loaded into a wagon and started toward a hastily improvised gallows. As the wagon paused, surrounded by a gathering throng of many hundreds, one of the convicted men delivered an impassioned plea for mercy and persuaded the crowd to let a friend read them a contrived letter of farewell to his mother. At this the women in the throng began to weep. Cries for a new trial arose. A tremendous argument ensued. During the confusion the two murderers, helped by their friends, managed to get aboard a single horse and gallop away amidst howls, cheers, and general excitement over what was conceded to be a bully show. The point of the tale resides, of course, not in the ingenuity of the outlaws but in the slaphappy frame of mind of the populace, a matter to be touched on again during further mentions of the affairs of Sheriff Plummer.

To the fluid, emotionally unstable inhabitants of Bannack and Alder Gulch, Conrad Kohrs became the principal butcher. He worked with intense concentration. At first he bought the cattle he needed. Sometimes he picked up trail-worn oxen at the auctions in Virginia City; sometimes he rode nearly a hundred miles to Deer Lodge to purchase a few head from the mountaineers over there; sometimes he dickered for a few of the animals that Mormons drove in from Utah. When a few hogs appeared, he acquired them, let them scavenge in the offal behind his butchershop, and sold the pork for 75 cents a pound. He acquired the first sheep ever trailed into Montana—he gave their pelts to miners to use as mattresses—and then discovered there was small demand for mutton. Like other traders to the unanchored prospectors, he lost painful amounts of money when his debtors simply vanished. So many of those who owed him for past bills moved to Alder Gulch that he followed them there and set up a branch shop at Summit, seven miles above Virginia City. Later he opened another store at Last Chance. During one hard winter at Summit he made candles out of beef tallow; when less odorous candles ran out of supply he sold his product for a dollar a pound.

Soon he had better contact with growers than did anyone else in Montana. Other butchers, who of course lacked refrigeration for storage and hence needed a continuing supply of animals, turned more and more to Kohrs for help in meeting their requirements. In order to preserve bargains on encountering them, he began buying against future prospects rather than on day-to-day needs. The little herds he acquired he left here and there to fatten where he knew conditions were good. He became a rancher, in short, before he stopped thinking of himself as a butcher.

The spring of 1864, two years after Crawford's departure, was a critical time. Kohrs did not yet own enough stock to meet deliveries. Supposing that he could pick up what he needed at the Blackfoot agency farm on Sun River, he rode there through the raw weather of March. Another buyer was ahead of him. On he hurried to Fort Benton—nothing. Back he went to

Deer Lodge, covering, he says, nearly 500 miles in six days, riding a single horse that had nothing to eat except the weather-cured bunch grass that it could crop at the end of a picket rope whenever Kohrs huddled down on the ground in his blankets for a few hours' exhausted sleep.

Hoping to take advantage of Kohrs's situation, the ranchers in Deer Lodge demanded more for their cattle than he was willing to pay. Desperate, he bought Johnny Grant's famous traveler, Woodtick, as a replacement for his own collapsed mount and rode 90 more miles to the Bitterroot, where finally he purchased the cattle he needed. One of the men he hired to help him drive the herd to Virginia City drowned while they were pushing the animals across a swollen river, but he reached Alder Gulch in time to meet his commitments.

In February, 1866, Woodtick's erstwhile owner, John Grant, ran into bad luck. First, fire destroyed his barn and hay near the town of Deer Lodge. Shortly thereafter Nathaniel Langford, an agent then for the United States government, seized several hundred gallons of whiskey that Grant intended for his Indian trade—an illegal stock that Grant had been using unchallenged for years. Disgusted, the old mountain man decided to remove to the Hudson's Bay colony at Red River, Canada. To Kohrs he sold for $19,200 his house with its twenty-eight glass windows and 365 head of cattle.

By counting his own animals with Grant's Kohrs oould boast of having more cattle than anyone else in Montana. The possessions immediately became a liability. Chinook winds started to melt the snow, then faded before a severe frost that turned the slush to a glittering sheath of ice. The gaunt cattle could not break through to grass, and Kohrs had only a little hay. But if a man is hard enough there is generally a solution.

"We killed the poorest," Kohrs recalled years later, "boiled the meat, and mixed chopped hay with it, making a broth, and saved some of the cattle by feeding them this slop."

When he wrote that account his holdings had spread from Deer Lodge to Sun River. He owned ranches in central Montana, in Wyoming, and for a time in Colorado; and no doubt he derived satisfaction from remembering how he had been able to lift himself to where he was. Admirable enough— but just the same there was a grim expediency to it that is difficult for modern readers to rest easy with, a make-do sort of ruthlessness which, as the next chapter will indicate, was one of the most depressing characteristics of the Rocky Mountain mining camps of the 1860's. Even today traces of the attitude have not wholly disappeared from the manner in which a few die-hard mountain dwellers still attack the remaining resources around them.

XIII  CASH IN AND GET OUT

ACCORDING to an estimate made in 1868 by J. Ross Browne, United States commissioner of mines, the impatient gold producers of the frontier—those of California and Nevada as well as those of the Rockies—allowed more than $300 million in mineral wealth—perhaps $3 billion in today's terms—slip irrecoverably through their fingers in less than two decades. Plaintively Browne added, "The question arises whether it is not the duty of the government to prevent, as far as may be consistent with individual rights, the waste of a common heritage, in which not only ourselves but our posterity are interested."

The development of lode mining in Colorado's Gregory Gulch is a case in point. As the workers dug down through the decomposed quartz that lay near the surface of the ground, the vein material grew harder and had to be blasted loose in chunks. The chunks then had to be ground into a powder that could be washed in the usual way in sluice boxes. Initially the miners resorted to the Mexican-style arrastra, a hard-surfaced basin in whose center stood an upright revolving post. Two horizontal arms protruded from this perpendicular shaft. A horse, mule, or ox was harnessed to one arm. An abrasive granite boulder was attached to the other. Around and around plodded the harnessed beast, revolving the shaft, which in turn dragged the boulder over the quartz that had been shoveled into the basin.

The process was slow and inefficient. In addition, as the mines went deeper, more and more of the "free" gold in the ore was replaced by gold in chemical combination with iron and sulphur, a substance to which the disgusted workers attached the derogatory adjective "refractory." Unable to handle it, they ignored it and concentrated impatiently on speeding the recovery of the remaining free gold by using steam-powered stamp mills—rows of heavy, iron-capped stems that could be lifted by revolving cam shafts and let fall with a crash on the ore. Dozens of these mills were imported from St. Louis and San Francisco, not just to Gregory Gulch but also to the quartz veins around Bannack and Summit in Montana and Boise Basin in Idaho.

The quartz mills crushed much more ore in much less time than arrastras did. Otherwise they were hardly more efficient, for they did little to meet the problem of refractory minerals, which were attacked, if at all, by various patented devices designed, in the words of one scornful commentator, "to physic" the gold out of the ore. Success was limited. According to Ovando Hollister, an early-day Colorado engineer, the early mills lost, in spite of their awesome roaring and steaming, between 60 and 85 percent of the gold in the ore.

Still, they seemed like progress. William Byers of the *Rocky Mountain News* exuberantly noted the advent of the first ones, and in February, 1861, rode up to Central City to see how they were doing.

As he noticed the black smear of smoke that their chimneys spread across the sky he experienced an uncharacteristic moment of doubt. Back in Denver he wrote soberly on February 16, "Of the fine forests that covered the hillsides [of Gregory Gulch] in the spring of '59, fully two-thirds has now entirely disappeared and a majority of the steam mills—the greatest consumers of fuel—have not yet been running twelve months." Very soon, he warned, wood for the mills, timber for mine props, and heating material for the "thousands of huge fire-places by which the habitations of the miners . . . are warmed" would have to be hauled long distances at steadily increasing costs.

Tomorrow's economics were as far as Byers' concern went. He did not raise the question, as J. Ross Browne had in connection with the waste of gold, whether today's rights might be legitimately curbed in the interests of posterity. His readers would have been outraged if he had. Thrift? What for? They labored dreadfully under wretched working conditions during short working seasons, and they wanted to produce as much gold within the time allowed as might be. If a dollar vanished so that another might be quickly gleaned, why, that was one of the facts of the mountain present. The future—if ever people arrived who really wished to live in such a land—would have to take care of itself.

And so the mills grew steadily larger, devouring more trees and spewing out more powdered rock that after its washing was either dumped as a gray sludge in the streams or else piled in careless heaps to blow grittily about the neighborhood with every wind. Sooner or later floods roared down the denuded slopes, destroyed a few jerry-built cabins here and there, and filled the streets with debris. Hurriedly then the miners cleared out as much as they had to, rebuilt what was necessary, and returned to their onerous digging. They could destroy forests and water. They could waste gold and work. But they could not afford to lose time.

The stamp of their carelessness lay on everything they did. The opening days of most rushes were marked by forest fires set by negligent campers. The alders that gave their name to Alder Gulch, Montana, were turned to embers within weeks of the discovery, and until the powdery mass compacted, the miners lived and worked in choking clouds of black ash. On June 17, 1859, less than two months after the stampede to Gregory Gulch had begun, Green Russell was writing, "It is reported here that the bodies of eighteen men have been found in the mountains, who were burned to death by the burning of the pine forest. . . . The forests are still burning and in all probability will continue to burn for some time."

Trout were seined by tubfuls out of Grand Lake, Colorado, now part of Rocky Mountain National Park, and hauled across the Continental Divide by packtrain to the towns along Clear Creek. In *Montana As It Is* Granville Stuart wrote that "barbarians" were hauling away fish by the wagonload and "murdering" game indiscriminately, even in the winter when the meat was too poor to eat, then throwing away the carcasses without so much as trying to salvage the hides.

Men lived with almost total thoughtlessness toward anyone except immediate friends. In some of the smaller camps they never got around to removing stumps and boulders from the streets. In the larger "cities" the unpaved thoroughfares alternated between powdery dust and wheel-churned morasses of mud. Pedestrians took their chances: excavations were seldom fenced off; abandoned claims were never filled in. Stacks of firewood and of merchandise awaiting storage cluttered the gaping, splintery planks of the sidewalks—if there were sidewalks. Butchershops often let the offal of their trade lie where it fell; Conrad Kohrs, it will be remembered, let hogs fatten around his establishments. Manure from hundreds of head of livestock disappeared only by being trampled into the earth. No one considered it his duty to remove dead animals or garbage; the stench from the shallow privy behind each building was a countertheme to the warm, dreamy mountain afternoons. Packs of dogs bayed and fought through the alleyways under the star-hung nights.

Make-do: many a grocery began in a tent, many a bakery in a log shanty. The first hotel in a camp generally created "rooms" by partitioning off sleeping cubicles from each other with sheets of muslin faintly fireproofed by being soaked in alum water. Mattresses and pillows were of straw, there were no washbowls in the rooms, and at the washstands out back one used a community towel and community comb. "Homes" were equally comfortless. A pair of miners would willingly whipsaw planks for their sluice boxes but seldom as flooring for their cabin, where the trampled earth sufficed.

Stoves were rare and most cooking—flapjacks, bacon, beans, beef, and potatoes—was done in the fireplace. Because water unfouled by the mines either had to be carried long distances in buckets or purchased from a wagon that hauled a few barrels through the streets, washing of persons or plates was niggardly. Rats and mice abounded. Tall tales in many a hamlet revolved around the profit—and misadventures—involved in importing the first wagonload of house cats.

Although early journals frequently grew ecstatic about the healthful climate and invigorating air, respiratory diseases were common. Men came wet and chilled from their claims into overheated cabins. Gambling parlors, saloons, and dance halls were overcrowded on Saturday and Sunday nights and ill-ventilated always. Spitting in the general direction of sandboxes and cuspidors in private homes or directly onto the floor in public buildings was a common American custom of the time. In the mining camps the habit became an acute, but apparently unrecognized, hazard to impoverished workers who, as the crowds in the saloons thinned out toward morning, were allowed by kindly proprietors to sleep on the sawdust floors. Coughs, colds, sore throats, runny eyes, pneumonia, and tuberculosis flourished.

A common ailment of the times was "mountain sickness." (A form of typhoid or undulant fever, perhaps, it disappeared about 1880.) Symptoms included a foul-tasting mouth, lassitude, constipation, headache. Then came chills followed by high fever. Fatalities have been estimated at 2 percent. One treatment was to boil sagebrush in a big kettle until a thick syrup resulted, add whiskey, and dose frequently. Indeed, home concoctions supplemented by purges and pills bought by label or word-of-mouth recommendation from fancy bottles in the drugstore were the prevailing response to any spell of feeling poorly—as was true in rural areas throughout the rest of the nation.

Morale was as subject to damaging shocks as was physical health. One undermining factor for many stampeders was the predominant maleness of the mining districts. An immediate coarsening of language was inevitable; it still happens among inductees into army boot camps. Another factor was monotony. Work routines and food had a gray sameness. Evenings were generally boring, save for occasional visits back and forth to spin yarns and perhaps sing to the accompaniment of rare fiddles, flutes, or jews'-harps. Generally, though, a man was tired and stayed home, and then what was there? Illumination was poor and in most cases he did not have very much to read anyway. His impatience tightened; his attitude toward community affairs tended to become a growled "to hell with it."

Still another part of the context was the intense concentration of the work. A placer miner bent on hurrying home with a fortune as soon as possible forced himself to the limits of his energy six days a week. He needed time occasionally to catch up on his chores. Custom decreed Sunday. On that day, in the words of Matthew Dale, writing from the New Nevada district near Central City, Colorado, no work was done "except patching up, tinkering around the cabin, doing their trading, retorting quick Silver etc."

These chores completed, letters written home, and freshly laundered shirts hung out to dry, the men walked into town to pick up their mail, buy their groceries, and learn what was going on in other parts of the district. Business houses made ready for the influx by hiring extra clerks, waitresses, bartenders, and hurdy-gurdy girls.[1] The main intent was social—to meet with friends, talk over rumors of new strikes, make plans, and above all escape briefly from the sinking feeling of apartness that threatened to overwhelm so many of them on their lonesome claims.

During the course of these Sunday gatherings there was a great deal of drinking (the routine gulping of cheap whiskey was common frontier custom), gambling, and fighting. Such affairs have been exaggerated until today they read like stereotypes. The point to remember about them, however, is not their own inherent wickedness, if any, but the fundamental social malaise of which they were symptomatic.

The week-long verve with which the men worked in their drive for gold seemed to create in many of them a tensity that could be released only by excitement. Some found it in the saloons and gaming tables. Others who lacked the funds or taste for those escapes gathered in noisy, nervous groups and spent much of their free Sunday time simply tramping up and down the middle of the town's main street, jostling for room with horsemen and wagons as they looked for something to divert them. Outdoor auctions of work animals and equipment drew large crowds. One Helena auctioneer, shrewdly aware of the taste of his audience for practical jokes, became famous for every now and then passing off an unbroken bronco on a green customer who wanted to try his prospective purchase. The wild bucking into the crowd would scatter people all over the street and was, Robert Kirkpatrick declared, "as much fun as a good circus."

Spectator sports like horse racing, wrestling, and boxing were well attended and drew forth feverish betting. Violence was wildly applauded. A certain John C. (Con) Orem, a nondrinking saloonkeeper and boxer, who stood 5 feet 6 inches tall and weighed 138 pounds, achieved mountainwide fame by whittling down massive opponents first in Denver and later in Virginia City. The climax of his career came in a specially erected arena in the latter town on January 2, 1865. Heralded by a brass band and watched by a thousand people, Orem fought a man who outweighed him by 50 pounds to a draw in a battle of 185 one-minute rounds that produced 68 knockdowns.

When the Hungate family was massacred by Indians near Denver in 1864, the mutilated bodies were hauled into the city and placed on public

---

[1] Not all hurdy-gurdy girls in the early mining camps were prostitutes. To many a lonesome man the opportunity just to dance with a woman was worth 50 cents or $1 a round, and tales can be found of respectable housewives who, without loss of standing, helped balance the family budget by working in the dance halls during busy weekends. A few dance houses did not even serve liquor. "A strictly temperance house" was a not uncommon lure in their newspaper advertising.

display. The general reaction amazed Nathaniel P. Hill, a professor of chemistry at Brown University, Rhode Island, who was en route to Central City to study the refractory ores of Gregory Gulch. "So fond are these Westerners of excitement," he wrote home, "that all the people in town with a few honorable exceptions went to see them."

A full decade later, after Denver had supposedly become a settled city of "elegant residences . . . furnished with rare and costly furniture" (the words are those of Frank Hall, acting governor and early historian), the morbidity still prevailed. In July, 1874, an enterprising entrepreneur discovered that a war party of Ute Indians had recently defeated a band of Cheyennes and had taken three scalps. He persuaded the women of the Ute band to edify their white brethren by staging one of their traditional dances with the fresh scalps dangling, as was customary, at the end of willow wands. According to the *Rocky Mountain News* of July 16, 500 Denverites attended the show. It was, the report concluded, "disgusting to notice among the spectators, lots of ladies prominent in church and society circles straining for a sight of the reeking scalps."

For women, the feeling of apartness, of being cut adrift from familiar anchors and of being crushed by the physical and spiritual hardships of the land, was even more acute than for men. Two instances will suffice: Ellen Kellogg Hunt, who went to Colorado, and Emily Meredith, who went to Montana. Both were married to men of some attainment—and in this connection it is worth noting a letter which Frank Hall wrote to his mother in 1861 in an effort to reassure her about mountain society. It was composed, he insisted, "of high-minded, intelligent men, men of talent who have graced higher spheres than those in which misfortune has compelled them to move in this country. They are here for the purpose of repairing as much as possible past adversities." Hall's generality was, as usual, a little too sweeping. Still, in the case of Ellen's husband, Alexander Cameron Hunt, and of Emily's husband, Frederick Meredith, he was right.

Ellen Kellogg had married Cam Hunt, as she called him, in 1853, when she was seventeen and he twenty-six. It had seemed a good match. A. C. Hunt was mayor of Freeport, Illinois, and a successful businessman—until ruined by the depression of 1857. Hearing of the Colorado strikes in the fall of 1858, he rushed west to look over the field. Deciding that his future lay there in the mountains, he returned for his family: his wife and two children (a girl not quite three, a boy one and a half), his father, who was a doctor, and his brother. For Ellen, aged twenty-three, the trip in the covered wagon was a nightmare. She caught cholera, started to recover, and was felled with an attack of what her father-in-law diagnosed as erysipelas.

As soon as they reached Auraria on June 27, 1859, Cam rented a cabin at the edge of town and went off looking for something to do. Burdened with two small children and scarcely able to drag around, Ellen took in boarders—but they were broke, too—and sold milk and butter from their cows. The diary she started dwindled to summaries: "Second, third, and fourth weeks. Weary days of labor and pain. Have made 175 loaves of bread and 450 pies." In August she wrote, "I have been away from this dreary cabin but twice since I came, once to take a walk and once to meet the ladies at the Hotel. Did not enjoy the ladies much, was too tired." When Cam sold their best carpet and mirror in order to buy flour for more pies, she noted, "After all our hard work and the humble position we have assumed we are poorer than when we began. . . . I am tired, tired, always tired."

Emily Robinson Sorin, only six months younger than Ellen Hunt, was a member of the first class to graduate from Hamline University, Minnesota. After her graduation she taught at her alma mater and contributed articles to Minnesota newspapers. In the fall of 1860, aged twenty-four, she married Frederick Meredith, publisher of one of the journals for which she wrote. Partly because of the Civil War, business fell off; and in the spring of 1862 the young couple, who as yet had no children, started for the Salmon River mines.

Like other Idaho immigrants whom we have met in this account, the Merediths ended up with the distracted throng on the Lemhi. After agonizing uncertainty, the couple turned their wagon with forty others toward what Emily called "a shadow of a hope of mines at Deer Lodge." Along the way someone spotted beside the Beaverhead River a board containing a barely legible message: "Tu grass Hop Per digins 30 myle Kepe the Trale nex the bluffe." Changing their destination once more because of that signpost, they landed in Bannack on Grasshopper Creek early in September, 1863. While Emily stayed alone much of the time in a two-room, $400 cabin in town, Meredith set himself up in business as a herder of oxen for the miners.

"I have often felt," Emily wrote her father, "I would go without food a week for the sake of a letter from home . . . and would be willing to die for the sake of having my spirit revisit you again." Inviting another family into her cabin's second room helped the lonesomeness, and she wrote more cheerfully, "If I only had a house with a floor in it and a stove, I should consider myself quite fixed." She could be tart in her observations. "I don't know how many deaths have occurred this winter, but that there have not been twice as many is entirely owing to the fact that drunken men do not shoot well." She recognized well enough why most people were in Bannack —money and, indeed, "a person ought to make money pretty fast here to pay them for living in such a place." Things of the spirit? "If 'Labor is worship' this is the most worshipful community, but of any other kind of worship there is no public manifestation whatsoever."

(A parenthetical question becomes inevitable: did those two women and their husbands find what they had reached for? Well, Alexander Cameron Hunt was appointed United States marshal for Colorado, then territorial governor, and afterwards was a successful official in railroad and land companies. Frederick Meredith moved from Bannack to the still newer town of Bozeman, Montana, at the foot of Bozeman Pass on the East Gallatin River. Indian troubles in 1867 frightened him and Emily east to St. Louis, where Meredith returned to newspaper work. Eventually he landed in Denver as a crusading editor in favor of bimetallism during the years when that economic theory was a burning mountain issue. His wife, still writing busily, became a leader in the woman suffrage movement. If she and Ellen Hunt ever met, which is geographically and chronologically possible, and showed each other their scars, there is no record of it.)

It is debatable, of course, whether living in the mining camps of the 1860's was really more deplorable than the living endured by laborers in the slums of the newly industrialized East or by squatters in the malaria-ridden, lackluster river bottoms of the Mississippi Valley. Ultimately, the factor which distinguished the Rocky Mountain towns was not their crudeness but the willingness of men who knew better and who often had appreciable amounts of money at their command not only to accept but even to utilize cruelty, waste, and wantonness as a means of gaining their ends.

This is not what one would have expected. Most observers agree that *as individuals* the miners were hospitable, sociable, helpful, and completely democratic in their relationships with each other. As individuals many of them rebelled against the personal degeneration brought on by saloons and gambling tables and sought earnestly for familiar group activities that would re-establish a feeling of identity and of security in this alien land. They held impromptu dances whenever they could, laughing the while at the necessary awkwardnesses that occurred. "Boots O such Boots as graced the floor!" writes Frank Hall of an 1860 New Year's Eve party near Central City. "Why bless you they were nearly as ponderous as the Stamps used for crushing quartz and as they scraped across the floor they left traces of hobnails firmly imprinted on the stout planks."

In Bannack during the winter of 1862–63 there were two fiddlers and thirty white women, including Emily Meredith. Amazingly, a few starched white dress shirts appeared, "but," wrote Granville Stuart, "the majority wore flannel shirts with soft collars and neckties. . . . No man that was drinking was allowed in the hall. The young people danced the waltz, schottish, varsoviane, and polka, but the older ones stuck to the Virginia-reel and quadrille. There were usually about ten men to every woman. . . . Tickets were $5.00 gold and there was no supper served."

Theatrical productions appeared quickly in the larger towns. Most were clumsy affairs with second-rate actors, sleazy costumes, and candles for footlights, but they awakened recollections of similar if more polished performances at home. Best known of the mountain troupes was Jack Langrishe's, which traveled regularly from Denver and Central City to Helena and Virginia City, catering deftly to the taste of the high-altitude audiences for farce, variety acts, and the more declamatory of Shakespeare's dramas, notably *Richard III*.

Familiar fraternal organizations flourished, the Masons being particularly strong. Young clerks without such ties formed their own groups to stave off emptiness. As winter congealed around Virginia City in 1865, young James Knox Polk Miller, newly arrived from Salt Lake City, helped launch the Young Men's Literary Association. One of the purposes of the group was to make available in a central place the Eastern newspapers and magazines for which the members hungered. It was also highly social, presenting an occasional ball for the young ladies of the town and now and then going on stag sleigh rides with a singing group called the Amphion Serenaders. "Had a *carousing* time generally & most of us got two thirds 'Over the bay' " is one of Miller's diary descriptions of a sleigh party. The tone, however, is not wantonness but fellowship. Such an evening was worth $55 out of Miller's monthly salary of $125.

These things were group activities, not community activities, and in the latter situation the collapse of normal social bulwarks became marked. Town councils, to be sure, struggled feebly to improve the more obvious flaws. They passed safety ordinances regulating the construction of chimneys; they authorized fines for the committing of nuisances, for failing to maintain the sidewalk in front of one's store, for riding recklessly through the streets. They sometimes used prisoners from the town jail to repair roads. They appointed scavengers and marshals, but since their treasuries were generally balancing along the edge of bankruptcy, they could seldom offer salaries large enough to lure dependable men away from the mines.

Real estate values fluctuated so erratically that property taxes were impractical as a source of revenue. Bonds were almost unheard of; before redemption date came around the town might have ceased to exist. Inevitably, therefore, the councils turned for their income to licenses assessed against business enterprises, the highest fees being attached to the surest sources—bawdyhouses, grogshops, and gambling halls. Limitations were obvious. Jails and water systems, the latter sometimes consisting of wooden pipes, were about as far as any but the largest and most enduring towns could go. Other long-range community institutions were left to private enterprise. Being long-range in a shortsighted milieu, they fared poorly.

Although Denver-Auraria founded a public hospital in 1859, it met with such indifference that it disappeared in 1861. Montana's first hospital, built in 1864, was for the Indians of St. Ignatius Mission in the Flathead Valley. The whites had nothing until January, 1866, after a baseless rumor of gold on Sun River had started a stampede from Helena. Temperatures dropped to 40 below zero. As starved men came staggering back with frozen feet and hands, private individuals were at last shocked into seeking subscriptions to establish temporary relief quarters in an empty cabin. There local doctors amputated several fingers and toes, and so Montana's first hospital for whites came into being—four years after the beginning of the rush to Bannack. Gradually religious and fraternal groups sponsored other hospitals throughout the Rockies. They were too few, however. For years most men who were sick or hurt had to rely on their friends.

The first schools also began as the result of private effort—sometimes private opportunism. Consider, for instance, Owen J. Goldrick, a flamboyant, magnificently bearded Irish emigrant who reputedly had attended both Dublin and Columbia universities. Chancing to be in St. Louis in 1859, he was hired to travel to Huerfano Creek near Pueblo and there undertake the education of the children of J. B. Doyle, one-time mountain man, co-founder of El Pueblo, and more lately a successful trader and rancher. The gold rush diverted Goldrick, however. In or near Pueblo he hired out as a bullwhacker to a caravan bound for Denver. A born ham, he paused outside the town limits and donned a broadcloth suit, starched white shirt, tall silk hat, and kid gloves. In this garb he strode down the dusty street swinging a huge bullwhip and booming at his oxen words which the startled residents took to be oaths in purest Latin. Though it soon became evident that he had a marked penchant for the bottle, he nevertheless beguiled enough parents that in October, 1859, he was able to open a private school, charging $3 a month each for thirteen children—nine whites, two Mexicans, and two half-breeds.

Because teaching paid after a fashion, private schools soon opened in most of the towns, aided occasionally by church support. Public schools generally had to await the drive of some unswervable soul like Abner Brown, who passed through Boulder, Colorado, nearly two years after its founding and noticed forty or so children running loose through the streets. Learning that they had no school, he, an outsider, prevailed on several of the parents to let him start classes in the "spare" room of a two-room cabin occupied by a family of five. After three months of this Brown was able to shame the city into erecting an uncompromisingly rectangular lath-and-plaster building 36 feet long by 25 feet wide. During the process of building he did the carpentry work himself in exchange for free board, and manufactured the stove out of scrap iron he found near an abandoned placer digging.

The building opened its door to every child in Boulder on October 15, 1860, the first public school in the Rocky Mountain mining region. In time others followed in nearly every camp that gave the least promise of permanence, but financial support from town councils was, in the main, so limited that textbooks were a sad and tattered mélange, and equipment was limited to whatever the ingenuity of the teacher could provide. One reminiscence tells of a pair of rubber boots being split open and nailed flat to a wall to serve as a blackboard.[2]

Churches too waged a determined but often ineffective battle against the prevailing indifference. Their best success came in the foothill supply towns, where real estate promoters tried to lure them in as signs of stability. The rival log clusters of Auraria and Denver both offered free lots to the first congregation that would build a place of worship. As a result Denver was able to boast a Methodist Episcopal establishment as early as the fall of 1859. In the days when Virginia City was struggling to maintain itself as capital of Montana Territory, the Episcopal diocese there paid Bishop Daniel Tuttle the almost unheard-of salary of $2,500 a year.

It was otherwise in the mountains. The churches themselves, both Catholic and Protestant, realized the folly of erecting permanent buildings in temporary towns, and hence treated the mining regions as missions. The missionaries they sent into the high camps were for the most part well adapted to their thankless tasks—physically tough, warm-hearted and persevering, but not particularly intellectual.

They lived as crudely as their parishioners. The Rev. A. M. Hough's cabin at Bannack had three windows, one covered with glass, two with muslin; it was, he wrote, "very uncomfortable" when temperatures dropped to 50 below zero. John L. Dyer, fifty years old at the time and a Methodist, rented a cabin 18 feet square in the Breckenridge district of Colorado. He carpeted it with gunnysacks and cooked by the fireplace. "My bed was made of pine poles, even to the springs. The bed was hay, with blankets for covering. . . . My furniture was primitive and limited—a table, and a couple of boards against the wall for a cupboard, six tin plates, half a set of knives and forks . . . a coffee-pot, a tin cup, and a pot for boiling vegetables—when I had them—and a frying-pan."

Lacking anything else to serve his congregation as a meeting place, Dyer preached his sermons in his home. A. M. Hough, after moving from Bannack to Virginia City in its early days, used a log cabin with an earthen roof, which, he said, "gave much trouble."

Those who made circuits, as Dyer did, were sometimes sorely taxed. On one occasion he had to shovel snow for three and a half days in order to go three and a half miles, but "by the blessing of God I made the riffle." In all "I traveled near 500 miles on foot, by Indian trails, crossing logs, carrying my pack, and preaching about three times a week. . . . My clothes were

---

[2] For the sake of perspective it is perhaps well to note the attitude of New Mexico's nonmining Spanish Americans toward education. The legislature of 1856 referred to the voters a bill that proposed to support public education by a tax on property. It was defeated 5,061 to 371. Muddying the problem were the tensions over parochial education; though the citizens were predominantly Catholic, their federally appointed officials were mostly Protestant. As late as 1880, 42,000 New Mexicans were illiterate.

worn out; my hat rim patched with dressed antelope skin; my boots half-soled with rawhide."

Invariably the miners treated these pioneer ministers with respect. Men would stop gambling to listen to them, and one saloonkeeper in Montana's Nevada City (two miles down Alder Gulch from Virginia City) offered Hough the use of his building as a meeting place at any time—except Sundays, when, as Hough would of course understand, the place was much too busy. Respect, however, did not mean interest from the miners or financial support from church headquarters. In spite of his handsome salary, Bishop Tuttle, who had been used to large audiences before coming to Montana, at times found his congregation in Virginia City limited to five men and five women.

Dyer's home mission board allowed him, on occasion, as little as $100 a year. Collections did not make up the deficit. Once a friendly Jew passed the hat for him and raised $22.50. In February, 1862, he walked a hundred miles from Buckskin Joe in South Park to Denver because he lacked $10 for stage fare. Obviously he had to rely on odd jobs to keep going—locating claims for tenderfeet, hauling logs, building houses. During the winter of 1863–64 he carried mail on skis across the Mosquito Range. On one trip he frosted his feet and as a cure applied a poultice made from the bark of a balsam sapling. "Half my toenails sloughed off with considerable skin." When finally he got around to writing his reminiscences, *The Snow-Shoe Itinerant* (by snowshoes Dyer meant the long Norwegian-style skis of the time), he concluded almost as if in surprise, "The unsettled condition of the mining camps is unfavorable to the keeping up of religious societies."

The miners were equally indifferent to legal institutions. At times they were even hostile. James Morley, a well-educated man, voiced a common sentiment when he expressed in his diary a wish that "the government would let us severely alone, for it is a fact that miners can make their own laws so as to get along smoothly with each other, better than government laws."

Ordinances that seemed unrealistic were ignored. On April 28, 1860, the miners of the New Nevada district near Central City adopted a constitution that declared, "There shall be no Bawdy Houses, Grog Shops, or Gamboling Saloons" under penalty of a $50 fine. Its effect can be gauged by young Matthew Dale's declaration four months later in a letter home that "The saloons, groceries, gambling halls, etc. are always in full blast on Sundays." Even issues as large as murder were often overlooked if the brawlers were from the town's shiftless element and confined their attentions to each other. After the first winter in Bannack, Emily Meredith wrote her father, "There are times when it is really unsafe to go through the main street on the other side of the creek, the bullets whizz around so, and no one thinks of punishing a man for shooting another."

This does not mean that those who worked their claims and shops, in contrast to the idlers who flocked after them, were themselves disorderly. Quite the contrary. Most of them came from areas of stable government and expected to go about their business without offering, or being subjected to, any more interruptions than had occurred at home. Back home, however, local government had handled such interruptions as arose. In the mountains the only government was their own people's courts. If these were to work, the community at large had to pause long enough in its fierce concentration on getting rich to hear the case concerned. Only in situations where public opinion was severely shocked would they consent to do this.

As noted earlier, Charlie Reeves, William Mitchell, and Augustus Moore were finally run out of Bannack for shooting into an Indian tepee and killing four people. When a young German murdered and robbed his brother-in-law in Denver in the spring of 1859 a people's court found him guilty in an open-air trial; after he had amused the attending crowd by delivering his last words in broken German, he was hanged to a cottonwood tree beside Cherry Creek. It was the last execution for more than a year, although Horace Greeley in June said in disgust that there were "more brawls, more fights, more pistol shots with criminal intent in this log city of one hundred and fifty dwellings . . . than in any community of equal numbers."

Early in 1860 a group styling themselves the Bummers stole a wagon-load of turkeys, defied Denver's sheriff, W. H. Middaugh, to do anything about it, and whooped drunkenly about town until a gathering of citizens gave them five hours to leave. Some did—but not enough. In April those who remained invaded a traveling village of Arapahoe Indians that had paused at the edge of town, raped all the women, including small girls, and departed with several stolen horses. After a perfunctory investigation the Denver town council closed the matter by requesting an old trapper who knew the chiefs to offer apologies.

Although no other action followed the affair, the citizens were growing impatient. Late in the summer they reactivated the people's court. During the remainder of the year it heard six murder trials. One dealt with a man named Gordon who had gone on a monumental drunk during which he killed a bartender in a brothel, shot a dog, and then knocked down a stranger, held him by the hair with one hand and shot him through the head with the other. Sobering, Gordon fled to Kansas. Indignant citizens subscribed a purse to send Sheriff Middaugh and a posse after the killer. He was given a full and open trial, complete with defense attorneys, before a people's court presided over by Ellen Hunt's husband, Alexander Cameron Hunt. The jury's verdict of guilty was referred, as was customary, to the multitude in the street. It roared back a thunderous confirmation, and Gordon was thereupon executed in full view of thousands of people who gathered along the Platte River bluffs to watch the spectacle—"a craving for excitement," Nathaniel Hill might have said.

All told, four of the court's murder trials ended in well-attended executions, two in acquittals.[3] Commenting on the trials some years later, William Byers insisted that they were fair. Witnesses were always allowed and could be cross-examined by attorneys for the defense. But that ended it. "When they were proved guilty," Byers said, "they were always hanged. . . . There were no appeals in those days, no writs of error, no attorneys' fees, no pardons in six months."

The wrongs handled by these people's courts were for the most part crimes of passion. On the appearance of organized crimes the reaction was viciously different—the vigilante. Aroused by widespread horse stealing during the late summer of 1860 citizens never identified formed a secret Committee of Safety. After pouncing on a suspect called Black Hawk, they tried him—no outsider ever knew of what the trial consisted—and won from him—no one ever knew how—a confession implicating John Shear and an attorney named A. C. Ford. This information gleaned, the committee hanged Black Hawk to a cottonwood limb before the men whom he had accused had an opportunity to face him.

Shear too was hanged. Lest anyone assume suicide, a note was left on a nearby stump: "This man was hung. It was proved that he was a horse thief." No details of the proof were appended,

Ford tried to escape by stagecoach. The vigilantes overtook the vehicle, removed their quarry, led him a mile away from the road, and executed him with shotguns. They were sentimental souls, however. When it developed that a thief had pilfered the corpse of a fine gold watch before the body was officially "found," one of the Committee of Safety followed the culprit 800 miles to El Paso, recovered the heirloom, and returned it to the grieving widow.

Similar distinctions marked justice in early Montana. People's courts handled the cases of Reeves, Mitchell, and Moore in Bannack and of honest Dillingham's murderers in Virginia City. The shift began to appear when a people's court was summoned in Nevada City, near Virginia City, on December 19, 1863, to try a handsome, smooth-shaven, blond six-footer named George Ives, accused with two lesser confederates, Gus Hilderman and Long John Franck, of murdering and robbing Nicholas Thiebalt, a young muleskinner.

Charles S. Baggs and Colonel Wilbur F. Sanders handled the prosecution

[3] One acquittal involved a popular bartender named Charles Harrison, who pleaded self-defense after shooting down in his saloon an intoxicated and obstreperous rancher. A little later, highly insulted because a Negro bullwhacker dared address him familiarly as "Charley," Harrison, a Southerner, told the man to go for his gun and then—self-defense obviously—shot him three times. The court took no notice of that affair.

in front of a jury of twenty-four men. Two lawyers represented the accused. The weather being mild, the proceedings were held in Nevada City's main street, where they could be observed by some 1,500 citizens gathered from up and down Alder Gulch. It would be the responsibility of this gathering to confirm or reject the jury's verdict. So that all could see and hear the principals, the judge and witnesses sat above the crowd level on one wagon bed, the jurors on another.

Long John Franck bought his own life by testifying against Ives. In the face of that damaging evidence the defense attorneys resorted to so many delaying tactics (as it seemed to the crowd) that on the morning of December 21 the restive miners ordered that the trial be completed by three o'clock that afternoon. In spite of the injunction, matters dragged on until dark, at which time huge bonfires were lighted both for illumination and for warmth.

After half an hour's deliberation, the jury by a vote of 23 to 1 returned a verdict of guilty. At once voices from the crowd began calling out motions whose aim was to delay the hour of execution. Suspecting that Ives's friends were trying to gain time to arrange a rescue, Sanders leaped onto one of the wagon beds and proposed immediate hanging. Uproar followed. Threats were howled at the officials and loud attempts were made to shift the blame for Thiebalt's murder onto the despised informant, Long John Franck. The tactics had worked in the case of the Dillingham murder. Here they did not. Sanders held fast; the crowd swung his way. A beam was thrust out over the top of the front wall of an unfinished building nearby, and there, in the mingled light of the full moon and the flickering fires, George Ives dropped into darkness.

That same night Sanders, who was a Mason, met with three or four other Masons in a Virginia City hardware store to discuss the revelations of the trial. Given a bit more time a cohesive gang of ruffians might well have upset the proceedings and have rescued Ives. Moreover, it was becoming evident that a cohesive band of outlaws, controlled probably by Sheriff Henry Plummer, did in fact exist and was responsible for the region's growing spate of robberies and murders.

What should be done?

It is not quite accurate to say, as some apologists do, that no legal jurisdiction existed to which the citizens might have turned—a statement that requires a brief review of the absurdities of territory making in the northern Rockies.

Before the gold stampedes, Washington Territory, whose capital was Olympia beside Puget Sound, had extended east to the Continental Divide (Everything between the Divide and Minnesota was Dakota.) During 1861–62 the Idaho gold rush shifted the bulk of Washington's population across the Cascade Mountains to the Walla Walla–Lewiston–Oro Fino area. Ambitious politicians at once raised a cry for a new territory, alleging among other things that communications between the mines and Olympia was difficult at all seasons and in winter impossible. Leader of the separatist movement was Washington Territory's delegate in Congress, William H. Wallace, a nimble-footed politician who kept hopping hither and yon without seeming to know where he wanted to land.

Eager to build strength by creating as many Republican bailiwicks as possible, the war-beset Congress in Washington, D.C., listened sympathetically to Wallace and in March, 1863, created Idaho Territory. A geographical monster, it stretched far enough east to include all of present-day Montana, Wyoming, and a bit of Nebraska. Obstetrician Wallace was appointed territorial governor of his own creation.

As soon as Wallace arrived in Lewiston he began campaigning for election as Idaho's delegate to Congress! His political maneuvering, too intricate to detail here, involved a reshuffling of the federally appointed judiciary. As part of his planning he ordered Idaho's new chief justice, Sidney Edgerton, one-time Republican congressman from Ohio and an acquaintance of President Lincoln's, to establish himself not in Lewiston, as was Edgerton's due, but in the new stampede town of Bannack.

Edgerton and his wife reached the out-of-the-way post in September, 1863. Traveling with the chief justice as a member of his retinue was his nephew, Colonel Wilbur Fisk Sanders, an attorney by training. Sanders had recently won a discharge from the Union Army because of poor health and was planning to begin anew as public prosecutor for Idaho Territory. Wallace's antics, however, had clouded Sanders' prospects along with Edgerton's, and he too settled in Bannack.

By that time questing politicians were talking of separating Montana from Idaho. In November, 1863, Nathaniel Langford and Samuel T. Hauser started for Washington, D.C., with a petition urging the step. Because their influence was limited, Sanders and certain new acquaintances began raising money to dispatch Edgerton east on the same errand. At the time of the Ives trial, however, Idaho still retained jurisdiction. Sidney Edgerton, resident of Bannack, was still Idaho's chief justice—a lawful representative, surely, of long-established American principles of fair and open trials.

In spite of the justice's availability, Sanders and his fellow Masons did not turn to him for leadership. The difficulties that would beset him perhaps seemed to them too formidable, too time-consuming. What due processes could Edgerton invoke? Idaho's criminal statutes had not yet been printed; even if they had been, no one in Bannack could have received a copy of the laws before spring. Wallace meantime had won his election and had departed for the East, leaving affairs in the hands of his incompetent territorial secretary. If Edgerton did move to take command of this crisis, what support could he anticipate from Lewiston—and how soon?

No one seems to have proposed that Justice Edgerton assume leadership of the people's courts. Perhaps their indifferent accomplishments to date made them seem too frail a reed. And how could they be strengthened? No newspaper or any other unifying system of communication existed to rally popular opinion either around the people's courts or behind the symbolic figure of the chief justice.[4] Besides—and this is Sanders' own recorded objection to people's courts—it seemed unreasonable and impractical to pull so many miners away from their work every time some cheap crook had to be tried. A swifter, more efficient method had to be found.

Further discussion with other leading citizens of Alder Gulch led to Montana's notorious Vigilante Committee, a monolithic organization designed to save everyone's time and money by having its seventeen-man executive committee secretly indict and pursue suspected criminals, try them (unless the indictment alone was deemed sufficient), and if they were found guilty, either banish or execute them without recourse to appeal.

The first posse to ride forth under the captaincy of James Williams (Sanders kept in the background) was fortunate in laying hold of one Erastus Yeager, better known as Red. We are told that Yeager confessed, but no documentation exists. He was then hanged before the twenty-odd men whom he had accused could confront him. Largely on the basis of Yeager's word, vigilante bands swept remorselessly through Alder Gulch, Deer Lodge, and Hell Gate Ronde, hanging their prey to trees, rafters, corral gates, any upright that was handy.

Plummer's turn came on Sunday, January 10, 1864. Toward dusk, fifty or more members of the Bannack branch of the committee marched past the cabin of Justice Edgerton, where the household was preparing to go to choir practice, and stopped at the dwelling of Mr. and Mrs. A. J. Vail, Plummer's in-laws. His wife Electra had left him by then, in tears it is said; but the rupture had caused no apparent trouble with the Vails and the sheriff was still boarding with them. He offered no resistance when ordered to come forth, nor did two of his deputies who were taken simultaneously in nearby houses. All were hanged near the church meetinghouse on a gallows that Plummer had erected for the execution of another criminal.

Protests were ineffective. Two lawyers in Virginia City who raised the issue of trial by jury were told by the vigilantes to keep quiet or leave. In general, the entire frontier approved of these summary actions. In New Nevada, Colorado, Matthew Dale shrugged aside the whole problem of fundamental rights. Only criminals needed to fret. "No one who follows a legitimate business, tends only to his own affairs, or has any moral proclivities is in danger of these self constituted vigilance committies." Young William Bell, an Englishman enthralled by the West, declared after witnessing the tree-hung fruit of a lynching at Trinidad, Colorado, ". . . my horse is safer in a coralle in Trinidad, than in an [army]

---

[4] One suspects Edgerton did not want to be a rallying point, for he must have known what his nephew was up to and yet made no protest.

officer's stable in Fort Union." Or, as Robert Kirkpatrick summed up the feeling, "The Vigilante Committee always purifies a new country."

Well, let's define purity. The day after Plummer's execution—"a stinger of a morning for cold," Kirkpatrick remembered—the Bannack committee decided to investigate Joe Pizanthia, a 125-pound Mexican 5 feet 2 inches tall. No charge of association with Plummer was involved; it was just that Pizanthia, an alien, had a bad reputation.

Pizanthia of course knew of the execution the evening before. When he saw the hangmen marching toward his cabin, he gave way to panic, shot at them, and wounded two men, one of whom later died. This triggered a mob fury that the vigilantes, defenders of law and order, were powerless to control. Several hundred men rushed to Justice Edgerton's yard and secured a small, dismounted cannon that for some unexplained reason was lying there. With it they blasted Pizanthia's house apart, dragged him out badly hurt, hoisted him with a clothesline to the top of a pole, and riddled his body with bullets. Razing the cabin, they set it afire and tossed the corpse onto the blaze. The next day men were observed panning the ashes for whatever gold dust Pizanthia might have secreted around the place.

Power, however pure, sometimes tends to excesses. In 1860 in Golden, Colorado, a disreputable character named Edgar Vanover was executed not for what he had done but for what a vigilante committee decided he might do. Somewhat similar was the case of Virginia City's Joseph Slade. Though an able freighter and rancher, Slade was known to have killed men during his time as a stage-station manager on the Overland Trail. During his periodic drunks he was given to smashing up the furniture in some of Virginia City's less savory establishments. He was a nuisance, no doubt of that, and someday he might hurt someone. The Vigilantes warned him to mend his ways. Defiantly he went on another drunk. Sobering, he offered to pay for the destruction he had wrought, but by then the committee was out of patience. So they hanged him.

In the mid-1860's Boise and Ada counties, Idaho, also were in need of purifying. The sheriffs were rogues fully as outrageous as Henry Plummer and far more capable. Vigilantes finally shook them loose—"The Idaho Inferno," one manuscript account by a participant labels the episode. One infernal aspect had to do with the political machines of which the sheriffs had been a part. To some people the whole thing smacked more of politics than of justice; suspicion and resentments, born of the secrecy, festered unpurified for years afterwards.

Power tends to perpetuate itself. In January, 1864, during the height of the vigilante activities in the northern Rockies, Sidney Edgerton went east, financed by $2,500 in gold nuggets, and saw Montana created a territory. In May he was appointed governor. In December his own chief justice, H. L. Hosmer, praised the past work of the vigilantes and then urged the committee to dissolve. "Let us inflict no more midnight executions." The committee declined, although at the time of its formation apologists had implied that it would disband on the appearance of responsible government agencies. Hosmer's presence, however, made no more difference than Edgerton's had earlier.

A large part of the community supported the intransigence. On January 20, 1866, the *Montana Post* reported with no apparent sense of incongruity, "On Tuesday evening last the citizens of Nevada [City] held a reunion of the happiest and most joyous kind, at the Adelphi Hall. The proceeds of the ball were devoted to the benefit of the Vigilance Committee. . . . We are happy to hear that . . . quite a respectable sum was realized."

Clothed in such respectability, the vigilantes went on to hang at least twelve more men in Helena alone. Protests grew. After the *Montana Post* had moved to Helena, anonymous objectors ran a paid advertisement in the paper: "We are American citizens and you shall not drive and hang whom you please." In spite of that, the committee did not formally disband until 1870.

The precedent stayed. Here was a quick and easy way to solve hard problems. Inevitably an occasion arose when the wheel turned full circle and vigilantes sprang alive not to fill a judicial vacuum but to replace what already existed. The setting for one such affair was a pioneer farming area around Gas Creek, a small stream that drains eastward into the Upper Arkansas River from one of the vast gray 14,000-foot peaks of the Continental Divide in Lake County, central Colorado. The time, 1874.

As part of a larger feud whose details are unrecoverable now, a certain Harrington quarreled with Elijah Gibbs over an irrigating ditch and struck Gibbs with a shovel. Late that same night Harrington saw that one of his outbuildings was afire. When he rushed from the house to quell the flames he was shot from ambush and killed.

Gibbs was arrested and charged with murder. Because of the larger feud, feelings in Lake County grew so inflamed that the trial was shifted from Granite, the county seat, to Denver. The jury there acquitted Gibbs. Considering that justice had miscarried, Harrington's partisans formed a Committee of Safety and rode to Gibbs's cabin to deal with him. He retorted by killing two of the visitors and wounding another. Another died from an accidental gun discharge. Fearing that he might not be so successful another time, Gibbs then fled.

The Committee of Safety next set up judicial quarters in a neighborhood gristmill. According to the *Rocky Mountain News,* "Citizens were marched 3, 4, and 5 miles over hills and through snow and lodged in this improvised calaboose." The intent of the committee evidently was to justify its attack on a man whom the law had cleared by proving, first, that Gibbs was a member of a secret organization formed for cattle stealing, "slandering neighbors," and so on, and, second, that he really had killed Harrington.

Witnesses in the calaboose who proved reluctant to testify had their necks placed in nooses and were even hoisted off the ground so that they might learn the discomforts of recalcitrance.

A few of these outraged citizens mustered enough courage to go to the county seat at Granite and swear out complaints against sixteen of the vigilantes. Lake County's probate judge, Elias Dyer, crippled son of the Rev. John L. Dyer (who has been quoted earlier), made out the necessary warrants. They were never served by the sheriff. Instead Dyer, who was now suspected of favoring the opposition, received the following note, dated January 29, 1875: "You are hereby notified to resign your office as probate judge, and leave this county within thirty days, by order of the Committee of Safety."

When summer arrived, rumors flashed through Lake County that Gibbs ("the vilest cutthroat," the Granite paper fumed, "that ever went unhung") was planning to return to his ranch. As a move to help him, perhaps, one of the men who had been brutalized during the winter's inquisition swore out fresh complaints against the vigilantes. Dyer, who had tried without success to elicit support from territorial officials, obligingly issued new warrants. In due time the sheriff reappeared from Gas Creek with several of the men named, plus several of their friends. There were about thirty of them, all armed. They clumped into the Granite courthouse to hold a meeting with Dyer in his own courtroom.

What actually transpired is unknown. The warrants, it was later said, were dismissed for lack of evidence. The meeting then broke up. Dyer, very pale, was observed limping across the street to a store. There he wrote two letters, one to his father: ". . . at eight o'clock I sit in court. The mob have me under guard. . . . I die, if die I must, for law, order, and principle." He then limped back to his office in the county courthouse. Five men followed him and killed him as he sat in his chair.

"He was well known," said the county paper, by way of an obituary, "to have been the associate and defender of midnight assassins, incendiaries, and thieves . . . a sneaking scoundrel." The coroner's jury declared that he had come to his death by hands unknown. Lake County citizens either feared the vigilantes or felt Dyer had got what he deserved. A wall of silence surrounded Gas Creek. A Denver detective charged by Territorial Governor John Routt with investigating the crime came up with no recommendations. Although the slain man's father spent years trying to open up the truth, he never gathered sufficient evidence to justify action. Yet there was uproar enough that the vigilantes too grew afraid; in time Gibbs returned to his ranch without a hand being raised against him.

Vigilantism, its apologists said, became necessary whenever the enforcers of order were either out of reach across the mountains or else hopelessly corrupt at home. What other recourse was possible? The rhetorical question prompts a second one in rejoinder: What other recourse did the citizens ever really try?

Efforts to restore order by legal channels would have taken time—time to rally opinion; time to present facts to responsible authorities, however far away; time to investigate the qualifications of the sheriffs and the temporary judges to whom the citizens entrusted their affairs. Since few of the stampeders expected to be around that long, why bother—any more than they bothered about fouled streams, burned forests, dead dogs in the streets, or lost gold in their careless mills? Let the vigilantes assume everyone's fear for his property and his hatred for those who threatened it. Let the self-elected become the protectors. After all, each citizen had his work to do. If one value disappeared in order that another might be gleaned as quickly as possible, why, that was just one of the hard facts of the mountain present. The future would have to take care of itself.

Eventually the future arrived with denuded hills and ravaged resources —and with minutemen ready still to take charge whenever a majority of the citizens preferred to exchange their responsibilities for the sake of their todays. It is a problem that has reached far beyond the Rockies, of course. Their usefulness in the matter consists merely in affording one more laboratory where the ingredients of democratic tyranny may be examined at leisure.

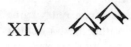

XIV

THOSE WHO STAYED

NOT EVERY summertime stampeder who visited the Rockies during the 1860's was so appalled by what he saw that he fled as fast as he could, with or without a stake. Here and there die-hard visionaries caught a glint of hope that defied reason. Recurrent disappointments afflicted them; an upsurge of Indian warfare threatened to paralyze their laborious transportation systems; their lopsided economy withered as the rich placers were worked out and their crude stamp mills proved inadequate for handling complex ores from the deep veins. Above all, the outrageous governments inflicted on them by the reconstruction Republicans in Congress and the bickerings of their own myopic politicians were enough to fill the stoutest optimist with dismay. In spite of those handicaps, however, a few incurable boosters decided to stay where they were and lift themselves into stability by their own bootstraps, if they possibly could.

The difficulties involved with government appeared first and most virulently in Idaho. After William H. Wallace had resigned as governor to run for Congress, Caleb Lyon was appointed in his place. A sharp-faced opportunist bearded somewhat like an Airedale, Lyon reached the territorial capital, Lewiston, in August, 1864. After promising redress to a delegation of Nez Percé Indians who came to see him about their overdue annuities, he began scheming how to get hold of some of their lands for himself. He also fell under the spell of certain calculating politicians who felt that since Idaho's fiddle-footed stampeders were then flowing south from Oro Fino and Florence toward Boise City, the capital should also shift in the same direction.

Although the legislature voted in favor of the move, the stubborn residents of Lewiston sought to retain the governmental seat by having the judge of their district court forbid the transferring of the state seal and archives. They also set a watch over Lyon. The governor fooled his guards by pretending a duck-hunting trip; on reaching the bank of the Snake River, he leaped into a waiting canoe and paddled furiously. His territorial secretary, DeWitt Smith, then obtained a detachment of soldiers from nearby Fort Lapwai and with them as an escort triumphantly carried the seal and records to the new capital. The Lewiston area retorted by trying to secede and join Washington, a move declared invalid by the Boise-oriented supreme court of the territory. Animosities engendered by the wrangle troubled Idaho politics for decades.

Having reached Boise, Lyon decided he did not like the new capital. Besides, he was under suspicion for misusing public funds. He either resigned or took a convenient leave of absence or was removed; the whole thing is fuzzy. Anyway, DeWitt Smith became acting governor in his place, but died in office on August 19, 1865, because, it is said, of excessive drinking. The territorial treasurer, H. C. Gilson, thereupon succeeded Smith just long enough to abscond with the entire territorial treasury, some $40,000.

Timing was unfortunate. The code of laws for the territory, as adopted by the first legislature, had not yet been printed and now could not be for lack of funds. Undeterred by an ignorance of what their predecessors had done, the second legislature went ahead at will. Then the first code was resurrected and Idahoans found themselves in a legal limbo marked, as a later governor put matters, by "perplexing discrepancies."

Meantime no one in the executive hierarchy was left to take over the vacated governorship. For that reason, perhaps, Lyon was reappointed in spite of the suspicions clouding his reputation. This time he stayed around Boise about six months and then departed with $46,418.40 that should have gone to the Nez Percé Indians as part payment for the gold-bearing lands they had relinquished to the United States.

Lyon was followed by David Ballard, honest enough but a radical reconstruction Republican of the type that dominated the federal Congress after the Civil War. He faced a legislature of Democrats. Many had arrived from the Georgia gold fields before the war; still more had fled west after the defeat of the Confederate Armies in the Mississippi Valley. They may not have constituted a majority of the population in the northern Rockies; and although their opponents charged them with wholesale balloting frauds, they were probably no worse than most others in an area where, one observer remarked, a large part of the electorate "cheated just for the love of it." The Democrats, however, were cohesive, whereas most of the other eligible voters were indifferent. As a consequence Democrats in both Idaho and Montana soon controlled the legislatures.

The feuds that boiled up between the elected lawmakers and the "foreign," federally appointed Republican executives paralyzed any attempt to solve the economic ills that came with the playing out of the placers. Census figures indicate the results. In 1863, according to one estimate, there were 32,343 people in Idaho, 1,089 of them women and 694 children. In 1870 the federal census showed a total of only 14,999.

Of those 15,000 residents, 4,247 were Chinese, in itself a significant commentary. Oriental miners, who could live on the gold the Americans wasted, were objects of violent antipathy. They were accused of taking work from native Americans, of being filthy (widespread legend said mice were a staple of their diet), and of indulging in unspeakable opium orgies. Whenever a camp began to decline, they were likely to appear, knowing that the impatient whites would sell out to them as a last source of revenue. With the inverted reasoning of intolerance, rabble-rousers took to seeing them as the cause rather than the result of poverty. A mob ran them out of Caribou, Colorado, in the early 1870's; the women of Helena declared Chinese laundrymen were working for unfair wages and ordered them to depart. Yet with infinite patience they persisted wherever placer mining had been wasteful, most particularly in Idaho. By 1873 they controlled the bulk of the paying claims in the territory—claims, be it noted, from which whites no longer could (or would) wring a living wage.

Montana fared but little better. The first governor, Sidney Edgerton, began his thankless task during the closing days of the Civil War. Although his first legislature, divided evenly between Republicans and Democrats, passed a resolution of loyalty to the Union, this was not enough for Edgerton's violent reconstruction sentiments. He excoriated all Southerners (presumably including those in his legislature) as "uncultivated savages." His nephew, Wilbur F. Sanders, campaigned for election to Congress on a similar platform, roaring to his listeners that Montana was infected with rebels "skulking in the gulches . . . inciting treason." Such talk alienated more votes than it attracted. Sanders was defeated and Edgerton found himself faced with an increasingly hostile legislature.

It was not an admirable legislature. "Venal, corrupt and shameless" is the description given it by the *Montana Post* (February 4, 1865), which, to be sure, was a Republican paper and Edgerton's principal organ. Most of the venality revolved around the lawmakers' choice of Virginia City to be territorial capital (they were sitting in Bannack at the time) and the issuance of some thirty-four charters awarding monopolistic toll-road and bridge-right charters over nearly every natural highway and river ford in the territory. The lawmakers' justification was pragmatic enough. If private enterprise was not encouraged to build the roads and bridges the territory needed, who would? On the strength of that argument, which probably was made still more glowing by an under-table passing of "gifts" and bribes, they whooped through so many unconscionable charters, which Edgerton signed, that if all the projects had been completed—and if travelers had heeded the tollgates—the burden on Montana transportation would have been overwhelming.

A more immediate financial problem lay in Washington's inability to find a man willing to exile himself to Montana as territorial secretary. No warrant authorizing the expenditure of federal funds in the territory was valid until signed by the secretary. Edgerton paid many necessary bills out of his own pocket. Despairing at last, he told his friends in September, 1865, that he and his wife were going to take their daughter east to school. On reaching his old home in Ohio he resigned his post.

His action precipitated years of trouble. Shortly before his departure he had vetoed on technical grounds an apportionment bill governing the election of subsequent legislators. This veto left Montanans with no legal way of holding an election, unless the governor ordered a special one. But after Edgerton's resignation there was no governor. At last, however, there was an almost unbelievable territorial secretary—Thomas Francis Meagher, a short, fat, forty-year-old, implacably ambitious Irishman.

In 1849, when he was twenty-five, Meagher had been sentenced by the British government to life imprisonment in Tasmania for his part in Irish revolutionary upheavals. By promising not to break parole, he had been allowed enough freedom that he was able to court and marry the daughter of a neighboring farmer. Finding that wedded bliss did not assuage his boredom, he wrote the chief magistrate that he intended to escape. He did, too, eventually reaching New York. There the Irish acclaimed him as a hero and he basked warmly in the limelight of sensationalism. Just as the luster was dimming, the Civil War gave him an opportunity to brighten it again by recruiting a brigade of Irish-Americans for the Union Army, himself as brigadier general. Peace brought new obscurity. Meagher, a citizen now, was already contemplating a move west when federal officers approached him as a last-ditch choice to be Montana's territorial secretary. Away he went, leaving his second wife to follow—his first had died in childbirth after he had packed her off to Ireland.

He arrived in Virginia City as a Republican. Realizing quickly that the Democrats ran Montana politics, he switched coats. This infuriated the local Republicans into frenzied outbursts. One letter writer declared that after arriving in Virginia City Meagher, who did like the bottle, had lain dead drunk in his hotel room for several days, "polluting his bed and his person in the most indecent and disgusting manner. . . . The Executive office is a place of rendezvous for the vilest prostitutes." And so on.[1]

He also annoyed the vigilantes. Not long after his arrival a ruffian named James Daniels stabbed a man to death in Helena after a card game. The vigilantes seized Daniels but during an uncharacteristic upwelling of civic virtue surrendered him to the new territorial authorities. The jury found Daniels guilty of manslaughter only and Judge Lyman Munson

[1] Such defamations, it should be noted, were standard weapons of political warfare in the mountains and not necessarily true. Political enemies of Wyoming's territorial secretary, Edward Lee, secured his removal in 1870 by a barrage of petitions that accused him of being "beastly drunk on several occasions in public, and . . . living publicly with a notorious prostitute."

sentenced him to three years in prison. Meagher capped this leniency by pardoning Daniels. Running out of patience, the vigilantes hanged him, Meagher's pardon still in his pocket. To the back of the dead man's coat the executioners pinned a note: "If our acting governor does this again, we'll hang him, too."

While still a Republican, Meagher declined to fill Montana's legislative vacuum by ordering the election of a new body, stating that his position as territorial secretary and acting governor did not give him adequate authority. After his conversion into a Democrat, he suddenly ordered the election. A Democratic legislature resulted. Promptly the federally appointed Republican judiciary declared the new body unconstitutional. The legislature retorted by cutting the judges' pay.

The new legislature also authorized a constitutional convention to meet in Helena and frame a state government. Seeing in the move a dastardly attempt by Democrats to seize still broader powers by making Meagher a Democratic United States senator, Wilbur Sanders rushed to Washington and warned the reconstruction congress that men "reeking with treason" (Sanders' words) were trying to smuggle a Democratic state into the federal fold.

Even Montana's Democrats realized that the territory was not ready for the financial burdens of statehood. Fewer than half the delegates who were elected to meet in Helena in January, 1868, bothered to fight the winter roads. Those who did assemble finally patched together the draft of a proposed state constitution, but when they sent it to St. Louis for printing, it somehow vanished and was never heard of again. No one seemed grieved.

Sanders, meanwhile, had alarmed Congress to such an extent that it passed an extraordinary law declaring that everything done by the "illegal" second and third Montana legislatures was null and void. Governmental chaos thereupon became total. Outraged citizens swelled Democratic ranks in protest and for a decade or more an unhealable legislative-executive schism racked the territory.

If Meagher could not be a senator, perhaps he could become a military hero once again. Convinced of imminent Indian uprisings, he bombarded army headquarters throughout 1868 with requests that he be allowed to raise volunteer troops for defending his people. However culpable his ambition may have been, his alarms, as a short digression will indicate, were not entirely baseless.

Indians throughout the frontier had taken quick advantage of the Civil War to strike at their oppressors. Wherever the army could spare troops to help the beleaguered settlers, the uprisings were quelled. Patrick Connor's 1863 crushing of the Bannocks of Idaho has already been noted. In New Mexico a California column commanded by General James Carleton found solace for arriving too late to fight the Confederates by waging a remorseless campaign against the Apaches. Kit Carson added to its effectiveness by breaking the Navajos. As a result of these drives New Mexico knew its first freedom from Indian attack (relatively speaking) since the days of the Spanish conquistadores.

The army, however, was not able to patrol the entire West. Sioux, Arapahoe, and Cheyenne raiders all but isolated Denver at times during the summer of 1864 by wiping out stage stations and occasional wagon trains on the plains. Dread of an alliance between Confederate guerrillas and Indian war parties intensified the nervousness of the mining camps—and indeed attempts to effect such a union were made by overzealous Southerners.

Into this emotional situation rode a band of Confederate raiders under James and John Reynolds. After seizing $42,000 from a wagon train on the Santa Fe Trail, they quarreled over the loot and fourteen of them returned to Texas. A mere six or seven continued with the Reynolds brothers to South Park. There they robbed several stages, adding piquancy to their success by telling their victims that they were the vanguard of 1,500 Texas Rangers on their way to sack and burn Denver. The effect was remarkable, considering the numbers involved. According to Nathaniel Hill, who rode through much of Colorado that summer, Governor John Evans packed a gun with him through the streets of Denver; even Catholic priests in far-off San Luis Valley went armed.

Posses combing the South Park area from the head of the South Platte River to Canon City quickly scattered the gang in a series of running fights. John Reynolds and one other escaped. A third was killed, his head cut off and taken to Fairplay, where it was preserved in alcohol. Jim Reynolds, who was wounded, and four more were captured and taken to Denver by United States Marshal Alexander Cameron Hunt. Because they were soldiers, not mere bandits, Hunt turned the five over to a detachment of volunteer militia for delivery to the military prison at Fort Lyon on the Arkansas River. They never arrived. In the pine forests at the head of Cherry Creek, on the divide between the Platte and Arkansas rivers, the captives tried to escape and were slain—or so their guards reported. Rumor insisted that they were actually lined up and executed. Such was the hysteria of the time—the late summer of 1864—that no investigation followed.

Shortly thereafter Governor Evans brought prominent Cheyenne and Arapahoe Indians to Denver for a peace conference. When the talks failed to produce tangible results, he tried to sow division among the enemy by suggesting that those who wished to lay down their arms should report to Fort Lyon, where they would be cared for. He then went east on territorial business. During his absence military affairs rested in the hands of Colonel John M. Chivington, hero of the victory over invading Confederates at the battle of La Glorieta Pass, New Mexico.

Chivington's command consisted of several hundred rambunctious miners who had enlisted at the height of the summer's hysteria to serve for a hundred days. They wanted a fight before disbanding. Chivington, who believed that only a summary lesson would persuade the Indians to behave, decided to let them have it. With four cannons and more than 900 men he marched toward Sand Creek, near Fort Lyon.

Between 500 and 600 Indians—men, women, and children—had followed Evans' suggestion and reported to the fort. Cynical whites scoffed that they simply wanted to live on government handouts during the winter and that when spring came they would rejoin their tribesmen, who were still beating war drums across the plains of eastern Colorado. Be that as it may, the officer in command at Fort Lyon fed them for a while and then sent them to Sand Creek, where they could hunt buffalo.

At sunrise on November 28, 1864, after a hard march through deep snow and intense cold, Chivington fell without warning on this camp. Ten of his men were killed and 38 wounded, 4 of whom later died. Upward of a hundred Indians, at least half of them women and children, were wantonly slain. The bodies of many were hideously mutilated.

At first Chivington was welcomed back to Denver with wild rejoicing, but after Congressional and army investigators had revealed the details of the massacre, a revulsion set in. When Chivington sought to justify himself by entering politics on a "Sand Creek" ticket, he was soundly defeated. Governor Evans, who had had nothing to do with the actual attack, was so badgered by criticism of it that he resigned his office.

In grim retaliation the Indians destroyed the hamlet of Julesburg in northeastern Colorado. In the spring of 1865 they moved on north into today's Wyoming, attacked several wagon trains, and killed at least twenty-six people. The army, skeletonized by the nation's demand for instant demobilization following the Civil War, responded with only limited success. Finally, however, after a long series of inconclusive skirmishes in the Powder River country east of the Big Horns, the Sioux and Cheyenne chiefs agreed to meet with government negotiators at Fort Laramie in June, 1866.

One of the Indian demands was for the closing of the Bozeman Trail through their hunting grounds to the Montana gold fields. They expected the matter to be discussed in good faith, but at the very moment of the talks Colonel Henry B. Carrington marched 700 troops past Fort Laramie to begin construction on three posts beside the hated wagonway. Incensed, the Indians broke off the discussion and began sniping at Carrington's work parties. On December 21, 1866, near brand-new Fort Phil Kearny a little south of present-day Sheridan at the snowy eastern toes of the Big Horn Mountains, Red Cloud's warriors obliterated Captain W. J. Fetterman's detail of eighty-one men.

Word of the Fetterman disaster sent a spasm of fear through the scattered farming communities of the lovely East Gallatin Valley, Montana, at the western end of Bozeman Pass. John Bozeman himself, who had settled near the town that now bears his name, became convinced that 11,000 Sioux warriors planned to go on the warpath as soon as spring arrived. On March 25, 1867, he wrote Governor Thomas Meagher an urgent letter, begging for protection for the community.

It hardly seems that he could have been as afraid as he sounded, for in April he and a miller named Thomas Cover crossed Bozeman Pass and rode toward the new forts in quest of flour contracts. Along the way they permitted five Indians to come into one of their camps on the supposition that the visitors were friendly Crows. They turned out to be Blackfeet. They killed Bozeman, wounded Cover, and ran off with the white men's horses.

It was a typical Blackfoot raid, not a Sioux uprising, but it looked like a harbinger of trouble to apprehensive Montanans. In great excitement Governor Meagher asked that the federal government underwrite the expense of a thousand volunteers, to be equipped by local merchants. Army officials dragged their feet. Peace advocates in Congress were growing increasingly critical; and, besides, military intelligence indicated that, although the new forts remained under intermittent siege, the Sioux had no serious intention of crossing Crow territory to attack the Gallatin Valley. The general in command of the department tried to calm Meagher down. This led the never-temperate *Montana Post* to charge the military, on May 2, 1867, with "unbearable and criminal imbecility, blundering nonsense, disgraceful and damnable cowardice."

Thus beset, the government reluctantly authorized Meagher to recruit 800 volunteers whom it would pay 40 cents a day. The department also promised to send him 2,500 muskets by the next river steamer. On the strength of this the acting governor flew about among the merchants of Helena, lavishly buying food, horses, clothing, and whatnot for his army, his Republican opponents sniffing the while that what he was really doing was providing a bottomless gravy bowl for Democratic contractors.

As the volunteers began to assemble, the governor and a small escort set out across the plains to Fort Benton under a blistering June sun to pick up the 2,500 muskets. On reaching the river town ill and feverish, Meagher boarded a docked steamer in hope of an undisturbed rest. During the moonlit night he splashed into the river. For two months thereafter his corpulent wife—James Knox Polk Miller described her in his diary as "an immense work . . . too large and unwieldy for a life companion"— prowled the riverbanks, looking. Promises of a reward turned out other searchers, but a corpse was never found. Enemies charged that Meagher had either fallen overboard while drunk or had committed suicide to escape the political mess he had created. Rumormongers whispered that only the vigilantes knew the truth. Others speculated that he had chosen this means to abandon his wife and seek, in a hidden rowboat, greener pastures under a new name. There were even a few who raised the simplest explanation—that he was sick and dizzy and lost his balance while searching for a breath of air. Readers may take their choice.

His army, which encountered no hostile Indians, was disbanded in October, 1867. In December the legislature accepted and sent to the federal government bills totaling $1.1 million. The cold eye of the inspector general reduced this to $513,000, which was still a neat sum for a bloodless war.

Farther south, meantime, the Indians won their point, not because they were victorious in battle but because the approach of the Union Pacific Railroad let the government find a compromise. As soon as the rails reached northern Utah, Montana traffic could disembark there and travel well-beaten wagonways to the northern gold fields in less time than was required to course the longer Bozeman Trail through Wyoming. So why fight to keep the Bozeman route open? The government ordered the trail closed, the forts abandoned, and the Powder River country set aside as a "permanent" hunting ground. These concessions lulled the Wyoming Indians sufficiently that they failed to recognize the graver threat implicit in the railroad. They gave up their raids (in 1867 they had killed several surveyors) and during the Union Pacific's rush toward Great Salt Lake they caused little trouble either to the construction crews or to the new army forts—Russell, Sanders, and Steele, plus old Fort Bridger—that were strung along the right-of-way to protect the workers.

The railroad created Wyoming. As 1867 opened, fewer than two thousand people lived in the area, most of them clustered about the stage stations and river fords on the old Oregon and Overland trails. An almost instantaneous change came with the creation, along the route chosen for the tracks, of a series of administrative centers called division points. Construction materials were assembled at those places; orders and workers were sent out. The division headquarters also became focal points for all who followed the construction crews.

Eager to squeeze cash from every possible source, the debt-saddled railroad located its division points on its own land, surveyed townsites around them, and sold building lots at $100 to $150 each to the incoming opportunists.[2] The town of Cheyenne was laid out early in July, 1867, while the rails still lagged more than a hundred miles to the east, near

[2] To repeat one of the more familiar facts of western history: the government encouraged the building of the Union Pacific and Central Pacific railroads by giving them alternate sections (a section is 640 acres) throughout a strip of land 40 miles wide straddling the length of the tracks. The idea was that by selling the land to settlers the railroads would eventually be partly reimbursed for their construction costs. This was delayed income, of course. A more immediate source of cash came from 6 percent government loans of $16,000 to $48,000 for each mile of track laid, the amount depending on the nature of the terrain.

Julesburg. The first settlers, six men and three women, arrived on the 9th. Behind them, during subsequent weeks, came trains of ox-drawn wagons loaded with planks from buildings that had been dismantled in Julesburg and would be reassembled in treeless Cheyenne. By November 13, when the rails reached the new division point, 4,000 people lived there. Three months later there were 6,000.

As soon as winter relaxed, the track layers pushed on over Sherman Summit, 8,236 feet above sea level, and down to the Laramie Plains, where Laramie City was laid out in May, 1868. There was no pause. On the graders toiled, around the northern snout of the Medicine Bow Mountains, over the Continental Divide near present Rawlins, on through still more overnight division points toward Utah—425 miles within the single year 1868, as the harried management raced to obtain as much public-domain land as was possible ahead of the eastward thrusting Central Pacific.

One factor that helped the Union Pacific crews attain this extraordinary rate was the timber in the mountains. On the plains there had been no trees to supply telegraph poles, bridge spans, or, above all, the 2,500 or so ties, each eight feet long, that had to be laid every mile. Until late in the summer of 1867 lumber had to be transported from the East at heavy expense. As soon as wagon hauling from the pine and spruce forests in the high country became practical, thousands of tie hacks swarmed into the Laramie and Medicine Bow mountains, south up Bear River into the Uintas, north up the Green to the Wind River Range. During the winter they felled the trees, squared out the ties with heavy broadaxes, and skidded them across the snow to the riverbanks. When the ice broke and high water surged, they chucked the wood into the streams and, soaking wet, followed it to the nearest grade crossings, where teamsters waited with their wagons.

It was a massive business, calling for thousands of draft animals, enormous tonnages of hay, quantities of food and clothing for the camps. Moreover, the ties would have to be replaced regularly. This was one reason why Laramie endured while division points located less conveniently to trees did not. In 1869 alone the railroad spent $2 million in Laramie for lumber. Many a glamorized gold camp did not fare so well with its placer bars.

The quick-blooming division points were very much like the mining camps. Isaac Alexander Banker, who left his family behind in the hope that he could make a stake as a surveyor by following the little towns westward to rails' end, gives something of their feeling in a letter written to his wife from Laramie on May 4, 1868: ". . . poorly cooked food sleeping on the ground or floor with people of all kinds . . . as yet no ladies or families of any account, all mixed as if shaken in a heap from a bag . . . all wickedness and strife and every body after money." He could not take it. After a few miserable weeks of trying he gave up and went home.

Brave little attempts were made to ameliorate conditions. Young men formed literary associations in Cheyenne as they had in Virginia City. Ministers built churches, then grieved over the smallness of their congregations, especially when the notorious Wyoming wind began to blow; people did not like to buck those dust clouds to go to church.

The same impatience with the law that had marked the mining camps put vigilantes into action in the railroad towns, their work often abetted by mobs. As in the affair of Joe Pizanthia at Bannack, these self-constituted enforcers of order sometimes lost control of things. The most notorious example occurred in short-lived Bear River City in the southwestern corner of the territory. After a vigilante-style mob had lynched three men under arrest for robbery and murder, a gang of roughs started smashing up the town in retaliation. Several were jailed, among them some railroad graders and tie hacks. Friends swarmed in from the construction camps to rescue them. Citizens banded to help the police and a wild melee resulted. During it the jail and newspaper office were burned down, and troops had to be called from Fort Bridger to restore order. No one knows how many were killed in the fighting—one citizen, evidently, and somewhere between nine and forty mobsters, depending on which of the different newspaper stories of the time a reader accepts as being closest to accuracy.

The construction boom was accompanied by a small gold stampede to the edges of the Continental Divide near South Pass on the old Oregon Trail. Several small towns appeared: South Pass City, Atlantic City, Miner's Delight. It is doubtful whether they produced throughout their brief lives as much money as Laramie garnered from timber in 1869 alone. The excitement was high for a time, however, and lent force to arguments for the formation of a new territory to be called Wyoming. Formalities were completed in 1868. The following year out from the East came the usual Republican officials to deal with the usual Democratic legislature.

The high hopes with which the government had been launched soon dwindled. Tourists and journalists who rode the new trains through the territory gave unflattering reports of Wyoming's agricultural possibilities, and settlers did not come. The South Pass gold excitement died. The hordes of construction workers were replaced (according to the 1870 census) by a mere 848 permanent employees. Cheyenne's population dropped by half. In the entire territory there were hardly 9,000 people, most of them huddled in the tie camps or in drab hamlets beside the main tracks.

During this time of stagnation someone fastened hold of an idea then current throughout the nation—female suffrage—and suggested that Wyoming gain needed publicity by granting women the right to vote and hold office. The move seemed safe. Men outnumbered women six to one. Even if most of the ladies proved bold enough to exercise the franchise, which was regarded as doubtful, it would hardly matter. In December, 1869, accordingly, a suffrage bill was presented to the legislature. It was good fun. Many of the legislators went along with it in the expectation that Republican Governor John Campbell, who vetoed most of the bills the lawmakers passed, would void this act as well. To their surprise he signed it into law, and thus Wyoming became the first political entity in the United States to allow women to vote. They took the privilege seriously and made their weight felt. Within little more than a year the territory had commissioned three of them to be justices of the peace and in Laramie women were granted the even more radical boon of being allowed to sit on juries.

The town boomers of Denver had been totally astounded by the decision of the Union Pacific to pass through the underpopulated regions to the north of them. Did not Colorado mines offer the only appreciable amounts of traffic available in the Central Rockies? Was not a line through their territory the shortest way from either Chicago or St. Louis to San Francisco?

As early as 1861, when talk had been swelling in Washington that the North must build a railroad in order to hold the West to the Union, a group of leading citizens had sought to prove that the central Rockies were not as formidable a barrier as was commonly supposed. Digging into their own pockets, they hired mountain man Jim Bridger and Edward Berthoud, a surveyor in Golden, to find a usable crossing directly west of Denver. After pushing up the difficult canyons of Clear Creek, the explorers located Berthoud Pass, 11,313 feet above sea level on today's U.S. Highway 40, and from there worked out a direct route to Salt Lake City. The promoters then tried to demonstrate the feasibility of the way by urging the powerful Central Overland California & Pikes Peak Express Company to run its stages via Berthoud Pass. The firm declined. The crossing was too high, the winter snow too deep. Though it meant adding many miles to the journey, stages continued rattling north from Denver to the Cache la Poudre River, then through the tawny foothills to the Laramie Plains, and across the Continental Divide at Bridger Pass.

Steadily thereafter Colorado's situation deteriorated. The opening years of the Civil War slowed immigration. Ore in the mines grew complex and hard to handle. Although an interim of feverish speculation seemed for a short while to promise floods of outside capital, it soon collapsed.

Precipitator of this unhealthful boom was a scandalous Irishman named Pat Casey, who found rich ore on a hill high above Nevada City in Gregory Gulch, built a big stamp mill for crushing it, and then set about making a local joke of himself with his riotous antics. Moreover, he was not as rich as his assay reports indicated, for his mill was no more efficient at recovering the gold in his ore than were the other thunderous contraptions in the neighborhood. Well, cats can be skinned in more than one fashion. Pat bit off another chew of tobacco, bought a new plug hat, and hied himself to New York City.

The luck of the Irish held. When he reached the East, Wall Street was agog over the soaring stock prices of the mines of the Comstock Lode in Virginia City, Nevada. Perhaps Gregory Gulch would do as well. In the fall of 1863 bemused investors paid Pat $150,000 for his holdings, to that date the largest mining transaction in the Rocky Mountain area.

The sale touched off a wild scramble for Gregory Gulch properties that could be capitalized and the shares marketed on the stock exchanges. Claims and fractions of claims changed hands several times a day, always at an increase in price—until April, 1864. During that month prices in the speculative Comstock companies broke disastrously. Colorado prices followed instantly. Scores of hopeful investors lost everything. Dozens of mines that before the craze had been offering employment and earning at least some income shut down to eerie silence.

The stagnation was deepened by the Indian troubles that followed the Sand Creek battle and by a mountain-style feud between the legislature and the governor who was appointed to succeed John Evans—Alexander Cummings, described by Frank Hall, an avowed enemy, as "stiff-necked, obstinate, willful and craftily able."

Hoping that home rule would rid them of Cummings and improve their destinies, Coloradoans narrowly ratified a state constitution that specifically refused voting rights to Negroes. Despite the discrimination, Congress in May, 1866, passed an act admitting the state. Andrew Johnson vetoed it. In explanation he cited the territory's insufficient population.

Outraged Coloradoans conducted a special census to prove the President wrong. To their dismay they learned that population, which had stood at 34,000 in 1860, had dropped to 28,000. Nevertheless, they tried again. Again Johnson vetoed admission, this time because of the continued disfranchisement of Negroes.

After so many discouragements the railroad shone like salvation; it *had* to come to Denver. But it didn't. In the fall of 1866 Union Pacific officials announced that the line would not continue along the South Platte past Julesburg but would veer instead up Lodgepole Creek toward what became Cheyenne.

Colorado's hopes shifted in desperation to the Kansas Pacific.[3] It was the child of expediency. After Chicago financiers had won their battle to have Omaha named the eastern terminus of the Union Pacific, St. Louis interests were placated by the chartering of an independent feeder line that would run from Missouri to a connection with the Union Pacific at the 100th meridian in south-central Nebraska. There was no traffic in Nebraska, however, but there was in Denver. Urged on by hopeful

---

[3] This road was known first as the Leavenworth, Pawnee, and Western, then as the Eastern Branch of the Union Pacific (with which it had no corporate connection), and finally as the Kansas Pacific. For the sake of simplicity I call it Kansas Pacific throughout.

Coloradoans, Kansas Pacific officials persuaded Congress to alter the road's charter so that it could continue to the edge of the mountains before swinging north to join the UP. The road's land grants, as generous as those awarded to the Union Pacific, were extended to cover this increased mileage.

As the road pushed west through Kansas its ambitions swelled. Why not ask Congress for additional land grants and loans and push on into Southern California, either by crossing Raton Pass into New Mexico or thrusting through the San Luis Valley? The K.P.'s aggressive general manager, young William Jackson Palmer, hurried ahead to examine the alternative routes, both of which ignored Denver. Faced with the paralyzing thought that no railroad whatsoever was coming, hundreds of the city's merchants and workers pulled stakes and late in 1867 streamed north to relocate in newly founded Cheyenne.

More resolute citizens formed a Board of Trade that met on November 13, 1867, to see what could be done. The Kansas Pacific tried to take advantage of the situation by offering to build into Denver if the tiny city of 3,500 people would subscribe $2 million to help construction. After recovering from the shock, the Board of Trade pointed out that they could build their own line a hundred miles north to Cheyenne and connect with the U.P. for no more than that sum.

The idea caught hold. Why not do it? "We were like drowning men," Frank Hall remembered later, "eagerly catching at every shred of hope." Leading residents, John Evans among them, chartered a road which they named with determined optimism the Denver Pacific. Impassioned rallies were held, bonfires blazed, oratory flowed. In a single day the 3,500 citizens of Denver pledged $225,000. Thinly populated counties along the proposed line voted bonds in support of the project, and in May, 1868, a thousand people marched behind a brass band to the city's edge to see the grading begin.

It was one thing to vote bonds, another to sell them. Investors in the East proved wary. Jealousies cropped up at home. The town of Golden, which was still the official capital of Colorado, had always dreamed that any transcontinental line which traversed the territory would pass through its limits and on up Clear Creek Canyon to Berthoud Pass. Obviously that hope was gone. Moreover, if Denver gained the sole connection with the outside, the legislature might yield at last to the rival city's importunities and shift the capital. In a desperate effort to head off such a disaster, W. A. H. Loveland energetically promoted a rival road to connect Golden with Cheyenne. He too appealed to the counties for bond issues on his behalf. During the bitter animosities that followed, the legislature moved the capital to Denver. The rivals both flirted with the Union Pacific for help; it played fast and loose with each, and in the end let each down. They would have to work out their own salvation.

The break came when Congress refused to grant to the Kansas Pacific the land and loan privileges it would need in order to reach California. Its castles tumbling, the road pulled its sights back to Denver and worked out a deal whereby some of its existing loan privileges with the federal government and its land grants between Denver and Cheyenne were transferred to the struggling Denver Pacific.

From then on work hummed on both lines. Tie hacks swarmed into the mountains, each one of them eating, someone calculated, 7½ pounds of meat, beans, stewed fruit, and bread every day. In the spring of 1869, 200,000 ties were floated down the Cache la Poudre River alone to the Denver Pacific camps. Farther south the Kansas Pacific hired 5,000 oxen and 600 mules, together with the necessary wagons and drivers, to haul ties from the South Platte–Arkansas divide to construction camps on the plains. Cattle ranchers like John Iliff in the northern part of the territory (he also supplied the Union Pacific) and Charles Goodnight in the south found new markets for beef that they imported in long, plodding trail herds from Texas. Farmers raised hay and vegetables; once-timorous merchants moved back from Cheyenne. The census of 1870 showed that the population sag had been reversed; the total had climbed from 28,000 in 1866 to nearly 40,000 within four years.

On June 24, 1870, the first passenger train came down the Denver Pacific tracks from Cheyenne. On August 15 service opened with Kansas City over the K.P. tracks. In December W. A. H. Loveland joined Golden and Denver and started pushing his Colorado Central up Clear Creek toward the mines in Gregory Gulch. Coloradoans were ecstatic. Adversity had turned into triumph and they had wrought most of the change themselves.

The Mormons of Utah showed comparable resilience. The main difference was that they began in relative prosperity. Though agriculture was difficult in their high, dry valleys, their hard-working farmers had found steady markets supplying army units, overland stage and freight stations, and the construction crews that built the Overland telegraph line in 1861. Population growth never faltered. From 1861 through 1868, 20,000 converts poured in from England and Northern Europe. Each year except 1865 and 1867 the church sent wagon trains loaded with food to meet these immigrants and bring them to Utah, along with machinery for making cloth, nails, and similar homely items.

Although Salt Lake City was as eager as Denver for a railroad, the church recognized the dangers that might come with it. Floods of cheap manufactured goods might destroy local industry and fasten commerce firmly in the hands of the Gentile (non-Mormon) merchants who already controlled much of the trade from the outside. Cheap freight might lead to mining developments that would attract roistering non-Mormon laborers who would corrupt local workers and then depart, leaving only ghost towns and scarred hills behind.

To counteract these threats, the church under Brigham Young developed its enormously effective School of Prophets, a propaganda agency with branches and women's auxiliaries in every town. Mormons throughout the territory were urged to attend these meetings, discuss the problems, offer suggestions, and hear explanations of the policies reached by the church.

Under the school's auspices a concerted drive was made to stimulate home industry. Women, for example, were urged to buy only clothing that was made locally—including silk; to that end the church imported hundreds of thousands of silkworms. The church-supported Zion's Cooperative Mercantile Institution, the famous ZCMI with its symbol "Holiness to the Lord" arching over the eye of Jehovah, was founded to swing trade as fully as possible into the hands of Mormon merchants. Mining prospects were deliberately underplayed, with the understanding that if and when ore bodies were opened, Mormon workers would be encouraged to take the jobs that were offered. None of these moves nor others like them were designed to continue the Mormon isolation from the rest of the world, but rather to make its ending as painless to their theocracy as possible.

The most immediate problem was the construction of the transcontinental railroad itself. Hoping to reap the economic gains for their own people while at the same time fending off the riotous construction men and the parasites they had seen in Wyoming, Mormon leaders, acting as trustees for the church, bid on and won 150 miles—$2 million worth—of grading, tie-laying, bridging, and tunneling contracts from the Union Pacific. They also obtained similar but smaller contracts from the Central Pacific, which was building eastward through Nevada. Laborers, teams, and other equipment were obtained by issuing "calls" throughout the territory, much as men were "called" to found new towns or go on proselytizing missions abroad.

The decision of the Union Pacific to avoid the rugged canyons leading into Salt Lake City and to go north through Ogden instead brought from the Mormons a retort like Denver's: they would build their own connecting link, the Utah Central, 37 miles long, from Salt Lake City to the main line at Ogden.

Neither the Central Pacific nor the Union Pacific kept faith with the church's contractors. Although the converging rails joined according to specifications at Promontory Point, north of Great Salt Lake, on May 8, 1869, the Central Pacific failed by $200,000 to pay its bills. The Union Pacific, caught in the tangles of the noisome Crédit Mobilier, declared itself unable to meet obligations in Utah of more than five times that amount.

To the men who had supplied work animals, grain, and food, to the laborers, and to the merchants who had supported them with credit, the announcement was catastrophic. They clamored for relief to the church, which had urged the work upon them. Did not some responsibility lie there?

The church was equally dismayed by the railroad's action. Its trustees had counted on profits from the Union Pacific work to finance the building of the Utah Central between Salt Lake City and Ogden. Without profits, how could that vital link be constructed?

An attempted answer to both problems was the issuance of 6 percent mortgage bonds secured by the anticipations of the Utah Central. These were offered for sale only to Mormons and were pushed hard, in the hope that enough would be taken up to finance not only the building of the Utah Central but also to meet the debts due the contractors for their work on the other roads. The burden was too great. Potential investors, doubting ability of the Utah Central ever to meet such heavy charges, kept their hands in their pockets. Even so, the church did not try to avoid its responsibility, but eventually paid every person who had worked on the Union or the Central Pacific road from its own hard-pressed treasury.

Meanwhile one windfall did come their way. The Union Pacific offered to settle its Utah debts for $200,000 in cash and $600,000 worth of surplus iron rail and rolling stock. The church trustees had little choice but to agree. At least the equipment let them complete the Utah Central (trains began rolling between Ogden and Salt Lake City in January, 1870) and freed cash for meeting other demands.

XV

BOOSTERS AND BOOMERS

MEN generally believe what they want to believe. Ever since the days of Zebulon Pike, government explorers had been telling the nation that the dry prairies along the eastern base of the Rocky Mountains were unfit for agriculture. As soon as settlers began coming into the area, however, they challenged the concept. Colorado's first territorial governor, William Gilpin, declared flatly that irrigation would turn the high plains into "the Pastoral Garden of the world." In 1869 traveler Samuel Bowles wrote that the irrigated gardens of the Denver area "riot in growth of fat vegetables. . . . Think of cabbages weighing from 50 to 60 pounds each. And potatoes from 5 to 6 pounds. . . . Yet here they grow, and as excellent as big."

Was such talk pure promotion? In October, 1869, Horace Greeley of the New York *Tribune*—he who had done so much to foster the Colorado gold rush of 1859—sent his agricultural editor, Nathan Meeker, west to learn.

Meeker was a literary agrarian, not a practicing one. Although raised on a farm near Cleveland, he had soon left for New York City, where as an intense young Bohemian he had published a few poems. He next joined a Fourierist Phalanx, one of the many communal colonies that flourished in America during the 1840's, and spent three years in that high-minded society with his plain-featured, devoted bride Arvilla. Although the colony's basis was agriculture, Meeker himself worked in the office.

After the failure of the phalanx, he ran stores in farming towns in Illinois, meantime scribbling energetically. He published a novel and turned out yards of copy about Midwestern agricultural matters for Eastern newspapers. Because he was in the right place at the right time, Horace Greeley hired him to cover Ulysses S. Grant's Mississippi Valley campaigns for the *Tribune*. The war over, Greeley brought him to New York to be the paper's agricultural editor. Thus Nathan Meeker, who had raised scarcely a parsnip with his own hands, came to be considered something of a national authority on farming matters.

On his way west in the fall of 1869 Meeker chanced to board a Kansas Pacific train that was pulling a special car full of wealthy Easterners on their way to Colorado to look over investment possibilities. Shepherd of the group was William Jackson Palmer, then in charge of the railroad's track laying. Palmer invited Meeker to join the party and continue with it by buggy from track's end through the Arkansas Valley to Pueblo and then north past Pikes Peak to Denver.

Palmer, then thirty-three years old, was already dreaming of a mountain railroad of his own. As a youth in Pennsylvania he had studied railroading and had been starting his career as private secretary to the president of the Pennsy when the Civil War interrupted. During the conflict he led a famous Pennsylvania cavalry regiment with such dash that he was mustered out a brigadier general at the age of twenty-nine. Because of his military experi- ence, the Kansas Pacific hired him to take charge of construction work through the dangerous Indian country of Kansas, and then had sent him on ahead to survey possible routes through the mountains to California. During the work he had fallen in love with the southern Rockies. Times were ripe for their development, he thought—or could be made ripe with the proper management. Although no record of his talks with Meeker remain, it would be strange indeed if he did not discuss the prospects of the area with the nation's best-known farm spokesman.

The tempo of migration was quickening again after the slowdown caused by the war. They must have picked up evidence of it, as they jogged through the Arkansas Valley, in the aspirations of two groups of land seekers known as the Georgia Colony and the German Colonizing Society.

The Georgia Colony had been set afoot by Joseph Decatur Patterson, called Cate, who had first come to Cherry Creek, Colorado, in 1859 with Green Russell's party of reinforcements from Auraria, Georgia. In the fall of 1862 Russell, Patterson, and several other Southern sympathizers had sought to slip back to their embattled homeland by following roundabout trails through the central Rockies. In their party was Joshua Potts, whose wife had just died, and Potts's six children, ranging from Martha, aged twenty, to a girl of four.

On the plains of northeastern New Mexico, Joshua Potts came down with smallpox. While the fugitives were halted in dismay, wondering what to do, they were caught by federal troops from Fort Union. Potts died. The rest of the party, the six orphans included, were taken to Fort Union as prisoners. In the spring of 1863 they won parole by promising not to bear arms against the North.

Most of the party continued to Georgia. Not Decatur Patterson, how- ever. All winter he had been remembering their ride south through the lush vales of Huerfano Creek near the foot of Greenhorn Peak, in the Wet Mountains southwest of Pueblo. When he asked Martha Potts whether she would like to live there with him, she agreed. They were married at Fort

Union—the officers and soldiers took up a collection of $300 as a wedding present—and off they went, with at least some of Martha's five orphaned brothers and sisters in tow.

Cate extolled the country so much in letters home that after the war his father, Sam Patterson, and a cousin came out to look over the country. Catching something of Cate's excitement, they went home to recruit a party. Any promise of a fresh start sounded good in Georgia in those days. In 1869, only weeks before Palmer's group came along, two hundred or so people followed Sam Patterson through Pueblo to the foot of the Wet Mountains. Another hundred, Green Russell and his family among them, were scheduled to follow in the spring.

No formal bylaws bound these Georgians together. On reaching Huerfano Creek they scattered out as individuals to select the land they wanted. Most settled near the head of the stream. To the south soared the Spanish Peaks, their green sides ribbed with upended dikes of rock that looked like Chinese walls. Westward the land rolled upward under cloaks of aspen and oak brush to La Veta Pass, a timeless gap through the Sangre de Cristo Mountains into San Luis Valley. A good country—some of their descendants are still there.

A more formal organization was the German Colonizing Society, creation of Carl Wulsten, editor of a German-language newspaper in Chicago. Horrified by the dreary conditions under which emigrants from Germany lived in the industrialized city, Wulsten too sought escape in the West—more specifically in Wet Mountain Valley, a magnificent basin between the Sangre de Cristo Range on the west and the Wet Mountains on the east. During the summer of 1869 he persuaded several dozen Germans to invest $250 each in a communal colony that would obtain land in the valley. For five years they would pool their labor to work it. Then they would divide the profits and disband, each to his own plot.

Wulsten sought to further the enterprise by asking the federal government for a grant of 40,000 acres, evidently feeling that his project was as meritorious an agency of settlement as were the railroads, and they were receiving millions of acres. Times had passed him by, however. The government's largess with the public domain was falling under sharp attack, and at about the time of Meeker's journey Congress rejected Wulsten's application. (To cast ahead: in March, 1870, the Germans emigrated to Wet Mountain Valley anyway and took up adjoining homesteads near a hamlet they named Colfax after the Vice-President of the United States. Crop failures caused by early frosts, penalties for cutting timber on government land without permission, and dissatisfaction with "King Karl" Wulsten's domineering ways led to a dissolution of the group before its five-year pact was ended.)

These signs of quickening immigration whetted not only Palmer's interest but also that of certain of his friends who had worlds of land to sell—Mexican land grants which Governor Manuel Armijo of New Mexico had awarded to certain favored citizens during the early 1840's. On formally taking over the Southwest the United States government had promised, through the treaty of Guadalupe Hidalgo, to honor all the grants that stood on sound legal footing.

Of the several that sprawled along both sides of the Sangre de Cristo Mountains, two were of particular concern to the Palmer group. One was the Beaubien-Miranda Grant, approximately 1.75 million acres, lying east of the Sangre de Cristos in present-day Colfax County, New Mexico, and extending northward a short distance into Colorado. The other, the Sangre de Cristo Grant, a mere 1,038,195 acres, stretched from the crest of the same mountains west to the Rio Grande in southern Colorado. As wildernesses they were not worth much. But if they could be populated with paying colonists . . . the thought was enough to make a speculator's pulse jump.

Lucien Bonaparte Maxwell, one-time beaver trapper and occasional guide for Frémont, had obtained part of the Beaubien-Miranda Grant in New Mexico through inheritance by his wife, Luz Beaubien. The rest he had picked up from the other Beaubien heirs and from Beaubien's one-time partner, Guadalupe Miranda, for a total cash outlay of $35,245. At about the same time William Gilpin of Colorado had bought the Sangre de Cristo Grant for $41,000, but had had to convey an undivided one-sixth interest in it to Wilson Waddingham, an Englishman, in exchange for Waddingham's timely loan. Though the land seemed cheap—none of it cost either purchaser as much as 5 cents an acre—it was not an unalloyed bargain.

In the first place, titles were clouded. Governor Armijo had made the initial awards in bland disregard of an old Mexican law that limited land grants to a single individual to 11 square leagues, approximately 48,800 acres, and twice that to a partnership. Since the original grantees of the estates under question had been partnerships, the United States was trying to hold Maxwell and Gilpin to 97,651 acres each. They of course hired lawyers to show that Armijo had not been bound by the old laws and that the government must fulfill its treaty obligations to them. Long and expensive litigation loomed.

In an effort to attract purchasers to the Sangre de Cristo Grant, Gilpin employed eleven prospectors to examine his mountain slopes. After they had tramped around for fifty-two days he issued a prospectus declaring that they had located twenty-two veins and two placer bars as rich as anything in Gregory Gulch. Grazing potentials, the prospectus continued, were superb and water for irrigation was plentiful. Unfortunately for the author, the prospectus reached the East shortly after the abysmal stock market crash of the Gregory mines. Big money sat on its hands. Small farmers, who could obtain free homesteads just outside the grant, saw no reason to pay for settling inside. As the 1860's drew toward a close Gilpin, heavily in debt by then, had not sold enough land to recover his initial purchase price.

Maxwell, by contrast, was troubled by too many people. Gold had been discovered at Elizabethtown—generally called Etown—on the western part of the grant in 1867, and New Mexico's only considerable placer stampede had filled the shallow valley of Moreno Creek with the usual confusion of sluice boxes, gravel piles, and ramshackle huts. In addition, a few squatters had invaded the grant lands near Fort Union to raise crops for the army and a few Texans had moved into the lower valleys with their longhorn cattle. Most of those people did not even know the grant existed. When informed of it by Maxwell's collectors they were unimpressed. No one in the American land of equal opportunity, they maintained, was entitled to hog nearly two million acres of land on the illegal whim of a defeated Mexican governor. The trespassers sat tight—and so did Eastern investors.

At that point the Kansas Pacific Railroad developed its brief-lived notion of pushing on to California, either by way of Raton Pass, which would take it alongside the Maxwell Grant, or through the San Luis Valley, which would run it across the Sangre de Cristo Grant. Investor interest promptly perked up. Through Wilson Waddingham, whose loan had brought him a sixth interest in the Sangre de Cristo Grant, Gilpin reached the ear of William Blackmore, an adroit and polished English lawyer long familiar with the West.

Blackmore divided Gilpin's grant into two pieces called Trinchera and Costilla Estates and sought to impress Dutch investors with their potentials by obtaining testimonials from high-placed persons. In December, 1868, Ferdinand Vandeveer Hayden of the United States Geographical and Geologic Survey indiscreetly extolled the area for him as "by far the finest agricultural district I have seen west of the Missouri River. . . . It is believed that sheep will yield an annual income of 90 per cent; cattle 50 to 60 per cent. . . . The lofty range of mountains . . . seems to be charged with ores of gold, silver, copper, lead, and iron." The Dutch firm of Wertheim & Gompertz listened longingly, but they were still worried about the title and for the time being held back.

Blackmore and Waddingham also joined a syndicate being formed to purchase the Maxwell Grant. Most of the other members were Coloradoans headed by Jerome Chaffee, who had made money in Gregory Gulch and then had plunged into politics. Chaffee's political connections gave him entrée to a smooth-functioning New Mexico machine called the Santa Fe Ring, and these intertwinings may have left the syndicate untroubled by so small a thing as a cloudy title. Anyway, the syndicate purchased Maxwell's holdings for $650,000 (not bad for a beaver trapper) and set up a selling agency called the Maxwell Land Grant Company. Figurehead president of this company was William Jackson Palmer, who, it will be recalled, had run surveys for the Kansas Pacific through both Raton

Pass and the San Luis Valley. Affairs looked prosperous enough that a group of English capitalists attracted by Blackmore and Waddingham promptly took an option to buy out the Maxwell Land Grant Company for $1.35 million.

Troubles then appeared. Congress rejected the appeal of the Kansas Pacific Railroad for additional land grants. Abandoning its California plans, the railroad swung into Denver, and the southern Rockies had no modern transportation in sight to help with their development, unless the Atchison, Topeka, & Santa Fe, which was bogged down in Kansas, somehow came to life. Or unless a new railroad appeared from an unexpected direction.

The brand-new road was Palmer's dream. When the Kansas Pacific's slowdown left the southern mountains open, he decided to jump in ahead of the Atchison, Topeka, & Santa Fe and build a line, to be called the Denver & Rio Grande, from Denver south across Raton Pass to Santa Fe and eventually to El Paso, Texas—the only north-south line in the West.

Denver businessmen applauded the plan because it would pull southern Colorado's yet-to-be-developed traffic toward them, away from the Kansas-oriented Atchison, Topeka, & Santa Fe. The Sangre de Cristo and Maxwell Land Grant people approved because they could not expand without a railroad—a matter of import to Palmer because he hoped that their interest would lead Blackmore and other Englishmen associated with the grants to push the sale of his railroad bonds in Europe.

To be free to further these ends Palmer resigned as president of the Maxwell Land Grant Company. He could not resign from the Kansas Pacific, however, until track laying had been completed into Denver. He was still nominally engaged on that work in October, 1869, when he escorted the Eastern financiers and Nathan Meeker along the Arkansas Valley to Pueblo, a hamlet of 600 people, and then north toward Denver. As they rode he talked freely of the nascent civilization he foresaw—he wanted publicity of course—and pointed to the area that appealed to him most, the smiling valley of Fountain Creek at the shaggy foot of Pikes Peak. It was not only good farm land, he insisted, but someday its stupendous scenery and the mineral springs bubbling in the canyon five miles farther west would make it a resort for vacationers and health seekers. The only thing necessary was to step up the flow of people—to the towns Palmer projected, to the grant lands, to the entire territory.

It was a heady vision. Meeker was full of it when they reached Denver, where he parted from his traveling companions. Seeking more information, he turned to a fellow journalist, William Byers, ubiquitous editor of the *Rocky Mountain News,* a Gregory Gulch acquaintance of Horace Greeley's, and the man best calculated, in the strange workings of providence, to fire Meeker's western fever still higher.

To sell the alternate, mile-square sections which had been granted them by the government, the Kansas Pacific and Denver Pacific railroads had established the National Land Company. Byers was the land company's general manager in Denver. Although he knew as little of practical agriculture as Meeker, he had already worked up an exuberant sales pitch. Colorado farming, he said, was bound to be profitable because of the unfailing market of the mines and because the distance from other agricultural areas precluded competition. As for that old canard about the Great American Desert, forget it. Dryness was a benefit. In the rainless West weather did not interfere with planting or harvesting. A man applied water by irrigation only when he needed it, in amounts exactly suited to his crops. Moreover, so Byers and other enthusiasts believed, the waters of the mountain rivers, like the waters of the Nile, carried fertilizing chemicals that would perpetually renew the soil.[1]

When Meeker continued north to board a Denver Pacific train—its workers were currently laying its rails south from Cheyenne—Byers went with him and showed him what he declared were the best railroad lands available in Colorado, those near the junction of the Cache la Poudre and South Platte rivers, some 20 miles out on the plains from the foothills. This visit, together with what he had heard from Palmer about immigration, about land grants, and about the Georgia and German colonies, mixed in Meeker's mind, as he journeyed back to New York, with his memories of the Fourier Phalanx. Out of the stew came a dazzling dream. Why could not he, Nathan Meeker, form the ideal cooperative colony, move it somewhere onto those lands he had learned of, and there capture for his followers the golden hope that was America?

He broached his idea in the New York *Tribune* on December 4, 1869. Heart of the colony would be a town called Greeley. Its physical plan, derived from Meeker's reading, sprang straight from the New England townships of colonial times and from the Mormon villages in Utah. In his town, as in theirs, a 10-acre central plaza would be surrounded by 10-acre blocks, each divided into business and residence lots. Outside the town were the farmsteads, their size increasing with their distance from the plaza.

A colonist could own both a town lot and a farm, but individual title would not pass until he had erected a building on his property. Intoxicating beverages were prohibited. A membership fee of $155 would be used to underwrite initial expenses, including communally owned and managed

---

[1] The mineral in the soil of the dry mountain benchlands had not been leached away by eons of heavy rain, and when irrigating waters were first turned onto the fields, production was extraordinary—but not because of the chemicals in the water, as boosters supposed. Actually, the irrigating waters also acted as leaching agents, and at times deposited harmful alkalis in the place of the beneficial phosphates they removed. Sanity about irrigation, upon which most Western agriculture depends, was achieved slowly, painfully, and expensively.

irrigation ditches. Once launched, the colony would support itself by selling land on a rising market to latecomers.

Response was fervent. Eight hundred letters arrived within two or three weeks. Scores of people attended an organization meeting held December 23, 1869, at the Cooper Institute in New York City. Horace Greeley was elected treasurer and Nathan Meeker president of what was named Union Colony. Vice-President was Robert A. Cameron, a jovial six-foot, 206-pound Indiana newspaperman and politician, one-time major general in the Union Army.

Meeker talked in terms of 70,000 acres. Although he did not pinpoint the location of this sizable block of land for fear that speculators would move in ahead of him and raise prices, he seems to have had from the beginning a preference for the area Byers had shown him near the junction of the Cache la Poudre and South Platte rivers, midway between Denver and Cheyenne.

As soon as news of the colony was spread, other interests clamored for a hearing. The Union Pacific wanted to show Meeker its lands in the Bear River Valley of southwestern Wyoming; Gilpin extolled the Sangre de Cristo Grant; Palmer spoke up for Fountain Creek at the foot of Pikes Peak. To placate them, as well as his own members, Meeker formed a locating committee composed of himself, one of his grown sons, vice-president Robert Cameron, and two other men. These site-seers started for the West on February 3, 1870. It was a perfunctory visit. They never reached the San Luis Valley, being turned around near Pueblo by reports of impassable snowdrifts in the mountains. On March 11 they were back in New York City, recommending the purchase of the lands along the South Platte.

The transaction, completed April 5, proved more expensive than anticipated. The 9,324.6 acres obtained from the Denver Pacific cost $31,058.58, an average of $3.44 an acre. The purchasers also had to buy out several homesteaders who had settled here and there on the public domain between the railroad sections. These 2,592.2 acres cost $27,982.30, roughly $10.80 an acre.

Instead of 70,000 acres Meeker had thus acquired fewer than 12,000. The fact that he held an option on another 50,000 acres of Denver Pacific land (never exercised in full) and had initiated homestead procedures in the names of individual colonists for several thousand more acres (few of the homesteads were ever "proved up") did not calm his more virulent critics. They felt cheated. So did many others when they reached the site.

The vanguard, some three hundred strong, appeared late in April and early in May. In their innocence many had expected a town to be ready. All they saw was an endless expanse of gravelly soil thinly covered with buffalo grass and cactus. Streets had not been laid out; no ditch was dug.

Meeker was still in the East, completing financial details, and Cameron, who looked to one of the new arrivals "like a seedy, cast-off, played-out, third-rate politician," failed to inspire confidence. Crying swindle, fifty or so of the new arrivals left for home on the next train.

The remainder, inspired by Meeker's belated appearance, settled down to the hard facts of town building. For shelter while working they obtained nine surplus army tents from Fort Russell near Cheyenne and imported some abandoned shacks from the one-time railhead at Evans, four miles away. These proving inadequate, the town officials purchased in Cheyenne, for $1,050, a wooden hall 64 feet long by 34 feet wide, knocked it apart and shipped the planks to Greeley. Reassembling them, they divided the shelter into two rooms, the larger for men, the smaller for families. (Most married colonists had left their families at home while creating new dwellings.) Inside the hall were rows of bunks filled with hay. Meals were cooked on stoves set up outdoors or over fires built on the ground. The proud providers of the building called it Hotel De Comfort. The occupants promptly renamed it Hotel Discomfort.

Timber cutters went into the hills to chop down trees and float the timber along the Cache la Poudre to a sawmill in Greeley. The stream, shrunken by a dry spring, proved inadequate and sawn lumber had to be brought from as far away as Chicago. Meanwhile a miner named Mc-Donald, who had built ditches for placer operations in the mountains, took a contract to bring irrigating water to the vegetable gardens in Greeley. (The fields outside would have to wait for a second ditch.) Because construction theories current at the time said that water run through a few parallel plow furrows would do most of the digging by erosion, McDonald contented himself with scratching out a canal 10 miles long, 8 feet wide, but only 15 inches deep. In following the bluffs along the river, he made his bends too sharp. In coming down hills he built no checks. As a result the water did not erode anything in some places, too much in others.

While thirsty gardens panted and shade trees imported from Illinois for $1,500 died of thirst, McDonald straightened bends, filled hollows, deepened cuts through flat places. Before the ditch was working adequately bills had reached $25,000. It was an unhappy omen. The first farm ditch, built during the winter and spring of 1870–71, reached the outlying fields too late to save most of the 2,000 acres that had been sown in anticipation of its arrival. Its ultimate bill was $87,000. All told, Meeker had projected four canals to cost an estimated $20,000. Before the four were constructed, the last two by outside capital, expenses had reached $412,000, a burden on the farms twenty times greater than expected.

There were other troubles. The snowless winter of 1870–71 dried the range and drove starving cattle into the towns—into Denver as well as into Greeley. In Greeley they ate the last of the struggling trees, 250,000 new strawberry plants, even the tarpaper off the sides of the shacks. Angry residents impounded as many steers as they could catch and held them for damages in an unused barnyard. One Sunday morning while nearly everyone was at church and only a single guard was on duty at the pound, masked men rode up and made off with the herd. In the end the only recourse the colonists found was to build a fence entirely around the town and the outlying fields. The cost—an unanticipated $20,000.

There were bitter complaints. Mrs. A. M. Green, who later achieved local notoriety for writing and producing a satiric play called *Ten Years on the Great American Desert,* proclaimed snippily to the world that she knew the cause of a mysterious house fire in Greeley; dismayed at its prospects, the unhappy building had committed suicide. And yet . . . the morning air did tingle, afternoon cloud banks did tower with almost unbearable brightness over Longs Peak to the west, evening primroses did open wide to the summer dusk. Water ran; the miracle of greenness came. More colonists arrived than left, and they believed fervently in the promise Meeker had given them. Within a year Greeley boasted 1,500 people, "a city well laid out," reported the Denver *Tribune* on May 16, 1871, "well built, with all literary and religious advantages, all industries thriving, raising products enough to be more than self-sustaining . . . needing no courts, no calaboose, one of the most thoroughly alive and stirring, and yet the quietest community in the west."

The influx impressed William Palmer. On October 27, 1870, he had incorporated the Denver & Rio Grande Railroad. On November 7, in Flushing, Long Island, he married his twenty-year-old fiancée, Mary Mellen, called Queen by her doting father, William Proctor Mellen, a prominent New York lawyer and financier. On November 9 the couple sailed for England on a honeymoon, or so Queen Palmer supposed. Actually her husband spent most of his evenings with a young friend, Dr. William Bell, who, for a lark had joined Palmer's Kansas Pacific surveys to California some years earlier and who now arranged, along with William Blackmore, an endless series of meetings with British capitalists. After all, a honeymoon could wait; raising money for the West's only north-south railroad could not.

The federal government had refused to give the D&RG any more public domain land than a strip 200 feet wide along its right-of-way. Forced thus to stern economies, Palmer adopted for his railroad the light narrow-gauge tracks (3 feet between rails) that had been tried successfully in parts of Europe. The diminutive rails, cars, and locomotives were not only much cheaper than the equipment used by the American broad-gauge roads (4 feet 8½ inches between rails) but they would allow tighter curves, steeper grades, and hence more economical construction in the mountains. By thus shrinking his ambitions, Palmer raised money enough to make a beginning. He hurried Queen back to Flushing, left her there, and sped on west to begin his great adventure.

One of the D&RG's new directors was Ellen Hunt's husband, Alexander Cameron Hunt, fired the year before as territorial governor of Colorado to make room for one of President Grant's political hacks. During Palmer's absence, Hunt and young Irving Howbert, clerk of El Paso County at the foot of Pikes Peak, had obtained for Palmer some 9,300 acres where Fountain Creek and Monument Creek run together—the very land in which Palmer had once tried to interest Meeker. They had done it shrewdly, by buying up all the agricultural scrip they could lay hold of. Agricultural colleges were financed in each state of the Union by the sale of public domain lands. Eastern states with no public land left within their borders were granted acreage in Western territories. Nominally worth $1.25 an acre, this land was traded by means of scrip, which in 1870–71 was selling at 80 cents. By dealing in this and by buying out homesteaders who had settled in the vicinity, Hunt and Howbert secured the 9,300-acre tract at an average cost of $1.07 an acre.

Palmer sold 2,000 of these acres at $15 an acre to what he called the Colorado Springs Company, although the nearest mineral springs were five miles away up the canyon of Fountain Creek. This gave him a gain of $20,000 on his purchase price. The idea was that the Colorado Springs Company (of which Palmer was president) would divide each $15 acre into several business and residence lots and sell each lot for $50 to $100 to members of a group to be called Fountain Colony, each of whom paid a $100 initiation fee. Profits from these sales were to be devoted by the town company to public improvements—ditches, parks, graded streets, schoolhouses, and so on. Besides these things the members also gained the advantage of living in a town whose property values would soar by virtue of its being the first target for the Denver & Rio Grande Railroad. The chief gain for Palmer (and his backers) would lie in the 7,300 acres he still held just outside the town. If the town succeeded, the value of the adjoining land was bound to skyrocket.

To run Colorado Springs, which obviously drew part of its inspiration from Meeker's more altruistic colony, Palmer hired three Greeley citizens, Robert A. Cameron, William E. Pabor, and E. S. Nettleton. They drove the first survey stake on July 31, 1871. By year's end Engineer Nettleton had nearly finished two ditches totaling 25 miles in length. One hundred and ninety-seven members had paid the Colorado Springs Company $36,059 for farm lands and town lots, and had erected 159 building to shelter approximately 750 people, all before the first little passenger train steamed in on January 1, 1872.

Among the passengers who rode subsequent trains were a breed of people who seldom stopped at Greeley—tourists. Much of Palmer's railroad and colony money was provided by Philadelphia and London investors, among whose stately mansions he moved with easy grace, telling them fascinating tales of the thrilling new West he was opening with his droll baby railroad. They came in droves to see, to sip the mineral waters at Manitou Springs, where a fine new hotel had opened, and to tramp and ride horseback through the dusky canyons and beside the glistening waterfalls. Though they constituted only a minor part of the population, they were so noticeable that soon Colorado Springs was being called, half satirically and half enviously, Little Lunnon.

Many of these outsiders were so captivated by the area that they built summer homes back among the crags and evergreens. Emulating them, Palmer slowly created in the rough wilds of Queen's Canyon a vast, turreted pile that he named Glen Eyrie. Queen never liked it. In the 1880's she packed up their three daughters and left her husband—a polite separation, not a scandalous divorce—and lived thereafter first in Newport, Rhode Island, and later in Surry, near the trimmer refinements of big London.

From Colorado Springs, Palmer straightway pushed the D&RG south to Pueblo, then west up the Arkansas toward Canon City at the mouth of the Royal Gorge. By threatening to bypass both towns unless they helped him, he persuaded the voters to authorize a total of $250,000 in municipal bonds for his benefit. Instead of building into the hearts of the towns, however, the Denver & Rio Grande put its depots on lands its agents had secretly purchased outside the city limits. There it created new colonies to sell more building lots, much as it had in Colorado Springs. True, the old towns benefited also. As Palmer pointed out to the stony-mouthed voters, stagecoaches in 1870 had carried an average of thirty passengers a week along the Front Range. In 1872 the stubby little passenger coaches of the baby railroad averaged more than twice that figure every day, to say nothing of freight. In little more than a year Pueblo's population rose from 600 or so to more than 3,000. But to men who were paying taxes on the bonds none of those statistics made up for the railroad's arrogant disregard of its implied promises.

Meanwhile the magic of the tracks was rippling out far ahead of construction to the one-time Mexican land grants. William Gilpin and William Blackmore, it will be recalled, had hoped to speed the development of the Sangre de Cristo Grant by dividing it into two pieces, the Costilla Estate in the south, the Trinchera Estate in the north. This alone had failed to impress the Dutch firm of Wertheim & Gompertz, to whom they had turned for financing, but on the approach of the railroad the Hollanders bought $1 million worth of stock in Costilla Estate, to be disposed of in Europe.[2] The same firm also interested itself in the Maxwell Grant. The prospect of the railroad had led the English company to take up its option with Chaffee's Colorado syndicate. That done, the new Maxwell Land Grant Company issued $3 million worth of stock on the holdings, and Wertheim & Gompertz also agreed to underwrite this.

[2] In the 1880's Palmer bought Trinchera Estate.

At that point the Panic of 1873 halted railroad building everywhere. The Denver & Rio Grande stalled at Pueblo, the Atchison, Topeka & Santa Fe near the Kansas border. Dolefully the grants tried to struggle on without them. On the Costilla Estate, Blackmore, Gilpin, and the anxious Dutch representatives dug ditches, erected flour mills, brought in sheep, but the land was less amenable and the supply of water shorter than Gilpin had said in his exuberance. Even renewed railway construction—the D&RG spiraled over La Veta Pass to Garland City near old Fort Garland in 1876—failed to help very much. But at least the year '76 brought one success. The United States Supreme Court belatedly confirmed the full 1,038,195 acres of the grant.

This reinspired the British owners of the Maxwell barony. Expecting Congress to whittle down the area claimed by the owners from 1,714,764 acres to a "legal" 97,651, squatters had swarmed across the domain. When collectors for the company ordered them either to pay for the land they occupied or get out, they banded together behind their Methodist minister, F. J. Tolby, and defied the owners.

In September, 1875, Tolby was murdered near Elizabethtown, supposedly by two Mexicans in the employ of the Maxwell Land Grant Company. Another Methodist minister, Oscar P. McMains, thereupon rounded up a mob that lynched one of the suspects. The other was shot from ambush. Martial law was then declared, possibly at the behest of the company, which had potent political connections, and troops from Fort Union restored uneasy order.

During this period the Maxwell people heard that Gilpin had won his fight. Hang on . . . but they could not do it. Investors would not come into such a mess. The owners skipped another interest payment on their bonds, and the Dutch took over.

Eventually, in 1879, Congress confirmed the grant in full.[3] Charges of corruption resounded; countersuits to the grants' eviction orders were entered in the U.S. Supreme Court. Meantime the Santa Fe Railroad built across Raton Pass and south along the grant's eastern border. Land values jumped; squatters grew still more defiant. The enraged grant owners imported thirty-five gunmen led by Bat Masterson to eject the trespassers. Before a clash could develop, the government marched in troops and checked the violence, except for two soldiers who were shot in brawls. After years of suspense the Supreme Court finally, in 1887, declared in favor of the grant. Government agents were then ordered to enforce the edict in favor of a hated foreign corporation—a situation that led the

[3] Gilpin and the Maxwell Land Grant people were more fortunate than the claimants of the gargantuan 4,000,000-acre Vigil–St. Vrain Grant that ran from the Sangre de Cristo Mountains east to the Purgatory River, north and northeast of the Maxwell Grant. Congress and the Supreme Court held that one to the maximum of 97,651 acres allowed under old Mexican law.

settlers of Stonewall Valley, under square-topped Fishers Peak near Trinidad, Colorado, to burn down a building occupied by U.S. marshals and then barricade themselves in their homes to fight off the posses that came after them.

Eventually the grant owners liquidated their troublesome holdings in good order. . . . But all this has taken us a long way from what turned out to be the more significant developments farther north.

Deciding in mid-1872 that Indian troubles had ended in eastern Colorado, the army threw open to purchase its military reservation at Fort Collins on the Cache la Poudre River 25 miles northwest of Greeley. Scenting opportunity, those compulsive town-formers, R. A. Cameron and W. E. Pabor, first of Greeley and then of Colorado Springs, stirred together a hash of Meeker-style, Palmer-style promotion, called it the Fort Collins Agricultural Colony, bought 3,000 acres of the reserve, and offered memberships, at a price, to still more hopefuls.

To wet their dry acres they dug two ditches. Both tapped the Cache la Poudre above the headgates of the Greeley canals. The first water was turned into them in the spring of 1874, a desperately dry year. By the time the Fort Collins farmers had taken the water they felt they needed, none was left for Greeley.

Representatives of the two towns met in a schoolhouse in neutral Eaton, north of Greeley, to seek a solution. The Greeley men demanded that the Fort Collins ditches be closed; *they* owned the water by right of prior appropriation. If their demand was not heeded, they would extend their canals above those of the rival town and choke them off. The Fort Collins people retorted that the Greeley colony had not placed any definite claim on record, but had simply taken what was coming along, and that anyway water belonged, by common law, to the land next to it. No one at the bottom of a stream could dictate what happened 25 miles farther up.

According to David Boyd, who was at the meeting, the talk was growing excited when a providential rain cooled both the parched fields and the hot tempers. Later meetings worked out a temporary division of such water as existed that year. Storage reservoirs were promulgated for the future. Their own battle solved, the town leaders then took long overdue cognizance of the far greater flood of water troubles that was likely to overwhelm them if the irresponsible promotions sweeping the territory were not checked.

The year before, William Byers and the editors of the *Star of Empire,* a publicity organ for the National Land Company, had dreamed up a dazzling stunt to draw attention to the railroad lands they were pushing. They summoned the world's first Irrigation Congress to meet in Denver on October 15, 1873. Delegates attended from six states and territories— Kansas, Nebraska, Wyoming, Colorado, New Mexico, and Utah. Soaring oratory cried for government land grants to aid a canal company in building a ditch 550 miles long from the point where the South Platte emerged from the mountains to the Missouri River. While this was being built, said engineer Fred M. Stanton, a stopgap could be provided by a ditch only 100 miles long, 12 feet wide, and 3 feet deep that would irrigate 25 million acres in eastern Colorado, 1.15 million of them owned by the Kansas Pacific.

At this point J. Max Clark, the delegate from Greeley, rose in protest. He'd had experience in these matters, he said. "I am accustomed to carry the mud of the waters of irrigation on my boot heels, and the brown dust of the desert in my hair." He produced statistics. In order to irrigate 750,000 acres—one thirty-fourth of what Stanton was talking about—a ditch would have to be built capable of carrying 11,362 cubic feet of water per second, a ditch 200 feet wide and 9½ feet deep. Even if Stanton raised the money to build such a monster, he would never fill it. The watershed of the South Platte River did not produce that much.

Byers' *Rocky Mountain News* attacked Clark savagely, sneering that before he ventured into such company again he had better clean his boots, shampoo his hair, and tidy up his "wordy bundle of absurdities." Shouting the Greeley delegates down, the rest of the convention passed and sent to President Grant resolutions urging government support of a canal from the mountains to the Missouri. Grant referred the proposal to Congress. Enthusiastically backed by the *Rocky Mountain News,* Stanton and other promoters promptly incorporated the Colorado Canal, Irrigation, and Land Company. Their plan was to launch a modest ditch, 50 feet wide and 6 feet deep, for transporting 7,960 cubic feet of South Platte water to 10.25 million acres of government and railroad land. Of course that much water existed —their prospectus said. At its lowest stage in the fall the South Platte carried 3,665 cubic feet per second. During the irrigating season it flowed 10,000 feet or more.[4]

At the very time the company was printing these figures the South Platte's principal tributary, the Cache la Poudre, was proving incapable of supplying the two hamlets of Greeley and Fort Collins. One critic chortled that at least the eastern end of Stanton's ditch would be a fine storage place for the army's gunpowder; it would never get wet there. Congress ignored the Western effusions, and the canal company perished from inattention.

The farce brought home to thoughtful Coloradoans the perils of ignorance. How much water were they going to need in the future to feed their growing population? How much water did they have? How far could it be stretched by means of storage and improved distribution?

It was a shock to discover that no one could answer, not even the

---

[4] The facts: the normal high of the South Platte at Denver is 1,500 cubic feet per second. During the drought of September, 1888, it shrank to 100 feet.

Mormons or Spanish Americans, who had been practicing irrigation the longest. They could talk in rule-of-thumb fashion about their own fields, but they could not produce dependable statistics that would help an entire district gauge the amounts of water used, at what intervals, by different crops in varying soils. No one had the faintest notion of how many additional gallons a miner, manufacturer, or domestic user might drain from the creeks. Since no one had yet devised an accurate method of measuring stream flow, no one really could say how much water did come out of the mountains. No social theories had yet faced the problem of allocating priorities when streams ran shallow and interests clashed. How, then, could realistic laws be established to protect individual hay growers, housewives at their laundry tubs, blacksmiths in their foundries when future promotions, more modest perhaps than the Colorado Canal, Irrigation, and Land Company and hence more dangerous, really began to roll?

Times were propitious for grappling with the problem. Republicans controlled Colorado politics at the time, and the Republican Congress felt the need of more Republican electoral votes to assure a Republican President in 1876. Accordingly a new enabling act was passed in 1875 to allow Colorado Territory to apply again for statehood. This involved the drawing up of a state constitution, and that in turn gave anxious farmers along the Front Range an opportunity to insist that their organic laws come face to face with the realities of water in the arid West.

Custom among farmers and miners from Colorado to California had long since defied common law in granting a man the right to take water out of a natural stream channel and to transport it as far as he wished, providing always that he used it beneficially at the end of his ditch and did not simply try to keep control of it for speculative purposes. Custom further decreed that a man could assure himself of the water he needed by posting a notice beside a headgate which said that he claimed so many inches of its flow, just as he could post a notice on a placer bar, saying that so many feet of its earth were his. Water, in other words, was property, to be surrounded like other forms of property with a corpus of protective laws. Chief among the rights adhering to it was the common American privilege of owning a part of the country's natural resources by virtue of getting there first—the doctrine, to state matters more formally, of prior appropriation.

Mining districts had long since verbalized one or another of the practical phases of this principle in their code books, crudely enough sometimes.[5] A

[5] From the 1859 code of a mining district in Gilpin County, Colorado: "It shall be the previlege of enny miner or Miners to take the water out of North Clear Creek in a ditch or floom around enny mans Claim or over his Claim for the purpose of washing Dirt on the Hill Side by Hydraulic power or Slusing not ingering the claims passing thare over." The Wisconsin district of Gilpin County declared, July 12, 1860, that "all water claims shall be held as real estate and not jumpable."

few courts had tiptoed around the edges of the problem. The Colorado state constitution was the first to express it as a matter of organic law, however, and so, as the principle extended in writing throughout every Western state, it became known as the Colorado Doctrine. Stump orators are inclined to view it as a majestic milestone. Possibly it was not, as we shall see when we come to the clash between social need and private rights that still torments Western water policies. But at least the doctrine was a recognition by mountain dwellers that they had moved into a new environment and needed a new body of laws to express their adaptations to it.

Colonies, land-grant companies, railroads, the prophets of irrigation, and the immigration boards which both Colorado and Wyoming supported out of public funds inundated the East with rhapsodies about the glories of the West. A subtler, less commercial propaganda came from the annual reports of the government's Geological and Geographical Surveys headed by Ferdinand V. Hayden.

The most striking example was Hayden's espousal of the Yellowstone Park idea. Although the region's mud pots, geysers, towering waterfalls, and chromatic canyons had long been known to fur trappers, prospectors, and random wanderers, and were the source of Jim Bridger's tallest tales— petrified birds singing petrified songs on petrified trees—no widely distributed description of the area appeared until the spring of 1871. In May and June of that year Nathaniel Langford published in *Scribner's Monthly* two exuberant articles, "Wonders of Yellowstone," describing the sights witnessed by two parties of amateur Montana explorers during 1869 and 1870. Even before the article appeared the editors were sure it would create a sensation and they wanted more.

Hayden meantime had been stirred by Langford's lectures in the East and by accounts prepared for the government by H. D. Washburn, surveyor general of Montana Territory, who had been on one of the early trips. Captivated by the excitement, he laid plans to examine the area officially during the summer of 1871. Learning of this, the editors of *Scribner's* prevailed on him to take along their top artist, Thomas Moran, so that future articles could be illustrated with worthy drawings.

During the trip Hayden picked up an idea developed earlier by Montana citizens familiar with the region. Why not keep its scenic wonders out of the grasp of private exploiters by setting the area aside as a national park, emulating a step already taken in Yosemite by joint action of the federal government and the state of California? The thought appealed to Hayden. Fortifying his arguments with Moran's sketches and the magnificent wet-plate prints of the expedition's photographer, William Henry Jackson, he aided Montana's delegate to Congress in pushing through the necessary legislation.

Another exploration of both Yellowstone and the Grand Tetons, vaulting above Jackson Hole, followed in 1872.[6] The next three years Hayden spent in Colorado, creating superb economic and topographic maps. Developers of all kinds seized eagerly on them. The general public was equally fascinated by Jackson's photographs of the Mount of the Holy Cross, of the ancient cliff dwellings along the edges of present Mesa Verde National Park, of the romantic pueblo of the Taos Indians, all of which and more became firmly planted in the nation's awareness.

More romance rained down from the weather station which the U.S. Signal Corps, parent of the Weather Bureau, placed atop Pikes Peak in 1873, constructing a horseback trail in the course of doing it which tourists immediately appropriated. In 1873 a house atop a Rocky Mountain peak was a space-age adventure. Feature stories about the weather station filled the Eastern newspapers. Still more publicity resulted from the fertile imagination of Sergeant John Timothy O'Keeffe, who manned the lonely post from 1875 to 1881. When he grew bored on his lofty perch he amused himself by concocting tall tales about his mule Balaam, a sea serpent stranded in one of the timberline lakes, a midwinter volcanic eruption amidst the ice and snow.

Climax of his inventions was an account of an attack on his station by famished pack rats. For desperate hours he and his wife (O'Keeffe had, in truth, no wife) fought the vermin with blazing discharges of "electric fluid" from a battery. Eventually they won, only to find that the rats had devoured their baby Erin, leaving naught but a "peeled and mumbled skull." A friend in Colorado Springs, Eliphalet Price (that's truly his name), gave these tales a literary flourish and placed them in a British newspaper. From there they spread throughout the world. So many of the tourists who by then were climbing and riding up the trail to the station wanted to revel in the disaster that O'Keeffe heaped up a grave, carved a touching headboard, and sold pictures of it to the shivering dudes for 50 cents each.

How many people were moved by these varied outpourings to seek new lives in the West is impossible to gauge. It may have been an appreciable total, for the vibrant descriptions, however fanciful, served to confirm what many a restless individual was already feeling. Release, opportunity, and excitement lay out yonder. As the belief mounted, the boom years of the Rockies began to roll.

---

[6] During the 1872 trip Langford and James Stevenson scaled the Grand Teton, or at least Langford said they did. William Owen of Laramie, who mastered the Grand with another party in August, 1898, came down swearing that nothing on the peak matched Langford's descriptions and obviously he had not climbed it. The controversy became so noisy that the Wyoming legislature at last passed a resolution awarding the laurels to Owen. The diary of another member of the 1872 trip, Sidford Hamp, though not conclusive, would seem to indicate that Langford and Stevenson really had succeeded. See Herbert O. Brayer, "Exploring the Yellowstone with Hayden . . . ," *Annals of Wyoming,* October, 1942.

XVI

SILVER THREADS

SOMEWHERE or another in the course of his hyperbole every promoter of railroads and agriculture in Colorado glanced toward the mines. There his confidence was renewed. No matter how stringently doubters might shrink his estimates about water, they could not contradict official statistics about the jump in mineral production. In 1868 the miners of the territory had turned out $2,010,000 in gold and $406,139 in silver. In 1871, when the population was little more than 40,000, the figures rose to $3,633,951 for gold and $1,029,059 for silver. Moreover, the increased wealth was coming from deep veins, with all that this shift toward permanence implied for the providers of food, equipment, and transport.

The upsurge owed much of its vigor to Nathaniel Peter Hill. In 1864, at the time of the collapse of Gregory Gulch mining stock, Hill was a thirty-two-year-old instructor in metallurgical chemistry at his alma mater, Brown University in Providence, Rhode Island. Eastern investors hurt by the Gregory debacle employed him to take a summer trip to Gilpin County, Colorado, and estimate the future.

He was a prim New Englander with a walrus mustache and straight, fine-spun hair that he parted neatly on the left. He did not drink, smoke, or swear. Worried about the food and water in the wilderness, he journeyed west with twenty-four bottles of concentrated lemon juice as a guard against scurvy and a jar of cayenne pepper for purifying water, one pinch per glass. His chemicals and scientific paraphernalia he sent ahead in several trunks.

In Denver he fell into the clutches of William Gilpin, who personally escorted him through scenery "grand and sublime beyond description" to Central City. His examinations completed, Hill went with the ex-governor to the Sangre de Cristo Grant to report on whatever ore Gilpin's hired prospectors turned up. Tired of waiting for them to come in and suffering indigestion from the Mexican food, he returned abruptly to Denver in a buggy driven by an officer from Fort Garland, who solemnly apologized to his solemn passenger each time he swore at the mules.

From Denver, Hill returned to Central City. There he rented a house, an action which suggests that he, like Nathan Meeker, had caught a new vision in the West quite apart from his original assignment. Then, almost as though reluctant to return east, he rode with his lemon juice far and wide through the central part of the territory, ending up in a blinding October snowstorm on the shoulder of Mount Elbert, highest peak in the Rocky Mountains, whither he had been lured to examine what its owner declared was the richest gold property in the world. No one has heard of the mine since.

Returning finally to Providence and Boston, Hill pinned down several financiers and told them about a plan which, to his thinking, offered greater possibilities than any hole in the ground. Colorado miners, he said, were throwing away as much as three-quarters of their gold because, no matter how finely they pulverized ore in their stamp mills, they could not break down the chemical combinations that locked up the metal. Smelting was the answer. A few Coloradoans were struggling with crude plants, but they lacked the technology necessary to deal with their highly complex ores. Hill thought that with proper backing he could succeed.

The men to whom he talked sent him back to Colorado by stagecoach through the bitter weather of February, 1865, to study the economics involved—the terms he could make with mineowners, the costs of labor, fuel, and transportation, the availability of building sites, and so on. The upshot was the formation, in the East, of the Boston and Colorado Smelting Company.

The papers drawn up, Hill once again rode jouncing stagecoaches back to Gregory Gulch. This time he bought several wagonloads of ore from the Bobtail mine high above the town of Black Hawk, where the gulch runs into the North Fork of Clear Creek. Slowly he creaked with his purchase to the Mississippi River and from there sent it by steamer and freighter to the great smelting center of Swansea, Wales. In that "filthy, crowded, smoky, dingy town" (Hill's words) he joined talents with some of the world's best industrial metallurgists to work out the problem that had all but strangled Colorado mining.

Egyptians had learned the basic steps of smelting sulphide copper ores millennia ago. A man threw broken ore and fuel into a furnace—coke and charcoal were the best fuels since they allowed free passage to air—added a flux of limestone to promote liquidity and to float off impurities, and fired up. The sulphur burned away as an acrid gas. The copper picked up the gold in the ore, together with a few stubborn impurities, and formed a "matte" from which the gold could later be removed by more delicate refining. The presence of copper in the Gregory Gulch veins had led miners to try to capture their gold in a copper matte, but the process was not working because of strange chemical reactions set up by other elements also present—traces of arsenic, antimony, zinc, lead, and whatnot.

Schoolteacher Hill had figured out on paper how to overcome these obstacles. The engineers at Swansea helped him adapt one of their furnaces so that he could determine whether his theories would prove out in practice. They did, after several bugs had been smoothed away, and back to Colorado he went.

In 1867 he imported iron and firebrick from the East, bought a flat piece of ground in the pinched canyon bottom at Black Hawk, and out of stone built a multichimneyed plant that for the next decade filled Gregory Gulch as far as Central City with a noxious yellow smoke. For fuel he used charcoal. Vast ore and lumber wagons churned the roads into endless booby traps. Woodcutters, charcoal burners, and fumes from the chimneys made ghastly deserts of the miles of hillsides over which William Byers had lamented as early as 1861.

Near the plant which was the center of this dreariness Nathaniel Hill built a fine house for his family. Around the home, pretentious behind gingerbread scrollwork on the eaves and the porch, he planted spruce trees, apparently unaware of the irony involved. They were the only vegetation visible. But who cared? Through the magic of science Gilpin County had learned to save its mineral.

Timing was propitious. Almost from the beginning of the Colorado mining rush prospectors had realized that silver existed with the gold in many of the mines. Generally it occurred in chemical combination with other elements, however, and so the impatient prospectors had let it go while concentrating on the free gold. Then, in 1864, such rich silver ore was found in veins near what became Georgetown, in the deep russet canyon of the South Fork of Clear Creek, that crude recovery processes were established. A rush into Clear Creek County followed. Again expectations were dashed by inadequate recovery, as they had been in Gilpin County to the north.

Baffled investors called for help on a renowned Cornish metallurgist who had been trained at Swansea, Richard Pearce. Pearce soon saw what needed doing but he could not bring it to pass, partly because the ores on the South Fork did not contain sufficient copper for a matte and partly because cheap fluxing materials were not at hand. Nathaniel Hill had both at Black Hawk, a few precipitous miles away. They joined forces, Hill as business manager and Pearce as engineer. By the end of 1872 they had worked out methods for smelting silver ores as well as gold at their Black Hawk plant. At first they sent the mattes outside for refining, but Pearce soon devised ways of handling them, too.

By no means every mine in the district used the Black Hawk facility. Capacity at first was limited to about ten tons of ore a day, which Hill purchased outright from the miners. Because his costs were high he did not pay what many of them thought they should receive on the basis of their assay reports. They kept stubbornly on in their old ways. Others found it more economical to crush their ore in stamp mills, recover what free gold they could by amalgamation, then send the concentrated residues to the Boston and Colorado plant for final smelting. Volume, however, was not the significant thing about Hill's and Pearce's accomplishments. Once they had broken through the technological barriers, other men followed and Rocky Mountain smelting was launched on the smoky career which made possible the development of a multibillion-dollar mining industry.

The first notable silver mine discovered outside of Clear Creek County was the Caribou, on North Beaver Creek in Boulder County. In the summer of 1869 hunters scrambling through thick evergreen forests 10,000 feet above sea level on the eastern slopes of the Continental Divide chanced to pick up pieces of float ore—fragments that had rolled down the hill from some vein higher up. Emerging at a ranch near Central City several miles to the south, the finders showed the specimens to William Martin. Having worked on the Comstock Lode in Nevada, Martin knew what silver was. He got hold of a piece of the float, learned where the hunters had found it, and hurried to an assay shop in Central City. Just as he'd thought! He persuaded three neighboring ranchers to put up a grub-stake and with George Lytle, an experienced miner, as helper followed the hunters' trail back to North Beaver Creek. They found more float, traced it up the hillside to the vein from which it had tumbled, and on August 31, 1869, opened the great Caribou Lode.

Snow soon drove them out. When they returned in the spring of 1870, carrying their supplies on their backs, three or four hundred people dogged their footsteps—twenty-four of whom they soon hired. Part of this work force they set to hacking out a wagon road through the trees so that they could ship their ore to the Black Hawk smelter. More mines opened, and a town appeared almost overnight. By September 1, 1870, one year after the discovery, three stages a day were arriving from Central City. The Caribou House, which could seat only twenty persons at a time in its dining room, ran nine shifts each meal.

Investors arrived almost as fast as prospectors. After lengthy dickering with Martin, Lytle, and their grubstakers, A. D. Breed of Cincinnati formed a company that paid them, in the fall of 1870, $50,000 for the western half of the original Caribou. Satisfied with their year's accomplishments, the discoverers kept on working the eastern half modestly and profitably.

Breed was more ambitious. He found a meadow five miles away beside Boulder Creek, where water and trees for fuel were plentiful. There at a cost of $200,000 he erected a mill five stories high, resonant with crushers, stamps, roasting cylinders, and amalgamating pans. He then devoted himself to the mine, turning out 3,650 tons of silver ore during 1872. The richest portions of the complex ore—it contained from 235 to 666 ounces of silver per ton, and silver was then worth $1.32 an ounce—was sorted out by hand and sold to the Boston and Colorado smelter. Ores of lower value went through the mill on Boulder Creek.

So far, so good—but expenses were high and Breed decided to try mining gullible foreigners instead. Somehow he made contact with Dutch capitalists. Their examining engineers arrived in Caribou, through deep snow, in March, 1873, and were impressed—as well they might have been. Breed had cleverly opened several exploratory drifts (tunnels) to display 34,000 tons of ore still in place. It was worth, according to the examiners' own valuation, an average of $169 a ton.

Cables hummed and the Mining Company Nederland was capitalized in Holland for $3 million to buy the mine and mill and start large-scale operations. The actual purchase price remains unknown, but it was more than $1 million, a record sale, to that date, for a Rocky Mountain mine. Breed meantime was frenziedly stripping away the best ore. Since he had only six or seven weeks available, it seems unlikely that he could have taken out as much as a thousand tons. They were the richest tons in sight, however, and their gross worth may have approached half a million dollars, though no one actually knows.

The best of this ore he sold to Nathaniel Hill and Richard Pearce. They were delighted with it, and when they heard that President Grant, his wife, and his daughter were about to visit Central City they were struck with a dazzling inspiration. They cast part of the refined silver into several bricks worth $13,000 and with them paved a sidewalk in front of the new Teller House, where Grant was to stay. At first the President did not believe that the silver was real. Assured it was, he remarked that it was very pretty and walked somewhat self-consciously across the gleaming sheen to the door. All America heard of that sidewalk.

That was on April 28, 1873. On April 30 Breed turned the Caribou Mine over to its new owners. Very pretty, he too might have said as he boarded a stagecoach for elsewhere.

The Hollanders always blamed Breed for their inability to make the mine pay. But the excessive optimism of the first examining engineers and the bickerings of high-paid managers seeking to shift onto each other's backs the blame for disappointing returns were equally responsible. In 1875 creditors foreclosed. Jerome Chaffee bought the property at a sheriff's sale and showed that the Caribou, like the other mines in the area, could be made to pay. About all the Dutch got out of it was a memento. The hamlet that grew up around their mill is still known as Nederland, center today of a lovely vacation area.

Europeans hungry for profit seemed particularly susceptible to fast-talking promoters from the Rocky Mountains. Another notorious example with a star-studded cast is the Emma Mine in Alta Basin at the head of Little Cottonwood Canyon in the Wasatch Mountains. The site is even more spectacular than Caribou's. The lower canyon climbs steeply between walls of pale granite from which summer sunlight lances blindingly. Great masses of broken rock have fallen from the cliffs; the creek purls among them with a delicious sound. Here, beginning in 1855, Mormons obtained huge granite blocks for their stately, six-spired, $4 million Temple, still the most striking building in Salt Lake City.

Higher up, the canyon widens into a basin whose sides, as tens of thousands of skiers know, soar in majestic swells toward the peak tops. During the mid-1860's this vast cup was visited by some of Patrick Connor's prospecting California volunteers. They found silver, but not enough to pay for the struggle of getting it out.

Finally only two penniless prospectors, Robert Chisholm and J. F. Woodman were left to scratch away, during successive summers, at a hole they called the Emma. From time to time they talked grubstakes out of various people; this gave each of the suppliers a claim to an interest in the mine. Slowly, meanwhile, the two miners stockpiled a little ore. As soon as the Union Pacific reached Ogden they sorted out the best of the mineral and dragged it on untanned cowhides to the quarry road. There they transferred it to wagons, hauled it to the newly completed railroad, and shipped it to Swansea.

In spite of high expenses, the ore netted $180 a ton.

The rush was on. Many people bought or claimed interests in the Emma. At least seventeen lawyers were involved in the suits, led by Senator William M. Stewart of Nevada, who during the course of the litigation abruptly switched sides and helped squeeze out his original client. In March, 1871, a pair of sharpers named Parks and Baxter obtained control at a cost of $375,000. They paid Professor Benjamin Silliman of Yale University $25,000 to examine the mine, and carried his eulogistic report to England, where they won still more favorable comment from the United States minister, Robert Schenck. Next they set up a company capitalized at £1 million ($5 million). Aided by a notorious promoter called "Baron" Grant, they flooded England with £20 shares.

Prices climbed swiftly to £31, and for thirteen months the company paid monthly dividends at the rate of 18 percent per annum. Then rumblings of trouble began. Lawsuits multiplied as neighboring mines in Alta Basin charged trespass. In the midst of these difficulties came the devastating word that the Emma's vein had disappeared into barren rock. In the spring of 1873, while A. D. Breed was simultaneously stripping the Caribou Mine in Colorado, the company collapsed. When its affairs were liquidated ten years later, each £20 share returned its holder a shilling.

It wasn't a swindle exactly. The Emma's ore had been good, and Professor Silliman could hardly have detected, on the basis of his perfunctory investigation, the geologic faulting which interrupted the vein. Although Congress was suspicious enough of Schenck that it investigated his part in the fiasco, he was not so much dishonest as the victim of his own enthusiasms; hoping for a killing, he too had invested in the mine and had lost $50,000. Still, to burned investors, the Caribou and Emma affairs looked like deliberate cheats. Coupled with the Panic of 1873, the resultant chill helped dry up, for a time, the flow of foreign funds on which other mining companies and other mountain industrialists—Palmer of the Denver & Rio Grande, Jay Cooke of the Northern Pacific, and so on—were counting for the completion of their own projects.

Within the mountains themselves, enthusiasm continued unabated. Prospectors roaming east of Alta, on the opposite side of the Wasatch Range from Salt Lake City, opened what became the fabulous Park City district, now another popular skiing area. There, in 1872, Marcus Daly first proved his worth as a mine scout. He was squat, red-faced, bluff, and uncouth. He had landed in the United States from Ireland at the age of fifteen, and most of his education had been acquired in the mines of California and at the Comstock Lode in Nevada. It was enough to sharpen an uncanny instinct for estimating the potentials of unpromising ore bodies. In Park City Daly examined a modest property named the Ontario, available for $27,000. He recommended it to George Hearst of San Francisco, father of William Randolph Hearst, and to Hearst's lawyers, Lloyd Tevis and James Ben Ali Haggin, son of a Kentucky barrister and a Turkish beauty. The trio spent $325,000 building a mill and then settled back to take out $8 million in clear profit.

This coup, together with his successful management of a smaller Park City mine, brought Daly to the attention of the Walker brothers of Salt Lake City, apostate Mormons and successful competitors, as few other merchants in Utah were, of the church-backed ZCMI (Zion's Cooperative Mercantile Institution). The Walkers were also bankers. In both capacities, financing and merchandising, they had developed a considerable trade with Montana businessmen. In that way they came across promising samples of ore from one of the new silver properties that were replacing the moribund gold placers at the head of Silver Bow Creek at a place called Butte. In 1876 the Walkers sent Daly there to look over possible investments.

He carried with him a letter of introduction to a slight, sharp-faced, red-whiskered local potentate named William Andrews Clark. Intellectual, avaricious, and ice-blooded, Clark had studied law in Ohio and had taught school in Missouri before joining the gold rush to Colorado. He worked briefly on the Bobtail Lode in Gregory Gulch—the same Bobtail from which Nathaniel Hill later took ore to Swansea—but the prospects seemed so poor to him that in 1863 he followed the crowds north to Bannack. Though in time he switched from mining to storekeeping in Helena and banking in Deer Lodge, he never lost his interest in swapping for mining claims. When interest in silver picked up, he realized that smelting would be the key. With more foresight than most Rocky Mountain mine dealers ever possessed, he went east to Columbia University to study metallurgy.

On his return Clark used his new knowledge as a guide in acquiring several small silver mines on the sloping hill north of the hamlet of Butte, named for Big Butte, a squarish summit to the northwest. Some one-horse smelters were perking away in the neighborhood; Clark himself finished building one that he obtained by foreclosing on William Farlin, the man whose discoveries had started the silver rush to Butte. None of the plants worked well, however. Searching for improvements, Clark shipped ore to various places, including Nathaniel Hill's Boston and Colorado Smelting Company in Colorado. He wanted Hill to take particular note of the copper in the ore. It made a fine matte for picking up silver, did it not? Hill, who was just then moving his smelter from cramped, fuelless Black Hawk to Argo, near Denver, agreed and in 1879 joined Clark in establishing a branch of the Boston and Colorado at Butte—for handling silver from Clark's properties and not primarily for treating copper, as yet.

How much help Clark actually gave Daly in 1876 is unknown. In any event Daly bought two mines for the Walkers, the Lexington and the Alice, high on the hill back of Butte. He acquired a small interest in the Alice for himself, built a mill at what he called Walkerville, due north of Butte, and settled down to run the properties. Clark owned a cluster of small mines nearby. They both made a little money and dreamed of more hidden somewhere in those vein-seamed, heavily mineralized hills just north of Silver Bow Creek. In spite of their antithetical natures, they were good friends. Clark's brother married the sister of Daly's wife. But all friendliness ended, as we shall see, after Daly unearthed, in the early 1880's, the gigantic ore bodies that lifted Butte to pre-eminence as one of the world's richest producers not of silver but of copper.

In Colorado, meanwhile, other prospectors were pursuing silver to the top of the highest peaks in the land. The first of these lofty holes, discovered in 1871, was located in the northwest corner of South Park, where the Mosquito Range rolls south from the Continental Divide.[1] There, 13,860 feet above sea level on the massive shoulder of Mount Bross, a prospector named Plummer located the Moose, producer of some $3 million during the next two decades.

Mount Bross, incidentally, had been named during an emotional moment for a tourist, William Bross. In the summer of 1868 Bross, who was lieutenant governor of Illinois, had been traveling across Colorado in company with Schuyler Colfax, Speaker of the House of Representatives,

---

[1] The Mosquito Range is the southern extension of the 200-mile long Park Range, which forms the western border of three of Colorado's great interior basins—North, Middle, and South Parks.

soon to be elected Vice-President of the United States. Also in the party were Samuel Bowles, editor of the Springfield, Massachusetts, *Republican,* Governor A. C. Hunt of Colorado, and various other dignitaries, plus several wives and sweethearts. For a lark the group decided to "climb" Mount Lincoln, 14,297 feet high, culminating point of the Mosquito Range. It was a stormy ride. Snow and hail spat at them as they zigzagged their horses past the ground pine at timberline and on across tough alpine tundra spangled with paintbrush, gentian, and lupine. Five hundred feet from the peak's gently rounded top they had to dismount and scramble the rest of the way over piles of shattered talus, their lungs gasping in the thin air.

The view from the top, caught in tantalizing glimpses through the cloud scud, exhilarated William Bross to such an extent that he pulled the shivering group together and led them in singing the Doxology. Caught up in their turn, the chorus spontaneously declared that the big (14,170 feet) hump to the south should evermore be known as Mount Bross, as it still is. still is.

Though the mountaintop singers who praised God for His blessings did not realize it, the area underneath their feet was laced with veins of silver ore. One lode, the Present Help, was opened on Mount Lincoln within 90 feet of the summit. Two hundred feet below that was the rich Australia. South of Bross, above timberline in Mosquito Gulch, was the greatest of them all, the London, which during its early years was ingeniously powered by a windmill with 60-foot vanes. Supply town for this burgeoning activity was Alma, located where Buckskin Joe Creek runs into the Middle Fork of the South Platte. There, in 1873, Hill and Pearce built another branch of their smelting company.[2]

This spreading rush for silver led inevitably to an invasion of the Ute reservation. In 1868 Alexander Hunt had negotiated with the tribe a solemn treaty that guaranteed them forever and ever the full western quarter of Colorado, save for a bit at the north. The next year the San Juan Mountains in the southern part of the reservation were scoured by Arizona prospectors urged on by Governor Pile of New Mexico in the hope that a rush would stimulate trade in Santa Fe. The scheme did not work. The small stampede that developed after the discovery of gold veins near peak-rimmed Baker's Park (named for Charles Baker, who first risked the remote area in 1861) came from the east, from Colorado's San Luis Valley—up the Rio Grande to its source, over the Divide at Stony Pass, 12,594 feet, and down Cunningham Gulch, so awesome a slit that today's jeep drivers are half persuaded that the wagon freighters of a century ago could not have negotiated it without the aid of some strange black art.

The Utes, led by Chief Ouray, demanded that the government eject those early trespassers, as required by Hunt's treaty. Reluctant troops were

[2] It was abandoned in 1875 because of technical difficulties.

ordered to march against their own people. Before a clash could develop, a government negotiator, Felix Brunot, called for an armistice and asked the Utes to sell to the government a block of land 65 miles long east and west and 35 miles wide, embracing the most rugged part of the San Juan Mountains.

It was a country of soaring pinnacles and plunging gorges more than a mile deep, of such towering and barren slopes of red and yellow volcanic rock that game did not frequent it. Hence the Utes were not particularly concerned. They agreed to part with the mountainous section—but only with the mountains. The whites were to stay away from the valleys and rolling foothills where farms and livestock might destroy the Indians' favorite hunting grounds.

Each side thought it had made a bargain. Certainly the whites got what they wanted. Hard on the heels of the original gold discoveries came the opening of vein after vein of silver. Hordes of miners poured in to found towns in every available mountain cup: Silverton (in Baker's Park), Lake City, Ouray, Telluride, Ophir, Rico, and dozens of smaller camps. Supplying them, mostly by way of Stony Pass, was a frightful problem in logistics yet the ore was rich enough to make prodigies of effort worthwhile. Even the equipment for an entire smelter, fire brick included, was carried over Stony Pass to Silverton on the backs of donkeys.

Clamor for better transportation inevitably arose and caught the sensitive ear of General William Palmer, president of the Denver & Rio Grande Railroad. As noted earlier, Palmer had managed in 1872 to push the road's narrow-gauge tracks as far south as Pueblo. From there he had gone up the Arkansas to Canon City at the lower end of the river's spectacular Royal Gorge. Pinched by one financial crisis after another, he had inveigled help from both Pueblo and Canon City, and then had offended them by locating his depots where his land companies would benefit at the expense of already established businesses.

His original intent had been to drive from Pueblo to Santa Fe—the railroad's charter from Congress specified that it must reach the New Mexico capital by 1882—and from there to El Paso. Gateway to those southern lands was Raton Pass, a 7,888-foot saddle in the east-west wall of the Raton Mountains. This same gateway was also the goal of the Atchison, Topeka, & Santa Fe Railroad, which was developing transcontinental aspirations. Since there was not room enough in the steep, narrow approaches to Raton Pass to accommodate double tracks, prior possession could be a matter of prime importance. Before a race could gather headway, however, the Panic of 1873 halted construction on both lines.

Late in 1875, about the time the rush to the San Juans was picking up momentum, the AT&SF began moving again. The activity frightened Palmer into a desperate effort to raise more money and push south from Pueblo toward Raton Pass. To help speed him on his way, influential citizens in Trinidad, a hamlet near the northern entrance to the pass, bought $20,000 worth of D&RG bonds. Palmer repaid the gesture in characteristic fashion: he created a new town, El Moro, on coal-bearing lands owned by himself and his associates outside of Trinidad, and built his depot there. The infuriated residents thereupon began making overtures to the AT&SF. At the moment this did not worry Palmer. The rival road had run out of money again and had paused in Pueblo.

The breathing spell should have let Palmer move without opposition into vital Raton Pass. The growing traffic of the San Juan mining country diverted him, however, and he sent two of his directors, William Bell and ex-governor Alexander Cameron Hunt, across the Divide to investigate. They returned enthusiastic. His friends William Blackmore and William Gilpin of the Sangre de Cristo Grant added more urgings about the potential riches of the San Luis Valley.

Encouraged thus, Palmer in 1876–77 ran a spur line westward toward the upper reaches of Huerfano Creek. By dint of steep 4 percent grades and tight curves called muleshoes, he surmounted La Veta Pass (9,383 feet, the highest point yet reached by an American railroad) and spiraled down to Garland City near Fort Garland. The next year he crossed the flat San Luis Valley to the company-formed town of Alamosa on the banks of the Rio Grande River—the first time the railroad had touched the stream for which it was named. It was a strategic spot. From Alamosa the D&RG could thrust either west into the San Juans, south down the river to Santa Fe, or both.

The directors of the Santa Fe Railroad watched all of this unhappily. Their emaciated treasury needed the sustenance of mining traffic that could be diverted from southern Colorado over their tracks toward Kansas City and the smelting centers that had grown up around the lead mines of Missouri. At the moment, however, they hadn't money enough to fight for revenue. Their only riposte to Palmer was a feeble subterfuge. Using as a front certain residents of Canon City who disliked the D&RG, they created in 1877 a dummy corporation called the Canon City & San Juan Railway. Their idea was to monopolize, in case of future need, the deep slit of the Royal Gorge as a gateway through the Front Range. The construction of rails in the chasm's narrowest stretch, if ever construction came about, would be difficult and expensive, but no worse than climbing a 9,000-foot pass.

Palmer of course was aware of the advantages of the Royal Gorge as an entry into the mountains. His engineering crews had run surveys through the canyon as early as 1871 but no construction had followed because at that time nothing existed in the high country to lure the rails westward. Afterwards, Alamosa's strategic location made a climb over La Veta Pass seem preferable to an onerous grading job through the Gorge. These preoccupations made the D&RG directors forget their first essential survey, and they neglected to file with the government's General Land Office in Washington a plat of their proposed line through the canyon, as a national law, passed in 1875, required them to do. Thus the Canon City & San Juan, acting for the Santa Fe, was in a position to test the validity of the law by running its own survey along the footsteps of the D&RG engineers, file the plat according to statute, and claim prior possession ahead of the enemy.

There would be a struggle about it, of course. The advisability of launching the fight depended on many things: developments in New Mexico, the growth of the San Juans, and the extent of a new silver field just being opened near the head of the Arkansas River, beside the old placer workings in California Gulch. In 1877, when the Canon City & San Juan Railway was created as a maybe-so counter to Palmer, the new camp at California Gulch did not even have a name. In January, 1878, the place was finally christened: Leadville, destined to be the first of the Rockies' huge industrial complexes.

Traffic indeed! As coming chapters will indicate, the avidity to control the ores produced in Leadville and its successors touched off titanic struggles involving not only the railroads but the mineowners as well. Bitterest bloodletting of all would be the ferocious, ten-year struggle between the owners and a new class of unionized workers brought to the high country by industrial developments which the railroads made possible. First, though, it is well to note the spasms that introduced this long era of strife to the mountains—the elimination of the Indians as contenders for the last open places along the toes of the Divide.

In the early 1870's, when surveyors for the Northern Pacific appeared on the north bank of the Yellowstone River in eastern Montana, the Sioux sensed what the newcomers portended. In theory neither the Sioux nor the rebellious bands of northern Cheyennes and Arapahoes who joined them should have objected; the hunting grounds that had been allotted the tribes by treaty lay south of the Yellowstone. Nevertheless, they struck hard, harrying the surveyors throughout the summers of 1872 and 1873 and in the process creating for themselves a favorite enemy—General George Armstrong Custer, whose 7th Cavalry functioned as guards for the beleaguered railroad locators.

The panic of 1873 halted the Northern Pacific's track laying at Bismarck, North Dakota, but this brought no relief to the Indians. The discovery of gold in the Black Hills of South Dakota triggered another rush onto Indian land. In final exasperation many of the Sioux defiantly left their South Dakota reservation and struck at settlers throughout the northern plains. In the spring of 1876 three columns of soldiers set about chastising the hostile bands, which were then hunting buffalo in southeastern Montana. As every schoolboy knows, the incident in that campaign which stunned all America was the obliteration of Custer's command—224 men plus the general—on the Little Bighorn River. Although the victory excited the Indians throughout the West, it actually served only to quicken the white juggernaut. The army massed fresh troops, rolled methodically over the Indians, and forced the Sioux to cede the Black Hills. As a side issue to the arrangements, the Shoshoni of Wyoming, who had done no fighting, were required to yield half their Wind River reservation to the defeated Arapahoes.

This war was immediately followed by another against those bands of Nez Percés that had refused to sign the 1863 treaty surrendering nine-tenths of their canyoned country for the benefit of Idaho placer miners. Leaders of the recalcitrants were Chief Joseph and his brother Ollokot. They clung to their ancient homelands in the lonesome Wallowa Mountains, where Oregon, Idaho, and Washington come together, insisting that since they had not acquiesced to the treaty, title to the Wallowas still remained with them. Whites who coveted the area retorted that a minority could not abrogate a document subscribed to by the majority of the chiefs. A long series of discussions got nowhere. Finally the government's chief negotiator, white-bearded General O. O. Howard, described by one army officer's wife as "ferociously" religious, lost patience. Bluntly he told the objectors that within the next thirty days they must gather up their live-stock, leave their Wallowa homes, and resettle themselves on the reserva-tion with the treaty-signing part of the tribe.

Bickering among themselves, the unhappy people prepared to obey. Suddenly, almost blindly, one young warrior responded to a slur on his courage by rounding up two friends and killing some whites who had been involved in the murder of his father several years before. Other braves caught the fever, fired it higher with alcohol, and began a series of random attacks that resulted in the deaths of eighteen settlers.

A hundred hastily summoned cavalrymen trotted south from Fort Lapwai, near Lewiston, Idaho, to protect refugees who had huddled together for safety in the hamlets of Grangeville and Mount Idaho. Mere protection, however, was not enough to placate the angry whites. They urged the troops to pursue the Indians on south across White Bird Hill, the route that young John J. Healy had followed fifteen years earlier during the prospecting trip that had led to the opening of the Salmon River mines.

The Nez Percés whom the soldiers met in White Bird Canyon would have parleyed had not a civilian scout with the troops fired a nervous shot. At that the armed Indians dropped out of sight in the tall grass or ducked behind the big rocks that studded the hillsides. Taking careful aim, they began to shoot. Within minutes thirty-four whites were dead and the rest of the soldiers were in full flight back to Mount Idaho.

General Howard's first fear was of a general uprising throughout north-ern Idaho and eastern Washington. Catholic historians suggest that Jesuit Father Joseph M. Cataldo and his fellow missionaries persuaded the northern tribes to reject the blandishments of Nez Percé emissaries and maintain a strict neutrality. Anyway, they did not fight. The treaty-signing part of the Nez Percés also held aloof. As a result a desperate flight toward Canada became the only recourse for the outnumbered belligerents—some 200 warriors, burdened by perhaps 500 old men, women, and children, and 2,000 horses for carrying their goods.

Outfighting and outmaneuvering the soldiers Howard led after them, they flowed east along the same rugged Lolo Trail that Lewis and Clark had followed into their homeland three-quarters of a century earlier. Almost contemptuously they skirted a log barricade that soldiers from undermanned Fort Missoula, Montana, had erected at the end of the trail to keep them out of the Bitterroot Valley. In the valley itself they did no harm, partly because of lack of sympathy from the Flatheads.

The Nez Percés and the Flatheads were ancient friends. Their young people intermarried frequently, and probably the Nez Percés expected help from their old allies. Certainly the Flatheads had grievances against the whites. No less a person than James Garfield, who one day would be President of the United States, had helped push many of them out of their beloved Bitterroot lands by forging Chief Charlot's signature to a treaty of cession. In spite of that, the Jesuit missionaries among them were able to persuade the Flatheads to stay neutral. They would not even let the fugitives follow the short route north to Canada through Flathead Valley.

Miserably the fleers turned south and west. In the Big Hole Valley they fought off, with heavy casualties, a surprise dawn attack by pursuing soldiers and limped on west through Yellowstone Park. It was a hopeless race. The Sioux wars had resulted in the founding of several forts in eastern Montana. Troops from these posts converged on the Nez Percés and finally forced the remnants of them to surrender almost within sight of the Canadian border—the bleak end of a 1,700-mile zigzag retreat through some of the most difficult mountain terrain in the land.

And still the spasms were not over. In Colorado, Nathan Meeker sought to work his way out of the debts that had piled onto him in Greeley by applying for a job, in 1878, as agent to the White River Utes in the northwestern part of the state. He took his wife Arvilla and one of his grown daughters, Josie, with him to the remote, sage-gray valley beside the piñon-dotted Danforth Hills. There, he hoped, the two women could pick up a few more dollars for him by teaching in the Indian school and running a boardinghouse for agency workers and visitors.

He was sixty-one, too old, too stiff-necked, too idealistic for such a job. He was determined that the Indians should settle on farms and learn the advantages of civilization even if he had to force them. They declined to be forced. During the dry summer of 1879 they set gigantic forest fires at various spots between the Wyoming border and New Mexico. They raided ranches in Middle Park, where William Byers was trying to promote a resort at a place called Hot Sulphur Springs. Because Byers had an influential voice, the government answered his request for protection by ordering into Middle Park a company of Negro soldiers under Captain Francis S. Dodge. Although Hot Sulphur Springs was a hundred miles from White River, the threat behind the gesture was enough to enrage the Utes still more.

In order to grow the winter wheat he would need the next spring, Meeker in September, 1879, directed his workers to plow up 200 acres of the best grazing land near the agency, including a race track which the Indians did not want plowed. A heated quarrel broke out. During it, one of the chiefs picked the stubborn old man out of his chair in the agency office, carried him kicking and struggling across the porch, and hurled him against a hitching rack. Alarmed but as grimly determined as ever, Meeker rushed a message 150 miles north to Fort Steele, near Rawlins, Wyoming, asking for more help than Dodge's soldiers in Middle Park could provide.

Major Thomas T. Thornburgh responded with 150 cavalry and 25 civilians: scouts, interpreters, mule handlers. To the Utes at White River the approach of this additional column looked like a declaration of war. They demanded that Meeker halt the soldiers for a parley. Hoping to calm the Utes, he sent the requisite message and Thornburgh agreed to camp at the edge of the reservation in the almost treeless valley of Milk Creek. Indians rode out to meet them. As had happened with the Nez Percés in White Bird Canyon, someone—no one in authority ever learned who— pulled a trigger.

By the time the command could group behind its supply wagons and slain horses, Thornburgh and thirteen soldiers were dead and several were wounded. A scout named Joe Rankin broke through the cordon and rode hell-bent for Fort Steele. Telegraph keys clattered and troops began converging on White River from every direction.

The Utes did not know any of that. While some of them kept Thornburgh's men under siege, others galloped back to the agency. There they killed twelve white workers and seized Arvilla, Josephine, and Mrs. Price, wife of the agency blacksmith, and the two Price children.

There was no climactic battle. Chief Ouray, leader of the peaceful Utes, managed to stop the fighting; ponderous Charles Adams, a long-time friend of the mountain Indians, managed to free the ravished women. No one could save the tribe. Colorado's outrage over the atrocities gilded with apparent dignity the centuries-old, unquenchable American desire for more land to develop, farm land needed now for feeding the silver miners pushing ever deeper into the mountains. "The Utes must go!" became the slogan of dozens of editorial writers. Protesters who argued against punishing an entire tribe for the wrongs of a part were hooted down. "Humanitarianism," declared the Denver *Times,* "is an idea. Western Empire is an inexorable fact. He who gets in the way of it will be crushed." Except for one band that was allowed to remain on a strip of land along the Colorado-New Mexico border, the whole Ute nation was swept out of the state onto a bleak desert reservation in eastern Utah.

Almost blatant ironies attached to the crushing. The first men to reach the devastated agency on White River found that Meeker's murderers had worked off their hatred against the mysteries of extinction by putting a log chain around the neck of the old man's corpse, which was clad only in a shirt, and dragging it around behind their horses until the fun wore off. They then had pinned it to the earth, which the whites craved so ardently, by placing the body on its back and driving a barrel stave through the mouth into the ground.

Nathan Meeker, exponent of Western Empire as it had manifested itself in the agricultural colony at Greeley, had, by the strange involutions of history, got in the way of his own destroying angel.

XVII

RAILROAD WRANGLES

LEADVILLE, sometimes called the Cloud City because of its 10,000-foot elevation, came about in this fashion. During the year of the panic, 1873, when Palmer and Jay Cooke had to stop work on their railroads and while the Utes were selling the San Juan Mountains to the United States, a squat, florid, one-eyed mining scout named William H. Stevens rode up Mosquito Gulch to Mosquito Pass, 13,188 feet high. Looking west from the top, he admired the view of the Sawatch Range, rising high and cold beyond the alternate meadows and spruce forests that carpeted the valley of the Upper Arkansas River. Then, his horse rested from its hard climb, he wound on down the hillside and swung south into California Gulch.

The steep-sided ravine was a waste of gravel piles and rotted stumps left by the thousands of placer diggers who had mined the district during the early 1860's. When Stevens arrived only a few workers remained, buying their supplies and getting their mail at Horace A. W. Tabor's rundown store in dejected Oro City, its line of abandoned shacks elbowing each other for room along the little string of level ground in the gulch's bottom.

The ugliness did not bother Stevens. In fact, he intended to increase it. He followed the trickling creek down out of the hills, and where the land flattened somewhat he dug several test holes. Sure enough, particles of gold were dusted widely through the gravel—too widely to be retrieved with pick and shovel. But by shattering the gulch bottom with powerful jets of water from hydraulic nozzles and washing the muck into long batteries of sluice boxes, perhaps he could gather enough mineral to make the operation pay.

He raised $50,000 among mining men who trusted his judgment, hired a metallurgist named Alvinus B. Wood as helper, and in the summer of 1874 set a crew of men to work building a 12-mile ditch to the Arkansas River to augment the trivial flow in California Gulch. While waiting for the water, Stevens and Wood began pilot operations. Annoyances immediately appeared. Heavy dark sand settling into the riffles of their sluice boxes hindered the extraction of the specks of gold. Although the problem had bothered hundreds of placer miners before them, they were the first to assay the bothersome stuff. It turned out to be a carbonate ore rich in lead and shot through with tantalizing gleams of silver.

Because they had to make that $50,000 ditch pay in a hurry, the two men could search for the source of the sand only at intervals. It took them until the summer of 1876 to obtain six likely claims, located in groups of three on either side of California Gulch. Each was 1,500 feet long and 60 feet wide, and represented a marked change in the West's attitude concerning mining practices.

At first the nation's placer miners had sought to distribute the gold in the gravel bars among as many men as possible by limiting the length of gulch claims to 100 or 200 feet. Lode claims were, on the average, even smaller —200 feet along the vein and 25 feet to either side. Title lapsed whenever a claimant ceased to work the holding.

Although the system had brought order of sorts to the first frenzied stampedes, it had fallen into disrepute with the spread of silver mining. Almost invariably silver was found in veins. Until 1873, when the price of the white metal began to drop, silver was worth only one-sixteenth as much as gold and therefore it was often necessary (depending on the amount of precious mineral per ton of ore) for a silver mine to handle more material than a gold mine did in order to achieve the same net profit—an increase in production that became possible with the development of sophisticated machinery. A 200-foot claim amounted to less than one acre. It did not yield sufficient ore to meet the requirements of mass production, nor did it allow room on the surface for milling, hoisting, and storage facilities. Claims, the mining states insisted, should be larger. Furthermore, miners should have the same privileges concerning title that farmers had: the right to obtain from the government clear and permanent possession, whether they worked their claims an arbitrary number of days per year or not.

Between 1866 and 1872 Congress produced a set of laws to meet these demands. A man was given a patent to his ground if he completed in sixty days $500 worth of improvements—the sinking of a shaft or the driving of an adit toward the vein—and then paid the government $5 per acre. Claim bounds were increased to 1,500 feet along the vein and 300 feet to either side of it, a total of almost twenty acres. Since even this was not as much as most practical miners wanted, they were thrown a sop. The new law allowed a single individual (or a partnership) to file on more than one claim. Obviously he would do this only if the ground looked good enough to warrant his undertaking the required $500 worth of development work within the time prescribed.

At that point tradition intruded most mischievously. During the first placer stampedes the discoverer of a district had been rewarded by being allowed two claims, whereas everyone else had been limited to one. How was the discoverer of a vein to be recognized under the new laws, which allowed multiple filings? As a substitute Congress devised an absurdity which no other mining nation on earth allows—the so-called apex law.

The apex of a vein is the point closest to the surface. Veins seldom rise to this point in perpendicular planes. They slant, like a leaning plank. The degree of the slant is called the vein's dip. If the dip diverges markedly from a vertical plane, obviously the ore body will soon extend beyond the 300-foot lateral limit set by the Congressional law of 1872. Here entered tradition, with its insistence that the discoverer have something extra. Why not let the locater of an apex follow the sloping vein sideways (not lengthwise) as far underground as the ore lasted?

Even if the pursuit involved crossing the vertical boundaries of another man's claim? Yes, even if it did. By right of discovery, 1,500 feet of the vein should be the finder's all the way to its roots. That was fair, wasn't it?

If veins had lain in clear planes, like sheets of paper inserted into a pudding, the provision might have worked. Veins are not that neat, however. Throughout geologic ages they have been faulted, twisted, and shattered by any number of the earth's inner rumblings. New planes strike rudely across old ones. Lateral stringers may wander off from the main lode in any direction, and sometimes they are very rich. Often it is not possible to say, far underground, whether a stringer or a faulted vein is a true continuation of the vein that apexes hundreds of feet above. Yet whenever disputes developed between exuberant followers of the dipping vein and their neighbors, the courts were obligated to reach a determination. The best approach they had was to listen to highly technical testimony offered by experts who, in cases of expensive litigation, were marshaled from all over the earth by the opposing lawyers. Since geology is not a precise science, appeals from the decision invariably followed. New experts were summoned, and when the multimillion-dollar quarrels eventually ended, the only ones who really benefited were, often enough, the attorneys.

All of which is not really a discursion, as future pages will show. But it has taken us a long way from the six claims, each 1,500 by 600 feet, which Alvinus Wood and William Stevens filed in groups of three on either side of California Gulch between the years 1874 and 1876.

Each group of claims covered nearly sixty acres. Right there the concept of the happy toiler doing his own mining on a one-man piece of ground vanishes. Sixty acres of rock reaching hundreds of feet into the earth could be handled only by several laborers operating expensive machines.

The first power drill to be used underground in America had appeared, significantly enough, only eight years before, in 1868, in a mine near Georgetown, Colorado. Power drills enabled a single miner to punch as many blasting holes into an ore body as five or six men had punched previously with hand drills. The greater amounts of ore broken loose by the faster blasting required more shovelers, plus trammers to push loaded cars along the drifts to the shafts, and steam-powered hoists to lift the ore up the shafts to the surface. There also had to be steam-powered pumps to keep water from accumulating in the deeper workings. Once the ore was on the surface it had to be run through concentrators. A concentrator was a mill which pulverized the material, mixed it with water, and then passed it through various jiggling and settling processes. These eliminated a large part of the nonmetallic waste rock and left the valuable residue in light enough form to be transported without undue expense to the nearest smelter.

Unit costs went down as volume went up—a mass-production approach to metal mining first tested in the copper and iron regions around Lake Superior. In the mid-1870's the concept was just beginning to reach the Rocky Mountains in the areas around Central City, Colorado, Park City, Utah, and Butte, Montana.

William Stevens, it is worth noting, had done his first work in the Great Lakes area. After he had proved himself there, investors on the lookout for mines to develop had sent him to Central City and into Utah, where he had watched the early attempts to put the new industrial theories into practice. Thus his importance to Leadville lies not just in finding silver, along with Wood, but in realizing immediately what would have to be done to make its extraction profitable, even to the point of taking out claims in blocks of three. From the beginning he envisioned large-scale production.

The first problem was to raise money. The only way to do this was to prove the worth of the claims. It was not easy. The property was located in a distant, isolated, moribund placer district remembered as a short-lived producer of free gold, not of lode silver. Besides, the recent Caribou and Emma fiascoes had left capital wary of silver promotions. A few samples of ore and a fancy prospectus were not going to be enough. Patiently, therefore, and financing the work out of their own funds (actual records of these initial steps seem not to have survived), Wood and Stevens set about mining several hundred tons of ore.

In the autumn of 1876 and again in the spring of 1877 they sold the best of this ore to young Augustus Meyers, who was stationed across the Mosquito Range at Alma in South Park as a representative of the St. Louis Smelting and Refining Company. That firm, having achieved success in the Missouri lead mines, was considering expanding into the Rockies.

Meyers sent the ore by wagon and rail to St. Louis for treatment. Results created such a stir that Alvinus Wood was able to sell his interest in the six claims and in the hydraulic ditch for $40,000 to a Chicagoan named Levi Leiter, a partner of Marshall Field.

By then Stevens, who preferred to stay with the mine, had learned that the best claims were the three that stretched in a line 4,500 feet up the slopes of Iron Hill, directly north of California Gulch. With Leiter he formed the Iron Mining Company and plunged into extensive operations. During the next decade the concern netted $2.5 million from ore that grossed $12 million—1880 prices.

The ore which Augustus Meyers sent to Missouri also brought Edwin Harrison, president of the St. Louis Smelting and Refining Company, west to look over the field. On the surface not much was visible. The still-continuing hydraulic operations had given birth to an unnamed straggle of shacks along the north side of the ravine. Prospectors arriving from neighboring areas to investigate the insistent rumors of silver were adding more buildings. Impecunious Horace A. W. Tabor moved down from Oro City and opened a grocery store in the cluster. To help make ends meet, his wife Augusta ran a boardinghouse, as she had been doing on and off ever since Tabor had dragged her to Gregory Gulch in 1859. The only other place to eat was the new City Hotel, a two-story building of logs, its eight sleeping cubicles upstairs divided one from the other by sheets of muslin.

After looking at every prospect hole in the vicinity, Harrison, acting on behalf of the St. Louis Smelting and Refining Company, paid three brothers named Gallagher $250,000 for their undeveloped Camp Bird claims. These were located on Carbonate Hill, a knob a little lower than Iron Hill and north toward a ravine called Stray Horse Gulch. The transaction completed, Harrison built a smelter for treating not only the Camp Bird ore but also that of the other mines in the district, including the Iron; a new claim was opening every day or so.

Part of Harrison's planning was predicated on the swift approach of rail transportation. The premise seemed safe, for three railroads wound within a hundred airline miles. The nearest was the narrow-gauge Denver, South Park, & Pacific, crawling painfully up the South Platte Canyon from Denver. In spite of its proximity, it was a frail reed. During five years of continuing crises, it had advanced fewer than forty miles. Even if it did reach South Park, it would still have to surmount or circle the formidable Mosquito Range.

A railroad that breached the Front Range at the Royal Gorge and then followed the Arkansas River north to the new camp would avoid the Mosquitos. Realization of that advantage turned Harrison's thinking toward the rival roads at Pueblo, the Denver & Rio Grande and the Atchison, Topeka, & Santa Fe.

This was late in 1877. By then, as we have seen, General Palmer had pushed the D&RG's narrow-gauge tracks as far south as El Moro, near Trinidad at the foot of Raton Pass, and west to Garland City in the San Luis Valley. The only answer the Santa Fe had been able to make was to incorporate the dummy Canon City & San Juan Railway. This was purely a paper concern, however. The Santa Fe itself had not passed Pueblo, whereas D&RG tracks were already in Canon City. For that reason

Harrison selected the D&RG as his best bet and approached Palmer with tales of the great freight potentials awaiting whatever aggressive railroad would build to California Gulch.

Intrigued, Palmer and some of his engineers rode to the yet unnamed camp to check. They were disappointed. There were still fewer than three hundred people clustered around Tabor's store, and although ore was dribbling out of several workings, none of the claims was far enough developed for the visitors to make a sound estimate about future tonnage. By contrast, Palmer did know how much tonnage was coming out of the San Juans. He was also faced with the problem of reaching Santa Fe in time to meet his charter requirements. Under the circumstances he decided that he had best devote his skimpy funds toward those goals. The first steps were extending the D&RG's San Juan spur to Alamosa, as mentioned in the preceding chapter, and pushing his main line south.

In February, 1878, he ordered his chief engineers to occupy Raton Pass with a grading crew. Somehow, perhaps through tapped telegraph wires, the Santa Fe management learned what he was up to. Since that road as yet had no tracks south of Pueblo, its locating engineers made themselves as inconspicuous as possible and traveled by D&RG train to El Moro—the same train that carried the D&RG party. Unaware of the enemy's presence the D&RG people spent the night in El Moro. The Santa Fe men rode on to Trinidad, where the Rio Grande was detested. Easily they rounded up a willing work crew and galloped on. When the D&RG men arrived in narrow Raton Pass, they found the rival graders joyfully shoveling up the earth ahead of them, secure both in possession and in plats which Santa Fe explorers had filed earlier with the government, as required by the law of 1875. To reach Santa Fe, New Mexico, the D&RG would now have to follow the Rio Grande Valley south from Alamosa. Grimly Palmer prepared to do just that.

Meanwhile Edwin Harrison was traveling to St. Louis aboard the special car of the AT&SF's new general manager, William B. Strong. Because both railroads spied busily on each other, officials of the D&RG learned at once of the trip. All too easily they guessed what Strong and Harrison talked about. In January, 1878, the camp at California Gulch had at last acquired a name, Leadville, and an official mayor, H. A. W. Tabor. Meantime the boundaries of the known ore deposits were expanding spectacularly from Iron and Carbonate hills across Stray Horse Gulch to Fryer Hill. Harrison, it was reported, was already promising the Santa Fe Railroad 24,000 tons of ore and matte a year from his operations alone. There would be other smelters—young Meyers had already opened a sampling works—and none of this took into consideration the supplies that would be needed by the hundreds of electrified people who were even then trudging along snowy trails over the lofty Mosquito Range to the new city.

Given redoubled energy by his stinging defeat in Raton Pass, Palmer in April, 1878, decided to jump into the Royal Gorge before his rivals could respond to Harrison's blandishments. Out went the necessary orders—and again the Santa Fe discovered the plan. In a Paul Revere midnight ride during which his horse dropped dead beneath his spurs, W. R. Morley of at AT&SF rushed to Canon City ahead of the Rio Grande crews. There he sought out the nominal officers of the Santa Fe-owned Canon City & San Juan Railway. With their aid he was able to hurry a grading crew into the mouth of the gorge a jump ahead of the Rio Grande workers.

Prior possession thus achieved, the Canon City & San Juan calmly "surveyed" a line through the chasm by following the stakes set out in 1871 by Palmer's first locating crews. The dummy corporation then filed in the General Land Office the plat of their line, as required by the law of 1875, and blandly said that since the D&RG had not entered a record of its own early examinations, the route was as open to jumping as was any derelict mining claim.

In a fury of frustration, Palmer ordered his grading continued. The rival crews built barricades under the towering cliffs, jeered each other, brandished weapons, and drew "dead lines" that supposedly could be crossed only at peril. These things were mere sound effects. The real battling was confined to the courts.

Filing or no filing, Palmer believed that his rights to the gorge were better than the spurious claim which the Santa Fe was endeavoring to establish through its bogus subsidiary. He straightway sued his rival for trespass—and just as immediately was haled into court by his own disgruntled bondholders!

For years they had received no interest on their investment. Their thinking was completely oriented toward Santa Fe, New Mexico, and toward the San Juans. They were outraged over the loss of Raton Pass, and to them it seemed the depth of folly to pour money into a battle for a canyon that until recently had not figured in the railroad's planning. Forget Leadville, they said, and drive on down the Rio Grande into New Mexico.

Palmer demurred. To check him they took control of the D&RG away from him and leased the entire system to the Santa Fe! At once the Rio Grande's depressed stock doubled in price on the New York Exchange.

A stubborn fighter, Palmer delayed surrendering the D&RG's physical plant to the Santa Fe until December 13, 1878, a Friday. Meantime he carried his intricate legal battles to the Supreme Court of the United States. Although both roads continued grading at spots along the Arkansas, both were enjoined from laying track in the narrowest section of the gorge until the law had settled the dispute.

On April 21, 1879, only four months after the reluctant surrender of the leased property to the Santa Fe, the Supreme Court ruled that the Rio

Grande held prior rights to the Royal Gorge.[1] The legal victory was meaningless to Palmer, however, so long as the AT&SF held the lease. He promptly attacked the document, charging among other things that the Santa Fe had violated the terms of the lease by manipulating freight rates in such a way as to discriminate against the city of Denver. Evidence to that effect was presented to a district judge in remote Alamosa, a D&RG town, and he obligingly declared the lease void. But would the enemy obey the ruling before resorting to lengthy court appeals?

In anticipation of the judge's favorable ruling, the D&RG had collected pistols, carbines, shotguns, and ammunition for the use of sheriffs' posses charged with enforcing the court order. As soon as instructions were flashed by telegraph along the line at dawn on June 11, small armies marched against the depots and roundhouses held by the Santa Fe. Most of the buildings were manned by hastily assembled toughs. There was a great deal of belligerent shouting, but a sheriff's star and a legal-looking writ proved to be powerful psychological weapons. Most of the defenders sheepishly abandoned their posts on order. The only overt resistance occurred in Pueblo, where a melee developed over the railroad's telegraph office. Several men were sorely bruised; one died. By nightfall the entire D&RG line was back in its owners' hands.

The Santa Fe fought back. Court battles more decorous but no less intense than the assault on the depots raged in Colorado and Washington, D.C. Injunctions flew. Tied tight by these legal snares, not a wheel turned in the disputed sections of the canyon throughout the rest of 1879 and on into 1880.

During this long delay Leadville went wild. Because the ore there occurred in horizontal beds rather than in more or less upright veins, practically anyone, however untrained, could dig straight down almost anywhere on Iron, Carbonate, and Fryer hills and make a strike, though whether or not the ore would prove rich enough to meet the high costs of development where railroads did not exist was a determination attended by considerable suspense.

In October, 1877, John Routt, the last appointed territorial and the first elected state governor of Colorado bought, on Carbonate Hill, a part interest in a prospect hole 12 feet deep called the Morning Star. Donning copper-riveted overalls, he helped deepen the shaft with his own hands whenever he could slip away from the executive mansion in Denver. In April, 1879, the Morning Star hit ore. During what was left of the year it produced $290,000 and then was sold for a million. Nice enough—but the man who really set the state abuzz was Leadville's grocer and mayor,

---

[1] The decision also stated that the AT&SF could build its own tracks in the can-yon. Where the bottom was too narrow for a double line, the Santa Fe should be allowed, if it wished, to use the D&RG tracks.

Horace Tabor. In April, 1878, he provided two down-at-the-heel prospectors, August Rische and George Hook, with tools, food, and whiskey
valued at about $60. In return they assigned him a third interest in what-
ever mine they found. It turned out to be the Little Pittsburgh on Fryer
Hill. By July it was showering $8,000 a week on its owners. In September,
frightened at his own prosperity, Hook sold his third of the mine to Tabor
for $98,000.

All this had come from one claim 1,500 feet long and 600 feet wide.
Eager to spread, Rische and Tabor bought several adjoining claims. One
was George Fryer's discovery claim. Fryer had scratched away in it for a
few weeks and then had sold it to Jerome Chaffee for $50,000. Shortly
thereafter Chaffee, who had done very little work on the property, sold it to
Rische and Tabor for $125,000. Inflation, Leadville style. Chaffee wasn't
happy about the deal, however. The expanded holdings of the Little Pittsburgh were pouring out silver now. Two months after selling Fryer's
discovery claim, Chaffee joined forces with David Moffat, Denver banker
and mine speculator, to buy Rische's one-third interest in the enlarged
Little Pittsburgh for $263,000. The new owners, Chaffee, Moffat, and
Tabor picked up still more ground and put two hundred men to work at $3
a day. This, it should be remembered, had all occurred within seven
months.

Tabor meantime was adventuring on his own. Early in the course of
Fryer Hill's hectic career he had been attracted by a hole whose ore looked
like that in the Little Pittsburgh; in fact, one story says that ore stolen from
the Little Pittsburgh was dumped into the Chrysolite shaft to make it look
good. Be that as it may, Tabor paid a reputed $900 for the mine, sank the
shaft another 20 feet, and ran into carbonate ore that enriched him at the
rate of $100,000 a month. Dizzied by the success, he grew reckless and late
in 1878 paid $117,000 for the Matchless, named for a popular brand of
chewing tobacco. Good engineers had earlier reported it worthless. For two
years, while wise miners sniggered, Tabor stubbornly kept his crews
working in the supposedly barren drifts. Late in 1880 they began taking
out $80,000 a month.

Between mining ventures Tabor dabbled in real estate, life insurance,
illuminating gas, a hotel. He built an elegant opera house that attracted
talent from throughout the United States. He founded a bank. In order to
mark the building, he hired a destitute prospector-carpenter named Winfield Scott Stratton, of whom we shall hear later, to carve, gild, and place
on the roof an enormous replica of a silver dollar.

By this time Lake County, in which Leadville was located, was the
second most populous district in the state. Hoping to appeal to the voters
by selecting a local man as candidate for lieutenant governor, Colorado
Republicans let their eyes fall on shambling Horace Austin Warner Tabor,
with his oddly shaped cranium and his drooping, soup-strainer mustache.

He nodded agreement and, because he lived in a land where being lucky was equated with being smart, he was elected.

It was difficult, off there at the state house in Denver, to attend to his mines. He sold his two-thirds interest in the Little Pittsburgh to Chaffee and Moffat for a million dollars and the Chrysolite to Eastern promoters for $1.5 million. The Matchless he kept; it was a pet. The purchasers of the other two properties at once capitalized their acquisitions—the Little Pittsburgh for $20 million—and floated stock issues that were soon over-subscribed.

Women began to find the fifty-year-old Tabor irresistible. He developed illusions of romantic and political grandeur. He poured tens of thousands of dollars into Republican party coffers and in 1883 was rewarded with a thirty-day appointment as U.S. senator to fill the unexpired term of Henry Teller of Central City, who had been elevated to President Arthur's Cabinet. Tabor also put aside his wife Augusta and secretly married, before his divorce became valid, his curly-haired blonde mistress, Lizzie McCourt Doe, called Baby Doe. Later, his divorce having become final, he and Baby Doe went through an elaborate public ceremony in Washington's stately Willard Hotel, as if for the first time. The wife of Colorado's full-term senator, smelterman Nathaniel Hill, refused to attend. But Chester Arthur, President of the United States, did and was thoroughly mortified later when details of the scandal hit the newspapers. Baby Doe, let it be said, loved her husband. And they knew well enough from whence stemmed their bliss: they named their third child and second daughter Silver Dollar—Rose Mary Echo Silver Dollar Tabor, called Silver all her life, in spite of dark, dark hair.

The dollar value of Leadville's output soared from $60,000 in 1877 to $11,285,000 in 1879—enough silver, one statistician figured, to run a wire a sixteenth of an inch in diameter from New York to San Francisco by way of Leadville. In 1880 the output climbed another 35 percent, to $15 million. The Little Pittsburgh paid dividends of $100,000 a month. In a promotion stunt the Robert E. Lee produced during a single seventeen-hour day in January, 1880, $118,500—like scooping up dollars with a shovel, someone said. The 1880 census counted 14,800 people in the town, 10,626 of them white males mostly under thirty years of age. Local boosters complained that the census takers missed many prospectors and timber cutters at work in the hills, which is likely; actual population, these boosters trumpeted, was 40,000. A figure halfway between is a reasonable compromise.

Seventeen smelters ringed the town. Two thousand lumberjacks method-ically sawed down the surrounding forests to provide fuel for the steam-powered machinery, for restaurants, hotels, and ordinary dwellings. The smelters gulped uncounted bushels of charcoal; there was no way yet to obtain coke. In spite of competition, smelter charges stayed so high that they annoyed old Meyer Guggenheim of Philadelphia, a Swiss-born importer who had put money into two Leadville mines. He sent Benjamin, one of his seven sons, to the cloud city to study the problem.

Taking advantage of the D&RG–AT&SF stalemate, the Denver, South Park, & Pacific quickened the pace of its climb over Kenosha Pass into South Park. Endless lines of freight wagons carrying ore, concentrates, and matte creaked out of Leadville to meet the advancing railheads and returned with supplies. Speed was more important than efficiency. During the mild winter of 1878–79, Tabor and several other impatient mine-owners formed a company that built a cliff-hung road of 8 percent grades over Mosquito Pass, 13,188 feet above sea level, the loftiest wagonway in America. (It is an easy and lovely jeep ride today.) It was the short route to Leadville, but not the easy one. In that rarefied air, freight horses and oxen could drag wagonloads of machinery, stoves, or beer upward only a few rods at a time before having to stop and gasp for breath. Teams going in opposite directions inched past each other on the narrow shelf only with the aid of superlatives in skill, luck, and it would seem, profanity. One traveler wrote that he was "rarely out of sight of dead horses and mules that have broken legs or died of overwork, and every precipice along the way shows the wrecks of wagons that have slipped over the edge."

Railroads *had* to come!

Early in 1880, as a part of his nationwide railroad manipulations, Jay Gould finally forced a division of territory among the rivals. Under terms of the agreement the Atchison, Tokepa, & Santa Fe surrendered the track it had completed in the canyons of the Arkansas to the Denver & Rio Grande for $1 million and promised to build no farther into Colorado. In return the D&RG halted its New Mexico track laying at Española, 34 miles north of the city of Santa Fe, and promised to do no more building to the south save for a branch line that dipped into New Mexico while skirting the San Juans on the way to Durango and Silverton.

The agreement completed, the D&RG pushed for Leadville as fast as it could go. Economic cataclysms were meantime shaking the town. The managers of the Little Pittsburgh had been stripping the mine of its high-grade ore in order to maintain dividends. Sensing trouble, the principal stockholders unloaded 85,000 shares at top prices. When the collapse came shortly thereafter it shook all Colorado. Almost simultaneously there were labor upheavals at the Chrysolite. And the price of silver, which had been demonetized in 1873, was dropping steadily, from $1.32 an ounce in 1872 to $1.15 in 1880. It would keep skidding, to $.99 in 1886 and to $.84 in 1889.

The glorious frenzy was gone. To survive, big-scale mining would have to become as alert to economy and efficiency as was any other industrial complex. The railroad helped. It brought coal to the smelters, several of which combined. Others moved out of the mountains, letting the ore come downhill to them. Among the latter were the Guggenheims, who built a $1.25 million plant in Pueblo, the beginning of their worldwide smelting trust. Leadville became orderly—like a provincial English hamlet, said a tourist who arrived in 1882 in search of the wild life. "The men," he wrote unhappily, "would not have looked out of place in the street, say, of Reading, while the women in their quiet and somewhat old-fashioned style of dressing reminded me curiously of rural England. Indeed, I do not think my anticipations have ever been so completely upset."

Jay Gould, manipulator of railroads, was a peacemaker only at convenience. Though it had pleased him to stop the tomcat fight between the D&RG and the Santa Fe, he almost immediately started another one between Palmer and the Goliath of the West, the Union Pacific. The catalyst in the stew was John Evans' struggling narrow-gauge line, the Denver, South Park, & Pacific.

Buoyed by the traffic coming out of Leadville to meet it, the DSP&P worked almost due south across South Park and circumvented the Mosquito Range at low Trout Creek Pass, a mere 9,346 feet high. Trout Creek brought the rails into the great, peak-backed Arkansas Valley near the hamlet of Buena Vista. Buena Vista was only 35 relatively level miles south of Leadville, and now Palmer's D&RG was faced with still another competitor for the silver freight of Lake County.

To stave off trouble he suggested a division of riches. Prospectors inspired by the Leadville story had spilled across the divide and were opening new golcondas on the headwater streams of the Gunnison River. Moreover, a land stampede was developing. The Utes were about to be driven from the state because of the Meeker massacre, and their departure would open the wide, sage-gray valleys of the Gunnison and Uncompahgre valleys to farmers eager to raise crops and beef for the expanding mines.

All that and Leadville, too: Palmer and John Evans worked out an agreement whereby the Denver, South Park & Pacific would build a line into the Gunnison country. The Denver & Rio Grande would press on into Leadville. Each company would lease to the other transit rights on its tracks and would share the freight.

Gould upset this agreement by buying control of the Denver & South Park and transferring it to the Union Pacific. Palmer said that though he trusted John Evans he did not trust Jay Gould. The agreement was off and he would build his own line into Gunnison. Union Pacific officials suspected quite rightly that blooming ambitions lay behind the intransigence. Deprived of New Mexico, the D&RG was now eying Utah—and that very definitely made the baby road a potential competitor of the continent-spanning Union Pacific. One way to check such delusions would be to use the DSP&P for choking off the D&RG in the Gunnison country. And so another race began, this one across the Continental Divide.

Because Palmer pretty well controlled the Arkansas Valley, the DSP&P decided to push west from Buena Vista up the magnificent canyon of Chalk Creek into the heart of the highest mountains in the Rockies, the Sawatch Range. The divide there was a sharp gray ridge 12,000 feet high; the plan was to pierce it with a tunnel 1,845 feet long at an elevation of 11,608 feet above sea level. It was a staggering project, but on the other side of the range sat the booming town of Pitkin, which some optimists thought would turn out to be as rich as Leadville.

Palmer concentrated on the supply camp of Gunnison, which lay in the heart of the sweeping meadows and aspen groves that dotted the valley of the same name. Gunnison lay only 70 miles west of Salida, a town at the upper end of the Royal Gorge, which by then was fully under D&RG control. The 70 miles were interrupted by relatively low Marshall Pass, 10,846 feet. A toll road for wagons already crossed Marshall, built by whiskery, pint-sized Otto Mears, the Russian-born offspring of an English father and a Slavic mother. Mears sold his wagonway to Palmer for $13,000. By pressing parts of it into service as a roadbed, D&RG engineers corkscrewed their tight little rails into Gunnison (they arrived in August, 1881) while DSP&P workers were still pecking away at Alpine Tunnel at the head of Chalk Creek.

Though financially foolish, the tunnel caught the imagination of the nation. The first bore to pierce the Continental Divide, it sheltered the highest rail line at the time in North America. Union Pacific publicists made the most of it. According to one brochure, trains emerging from Alpine's west portal halted on a hair-raising curve that commanded a stupendous view to the west, whereupon the passengers, as elevated spiritually as William Bross had been in the Mosquitos, burst spontaneously into a hymn, "Nearer, My God, to Thee."

Less was said of the fifty or so men killed by accidents during the tunnel's construction, and of the rock and snow avalanches that intermittently swept the approaches. The most severe of the early snowslides was triggered in 1884 by the rumbling of a train emerging from the tunnel's western portal. It roared down the long hill into the town of Woodstock and killed thirteen people. Maintenance expenses were fearsome, and although Pitkin was a prosperous camp for a few years, it was no Leadville. And so ended the grand scheme to cut Palmer off at the Divide. By the time a Denver and South Park train finally limped into Gunnison on September 1, 1882, D&RG grading gangs were well on their way to Utah.

The abrogation of the agreement with Palmer doomed the Denver & South Park to high passes and snow trouble in every direction. Denied the right to use the D&RG tracks between Buena Vista and Leadville, the UP subsidiary contemplated the Mosquitos, found them too formidable, and instead crawled north up South Park's Tarryall Creek to Boreas Pass, a saddle 11,428 feet high in the Continental Divide, which there runs east and west. Boreas, named for the rude god of the north wind, opened a way to the mining country around Breckenridge. Below Breckenridge at lovely Dillon, named for the president of the Union Pacific (the original townsite is now underneath the waters of a monstrous reservoir), the tracks bent in a hairpin curve to another crossing of the Divide, Fremont Pass, 11,318 feet high.[2] From Fremont it was able, finally, to stepladder a way down into Leadville.

In spite of the erratic double crossing of the Divide, the distance from Denver to Leadville by way of the Denver & South Park was only 150 miles, compared to the D&RG's 280-mile swing through the Royal Gorge. (Seventy-seven air miles separate Denver and Leadville.) Distance was not the only criterion in mountain railroading, however. The DSP&P had to build ten miles of wooden showsheds to protect the approaches to Boreas Pass alone. Fantastic expedients were sometimes necessary to keep traffic moving. Once when a circus train was stalled by drifts, so the tale runs, elephants were unloaded and put to work pushing from behind. Under such conditons the UP subsidiary never became an effective competitor of the D&RG, not even inside Colorado.

Palmer's energies during this period are exhausting to contemplate. He pushed the San Juan branch over rolling Cumbres Pass (10,022 feet) to the new smelter town of Durango and on up the mile-deep gorge of the Animas River to Silverton, arriving there July 10, 1882. Far west in Utah, meanwhile, he and William Bell formed a subsidiary, the Rio Grande Western, and with it purchased the half-famished local railroads that ran part way up Little Cottonwood Canyon toward Alta, into the silver fields of Bingham Canyon south of Great Salt Lake, and over the Wasatches to booming Park City. These secured, the Rio Grande Western pushed west to meet the Denver & Rio Grande, a junction achieved near Green River, Utah, in March, 1883.

D&RG publicists boasted that the road had more men at work during this period than there were in the United States Army—35,000 surveyors, graders, tie cutters, bridge builders, tunnel blasters, teamsters, track layers, and whatnot. The figure seems grandiloquent. Perhaps it includes the prodigious turnover in the work force. Labor recruiters in the East advanced traveling expenses to newly arrived immigrants, only to have them desert in droves on nearing the mines.

Hoping to turn the D&RG into a vital link in a new transcontinental route, Palmer made arrangements to join the Central Pacific at Ogden. This annoyed the Union Pacific. When the D&RG laid its diminutive narrow-gauge iron into the huge Ogden railroad yards, owned jointly by the

[2] Fewer than twenty airline miles separate Boreas and Fremont passes. Rail distance was upward of 50 miles.

Today a major automobile highway crosses Fremont Pass. At its very top tourists can glimpse the world's largest molybdenum mine methodically chewing down an entire mountain, Bartlett Peak.

UP and CP, a Union Pacific crew put chains around the tracks and uprooted them with a switch engine. Palmer retorted by circling the yards and meeting the Central Pacific on the west. In order to accommodate his narrow-gauge rolling stock, he laid a third rail inside the CP's broad-gauge tracks and steamed triumphantly into the depot that way. Now there was a second transcontinental crossing of the Rockies—slow and roundabout, to be sure. Passengers spent thirty-five hours covering the 735 miles between Denver and Salt Lake City, but the scenery was spectacular enough so that for its sake many travelers submitted to the long boneshaking.

To the holders of D&RG stocks and bonds, who for years had received neither interest nor dividends, Palmer's construction feats seemed like financial disasters rather than railroading triumphs. Though he retained control of the Rio Grande Western, they forced him out of the presidency of the Denver & Rio Grande. If they expected this to bring relief from further building they were immediately disabused. During the mid-1880's a new competitor appeared, the Colorado Midland, presided over by John J. Hagerman, who had made a fortune in the Michigan iron mines.

Wasted by tuberculosis to a wispy 120 pounds, Hagerman had gone to Colorado Springs to die. To while away the time he bought some silver claims in the remote town of Aspen beside the Roaring Fork River, west of Leadville across 12,000-foot Independence Pass. To Hagerman's surprise, his health improved and his mines developed beautifully—but not profitably because of appalling transportation costs.

Hoping that a railroad would improve *their* health, Hagerman raised $7 million among eastern friends. With this money he wound a broad-gauge track from Colorado Springs up fierce 4 percent grades in Ute Pass to South Park and thence via Trout Creek to Leadville. He pierced the Continental Divide west of Leadville, and just north of Mount Massive, with a 2,200-foot tunnel 11,528 feet above sea level, almost as lofty as the Denver & South Park's Alpine bore. Snow plagued the Midland too. Wearied of the endless battle with the weather, the line built a longer, lower tunnel, the Busk-Ivanhoe, at 10,930 feet. This drop of 590 feet in altitude eliminated thirteen snowsheds and enough curves to make five and a half full circles.

The Midland threat aroused the debt-ridden D&RG to still more construction. Its tracks already ran north from Leadville across Tennessee Pass (10,424 feet) to the mines on Eagle River. It now pushed on down the Eagle to the bright red canyons of the Colorado, followed the Colorado to the sparkling Roaring Fork at Glenwood Springs, and pushed up the Roaring Fork to Aspen. Though this giant V ate up more than twice as many miles as the Midland's route, the baby road reached Aspen first, in October, 1887, to a wild welcome of gunfire, dynamite blasts, and whistle toots from every mine in the vicinity. The Midland did not arrive, anti-climactically, until the following January.

The Midland, however, was a standard-gauge road and could offer fast connections with broad-gauge lines in eastern Colorado. Moreover, the AT&SF was about to buy it from Hagerman at a thumping profit. These factors persuaded the construction-weary D&RG to strain itself still more and standardize its tracks through the Royal Gorge, over Tennessee Pass, and down the Colorado River to a junction point with the Rio Grande Western. That line in turn broad-gauged its tracks to Salt Lake City and Ogden.[3] The stimulus these new outlets gave to Aspen mining is indicated by the camp's immediate jump in production—to $10 million in 1889, even though silver was selling at an abysmal $.84 an ounce.

And there were still a few surprises left. In 1894 workers in Aspen's Smuggler mine uncovered the largest "nugget" of silver ever found in the Rockies, a chunk weighing 2,060 pounds, 93 percent pure metal. That's a lot of teaspoons.

[3] Part of the broad-gauging along the Colorado River was a joint undertaking of the D&RG and Midland. Meanwhile the Denver & Rio Grande and the Rio Grande Western, though physically a single line, remained split by violent economic schizophrenia. Gould's son at length merged them forcibly into the Missouri Pacific system as the Denver & Rio Grande Western. The Denver & Rio Grande Western did not emerge as an independent mountain entity until after World War II.

XVIII

THE RUSSET HILLS OF BUTTE

FAR to the north more railroad battles loomed. In 1875 Frederick Billings reorganized the Northern Pacific and during the next four years raised enough money to start construction from both east and west toward a junction in Montana. The Union Pacific reacted by creating two narrow-gauge subsidiaries. One, the Utah & Northern, was designed to snatch as much of Montana's mining traffic as possible away from the new trans-continental rival. The other, the Oregon Short Line, was, as the name suggests, an implicit promise to the nation of a quicker way from the East to the Pacific Northwest than the Northern Pacific could offer. The whole business was complicated by the railroad empire being created in Oregon by Henry Villard—the same Villard whom we met earlier as a newspaper reporter touring the infant gold camps in Colorado's Gregory Gulch—but those reverberations lie outside the scope of this work. The main concern here is the effect that the burst of railroad building had on the northern Rockies.

Mormons had made the first effort to move north by rail. Starting at Ogden, a cash-starved company called the Utah Northern had struggled as far as Franklin on the border between Utah and Idaho before bogging down in a financial morass. Jay Gould absorbed the company's charter and rights-of-way by picking up its bonds at 40 cents on the dollar. He re-incorporated his acquisition as the Utah *and* Northern, named Sidney Dillon of the UP as its president, and in 1879 began construction north toward Montana.

Dillon was also president of the Oregon Short Line, which began work two years later. The Short Line left the main tracks of the Union Pacific at dusty, sage-gray Granger in southwestern Wyoming and more or less paralleled the old covered-wagon trail through southern Idaho to Oregon. En route its tracks crossed those of the Utah & Northern at the edge of the Fort Hall reservation of the Bannock Indians. The Bannocks, who had lost another war with the United States in 1878, were no longer feeling resistant. They obligingly sold the crisscrossing railroads permission to build a junction town, Pocatello, on their reservation and to lay tracks across it in return for a promise of free train rides and 500 head of cattle. The payment in kine was later commutated into a somewhat more equitable cash settlement.

About the time the Oregon Short Line emerged from the reservation onto the blistered deserts bordering the black lava canyons of the Snake, silver was discovered 75 miles northward along the Big Wood River, where it emerges from the lower reaches of Idaho's sky-scratching Sawtooth Range. Delighted by this unexpected bonus, the Short Line delayed construction toward Oregon long enough to throw a spur up Wood River to the overnight towns of Hailey and Ketchum, jumping-off places for huge high-sided freight wagons and trailers bound into the mountains beyond. As time passed, the officers of the railroad realized that the area offered other traffic possibilities than ore. The hills abounded with game, and Wood River was full of trout. Tourists began coming in. Both Jay Gould and E. H. Harriman of the UP spent several summers in lovely mountain vales with their families. Many years later when skiing became popular, the railroad cashed in on that interest too by developing a winter sports area under the carefully contrived name of Sun Valley.

Land-hungry farmers followed the Utah & Northern into eastern Idaho as swiftly as silver miners followed the Short Line. The majority of them were Mormons, and their invasion of the fertile valleys coincided with an upsurge of anti-Mormon feeling throughout the nation. In 1882 and again in 1887 Congress passed repressive laws designed to break the political and temporal power of the Mormon Church. Under these acts persons who believed in polygamy as a religious principle, and that meant the generality of Mormons whether they had actually contracted plural marriages or not, were declared ineligible to vote, sit on juries, or hold public office. Church property was confiscated and placed in receivership; children of polygamous marriages were disinherited. Federal agents, often striking at night, sought to run down and jail persons who dwelt in unlawful cohabitation—"this leprous legacy of barbarity and sensual riot," one Idaho politician trumpeted in 1884.

In Utah the Mormons had their own political group, the People's party, to lend solidity. In western Wyoming and in Idaho they had no such recourse. In the latter state they sought relief by forming undercover, opportunistic alignments with whatever splinter group promised relief, however indirect. The matter was further complicated by violent quarrels between anti-Mormon parties, and the whole sorry business became entwined with other hate-breeding local feuds, including northern Idaho's persistent but unsuccessful attempts to secede from the rest of the state and unite with Washington. Eventually, after the Supreme Court of the United States had upheld the repressive laws, the Mormon Church admitted defeat and in

1890 officially advised its people to contract no more marriages contrary to national law. In Utah the People's party was dissolved. In Idaho, in 1894, Mormons finally were allowed to go again to the polls.

The Utah & Northern, which quite unwittingly had done so much to spread the geographic scope of the agony, meantime went on about its business. Near midnight on December 21, 1881, the first train entered Butte. One excited publicist declared that the line was now "the most important narrow-gauge road in the world," a statement which, if it reached him, surely lifted the eyebrows of William Palmer of the D&RG. Other observers, less impressed, declared that the roadbed over Monida Pass between Montana and Idaho was so rough that boxcars now and then tipped over in the middle of freight trains and passengers were occasionally shaken out of their plank-sized upper berths in the tiny sleeping cars.

To Marcus Daly the timing could not have been more opportune. In 1880, while Utah & Northern track layers were struggling over Monida Pass, he had found near the top of the ruddy hill behind Butte a small mine named Anaconda whose looks appealed to him. Its shaft was only 65 feet deep and it could be picked up for $30,000. He suggested to the Walker brothers in Salt Lake City that they buy it.

They demurred. The expensive development work that Daly had done for them on the Alice and Lexington mines was lifting those properties into the front ranks of Butte's silver producers, a position which the Alice would hold for several more years. Rather than buy the unproved Anaconda, they preferred to take over Daly's quarter interest in the Alice and reap their profits without further outlay.

Daly used the proceeds of the sale to acquire the Anaconda for himself. Unable to expand the shallow workings out of his own pocket, he offered a three-quarter interest to George Hearst, Lloyd Tevis, and James Ben Ali Haggin of San Francisco. The trio were feeling expansive. In 1877 they had used some of their profits from Park City's Ontario mine, which Daly had located for them, to buy and develop the Homestake mine in the Black Hills of South Dakota, and were just beginning to see signs of its blossoming into what it later became—the greatest single gold mine in the world, producer up to the present time of half a billion dollars. Thus it was no particular strain on them to pick up three quarters of the Anaconda and tell Daly, who retained a quarter interest, to go ahead with its development.

They thought they had bought a silver mine. At first Daly thought so, too. He rented a stamp mill from William Andrews Clark for treating the Anaconda's oxidized silver ore and then found, as he deepened the shaft during 1881, that the copper content was increasing. This was not surprising. Other Butte properties had encountered the same feature, and the local smelters were geared to picking up the sought-for silver in mattes of copper. When the matte was shipped east, or even to Swansea, Wales, for refining, the producers received payment also for the copper. In all cases, however, they considered this a mere incident to the more valuable metal.

Alone of all the mineowners in Butte, Marcus Daly was able to revise his thinking. As soon as railroads reached Butte and freight rates tumbled, might it not be possible, through the use of mass-production techniques (shades of William Stevens and Ed Harrison at Leadville!) to shift emphasis—to make copper his goal and silver the by-product?

The folklore of Butte suggests that bluff, uneducated Marcus Daly came to his revolutionary decision through an almost mystic insight into the coming importance of copper to electricity. Bell had invented the telephone in 1876, Edison the incandescent light bulb in 1879. George Westinghouse, William Stanley, and Nikola Tesla were experimenting with motors and copper wires for the transmission of power. In 1881, however, Marcus Daly could not have heard of the experiments with power. And, like most of his contemporaries, he almost surely considered light bulbs and telephones as curiosities with limited application.

What he did grasp, down to their finest details, were the potentials of his own craft. To his backers in San Francisco he gave an estimate, based on years of experience, of the amount of ore available in the mine and its neighboring claims, the metal content, and the cost of extracting it. He let them balance what he said against the prices prevailing in 1881—copper at 18 cents a pound and silver, the sweetener, at $1.13 an ounce.

After listening to him, Hearst, Tevis, and Haggin conceivably discussed the possible effect of electricity on the demands for copper, but their ultimate decision was probably based on nothing more abstruse than the arithmetic of the situation—and on their well-justified faith in Marcus Daly as a first-class miner. They put up the $4 million he wanted.

His first step was to shut down the Anaconda. This led his neighbors to fear that the vein had pinched out and that its extension onto their properties would also vanish at depth. They panicked, and he was able to buy their claims at bargain rates—or so says another item in Anaconda folklore. Having thus obtained the extra ground he needed for large-scale production, Daly installed new hoists capable of lifting heavy loads of ore from such unheard-of depths that the town thought he had lost his mind.

He needed a giant smelter to handle all the ore he envisioned, and not enough water was available in Butte for running it. After a careful search he found the site he wanted on the bank of Warm Springs Creek, 26 miles northwest of Butte. Late in 1882 a friendly rancher quietly picked up the necessary acreage. Water proved harder to come by—at least according to still another item in Montana folklore. This tale says that William Clark controlled the rights and charged such an outrageous price for them that Daly never forgave him.

The next step was to assure himself of ample wood for the smelter furnaces and for timbers to shore up the drifts and stopes of the enlarged mine. That consideration brought the Northern Pacific Railroad into the picture, not because of its carrying capacity but because of its land. It held the most generous grant ever awarded by Congress—a checkerboard of alternate square-mile sections throughout a strip of territory that extended 40 miles to either side of the main line. That is to say, for each mile of track completed, the NP received 25,600 acres. The Utah & Northern, by contrast, had no land grant whatsoever.

The Northern Pacific was in a tearing hurry to capture every acre possible. Public opposition to the overly generous land-grant program was gathering headway, and Congress, yielding to the pressure, just might declare some of the acreage forfeit because the track had not been completed within the time limits prescribed by earlier laws. No one was more aware of this danger than Henry Villard of Oregon. In pursuit of his own ends Villard had raised enough millions to oust Frederick Billings, the president of the NP, and take over the running of the railroad. That done, he intensified the pace of construction. Crews pushed westward up the Yellowstone River and over Bozeman Pass, where Lisa's fur men had hunted three quarters of a century earlier. Other gangs simultaneously chopped westward through the dense forest beside Clark Fork and in Hell Gate Canyon, a route David Thompson had long ago exploited for the North West Company.

(To cast ahead a bit: the rails came together in September, 1883. The junction point was Gold Creek, once called American Fork, near the vanished log cabins of James and Granville Stuart, and the shallow prospect holes where Francois Finlay, nicknamed Benetsee, had discovered the first traces of Montana gold. It was an amazing feat of building—and it put the Northern Pacific $9 million in debt. Like Palmer, Villard was forced by his angry bondholders to resign. This was early in 1884, and by that time the Utah & Northern was pushing from Butte north through Deer Lodge Valley to join the Northern Pacific at the hamlet of Garrison. The U&N hoped, of course, to keep Butte traffic in its own hands. Had Villard stayed in office he might have fought, building his own spur to Butte. That speculation is idle, however, for both lines were weary. They compromised by forming a jointly held subsidiary, the Montana Union, and through it divided the traffic from the north. And now Butte, like Leadville, was served by two railroads.)

Well before this, in the fall of 1882, Daly made his move to get the wood he wanted. He worked through Villard and the Northern Pacific, whose checkerboard of grant land in western Montana and in the panhandle of Idaho contained some of the finest stands of commercial white pine, spruce, fir, and larch in the nation. The railroad, too, needed enormous quantities of wood for ties, bridge timbers, and buildings along its 925 miles of track between eastern Montana and the Columbia River; in Montana alone the line used (according to the 1884 forestry report of the U.S. commissioner of agriculture) 2,228,160 ties and 777,798,600 board feet of lumber.

An organization known as the Montana Improvement Company was formed to facilitate the handling of the railroad's timber—cutting it, snaking it out of the woods, sawing it, and delivering it. Half the stock in the Montana Improvement Company, plus one share, was owned by the Northern Pacific Railroad. The other half, less one share, was held by E. L. Bonner, R. A. Eddy, and A. B. Hammond, Missoula lumbermen, and by Marcus Daly, financed by his California capitalists. The Northern Pacific not only paid the Improvement Company for handling the wood but also agreed to ship forest products for its stockholders at less than normal freight charges. Thus Daly not only obtained an almost limitless supply of lumber from the biggest timber operation in the Rockies, but also got it at a lower over-all cost than was available to any other mining interest in Montana Territory.

Rumors of what he was up to spread rapidly through the mining world. At first the seventeen copper producers of the Lake Superior area, who sold their output through the great Calumet & Hecla combine, were amused. They all but controlled the market. Their ore was of higher grade than Daly's; their transportation costs by water were lower than his by rail from the Rockies; and it did not seem possible that mere mass production would be enough to overcome the differential. Early in 1883, as a warning to him to keep out of the field, they cut the price of copper.

Daly went right on working. In the spring of 1883 he journeyed to Warm Springs Creek to select the exact site for the smelter and for the town that would grow up around it. The valley was lovely then. The richly timbered hill to the south culminated in a 10,000-foot summit that he named Mount Haggin. In the bottom lands beside the curling stream cattle grazed in grass to their knees. We'll put Main Street there, north and south, he said, and it was never lovely again. In 1884 yellow sulphur smoke tinged with arsenic began coming from the stacks. The creek turned opaque. Vegetation nearby withered; grass at a distance became so impregnated from the fumes that cattle are said to have copper-plated their teeth just from grazing on it—before they died, that is. Trains chuffing in to haul off freight cars full of matte spewed more smoke. Buildings, clothing, skin, everything bore the taste and feel and smell of grit.

The remodeled mine was ready to produce ore before the smelter was prepared to handle it. To keep it from piling up and to raise money that he needed in a hurry, even at a loss, Daly shipped 27,370 tons by rail and ocean freighter to Swansea, where it sold for $1.7 million. These figures led William Clark and the lesser mineowners and smeltermen of Butte to join

Daly in defying Calumet & Hecla and adapt their own properties, like his, to large-scale production.

Amusement fading, the Lake mines in November, 1884, cut the price of copper once again. Daly and the others just mined a little harder. Butte's population rose toward the 20,000 mark. Boston financiers who were experienced in copper production sent scouts to Montana to look over the russet hills. The result was a wholesale purchasing of claims back of Butte and the formation of two huge new combines, each with its own smelting works, the Boston & Montana Consolidated Copper and Silver Mining Company and the Butte & Boston Consolidated Mining Company.

In 1885 Daly's Anaconda turned out 36 million pounds of copper. Twenty-five other Butte mines, led by Clark (the Boston companies were not fully under way as yet) produced 32 million pounds. The total was not a great deal less than the 77 million pounds turned out by the seventeen Lake mines. Clearly Daly had discovered techniques of production which, with the help of the silver in his ore, made him formidable indeed.[1] In 1886, in final grimness, the Lake producers cut prices to a rock-bottom 10 cents a pound. Let Butte Hill try meeting that, even with the support of silver—for its price, too, was dropping: from an average of $1.07 an ounce in 1885 to 99 cents in 1886.

The winter that followed (1886–87) was disastrous, and not just for the miners. Eastward on the high plains of Montana and around the Big Horn Mountains of Wyoming drought had shriveled a range overstocked by cattle imported by careless plungers, many of them English, who hoped to make quick profits on a perpetually rising market. Instead, prices dropped sharply, a blow followed in the fall of 1886 by early snows, long spells of below-zero weather, and paralyzing winds. Some outfits helplessly watched two thirds of their drought-thinned animals perish in the bottomless drifts. Only the hardiest, like Conrad Kohrs, who had moved from Deer Lodge onto the plains, managed to survive and adapt to new conditions brought by railroads, barbed wire, and a slow influx of farmers cutting up the sod with their plows.

In Butte many mines shut down. Daly did, too—but only so that he could, by drawing on his backers for more millions, enlarge the smelter at Anaconda town, buy more ground on Butte Hill, and increase the mine's output to the then astounding figure of 115 tons a day. (Today the Anaconda mills at Butte gulp down that quantity in a matter of minutes.) During the shutdown the unemployed miners, to whom no one considered sending anything so radical as a welfare check, pulled in their belts, huddled around their stoves, and dully waited out one terrible blizzard after another. In the spring, when the Anaconda reopened and they filed thankfully back to

---

[1] In 1885 the mines of Montana produced $7,322,000 worth of copper and $10,-060,000 worth of silver. Much of the silver came from Butte and obviously played no small part in sustaining the mines during the long price war.

work, the mine was able to turn out copper three quarters of a cent per pound cheaper than before. The war went on.

Though the users of copper reveled in 10-cent metal, the producers were growing desperate. Sensing this, a group of French speculators led by Hyacinthe Secretan raised $13.5 million and set out to corner the world's supply of the red metal. Every major producer was offered 13 cents a pound if he would limit his output according to a prescribed scale and sell only to the syndicate. Once the supply was monopolized, so the plan went, the syndicate would release the metal to users at from 17 to 20 cents a pound.

Weary of the cutthroat war, mines throughout the world fell into line. Haggin signed a contract with Secretan for Anaconda, as did the management of Calumet & Hecla for the Lake Superior mines. For Daly this meant no rest, however. Almost at once he had to face a new threat raised by his own government in the form of a series of civil and criminal suits filed against the Montana Improvement Company for depredations on the public forests.

The company was not alone in its brazen disregard of regulations concerning the timberlands of the public domain. Most Westerners were hostile toward conservation of any kind. They came by the trait honestly enough. Forests in the East had, in general, been obstacles that needed clearing away before crops could be raised. Although the evergreen forests of the Rockies stood on ground too high and rough for agriculture, the old disdain for forests still prevailed in pioneer thinking.

Hand in hand with the attitude went the assumption that all pioneers were entitled to exploit at low charge or no charge at all the resources of whatever countryside they helped to open and tame—its beaver fur, its game animals, the precious metals, the water, and even, after the passage of the Homestead Act, the richest farming land. They asked only that the good things of the earth be put to beneficial use. They did approve of limiting, by compact or by Congressional action, the amount of agricultural or mining land an individual or company could obtain free from the public domain; otherwise distribution was to be determined largely on the basis of first come first served. Beyond that, they were loath to accept any restraint whatsoever, even for the sake of their own posterity.

When the first miners and settlers in the Rockies needed fuel or mine timber they simply chopped down the nearest trees. As their construction work expanded, however, they became too busy to do their own lumbering, and turned to commercial suppliers. About the only timber available to these men was in the public forests, and the forests were hedged in by unrealistic restrictions. It was impossible, for one thing, for a man or a company to obtain title to an unsurveyed block of forest land—and, anyway, the sawyers did not want title to land; they simply wanted the right to fell the trees on it. Though it was possible to obtain lumbering permits, the costs and the red-tape involved seemed unutterably picayune and anachronistic to the free-wheeling timber contractors, whose markets with the mines and railroads were, in certain sectors, next to insatiable.

Like the placer miners, accordingly, the lumbermen openly invaded the public domain and took what they wanted, but with even less sense of permanency. Because there seemed room enough for all, they did not even work out a self-imposed system of establishing "claims." Reap and go—like the early beaver trappers.

At first they met little opposition, for Congress did not vote funds for adequate policing. Finally, however, the depredations in the Great Lakes area and along parts of the Pacific coast reached such an extent that the government roused itself after a fashion. It reaffirmed the policy that cutters must have permits and ordered its timber agents to collect the license fee *ex post facto,* by levying at the mills a "stumpage" tax of 16⅔ percent on the value of the finished product. Wood cut without permit was to be seized and sold at public auction, the proceeds going to the U.S. Treasury.

Westerners reacted wrathfully. "The collection of this tax is a wrong and outrage on the pioneers of the west," editorialized the Laramie (Wyo.) *Daily Sentinel* on July 17, 1872. The rumbling was more than newspaper talk; feeling in Laramie ran so high that when N. K. Boswell, the government timber agent there, was ordered to tighten the screws, he refused and telegraphed his superior to come try it himself, if he dared.

During Colorado's transition to statehood in 1876, her legislators went so far as to try to inveigle control of her forests away from the federal government by slipping into Article XVIII, Section 6, of her proposed constitution a clause stating that the state would enact laws to preserve the timber "upon the lands of the public domain, *the control of which shall be conferred by Congress upon the State."* [Italics mine.] When Congress refused the bait and government agents continued their crackdown, the *Rocky Mountain News* fumed on March 24, 1877, that "Mr. Secretary Schurz [of the Department of the Interior] may as well understand first as last that his new 'orders' are useless and that it will not do to send any spies or informers to Colorado on such a mission. The people of this state must have timber."

Part and parcel of the *News*'s continuing attacks on Schurz was an argument that swelled ever louder throughout the mountains. If the government wanted to stop depredations on its forests, let it sell its timberlands to the people—providing, always, that the price was right. After federal agents had seized 120,000 ties belonging to influential Colorado citizens, the *News* insisted (October 10, 1877) that the only fair solution was to sell timberlands to cutters at a price of $1.25 an acre, hardly the cost of a single mature yellow pine. Otherwise, let the government beware. "The standing army of the United States is not half big enough to drive out the settlers from Colorado and that is the only thing that will stop woodcutting on government land."

A similar clamor from Wyoming, Utah, Montana, Idaho, and the Coast states led Congress in 1878 to pass two foolish laws. One, the Free Timber Act, legalized what individual miners and ranchers had long been doing; removing wood at will from the public domain for their own mining and domestic needs. The far more acute problem of commercial cutting for the benefit of those same ranchers and miners was ignored. Lumbering of that sort could continue only under the same old "stumpage" provisions, which led the Laramie *Sentinel* to grumble in the same old vein, "The proper thing to do would be to take these 'stumpage collectors' and duck them in the horse pond for the first offense and hang them out to dry for a second."

The other law of 1878, the Timber and Stone Act (applicable at first to the Coast states but later extended), allowed a citizen to buy for his own use up to 160 acres of *surveyed* land, provided that it was unfit for agricultural purposes, at the price of $2.50 an acre—double the *News*'s recommendation but ridiculously low even so. Congress, of course, was still bemused by the Jeffersonian philosophy of a nation of small freeholders, of land distributed to all comers in plots of 160 acres each, which had been quite enough for a single family to handle in the humid East before the days of mechanized farming. Under the arid condition of the West, this theory simply did not work out in practice—nor did the notion of small, one-family sawmill operations work out any better in areas where railroading and big-scale mining were creating voracious demands for wood.

What better approaches might have been devised is hardly the point here. What did happen is that the impatient West, prone anyway to taking matters into its own hands, reacted with ruthless disdain for what it considered to be nonsensical regulations. The big timber operators, imitating methods of fraud already perfected on the plains by land speculators circumventing the homestead requirements, simply paid their employees a few dollars to buy forest land (if it was surveyed) under the terms of the Timber and Stone Act and transfer it in wholesale lots to the company. Where the land wasn't surveyed—and in the 1880s that was much of the West—they just went ahead as before and bribed, intimidated, or simply ignored whatever underpaid, overworked government agents happened at rare intervals to object.

Ordinary settlers regarded all this with mixed feelings. They wanted the timberlands open. They believed that railroads, smelters, and mines were necessary to the prosperous building of the West. At the same time they were fiercely opposed to letting great blocks of any kind of public land—farming, grazing, or timber—slip by fraudulent means into the hands of speculators or mighty corporations.

In their opposition they found staunch allies in President Cleveland and in Cleveland's humorless, unbending land commissioner, William Andrew

Jackson Sparks. As soon as Sparks was appointed he plowed headlong into the thickets of corruption with a wildly swinging ax. He ordered cattlemen to remove every illegal fence from the public domain and threatened to send out troops to see that they did. He vowed to take away from the land-grant railroads the acreages that they had not earned within the time limits set by their charters and to redistribute the holdings to homesteaders. As for homesteading itself, he suspended throughout most of the West final action on entries (that is, on passing full title to claimants) until his investigators could run down charges of widespread fraud.

Still other investigations revolved around the Timber and Stone Act and around alleged trespasses onto the public forests. The findings that emerged horrified Sparks and led him to institute criminal and civil suits against several lumber companies. A particular target of his ire was the Montana Improvement Company, owned by the Northern Pacific Railroad in conjunction with Marcus Daly of Anaconda and lumbermen Hammond, Bonner, and Eddy of Missoula. What made their frauds and trespasses doubly objectionable was the fact that they could have confined their cutting to Northern Pacific grant lands if they had chosen. But sometimes there was better or more convenient lumber on nearby public land. Besides, the railroad wished to hold the good timber on its land for high prices in the future. Thus, though the Montana Improvement Company had been formed to handle trees rightly belonging to the Northern Pacific, it soon took to ignoring these and, in the main, cutting government trees instead. It made no effort to ask for licenses, of course. For one thing, the permits probably would have been refused. For another, the 16⅔ percent fee would have added nearly half a million dollars a year to Anaconda's wood bill alone.

And now, suddenly, here was the land commissioner himself, firing charges right and left.

Unhappily for himself, Sparks plunged too fast and stepped on too many toes. Would-be settlers, bewildered by the abrupt suspension of normal homestead routines, raised cries of pain. The major railroads, the cattlemen, and the big landowners brought subtler but more effective pressures to bear through their congressmen and senators. The uproar reached such proportions that in November, 1887, Sparks was removed from office. Many of the suits that he had initiated stayed on the dockets, however, including those against the Montana Improvement Company. As additional assurance, Daly and the other owners decided to seek not just a friendly but also an effective voice in Congress.

About this same time, the spring of 1888, William Andrews Clark entered the lists for Congress as a Democrat, in Montana an almost sure guarantee of success. Because he was a mineowner and a heavy user of wood, he presumably would raise a friendly voice on behalf of his fellow industrialists. Prognosticators, however, were predicting a Republican administration in Washington. A Republican President would naturally appoint Republicans to serve as Secretary of the Interior and as land commissioner, and those were the men with whom Montana's delegate would have to deal in respect to the troublesome suits.

Searching their souls by the grim light of the writs that had been served on them, Daly, Hammond, Eddy, and Bonner—Democrats all—decided to desert Clark and work for the election of the Republican nominee, young Thomas H. Carter. Furthermore, legend adds, bluff, jovial Marcus Daly had been out of sorts with frosty little William Clark ever since Clark had overcharged him for the water rights needed by the smelter on Warm Springs Creek. And so out went the word to the mine foremen at Anaconda, to the timber bosses of the Improvement Company, to the train crews of the NP—Carter. A glass of beer here, a cigar there, veiled threats about keeping a job, sample ballots obligingly marked: to Clark's utter amazement counties that always before had voted Democratic went Republican and he was roundly defeated by a virtual unknown.

He never got over the hurt to his pride or the self-righteous feeling that he had been the victim of unforgivable political treachery. The undying resentment would lead, as we shall see in a later chapter, to multimillion-dollar personal vendettas against Daly and eventually into a tangled power struggle for the economic and political mastery of most of the northern Rockies. For the moment, however, expediency led him to hide his fury.

Under the aegis of the new Republican national administration, which had indeed been elected, Montana was again seeking statehood, and in the spring of 1889 a convention gathered to draft a constitution. The mineowners of the would-be state hoped that by banding together against the cattlemen, sheepmen, and ordinary small businessmen they could slip into the document certain clauses which would give them tax advantages possessed by no other industry in Montana. Clark, who was chairman of the convention, spearheaded the drive. To his fellow delegates he cried in his high thin voice that theirs was now the glorious opportunity to "protect those brave pioneers who came out here and . . . opened up these great mountains and brought their hidden wealth to light; yea, I say it is the duty of the members of this convention to throw such safeguards around this great industry as are proper and just; this great industry that . . . has made all the valleys and mountains of Montana productive."

By maintaining an appearance of unity the mineowners pushed the desired clauses through without trouble, and now Anaconda had two assets—a friendly state constitution so far as taxation was concerned and a friendly Republican congressman who soon moved on to a senatorship.[2]

On other fronts the company was still sore-pressed. On March 14, 1889,

[2] The suits that Sparks had initiated were duly laid to rest, as planned. When others were instituted later during McKinley's presidency, Senator Carter, helped by Henry Rogers of Standard Oil and by President-maker Mark Hanna, managed to quiet them, too.

arsonists (or so Daly believed) burned the smelter at Anaconda down to the ground. Almost at the same moment he learned that the plan of the French syndicate to control the copper market had gone awry. After buying 400 million pounds of the metal at 13 cents a pound, the schemers discovered that they could not pass it on to users at the increase in price that they had anticipated. There was too much secondhand copper floating around, too many copper mattes from small gold and silver smelters, too many possible substitutes like iron and zinc. Users turned to these cheaper sources, one of the bankers supporting the syndicate committed suicide, and the price of newly mined copper crashed suddenly to 7½ cents.

Frightened Parisian bankers seized the only security they had for loans made to the syndicate—the 400 million pounds of copper. If that much metal were dumped onto the market at once, the catastrophe would be complete. Haggin and the directors of Calumet & Hecla rushed to France. Uniting with the rest of the world's producers, they persuaded the bankers to release the copper a bit at a time at a pegged price of 12 cents a pound, only a penny less than the syndicate had been paying.

The future shone again. When Daly rebuilt the smelter at Anaconda he enlarged its capacity to 3,000 tons a day (he planned to handle ore for other producers, too) and emerged strong enough that when the Montana Union Railroad would not carry the freight involved at the prices he suggested, he snapped his fingers at the company, built his own line from Butte, and cut haulage costs by two thirds. Other mineowners received comparable relief in 1889 when the Montana Central, a subsidiary of J. J. Hill's Great Northern Railroad, built south from Great Falls to Butte and entered the competition for a share of the camp's booming traffic.

Even the vacillating policy of the national government concerning the coinage of silver helped shovel profits into the pockets of the mineowners. Until 1873 the U.S. Treasury had maintained a bimetallic money standard by buying and coining into dollars all the silver offered to it. The price it paid was arbitrarily set in terms of gold at a ratio of 15.998 to 1; that is, approximately sixteen ounces of silver were equal in value to one ounce of gold. Until the early 1870's silver was worth more than that on the world market and relatively little was presented for coinage. But then great new deposits of white metal were found, many in the United States, and at the same time most of the nations of Western Europe went onto a straight gold standard. As an inevitable result, the price of silver began to slip. Foreseeing a flood of offerings at the 16 to 1 price, the government in 1873 quietly removed the coinage provision from the books and silver prices were then free to seek their own level without artificial checks.

The prices of other commodities also were declining. Debtors, and that included most of the mortgage-carrying farmers in the country, found themselves forced to pay off their obligations with more money, in effect, than they had borrowed. Radicals blamed the government for restricting the amount of money in circulation. Impassioned orators began crying out against what they called the Crime of 1873: "a crime, because it has confiscated millions of dollars worth of property. A crime, because it has made tens of thousands of tramps . . . thousands of suicides . . . has brought tears to strong men's eyes and hunger and pinching want to orphans."

The remedy, argued these radical theorists, was controlled inflation, a pumping of silver money back into the economy which would cause the prices of all commodities to rise. In 1878 Congress yielded enough to pass what radicals considered a timid half measure, the Bland-Allison Act; under its provisions the Treasury was required to buy, at the prevailing market price, a minimum of 2 million ounces of silver per month. In spite of this, the price both of silver and of most other commodities continued to decline. Declaring that the Bland-Allison Act had not been strong enough, senators and congressmen from six new Western states (the Dakotas, Washington, Montana, Wyoming, and Idaho) launched a drive for heavier purchases. In 1890 they managed, by trading votes on a tariff measure, to push through the Sherman Silver Purchase Act. Now the government had to purchase 4.5 million ounces of silver each month.

The price jumped from 84 cents to $1.05. Foreign silver then began to roll onto the market. Battered by this and by other dislocations to the economic machine, the slump resumed; by 1892 the price was down to 87 cents. Their fervor intensified by spreading hard times in the farm belt (and their earnestness supported by the mineowners, a strange love affair between haves and have-nots), militant theorists insisted once again that the remedy had not been sufficiently bold. Success would come only when the government had courage enough to forcibly peg the price of silver at the old ratio with gold of 16 to 1 and bought without limitation all the metal offered at that price.

The mountain West really thought it might win the battle. Optimism boiled through the mining camps. In 1890, when Montana had a population of 143,000 (up 265 percent from 1880), her mines turned out $17,625,000 in copper (a value that presumably would rise under inflation), $16,537,000 in silver, $3.3 million in gold.[3] By 1892 the copper producers of Butte had outstripped those of Lake Superior by a thumping 57 million pounds. With that much volume, even a fractional rise in prices would be significant.

Most of Butte's copper was dug from a small area by relatively few people. To aggressive personalities—and the capitalistic world was full of those in the 1890's—the concentration offered alluring enticements to seize control of the whole. Before considering those battles, however, it is well to consider two other explosive centers that were developing simultaneously in other parts of the Rockies: Coeur d'Alene, Idaho, and Cripple Creek, Colorado.

[3] Colorado's mines produced that same year $19,740,000 in silver, $4,913,000 in lead, $4,151,132 in gold, a mere $559,368 in copper.

XIX

THEY MISSED MILLIONS

ANDREW J. PRICHARD was a loner—poor, morose, secretive, at odds with the order of things. Though he had a wife and son, they are shadowy in his accounts, which somehow don't quite have the ring of candor to them. Footloose and dissatisfied, he wandered out of New Mexico into Colorado, out of Colorado into the Gallatin Valley of Montana. During his stay in the Gallatin Valley he joined one of the scattered small chapters of the Liberal League, a loosely knit, continent-wide, numerically insignificant group of socialistic, atheistic Free Thinkers. Then on he went, west along the Mullan Road, across the Bitterroot Mountains and down into the heavily timbered South Fork of the Coeur d'Alene Mountains in the Idaho Panhandle. It was November, 1878. His family seems not to have been with him.

During the preceding two decades tens of thousands of people, many of them experienced miners, had followed the same Mullan trail along the Coeur d'Alene's South Fork. Some had noticed traces of gold, but nothing exciting, and because they were bound for other places they had hurried on, sticking close to the cleared path. Not Prichard. He was in no hurry. Wherever the terrain and trees allowed, he contoured along the sides of the valley's steep northern hills, looking for quartz outcroppings. A little west of the present town of Osburn, so he said later, he found a vein and named it, as a sign of his Free Thinking, the Evolution. There is no evidence that he made any effort that year to file a claim to the lode.

He spent most of the next year logging near the tiny settlement of Spokane, Washington. In the fall of 1879 he returned to the Evolution. He arrived, he says, with only a single dollar in his pocket and no tools adequate for developing a hard-rock mine. He built a cabin a little less than half a mile southwest of the claim, on a flat at the foot of the steeply rising mountain. As often as snowstorms allowed, he worked at placer mining in a nearby ravine that he named Prospect Gulch. He took out his first gold in March, 1880, he reported later. Yet he made no apparent effort to record that claim either, although he must occasionally have gone for supplies to the lakeside hamlet of Coeur d'Alene, county seat of Kootenai County, where the recorder's office was located.

Nearly two years went by, during which time either claim could have been jumped. Late in 1881, the tale resumes, Prichard cut a trail up the steep mountain behind the Evolution, crossed its top and came down into the valley of the North Fork of the Coeur d'Alene River near its junction with a tributary later called Prichard Creek. He followed Prichard Creek east. Where it forked he turned up the Eagle Creek branch and wound among enormous trees toward the Bitterroot Divide. He said later that he found gold in several places—one pan yielded $42—and that he worked the streams until snow drove him out.

On April 25, 1882, he visited the office of the Kootenai County recorder. He registered two claims there—not to ground along the North Fork, where he reputedly had found rich diggings a few months earlier, but to his original workings on the South Fork—the Evolution and the placer ground in Prospect Gulch.[1]

The plot thickens. One tale has it that Liberal Leaguers to whom he wrote about his discoveries leaked the news and that in June, 1882, a small party of opportunists appeared at his cabin near the Evolution. He yielded to their threats and cajolery and led them to the North Fork—but not, perhaps, to the spots where he had found gold. In any event, only one of the party seems to have been excited enough to go through the formality of filing claims. This was an old man named Gillett. Though Gillett was sixty-five years old, he left the others and prospected alone. He found gold on Prichard Creek a little below present-day Murray. Amidst the obscurity one wonders, at times, whether anyone other than Gillett really did visit the North Fork during those years.

Then, in March, 1883, presumably long after his captors had gone their ways, Prichard at last began staking out claims on the North Fork—exuberantly, as if to make up for lost time. Four of these recordings he called the Discovery Claims. They lay contiguous to what became Murray, not far from Gillett's strike. Possibly they were on ground Prichard had tested as early as 1881. Or possibly he went to the North Fork after hearing of Gillett's find. The belated date of filing tells nothing about the time of actual location.

Prichard took a half interest in each of these "discovery" claims for himself. The other halves went to his own absent son, to the son of a friend, and to two poor Liberal widows, one in Michigan and one in Illinois. He also staked out, either then or later, several claims for other friends in the Liberal League, using their powers of attorney to justify the

[1] These workings actually lay east of Kootenai County in Shoshone County, whose seat was the moribund town of Pierce, 150 or more difficult miles to the south. Other claimants along the Coeur d'Alene River made the same mistake. Prichard rectified his by refiling the claims on April 30, 1885, shortly after the Shoshoni County seat had been transferred to the new town of Murray on the North Fork.

extralegal procedure. His motives appear in a letter he wrote to one of them:

> I have made a discovery of a gold-bearing country that will give employ-ment to at least 15,000 to 20,000 men. There are two good and natural townsites where will be built cities representing thousands in less than two years. . . . I would like to see as much of this go into the hands of Liberals as possible, and also see them build a city where they can have their own laws and enough of this vast mining region to support it, which they can do if they will go at it cool and work together.

Some Liberals appeared; how many is open to question. By August, 1883, Prichard felt sure enough of control that he risked boasting of his discovery to the editor of the Spokane newspaper. The rush was on then, and the Liberals had no chance.

As had happened before in stampedes, there was not enough ground to go around. Belligerent latecomers tried without success to reduce the size of claims from the 20 acres specified by federal law to 10 acres. They jumped the claims Prichard had recorded for absentee friends and defied him to do anything about it; claims could not be filed by proxy. They also attacked his right to share in as many as four discovery claims; he was hogging things. One can't help wondering, in view of the way he was gleaning hostility instead of money, whether he invented at least part of his involved tales of long searching—tales uncorroborated by the indirect evidence of filings—in the muddled hope that they might stir sympathy. If so, the effort failed.

The first stampeders arrived from the farming regions of eastern Washington. Small steamboats carried them across Coeur d'Alene Lake and ten miles up Coeur d'Alene River. They disembarked at Cataldo, a settlement at the foot of a ridge on whose top loomed an amazing, white, baroque building 60 feet tall, its façade decorated with tall pillars and triple arches topped by crosses—the Sacred Heart Mission, recently abandoned for a new site, that had been built in 1846 by Jesuit priests. Near Cataldo the North and South forks of the river came together—smiling valleys winding out of dusky mountains. At the junction some of the stampeders trans-ferred their belongings into awkward bateaux and laboriously poled their way up the North Fork. Others bought horses at Jackass Prairie and followed a tortuous riverbank trail that crossed the deep stream thirty-six times. On arrival at the gold fields each group swore that the other's way of going surely had been preferable.

On the completion of the Northern Pacific in the fall of 1883, throngs from the East began traveling by train to Thompson Falls, Montana, site of David Thompson's vanished fur trading houses, where the Clark Fork dropped in a white thunder down gray-black ledges of stone. From the falls they climbed west across the Bitterroot Mountains into Idaho, under a sweet-smelling, moss-hung canopy of evergreens so dense that for miles not a glimmer of sky appeared. Winter scarcely slowed the rush. During the early months of 1884 a reputed 5,000 men donned snowshoes, hitched themselves to toboggans, and slogged on. With them, wrote one visitor, were "scores of women of a certain class, dressed in men's clothes and hauling their feminine wardrobes on sleds."

Supplies came in the same way—200 pounds per toboggan, dragged by human horses across the 40-mile trail for an average wage of $50 per trip. It took three to four days, depending on the weather. Lucky wayfarers could spend one night en route in a crude halfway house, its two rooms lined solidly with tiers of bunks whose only mattresses were pine boughs. Most travelers had to sleep on top of the snow beside fires built on platforms of green saplings; by morning the embers generally glowed forlornly in the bottom of pits fifteen feet deep.

The boom collapsed almost as quickly as it had begun. During the winter, town lots in Eagle, at the forks of Prichard Creek, sold as high as $1,500 each; by late summer they were being offered for $50 with few takers. Murray, a little farther downstream, was only slightly more prosperous. Throughout 1884 and 1885 only a meager $635,000 in placer gold came from the twenty miles or so of creek that Prichard had hoped would support 20,000 men.

Sensing as early as the spring of 1884 that the North Fork diggings would not amount to much, disgusted prospectors began to fan out to the south, looking for more enduring quartz leads. On May 2, in a thin slash called Canyon Creek, which flowed southwest to join the South Fork seven miles away, John Canten and Almeda Seymore found the Tiger lode—not gold but a fabulous streak of lead and silver. Three days later Scott McDonald and George Carter climbed farther up the same lode and staked what they called, with wry reference to their own condition, the Poorman. Soon the mines combined, the Tiger-Poorman, poor no longer. Other prospectors pressing down Canyon Creek quickly turned up other veins equally fabulous—the Gem, the Frisco, the Hercules, bloody names of which we will hear again.

Seven miles up the South Fork from the entrance of Canyon Creek was Mullan, outgrowth of discoveries that began during that same merry month of May. Climax was the Morning, found a bit later (July 2), two miles up the rough timbered mountainside north of Mullan. Since its opening in 1884 generations of Morning miners have chewed downward more than a mile and a quarter into the deepest lead-zinc ore body in the world; the workings, which began high in the hills, are now considerably lower than sea level. A few miles below (west of) the mouth of Canyon Creek, across the South Fork from Prichard's Evolution claim, other prospectors found still more veins of silver, lead, and zinc.

The center of the South Fork activity was the junction of Canyon Creek with the river. There the hills rounded out to make room for a swampy hollow filled with giant cedar trees. On dry ground nearby a certain Colonel Wallace built a store. Other merchants and teamsters, recognizing the place's advantage as a supply center, soon followed. They drained the swamp, built the usual hasty log cabins and false-fronted stores of raw planks, and named the town Wallace. It soon became the metropolis of the district.

In September, 1885, a full year after Colonel Wallace had built his store, along came sixty-five-year-old Noah Kellogg, a carpenter left unemployed by the fading of the Murray placers. To pass the time he was prospecting, supporting himself on a skimpy grubstake—a $3 donkey and $17 worth of bacon, beans, and flour, furnished by two residents of Murray, O. O. Peck and J. T. Cooper. The upper South Fork being staked solid with claims, Kellogg turned west, downstream, and eventually worked his way into Milo Gulch, a tributary that came into the river from the south. He ran out of food there, he testified later, and went back to Murray.

He reported not to his original backers, but to Dutch Jake Goetz, a jovial Murray saloonkeeper, and to a pair of Irish friends, Con Sullivan and Phil O'Rourke. They put up another grubstake and went with Kellogg straight back to Milo Gulch. Within twenty-four hours, they said, they found one of the great silver mines of the world, the Bunker Hill and Sullivan. As soon as the news was out, a nimble-footed promoter, Jim Wardner, who had come to Murray dragging a sledload of butterine, an early-day margarine product, rushed over the ridge, took up all the water claims within reach, and filed on a townsite below the lode, naming it for himself, Wardner. Within two months there were 4,000 people in the cramped village and the excess was spilling out onto the broader flat where Milo Gulch entered the South Fork. The new town, first called Wardner Junction, soon changed its name to Kellogg.

Suspecting trickery, Peck and Cooper, the original grubstakers, hired lawyers. They unearthed evidence tending to show, in their minds at least, that Kellogg had made his strike while still living off their provisions. If so, they, and not Goetz, Sullivan, and O'Rourke, were the ones entitled to the grubstakers' share in the mine.

Thunderous litigation began. During it along came Simeon Reed, a Portland capitalist, who offered $650,000 for the property. The disputants quieted their differences long enough to make the sale—Kellogg came out with the lion's share, $300,000—and Reed began developing the mine. Other suits followed. Old and in failing health, the new owner wearied of the constant bickering and sold the mine for a pleasant profit to a syndicate pulled together by famed mining engineer, John Hays Hammond. Since then the Bunker Hill and Sullivan has cleared some $75 million.

By 1890 competing railroads had swept into the district from both east and west, and soon the South Fork of the Coeur d'Alene was supporting the 20,000 people Andrew Prichard had envisioned for the North Fork. During five dreamy years he had shambled close to, at times even across, lodes that since then have produced silver, lead, and zinc with a gross value of upwards of $1 billion and have paid dividends of more than $200 million. As matters turned out, one of the few mines in the district that never amounted to much was Prichard's Evolution.

But, anyway, he started it all.

A search even longer than Prichard's and equally unrewarding to the discoverer was Crazy Bob Womack's quest for the gold of Cripple Creek, a little stream that bubbled out of a spring high on the grassy southwest shoulder of Pikes Peak. Big and rawboned, Bob had come in 1861 at the age of seventeen with his family from Kentucky to Clear Creek west of Denver, when all of Colorado's Front Range was still being called the Pikes Peak region. Ten years later, after making a little money in the mines around Idaho Springs and Georgetown, the father, Sam Womack, had switched to cattle ranching in the foothills a bit southwest of the spot where General Palmer would shortly create Colorado Springs. This truly was Pikes Peak country, dominated by the swollen gray summit that rose 14,110 feet high to the northwest of the ranch house.

For the rest of his life Bob was rarely out of sight of the mountain. When his younger brother William married and took his wife from their father's ranch due west across the tangled hills and purple-shadowed canyons to a cabin on Cripple Creek, Bob, a confirmed bachelor, followed. It was a country of almost limitless vistas, especially southwest across lower South Park to the Sangre de Cristo Range. Though several small outfits ran cattle in the district, the world looked, from the ridgetops, as untouched as it had ever been. Actually, Colorado Springs was only 18 miles away as the crow flew—44 miles by the wagon road that circled the north side of the peak through Ute Pass—and prospectors had trampled back and forth over practically every foot of the area.

Bob had caught gold fever from his father during their early years on Clear Creek. It was fanned alive again in 1873 when geologist Ferdinand Hayden reported that the area around Cripple Creek had been convulsed eons past by volcanic activity and that some of the rock showed indications of gold. The next year one of the Hayden party formed a mining company and drove a short adit into a hillside south of the Womack cabin. The workers found nothing that looked to them like gold ore, and they soon left. The activity stirred Bob's imagination, however, and as he rode the range thereafter he watched the ground for signs of ore more intently than he watched for cow tracks.

In the spring of 1878 he picked up a dull gray piece of float rock that he impulsively mailed to an assayer. It proved to be sylvanite, an ore of gold and tellurium. A ton of sylvanite comparable to the specimen Bob had sent in would be worth $200—if he could find a ton.

Where was the source of that little piece of gray stone? No outcrop was visible anywhere, which meant that erosion must have covered every vein apex. To find the lode Bob would have to dig, with nothing to guide him.

For twelve more years, while the rest of the family moved away and the nearby ranch lands fell into the hands of Horace Bennett and Julius Myers, Denver realtors, he pocketed the hillsides with shallow pits. The shirking of his ranch duties annoyed his employers, Bennett and Myers, and in Colorado Springs, where he went now and then to tie on a drunk and expound on his mining theories, he came to be something of a joke. Crazy Bob Womack, forty-six years old and nothing to show for his feckless life.

In October, 1886—new snow was gleaming on the distant peaks of the Sangre de Cristos—he once again took his shovel into what he called Poverty Gulch, the uppermost tributary of Cripple Creek, and dug another hole. He did not find a vein, but he unearthed traces of sylvanite that made him feel a vein was near. To press his search he would have to leave his job and that meant finding a grubstake. Finally he talked a Colorado Springs dentist named John P. Grannis out of $500—money which Grannis had to borrow. With that Bob kept pecking away. At last, on another brisk October day in 1890, sixteen years after the first tunnelers had given up and left, he touched the edges of the El Paso lode.

Locating money for development threatened to be as hard as locating the claim. Colorado mining men had a fixation that ore did not occur in quantity unless associated with quartz veins. No quartz was visible around Cripple Creek—just that dull gray sylvanite. A highly complex ore, it obviously would require extensive milling and smelting—volume operations. Without quartz, how could one be sure of the necessary volume? Be cautious!

But if money did not come, prospectors did, as always at the smell of gold. Among them was Winfield Scott Stratton, the wandering carpenter who a decade earlier had made the big wooden silver dollar that H. A. W. Tabor had hoisted as a sign onto the top of his new bank at Leadville. Stratton visited Poverty Gulch and then moved south to the slopes of a hill called Battle Mountain. There on July 4, 1891, he took up two claims that he called, because of the date, the Washington and the Independence.

A scratch here, a scratch there: sluice boxes and their accompanying rubble began to scar both slopes of the ridge that formed the east side of Cripple Creek's valley. Nine miles northeast was the elephantine back of Pikes Peak. Thousands of people rode up there that summer on a new cog railroad of exciting 16 percent to 25 percent grades. They felt dizziness clutch them as they stepped out of the cars onto the lofty summit, caught themselves, and as their breathing steadied let their stunned eyes sweep across the panorama that rolled scores of miles in all directions. Few, if any, of them noticed the little huts tucked far below in the folds of the undistinguished hills rolling down from their toes. The railroad, which had cost Wisconsin mattress-maker Z. G. Simmons and his fellow capitalists $1.25 million to build, was much more exciting—the tourist marvel of the 1890's. Gold, they supposed, had had its day in Colorado, and now a new era was on its way.

And so the overlooked placer miners kept on working as best they could without machinery or capital. During the entire year of 1891 a few hundred of them produced no more than $200,000. Even the short-lived North Fork of the Coeur d'Alene River had yielded more than that during its first year.

The break came in November. That month a German count, Louis Otto de Pourtales, who owned the Broadmoor dairy farm just outside Colorado Springs and who hoped to subdivide part of it after developing a glittering European-style casino nearby, went up to Cripple Creek with an artist friend, Thomas Parrish, who prospected as a hobby. After tramping around from one drab cluster of shacks to another, they dumfounded Cripple Creek—and Colorado Springs too—by paying $80,000 for the Buena Vista claim on Bull Hill, east across the ridge from Poverty Gulch. Suckers! Or were they? The next spring they persuaded canny James J. Hagerman, owner of the Mollie Gibson mine at Aspen and builder of the Midland Railroad, to spend $225,000 buying up the adjoining ground and building a mill.

Meanwhile other knowledgeable mining men were quietly looking around, reassessing their beliefs about quartz. Rumors flew. Prospectors who had been trying in vain to sell shallow pits for a few hundred dollars raised their prices to tens of thousands. With renewed eagerness they deepened their shafts, and mine after mine began breaking into ore. Production amounted to $500,000 in 1892, $2 million in 1893, $8 million in 1900, all from gold ore that contained less than 1 percent silver.

Ranch owners Bennett and Myers split up a pasture into building lots, named the townsite Cripple Creek after the trickling stream that bisected it, and made a million dollars selling real estate. Soon the ridge to the east (an oval area of about 10,000 acres) was ringed with towns—Cripple Creek itself, Victor to the south near Stratton's Independence, and then, running north, the hamlets of Goldfield, Independence, Altman, 10,000 exhilarating feet high on the slopes of Bull Hill, and finally Cameron. The population of the district, which soon was knit together by trolley cars, jumped from 15 in 1890 to 50,000 in 1900.

Three railroads pushed into the area from three different directions. They competed for the ore from 475 mines. Many of these mines were specious holes that worked only until the promoters could unload stock on gullible investors. Others produced fantastically. During the course of eight years Stratton, who held down production because he had no desire for great wealth, cleared $2.5 million and then, in 1899, sold reluctantly to the Venture Corporation of London for a tax-free $10 million in cash—the biggest mining transaction completed by a single man in the Rocky Mountains.[2] Verner Reed, a promoter who wrote novels between jobs, picked up another million from the Venture Corporation for swinging the deal.

At least twenty-eight men cleared a million or more dollars from Cripple Creek's gross production of more than $400 million and from the related pursuits of milling, real estate, and transportation. Most, like Stratton, were humble men—carpenters, plumbers, druggists, grocers, butchers, schoolteachers, prospectors. A few, like Spencer Penrose, whose brother Boies was a United States senator from Pennsylvania, were bluebloods who had wandered out to Colorado Springs because it was a pleasant place to work off the energies of youth.

Womack? He never had been practical. He sold his part of the El Paso claim for a few hundred dollars; it was incorporated into the Gold King properties, producer of millions. After he had spent that money and a pittance or two he picked up on other transactions, he went down to Colorado Springs to work as a kitchen helper in the series of boarding-houses run by an old-maid sister of his four years his junior. In 1904, when he was sixty-one, he suffered a paralytic stroke and was bedridden the rest of his life. Learning of his troubles in 1908, a Colorado Springs editor launched a relief fund drive. Four hundred million dollars—say $2 billion today—because Crazy Bob Womack had spent sixteen years looking for gold where smart miners knew perfectly well there was no gold . . . they managed to scratch up $812 for treatments that failed to help very much. The next August, 1909, he died. By then Cripple Creek's production was falling off—a mere $11.5 million that year.

Add one more spin-off. Among the mining men who traveled the Rockies looking for properties to develop was Joseph De Lamar, a one-time Dutch ship captain. For a brief time De Lamar tried running a gold mill at Cripple Creek, but was defeated by the complexity of the ores.

[2] Stratton's only close rival in Colorado was Tom Walsh, an Irishman who had been fiddling around the mountains since 1872—Central City, the Black Hills of South Dakota, Leadville, Cripple Creek, Silverton in the San Juans. In 1896 he picked up the Camp Bird Mine above lovely Ouray. He cleared a million from it, then sold it for $6 million to the Venture Corporation, the same company that had bought out Stratton. The Camp Bird proved the better buy, yielding a gross of more than $30 million. The Independence did not return its purchase price to the buyers.

Walsh used his share of the money to buy, among other things, the Hope diamond for his daughter Evalyn. It is now on spectacular display in the Smithsonian Institution, Washington, D.C.

Shifting to Utah, he bought in 1899 a substantial interest in 200 acres of copper claims owned by Enos Wall in Bingham Canyon south of Great Salt Lake. The ore, dusted in specks throughout an enormous mass of porphyry rock, was a low-grade sulphide—less than 2½ percent copper. The price of copper had recently climbed back to 18 cents a pound, however, and De Lamar began wondering whether, under the circumstances, a volume operation might turn a profit.

To help him determine he employed as his consultant a husky, red-faced, hard-drinking thirty-year-old mining engineer named Daniel C. Jackling. A graduate of the Missouri School of Mines, Jackling had come to Cripple Creek in 1894 so poor that he could not afford stage fare and had walked the last 18 miles. In Cripple Creek he and another young engineer, Charles MacNeill, took over the mill that had defeated De Lamar and made a success of it. To De Lamar that was recommendation enough.

Assisted by Robert Gemmell, state engineer of Utah, Jackling ran exhaustive tests on the copper property in Bingham Canyon. The report they came up with was far more sweeping than De Lamar had bargained for when mentioning "volume." They suggested not the tunneling and stoping operations normal to hard-rock mining but the stripping away of the over-burden and the removal of the ore with newfangled machines called steam shovels. The shovels would dump the ore straight into gondola cars travel-ing on tracks that followed the operation from spot to spot. Each day several trains would haul the rock over a specially built railroad to a mill and smelter site near the shore of Great Salt Lake. There it would be run through a larger mill than De Lamar had ever seen.

The very thought of the expenses involved appalled him and he dropped the project, thinking probably that he had hired a madman. Finding himself abruptly unemployed, Jackling built a mill in Washington state and then returned to Cripple Creek. There he approached several prosperous friends —millman Charles MacNeill, mineowner Charles Tutt, Spencer Penrose, and a few others. After talking himself hoarse he persuaded them, in May, 1903, to go to Utah with him and ride up Bingham Canyon in a buggy. By dark MacNeill was convinced, and that swung the others. They formed Utah Copper Company and bought 80 percent of Enos Wall's original holdings; Wall retained a 20 percent interest; De Lamar dropped out entirely.

To raise money the new owners carried their figures to John Hays Hammond, chief engineer of the Guggenheim Exploration Company in Denver. After seventeen engineers of Hammond's staff had spent $150,000 testing the property and analyzing Jackling's wild ideas, the Guggenheims agreed to go ahead. They underwrote a $3 million bond issue and bought 232,000 shares of Utah Copper Company stock at $20 a share. This gave them a quarter interest in the enterprise and the right to smelt all the copper it produced.

With the money thus raised, the company purchased more ground, brought in steam shovels (the original one took its first bite in 1907), purchased seventeen locomotives for their railroad, and built a mill with the then-unheard of capacity of 6,000 tons per day.

It was the beginning of the Southwest's most notable heavy industry, the open-pit mining of low-grade porphyry copper ores. During Utah's first thirty years of operation, it produced more than 3 billion pounds of copper. Today its mills (now owned by Kennecott) can handle 100,000 tons of rock every twenty-four hours. The batteries of trains that crawl around on the gorgeously hued terraces of the demolished mountains look, on the sides of the gigantic pit, as tiny as caterpillars.

Today more than 85 percent of all the world's copper is produced from porphyry ores by the open-pit methods envisioned by Jackling and Gemmell. Undoubtedly the industry would have evolved sooner or later without the intervention of Crazy Bob Womack, the maverick, boozy cowboy who liked to prospect, and the ranch land that he turned into one of the world's great gold fields. Still, if one wants to stitch the chain of cause and effect toward that preconceived end, it is possible to argue that, since many of the men and some of the initiative and training and money that produced Utah Copper came from Cripple Creek, Bob ought to receive a little of the credit. But he never does.

XX

AMONG THESE DARK SATANIC MILLS

DURING the early 1880's the little town of Gunnison, Colorado, sought in typical frontier fashion to draw attention to herself with a grandiose brag. She built a sprawling four-story hotel graced by what the citizenry considered a dazzling wrought-iron portico, and then began plans for a steel mill that, in the words of the local newspaper, "has thrown a bombshell into Denver's future."

Denver managed to survive. The Gunnison hotel was seldom full and the steel mill was never built. The point, however, is not the hollowness of the boast but the psychological need that it filled. When a newspaper editor inflated his town, he was not merely trying to lure in new subscribers for his journal and new customers for his advertisers. He was also justifying to the world his own wisdom and the wisdom of his readers in choosing so fine a home. The town's identity became, in part, the people's identity. And that was what made the deep-vein mining camps of the Rockies so malignant a spiritual shock to so many newcomers—the towns had no firm roots. Like other adolescents, they grew too fast, and although they seemed strong their total orientation toward a single resource made them easily vulnerable. While the first citizens were still trying to determine what they stood for, the towns they yearned to be proud of were captured by outside corporations whose sense of responsibility lay, naturally enough, toward the absentee stockholders who had created them and not toward the localities from which the profits came.

The early placer camps had been rootless too—but with this difference: few of the people swarming into them had arrived with the least intention of staying. By contrast, those drawn to the industrialized mining towns were ready to be persuaded. If the veins were deep enough to last (and thanks to steadily improving technology some of them have lasted for three quarters of a century), then perhaps a man should adjust his life and his town's life accordingly. But adjust in the light of what values?

An urban schizophrenia developed. One element in each of the new towns sought reassurance by trying to make its new home as patterned and as orderly as was any other American city. On the other hand, many residents clung to attitudes bequeathed them by the impatient and careless placer camps. They liked to think of themselves as carrying on the torch of those wild, free (and partly mythical) days when every prospector, no matter how poor, was deemed to be a potential millionaire and free to act accordingly. No one could trammel *him*.

An assertion of this attitude helps account for some of the rather extraordinary statistics openly flaunted by the latter-day high-altitude cities. In 1890 Wallace, Idaho, boasted of twenty-eight saloons serving 913 inhabitants, plus an untallied number of miners back in the hills. In June, 1879, the Leadville *Daily Chronicle* announced proudly that her population, then about 10,000, was supporting 120 saloons, 115 gambling houses, 35 houses of prostitution, and 19 wholesale liquor dealers. Plus, the paper added with a hasty twinge of conscience, 51 groceries, 17 hardware stores, 12 shoe shops, 4 banks, 3 newspapers, 9 book and stationery shops, and a music store.

The kind of theater the citizens relished provides another yardstick of their ambivalent attitudes. Since men still outnumbered women by more than two to one, "box houses" flourished. A lurid combination of saloon, variety theater, and bordello, a box house consisted of an auditorium floored with sawdust and dotted with tables. A sleazy stage occupied one end of the drafty hall. The other three sides were surrounded by a double tier of boxes which, if the occupants so desired, could be locked from behind and curtained off from prying eyes outside while still commanding a view of the floor. Scantily clad waitresses hustled drinks in the boxes and at the tables and every now and then assembled as a chorus line in support of more professional performers.

"Beautiful Dizzy Blondes . . . Naughty Blondes" was the advertisement which the Grand Central box house at Leadville ran in the *Chronicle*. To obtain these blondes the management promised through want ads in the same paper to pay salaries in gold, plus tips, and added, in capital letters, probably for the titillation of male readers rather than for the edification of the applicants, that those who were hired "Must Appear in SHORT CLOTHES." Similar costuming, together with the nature of the entertainment, led one observer to declare of the Comique in Butte that "hell, itself, might have been used as a model." Resorting to homier metaphor, the Spokane *Spokesman-Review* sniffed that the Coeur D'Alene box house in Spokane, where the miners of the Idaho Panhandle went to relax, was "a department store of vice and immorality."

Box houses were by no means the whole of the story, however. The educated personnel who ran the mines and mills and larger mercantile establishments wanted a different kind of entertainment for themselves and their families, even if they had to provide it themselves. Inspired by their own successful production of *The Bohemian Girl,* the cultural elite of Central City, Colorado, staged a drive that in 1878 resulted in the building of the famed Central City Opera House as a base for future efforts, both home-grown and imported.[1] In other towns patron saints waved the necessary wands. H. A. W. Tabor provided both Leadville and Denver with elegant theaters. They too were known, according to the universal custom of the mountains, as Opera Houses. Whether or not opera appeared was immaterial.

Butte's Maguire Grand Opera House was built by a professional showman, John Maguire. So that his theater could live up to its name, he tried to persuade Melba to sing there but she declined, giving as her excuse fumes from the smelters. Sarah Bernhardt was less susceptible. In return for $3,000 she performed *Theodora* in Maguire's palace, in French, one night only. For the privilege of watching her Montanans dumped $5,000 into Maguire's tills. According to the Anaconda *Standard,* "The mere trifle of not having understood a word that was spoken during the entire play makes no difference to those who sat through the performance. They 'saw Bernhardt' and that of itself is enough to stamp them as people of culture and endowed with an appreciation of the artistic."

To be Eastern—ah, that was the accolade desired most by those citizens who combated the placer-camp element of the towns. In the eyes of the Cripple Creek newspaper, the ball that marked the opening of the National Hotel was superb to the extent that it matched anything that "might have been witnessed in any eastern metropolis garnished with wealth and polished by age. . . . That it could have taken place in a supposedly crude, uncultured mining camp in the West was, in this reporter's opinion, a matter of pride. The cream of Cripple Creek society was present. The exquisite gowns of the ladies . . . the sober black swallow-tails of the gentlemen . . ." And so on and on.

When these amusements failed, it was still possible to escape briefly by "going outside," as the mountain dwellers put it, a relief which had not been available to the residents of the early isolated placer camps. The bustling narrow-gauge railroads ran excursion trains to all sorts of special events and special places. When a notable production of *The Mikado* was staged in Durango, Colorado, theatergoers from all over the San Juan Mountains were able to board the coaches of the D&RG and travel there to see it. The inauguration of a governor always drew throngs of party faithful to the state capital for a week of celebration. Quieter relaxation was available in the combination hotels and bathhouses that sprang up at every rail-served hot springs, each of which compared itself to some famous Eastern or European spa. Stomach disorders reputedly yielded on the instant to the "thermal alkaline purgative waters" of Pagosa Springs, Colorado; muscular pains were relieved at the same resort by immersing

[1] Lavish productions are still offered in the same opera house each summer.

the sufferer in hot, white mud. M. L. DeCoursey, one of the early promoters of Glenwood Springs, also in Colorado, wrote earnestly that baldness could be ended at his establishment "inside of 3 mos. by rubbing with the water once daily. This is a literal fact."

Such moments of relief were often essential. Especially during their formative days the new mining cities seemed to pay as little attention to municipal problems as the early placer camps had. The cause was the same—inadequate revenue. Bond issues attracted scant support; real estate assessments never came close to catching up with the swiftly soaring property values. Desperate for income, the municipal governments resorted to unsavory sources similar to those that had served their predecessors. Although Colorado statute outlawed prostitution and gambling, followers of both professions openly lined up on the first of each month in Leadville's city hall and gained thirty days' immunity from the police by paying their fines in advance. Otherwise the town could hardly have survived.

Throughout much of America in those days municipal services were sketchy at best. In the mining camps the inadequacies must have been next to intolerable. Schools were underequipped and overcrowded. Police were underpaid. Fire was a perennial threat, as it was in many other cities of the time—witness Chicago. Repeated disasters seldom made the mining centers careful, however. Ramshackle Helena was gutted at least six times between 1869 and 1874. One brewery saved itself in 1870 by wetting down its building with its own beer; in that same year the town finally got around to replacing its wooden water mains with iron pipes. They were not protection enough. In January, 1874, 150 buildings disappeared in a belch of spark-twinkling smoke. The next year the Helena city council at last ordered an up-to-date steam fire engine.

Central City, Colorado, founded in 1859 and jammed wall to wall in narrow Gregory Gulch, experienced no serious blaze until May, 1874, even though it possessed neither fire engine nor storage reservoir—just buckets for volunteer water carriers. As matters turned out, drought had left the creek almost dry that disastrous spring. The mines sucked up what water there was—and so there the brigade stood with its empty buckets. Damage, half a million dollars, or six times that in today's terms.

Cripple Creek, Colorado; Wallace, Idaho; and Park City, Utah, did have reservoirs but were careless about keeping them full. Because of that each town nearly vanished, Wallace in 1891, Cripple Creek during two fires in April, 1896, and Park City in 1898. Pandemonium accompanied the holocausts. Wagons, wheelbarrows, even washtubs dragged screeching across the gravel were pressed into service for carting away belongings. Horses bolted; disheveled mothers ran to and fro calling for lost children; strong men strode purposefully ahead through the smoke, clutching unlikely objects—"picture albums, chamber pots, looking glasses . . . a kettle of beans," according to the recollections of Mabel Barbee Lee, who went through the Cripple Creek fires as a young girl. Over it all roared the crash of giant powder and the splinter of wood as volunteers made up for the lack of water by razing buildings to create firebreaks.

Butte added her own special twist to a fire catastrophe. At ten o'clock one cold night in January, 1895, a blaze that began in a flour warehouse spread to a hardware store next door, where 350 boxes of dynamite were illegally cached. Just as the firemen were setting their ladders and dragging up their hoses—Butte did have relatively up-to-date equipment by then— an indescribable blast shook the town, shattering windows as far away as Walkerville. Stones, huge timbers, and mangled bodies hurtled hundreds of yards through the air. The entire fire department—except for one horse and two men working on a hose coupling some distance away—simply disappeared. More blasts followed, creating havoc among spectators who had rushed up to help the injured. So far as could be determined—there was not much recognizable flesh left to go on—fifty-seven men died; hundreds were hurt by the rain of debris. When a million-dollar blaze took out much of the business district ten years later (September 24, 1905), it seemed almost like an anticlimax.

Filth was a less dramatic but a more pervading danger. None of the towns, for instance, had animal pounds. At the approach of winter, prospectors came in from the hills and calmly turned their hard-worked donkeys loose to fend for themselves. (Actually, no prospector ever spoke of a donkey but referred to the animals as burros, jackasses, or, most generally, as jacks.) By day householders drove the forlorn creatures out of their yards with dogs. By night the famished jacks roamed the alleys in search of anything edible, occasionally shattering the sleep of the residents with disconsolate brays that David Day, editor of the wondrous *Solid Muldoon* of Ouray, Colorado, described as a cross between the roar of an earthquake and the yell of a woman who has stepped on a mouse.

The fact that the jacks survived is in itself a commentary on the towns. Scavenging, including the nighttime emptying of backyard privies by "honey men" driving coal-black wagons, was never properly attended to. Garbage, dead animals, and offal from the butchershops were dragged at irregular intervals to pits dug around the edges of the towns. Those that ringed Leadville on three sides were burned when convenient. Those on the flats outside Butte were left open until full and then covered with a skim of earth.

During winter collections lagged. Signs of spring were predictable: the newspapers began to editorialize about the effluvia. In August, 1880, the Leadville papers added the town cemetery to the list of offenders. In March, 1890, the *Solid Muldoon* complained bitterly of the six dead animals awaiting cremation on the cliff-girt Ouray dump—probably the loveliest dump so far as natural setting went as existed in the United States. Regularly editor Day cried out that "garbage fiends" should be made to burn their output. He bemoaned castoff clothing lying about in such quantities that it "invites the spread of pestilence." He suggested hopefully that the D&RG railroad might contract to haul horse manure five miles beyond the city limits for $5 per loaded freight car. Results both in Ouray and in other mountain towns were negligible. When federal troops occupied Wallace, Idaho, during the first labor troubles of 1892 (of which more later) they could not stand the stench and voluntarily did what the residents neglected; they swept out the town.

The curtains of flies passed belief. Typhoid, diphtheria, and scarlet fever flourished. "Put lime around privy vaults to fight typhoid," the *Solid Muldoon* urged its readers on July 23, 1889. The next year the outbreak of diphtheria was so severe that even funerals were unattended—not from lack of sympathy, editor Day reported, but as a common-sense precaution to check the spread of the disease.

Chemical fumes were Butte's principal health hazard. The cheap way to start removing sulphur from copper sulphide ore was to lay down alternate layers of logs and crushed ore and set the mass afire, a process called heap roasting. Combustion drove off sulphur dioxide and sulphur trioxide in clouds of acrid, brown-yellow smoke so dense that when atmospheric conditions were wrong, housewives had to light their lamps at midday.

Hoping to lift the fumes above nose level, the Butte city council decreed that no ore should be roasted except under chimneys at least 75 feet tall. The Boston and Montana Mining Company, which operated just outside of Butte in Meaderville, ignored the edict until mid-December, 1891. That month fumes from its heaps settled over the town in uncommonly heavy clouds. Fifteen people died, a higher rate of fatalities than normal. Convinced that the fumes were responsible, outraged citizens demanded action. Yielding to the clamor, the mayor deputized a hundred men and sent them to Meaderville to bury the offending heaps under two feet of sand.

He deputized them, notice. Until the turn of the century, when labor warfare once again swept away restraint, the citizens of the hard-rock towns showed more inclination than their predecessors to stay within the framework of the law. There were, to be sure, occasional outbreaks of vigilantism, especially in the early days of the camps, and these acts of violence were justified, as one might expect, on the same old grounds of expediency. On April 16, 1881, the editor of the Durango, Colorado, *Record* (who incidentally, was a woman, a Mrs. Romney), described a local hanging with some relish—"the pale moonlight glimmering through the rifted clouds clothed the ghastly face with a ghastlier pallor"—and then added defiantly, "Thus the Powers that Be . . . have proclaimed to the world that good order, peace, quietude, and safety must and shall prevail in Durango." Leadville lynchers hanged side by side to the roof joists of an unfinished building a twenty-year-old youth suspected of burglary and a man named Frodsham, who was accused of moving onto town lots belonging to someone else—property records were chaotic—frightening off protesters with a show of truculence, and then selling the property for his own gain.

In spite of these instances, vigilantism was not the problem it had been earlier. During the same fall that Frodsham was lynched the merchants of Leadville tried to help the town's understaffed police force in a somewhat more responsible way by hiring a protective patrol of their own and asking the county sheriff to legalize the action by deputizing the watchmen. This private force was then ordered to cooperate with the town constabulary. And it did. The patrol's own records show that during their first month of activity, the watchmen quenched several fires, checked three attempts at burglary and "two of hold up your hands," escorted twenty-one drunks home, recovered six strayed horses, and assisted the city police in making fourteen arrests.

Citizen groups undertook still other municipal obligations. Merchant associations hired water carts to sprinkle the streets in front of their establishments. Fraternal, church, and labor union groups solicited money for hospitals and staged subscription suppers and dances to raise book funds for schools and circulating libraries. Mine employees, many of whom were quite musical, formed brass bands, string bands, and, in particular, cornet bands. Cornish and Welsh miners were famous for their choral singing. All these groups, often uniformed by the mining companies for which the men labored, could be counted on to give concerts in support of worthy causes. Wealthier individuals donated hose carts, hook and ladder wagons, and other equipment to the volunteer fire companies.

The sense of community pride inherent in these activities was reinforced, as in other American towns of the time, by sporting events that the whole camp could cheer. Every municipality that was able to level off the necessary amount of ground supported a baseball team and a race track, the latter of which featured fancy thoroughbreds owned by local tycoons— Marcus Daly's famed Tammany at Anaconda town, for one instance. Volunteer fire fighters flamboyant in spangled tights hitched themselves to their two-wheeled hose carts and raced units from rival towns along the main street to a specified hydrant to see who could draw a stream of water in the shortest time. Two-man teams of brawny miners, elevated on platforms in the center of the main street so that all could see, vied in punching holes into blocks of granite with drill steel and sledge hammers. Favorite time for these games was the afternoon of July Fourth, when they furnished a stirring climax to morning parades resplendent with evergreen floats, brass bands, militia companies, mounted sheriffs' posses, and beplumed, besworded, stiffly self-conscious members of various fraternal organizations, all striding ahead to the bang of blasting powder fired between blacksmiths' anvils, one turned upside down on top the other.

The local newspapers sought to elevate their towns still more by assiduously insulting the neighbors. Any sort of nonsense would do if it sounded contemptuous enough. Ouray's *Solid Muldoon* pleased its readers by asserting that the vibrant energy of *their* town was shaking even the bedbugs loose in the somnolent dwellings of outclassed Lake City to the east. As for Silverton, across Red Mountain Pass to the south, masked balls were the favorite entertainment over there (said Day on September 9, 1884) because "the average Silverton woman never appears half so attractive as when masked. The majority of them are so dumpy they have to stand on a chair to scratch their backs, and the remainder are so lofty that the average masher would have to hook his toes in the kilt plaids on their basques to get in a good square bite. It's in Ouray you find symmetry in human architecture."

Side by side with such trivia went a continual run of items that indicate how eagerly the mountain dwellers turned to their newspapers for local "flavor" as well as for gossip and information. From the *Solid Muldoon* of November 10, 1879; "One or two weddings are on for next week. This weather does kind of suggest two in a bed and spoon fashion." January, 1881: there had been a snowstorm and (how Day loved puns!) the young people could now "indulge in street sleighing and heart slaying sighed by side." A little later: "J. R. Foster brought his daughter 80 miles over rough mountain roads to have doctor LeLange fix her teeth, and was so well pleased that he had a few of his own molars tunneled under and blown out." Mixed into this mélange were lumps of dreadful doggerel, composed by Day and attached as a reader-pleasing sort of practical joke to some local personage. A certain Ouray belle, for example, was supposedly the source of this quatrain in the issue of April 23, 1889:

> *If aught but water you e'er taste,*
> *Just keep your arm from off my waist!*
> *If you drink wine or other slop,*
> *You'll ne'er hear my corset pop!*

From the day-to-day attitudes on which these trifles were based, from deeper tensions and pretensions, from the juvenile struttings and the more mature efforts to alleviate the worst of conditions, a rooted pattern of mountain living might have emerged—if there had been time. There was no time. The gray fist of industrial urbanization, a continuing pang to the American psyche, closed in on the mountain towns with brutal swiftness. Choked into silence, the indigenous voices that were developing gave way to the acrimonious dialogue between labor and capital that at the turn of the century was tormenting the entire nation. In the high-altitude camps of the Rockies, where every economic pursuit focused eventually on a single resource, there was no dilution. Even the commercial and professional men had to take sides. Unarbitrated and untamed, the fights raged horribly, without compromise and, indicative of the bleakness of the struggle, even without heroes.

A deep sense of betrayal filled the workers. In every major center they could hear names and see faces that epitomized the hope that had lured them to the mountains—Tabor, Daly, Clark, Stratton, Walsh, and lesser fry like Noah Kellogg of Coeur d'Alene, men once as poor as they who had found self-sufficiency and the dignity (presumed at least) that went with it. Instead of being examples, however, the names had become mockeries. Outsiders who happened to have money enough for mine development had absorbed the promises, and in a twinkling nothing remained for the majority, many of them immigrants from abroad, except grueling labor under miserable conditions paid for at a rate of from $2 to $3.50 a day.

A "day" ranged from eight hours in a few favored mines to as much as twelve in some of the reduction works. Special circumstances had little effect. The water in the mines at Butte was so hard on shoes that the town kept sixty-five cobblers busy, yet no adjustments in pay were made because of exorbitant shoe costs. Although laborers in the wet mines at Leadville or Coeur d'Alene had to provide rubber suits and rubber hats, they seldom were paid any more than workers in dry mines nearby. Quite naturally these many variations were in themselves sources of dissatisfaction.

Men who labored in mines close to town lived with their families in rows of drab, sooty, almost identical houses jammed side by side behind weedy yards overlooking ironically magnificent panoramas. Those employed in mines too far from town to be able to walk to their jobs were forced to live in company boardinghouses and buy their necessities in company stores that charged all the traffic would bear.

Illness was a perennial dread. In addition to the diseases spread by contagion in the filthy towns, miners faced accidental blasts, cave-ins, underground fires in heavily timbered workings, pneumonia that at high altitudes was often fatal, and silicosis produced by breathing in the rock dust that billowed out from their heavy power drills, the aptly termed "widow-maker" of the Rockies.

The sole defense against the economic disaster of sickness was one of the medical programs offered by the larger companies and supported by compulsory pay deductions. The workers bitterly resented these enforced benevolences. In their minds the programs were not designed to aid them so much as to let the company escape liability for injuries. The suspicions were not without foundation. Many company doctors were incompetent timeservers. Underpaid themselves and lacking adequate facilities, they often were tempted to conduct perfunctory examinations, provide the sufferer with a splint or a few pills, send him home, and mark the case completed—which was enough for the state laws.

Still, so long as a man stayed healthy and his wages remained constant he could get by. The squeeze came when mine profits fell because of sagging metal prices or increased costs of production. Stockholders complained and the unhappy local managers were then tempted to adjust matters by trimming wages. In self-defense the workers retorted by forming autonomous little unions and affiliating, generally in dark secrecy, with the Knights of Labor, in that era the main national organization of workers.

One of the first Knight-chartered groups in the Rockies was the union at Butte. Its test came quickly. In the spring of 1878 Marcus Daly cut wages in the Alice and Lexington mines, the silver properties he was then managing. By calling a strike the union easily won a uniform rate of $3.50 a day for all underground workers, whether skilled or unskilled. At the time this was an extraordinary triumph and the anniversary of the victory, June 13, became an annual holiday at Butte, complete with parades, soaring oratory, and a grand labor ball.

Daly lived in Butte. The corporation which purchased Leadville's Chrysolite mine from H. A. W. Tabor had its headquarters in the East, and that difference may account for the different outcome in Colorado's first major confrontation. Management at the Chrysolite first antagonized the workers by an attempt to dock their pay for medical services and then by posting an order against smoking, talking, or loitering on the job. On May 26, 1880, the men laid down their tools to hold a protest meeting. An organizer named Michael Mooney diverted the discussions with a ringing demand for an eight-hour rather than a ten-hour day at a uniform wage of $4, instead of the prevailing $3 to $3.50, a differential depending on skills. Forming a long serpentine, the chanting Chrysolite workers marched to other nearby properties, and soon most of the mines in Leadville had shut down.

It was like a holiday at first—street parades led by brass bands, speeches, and considerable carousing in the saloons. After two weeks of this the mineowners retorted by forming what they called a citizens' committee. With considerable lack of originality the committee scheduled an answering parade and sought to swell its ranks by requesting businessmen to close their stores and join the march. Military semblance was added by calling out volunteer militia units that had been formed a few months earlier during the Ute uprising when Nathan Meeker had been killed, and by urging all marchers who owned guns to carry them.

This naked threat infuriated the workers. There were street scufflings, a shot or two, name calling, and then a charge by mounted paraders against the hostile spectators on the curbs. In the words of our old friend Frank Hall, then serving as Colorado's secretary of state, tempers were "about to burst forth in the red flames of war," or so Governor Pitkin was advised. He put Leadville under martial law and ordered in the state militia.

Under the protection of the troops the mines reopened. One hundred and sixty-five "vagrants," a term that included anyone out of work, whether strike leader or congenital bum, were offered a choice of paying a fine, serving a jail sentence, or leaving town. "Tramp, tramp, tramp, the boys went marching," reported the *Democrat* with relish and added the next day that the governor's action had been wholly justified: if the demands of labor had been met, "the Mine Owners might as well have deeded their property to the Miner's Union."

The next clashes came in the Coeur d'Alene section of Idaho, where crusading organizers from Butte helped found locals at Mullan and Wallace beside the Coeur d'Alene River and at Gem and Burke in the deep gash of Canyon Creek. At first the pay in those towns had been the same for everyone—$3.50 per ten-hour day. Then, as the price of silver continued to drop, the mineowners pushed through the Leadville differential, $3.50 for skilled labor, $3 for unskilled. The latter group of course constituted the greater part of the work force.

When the Sherman Silver Purchase Act of 1890 lifted prices, the autonomous unions banded together to demand a return to the uniform $3.50 scale. They also hoped that by building and maintaining their own hospital out of union dues they could end company pay deductions for medical services. A relatively peaceful strike early in 1891 carried the day—or seemed to. Metal prices were dropping again, however, and management, uniting in a counterunion called the Mine Owners' Association, began secret plans to defeat the new scale.

First they planted an adroit Pinkerton detective, Charles Siringo, in the Gem mine, four miles up Canyon Creek from Wallace. Within a very little while Siringo gained such confidence from his fellow workers that they elected him secretary of the Gem Union, where he was privy to every strategy meeting.

Whether luck or conspiracy dictated the next move is unknown. Anyway, the two railroads that served the Coeur d'Alenes, the Union Pacific and the Northern Pacific, announced an increase in freight rates on concentrate shipped from the mines to outside smelters. Announcing publicly that they could not meet the added costs, the owners on January 1, 1892, shut down every mine in the section. Sixteen hundred unemployed miners tightened their belts and with their families shivered out the winter as best they could. In March the railroads yielded and restored the old rates. The owners then announced that the mines would reopen on April 1 at the prestrike differential of $3 to $3.50.

Rightly or wrongly, the workers were convinced that the railroad episode had been staged to starve them to the point that they would accept work at any rate. Defiantly they called another strike. This time they were supported by a relief fund of $30,000 a month sent in by Montana unions under the leadership of the Butte local.

The owners retorted by importing non-union workers. Some of these newcomers the unionists converted, some they frightened away. The frustrated owners thereupon devised another weapon soon to be familiar throughout the mountains, a court injunction restraining the union from interfering with the operation of the mines. Protected thus by the law, they brought in 800 scabs and put them to work behind armed guards.

Obviously no strike could succeed if this maneuver went uncontested. But how fight back? On July 9, 1892, as the frantic union officials were seeking a solution, a visitor from Butte chanced to recognize Charles Siringo, secretary of the Gem local, as a Pinkerton spy. At that point the unionists lost their heads. A mob started after Siringo. He escaped through a prepared hole in the floor of the house where he lived and scrambled up the heavily timbered hillside to the Gem mine directly above town. Other union men meanwhile beat up some scabs they had caught in a saloon. In retaliation the nervous guards in the mine on the hillside began shooting down into the main street. Nearly every building in town was punctured; several men were wounded; three died.

Attackers swarmed up the slope against both the Gem and the barricaded Frisco, another mine nearby. They blew the Frisco mill to bits by shutting off the water in the penstock and scooting a case of dynamite down the dry slide. Meantime one of the guards at the Gem had been slain. Hearing the blast at the Frisco and terrified by a more violent kind of fighting than they had bargained for, the non-union workers surrendered. Siringo, a brave man whatever else he may be called, once again escaped into the trees.

Every scab along Canyon Creek was ordered out of the district. There still remained the most intransigent of the mines, the mighty Bunker Hill & Sullivan, located some miles down the river from Wallace. The unionists marched there, seized the mine's concentrator mill at Kellogg and threatened to destroy it unless every non-union worker was fired forthwith. Bethinking themselves of the ruined Frisco, the managers complied. Congratulating themselves on winning their point, the workers returned to Wallace. After burying their slain comrades at a gigantic, emotional funeral, they went to dancing through the streets in gala celebration.

It was a short-lived triumph. Were duly issued court injunctions to be obeyed or not? Acting (they said) to prevent anarchy, government officials dispatched several companies of the Idaho National Guard, supported by 1,500 U.S. troops, eastward up the Coeur d'Alene River from Fort Sherman beside Coeur d'Alene Lake and westward across the Bitterroot Mountains from Missoula. With them the commanding officers brought nearly five hundred indictments for contempt of court, issued because of the defiance of the injunctions. Though many miners fled before the papers could be served, about 350 were incarcerated in what became still another institution of mountain warfare, the bull pen. In Wallace and Wardner these pens consisted of boxcars and unsanitary, cavernous warehouses surrounded by wooden stockades 14 feet high. Union halls were closed and the county sheriff, a one-time miner, was replaced by a man whom the owners favored.

Under the firm hand of the military, excitement simmered down into sullenness. As the troops gradually withdrew, most of the indictments were quashed. Not all, however. A handful of the leaders in the rioting were taken to Boise to be tried before the judge who had issued the injunctions. Eventually the men were freed—some paid fines or served short terms in prison—but not before they had thoroughly analyzed, while in jail, the plight of their broken local unions. The result was a convention in Butte and the formation, by delegates from various mining camps in South Dakota, Idaho, Utah, Colorado, and Montana, of the mountainwide Western Federation of Miners.

The date was May 15, 1893, a time of deep economic distress throughout America. During the preceding summer protesting farmers in the Midwest had joined other reformers in launching a new political group, the People's party, commonly called Populists. Although their nationwide vote in the fall elections was negligible, the Populists captured several state offices in the West. Among these was the governorship of Colorado, where the successful candidate was Davis H. Waite of Aspen. A tall, gaunt, humorless, sixty-seven-year-old radical with a long white beard, Waite was one of the very few high-placed friends the Western Federation of Miners ever knew.

Shortly after Davis' inauguration in March, 1893, the price of silver collapsed abysmally, dropping in four paralyzing days from 87 cents an ounce to 62 cents. More than half the mines in Idaho's Coeur d'Alene district and in Colorado's San Juan Mountains closed their doors. The brand-new camp of Creede, Colorado, near the head of the Rio Grande, which the year before had turned out 5 million ounces of silver, and where the optimistic owners of the Holy Moses mine had just refused $1.5 million for their property—infant Creede was forever maimed. In Leadville marginal properties shut down. Those with better ore combined for the sake of greater economy, discharged some workers, and asked the remainder to accept a cut from $3 a day to $2.50, tempering the blow with a promise that when the price of silver climbed back to $83\frac{1}{2}$ cents an ounce the former wage scale would be restored. Many men refused and joined their discharged fellows in forlorn wanderings. The flow of concentrates shrank to such a trickle that the Guggenheims suspended operations in their huge new smelter at Pueblo, opened less than two years before. In Denver twelve banks closed their doors.

Distraught officials from thirty-nine Colorado counties gathered in Denver to wring their hands and seek remedies. In the course of addressing the group, Governor Davis Waite uttered another of a long series of unfortunate remarks, crying out against threats that no one had made: "It is infinitely better that blood flow to our horses' bridles than our national liberties should be destroyed." Conservatives guffawed nervously at the gruesome image and attached to the governor a nickname still remembered in Colorado, though nearly everything else associated with him has been forgotten—"Bloody-Bridles Waite."

Hundreds of unemployed swarmed into Denver. To keep them quiet the harried municipality set up a refugee camp of tents and soup kitchens in a park beside the South Platte River. Railroads were persuaded to keep the horde moving east by charging minimum fares for the trip—finally no fare at all. To speed the exodus—crime rates, be it noted, had jumped alarmingly—the city hauled lumber into the park and let the men build an armada of crude, flat-bottomed scows for floating down the Platte out of sight and mind. It was a cruel experiment. Some of the ungainly craft foundered along the way; more hung up on one or another of the sandbars that ribbed the shallow stream's long course. Destitute men were stranded here and there in helpless little knots as far away as eastern Nebraska.

Mineowners and laborers shared one worn hope—that inflation, brought about by pumping silver money into the economy, would lighten the universal distress. Ignoring their arguments, Congress in November, 1893, repealed the Sherman Silver Purchase Act. The West was outraged. The city council of Georgetown, Colorado, voted to secede from the Union. Governor Waite alarmed conservatives still more by threatening to ship Colorado silver into old Mexico and there, outside the jurisdiction of the federal government, coin the state's own money, labeled "Fandango Dollars" by his scornful opponents.[2]

The one break in the gloom was Cripple Creek, where Crazy Bob Womack had discovered gold late in 1890. Though the price of all other commodities was collapsing, that of gold remained constant. During the grim year of 1893 the hustling young mines on the back side of Pikes Peak quadrupled their production, from $500,000 in 1892 to $2 million in 1893. By 1900 the annual output would be $18 million.

Unemployed miners flocked in, hoping for jobs. With them came John Calderwood, who in May, 1893, had been one of the organizers of the Western Federation of Miners in Butte. He earnestly went about establishing local unions in the different towns of the Cripple Creek district and agitating, as did all affiliates of the Western Federation, for an eight-hour day.

A few Cripple Creek mines had already adopted that standard. Others used shifts of nine hours. All paid the same, $3 a day. A strike for a uniform eight-hour day broke out in February, 1894, and centered around

---

[2] Although Waite could not persuade a special session of the state legislature to adopt his coinage schemes, he did push through another radical act that granted the women of the state equal political privileges with men. Colorado thus became the second state in the nation (Wyoming was the first) to adopt female suffrage.

little Altman, 10,620 feet high on Bull Hill. For several weeks the owners sat tight, hoping to starve the recalcitrants into submission. That failing because of relief funds sent in from other unions, management next employed the maneuver that had broken the 1892 strike in the Coeur d'Alenes. They obtained court injunctions ordering the union and its officials not to interfere with the operation of the mines. That done, they hired some of the many unemployed workers in the district and reopened their workings.

The union did what it could to intimidate the scabs. Armed patrols paced the roads leading to the mines. Other men collected all the rifles and pistols they could find and stored them in a log fort built on the top of Bull Hill. To add to the bastion's martial appearance, they whittled a cannon out of wood and aimed it in sham menace at one of the nearby mines.

Because of this defiant activity, eighteen union officials were imprisoned in Colorado Springs for contempt of court. Almost at once they were freed through the efforts of lawyer Thomas T. Tarsney, a somewhat questionable helper since Davis had recently appointed him adjutant general of Colorado and in theory he should have been more impartial in the struggle.

Learning from Tarsney's actions that they could not count on help from the state, as the mineowners in Idaho had, the Colorado capitalists decided to work through Sheriff Frank Bowers of El Paso County, whose seat was Republican-dominated Colorado Springs. Opportunity was afforded by a rampaging gang of toughs who were using the strike as a mask for vandalism. Bowers was instructed to restore order by seizing the fort on Bull Hill, suspected of being headquarters for the thugs. The mineowners promised the county administrators to meet the expenses of as many extra deputies as Sheriff Bowers needed.

Bowers did his recruiting in Denver among recently discharged policemen and firemen. They were violently anti-Waite. On assuming office the governor had named new police and fire boards for the city (municipal appointments which, oddly enough, the state then controlled) and ordered them to clean up the corrupt municipal government. Reform lagging, he lost his temper and fired his own appointees. They declined to depart, saying that only the legislature, which had confirmed their appointments, could oust them.

His passion towering still higher, Waite called on the militia to drive the rebels from the city hall. They answered by barricading themselves in the building with the entire police and fire departments, plus several grinning underworld figures led by a notorious bunco artist called Soapy Smith. As bugles tooted and the militia marched, 10,000 Denver citizens packed the streets around the city hall to watch the fun. There was none. Calmer heads persuaded the antagonists to submit the disputes to the courts. The law upheld the governor. Triumphantly he fired every member of both departments.

The deposed rank and file ached to retaliate. Humbling the Cripple Creek unions, which the governor was deemed to favor, seemed a good way. One hundred and twenty-five of the recently discharged policemen and firemen signed on with Sheriff Bowers and rode by train to the wars—first the D&RG to the town of Florence on the Arkansas River, and then north on two or three flatcars of the still-building narrow-gauge Florence & Cripple Creek Railroad, which had just reached Victor at the south end of the district.

The union prepared a reception. As the diminutive freight engine labored with its jampacked flatcars up the hill beside the Strong mine, a terrific blast shattered the workings. Debris rained down on the dumfounded deputies. In panic the locomotive engineer put his train into reverse. The jubilant strikers, or perhaps the thugs who operated among them, tried to clinch the victory by loading a handcar with dynamite and giving it a shove along the downhill track after the retreating train. Fortunately the traveling bomb jumped the rails before overtaking its quarry. Some of the more excitable strikers then stole a work train and set out to remedy matters directly. A confused midnight battle at the deputies' camp ended in a draw, with two men killed.

Alarm swept Colorado Springs. One fevered orator cried out to a mass meeting that the "insurrectionists" were even then sweeping around Pikes Peak to "despoil the Springs' fair womanhood and slit the throats of its little children." Eleven hundred men joined Bowers' deputies, and the reinforced army again marched forth to capture Bull Hill.

Before it could attack, Governor Waite rushed onto the scene, engineered a truce, and worked out a compromise that both the mineowners and the union accepted. The peace threatened to expire, however, when the fire-breathing core of the deputy army, furious still at Waite and embarrassed by their recent flight from the exploding mine at Victor, refused to lay down its arms. Again they started toward Bull Hill to capture the men for whom the sheriff still held warrants. By that time, however, the state militia had appeared. It put itself between the would-be combatants, and with the suasion of bayonets behind him, Adjutant General Tarsney was able, on June 10, 1894, to disperse the deputies and end the 130-day strike with a contract that by and large favored the union.

Although the Western Federation of Miners gained prestige among workers everywhere for the victory, it was no portent of better things. Conservatives rallied. In Colorado their first blow, as irresponsible as the one that had sent a handcar of explosives after a trainload of men, was struck at General Tarsney. Twelve days after the settlement of the strike parties not unknown but never publicly named lured him from his room in a Colorado Springs hotel, rapped him over the head with a pistol butt, lugged him to a barn on a ranch belonging to a Cripple Creek mine official, and there methodically tarred and feathered him. A little later the voters of the state turned Governor Waite out of office and replaced him with a Republican, a rejection brought about more by Waite's antics in such affairs as the city hall war than by his labor stand. Still, the trend was away from radicalism, as Bryan's defeat on the free-silver issue in 1896 indicated, and soon the Federation found itself on the defensive again. The battles that ensued brought the mountains the grimmest decade they ever knew.

The new outbreaks began at Leadville in 1896. Partly because gold had been found on Breece Hill nearby, the town's prosperity seemed to be returning. During the winter of 1895–96 the citizens celebrated by building a towered and turreted palace out of blocks of ice—five acres of frozen wonderland sheltering ballrooms, skating rinks, and a series of a carved ice sculptures depicting the story of Leadville. Wages had even risen a bit— back to $3.00 for skilled labor, even though the price of silver remained below 83½ cents, the point at which the union and the owners had agreed to negotiate. Thus the union's sudden threat of a strike in June, 1896, unless all underground workers received $3 looked to management like a breach of faith. They retaliated by closing every mine and smelter in Leadville.

From then on the pattern was familiar. After a period of waiting, the owners used non-union labor for reopening two properties at the edge of town. Shortly after midnight on September 21, 1896, unionists attacked both mines. Though they managed to destroy some of the surface buildings with dynamite and fire, the workers inside soon dispersed the attacks with rifle fire. All told five men died, one of them a deaf city fireman who had not heard the unionists order him and his fellow firemen to stay away from the hydrants.

On the request of the owners, in came the state militia to restore order and protect property. After a winter unrelieved by any such gaiety as an ice palace, the strike collapsed.

Two years later a similar course of events disrupted the Coeur d'Alenes. Beginning as a contest over wages, the quarrel soon ballooned into a struggle between the Federation and the Bunker Hill and Sullivan Mine over union recognition. An instructive way in which to view it is through the eyes of Levi Hutton, a locomotive engineer for the Northern Pacific Railroad.

Each day Levi, an Iowa orphan, ran a mixed freight and passenger train from Wallace up Canyon Creek to Burke, a town pinched so tightly between the walls of the ravine that both the hotel and the Tiger-Poorman mill were built over tracks. In 1897 Levi married May Arkwright, a fat, homely Irish girl, also an orphan, who cooked in the boardinghouse where he ate. Shortly after the wedding the Huttons invested their savings, $500, in the hard-luck Hercules mine at Burke. This made them capitalists, but in 1899 the Hercules did not amount to enough for it to attract attention from the strikers, and Levi Hutton's ambiguous position probably did not bother him as he donned his overalls on the morning of April 29 and chuffed up the canyon on his regular run.

Masked men seized the train, loaded on several hundred pounds of dynamite stolen from the powder magazines of two different mines, and then waved scores of armed workers into the cars. Levi was ordered to drive to Wallace. There several hundred more unionists from Mullan climbed aboard. Levi was then told to head downstream to Kellogg. He demurred. Those were Union Pacific tracks; he had no orders and since every telegraph line in the Coeur d'Alene district had been cut, he could not learn what might be coming toward him. Objection overruled. Slowly he crept ahead, more than a thousand men packed inside the cars and clinging to their tops.

On reaching Kellogg he was directed to stop near the new Bunker Hill and Sullivan concentrator, one of the biggest buildings of its kind in the world, recently completed at a cost of what today would amount to more than a million dollars. After a little sporadic shooting the non-union workers in the plant fled. During it two men died, James Cheyne, a scab, and one member of the Federation, who was killed either by mistake or as the result of a private feud. The attackers then blasted the concentrator into rubble and burned down the superintendent's home. That done, Levi took them back to Wallace.

Reactions were predictable. The mineowners appealed for help to Governor Frank Steunenberg, a heavy-jowled man who neither drank nor smoked nor, for some unexplained reason, wore a necktie above his naked gold collar button. A Democrat who had been elected with Populist support, Steunenberg appealed in his turn to the President of the United States (the Idaho National Guard was serving in the Philippines) and sent the soldiers granted him, many of them Negroes, into the Coeur d'Alenes under the domineering direction of State Auditor Bartlett Sinclair.

Seven hundred unionists, most of whom took deep umbrage at what they described as unnecessarily rough handling by the Negroes, were thrown into miserable bull pens. Sinclair next established a rigorous permit system; under it no one was allowed to work in the area unless he first proved that he had not participated in any way, however indirectly, in the dynamiting and then promised to resign from the Federation, if he was a member. The state then set out to convince union officers everywhere that they were responsible for the actions of the rank and file. To make the point clear a rising young prosecuting attorney named William E. Borah tried Paul Corcoran, secretary of the Burke union, for the murder of James Cheyne at the concentrator, even though Corcoran evidently had not been in the neighborhood of the shooting. Convicted, the union leader was sentenced to seventeen years in the penitentiary (but was pardoned after one year). The success of this relentless drive broke the Federation in Idaho. The antipathies it raised also defeated Steunenberg's campaign to be re-elected in 1900.

Among those who had been roughly thrust into one of the bull pens was Levi Hutton. He was held there twelve days without recourse simply because his questioners refused to believe his statement that he had not recognized any of the masked men who had taken command of his locomotive cab. Aroused by his treatment, his wife, May, roamed the district collecting other atrocity tales and put them into a scathing book entitled *The Coeur d'Alenes, a Tale of Modern Inquisition in Idaho.* Shortly after it was published, the Hercules mine struck bonanza silver and during subsequent years grossed an estimated $150 million. From this sum the Huttons netted, as their share of the property, $2 million. They moved to Spokane, lived lavishly, and, remembering their own bleak childhoods, built a splendid orphanage nearby. May also bought up and destroyed every copy of her book that she could locate. She explained the sudden censorship on the grounds that it was poorly written, though whether, in the light of her new milieu, she was criticizing its rhetoric or its anticapitalistic sentiments is not quite clear.

By this time Federation affairs were in the hands of admitted socialists, Charles Moyer, president, and Big Bill Haywood, secretary-treasurer. After the defeat in Idaho they moved Federation headquarters from Butte to Denver, took a deep new breath, and openly vowed that henceforth the union was committed not just to wage problems but to bringing about by whatever means served them best "a complete revolution in the present system of industrial slavery"—a statement ill-calculated to reassure Colorado industrialists.

High-flown theory notwithstanding, wage problems were what launched (May 2, 1901) a new strike at the Smuggler-Union mine, perched atop one of the vast gray-brown cliffs that ring the breath-takingly beautiful town of Telluride in the San Juan Mountains of southwestern Colorado. After a brief shutdown, Arthur Collins, the unnaturalized English superintendent of the Smuggler-Union, hired strikebreakers on exactly the terms he had refused the union. This singular affront led 250 armed strikers to surround the upper workers near timberline. At dawn on July 3, as the night shift came from the adit, the attackers poured out rifle fire. They killed three men and wounded five or six. The terrified scabs offered to surrender in return for a promise that they would be harmed no further. The word was given but as soon as they were disarmed several were beaten viciously and all were herded not into Telluride, where many had families, but up a rough horse trail to the top of Imogene Pass, 13,000 feet high, and told to keep on going down the far side to Ouray. A little later, in September, Collins worked out a compromise with the union, but it failed, as we shall see, to heal the festering animosities.

The Colorado labor situation drew top billing during the state's gubernatorial election of 1902. The Republican candidate, James Hamilton Peabody, a businessman of Canon City, campaigned on a platform of enticing outside capital into the state by guaranteeing order and the protection of property. Like the Democrats, he also advocated that the state constitution be amended so as to allow legislation establishing an eight-hour day for all mine, mill, and smelter workers. To the Western Federation of Miners, this plank in the platform was mere lip service, and the membership was urged to vote against the entire Republican slate.

Peabody, who had no cause to love the Federation for this stand, was elected on November 7, 1902. On November 19 someone aimed a shotgun through the living-room window of Arthur Collins' home near the Smuggler-Union mill outside Telluride and obliterated him as he sat talking with friends.

Was this the protection the new governor had promised? On top of that sarcastic question from his defeated opponents came heavy pressures from the United States Secretary of State. Collins had been an English citizen and the embarrassed federal government wanted his murderers brought to justice. Harried thus from all sides, Peabody let his bias against the union become a fixation.

Every officer of the Telluride local was arrested on no other grounds than that he belonged to the Federation. All were released because of lack of evidence. (The murder never was solved.) But if a unionist had indeed removed Collins, the act brought the Federation no gain. For he was replaced as superintendent of the Smuggler-Union by handsome, high-living, bed-hopping, scandalous Bulkeley Wells, glamour boy of Colorado mining. Wells was not only violently antilabor but was also a general in the Colorado National Guard and could reach Peabody's ear at practically any moment he chose.

Collins' murder also helped defeat the Federation's hope for eight-hour legislation. Although the necessary constitutional amendment had been passed by an overwhelming vote, Governor Peabody and the antilabor majority in the legislature let the necessary enabling acts be sidetracked into such quicksands of delay that they never came to a vote during his administration. That taste too was bitter in the Federation's mouth as it girded for a showdown in the summer of 1903.

Once again the struggle began over wages, this time on behalf of workers, some earning as little as $1.80 a day, in the reduction plants at Colorado City, a grimy suburb of Colorado Springs, where most Cripple Creek ore was treated. When the mill operators, led by Charles MacNeill, met the strike with non-union labor, the Western Federation of Miners determined to cut off their supply of ore by calling a sympathy strike in Cripple Creek. Thirty-five hundred union members who had no immediate grievances of their own reluctantly laid down their tools.

That same summer a somewhat similar mill strike closed the mines at

Telluride. The owners now had a moral issue of their own to trumpet through the mountains. Was this socialistic W.F.M.—they dubbed it the Western Federation of Murderers—to be allowed to turn satisfied workers into pawns in what amounted to a raw struggle for dominance over capital?

Although details varied in Cripple Creek and Telluride, the general pattern was the same. Strikebreakers were subjected to threats, boos, and sometimes violence. The owners thereupon appealed for the protection of troops and promised to finance the operation by purchasing the scrip which the state issued to raise the necessary money. (The cost to Colorado eventually exceeded half a million dollars.)

Having received the owners' appeal, Governor Peabody sent in investigating commissions that spent most of their time listening to the owners. On the recommendation of the commmissions Peabody dispatched militia under officers openly hostile to the union. "I'm here," declared General Sherman Bell on reaching Cripple Creek with a thousand men, "to do up this damned anarchistic Federation."

Bull pens were set up to hold arrestees. Even before martial law was finally declared the military refused to accept writs of habeas corpus for freeing the prisoners. Firearms had to be registered. Curfews were established; in Telluride even the Golden Star Temperance Society had to obtain permission to hold its annual dance. No man could find work unless he could produce a pass issued to him by the militia officers. Scores of unionists arrested on charges of vagrancy were ordered out of both towns.

All this was abetted by local businessmen organized into Citizens Alliances, a movement being fostered on a countrywide scale by the National Association of Manufacturers. (In Telluride, the local branch of the W.F.M. issued an ill-spelled manifesto describing Alliance members as "deciples of destruction" who believed that "broadcloth and fine linen can know no stain of crime . . . diseased in both mind and constitution.") In Colorado the Alliances became what amounted to old-style vigilante organizations. They not only fired clerks sympathetic to the strikers and refused credit to union families, but they also decided who was fit to dwell in their towns and who wasn't.

A foretaste of their methods came in Idaho Springs, where another strike was under way. In July, 1903, an explosion wrecked part of the surface workings of the Sun and Moon Mine. Fourteen unionists were jailed for investigation. Without waiting to hear the evidence an estimated 80 percent of the businessmen of Idaho Springs formed an alliance called the Protective League, seized the prisoners, escorted them to the city limits, and told them to keep going. The justification they published had a certain familiar ring: ". . . the higher and unwritten law of self-protection to which resort must always be had when there is no other speedy and adequate remedy at law."

Seeking redress, the deportees swore out warrants against members of the League. One hundred and twenty-nine of Idaho Springs' leading citizens were arrested. Clucking that it would cost the county too much to try so many, the district attorney entered a nolle prosequi and freed them all.

Southward in Telluride a superficial quietness returned, and on February 20, 1904, the militia were withdrawn. Dozens of the men who had been deported on vagrancy charges promptly returned to their homes. To deal with them the Citizens Alliance, led by Bulkeley Wells and Charles F. Painter of the local *Journal,* called a mass meeting, passed out National Guard rifles that had been left in Wells's charge, and in the dead of night invaded the residences of the returnees. Back down the road under leveled rifles went seventy-eight men.

The Federation then borrowed a device invented by the owners. They obtained an injunction against such antics and with their president, Charles Moyer, at their head prepared to test the Telluride Alliance. En route to the town Moyer paused in Ouray to talk to some of the deportees. There he was arrested for desecrating the flag: the union had passed out handbills bearing a likeness of the national emblem on whose stripes were printed such sentiments as "Union Men Exiled from Homes and Families in Colorado! Wholesale Arrests without Warrant in Colorado!" and so on.

Taken in handcuffs to Telluride, Moyer was delivered to Bulkeley Wells, manager of the Smuggler-Union, and to Sherman Bell, commander of the National Guard. They jailed him, refused a writ of habeas corpus, and were thereupon ordered to pay Moyer $500 each for false imprisonment. Bell and Wells declined. Eventually, on order of the Supreme Court of the state, they took their prisoner to Denver and surrendered him. On July 6, 1904, the court released Moyer and then in an involved 2 to 1 decision absolved his captors from legal responsibility!

At 2:00 A.M. on that same day, July 6, a dynamite explosion shattered the depot at Independence in the Cripple Creek district. Thirteen non-union workers who had just come off shift died; six were badly mutilated; twenty or more received lesser injuries. Wild indignation swept the area. The Citizens Alliance called a mass meeting. During it street fighting erupted between union and Alliance sympathizers. Two men were killed, five hurt. The ire of the crowd then turned against the nearby Federation hall, where some fifty men had taken refuge. A fusillade ripped it until, one of the refugees wrote, "it seemed to me the plaster of the walls fairly moved in on us from the hail of bullets." Surrendering, they were thrown into bull pens. Federation halls and union stores throughout the district were wrecked by howling mobs. The militia returned and with the help of the Citizens Alliance rounded up 1,569 workers (but no Alliance members) for "examination." Of these, 238 were put aboard special trains and hauled out of the area, some as far away as Kansas and New Mexico, and warned not to return.

The Federation was broken. Only sullen acts of vengeance remained. On

December 30, 1905, Frank Steunenberg, ex-governor of Idaho, was killed by a bomb attached to the gatepost of his home in Caldwell, Idaho; it was during his administration that the union had been defeated in the Coeur d'Alenes. Twenty-six months later, on March 2, 1908, another bomb exploded under Bulkeley Wells's bed on the second-story sleeping porch of his home near the Smuggler-Union mill outside Telluride. He was luckier than Steunenberg. Protected by the thick mattress on the bed, he survived.

No one was ever tried for the assault on Wells. A certain Albert Horsley, who went under the name of Harry Orchard, was arrested for Steunenberg's murder. In prison Orchard confessed not only to that crime but to blowing up the Independence depot, plus various other murders—and also various unsuccessful attempts on the lives of such people as Governor Peabody, Justice William Gabbert of the Colorado Supreme Court, and Fred Bradley, erstwhile manager of the Bunker Hill and Sullivan mine. Haywood, Moyer, and other officials of the Western Federation of Miners, he said, had hired him to undertake the assassinations.

On the strength of Orchard's assertion, Idaho and Colorado officials entered into secret arrangements under which three officers of the Federation—Moyer, Haywood, and George Pettibone—were pounced on in their Denver homes early one Sunday morning, hustled aboard a special train (Bulkeley Wells of the Colorado militia was one of their captors), and spirited out of the state before writs of habeas corpus could be issued freeing them. In Boise the trio vehemently denied the charges and cried out that the antilabor governors of Idaho and Colorado were using Orchard in an attempt to discredit what was left of the Federation. Orchard was willing to play along, they said, because he hated Steunenberg. In 1899 Orchard, like May and Levi Hutton, had owned a small part of the Hercules mine at Burke but because he had participated in the destruction of the Bunker Hill and Sullivan concentrator he'd had to abandon his share of the property and flee when Steunenberg's militia marched in. Thus, unlike the Huttons, he had never become a millionaire and was resentful enough so that he had been willing to kill the governor. Or so the union said.

In the summer of 1907, after long legal maneuvers, William Haywood's trial for conspiracy to murder finally opened in Boise. William Borah was a leading figure for the prosecution, Clarence Darrow for the defense. Reporters flocked in from throughout the world. Labor everywhere, remembering the nature of Haywood and Moyer's "kidnaping" from Denver, was in a paroxysm of excitement. No worker, the militant Socialists chanted, could possibly expect justice under the American capitalistic system.

After the decorously conducted trial was over, the presiding judge, Fremont Wood, who privately believed Haywood guilty, instructed the jury of grizzled farmers, eleven of them more than fifty years old, that under Idaho law a man could not be convicted of a crime on the unsupported word of an accomplice. There had to be corroboration of some sort. Having heard nothing that seemed to them to furnish such corroboration, the jury acquitted Haywood.[3] After a second official, George Pettibone, had also been acquitted in a later trial, the charges against Moyer were dropped.

The results, which considerably deflated critics of the American judicial system, also split the Western Federation. Conservatives, including a chastened Moyer, turned out the radicals, joined the American Federation of Labor, and in 1916 adopted a new name, the Union of Mine, Mill & Smelter Workers. Haywood and his radicals swept on into the notorious Industrial Workers of the World—and soon garnered two Rocky Mountain martyrs for the cause. One was a Swedish immigrant, Joe Hill (born Haaglund) who was famed as a writer of early twentieth-century protest songs. Largely on the basis of circumstantial evidence, Hill was convicted of and executed for the holdup murder of a Salt Lake City grocer and his son—a complete frame-up, charged the union; the "copper trust" wanted Hill convicted just because he was beloved by the I.W.W. The other martyr, Frank Little, an I.W.W. organizer, his broken leg in a cast, was kidnaped in August, 1917, during a strike in Butte and hanged to a railroad trestle—another example, the union charged, of undiluted malice on the part of the mine owners.

And so, though the unique settings of the mountain cities seemed to call for a culture as indigenous as that of the New England towns clustered around their village greens, it never developed. Torn and dehumanized by their own violence, the cloud cities became not cohesive communities but the gray locales of an unsightly, highly standardized industrial process—this in the free, unfettered West that during its tourist-oriented summer carnivals still boasts of the days of the gold rush when every man had a chance to strike it rich. A more eloquent commentary on the black side of America's hectic industrialization could hardly have been devised.

[3] A Telluride miner named Steve Adams repudiated a confession that might well have shed light on the Independence depot explosion, but not necessarily on Steunenberg's assassination.

XXI

BENEFICIAL USE REDEFINED

ECONOMIC GOSPEL, as revealed by the apostles of Western faith, was threefold. First, every man, however humble, was entitled to a share of the land's material bounty. Second, anyone who claimed a part of the nation's resources must use what he had and not store it away for future profit. Third, prior utilization of land, water, or mineral brought with it higher rights than those attaching to a later appropriation, however ethical or even necessary the second claim might be.

These precepts were turned into commandments by national law. A farmer or prospector received title to his ground from a benevolent government only after he had completed (or had pretended to complete) a specified amount of "development" work calculated to increase the usefulness of his property. In times of drought a haygrower who had arrived late beside a stream was obliged to let life-giving water gurgle coolly past his fields to a neighbor whose farming practices might be deplorable but who had filed his water claim earlier. If formal laws did not fit the case, then "unwritten law" came into play. Many a mountain sheepman, for example, was denied the right to graze his flocks where cattle ranches had been established first, even though the land actually belonged to neither group but to the government.

Because these laws were starkly utilitarian, a calloused clutch of raiders —mineral pirates, grass pirates, water, timber, and game animal pirates quickly learned how to pervert them to their own ends. Of these raiders none was more cunning, aggressive, or personally appealing than Frederick Augustus Heinze of Butte.

Born in Brooklyn, Heinze was the fifth child and third son of a wealthy, domineering German importer who sought to impose Old World notions of discipline on the lad by sending him for four years to rigid German academies. At the age of fifteen young Frederick entered the Columbia University School of Mines in New York City. After his graduation in

1889 his father urged him to continue his scientific education in Germany. Otherwise his only graduation present would be $100.00.

Young Heinze chose the money, wandered through Colorado, and in September, just turned twenty, landed in Butte. There he took a job as a junior mine surveyor with the Boston & Montana Consolidated Copper and Silver Mining Company.

Although each of the main copper companies had its own smelter and did custom work for the smaller mines, Heinze decided in the full flush of his youthful wisdom that there was room for still another independent plant and that he was just the man to provide it. Journeying to London, he sought the aid of the financial house of Baring Brothers. He was an impressive-looking young man, six feet tall and powerfully built; he had handsome brown eyes, a fine baritone voice, and a remarkable command of the English language. He interested the Barings, or thought he did, but the failure of the firm ended the discussions.

His father also declined to help, feeling that the lad was still too green for such a project. Battered into marking time, the embryo capitalist went to work for the august *Engineering and Mining Journal,* compiling copper statistics. He followed this with a year's intensive study in a German mining university.

On the death first of his grandmother and then of his father he inherited about $50,000. He raised a like sum from his older brothers, Arthur and Otto, the former a lawyer, the latter a partner in a successful dry goods firm. His sisters' husbands and other friends added smaller amounts, and with this money Frederick Augustus Heinze formed the Montana Ore Purchasing Company. On January 1, 1894, the firm opened its smelter at Butte. Through involved options and leases the company also acquired control of several small mines. F. A. Heinze, the president, was twenty-four years old.

From Butte he moved restlessly to British Columbia and in October, 1895, began building a smelter at Trail, just north of the Washington border. Bringing in ore involved him in railroad construction and a headlong conflict with the Canadian Pacific. Simultaneously, the Montana Ore Purchasing Company ran into trouble in Butte. One of its mines, the Rarus, was bordered on the south by two mines belonging to the Boston & Montana Company, the firm for which Heinze had worked as a surveyor on first visiting the copper camp. The B.&M. property that touched the southeast section of the Rarus was the Michael Davitt, named after an Irish revolutionary hero. To the west of the Michael Davitt, and south of the Rarus, was the B.&M.'s Pennsylvania mine.

While Heinze was in British Columbia, the B.&M. engineers decided that a vein which apexed on the Michael Davitt dipped northwestward onto Rarus ground. If this was true, the B.&M. as assigns of the original locater, could invoke the apex law (see page 260) and claim the ore in the vein even though it lay within the Rarus boundary lines.

Heinze rushed to Butte and descended into the Rarus to investigate. Today there is no way of determining what he found or what he really believed. This much is certain, however. Frederick Augustus Heinze, a consummate bluffer, always acted on the assumption that the best defense was a slashing offense. Emerging from the Rarus, he declared loudly that the B.&M. had things backwards: the veins involved apexed on the Rarus and *his* firm was entitled to the ore in the lower reaches of the Michael Davitt. He then journeyed to Massachusetts and blandly told A. S. Bigelow, president of the Boston & Montana, that in order to avoid the unpleasantness of an expensive lawsuit he would buy the Michael Davitt for $250,000.

Bigelow showed him the door and began suit in a federal court for the right, under the apex law, to invade the lower reaches of the Rarus. Heinze countered with a suit claiming ore in the lower part of the Michael Davitt. The judge, Hiram Knowles, who once had been an attorney for the Boston & Montana, thereupon enjoined both litigants from mining the disputed vein until the issue had been settled. The trial was scheduled for early 1898.

To obtain the money he would need for pressing the suit Heinze launched a colossal bluff against the Canadian Pacific Railroad. Frightened, the company got rid of him by paying him a million dollars for his smelter and railroad in British Columbia. Opening wide his purse, Heinze then captured the local Silver Bow Democratic county convention. (Butte was the county seat.) This enabled him to nominate for the office of district judge massive, gray-bearded, unwashed, uncombed William Clancy, whose only qualification for the job was an unswerving loyalty to F. A. Heinze.

During the subsequent campaign Heinze was everybody's friend. The miners liked him. He was handsome and generous and could sing sentimental Irish songs. More importantly he looked to them like a Western shepherd boy taking on Goliath corporations. By election time he was the most popular man in Butte and his chosen judge, William Clancy, was elected without trouble.

Shortly thereafter, in February, 1898, the Michael Davitt trial was held before Judge Knowles. After hearing the evidence, including that offered by Heinze's hired "experts," Knowles directed the jury to return a verdict in favor of the B.&M. Geologists familiar with the convulsed nature of Butte's veins were inclined to think that the instructions were proper. The pro-Heinze jurors, nevertheless defied the judge and decided in favor of their idol. This necessitated a new trial. Until the action could be completed, the injunctions against mining the disputed ground remained in force.

Meanwhile Heinze had sought to discomfit the B.&M. still further by instituting another suit against the company, this one in Clancy's court, claiming that the veins in the Pennsylvania mine also apexed in the Rarus and that he was therefore entitled to the Pennsylvania ore as well. Clancy obligingly issued injunctions ordering mining in the Pennsylvania to cease until he could hear the case. With two of its major mines closed by litigation, the Boston company began suffering pangs in the treasury.[1]

Almost immediately new complications developed. Early in 1899 Standard Oil bought Anaconda for $39 million and used its mines, timber holdings, stores, smelters, and what not as the basis for forming the well-watered Amalgamated Copper Company, capitalized at $75 million, nearly twice its actual value. Ailing Marcus Daly, founder and superintendent of Anaconda, became the new company's vice-president.

At once Amalgamated began reaching toward the Boston copper companies, in which some of Amalgamated's officers already held substantial interests. If the new firm succeeded in absorbing them, it would likewise absorb the Boston lawsuits. Frederick Heinze would then be faced with a formidable foe indeed.

Through a minority stockholder he set up such a round of suits in the Boston companies that he delayed the take-over for two years. Meantime Clancy was coming up for re-election. To ensure victory, no matter how much money Amalgamated poured into the fight, and to reinforce Clancy with still another complaisant judge, Edward Harney, Heinze joined forces with William Clark, mortal enemy of Marcus Daly.

As was mentioned earlier, Clark's enmity had been sparked by Daly's support of Republican Thomas Carter, who in 1888 had defeated Clark in an election for Montana's last territorial delegate. When the territory achieved statehood in 1889 Clark sought to assuage his wounds by becoming a senator. He was beaten this time by disputed election returns. Republicans set up one legislature (in those days state legislatures elected U.S. senators), Democrats the other. Each sent two senators to Washington. Congress seated the Republicans; the Democrats, one of them William Clark, had to wait for the election of 1893 for another chance.

During the waiting a vicious fight broke out over the location of Montana's capital. By decree of the new state constitution, Montana voters were to cast ballots in 1892 among half a dozen contenders. The top pair in the voting would face each other in a runoff election in 1894. Daly

---

[1] Later in the course of the suits Eastern financiers—Henry Rogers and William Rockefeller of Standard Oil, Thomas Lawson, a Boston broker, and James Stillman, president of New York's National City Bank—began their intricate maneuvers to corner the world's copper market. As one tiny maneuver in the campaign they transferred ownership of the Michael Davitt to the Butte & Boston. Heinze thus was fighting two firms, the Butte & Boston over the Michael Davitt and the Boston & Montana over the Pennsylvania. For simplicity this account lumps the two companies together as the "Boston group."

aspired to name Anaconda town. It had been his pet since he had brought it into being with his smelter a decade earlier. He had graced its griminess with a plush hotel and a race track, and he relished the thought of having the state government housed like trained bears in his company-dominated town. He took umbrage when Clark not only opposed him but made slighting remarks about his intelligence.

In 1892 the voters chose Helena and Anaconda for the runoff. Clark declared in favor of Helena. Daly retorted by spending enough money in 1893 to defeat Clark's senatorial aspirations. Wildly vengeful, Clark thereupon poured forth a reputed million dollars to down Anaconda's bid to be Montana's capital. The feud was still white hot in 1898 when Clark opened another drive for a senatorship.

At first Daly seemed to be triumphant in that his men won more seats in the legislature than did Clark's supporters. The loyalty of the Daly contingent was not impregnable, however. At a cost of $431,000 Clark purchased the forty-seven extra votes he needed to be declared, on January 28, 1899, Montana's new senator.

Through Montana's other senator, Republican Thomas Carter, Daly challenged the election and presented such lurid evidence of bribery (much of it gathered by highly corrupt means) that the Senate of the United States prepared to refuse Clark his seat. He resigned before the blow could fall. This created a vacancy that could be filled only through appointment by Montana's governor, Robert Smith. Smith, a Daly supporter, was lured to San Francisco as counsel in a trumped-up mining suit. The absence allowed the lieutenant governor, a Clark supporter, to name William Clark as senator to fill the vacancy caused by William Clark's resignation. At that such a hue and cry went up throughout the land that Clark again resigned. It was then decided that the new legislature, scheduled for election in November, 1900, should fill the empty seat. Clark, his hide quite impervious to shame, decided to elect legislators who would support his candidacy for the seat he had twice abandoned. In pursuit of that end he joined hands with the idol of Butte, Frederick Augustus Heinze.

The pair drew thunderous plaudits from miners everywhere by instituting an eight-hour day in their properties. Heinze bought a newspaper, the *Reveille,* and joined Clark's *Butte Miner* in a scurrilous campaign against Amalgamated, the creation of Standard Oil. He imported a star of the day, Cissy Loftus, to sing at rally after rally, to the tune of "The Wearing of the Green": "We must down the kerosene, boys, we must down the kerosene."

They won. Heinze elected his judges and Clark a legislature committed to sending him to the Senate.[2] There was no true union of hearts, however. When Henry Rogers of Standard Oil approached Clark in Washington with word that through Mark Hanna he controlled thirty votes in the Senate and threatened to unseat Clark unless he played ball, the fledgling lawmaker

[2] A week after the election Daly died of diabetes in New York City.

deserted his ally without a tremor. He fought Heinze ruthlessly in the elections of 1902. Though Heinze's charm was such that his men were elected, it was obvious that from then on Sir Galahad was to be utterly alone in his fight against one of the most powerful industrial combinations ever formed—for by then Amalgamated had absorbed the Boston companies and only Heinze stood free of the tentacles.

He liked his enemies big. With booming relish he sent up a barrage of court actions. At one time he had thirty-seven lawyers, including his brother Arthur, on his payroll. Some of his scores of suits were diversionary, some were exploratory. The main ones centered about the apex law. He added other key claims to the Rarus, hired experts to testify, often in outrageous contradiction of geologic fact, that valuable veins surfaced on the holdings and that he was therefore entitled to rich ore underlying the best of the opposition's property. On the basis of the flimsiest testimony, Clancy or Harney would then issue injunctions and the mining of the disputed ground would stop.

Each litigant was permitted inspectors to see that the injunction was obeyed, but when Heinze refused entry to men from the other side, legal compulsion to make him accept them was remarkably slow in coming. Meanwhile, acting through dummy corporations, he robbed the disputed workings of millions of dollars' worth of ore.

To hide what he was doing he had his workers build great bulkheads of concrete designed to look like native rock. After a stope had been stripped of ore, the men hid the extent of their pilfering by blasting worthless rock into the excavations. One such explosion accidentally killed two enemy workers nearby. There might well have been more deaths, for Amalgamated men occasionally broke through from their workings into Heinze's illegal underground chambers and tried to drive the raiders away with stinkpots, floods of water, and powdered lime blown through air hoses. Heinze's men replied in kind, and histories like to describe the annoyances as Butte's underground war. Actually, both sides stopped short of deliberate murder, for fear perhaps that the government might come onto the scene.

Unable to break through the legal thickets that screened the robberies, Amalgamated in October, 1903, suddenly put 20,000 men out of work by shutting down every mine, smelter, colliery, lumber camp, and store that it operated in Montana. The company then notified Governor Joseph K. Toole that it would not reopen until he had summoned a special legislature to pass a Fair Trials bill that would permit either party to a civil suit to obtain a change of venue simply by charging the judge with prejudice.

In a famous speech of extraordinary eloquence—"They will force you to dwell in Standard Oil houses while you live—and they will bury you in Standard Oil coffins when you die!"—Heinze urged the miners to hold out. But how could they, without work in the face of a Montana winter?

Though the *Reveille* sneered that his enemies were boasting of being able to make Montana's voters "think through their stomachs better than through their brains," the legislature was summoned and the bill passed.

Heinze wasn't licked exactly. He hung onto enough property and won enough suits (as 1906 opened he had 110 cases pending!) that in final desperation Amalgamated bought him out for an estimated $10.5 million. He should have let well enough alone. But that wasn't Heinze's way. He took his money to New York, formed a copper trust of his own, and tried to beat Amalgamated at its own game. He couldn't swing it. Even though the doing helped precipitate the nationwide Panic of 1907, Standard drove down the price of his stock, shattered his banks, and broke him flat.[3] He was thirty-seven years old, white-haired, hollowed out with weariness. Seven years later he died.

He had succeeded in the West because there he had been able to bend to his own ends the ideals of a simpler time. He had perverted judicial safeguards, had plundered and lied without scruple. His weapon, the apex law, had been based on the most naïve of pioneering urges—a desire to give the discoverer of a vein a bonus for his success. What could be fairer, the miners demanded, and cheered Heinze's rapacity to the skies.[4] Unable to rise themselves, they triumphed vicariously through him. He was a symbol of lost dreams. As such he did not have to make logical or even ethical sense.

A share for everyone who would use it, the gospel said. But what good was a share so small that it served only to mock the possessor? Except in cases of bonanza ore, a mining claim 1,500 feet long by 600 feet wide was not big enough to justify the capital outlay necessary for volume production—even assuming a poor man could raise the money. A timber claim 160 acres in size would not support a heavily mechanized sawmill, yet no other kind of mill could meet the competition of big operators moving into the northern Rockies from forests around the Great Lakes. An agricultural homestead, also 160 acres in size, could not possibly carry enough cattle to keep a rancher's family alive. True, the Desert Land Act of 1877 let him buy 640 acres for $1.25 an acre, 25 cents down at the time of filing and the balance after three years, but he had to irrigate the holding within that time, and the expenses involved made this form of land acquisition all but impossible for most would-be ranchers—unless they resorted to fraud, as many of them did.

Recognizing the deficiencies of Eastern land laws in the arid West, John

---

[3] A few years later government trustbusters forced Standard to shed Amalgamated, which reverted to its old designation, Anaconda.

[4] Though the master of the apex law, Heinze was not its only manipulator. Every mining camp learned its disruptions. The initials of A. E. Carlton of Cripple Creek, for instance, were said to stand for "Apex Everybody" because of the abandon with which he cashed in on its opportunities.

Wesley Powell of the United States Geological Survey urged in 1879 that the nation's homestead program be given a thorough overhauling. The most far-reaching of his proposals concerned grazing lands. Let small ranchers obtain pastoral claims of 2,560 acres each, he urged, their boundaries arranged not in rectilinear lines, as was customary, but in accordance with the land's natural contours and in such a way that every owner would have access to a stream.

The notion appalled Easterners. A century earlier the United States had ceased surveying claims according to contours—a quarrel-breeding system in use in early Virginia and Kentucky—and had instituted the grid pattern. A little later Congress had decided that 160 acres was the optimum plot for a single family. Although Powell presented a mass of figures to show that geographic and climatic conditions west of the 100th meridian were radically different from those in the humid East, he could not budge the weight of so much tradition. The government clung to the old patterns, and would-be cattlemen, sheepmen, and farmers had to get along with the inadequacies as best they could. The result was confusion, heartbreak, open violation of the law, and clashes of interest that at times erupted into horrifying violence.

The common way for a man of modest means to launch himself as a cattle, sheep, or crop grower was to homestead a likely quarter section of meadowland near a mountain stream. He then dug a short ditch for irrigating wild hay, alfalfa, or grain, acquired a few animals which he fed during the worst of the winter weather, and the rest of the time grazed them on the public land surrounding his homestead. A few such people were no particular trouble to the big-time cattlemen who ranged their herds across the same land. But the homesteaders tended to cluster together—in Cassia County in southern Idaho, say; along the White River and in the San Luis Valley of Colorado; beside the sparkling tributaries of Powder River, flowing eastward out of the Big Horn Mountains of Wyoming. Such clusters meant trouble. Homestead fences disrupted normal grazing patterns and sometimes cut the range cattle off from water entirely. And, although one small herd did no great damage to the grass, several of them added to a big rancher's stock could badly overgraze a choice valley.

If the herds were sheep, the problem was intensified, because (so the cattlemen said) a gland between the animals' toes exuded an odor cattle could not abide. In addition those sharp little hoofs tramped out the grass roots. Out with the woollymonsters! Cattle had arrived first, the ranchers said, and therefore, in the Western code, cattle held prior rights.

Actually sheep had appeared as soon as cattle in the valleys around the mining camps. Because of the helplessness of the animals, however, and the danger from predatory killers, most of the flocks were kept under close supervision near the home ranch and did not establish claims to such sweeping extents of open range as cattle did. During the late 1870's and early 1880's, moreover, the spread of cattle was quickened almost to stampede proportions by steadily rising beef prices. Ranges became over-crowded, and the cattle barons, fighting for space, began talking as if they really did own the public lands.

As early as 1879 rancher E. W. Smith of Evanston in southwestern Wyoming was speaking angrily about the "aggressors"—Mormon sheep-men pushing out of the Utah deserts into summer grazing country in the upper Bear River valley. Coloradoans were more direct. In 1884 various groups, presumably cowboys, tied up and beat sheepherders in Rio Blanco County in the northwestern part of the state, burned sheepmen's cabins near Colorado Springs, and vandalized the home and slaughtered several animals belonging to one Teofilio Trujillo in the San Luis Valley farther south.

In 1883 Idaho cowmen rammed through their territorial legislature an extraordinary Priority Rights bill that forbade sheep from grazing in any locality where cattle had ranged first. And in Wyoming, where cattle raising was the dominant industry, the Wyoming Stock Growers' Association, composed mostly of wealthy cattlemen, captured the territorial government and through it managed range conditions to suit its members.

As the grasslands grew increasingly crowded, the cattlemen also had to protect themselves from each other. Landownership was one possibility; and, indeed, the government would, under certain circumstances, sell sizable blocks of the public domain to high bidders. Unhappily, the initial expense was heavy and after that there would be taxes. The cattlemen suggested therefore that the government lease the public land at a mini-mum fee. This proposal brought forth violent objections from other Westerners, particularly sheepmen, lest the system enable monopolists, meaning cattle barons, to engross undue amounts of grass. Heeding the protests, the government rejected the scheme.

Nature offered another solution. Streams in the West were widely spaced. If a man controlled land along a creek, he also controlled the grazing as far back from the water as a cow could walk. By filing on an agricultural or desert homestead himself and by having his employees file on others that they immediately (and illegally) conveyed to him, a rancher could lay hold of miles of stream. With that in his pocket he could then master enormous acreages to the right and the left. Why not? He was using the grass, he had been there first . . .

The process was just getting well under way when catastrophe struck the cattle industry. During the summer of 1886 a severe drought shriveled the already overgrazed ranges of the high plains east of the mountains. The next winter unprecedented blizzards hammered at the emaciated herds, killing cattle by the tens of thousands. At the same time prices dropped alarmingly, precursor to the disastrous depression of the early 1890's.

Painful readjustments followed. Some ranchers, among them many highborn Englishmen who had thought cattle raising a jolly way to make a fortune, quit the business entirely. Some concentrated their herds, upgraded quality, and sought out permanent hay lands where they could raise winter feed. Others horrified their neighbors by turning to sheep.

Sheep were cheaper to buy than cattle and quickly yielded double returns, on wool and mutton. They could be moved readily from spot to spot as conditions demanded; and they fared better on winter ranges where water and forage were skimpy. Or so ranchers told each other, and the results of the new optimism were marked. Before the blizzards of 1886–87, Wyoming grasslands had supported about 400,000 sheep and 900,000 cattle. During the next four years the sheep population nearly doubled while the number of cattle shrank by 25 percent. (In Montana during those same years the sheep count jumped fourfold, from 875,000 to 3,327,000.) By 1901, when the prices of all livestock were rising again, Wyoming tallied 769,000 cattle and 5.5 million sheep. These, be it noted, were sheep on the tax rolls. Uncounted migrant herds that wintered on the deserts of eastern Oregon, Nevada, and Utah also pressed into the high country each summer.

Cattle ranchers who were trying to recoup after the catastrophe of 1886–87 bitterly resented the intrusion. The Meeker (Colorado) *Herald* warned grimly on January 14, 1888, that cowmen along the White River were in no mood to be "imposed on." In other areas prose grew downright purple. A correspondent from Mountain View, Wyoming, near old Fort Bridger at the foot of the handsome Uinta Range, wrote in the Evanston *News-Register* for January 27, 1894, that "this little valley . . . was at one time the garden spot of our state. Springs were to be found bubbling from our hillsides, wild flowers bloomed in profusion, and succulent bunch grass grew in abundance. . . . But now this beautiful country is so badly beaten down with sheep that there is scarcely enough grass to support a sage hen. The sheepmen [two thirds of them nonresidents of the state, the author added later] say they have as good a right to this range as the first settlers. Of course under our laws they have, but when it comes to rights existing between man and man they have not."

Man to man, and the gospel: cattlemen meeting at Fort Bridger in the spring of 1895 mapped out a strip of territory at the base of the Uintas 55 miles long and 28 miles wide, nearly a million acres of *public* land, and ordered sheepmen to stay out. That same year cattlemen farther north at Big Piney in the Green River Valley established a deadline and told sheepmen not to cross it. Four or five flockowners banded together, hired armed guards, and went defiantly ahead. Nothing happened. Then when their vigilance relaxed masked riders attacked, clubbed 2,000 sheep to death, scattered the rest, burned camp equipment, and ran the herders out of the country.

In Idaho a few months later (February, 1896) a tough called Diamondfield Jack Davis, hired by the Shoe Sole outfit, killed two sheepmen who dared cross a deadline near Goose Creek in Cassia County. His employers went all out for him. After the prosecution, led by William Borah, had convicted Davis, largely on circumstantial evidence, they carried the case to the Supreme Court of the United States, which upheld the verdict. And still the ranchers fought—no sheepman must win anything. Governor Steunenberg of Idaho commuted Davis' death sentence to life imprisonment. After serving seventeen months of this Diamondfield Jack was pardoned.

So it went—sheep clubbed to death, killed with poison bran, driven over cliffs, shattered with dynamite bombs. In 1887, at Tie Siding, Wyoming, 2,600 head were crowded through a ring of fire so that the flames would set their wool ablaze. Sheep dogs were wantonly shot, wagons were destroyed, herders were abused and occasionally killed. Even today old-timers at Collbran, Colorado, will tell you that there are still no sheep on that part of Grand Mesa because of the ferocity with which woollymonsters from Utah were driven out during the war that raged there between 1892 and 1894. Well, possibly. But, although sheepmen may not have returned to the Collbran area, they persistently revisited most other parts of the Rockies. There was profit in the pursuit. Under those circumstances they rejected the doctrine that first in time necessarily meant first in right. Nor were the increasingly impatient bystanders who watched all this willing to continue forever with so inflexible a theory . . . but more of that later.

A similar rejection of old-line pretensions occurred among small ranchers in Wyoming. Left unemployed by the disaster of 1886–87, many cowboys turned to doing for themselves what they had first learned to do for their bosses. They filed land claims along the streams and took to putting their own brands on stray calves called mavericks. Big ranchers nearby invariably insisted that most of these "mavericks" really belonged to them.

When increasingly stringent brand inspection laws failed to help, reactionaries among the cattlemen sought relief in vigilantism. In July, 1889, six or seven masked men seized two homesteaders on Sweetwater Creek near Independence Rock on the old Oregon Trail. One, Jim Averill, ran on his claim a store that was considered a rustlers' hangout; he had also written letters to newspapers protesting the way in which three big ranchers in the vicinity were freezing out would-be settlers by illegally homesteading every hay meadow for a hundred miles along Sweetwater Creek. Captured with Averill was a neighboring homesteader, Ella Watson, commonly known as Cattle Kate. Ella was a prostitute, not a rustler, but she exchanged her wares for cattle that had been stolen, and that was enough for the vigilantes. They hanged both Jim and Ella, and were astonished by the nationwide outcry that followed.

Six men were arrested. Long delays then occurred. As the excitement died down, witnesses against the accused vanished and the case was dismissed. It had all been "a horrible piece of business," admitted John Clay, president of the Wyoming Stock Growers Association, who was not personally involved. But "what are you to do? Are you to sit still and see your property ruined with no redress in sight?"

From Sweetwater Creek the trouble shifted to Johnson County, east of the Big Horn Mountains. Once the area had been marvelous cattle country. During the 1883 roundup 400 cowboys fed by 70 chuck wagons and using 1,400 saddle horses had worked 181,000 cattle along Crazy Woman Creek, a branch of Powder River. After 1886–87, however, cowboy-settlers arrived in such numbers that within five years they were able to elect one of their fellows, Red Angus, sheriff of the county and establish their own roundup district in flat defiance of the Association, which by Wyoming law had charge of all the state's roundups.

Times were hard. Cowboy-settlers who could not get jobs on big ranches because they had been blacklisted by the Association felt they had to steal to stay alive. Men not involved in the thefts sympathized with those who were. As a result rustling in Johnson County generally went unpunished by local officials.

Utterly frustrated, twenty-five leading members of the Association (which officially kept aloof from the goings-on) hired a gang of professional gunmen in Texas and Colorado. In April, 1892, they rode north through flurries of snow toward Buffalo, the county seat, to put things to right. They were so thoroughly convinced of the justice of their cause that they allowed a newspaper reporter to accompany them.

Exactly what they planned remains unknown. One reminiscence suggests that they intended to capture the Buffalo courthouse, in order to keep settlers from seizing guns belonging to the state militia that were stored there. After summoning a town meeting to assure law-abiding citizens that their rights would be respected, the invaders would then post a list of known outlaws, with orders that they leave the country in twenty-four hours. Or perhaps the cattlemen carried a death list with them from the outset and meant to be executioners as well as accusers. For on learning that two of the men they wanted were at the KC ranch house 50 miles south of Buffalo, the Regulators, as they have been called, swung that way and, after a daylong, badly managed siege, killed both.

Word of the shooting had meantime reached Buffalo. Sheriff Red Angus, bearing warrants for murder, marched south at the head of several hundred deputies and citizens, and trapped the Regulators in still another ranch house. One managed to slip loose and ride for help. Telegraph wires hummed and on order of the President of the United States himself in came the cavalry from nearby Fort McKinney to take the Regulators into protective custody.

The accused were transferred from hostile Buffalo to Cheyenne for trial—the expenses of their incarceration to be met by impoverished Johnson County. As in the Averill-Watson affair, long delays ensued, witnesses vanished, expenses soared. His county hopelessly in debt, the despairing Johnson County prosecutor finally let the proceedings drop.

The cattlemen were winners in the sense that no one went to prison for the twin killings. It had been a narrow escape, however, and an expensive one—upwards of $100,000 before the accused went free. In the face of outraged popular sentiment, the ranchers grew meek. Although settlers were still harassed at times by cut fences and broken ditches, there was no further effort to use vigilantism for maintaining the rights of prior appropriation.

All this while railroads, territorial and state immigration bureaus, irrigation companies, and even travel writers were upsetting range patterns still more by luring farmers onto the benchlands beside the mountain streams. What a way to live! "Sunshine, Irrigation, Independence!" rhapsodized an 1895 promotion pamphlet of the Alamosa Land and Canal Company of Colorado's San Luis Valley. "To breathe in that atmosphere, is a source of constant delight," declaimed an 1891 prospectus of the Dearborn Canal Company of Helena, Montana. According to these and scores of other brochures, a steady source of water forever exorcised agriculture's erstwhile demons of drought at planting and excess moisture at harvest.[5]

In practice, the supply of water proved highly uncertain mainly because of the varying depth of each winter's snow pack in the high basins. In the dry year of 1889 the Snake River carried 2,200 second-feet of water past Eagle Rock in southeastern Idaho. In the wet year of 1894 the river was thirty times that big, 70,000 second-feet. At Blackfoot in 1905 it was completely dry—and what good is a water right to a dry stream?

The excessive claims that had been made by the pioneer appropriators of water were further confused by inadequate records. Local courts in both Colorado and Utah were clogged with water litigation. Wearying of repeated suits that settled nothing, David Boyd of the Greeley (Colorado) *Tribune,* cried out on April 23, 1880, for legislation that would cut the knot by compelling state-supervised arbitration. "How long, my fellow sufferers, are we to be the playthings of these quibbling lawyers, these men . . . of blind conservatism, of narrow routine, of crass stupidity?"

---

[5] In 1889 the Colorado State Agricultural College at Fort Collins released the results of experiments that completely debunked the early-day theory of irrigation water as a renewer of the soil. In spite of that evidence promoters continued to trot out the same old sales pitch. The mountain water carried beneficent fertilizer to the roots of each individual plant, said the Dearborn prospectus in 1891. "Irrigating water is a grand fertilizer," insisted the Alamosa company's promotion in 1895. In 1909 B. C. Buffum of Worland, Wyoming, wrote in *Arid Agriculture* that with irrigation "only in special locations or with special crops will the use of any artificial fertilizer be found advisable." People, it would seem, persistently believe what they want to believe.

And yet Utah, where irrigation by Anglo-Saxons had first begun, and Colorado, where the struggles of the Union Colony at Greeley had long since flashed a precautionary light, were in good shape compared to Montana.

For specifics, consider the West Gallatin Valley. Diversion had begun there, near Bozeman, in 1864. By the turn of the century the office of the county clerk housed fifteen volumes setting forth 2,500 recorded claims. Scores of those filings were far too vague to be useful in establishing precise rights: "All my ditch will carry," for example, or "sufficient for my land." Five different companies claimed *all* the water of West Beaver Creek; six separate registrants demanded *all* of Lyman Creek. As was common throughout the arid West, the worst offenders were corporations that entered unconscionable claims, promised for a fee to deliver water to distant customers, and then found that in times of shortage they could not meet their obligations.

Naturally there were quarrels. Samuel Fortier, engineer of the Pacific District of the U.S. Department of Agriculture, who studied Montana's scrambled situation shortly after the turn of the century, wrote in discouragement in 1906 that throughout the state's agricultural regions, "The division of water is the chief topic in farmhouses from seed time to harvest, and communities seem willing to spend the greater part of their earnings in protracted litigation."

Like David Boyd of Greeley, Fortier recommended enforced arbitration. Decision, he said, should be based not only on prior appropriation (which in Montana was finally ruled to begin on the completion of a ditch and not on the filing of a claim), not just on beneficial use (witnesses described in court what the water had been used for and were asked to estimate whether there had been any waste), but also on a consideration of other users, domestic and industrial as well as agricultural, no matter how late they had arrived.

What finally slowed but never stopped the wrangling was the interest of distant states in the rivers that rise in the mountains. Belatedly realizing they could not defend the priority of their rights against outsiders unless they put their own records in order, the mountaineers began a grudging readjustment. Legislatures established procedures for adjudication, state engineers and other water czars set up precise measuring devices in each of the multitudinous irrigation districts, and settlements were slowly ironed out—within each state.[6] Disputes still rage between the mountain states and outsiders, however, with the Supreme Court of the United States more and more assuming the role of arbiter and refusing to place the once-

---

[6] Intrastate settlements were of particular importance in Colorado. There huge transmontane tunnels are whisking all possible amounts of unappropriated water from the western slopes of the mountains, where precipitation is heavier, to the dry eastern slopes, where farming is more extensive and where the larger cities lie.

sanctified Colorado doctrine of prior appropriation ahead of all other social needs.

Long before the difficulties of apportionment had come to a head proponents of irrigation were arguing that massive reservoirs were needed to stabilize stream flow and to bring more land into cultivation. Despite, or perhaps because of, the country's increasing urbanization, an intense emotionalism centered around the latter point. The sturdy American yeoman, the mystique held, had made the country great and would continue to do so as long as everyone who wanted a plot of arable land could obtain it—a matter of particular concern during the early 1890's, when an acute depression was creating longer and longer bread lines in the cities. If private capital could no longer meet the emergency, then let the government step into the breach.

Most eloquent of the agencies espousing federal aid were the Irrigation Congresses whose annual conventions were launched in Salt Lake City in 1891. A crusading fervor marked each gathering. Poverty, declared the president of the 1902 gathering in Colorado Springs, now grinds the people, but then "I see National Irrigation like a good fairy wave its magic wand, and lo! a new star of hope arises in the sky of our common humanity." Massed choirs (the singers from the Mormon Tabernacle in Salt Lake City were favorites) sang special hymns. Delegates wept and cheered. In Albuquerque in 1908 "in the middle of the ode the great audience [of 5,000 people] interrupted for nearly five minutes with applause before allowing the chorus to proceed."

Federal aid, however, was a touchy matter in a field hitherto dominated by private enterprise. Seeking to stave off government intervention with a compromise, Senator Joseph M. Carey of Wyoming in 1894 maneuvered through Congress a states rights sort of bill known as the Carey Act.

Under terms of the Carey Act the federal government would donate to each of seven Western states up to a million acres of irrigable land, which was to be sequestered in the following manner. Private companies selected an area of several thousand acres which they thought they could develop and presented to the state engineer concerned plans for dams and canals. If the plan was approved, and in general specifications were strict, the land involved was turned over to the state. The state then sold it to prospective settlers in 160-acre tracts at 50 cents an acre. The company, the stigma of "promotion" removed by state sponsorship, hoped to profit by selling the settlers water rights. Thus everyone came into the act—federal government, state government, and private effort.

As soon as a plan had been approved and the land set aside, the company tried to lure in settlers. A favorite method was an excursion trip from the East, drummed up by real estate agents, newspaper advertising, handbills, and special low fares offered by the interested railroads. On arrival in the vicinity, prospects were shown a green belt of already irrigated farms and then were taken to the sagebrush flats the water company hoped to convert. The first stop was the office shack. Brave maps shone on the drab inside walls. Arching over them like a rainbow was a printed motto, OPPORTUNITY. The prospects saw on the map what plots were available, then bounced off in buggies or sometimes in an early-day touring car to inspect them.

Sage, wind, barrenness—those who bought often gave up under the pressures of the long wait for water. The fault, Attorney General Joseph Peterson of Idaho told the National Irrigation Congress that met in Denver in 1914, was not the "sleek promoter slinking away with his pelf," but the nationwide back-to-the-soil propaganda spread by do-gooders trying to clear out the Eastern industrial slums. The underequipped, unprepared tenderfeet weren't ready for the experiment. "They became horror-stricken by the harmless, though blood-curdling yell of the coyote. . . . They fell into despondency; they failed; their suffering was piteous." Scores departed, and their experience frightened others into staying at home. This in turn hurt the companies who were trying to finance their work by selling bonds to Eastern investors. As the trickles of capital ran dry—well, not all the ghost towns of the Rockies were erstwhile mining camps.

The best known of the Carey Act projects was the one dreamed up by florid George Washington Thornton Beck, 6 feet tall, 200 pounds heavy, a fine amateur boxer, graceful and debonair withal. Son of a Kentucky congressman, Beck had prospected as a young man in Colorado, had surveyed for the Northern Pacific Railroad, and in 1879 had founded a successful sheep ranch on Goose Creek, near present Sheridan, Wyoming, on the northeast flank of the Big Horn Mountains.

One of Beck's favorite recreation spots—he was an ardent hunter—was the foothill country of the Absaroka Mountains, through which the North Fork of the Stinking Water (now Shoshone) River tore a spectacular canyon on its way out of Yellowstone Park. A hunting crony who shared his love for the region was Buffalo Bill Cody, one-time Pony Express rider, buffalo hunter, army scout, and founder, with Nate Salisbury, of a world-famous, highly profitable Wild West show. On the passage of the Carey Act, Beck began talking to Cody about a 25-mile canal from the Shoshone Canyon to the base of the hot, brown hills.

The idea appealed to the showman. His first dream, a grand ranch at North Platte, Nebraska, had gone sour. At the start he had left its affairs in the hands of his wife, Louisa, whom he called Lulu, and she had put the property in her own name. This caused bickering. So did Cody's heavy drinking, extravagant living habits, and repeated infidelities when he was on tour—infidelities that even embraced, Lulu thought darkly, no less a person than Queen Victoria!

Because of his unhappy home life, Cody more and more frequently sought refuge at a hunting ranch he owned in the Carter Mountains, over-looking the flats Beck proposed to develop. When Beck agreed to call the townsite near the project Cody, Bill was hooked. He poured money into the scheme, as did his showman partner, Nate Salisbury, and Phoebe Hearst of California, widow of George Hearst.

Hard luck plagued them. Supplies had to be hauled in over atrocious roads from Red Lodge, Montana. Landslides and breaks plagued the canal. By 1900 Cody had a population of only 87 and the state engineer was threatening not to accept such work on the canal as had been completed. And still Bill hung onto his namesake. Wind? he was accustomed to say. Why, no. The place was so close to heaven that it was just picking up the breeze made by the angels as they flapped their wings. He persuaded the Lincoln Land Company, a subsidiary of the Burlington Railroad, to buy a half interest in the townsite. The next year the railroad itself arrived. Bill erected a fancy hotel, named the Irma after one of his daughters, opened livery stables, and established excursion lines into Yellowstone Park. Even so, growth remained slow—1,200 people by 1905. And the irrigation company was bankrupt.

Beck, Cody, and their associates bailed out by surrendering their reservoir claims and canal rights to the United States Bureau of Reclamation. Such a bureau was what the National Irrigation Congress had wanted all along, and when it became obvious that the Carey Act would not suffice of itself to remake the West, they had resumed their agitation. President Theodore Roosevelt lent his aid, and in 1902 the Newlands Act put the federal government into the business of building bigger reservoirs, canals, and diversion tunnels than private corporations had been able to tackle.[7]

The Shoshoni project in the Big Horn Basin was one of the earliest assumed by the Bureau. At the time of its completion in 1910 the dam in the canyon was the largest in the world. But if the project's fortunes were looking up, Bill's were sinking. Lulu refused him a divorce. He lost money he did not have in Arizona mining speculations. Mired in debt, he let himself and his Wild West show fall into the hands of H. H. Tamman, one of the proprietors of the Denver *Post,* who also owned the Sells-Floto Circus.

On January 10, 1917, the old showman (he was seventy-one) died in Denver, still gripped in Tamman's toils. By special resolution of the Colorado legislature, and at the urging of the Denver *Post,* which knew a good publicity stunt when it saw one, his body was laid in state under the rotunda of Colorado's gold-domed capitol building. Twenty-five thousand people filed past the bier. Then, according to persistent but unauthenticated rumor, Lulu "sold" her husband to Tamman for $10,000—on the strength of prior appropriation for beneficial use, no doubt. That is, she allowed

---

[7] The Carey Act was not repealed; under its provisions Idaho in particular carried out several projects, but the giant was henceforth the Bureau.

him to be buried atop Lookout Mountain due west of Denver—fanfare by the *Post*. Interment was in a burglarproof vault of steel and concrete lowered into a granite boulder, lest the resentful people of Cody, who believed that he really wanted to be buried on Carter Mountain in Wyoming, try to steal him back.

Talk of artificial reservoirs to conserve and control stream flow turned attention to the natural reservoirs created by the spongy humus of the forests . . . where there was humus. It was disappearing at an alarming rate. Tie hacks, charcoal burners, and lumbermen chewed through the trees without regard for the government's unrealistic laws controlling the disposition of wooded lands. Even more destructive were the fires caused by their carelessness. Freak accidents contributed to the appalling losses. A horse used to haul underground cars in the Terrible Edith mine near Prichard, Idaho, escaped outside with the open flame of a carbide lamp burning on its harness. It wandered into a hay barn—and there went that forest. Sometimes fires were set deliberately by charcoal burners who were allowed to cut burned-over areas without permit, and by sheepmen desirous of using the lush grass that springs up rapidly in fresh burns. And always there was the hazard of lightning. On one exceptional July day in 1926, for example, lightning set 150 different blazes in the Kaniksu Forest of northern Idaho; on another day in the same month in the same forest a slightly less severe storm caused 72 blazes.

What this destruction meant not just to the mountains but to the farms and cities that drew their water from the high country was summed up by Elwood Mead, an early-day Wyoming conservationist, during an 1888 speech to the Colorado State Forestry Association: "If we can keep the sides of our mountains covered with timber we won't need a mountain reservoir for the next decade. But let the sun's rays fall directly on their bare and blasted sides, and all the reservoirs in Christendom would fail to give us a satisfactory water supply."

Opposed to this new kind of protective thinking was the West's laissez-faire economic philosophy. The region had been developed within a single generation, so the argument ran, only because the land had been opened wide to everyone. Continuing prosperity depended on continuing payrolls from mines, railroads, lumber camps, stock ranches, and (a new pursuit) electric power developments, all of which needed free entry to the woodlands. The fat East, which had sent its hungry people West and had profited from their work in extracting Western resources, had no business telling the frontier that now it should start saving what it had worked so hard to win.

The battle began quietly in 1891, during a sweeping revision of the country's hodgepodge of land laws. At the prompting of the American

Forestry Association and of the American Association for the Advancement of Science, Congress accepted an amendment to the General Land Revision bill that allowed the President to withdraw timberlands in the West from public use or entry. Under this authority President Harrison in 1891–92 established six forest reserves totaling 3 million acres. (The Yellowstone Forest Reserve in Wyoming was the first in time; the greatest number were in Colorado.) During the next five years President Cleveland added 16 million acres.

The reserves marked a radical shift in the nation's century-old policy of placing the public domain as rapidly as possible in the hands of small freeholders who would use it beneficially. By contrast, the 19 million acres of newly reserved land could not be privately owned or exploited at all, with one small exception: settlers and miners living outside the reserved areas could obtain, under rigorous conditions but without cost, permits that allowed them to enter the forbidden lands and cut timber for their own immediate use. Otherwise there was to be no trespass—no homesteading, no mining, no grazing, no cutting of timber for sale to others, and (something new and eagerly sought in sections of the West) no water developments for electrical power.

Although this was an extraordinary piece of legislation, it engendered little outcry at first. It came as a last-minute amendment to a complex bill and was offered, one proponent soothingly assured his colleagues, as a temporary measure so that "the water supply in that country may be preserved." Then, before the effects of the law were really felt, the depression of '93 slowed Western economic activity to an apathetic drag. Under those circumstances few exploiters coveted the relatively small area closed to them by the reserves. Those who did went ahead as always, reaping the grass and trees and minerals without leave. Penalties seldom followed, for Congress steadily declined to appropriate money enough for effective administration. Under the impact of the depression the sum allocated for both policing and fire fighting in the reserves was whittled from 1891's inadequate $240,000 to 1895's ridiculous $75,000; the number of agents dropped from ninety-five in 1892 to forty-two in 1895. When Representative T. C. McRae of Arkansas offered bills to remedy some of these defects, Rocky Mountain congressmen—Hartman of Montana, Coffeen of Wyoming, Bell of Colorado—joined the anticonservationist bloc in crippling the legislation with amendments and, finally, in burying it in committee.

Conservationists outside Congress stayed at work, however, and in 1896 prevailed on the Secretary of the Interior to request that the National Academy of Sciences make the first detailed study of the country's vanishing timberlands. The upshot was the Academy's recommendation that the reserve program be extended. In compliance, President Cleveland established, on February 22, 1897, just before his retirement from office, thirteen new reserves covering 21,279,840 acres. A total of 40 million acres of Western land were now closed to any sort of economic activity.

The country's economy meanwhile was picking up, and Cleveland's action at last drew forth the roars of protest that one might have expected earlier. The din in the Rockies was so great that some historians have declared that the mountain dwellers were solidly opposed to conservation. The charge is too sweeping. The Colorado State Forestry Association had vigorously promoted the creation of forest reserves in that state. Led by Colorado, all the mountain states had formed forestry departments to protect timber on state-owned land and fish and game departments to preserve the rapidly dwindling stocks of wildlife. Residents near Laramie, Wyoming, grew so incensed over illegal timber cutting in the Medicine Bow Mountains that they repeatedly petitioned the President to declare that area a reserve, a step finally taken in 1902.

Those were small voices, however. The deafening ones came from newspapers and congressmen supported by mineowners who needed wood to shore up their tunnels, railroads that needed ties, lumbermen who sold wood products to city dwellers and to farmers on the treeless plains, and from stockmen who, because of competition for the already overgrazed valleys, were more and more frequently seeking out the waving summer bunch grass of the high Rockies. Unanimously they decried this "foolish and sentimental regard of the forests"—or, as Senator Teller of Colorado put it (his nephew was the chief trespasser in the Medicine Bow Mountains), "Are not men better than trees?" To Senator Thomas (often called Slippery Tom) Carter of Montana the government's action amounted to a "contemptuous disregard of the people's interests."

The protests forced concessions from the government. During a special session of Congress summoned by McKinley after his inauguration in March, 1897, arbitrary reserve boundaries were redrawn so as to eliminate land fitted for agriculture. Prospecting was declared legal, and timber sales were authorized on the basis of competitive bidding, after rangers had decided which trees could best be cut without damage to the watersheds. Permits were issued without charge for the grazing of as many horses and cattle as the rangers decreed. Sheep, however, remained excluded from all the reserves except those in Washington and Oregon, where the climate was deemed to be moist enough and the soil deep enough that the watersheds could withstand the pounding of their sharp hoofs. This favoritism to cattle drew such wails from the National Wool Growers Association that in 1899 a few sheep were allowed on the Big Horn Reserve and, shortly thereafter, on the other protected forests.

Still another concession, the Forest Lieu Act of 1897, opened the way to massive frauds. Many homesteaders and miners held claims within the new forest boundaries. To eliminate the patchwork, owners were urged to trade their land inside the reserves to the government for land of equal value outside. Instead of benefiting the small freeholders, as intended, the act turned out to be a gravy bowl for speculators. The greatest landowner in the Northwest, thanks to its grants, was the Northern Pacific Railroad— together with certain dealers and lumber companies who, having noticed the depletion of the forests around the Great Lakes, had bought enormous acreages from the railroad in hopes of a rising market. This land, which was scattered across Montana and Idaho in mile-square checkerboards, had been transferred in unselected blocks to the purchasers. Some of it was located above timberline and some stood on end in steep canyons, but so long as it lay within the arbitrary reserve boundaries it could be called forest (even if it hadn't a tree on it) and could then be exchanged for easily logged timber on the outside.

By a diligent reshuffling of their holdings, the railroad and the speculators unloaded 3 million of their poorest acres on the government in exchange for some of the nation's prime timber country. An estimate of the unearned increment which the swaps brought to the jugglers can be made from the rise in value experienced by one Idaho plot as the depression lightened its hold: purchased in 1901 for $240,000 the land resold in 1909 for $2.5 million. No wonder that certain timber barons, like C. A. Weyerhaeuser, were inclined to observe piously, "The government is doing the right thing. It should save the timber"—at least from the little operator, whose only recourse was to bid high or trespass illegally.

Once the key to the wilderness had been the work a man did in pioneering it—prior appropriation for beneficial use. Now, abruptly, the past no longer counted for as much as did a vague future—"the permanent good for the whole people," in the words of Secretary of Agriculture James Wilson, "and not the temporary benefit of individuals or companies."

To much of the West such thinking was socialistic and shocking. "The pretext," shouted Governor Steunenberg of Idaho, "that our land and forests are the just inheritance of posterity is not only hackneyed but illogical and overdone."

Resentment increased in 1906 when the government began charging for grazing permits that until then had been issued without charge. Why, ranchers fumed, should they be expected to pay for grass on the reserves when everywhere else on the public domain it was open for the taking? President Theodore Roosevelt, moreover, was outdoing his predecessors in an energetic extension of the government's restrictive program. To check his hand Western congressmen early in 1907 tacked onto a Forest Service appropriation bill an amendment that took the power of creating new forests in the Rocky Mountains and the Pacific Northwest away from the President and gave it to Congress.

In order to obtain the appropriations that his forest program needed, Roosevelt signed the bill—and then two days before the law became effective established twenty-one new forests embracing 40 million acres. Upwards of 150 million acres were now under tight government supervision.

Wild protest at the President's highhandedness filled the Rockies. A Public Lands Convention dominated by graziers met in Denver on June 19, 1907, to work out ways of circumventing the action—but failed to produce a viable program because of conflicts among themselves. Gifford Pinchot, chief forester of the United States, took more wind from the ranchers' lungs by inviting two cattlemen, Fred Light of Aspen, Colorado, and Tom Shannon of Montana's Little Belt Mountains, to test the constitutionality of the forest laws by suing the government. In both cases the courts upheld the government.

The next year Roosevelt sought to put the entire public domain, and not just the forests, under direct federal control. Congress refused. (The step was not taken until the passage of the Taylor Grazing Act in 1934.) Fees for grazing permits stayed in effect, however—"the greatest calamity," cried *Field and Farm* magazine of Denver on December 26, 1908, "that ever befell the cattle interests of Colorado or any other mountain state." Hoping to apply direct pressure on Gifford Pinchot, the National Wool Growers Association invited him to attend their 1909 convention in Pocatello, Idaho, and "talk to sheepmen about cooperative matters pertaining to the national forest." Crisply the chief forester wired back, "Until I have additional evidence through formal action of the National Wool Growers Association showing an earnest desire to cooperate with the Forest Service along brighter lines than heretofore, I must decline to attend its convention." There was no relaxing of fees—nor of Rocky Mountain plaints. The land, *Ranch and Range* editorialized in its issue of September, 1909, groaned under the affliction of "a vast army of carpetbaggers and aliens, whose principal duty seems to be the collection of revenue from the unfortunate pioneers who are trying to hew a home out of the wilderness."

During these controversies the government's case for controlled grazing was inadvertently aided, in April, 1909, by a fresh outburst of violence between cattle and sheep interests in the Big Horn Basin of Wyoming. The climax of years of strife there came near some run-down ranches where Spring Creek flows into Nowood Creek close to the little town of Tensleep. Three sheepmen, Jules Lazair, Joe Emge, and Joe Allemand, and two herders, Pierre Cafferal and Charles Helmer, defied a local deadline and drove two bands of sheep through cattle country on their way to summer grazing in the Big Horn Mountains. On reaching their Spring Creek campground the men separated. Lazair, Emge, and Allemand cooked their supper in a wagon on one side of the stream. The herders camped in another wagon 1,341 feet away (measurement by the county sheriff) on the other side.

Several cattlemen followed through the dim moonlight, tied their horses out of sight in a clump of tall sagebrush, masked themselves, and walked along a ditch bank to the sheep camp. They took the two herders, Cafferal and Helmer, some distance away and forced them to lie face down on the ground while they burned the wagon and its equipment. The occupants of the other wagon were less fortunate. A fusillade ripped it. Emge and Lazair died. Allemand, wounded, dropped to the floor, but came outside with his hands over his head when the raiders set the vehicle afire. A man named Herbert Brink coolly gunned him down. The raiders then killed three sheep dogs and twenty-five or so sheep, crippled several more, freed Cafferal and Helmer with a warning not to talk, and rode off.

They were caught because of a distinctive boot track. For the first time in Wyoming punishment followed a sheep raid. Brink was sentenced to death, two companions were given prison terms of twenty to twenty-six years, others received lesser sentences.[8] Outraged citizens, reflecting on the affair, pointed out that such warfare, once common throughout the mountains, had been ended in the Forests by the government's strict division of the grasslands by means of its permit system. The only major outbreak of trouble in any National Forest came in 1918 when masked cowboys drove 500 head of sheep over a cliff into Oh-Be-Joyful Creek (that's really its name) in the Gunnison country of Colorado.

Timbermen, too, received an object lesson. One way to reduce the effectiveness of the Forest Service was to skimp its appropriations, a tactic performed with relish by Senator Heyburn ("The Objector") of Wallace, Idaho. Because of a barren treasury there was no way, in the dry summer of 1910, to prepare fire trails and tool caches, or to recruit adequate patrols for combating the hundreds of small blazes that began dotting northern Idaho during August.

On the 20th a gale whooped out of the west. Small blazes merged into an inferno. Trapped men hid in mine tunnels, burrowed into swamps, or crouched in river pools with blankets over their heads. Flames poured into Heyburn's home town of Wallace. Terrified residents either fled into the cleared, boggy land near the mouth of Canyon Creek or rushed to board the evacuation trains whistling urgently at the depot. Among the latter were Ranger Kottkey's wife and her just-born baby, Henry. The trestles were smoking as their train inched timorously across. Little Henry's first bed was the straw of a boxcar, his first bath was in a makeshift pan on a railroad siding. But at least he lived.

Eighty-five people, most of them fire fighters, did not. An uncounted number of ranch, mine, and lumber camp buildings, the four small towns of Taft, Deborgia, Haugan, and Tuscor, and 3 million acres of white pine

---

[8] Brink's sentence was later commuted to life. While in prison he helped fellow convicts lynch a Negro who had raped a white woman. Paroled eventually, he went to Canada. There, Wyoming rumor insisted, he lived with his sister and raised children by her.

forest with an estimated value of half a billion dollars disappeared entirely. After that, private timber owners banded into associations that set up cooperative patrols of their own, and the Forest Service experienced less trouble in obtaining funds for fire-fighting equipment, research, and personnel training.

Dramatic though the Tensleep killings and the Idaho fires were, a far more effective element in winning the West's grudging approval of the new order was the daily work of the Forest rangers. At first the men of the Service had been inclined to regard themselves as mere custodians, or "keepers" (to use President Cleveland's term), with little to do other than ward off despoilers, whether fire or human. Very quickly, however, the vision enlarged and the keepers became helpers, a shift epitomized by Theodore Roosevelt's changing the name "Forest Reserves," with its connotations of exclusion, to "National Forests," with its suggestion of the entire country's concern.

Forest personnel were given the status and protection of Civil Service. Riffraff who had signed on as rangers because they were not qualified for other work were replaced by dedicated men who believed enough in what they were doing to accept relatively low pay, long hours, primitive living, and comparative obscurity. Although Chief Forester Pinchot might be as frosty as a mountain morning with what he considered the intransigence of the Wool Growers, the Service in general sought out the cooperation of the suspicious mountain people whose living it now partly controlled. In 1906, for example, ranchers accustomed to running their animals on the more open parts of the Cochetopa National Forest in south-central Colorado were asked, to their amazement, to help work out an acceptable grazing plan for the area. They complied reluctantly, found that results did not hurt as much as they had anticipated, and spread the good word among other stockmen. Counties that feared the loss of property taxes were soothed by the government's agreement to turn back to them 25 percent of the money collected from timber sales, grazing permits, and mineral leases. Another 10 percent of the revenues was spent in the forests where it had originated for building fences, trails, bridges, and for eliminating predatory animals and poisonous plants.

Not all was sweetness, of course. Lumbermen who bid too closely for timber and then had trouble showing a profit often complained that restrictions on their logging practices were bureaucratic, arbitrary, and impractical. There were ranchers who grumbled that grazing permits were being used not just as protective devices for the watershed but as social levers, that small operators who happened to own supplemental haylands, however shoddy, near a forest's boundaries were given preference over bigger, more efficient ranchers from a distance, even though the latter may have been using the area for years and lacked anywhere else to turn. Was this free enterprise? Did it properly reward the man who'd had guts enough to lay hold of an empty land and make something of it? Sheepmen who felt the pinch fumed that green foresters who had studied about range capacity only in books were far more ready, on the basis of mere assumption, to cut allotments and hence profits than to increase them. Such things, the objectors told each other over and over, were not only contrary to the Western tradition but probably were un-American to boot.

And yet when pressed most of these nay-sayers were willing to concede that perhaps beneficial use should no longer be regarded as synonymous with quick profits and that figuring out ways to beat the law, as Heinze had in Butte and as Senator Teller's nephew did in the Medicine Bow Forest (he wriggled free from half a dozen suits for trespass), was not necessarily entitled to the accolade of old, "smart business." After all, the mountains were going to be around awhile yet—and be subjected, they soon learned, to far more strenuous demands than anyone could possibly have foreseen during the relatively calm days preceding the First World War.

EPILOGUE: THE NEW STAMPEDE

THE PERIOD between the First and Second World Wars was, for the Rockies, a time of cruel suspension and uncertain change. Not even children could pull the covers over their heads and pretend that the bogies were not there, for we were surrounded with the wreckage of hopes that once had blossomed as brightly as our own and then had withered, in spite of those who kept insisting that the old values were still sound.

The most graphic of the ruins lay in the Red Mountain district, a six-mile sprawl of abandoned workings along one of the headwater streams of the Uncompahgre River. By horseback across the intervening high ridges Red Mountain was not far from Telluride, but by car it was a long drive around through Ouray and up the resounding Uncompahgre Gorge. Occasionally my stepfather would go there to examine moribund mining claims in which he held an interest, and the trip gave my brother and me and perhaps a friend or two an opportunity to scamper off along the weed-grown bed of the silent narrow-gauge railway for an hour of delicious prowling amidst acres of junk.

Laced among the lifeless cabins were long dumps of waste rock, running like petrified tongues from the mouths of the deserted mines that once the railroad had served. Depressed by each winter's heavy snowfall, the mill and mine buildings, the stores, the little bell-towered church—everything leaned a little more perilously each year, until we returned one summer to find that another landmark had collapsed into a heap of splintered boards. Rusted pipes and cable, overturned ore cars, and detached chunks of machinery sprawled everywhere. Even the creeklets that oozed out of the gulches were rusty red. Actually the stain was caused by iron minerals inside the mountain, but as we wandered among the desolation it was possible to think that even the water, dismayed by its abandonment, was oxidizing down into nothing.

We never found much inside the cabins other than broken-handled implements, cracked dishes, and oddments of homemade furniture, for the

348

departing residents had removed whatever was usable. Now and then among the waterlogged layers of newspaper that had been tacked to the walls for insulation we would notice a section of print that was still legible, and we would read, without much interest, of what had been happening down in Silverton in 1906. We investigated the little wooden snowsheds that led from each house to its nearby privy. We stirred our shoe toes through the heaps of crumbling tin cans outside the kitchen doors and occasionally saw, without being aware of their value as collectors' items, old whiskey and catsup bottles whose glass had been stained a delicate purple by years of sunshine.[1] Then we'd hear my stepfather honking the car horn and we'd scurry back. We sensed vaguely that we had brushed across lost dreams, and after we had returned to Telluride we realized, during uneasy moments, that the stuff of our own lives was slipping away just as inexorably.

Even children could detect the grim note that came into the voices of our elders when they told that another mine up in Marshall Basin had closed. We stood around with our mothers, watching the neighbors across the street move away, leaving behind a For Sale sign that no one ever lifted from the desiccated lawn. Then another, and another, and pretty soon one of the groceries on Colorado Avenue closed, and after that the lace curtains disappeared from the windows of one of the huts, called cribs, down on Pacific Avenue, "the line" where the prostitutes lived.

By August, 1929, the Bank of Telluride was insolvent and the examiners were on the way in. At that point the bank's president had an inspiration. His name was Charles Delos Waggoner. He was thin and crisp, of medium height, with a neat little mustache. In spite of his somewhat dandified airs, everyone called him Buck. His sole concern that desolate August, he said later, was the protection of his depositors.

He arranged for forged telegrams to be sent in secret bankers' code over the signatures of certain Denver banks to their correspondents in New York City. These fraudulent messages, accepted as honest because of the code, instructed the recipients to place a total of half a million dollars in the Chase National Bank, to the credit of the Bank of Telluride. Buck was in New York City when the telegrams arrived. By a dizzy manipulation of cashiers' checks drawn on the Chase National Bank, he paid off his own bank's obligations and headed for western Canada, half a breath before the Denver banks discovered the forgeries and sounded the alarm. He was caught in Wyoming.

---

[1] Addenda for would-be ghost-town souvenir hunters. Snow has kept on flattening the buildings at Red Mountain. Fires have eaten up more. During World War II all available scrap metal was salvaged. The paving and widening of the spectacular Ouray-Silverton highway, which runs past the edge of the district, enabled local citizens to carry off usable door frames and window sashes. Tourists have scoured the kitchen middens. Today little remains of Red Mountain other than the old dumps of colored waste rock.

Telluride's only benefit was a brief lift in spirit. One of their back-country boys had outfoxed the city slickers and for a time the name of their town was on the front page of every major newspaper in the land. In the end, though, Buck went to prison and the doors of his bank never re-opened. By the beginning of the 1930's the *brump* of the stamp mills above the town had ended, and no amount of shouting could drive the silence away.

Those who were left in the town tried. After all, Telluride was the county seat and a certain amount of county business, financed by property taxes on the railroad and on the neighboring cattle and sheep ranches, had to go on until mining came back. All over the Rockies people were chanting that litany, as no doubt the inhabitants of Red Mountain once had chanted it, too: Mining will come back.

We leaned on frail reeds while we waited. A brief upswing in livestock prices ended in 1927 and the market resumed its long postwar slide into the depression. Desperate for revenue, many cattlemen took to crowding their animals onto smaller areas and renting the balance of their land to sheepgrowers. Equally desperate for revenue, the sheepmen let their herds crop both the rented forage and the grass on the public domain to the roots, reducing the range's carrying capacity and creating, with the cattle-men's help, serious problems of erosion.

The rangeland crisis in the mountains was intensified by the same fierce drought that during the early 1930's turned the high plains east of the Rockies into dust bowls. Spurred by the disaster, Congress passed the Taylor Grazing Act, named for Edward Taylor, a long-time congressman from western Colorado, and so placed the federal government in charge of whatever public domain still lay outside of the National Forests, the National Parks and Monuments, and so on. Thus the most vital single factor in the swift spread of the American frontier—free land—came to an end. Henceforth men could use the nation's natural resources only under the supervision of gigantic federal bureaus.

The mountain railroads were no better off than the depression-harried stockmen. All the lines had emerged from the First World War in debt; some were in receivership. The wretched physical condition of Colorado's principal mountain road, the Denver & Rio Grande Western, led local jokesters to scoff that its initials really meant Dangerous & Rapidly Growing Worse. In the early 1920's two cattle growers of the southern San Juan area found the yards at Durango in such a snarl of inefficiency that they were forced to drive their animals another 185 miles to Gallup, New Mexico, in order to ship them to market. The tale, needless to say, was repeated endlessly every time something went wrong with a livestock shipment anywhere in southern Colorado. This, a railroad!

The matter was no joke to the Rio Grande, either, or to its Ridgeway-Telluride-Durango subsidiary, the Rio Grande Southern. The company earnestly wanted to abandon the profitless, snow-heaped, flood-tormented narrow-gauge branches and concentrate on improving and shortening its main line between Denver and Salt Lake City. Heeding the howls of local businessmen who preferred a poor road to none, the Interstate Commerce Commission refused permission. Wretched compromises resulted. Although livestock and ore trains still ran into Telluride and on to Durango more or less as needed, passengers and mail were relegated to a hybrid called the Galloping Goose, a truck body mounted on railroad wheels. There were seats up front for five or six passengers, if ever that many appeared, a van-type body behind for miscellaneous freight, a cowcatcher for nostalgia, and gasoline for power. This unnatural offspring of an efficiency expert's mating with a balance sheet kept careening along the rusty rails until 1951, when the D&RG at last began to abandon its narrow-gauges. But at least the Goose had kept galloping until then. The Burlington-dominated Colorado & Southern, successor of the once high-climbing Denver, South Park & Pacific, gave up the struggle ten years earlier and sank out of existence.

Strangely enough, the depression that was suffocating the stockmen and the railroads brought a flutter back to the mining industry. Most of the large gold and silver properties in the mountains were controlled by absentee corporations whose directors seldom had either the opportunity or the inclination to sniff around the edges of the cold workings in quest of crumbs. But local men did. Wages were down, materials were cheap, and they hoped that by cutting corners they could dismantle the old mill and mine buildings and make a precarious profit by wringing gold dust out of the tons of debris that had accumulated during the years. For this privilege they paid the owners a royalty, so that no one lost too much in case of failure. Other men, backed by slightly more capital, poked inside the hollowed mountains, found pillars of ore that for one reason or another had not been removed by owners intent on bigger game, and secured royalty leases on those.

These cleanup operations were quickened in 1934 by President Roosevelt's abrupt devaluation of the dollar. Overnight the price of an ounce of gold leaped from $20.67 to almost $36. Lessors promptly intensified their work, building modern little mills to take advantage of newly developed techniques for removing metal from refractory chemical combinations. Relief agencies even conducted classes in gold panning, and here and there, during summers, one saw families camped beside the streams while the husband sought to eke out a dollar or two a day washing gravel as it had been washed three quarters of a century earlier by the first stampeders.

It was no true revival, however. The bonanza ores were gone, and the essential smallness of our operations was underscored by the giant bones among which we pawed. For a time in the early 1930's I worked for a lease company at the Camp Bird mine, 11,300 feet high above Ouray, just over

Imogene Pass from Telluride. Thirty or forty of us lived without a flush toilet or a shower in one corner of an enormous yellow boardinghouse that had been built to hold 300 men. Because neither Ouray County nor the lease company had money enough to repair the old aerial tramway or tame the wriggly little road up Canyon Creek, our supplies reached us as supplies had reached the mines in the 1880's—by mule train. Although the power company founded in Telluride by L. L. Nunn had once run the highest transmission lines in North America across Imogene Pass (13,114 feet) to electrify the Camp Bird's main haulage adit, the wires had been removed, and during the thirties the company never got far enough ahead of the red ink to replace them. So mules hauled our ore cars, too, by the light of carbide lamps hung to their harnesses. Gold mining, someone cracked wryly, wasn't coming back; it was going back.

Still, such operations provided a living for several people—until the Second World War. Instantly the gold mines were denied priorities for materials. Shortages closed them down—soaring costs would soon have had the same effect anyway—and eight decades of often overblown romance, wherein the tail seemed frequently to be wagging the dog, came to an end.

Mining of course did not stop. Emphasis merely shifted—to the copper of Butte, Montana, and Bingham Canyon, Utah; to the lead that accompanied the silver of the Coeur d'Alenes in Idaho; to zinc in the narrow canyon of the Eagle River below Colorado's Tennessee Pass; to molybdenum at Climax, high above Leadville; and, very mysteriously at the time, to the carnotite ores that pocket the plateau country bordering the San Miguel River a few dozen miles below Telluride. Carnotite yields both vanadium oxide (red cake) and uranium oxide (yellow cake), the latter of which had been briefly valued during the early years of the century as a source of radium. When the carnotite mines reopened late in the 1930's we assumed that the goal was vanadium oxide, to be used in hardening steel. We were wrong. Under impenetrable secrecy, yellow cake began moving to an ultramodern research complex at a place called Los Alamos in the Jemez Mountains north of Santa Fe. Years later, when the bomb went off at Hiroshima, we knew. And with that revelation, and on the ending of the war, a new rush of prospectors swarmed into the dry lands of Wyoming and the dry plateaus of the Four Corners country, where Colorado, Utah, New Mexico, and Arizona come together, looking for still more uranium— a story of the deserts really, rather than of the mountains, but one that for a time gripped the attention of the entire mountain area.

War-born improvements in technology turned the surviving metal mines into giants. By the mid-1960's Bingham Canyon, Utah, was turning out upwards of 80,000 tons of copper ore *each day*—more ore per twenty-four hours than the narrow-gauge railroad from Red Mountain had hauled away from that district in four full years! Miners delving underneath Butte reached sea level, a vertical mile below the surface, found costs at that depth to be excessive, and switched to a vast open-pit operation like the one at Bingham Canyon. A steady climb in the price of silver throughout the 1960's boomed the Coeur d'Alene mines of northern Idaho to such an extent that the area became the nation's leading producer of the white metal. Even Red Mountain and Telluride felt the impact of mass production. A company searching for lead and zinc (and later for silver) drove a long tunnel between the two localities and then, hauling ore from both openings, started excavating the entire interior of the divide range.

So far as annual tonnages were concerned, mining was back. It did not seem like the old days, however. The new effort was concentrated, leaving hundreds of once-active claims untouched, their tunnels and cabins slowly collapsing. The serpentine supply trains of livestock, their cavernous barns and profane herders, and the ranchers who once had grown fodder for the animals, all vanished. The little railroads disappeared. Automation eased the grueling labor inside the earth; when a new molybdenum mine opened in 1967 in Clear Creek Canyon, Colorado, a single worker could tell by a glance at a television screen which ore bin far underground he should fill by simply pushing a button. Work forces dwindled. The four thousand or more inhabitants that Telluride's strenuous demands had once drawn to the town had shrunk by 1967 to fewer than six hundred. Burdened with an outmoded tax structure, the decrepit town faced, as most of the reduced mountain communities did, harrowing problems in maintaining schools, hospitals, sewage-disposal plants, and other municipal services. That's what old-timers meant when they said that mining hadn't revived, no matter what the tonnage figures seemed to proclaim.

Timber operations followed a comparable pattern: increased production from a decreasing number of mills and lumberjacks. At first the trend was obscured by the postwar boom in construction. A long-pent demand for wood dotted the forests with sawmills, some of them in remote and unlikely places. In 1949–50 an epidemic of deadly spruce-bark beetles quickened the spread. The only effective check to the devastation seemed to be the removal of infected trees by logging. The Forest Service sold off big stands of red-barked Engelmann's spruce, once regarded as a weed tree, at bargain rates and encouraged the use of powerful, war-developed bulldozers for battering out roads to trouble spots in areas once regarded as inaccessible.

In 1957 a satiation of needs led to a collapse of lumber prices. Marginal mills failed. Others consolidated and sought to restore profits by diversifying their output—pulp wood, particle board, and whatnot. Highly automated giants emerged, particularly in northern Idaho and western Montana. The picturesque lumber camp of folklore vanished as completely as had the high-basin boardinghouses. Workers lived in town as sedately as anyone else and drove to their jobs over roads kept open during the winter by more muscular plows than had existed before the war.

The drift of people away from the high country was more than counteracted by the rapid growth of the cities near the foothills. Outpourings of federal money, the lion's share of it in the southern Rockies, stimulated the flow. A huge steel mill went up near Salt Lake City, missile factories invaded Denver, the Air Force Academy and the huge underground North American Air Defense Command settled at Colorado Springs, atomic installations proliferated in New Mexico. These new complexes attracted highly sophisticated research enterprises—the National Center for Atmospheric Research at Boulder, Colorado, to name but one. By their presence they upgraded the quality of education in the mountain colleges and universities, drew a host of service industries and spawned a full range of urban problems.

By 1960, 80 percent of Colorado's population dwelt in a 15-mile-wide belt of valley land east of the Front Range. Two thirds of the state's water, however, originated on the western slope of the Continental Divide. How were the two to be brought together?

Early in the twentieth century visionaries had suggested drilling conduits under the Divide, but the effort had not seemed economically feasible until after it had been connected with proposals for a railroad tunnel. The latter dream was an obsession with David Halliday Moffat, a splinter-thin gold rusher who had waxed fat, literally, while opening banks and mines throughout most of the state and in 1885 had been elected president of the Denver & Rio Grande Railroad. Moffat wanted to shorten the D&RG's looping route to Salt Lake City enough so that it could become an essential link in a new transcontinental system and effectively challenge both the Union Pacific to the north and the Santa Fe to the south. The key to the project, as he envisioned it, was a six-mile tunnel under James Peak, a mountain easily visible from the state capitol building.

Railroad manipulators in the East blocked his efforts. In ultimate disgust he left the D&RG, incorporated what became known as the Moffat Road, and pushed as due west toward Salt Lake City as the rugged terrain allowed. Unable at the outset to finance the James Peak tunnel, he built a "temporary" crossing over Rollins Pass (also called Corona Pass), 11,680 feet above sea level. After spending $9 million, all of it his own money, he died and his road limped to a halt out in the remote ranching country of northwestern Colorado.

Bond issues for financing the James Peak tunnel and thus doing away with the maintenance nightmares on Rollins Pass were repeatedly offered to the voters and repeatedly defeated by Denver conservatives who opposed public aid to private enterprise and by Pueblo citizens who wanted to keep the main line of the D&RG running through their city. Minds in southern Colorado were changed, however, by a 1921 flood in the Arkansas River that killed more than a hundred persons and broke gas mains that unleashed devastating fires throughout Pueblo. Stunned residents in the southern part of the state thereupon agreed to vote for tunnel bonds if Northerners would vote for flood-control projects designed to prevent a repetition of the disaster. Conservatives meanwhile were won over by a promise that as soon as the tunnel's pioneer bore had served its purpose as a railroad construction aid it would be transformed into a water-diversion conduit.

The Moffat Tunnel, as it became known, was holed through in 1927. A few years later the D&RG, which had gained control of the Moffat Road, built a 38-mile cutoff that linked the erstwhile Moffat tracks to D&RG tracks in the upper canyon of the Colorado River and shortened the run to Salt Lake City by 175 miles. Denver residents could then boast that they were on a transcontinental route that went through the mountains, not around them. They could also abandon their stringent water rationing and sprinkle their lawns whenever they wished. The success led every other city and irrigation district on the eastern side of the mountains to supplement its water supply with increasingly bigger diversion projects.

As the water-starved cities of Utah's population belt along the Wasatch Range followed suit, the drain on the Colorado River stirred apprehensions in California. To calm their coastal neighbors, the citizens of the central Rockies sought to maintain the balance of water in the huge river basin by building bigger and bigger storage reservoirs on every major stream in the area, gargantuan enterprises that swallowed towns and highways, altered the face of the land, created new patterns of recreation, and pumped hundreds of millions of dollars into faltering high-country economies. Whether or not the long-range gains will prove in every instance to be worth such massive dislocations is a matter still hotly debated.

Most of the newcomers who settled in the growing cities near the foothills responded enthusiastically to the dry climate and dramatic landscapes. College professors, said one wry bit of folklore at the University of Colorado, were even expected to take out part of their salaries in sunshine, scenery, and pleasantly informal styles of living. Indigenous folk celebrations—rodeos, Indian dances, Spanish fiestas—caught the fancy of many of the new settlers. In New Mexico the architecture of the Pueblo Indians, as modified by the Spanish Americans, completely won over the modern homebuilders settling around the new atomic plants. And only an hour away from every major center from Great Falls, Montana, to Albuquerque, New Mexico, lay the enthralling open-air playgrounds of the National Forests.

The salubrious climate and vigorous sports of the mountains had long been advertised, of course. Big-game hunters were attaching themselves to fur-trade caravans as early as the 1830's. In 1873 Denver's Committee of Asthmatics printed a hundred case histories in pamphlet form and broadcast the hope of relief to sufferers throughout the nation. Dwellers in the high basins learned as early as the 1860's to travel about on long Norwegian skis, balancing themselves with a single pole held slantwise in front of them; a few unconventional souls, banding into Outing Clubs, even used the devices for sport. Railroads eagerly promoted mineral-water spas where guests in ornate resort hotels amused themselves between sips by taking scenic drives in elegant coaches.

These things were exceptions, however. Until the advent of the automobile, outdoor recreation was limited to a few places and to a relatively few people. Then, released by the new mobility that developed after the First World War, venturesome families began visiting the Rockies in their own cars as fancy dictated, rather than aboard some train. At first most of the visitors sought out the National Parks. Later, in the 1930's, increasing numbers took to bumping over the new fire and supply roads which the Civilian Conservation Corps was building, partly as a relief measure, deep into forests where once only unmapped trails had led.

The surge was not limited to summer campers and autumn deer hunters. Stimulated by the success of the winter Olympics held in 1932 at Lake Placid, New York, skiers began prowling the Rockies, looking for runs comparable to those in Switzerland. Hoping to fill empty train seats, officials of the Union Pacific hired a Swiss expert to locate a site to meet the demand. The spot finally selected was the old town of Ketchum on the Wood River of southern Idaho, once a lively center for the distribution of mining supplies and, in the fall, for loading tens of thousands of sheep aboard freight cars for shipment to market. Turning up an eastern fork of the Wood River, the promoters built Sun Valley, first of the major Rocky Mountain ski resorts. The Denver & Rio Grande meanwhile promoted more modest sites within reach of Denver and Boulder: Winter Park at the western portal of the Moffat Tunnel; the long hills near Hot Sulphur Springs in Middle Park, where William Byers had tried, seventy years earlier, to develop a summer resort; and Steamboat Springs on the Yampa River, where some of the first American ski jump records were established. Other weekend enthusiasts drove automobiles to the top of Berthoud Pass on U.S. Highway 40, then skied down swaths cut through the forest for telephone lines, and were picked up at the bottom of the improvised runs by a friend who had volunteered to bring down the car. Lifts? You were lucky, during those years, to find even a rope tow.

The Second World War slowed the stampede of recreationists. Afterwards, the depression gone, it swelled even more prodigiously. Between 1946 and 1964 visits to the National Forests in Colorado increased from 1.5 million to 14,567,000; in New Mexico from 500,000 to 5,769,000; in

Montana from fewer than one million to more than seven million.[2] In the fall more than half a million Nimrods fanned out through the hills and harvested surprising amounts of wild meat—an estimated 88,000 deer in Utah in 1964, 81,000 in Colorado, 53,000 in Montana, plus 12,000 elk in Idaho, 11,000 in Colorado, 9,400 in Wyoming. The only other state in the Union which yielded comparable amounts that same year was Oregon; 55,000 deer and 15,000 elk.

In the winter the skiers came, seeking multimillion-dollar lifts that would enable them to plunge down as many miles in a weekend as some average prewar skiers had covered in a winter. To entertain and house these new sportsmen (and women) old towns were refurbished—Aspen, in Colorado, and Alta, Utah, are two of the better-known ones—and new ones appeared, for instance, the carefully planned Tyrolean-style village of Vail, Colorado.

Motels, restaurants, garages, filling stations, outfitters, and storekeepers in existing towns were staggered by the sharply concentrated demands of these fluid hordes. For a single example: the permanent population of Lake City, Colorado, seat of Hinsdale County, located in the heart of a popular trout-fishing and deer-hunting area, is fewer than a hundred. Then in July and August and for a while in October upwards of a thousand restless transients flow through each day, expecting food, beds, gasoline, and miscellaneous supplies. Since local facilities in Lake City and in a dozen towns like it can fill only a small portion of the requests, a new kind of supplier has appeared: the man and his wife who during winter operate a desert dude ranch or motel or store in, say, Scottsdale, Arizona, and who, at the beginning of summer load their trucks with saddle horses and dude wranglers, with gay stocks of Western clothing, with brooms, portable television sets, and mortgages, and head for the high country—Yankee peddlers, 1970 style.

Even the decrepit, 45-mile-long narrow-gauge branch railroad running from Durango, Colorado, up the awesome Animas Canyon to Silverton felt the shock. Tourists discovered the exotic little curiosity in the early 1950's, just when the D&RG was preparing, with a sigh of relief, to shed the profitless spur. Such a clamor against abandonment arose that the railroad reconsidered. By 1967 two ramshackle strings of yellow observation cars were being hauled up the wavering tracks each summer day—the so-called "Train to Yesterday," one of the most popular historic tourist items in the Rocky Mountain area.

Towns overwhelmed by these jostling crowds were not quite sure what shape they wanted their new identities to take. Some, like Montana's Virginia City, grew resolutely picturesque and reconstructed themselves to

[2] These figures include skiers as well as summer visitors and take into account repeat visits by the same persons. They do not include visits to National Parks, Monuments, Historic Sites, and visits to recreational sites supervised by the Bureau of Land Management. The increased use in those areas has been equally spectacular.

look, they hoped, as they had during the days of the gold rush. Others, like Colorado's Central City and Silverton, succumbed to the carnival trade and filled themselves with tawdry curio shops competing for attention by means of flamboyant signs and amplified barkers. Still others contented themselves with offering comfortable if somewhat standardized accommodations and entertainment. A favorite form of the latter was drama, ranging from serious experimental drama at places like Helena to old-time melodramas at Cripple Creek, Durango, and Jackson Hole. To all of which, critics of the scene are inclined to sneer, Samesville, U.S.A., Rocky Mountain style.

Inevitably a few of the people who rolled through the hills began to desire something more permanent than a motel room. Those with modest means obtained title to abandoned houses in the old mining towns by paying the back taxes, and then rebuilt the dwellings. More affluent visitors, especially skiers, began erecting second homes at Sun Valley, at Jackson Hole, at Aspen, and half a dozen other spots. Summer cabins oriented toward outdoor living dotted the eastern flanks of the Big Horn Mountains, the meadows of Montana's Bitterroot Valley, the mesas back of Santa Fe. A surprising cultural drift accompanied this movement into mountain camps once notable for their crudeness. Ouray sought to emulate Taos as an artists' colony; Central City produced lavish operas each summer; Aspen launched music festivals and intellectual seminars almost as rarified as the mountain air. Towns as isolated as Cody and Big Horn in Wyoming and Helena in Montana built handsome museums to glorify the work of such Western artists as Charles M. Russell and Frederic Remington.

Difficult though the problems of adjustment have been to the mountain hamlets, the strain placed by recreationists on the National Forests has been even greater. For one thing, the towns wanted the new rush. The Forest Service did not and, partly for that reason, was not nearly as well prepared for it as the National Parks were.

The Service was work-oriented. A notion clung to the Rockies, and to much of America, that there was something faintly reprehensible about grown men playing around in the outdoors like unemployed Boy Scouts— unless a man was hunting food, in the tradition of the pioneer provider. Thus it was culturally acceptable for rangers to join state fish and game departments in propagating wildlife, but otherwise their efforts were utilitarian. The guiding words were "multiple use" and "sustained yield." That is, water, trees, grass, and so on were to be distributed as widely as possible, without exceeding replacement potentials, in order to achieve the greatest good (generally in terms of dollars) for the greatest possible number of users.

The rangers had reason to be proud of their accomplishments on many fronts, particularly in fire prevention—Smokey Bear publicity, on the one hand, and aerial firefighting, on the other. On July 12, 1940, on the Nez

Percé National Forest of Idaho, smoke jumpers trained at the famed fire-fighting school at Missoula made the world's first jump from a plane to fight a blaze. Shortly thereafter the virtues of promptness were illustrated when three airborne firemen extinguished in the Selway Wilderness of Idaho a blaze that before the Second World War almost surely would have swept out of control, destroying tens of thousands of trees. In 1947 helicopters were pressed into service not only for ferrying men and supplies but for laying hose across rugged terrain. In 1953–54 bombers began dropping fire retardants mixed in water. And whenever a prime area did happened to burn, studies were launched about possible reforestation, either by means of seeds or by saplings grown on one of the Service's tree farms.

Checking the damage caused by the human users of the forests proved more difficult than combating fires or bark beetles. The original permits issued to ranchers for grazing the mountain meadows had been too generous and large blocks of land were slowly being hurt by overgrazing. But how could this be proved? Circumstances were clouded by several variables: fluctuations in weather, variations in the growth rate and nutrient value of different grasses, and the preferences that cattle and sheep showed for different forage. Before the problem could be lifted out of the cloudy realm of personal opinion, the Service had to train agronomists, devise methods of study and observation, and then spend years collecting statistics which failed to convince very many ranchers.

The stumbling block was an economic situation which had been created by the Forest Service itself. The number of animals that the government allowed a man to run on a section of National Forest land during a specified period of the summer was called his permit. Over the years permits had become vested rights. The selling price of mountain ranches was based not only on their normal agricultural assets but also on the size of the permits that went with them. Because permits had cash value, holders naturally did not want them diminished. The first hint that the government intended to make cuts stirred violent protests about socialistic confiscations of property rights. They had eyes, they flared. They could see the condition of the range. It was not deteriorating. After all, they too had an interest in maintaining the quality of the land on which they depended year after year. Were they foolish enough to jeopardize their own futures?

Yes, the rangers retorted, and the two sides began glowering as truculently as in the days when the Forest Service had started exacting fees for the use of grass. The issue came to a head in 1939 in the Uncompahgre National Forest of southwestern Colorado, with an announcement by the local forest supervisor that fifteen ranchers running a total of 14,652 head of cattle on the high plateaus would have to accept a cut of approximately 20 percent. (The reduction involved both the number of animals and the length of time they were allowed on the forest.) The ranchers refused, denying the necessity of the slash and suggesting alternatives that seemed to them fairer. Fourteen years of meetings, surveys, counterdemonstrations, arguments, and appeals followed—a cold war, the Denver *Post* labeled the stalemate on January 8, 1952. Finally, after a national board of appeals had personally viewed the range and had listened to the testimony of experts summoned by both sides, Secretary of Agriculture Charles Brannan ordered that the cuts be made. So far as the mountains as a whole were concerned, relatively few animal-days were involved. But a principle was settled that was enormous: no one could obtain so vested a right in the public lands as to be beyond the supervision of the government agencies concerned. A century earlier few men on the frontier would have believed such a development possible.

The value of the trees, grass, and watershed protected by the Forest Service could be expressed in good round figures preceded by a dollar sign. Accustomed to that kind of rationale, local supervisors at first looked sourly on the influx of recreationists brought by automobiles. During the early 1930's they complained bitterly in their reports about taking care of people rather than of forests—of hauling garbage, erecting directional signs, hunting for lost children, and answering foolish questions. Not until skiers began risking their lives en masse did a major shift in attitude occur.

To most dwellers in the high country these new sportsmen were incomprehensible. We were afraid of snow. The toll of disaster over two thirds of a century had been appalling. In 1874 an avalanche at Alta, Utah, killed 60-plus residents; the exact number was never determined. Between 1875 and 1910, when the last of the Alta mines closed down, another 67 died from the same cause, an average of two a year. Nor was Alta unique. At 7:30 A.M. on the morning of February 28, 1902, a slide tore away part of the workings of the Liberty Bell mine above Telluride. As rescuers toiled up from town, a second avalanche dropped on them. And finally, after the rescue work had ended and the weary volunteers were dragging the corpses and injured back to town on sleds, a third slide fired a parting shot. The triple blows killed 19 men, including my grandfather's brother, and cruelly hurt 11 more. My stepfather-to-be saved himself by seizing a tree as he was being hurled down a hillside; then he clung, deafened and semiconscious, almost suffocated by the snow that had packed like cement into his ears, mouth, and nose.

A rough count of the casualties mentioned in the Denver newspapers alone indicates that during the winter of 1905–6 at least 113 Coloradoans perished in snow avalanches, 22 of them at a single mine near Silverton. In 1910 a slide at Burke, Idaho, killed 21. "THE WHITE DEATH" summed up a jittery headline in Ouray's *Solid Muldoon* on February 8, 1883, "DEALS DEATH AND DESTRUCTION IN EVERY QUARTER."

The toll dropped as population thinned out, but even so we were given frequent reminders of what was possible. Not long after I left the Camp

Bird lease above Ouray, a slide swept away the boardinghouse and killed seven or eight of my erstwhile companions. And we had all listened to men like Harry Johnson, who had been trapped above Telluride at the Black Bear mine, where the cook and her husband had been crushed to death in their own bed, and whose tale of a dazed groping for help in the white wastes 12,000 feet high was by no means reassuring.

As skiers unfamiliar with the slopes began thronging them, the Forest Service, which issued special-use permits for the lifts that might carry the newcomers to disaster, took to worrying. The result was the establishment at Alta, during the winter of 1937–38, of the nation's first avalanche research center. The masses of information collected there during subsequent years enabled not only ski patrols but also highway departments and telephone and pipeline maintenance crews to design protective bunkers for vulnerable spots, to predict unstable conditions, to shoot down with cannons and special "avalaunchers" threatening accumulations of snow. If hazards warrant, slopes and highways are closed entirely. When accidents do occur, tested rescue procedures are put immediately into operation. Results were phenomenal. By 1965 the annual toll from avalanches, which once had killed a score or more people in the Rockies each year—more than a hundred some years—had dropped to less than six, although more users than ever were traveling the roads and coursing the slopes.

The guidelines for whatever the Forest Service did, whether in promoting outdoor sports or in developing utilitarian goals, were laid down as matters of administrative policy and hence were susceptible to amendment with each change of administrators. To give the programs the dignity and stability of law, Congress in 1960 passed a "Multiple Use-Sustained Yield" bill. In this new act recreational facilities were officially recognized for the first time as a national resource, and the Service was ordered to "manage" recreation along with trees and grass and water.

Budgets jumped; crash programs were instituted. Thousands of miles of road were built not only for timber cutters and stockmen, as in the past, but also for growing numbers of highly sophisticated mobile camping units. Visitor information centers, built in imitation of similar units in the National Parks, appeared in the more popular areas. Signs interpreting a region's history, geology, ecology, and whatnot sprang up beside the mountain highways. "Adventure" trails led from parking places into choice dells where viewers might glimpse animals in native habitat.

Census takers meanwhile stalked the gathering places with clipboards and pencils, trying to determine what the forest visitors really wanted. Most, it seemed, were not touring the forests per se but were passing through on the way to visit family members in another part of the country. They would leave the direct route if roads were good and afforded roomy turnouts where they could exclaim over striking views with a minimum of inconvenience. Fishermen among them hoped to be able to catch trout from the shoulder of the road and apparently saw no incongruity in ganging up elbow to elbow beside pools formed by bridge abutments. A significant majority of the passers-by insisted that when they "camped out" for a night in a mobile home they preferred doing it in tight clusters with others of their kind. They desired showers and laundromats with hot and cold running water, sturdy tables and prepared fireplaces, convenient toilets, and ready access to grocery stores and gasoline stations. When they returned at night from a day with the powerboats or motor scooters they carried with them, they were not averse to nearby entertainment—jukeboxes, bowling alleys, shooting galleries, cocktail lounges, and the like. They certainly expected to play their radios at full blast, ear to ear.

As more and more camping spots of this sort appeared, dissident voices began to sound. As long ago as 1872 naturalist John Muir of California's Sierra Nevada had spat out in a private letter about "the rough vertical animals called men, who occur in and on these mountains like sticks of condensed filth." But were modern recreationists really so enured to urban packing that they craved similar conditions in the mountains? Or were they answering out of ignorance of better things questions that led to conclusions already determined by the askers? Were their attitudes being subtly guided by the purveyors of an annual $4 billion worth of trailers, boats, scooters, sports clothing, and sports equipment—a new breed of exploiter as ruthless as any lumberman ever was?

Whatever the cause of the crowding—ignorance, exploitation, or inherent nastiness—its results seemed both disturbing and challenging to wilderness lovers. "We are entering a new era in land management," said Elizabeth Hannum, angry conservationist of the School of Forestry at the University of Montana, to a statewide Recreation Planning Conference at Missoula on April 28, 1966, "and I wonder how we are going to handle it. . . . Our burgeoning population is descending on every available acre to recreate . . . an army of family campers that crowds our public campgrounds every summer and makes Times Square look like a Buddhist retreat. . . . When the last wilderness trail has been cemented over; when the outdoor toilets are in mile-long rows, as close as houses on a Philadelphia street; and when parking lots cover 99 percent of every park, what then? . . . Are we civilized, or are we modern barbarians?"

One answer has been the closing of certain remote areas to roads and all forms of commercial activity except some grazing. It is not a new movement. In 1924 Aldo Leopold of the Forest Service, an eloquent crusader for the concept of "quality" in outdoor recreation, prevailed on the government to set aside as the Gila Wilderness Area half a million acres of mountain land in southwestern New Mexico. Dozens of comparable reservations followed during the next decade: wilderness areas that were more than 100,000 acres in size, wild areas that were smaller, primitive areas in which limited amounts of timber, forage, and water extraction might be allowed at some future date—a total of some 15 million acres.

Though the proliferation was a national phenomenon, the largest number of protected sections occurred, naturally enough, in the remote sections of the Rockies. One agglomeration of primitive and wilderness areas in Idaho, broken only by a single road corridor, stretches 130 miles from north to south. The next largest area, nearly a million acres, lies in Montana, south of Glacier National Park—the Bob Marshall Wilderness, named for another crusading Forest Service official, founder of the Wilderness Society. And in addition to these restricted areas the National Parks also contain large sections of unexploitable, roadless land.

Like other Forest activities prior to 1960, the preservation of these wilderness regions was a matter of administrative policy and hence subject to arbitrary change. As pressures on the forests increased, wilderness lovers began to fear such changes would occur. Even the Multiple Use bill of 1960 with its directives that recreation be "managed" like any other resource seemed a threat, and in example of what they meant preservationists pointed to the Lincoln Back Country, an isolated area northwest of Helena, Montana.

The Lincoln Back Country, which lies just south of the Bob Marshall Wilderness, is not a particularly beautiful region in comparison to other areas of mountainous Montana. Its timber is of dubious commercial value. Its great virtue, to protectionists, was that it remained, even in the mid-1950's, almost untouched by any sort of activity, except for a little horseback camping, hunting, and fishing. But it was not included in any of the Wilderness areas and hence was vulnerable.

In 1957 a new paved road was pushed through the hamlet of Lincoln, dozing under tall ponderosa pines 12 miles west of the Continental Divide. Neon lights flashed above new gas stations, cafés, motels, and outfitting centers. The Back Country was accessible now—and not only to increasing numbers of hunters and fishermen. Stirred to activity by passage of the Multiple Use bill, officials of the Helena National Forest, in which the Back Country lay, presented in 1963, without adequate public hearings, a "Long Range Plan, Northern Half Lincoln Ranger District"—a plan involving an extensive road system for access to marketable timber, campgrounds, picnic areas, and for the "dispersal" of hunters and fishermen.

Conservation groups rose in opposition, attacking the plan for specific flaws, for its method of presentation, and especially for what they called its unnecessary opening of a hitherto untouched area merely because of bureaucracy's chronic self-preserving twitch, the desire to justify itself by "doing something." Thus beset, the Forest Service withdrew its Long Range Plan for further consideration.

Meanwhile preservationists everywhere were attacking along a broad front, insisting that the entire Wilderness system be removed from administrative whim and given the protection of law. An intense emotionalism accompanied the campaign. The wilderness, its proponents argued, was a priceless heritage, the land as our pioneers had known it, fulfilling a spiritual need even for people who never saw it but derived abiding satisfaction just from knowing that it was there. Those who did seek it out found the country's last true solitude, with its powers to restore and sustain. Here, somehow, was the embodiment of what Henry Thoreau had meant with his paradoxical statement that "in wildness is the preservation of the world," as though civilization could best be maintained by periodically escaping from it. But the escape could not be true and wholesome unless nature remained undisturbed. The very sound of a chain saw, even if being used for clearing a hikers' trail, was an offense. Insect infestations and lightning-caused fires should be allowed to run their natural courses, except where they posed immediate threats to adjacent commercial areas.

To many mountain dwellers that kind of thinking was incomprehensible. Grazing and timber lands, they said, ought to be utilized under the sustained-yield program. Though lumbering caused temporary scars, eventually the land could be made more beautiful than before through scientific reforestation.

Emotionalism appeared in these arguments too. "The deep breathers," one Colorado congressman scornfully labeled the preservationists. Local businessmen trotted out a cliché as hoary as Thoreau's: "The economic strength of any nation lies in the exploitation of its natural resources." Wilderness bills were decried as class legislation—"the domination," said one lumberman of Grand Junction, Colorado, "of Public Land Use by . . . a minority group of the participants," and hence un-American.

The preservationists won. In September, 1964, President Johnson signed a bill which officially described the wilderness as "an area where the earth and its community of life are untrammeled by man, where man himself is a visitor who does not remain." More than 9 million acres of former wild, wilderness, and canoe areas were placed within a National Wilderness Preservation System and were to be managed in such a way as to keep them untrammeled by man—a paradox in itself, since the very word "management" is a denial of wilderness. Another 5.5 million acres of erstwhile primitive areas were ordered re-examined within ten years to determine whether they merited inclusion within the preservation system. Finally, methods were outlined whereby additional areas could be added to the total.

Within less than three years some three dozen proposals for additions, including the Lincoln Back Country, had been offered to Congress. Men who looked on the forests as utilitarian objects wrung their hands. "Some of our esteemed citizens," wrote Uncle Dudley in *Nation's Agriculture*

(July-August, 1967), "are going a little nuts about wilderness. Why, we just got done changing a wilderness into a fairly desirable United States of America." Anyway, most vacationists preferred the outdoors without primitiveness: "there is no waiting list," Uncle Dudley snorted, "for unimproved campsites." Enough was enough. Resist further exclusion; develop the lands as a majority, not a minority, of people wanted them developed.

So. It's a new stampede, but an old story. For example:

Not long ago my family and I, traveling horseback with friends, rode up Henson Creek above Lake City to American Flats, 12,000 feet high, mile upon mile of alpine tundra rolling around the feet of the peaks, two of them more than 14,000 feet high. Scars showed everywhere—colored splotches of waste rock beside old prospect holes, a network of paths eroded into the thin, friable soil by unguessable numbers of sheep, the slash of a mine road climbing across a distant pass. A bruised land—but the wind sang, the cumulus clouds piled dazzlingly. An occasional jeep ground past, following the mine road, its sunburned occupants staring wide-eyed. A family banged along on two scooters, children clinging to their parents' waists; probably they lacked money for jeep rentals or time and experience for horses, and this was the only way for them to see the highlands. Red flags fluttering from short yellow stakes showed where surveyors were contemplating a normal highway that would enable still more visitors to partake of the scene.

Then we veered away from the sheep trails and the roads, following the old Horsethief Trail through a gap in the rim. During the 1880's enterprising rustlers had stolen horses and mules in Lake City, had driven them across the range by this breathless route, and had sold them in Ouray —then had doubled their profits by stealing more stock in Ouray for sale back in Lake City.

Behind us Coxcomb Peak rose like a cleaver, Wetterhorn like a chisel snout. Ahead yawned Uncompahgre Canyon, 6,000 feet of blue-misted space from the top of Potosi down to the town of Ouray in the canyon bottom. High-antlered deer trotted along the near skyline, watching us as curiously as we watched them. One by one our horses came off a shale bank onto a sharp gray ridge. The lead rider made no sound. Neither did the next or the next, so that no preparation braced anyone. We rode dumbly, looking left into the stupendous gash of Uncompahgre Gorge; and all at once, abrupt under our right boot toes, as startling as a yell in the night, gaped the Cow Creek drop we had forgotten about, one more mile of collapsing cliffs and trees and tormented ravines sliding down, down, down, to soar again on the opposite side to the stark cliffs of Courthouse Mountain.

Long ago someone had named that knife-edged ridge between the chasms the Bridge of Heaven. We held our breath as the horses walked gingerly across. Devilish things reputedly had happened there in the past. Wind blew one prospector off to his death below. Lightning killed another. One sheepherder, crossing the narrows with a rival in love, gave the fellow a push. So they say, calling it the Bridge of Heaven. On Horsethief Trail.

We zigzagged down among stately blue spruce, through asters and paintbrush and grass as high as our stirrups, past deep-blue larkspur, among white aspen boles, lost in a murmur that we called silence but that in reality was only the absence of human sound. Early the next morning we drove from Ouray up the winding highway to the south. High above the town, we pulled out on an overlook and studied the northeastern rim of the gigantic amphitheater of cliffs, hoping to spot some part of the trail we had followed the day before.

There? Or there?

We could not be sure—so little a thread in the vastness.

"Never mind," Mildred said. "We'll remember: all of it was a bridge of heaven."

Our eyes dropped back to the town. Red sightseeing jeeps were leaving the garages to pick up the day's passengers. The strident thrum of a motorcycle reached even to where we stood. A huge sign, which we knew glared with lights by night, was stretched across a cliff face, showing the way to a local scenic wonder that everyone was invited to see—for a price. To the right a large white star and a large white cross gave man-made blessings to the dark spruce. Behind us, noisome as well as visual, a fluff of smoke rose from the town dump, surely the loveliest dumpsite in the entire nation, just as lovely as the old Ouray dump had been in the 1880's, when editorials in the *Solid Muldoon* had complained about its condition.

And above, in the high thin blueness, the Bridge of Heaven on Horse-thief Trail. Four hundred years of it—the plunder trail to heart's desire. So for Coronado's Spaniards and William Ashley's beaver hunters, for the miners and the stockmen and the utopian colonists, for tie cutters and ditchdiggers. So, too, for today's vacationists and dambuilders and the purveyors who batten on them—there are, after all, more ways than one to skin either a cat or a continent.

The jeepsters sang and waved as they passed, and who is to say they were any less happy than the backpackers heading for the Mount Hayden Hiking Trail, up Canyon Creek above the glaring sign? That's the hell of heaven: defining it to everyone's taste. Somehow, though, it has to be managed. For there simply aren't four hundred more years of plunder remaining, either in the Rockies or in the country as a whole.

WITH THANKS—

The repositories where I did most of my paper digging were the Wyles Collection, Christian Brun, director, University of California, Santa Barbara; and the Henry E. Huntington Library, San Marino, its reference room graciously presided over by Mary Isabel Fry. Not the least of the Huntington's stimulations were opportunities for discussion with several students of the Western scene: Allan Nevins, nimble leader of the postluncheon safaris through the Huntington gardens; Professor Rodman W. Paul, Division of Humanities and Social Sciences at California Institute of Technology; Dr. Doyce B. Nunis, Jr., of the History Department of the University of Southern California; and of particular note so far as my own labors were concerned, Dr. Ray Allen Billington, the Huntington's Senior Research Fellow and leading interpreter of the American frontier.

Archives in the mountain area that responded generously to my importunate calls include the library of the Colorado State Historical Society, Denver, Enid Thompson, director, Laura Ekstrom, librarian, and Louisa Arps, an old friend of mountain-climbing days; the Denver Public Library, Western History Department, headed by always-resourceful Alys Freeze, ably assisted by Opal Harber; and the same library's Conservation Department under Roberta Winn; the library of the Montana State Historical Society, Mary Dempsey, librarian, Helena, Montana. In Boulder I drew on the University of Colorado libraries, guided by Jack Brennan, curator of Western history materials, with assists from Henry Waltemade, associate director for Special Collections, and also from one of the better historians of the American West, Robert Athearn. In Laramie the University of Wyoming's Western Research Center, under its energetic director, Gene Gressley, proved a most pleasant place to work; while I was there I was given additional clues to useful material by James D. McLaird.

Between visits to the archives my wife Mildred, our daughter Leith, and I tried to see as much of the mountains at first hand as we could, a pursuit delightfully facilitated by many friends and acquaintances. In Missoula, Montana, Vi and Howard Foulger were indefatigable hosts; in the same city Elizabeth Hannum, R. W. Behan, and George Weisel dropped their work at the state university long enough to elaborate on conservation matters. Tony Thacher of the Anaconda Company steered us through the astounding clutter of Butte.

Aubrey Haines, historian of Yellowstone National Park, was a peerless guide on a tour of that region.

Wyoming museum directors, Harold McCracken of the Whitney Gallery of Western Art, and Richard I. Frost, of the Buffalo Bill Museum at Cody, and Jim Forrest, of the Bradford Brinton Museum at Big Horn, opened those vistas to us. Tris and Trudy Colket, then of the T Bar T Ranch at Goose Creek outside Sheridan gave us a new view of the Big Horn Mountains; their neighbor, Emmie D. Mygatt of Big Horn, provided more material relating to modern Indian affairs than the stringencies of space have let me use.

Coloradoans were equally openhanded with their time and knowledge, beginning with Professor T. M. Griffiths, Department of Geography, University of Denver, with whom I have roamed the high country since boyhood. Another old friend and a peerless historian of the West, Marshall Sprague of Colorado Springs, and his wife, Edna Jane, gave us a rousing introduction to the area they know so well, Cripple Creek. Ben and Barbara Draper opened Georgetown wide. As they have done in other connections, Don and Jean Griswold shared their unparalleled knowledge of Leadville; LeRoy Wingenbach of the Leadville newspaper helped, and John Pitts brought out his jeep for an exploration of the Mosquito Range and adjacent sections of South Park. Farther south, near Telluride, Harry Johnson spun his incomparable yarns; Homer Reid, still another old friend, and my son, David G. Lavender, and his wife, Val, then camped near Woods Lake, used their jeeps to remind us how hair-raising the old mine roads of the San Juan country really were. Joe Redd, with whom I once covered much of the Lone Cone-Disappointment country on horseback, whirled us about the same section by faster but hardly gentler means. Jim Houston of the Colorado Fish and Game Department provided material and guidance around the Lake City area.

Victor Palmieri of the Janss Corporation facilitated a study of modern resort development at Aspen and at Sun Valley, Idaho, where Dorice Taylor was a most charming guide. Gordon Weller introduced us to Vail, Colorado.

Personnel of the United States Forest Service went far beyond the normal call of duty. J. N. Hessel and E. F. Littlehales of the regional office in Denver patiently answered interminable questions. Julius Fullenwider of Norwood, Colorado, loaded me with materials. Howard Foulger unlocked western Montana and the Idaho Panhandle: he and Andy Arvish of the Clearwater National Forest made it possible for the three of us to follow Lewis and Clark's route along the stupendous Lolo Trail; later, with Henry Kottkey of Coeur d'Alene Forest, Howard showed us the mining country around Wallace and Murray and David Thompson's beaver preserve along the Clark Fork River and in the lower Flathead Valley.

Climax of the research were pack trips on horseback, first through the high Uncompahgre country back of Ouray, Colorado, with Bert Tucker, supervisor of the Uncompahgre and Grand Mesa National Forests, Ranger Ray Urbom of Montrose, and conservationist-journalist Becky Walker of Grand Junction. This was followed by a similar trip through the Needle Mountains south of Silverton, Colorado, with the same people, plus Rod Blacker, supervisor of the San Juan National Forest, and his son Mike.

To all of these people, a salute. Thanks to them we once again could feel the high reaches of the Continental Divide deep in our viscera. If some of it has managed to seep back through my fingertips, much of the credit is theirs.

A portion of this book's "Prologue" appeared in a different form in *A Vanishing America*, published in 1964 by Holt, Rinehart, and Winston, and is used here with their permission.

Besides sharing the wanderings in the field and the libraries, Mildred typed the finished manuscript. So in a very real sense this book, like all of them, is hers, too.

DAVID LAVENDER
Ojai, California

September, 1967

BIBLIOGRAPHY

PLACE HISTORIES

A handful of exceptional books for introducing the general reader to frontier history include Ray Allen Billington's threesome, *The Far Western Frontier, 1830–60* (New York, 1956), *Westward Expansion* (2nd ed. New York, 1963), and *America's Frontier Heritage* (New York, 1966); William H. Goetzmann's far-striding *Exploration and Empire* (New York, 1966) and Robert Athearn's literate account of the high plains and bordering ranges of the Rockies, *High Country Empire* (New York, 1960). Narrower in their geographic scope but not in their interpretive value are Leonard Arrington's *Great Basin Kingdom, an Economic History of the Latter-Day Saints* (Cambridge, 1958), Paul Horgan's two-volume study of the Rio Grande, *Great River* (New York, 1954), and T. E. Larson's *History of Wyoming* (Lincoln, Nebr., 1965), notable among state histories for its readability. Three first-rate sectional accounts that touch on the Rockies in part are Dorothy O. Johansen and Charles M. Gates, *Empire of the Columbia* (New York, 1957), Earl Pomeroy, *The Pacific Slope* (New York, 1965), and Howard R. Lamar, *The Far Southwest, 1846–1912* (New Haven, 1966).

Two useful and interesting special studies are Robert L. Perkin, *The First Hundred Years: An Informal History of Denver and the Rocky Mountain News* (New York, 1959), and Marshall Sprague, *The Great Gates* (Boston, 1964), which uses horseback, wagon, automobile, and jeep passes through the Rockies as a focus for the region's history. Finally Louise Barry's "Kansas Before 1854; a Revised Annals," *Kansas Historical Quarterly,* Vols. 27–29, 1961–1963, contains a wealth of detail concerning people who traveled to and from the Rockies in the early years.

Other regional and state accounts of varying degrees of usefulness to this study include the following:

ARPS, LOUISA WARD. *Denver in Slices.* Denver, 1959.

ATWOOD, WALLACE W. *The Rocky Mountains.* New York, 1945.

BAILEY, ROBERT C. *River of No Return* [The Salmon River in Idaho] Lewiston, Idaho, 1947.

BAKER, JAMES, and LEROY R. HAFEN. *History of Colorado.* 3 vols. Denver, 1927.

BANCROFT, CAROLINE. *Gulch of Gold, A History of Central City, Colorado.* Denver, 1958.

BANCROFT, HUBERT H. *History of Nevada, Colorado and Wyoming, 1540–1888.* San Francisco, 1890.

———. *History of Washington, Idaho, and Montana.* San Francisco, 1890.

BARTLETT, I. S. *History of Wyoming.* Chicago, 1918.

BASKIN, O. E. (compiler). *History of the Arkansas Valley, Colorado.* Chicago, 1881.

BEAL, MERRILL D., and MERLE WELLS. *History of Idaho.* 3 vols. New York, 1959.

BECK, WARREN A. *New Mexico.* Norman, Okla., 1962.

BIGGAR, HUGH J. *The Development of the Lower Flathead Valley.* Unpublished M.A. thesis. Montana State University, 1950.

BOWLES, SAMUEL. *Our New West.* Hartford, Conn., 1869.

BRIGGS, HAROLD E. *Frontiers of the Northwest.* New York, 1941.

BROSNAN, CORNELIUS J. *History of Idaho.* New York, 1935.

BROWN, MARK H. *The Plainsmen of the Yellowstone.* New York, 1961.

BURLINGAME, MERRILL G., and K. ROSS TOOLE (eds.). *A History of Montana.* 3 vols. New York, 1957.

CLARK, THOMAS. *Frontier America.* New York, 1959.

DICK, EVERETT. *Vanguards of the Frontier.* New York, 1941.

DONNELLY, THOMAS C. *Rocky Mountain Politics.* Albuquerque, 1945.

ELSENSOHN, M. ALFREDA. *Pioneer Days in Idaho County.* 2 vols. Caldwell, Idaho, 1947, 1951.

EMMETT, CHRIS. *Fort Union* [New Mexico] *and the Winning of the Southwest.* Norman, Okla., 1965.

FENNEMAN, NEVIN M. *Physiography of Western United States.* New York, 1931.

FETLER, JOHN. *The Pikes Peak People.* Caldwell, Idaho, 1966.

FRINK, MAURICE. *The Boulder Story: Historical Portrait of a Colorado Town.* Boulder, Colo., 1965.

FRITZ, PERCY S. *Colorado, the Centennial State.* New York, 1941.

FULTON, MAURICE, and PAUL HORGAN (eds.). *New Mexico's Own Chronicle.* Dallas, Texas, 1941.

GHENT, W. J. *The Early Far West.* New York, 1931.

GRISWOLD, DON and JEAN. *Colorado's Century of "Cities."* n.p. 1958.

HAFEN, LEROY R. and ANN W. *Colorado and Its People.* 4 vols. New York, 1948.

——— and F. M. YOUNG. *Fort Laramie and the Pageant of the West, 1834–1890.* Glendale, Calif., 1938.

HALL, FRANK. *History of the State of Colorado.* 4 vols. Chicago, 1889–1895.

HORN, CALVIN. *New Mexico's Troubled Years.* Albuquerque, 1963.

HOWARD, JOSEPH KINSEY. *Montana, High, Wide and Handsome.* New Haven, 1943.

HOWBERT, IRVING. *Memories of a Lifetime in the Pikes Peak Region.* New York, 1925.

ISCH, FLORA MAE BELLFLEUR. *The Development of the Upper Flathead and Kootenai Country, Montana.* Unpublished M.A. thesis. Montana State University, 1948.

JOCKNICK, SIDNEY. *Early Days on the Western Slope of Colorado.* Denver, 1913.

KELEHER, WILLIAM A. *The Fabulous Frontier, Twelve New Mexico Items.* Santa Fe, 1945.

LEESON, MICHAEL (ed.). *History of Montana.* Chicago, 1885.

LIVINGSTON-LITTLE, D. E. *An Economic History of Northern Idaho.* Serialized in the *Journal of the West,* Vols. II-III, 1963–64.

MCCONNELL, VIRGINIA. *Bayou Salado, the Story of South Park.* Denver, 1966.

MOKLER, ALFRED JAMES. *History of Natrona County, Wyoming.* Chicago, 1923.

MORGAN, DALE L. *The Great Salt Lake.* Indianapolis, 1947.

MULDER, WILLIAM, and A. RUSSELL MORTENSEN (eds.). *Among the Mormons.* New York, 1958.

PARKHILL, FORBES. *The Law Goes West.* Denver, 1956.

Pioneers of the San Juan Country. 4 vols. Colorado Springs, 1942, 1946, 1952, 1961. Compiled by the Sarah Platt Decker Chapter, D.A.R., Durango, Colo.

REYNOLDS, HELEN MARJORIE. *Some Chapters in the History of the Bitter Root Valley.* Unpublished M.A. thesis. State University of Montana, 1937.

ROBERTSON, FRANK C. *Fort Hall* [Idaho]. New York, 1963.

ROCKWELL, WILSON. *Uncompahgre Country* [Colorado]. Denver, 1965.

SANDERS, HELEN F. *A History of Montana.* 3 vols. Chicago, 1913.

SHOEMAKER, LEN. *Pioneers of the Roaring Fork* [Colorado]. Denver, 1965.

SMILEY, JEROME C. *History of Denver.* Denver, 1901.

————. *Semi-Centennial History of the State of Colorado.* Chicago, 1913.

SPECK, VIRGINIA. *The History of Deer Lodge Valley, Montana.* Unpublished M.A. thesis. Montana State University.

SPRAGUE, MARSHALL. *Newport in the Rockies, The Life and Good Times of Colorado Springs.* Denver, 1961.

STEGNER, WALLACE. *Morman Country.* New York, 1947.

STONE, ELIZABETH. *Uinta County* [Wyoming]: *Its Place in History.* Laramie, 1924.

STONE, WILBUR FISKE. *History of Colorado.* 4 vols. Chicago, 1918–19.

Tales of the Seeds-Ke-Dee [Green River Basin, Wyoming]. Compiled by the Sublette County Artists' Guild. Denver, 1963.

TAYLOR, FRANK C. *Colorado South of the Border.* Denver, 1963.

THOMAS, SEWELL. *Silhouettes of Charles S. Thomas, Colorado Governor and United States Senator.* Caldwell, Idaho, 1959.

TOOLE, K. ROSS. *Montana: An Uncommon Land.* Norman, Okla., 1958.

TWITCHELL, RALPH E. *Leading Facts of New Mexico History.* Cedar Rapids, Iowa, 1912.

UBBELHODE, CARL. *A Colorado History.* Boulder, Colo., 1965.

WALLACE, BETTY. *Gunnison Country* [Colorado]. Denver, 1960.

WARD, LOUISA A. *Chalk Creek, Colorado.* Denver, 1940.

WHEAT, CARL I. *Mapping the Transmississippi West.* 2 vols. San Francisco, 1957–58.

WINTHER, OSCAR O. *The Great Northwest,* New York, 1952.

INDIANS

Accounts dealing with particular battles and campaigns are noted in their chronological setting. General works consulted throughout the preparation of this book include Frederick Hodge (ed.), *Handbook of American Indians North of Mexico* (2 vols., Washington, D.C., 1907, 1910); Oliver La Farge, *A Pictorial History of the American Indian* (New York, 1956); and, particularly, William Brandon's fluent, magnificently illustrated *The American Heritage Book of Indians* (New York, 1961). The Indians of the interior Northwest have received noteworthy treatment in two recent volumes that brilliantly complement each other: Alvin M. Josephy, Jr., *The Nez Percé Indians and the opening of the Northwest* (New Haven, 1965), and Robert Ignatius Burns, *The Jesuits and the Indian Wars of the Northwest* (New Haven, 1966).

Other more or less comprehensive works dealing with various tribes, individuals, and Indian warfare in the Rockies include:

BAILEY, PAUL. *Walkara, Hawk of the Mountains* [A Ute chieftain]. Los Angeles, 1956.

DANIELS, HELEN SLOAN. *The Ute Indians of Southwestern Colorado.* Durango, Colo., 1941.

DUNN, J. P. *Massacres of the Mountains.* (Facsimile edition.) New York, 1958.

EWERS, JOHN C. *The Blackfeet, Raiders of the Northwestern Plains.* Norman, Okla., 1958.

GLASSLEY, RAY H. *Pacific Northwest Indian Wars.* Portland, Ore., 1956.

GRINNELL, GEORGE BIRD. *The Cheyenne Indians.* 2 vols. New Haven, 1924.

HAINES, FRANCIS. *The Nez Percés, Tribesmen of the Columbia Plateau.* Norman, Okla., 1955.

McWHORTER, L. V. *Hear Me, My Chiefs! Nez Percé Legend and History.* Caldwell, Idaho, 1952.

ROCKWELL, WILSON. *The Utes, A Forgotten People.* Denver, 1956.

RONAN, PETER. *Historical Sketch of the Flathead Indian Nation.* Helena, Mont., 1890.

TRENHOLM, VIRGINIA COLE, and MAURINE CARLEY. *The Shoshonis, Sentinels of the Rockies.* Norman, Okla., 1964.

THE FIRST COMERS (Chapters 1 and 2)

Bernard DeVoto's masterly *The Course of Empire* (Boston, 1952) is useful in relating French, English, and Spanish approaches to the Rockies to the overall pattern of New World exploration. An older summary, narrower in its view but more easily digested, is Herbert E. Bolton's *The Spanish Borderlands* (New Haven, 1921).

A handful of scholars have translated and assembled into running narratives a great number of documents dealing with the principal epochs in New Mexico's settlement. The following three collections by George P. Hammond and Agapito Rey were essential to my account: *Narratives of the Coronado Expedition* (2 vols., Albuquerque, 1940); *The Expedition into New Mexico Made by Antonio de Espejo, 1582–83* (Los Angeles, 1929); *Don Juan de Oñate, Colonizer of New Mexico, 1595–1628* (Albuquerque, 1953). The long introduction to Alfred B. Thomas' *Forgotten Frontiers* (Norman, Okla., 1932) is dull to read but necessary for an understanding of Anza, as are the documents that Thomas has translated. Herbert Bolton has done a more graceful job translating, editing, and introducing Escalante's diary, *Pageant in the Wilderness* (Salt Lake City, 1950).

See also:

BANNON, JOHN FRANCIS (ed.). "Defensive Spanish Expansion and the Significance of the Borderlands," in *Bolton and the Spanish Borderlands.* Norman, Okla., 1964.

BOLTON, HERBERT E. *Coronado, Knight of Pueblos and Plains.* New York, 1950.

———. "French Intrusions into New Mexico, 1749–1752," in *The Pacific Ocean in History.* New York, 1917.

DUNN, WILLIAM E. "Spanish Reaction Against the French Advance Toward New Mexico." *Mississippi Valley Historical Review,* II (1915).

FOLMER, HENRI. "The Mallet Expedition . . . to Santa Fe." *Colorado Magazine,* XVI (1939).

HALLENBECK, CLEVE, and JUANITA WILLIAMS. *Legends of the Spanish Southwest.* Glendale, Calif., 1938.

HAMMOND, GEORGE P. *Don Juan de Oñate and the Founding of New Mexico.* Santa Fe, 1926.

NASATIR, ABRAHAM P. *Before Lewis and Clark. Documents Illustrating the History of the Missouri, 1785–1804.* 2 vols. St. Louis, 1952.

THOMAS, ALFRED B. "Spanish Expeditions into Colorado," *Colorado Magazine,* I (1924).

———. "Massacre of the Villasur Expedition." *Nebraska History,* VII (1924).

———. "San Carlos: A Comanche Pueblo on the Arkansas River." *Colorado Magazine,* VI (1929).

SMURR, JOHN W. "A New La Verendrye Theory." *Pacific Northwest Quarterly,* XLIII (1952).

THE EXPLORATION OF LOUISIANA (Chapter 3)

The standard edition of the Lewis and Clark journals is Reuben G. Thwaites, *Original Journals of the Lewis and Clark Expedition* (8 vols., New York, 1904–5). Bernard DeVoto condensed these tomes into one and added a provocative introduction (Boston, 1953). A locating of the explorers' route and campgrounds in respect to modern place names is in Olin Wheeler's two-volume *The Trail of Lewis and Clark* (New York, 1904). An indispensable companion to these studies is Donald Jackson's *Letters of the Lewis and Clark Expedition with Related Documents, 1783–1854* (Urbana, Ill., 1962). Mr. Jackson has also brilliantly edited *The Journals of Zebulon Montgomery Pike, with Letters and Related Documents* (2 vols., Norman, Okla., 1966).

See in addition:

BAKELESS, JOHN. *Lewis and Clark, Partners in Discovery.* New York, 1947.

HOLLON, W. EUGENE. *The Lost Pathfinder, Zebulon Montgomery Pike.* Norman, Okla., 1949.

JOSEPHY, ALVIN M., JR. "The Lolo Trail." New York Westerners *Brand Book,* IV (1958).

THE BEAVER HUNTERS (Chapters 4, 5, and 6)

The literature on the Rocky Mountain fur trade is so voluminous that a detailed listing here would be impractical. The two standard reference works are Hiram M. Chittenden's pioneering but now outdated *A History of the American Fur Trade of the Far West* (2 vols., reprinted, Stanford, Calif.,1954) and Paul Phillips' overly ambitious *The Fur Trade,* completed after his death by John W. Smurr (2 vols., Norman, Okla., 1961). Three volumes of a projected six-volume biographic encyclopedia of *The Mountain Men and the Fur Trade of the Far West,* edited by LeRoy Hafen, had been published (Glendale, Calif., 1965, 1966) when I was working on the fur trade section of this book. I drew extensively on all three.

The key figure in the initial British invasion of the Northwest was David Thompson, whose *Narrative of His Explorations in Western America, 1784–1812,* was enthusiastically edited first by J. B. Tyrrell (Toronto, 1916) and, half a century later, more critically by Richard Glover (Toronto, 1962). Other standard accounts of early days in the Northwest are Washington Irving, *Astoria;* Ross Cox, *Adventures on the Columbia River* (new edition by Edgar I. and Jane R. Stewart, Norman, Okla., 1961); Alexander Ross, *Adventures of the First Settlers on the Oregon and Columbia River* (Cleveland, 1904); Gabriel Franchère, *Narrative of a Voyage to the Northwest Coast of America . . .* (Cleveland, 1904); and Philip Ashton Rollins' skillful presentation of Robert Stuart's diary of his return from Astoria to St. Louis in 1812–13, *The Discovery of South Pass.* The relationship between Astor and the North West Company of Montreal has been re-examined by David Lavender in *The Fist in the Wilderness,* pp. 118–145 *passim* (New York, 1964).

Of the books that deal with the middle period of the fur trade (roughly 1815–1830) the two pre-eminent ones are Dale L. Morgan's *Jedediah Smith and the Opening of the West* (Indianapolis, 1953) and the same author's monumental collection of documents in *The West of William H. Ashley, 1822–1838* (Denver, 1964). The feverish decade of the 1830's is covered by Don Berry, *A Majority of Scoundrels* (New York, 1961), and Bernard DeVoto, *Across the Wide Missouri* (Boston, 1947). For material on the fur trade farther south and on the Santa Fe trade, see the bibliography in David Lavender's *Bent's Fort* (New York, 1954). The flickering out of the trade during the 1840's is captured by two tourists who happened through the southern Rockies during the war with Mexico: Lewis Garrard, *Wah-to-yah and the Taos Trail* (new edition, Norman, Okla., 1955), and George Frederick Ruxton, whose autobiographical writings have been edited by LeRoy R. Hafen in *Ruxton of the Rockies* (Norman, Okla., 1950) and whose fictionized *Life in the Far West* (also edited by Hafen, Norman, Okla., 1951) is indispensable to any study of the life of the mountain fur hunters.

In addition to Garrard and Ruxton's volumes I have relied for "flavor" chiefly on Osborne Russell, *Journal of a Trapper* (edited by Aubrey L. Haines (Portland, Ore., 1955), Warren Angus Ferris, *Life in the Rocky Mountains* (edited by Paul C. Phillips, Denver, 1940), and Frances Fuller Victor's wide-eyed rendering of Joe Meek's recollections in *The River of the West* (Hartford, Conn., 1871).

A selected handful of other books bearing on beaver hunting and the Indian trade of the mountain West follows:

ALTER, J. CECIL. *James Bridger*. rev. ed. Norman, Okla., 1960.

CAMP, CHARLES L. (ed.). *James Clyman, American Frontiersman*. Portland, Ore., 1960.

———— (ed.). *George C. Yount and His Chronicles of the West*. Denver, 1966.

CLELAND, ROBERT GLASS. *This Reckless Breed of Men*. New York, 1950.

COUES, ELLIOTT (ed.). *The Journal of Jacob Fowler*. Facsimile ed. Minneapolis, 1965.

DAVIDSON, GORDON. *The North West Company*. Berkeley, 1918.

EWERS, JOHN (ed.). *Adventures of Zenas Leonard, Fur Trader*. Norman, Okla., 1959.

HAFEN, LEROY R., and W. J. GHENT. *Broken Hand: The Life Story of Thomas Fitzpatrick, Chief of the Mountain Men*. Denver, 1931.

HARRIS, BURTON. *John Colter*. New York, 1952.

IRVING, WASHINGTON. *The Adventures of Captain Bonneville*, edited by Edgely Todd. Norman, Okla., 1961.

JAMES, EDWIN. *Account of An Expedition . . . to the Rocky Mountains . . . in the Years 1819, 1820 . . .* 4 vols. Cleveland, 1905.

JAMES, THOMAS. *Three Years Among the Indians and Mexicans*, edited by A. P. Nasatir. Philadelphia, 1962.

MERK, FREDERICK. *Fur Trade and Empire*. Cambridge, Mass., 1931.

OGLESBY, RICHARD. *Manuel Lisa and the Opening of the Missouri River Fur Trade*. Norman, Okla., 1963.

PARKMAN, FRANCIS. *The Oregon Trail*. New York, 1849.

RICH, E. E. *McLoughlin's Fort Vancouver Letters*, 3 vols. Toronto, 1941–1944.

————. *Peter Skene Ogden's Snake Country Journals, 1824–26*. London, 1950.

ROSS, ALEXANDER. *The Fur Hunters of the Far West*. London, 1855.

SABIN, EDWIN L. *Kit Carson Days*. rev. ed. New York, 1935.

WHITE, M. CATHERINE. *David Thompson's Journals Relating to Montana and Adjacent Regions, 1808–12*. Missoula, Mont., 1950.

BEGINNINGS OF SETTLEMENT (Last of Chapter 6, Chapters 7 and 8)

Any study of the Catholic missions in Montana and Idaho should begin with the four-volume *Life, Letters and Travels of Father Pierre-Jean De Smet, S.J., 1801–1873*, edited by Hiram M. Chittenden and Alfred T. Richardson (New York, 1905). Affairs at Fort Owen, successor to St. Mary's Mission, are covered in *The Journals and Letters of Major John Owen . . .* , 2 vols., edited by Seymour Dunbar and Paul C. Phillips (Helena, Mont., 1927), supplemented by George F. Weisel's painstaking annotation of the Fort Owen Ledger, *Men and Trade on the Northwest Frontier* (Missoula, Mont., 1955).

For government explorations during this period see below under Beckwith (who finished Gunnison's work), Frémont, Stansbury, and Stevens. A dramatic rendering of Frémont's disastrous fourth expedition is William Brandon, *The Men and the Mountain* (New York, 1955).

Outstanding on the Utah War is Norman F. Furniss, *The Mormon Conflict, 1850–1859* (New Haven, 1960), supplemented by the documents collected in LeRoy R. and Ann W. Hafen, *The Utah Expedition, 1857–1858* (Glendale, Calif., 1959).

See also:

BECKWITH, E. G. *Report of Exploration for a Route for the Pacific Railroad. . . .* Vol. II of *Pacific Railroad Reports.* Washington ,1855–60.

BROWN, JAMES S. *Life of a Pioneer* [Autobiography of an early-day Mormon]. Salt Lake City, 1900.

CARTER, KATE B. "The Salmon River Mission" [Pamphlet]. n.p., 1963.

CARVALHO, S. N. *Incidents of Travel and Adventure in the Far West* [Frémont's Fifth Expedition]. New York, 1860.

FRÉMONT, JOHN CHARLES. *Narratives of Exploration and Adventure.* Edited by Allan Nevins [the first three expeditions and Frémont's "Geographic Memoir"]. New York, 1956.

HINE, ROBERT V. *Edward Kern and American Expansion.* New Haven, 1962.

HOLLEN, W. EUGENE. *Beyond the Cross Timbers: The Travels of Randolph B. Marcy, 1812–1887.* Norman, Okla., 1955.

LECOMPTE, JANET S. "The Hardscrabble Settlement, 1844–48." *Colorado Magazine,* XXXI (1954).

———. "Pueblo Massacre," *Brand Book* of the Denver Westerners, 1954.

MARCY, RANDOLPH B. *Thirty Years of Army Life on the Border.* New York, 1866.

MENGARINI, GREGORY. "Narrative of the Rockies," in John W. Hakola (ed.). *Frontier Omnibus.* Missoula, Mont. 1962.

NELSON, LOWRY. *The Mormon Village: A Pattern and Technique of Land Settlement.* Salt Lake City, 1952.

PALLADINO, LAURENCE B. *Indian and White in the Northwest.* Baltimore, 1894.

SCHAEFFER, CLAUDE. "The First Jesuit Mission to the Flatheads, 1800–1850. A Study in Culture Conflicts," *The Pacific Northwest Quarterly,* XXVIII (1937).

STANSBURY, HOWARD. *Exploration and Survey of the Valley of the Great Salt Lake . . .* Senate Exec. Doc. 3, 32nd Congress, Special Session. Washington, 1854.

STEGNER, WALLACE. *The Gathering of Zion.* New York, 1965.

STEVENS, HAZARD. *The Life of Isaac Ingalls Stevens.* 2 vols. Boston, 1901.

STEVENS, ISAAC I. *Narrative and Final Report of Explorations for a Route for a Pacific Railroad . . .* Vol. XII, part 1, of *Pacific Railroad Reports.* Washington, 1855–1860.

TAYLOR, MORRIS F. "Action at Fort Massachusetts: The Indian Campaign of 1855," *Colorado Magazine,* XLII (1965).

VANDENBUSCHE, DUANE. "Life at a Frontier Post: Fort Garland," *Colorado Magazine*, XLIII (1966).

THE EARLY GOLD RUSHES (Chapters 9 to 13)

Because mining dominated the economy of the Rocky Mountains for more than half a century, accounts of mining likewise dominate mountain historiography. Nearly every book listed above under "Place Histories" devotes considerable space to the topic—and yet, oddly, there is for the general reader no really sound, comprehensive account of mining in the Rockies. The best launching point, brief and scholarly, is Rodman Paul's *Mining Frontiers of the Far West, 1848–1880*—a closing date that stops short of some of the bigger bonanzas (New York, 1963). Other useful introductions, though the material extends far beyond the Rockies, are three accounts by Thomas A. Rickard, engineer and editor of mining journals: *A History of American Mining, Man and Metals* (both published in New York in 1932) and *The Romance of Mining* (Toronto, 1945). Highly useful but not generally available is Duane Allen Smith's unpublished doctoral dissertation, *Mining Camps and the Settlement of the Trans-Mississippi Frontier, 1860–1890* (University of Colorado, 1964). Good short studies on the same theme are August C. Bolino, "The Role of Mining in the Economic Development of Idaho Territory" (*Oregon Historical Quarterly*, LIX June 1958, S. J. Coon, "Influence of the Gold Camps on the Economic Development of the West" (*Journal of Political Economy*, 1930), and A. H. Koschmann, "The Historical Pattern of Mineral Exploitation in Colorado," in *Minerals and Energy*, (Western Resources Conference, Golden, Colo., 1962). To these should be added Clark Spence's *British Investments and the American Mining Frontier, 1860–1901* (Ithaca, N.Y., 1958).

Muriel S. Wolle's entertaining and handsomely illustrated twins, *Stampede to Timberline, the Ghost Towns and Mining Camps of Colorado* (Boulder, Colo., 1949) and *Montana Pay Dirt* (Denver, 1963) are helpful for setting the stage for those two states. The opening of the Northwest is ably covered in William J. Trimble's pioneering *The Mining Advance into the Inland Empire* (Madison, Wis., 1914). This should be supplemented by a series of documents published in *Idaho Yesterdays:* "Gold in 1860" (Fall, 1959), "News from the Nez Percé Mines" (Winter, 1959–1960), "Clearwater Gold Rush" (Spring, 1860), Ralph Burchams' presentation of Elias Pierce's story in "Orofino Gold" (Fall, 1960), "The Salmon River Mines" (Spring 1962) and "Fabulous Florence" (Summer, 1962).

Essential government reports include J. Ross Browne and J. R. Taylor, *Reports upon the Mineral Resources of the United States* (Washington, 1867), J. Ross Browne, *Report on the Mineral Resources of the States and Territories West of the Rocky Mountains* (Washington, 1868), and the series by Raymond Rossiter, *Statistics of Mines and Mining in the States and Territories West of the Rocky Mountains* (Washington, 1869–1874).

Newspaper files consulted include the *Rocky Mountain News* of Denver from its founding in April, 1859, through the 1870's and the *Montana Post*, first of Virginia City, then of Helena, 1864–1869.

Additional material came from the following:

ATHEARN, ROBERT. "Life in the Pike's Peak Region. The Letters of Matthew H. Dale," *Colorado Magazine,* XXXVI (1959).

BANCROFT, CAROLINE. "The Elusive Figure of John H. Gregory . . ." *Colorado Magazine,* XX (1943).

BANCROFT, HUBERT HOWE. *Popular Tribunals.* 2 vols. San Francisco ,1887.

BARNEY, LIBEUS. *Letters of the Pike's Peak Gold Rush.* Reprint edition. San Jose, Calif., 1959.

BARSNESS, LARRY. *Gold Camp: Alder Gulch and Virginia City, Montana.* New York, 1962.

BIRD, ANNIE LAURIE. "Portrait of a Politician" [William H. Wallace of Idaho and elsewhere]. *Idaho Yesterdays,* 1958.

BOWLES, SAMUEL. *Across the Continent.* Springfield, Mass., 1866.

BURLINGAME, MERRILL G. "John M. Bozeman, Montana Trailmaker," *Mississippi Valley Historical Review,* XXVII (1940–41).

CANNON, HELEN, "First Ladies of Colorado, Ellen Kellogg Hunt," *Colorado Magazine.* XXXIX (1962).

CLARK, C. M. *A Trip to Pike's Peak.* Reprint edition. San Jose, Calif., 1958.

CLARK, WILLIAM ANDREWS. "The Origin, Growth, and Resources of Montana," *Contributions to the Historical Society of Montana,* II (1896).

DIMSDALE, THOMAS J. *The Vigilantes of Montana.* Reprint edition. Norman, Okla., 1953.

DYER, JOHN L. *The Snow-Shoe Itinerant* [Pioneer Preaching in Colorado and New Mexico]. Cincinnati, 1890.

EDGAR, HENRY. "Journal, 1863," *Contribution to the Historical Society of Montana,* III (1900).

FLYNN, NORMA. "Early Mining Camps of South Park," *Brand Book* of the Denver Westerners (1952).

FOSSETT, FRANK. *Colorado, its Gold and Silver Mines. . . .* New York, 1879.

GREELEY, HORACE. *An Overland Journey . . . 1859.* Reprint, Charles Duncan (ed.) New York, 1964.

GREEVER, WILLIAM S. *The Bonanza West.* Norman, Okla., 1963.

HAFEN, LEROY R. (ed.) *Colorado Gold Rush: Contemporary Letters and Reports, 1858–59.* Glendale, Calif., 1941.

————. *Pike's Peak Gold Rush Guide Books of 1859.* Glendale, Calif., 1941.

————. *Overland Routes to the Gold Fields, 1859, from Contemporary Diaries.* Glendale, Calif., 1942.

————. "George A. Jackson's Diary, 1858–59," *Colorado Magazine,* XII (1935).

————. "Cherokee Goldseekers in Colorado, 1849–50," *Colorado Magazine,* XV (1938).

HALL, FRANK. Unpublished letters about Colorado affairs. Copies in Western History Dept., Denver Public Library.

HEALY, JOHN J. Two excerpts from his reminiscences, which ran in the Fort Benton *Record* from April 12 through July 17, 1878, are "Johnny Healy Strikes It Rich," edited by John L. Struble, *Idaho Yesterdays,* (Fall 1957), and "An Adventure in the Idaho Mines," edited by Clyde McLemore, *Frontier Omnibus.* Missoula, Mont., 1962.

HOLLISTER, OVANDO J. *The Mines of Colorado.* Springfield, Mass., 1867.

HUNT, ELLEN. "Diary," edited by LeRoy R. Hafen, *Colorado Magazine*, XXI (1944).

JACKSON, W. TURRENTINE. *Wagon Roads West*. Los Angeles, Calif., 1952.

KIRKPATRICK, JAMES. "A Reminiscence of John Bozeman," edited by Paul C. Phillips, *Frontier Omnibus*. Missoula, Mont., 1962.

KIRKPATRICK, ROBERT. *From Wisconsin to Montana and Life in the West, 1863–1869*, edited as an unpublished M.A. thesis by Michael G. Mc-Latchy, Montana State University, 1961.

LANGFORD, NATHANIEL PITT. *Vigilante Days and Ways*. Reprint edition. Missoula, Mont., 1957.

LONDONER, WOLFE. "Western Experiences in Colorado Mining Camps," *Colorado Magazine*, IX (1932).

MARSHALL, THOMAS MAITLAND. *Early Records of Gilpin County, Colorado, 1859–1861*. Boulder, Colo., 1920.

MEREDITH, EMILY. "Bannack and Gallatin City (Montana) in 1862–63," edited by Clyde McLemore, *Frontier Omnibus*. Missoula, Mont., 1962.

MORLEY, JAMES HENRY. *Diary, 1862–65*. Unpublished. Typescript in Montana State Historical Society, Helena.

MORLEY, JULIUS. *Reminiscences*. Unpublished. MS BM82, Montana State Historical Society.

MULLAN, JOHN. *Report on the Construction of a Military Road from Fort Walla Walla to Fort Benton*. Washington, 1863.

——. *Miners and Travelers Guide*. . . . New York, 1865.

OLSEN, BENTON CLARK. *The Vigilantes of Montana: A Second Look*. Unpublished M.A. thesis, University of Utah, 1966.

PAUL, RODMAN W. "Colorado as a Pioneer of Science in the Mining West," *Mississippi Valley Historical Review*, XLVII (1960–61).

PERRIGO, LYNN. *Social History of Central City, Colorado, 1859–1900*. Unpublished doctoral dissertation, University of Colorado, 1936.

——. "Law and Order in the Early Colorado Camps," *Mississippi Valley Historical Review*, XXVIII (1940–41).

RICHARDSON, ALBERT D. *Beyond the Mississippi*. Hartford, Conn., 1867.

ROLLE, ANDREW (ed.), *The Road to Virginia City (Montana), The Diary of James Knox Polk Miller*. Norman, Okla., 1960.

SASSMAN, OREN. *Metal Mining in Historic Beaverhead* [Montana], *1862–1940*. Unpublished M.A. thesis, Montana State University, 1941.

SMURR, J. W. "Afterthoughts on the Vigilantes," *Montana Magazine*, Spring, 1958.

SPAIN, DAVID S. "Diary . . . ," *Colorado Magazine*, XXXV (1958).

SPENCER, ELMA DILL RUSSELL. *Green Russell and Gold*. Austin, Texas, 1966.

STUART, GRANVILLE. *Forty Years on the Frontier . . . Journals and Reminiscences*. Edited by Paul C. Phillips. Reprint, Glendale, Calif., 1957.

——. *Montana As It Is*. New York, 1865.

STUART, JAMES. "The Yellowstone Expedition of 1863," *Contributions to The Historical Society of Montana*, I (1876).

TALKINGTON, HENRY L. "Mullan Road," *Washington Historical Quarterly*, VII (1916).

TAYLOR, BAYARD. *Colorado: A Summer Trip*. New York, 1867.

THOMPSON, FRANCIS M. "Reminiscences of Four Score Years," *Massachusetts Magazine,* VI (1913).

TOPONCE, ALEXANDER. *Reminiscences . . . 1839–1923.* Ogden, Utah, 1923.

TUTTLE, DANIEL S. *Reminiscences of a Missionary Bishop.* New York, 1906.

VILLARD, HENRY. *The Past and Present of the Pikes Peak Gold Rush.* Reprint, Princeton, N.J., 1932.

WATT, JAMES W. "Experiences of a Packer in Washington Territory Mining Camps During the Sixties," edited by William S. Lewis, *Washington Historical Quarterly,* July, 1928–January, 1929.

WELLS, DONALD. "Farmers Forgotten, Nez Percé Suppliers of the Northern Idaho Gold Rush Days," *Idaho Yesterdays,* Summer, 1958.

WILLARD, JAMES F. "Spreading the News of the Early Discoveries of Gold in Colorado," *Colorado Magazine,* VI (1929).

WILLIAMS, FRANCIS. "Trials and Judgments of the People's Courts in Denver," *Colorado Magazine,* XXVII (1950).

WILLING, GEORGE M. "Diary of a Journey to the Pike's Peak Gold Mines in 1859," edited by Ralph P. Bieber, *Mississippi Valley Historical Review,* XIX (1927–28).

WILLISON, GEORGE F. *Here They Dug the Gold.* New York, 1946.

WINTHER, OSCAR O. "The Mineral Empire," in *The Old Oregon Country, A History of Frontier Trade, Transportation, and Travel.* Stanford, Calif., 1950.

WOODY, F. H. "A Sketch of the Early History of Western Montana," in *Contributions to the Historical Society of Montana,* II (1896).

WRIGHT, AGNES SPRING (ed.). *A Bloomer Girl on Pikes Peak, 1858: Julia Archibald Holmes . . .* Denver, 1949.

GROWING PAINS: POLITICS AND PROMOTION (Chapters 14 and 15)

A wealth of documents concerning Colorado's early utopian colonies is gathered in James F. Willard (ed.), *The Union Colony at Greeley* (Boulder, Colo., 1918), and Colin B. Goodykountz and James F. Willard (eds.), *Experiments in Colorado Colonization. 1869–1872* (Boulder, 1927). Additional material on Nathan Meeker's days at the Union Colony, Greeley, can be found in Marshall Sprague's biography of Meeker, *Massacre: The Tragedy at White River* (Boston, 1957).

The Western History Department, Denver Public Library, possesses a large file of promotional pamphlets extolling early irrigation projects.

A start on the literature covering the endless controversy over Chivington's attack on the Indian camp at Sand Creek on the plains east of the Rockies can be found in two articles published in *Colorado Magazine* for the fall of 1964, a hundred years after the event: Janet Lecompte, "Sand Creek," and Raymond G. Carey, "The Puzzle of Sand Creek." For details concerning the Indian troubles that closed the Bozeman Trail in the 1860's, see Dee Brown, *Fort Phil Kearny: An American Saga* (New York, 1962).

Books on the building of the Union Pacific are legion. Two good recent ones are Wesley S. Griswold, *A Work of Giants* (New York, 1962), and James McCague, *Moguls and Iron Men* (New York, 1964). The definitive account of the Denver & Rio Grande Railroad is Robert G. Athearn's *Rebel of the Rockies* (New Haven, 1962).

Government surveys of the Rocky Mountains and a detailed citation of documents dealing with the formation of Yellowstone National Park can be found in Richard A. Bartlett's *Great Surveys of the American West* (Norman, Okla., 1962).

Still more detail on the period came from:

ALBRIGHT, ROBERT E. *The Relations of Montana with the Federal Government, 1864–1889.* Unpublished doctoral dissertation, Stanford University, 1933.

ATHEARN, ROBERT G. *Thomas Francis Meagher, An Irish Revolutionary in America.* Boulder, Colo., 1949.

BANKER, ISAAC ALEXANDER. Unpublished letters from early Wyoming. Western History Research Center, University of Wyoming.

BELL, WILLIAM A. *New Tracks in North America.* London, 1869.

BOYD, DAVID. *A History: Greeley and the Union Colony of Colorado.* Greeley, Colo., 1890.

BRAYER, HERBERT O. *William Blackmore: The Spanish-Mexican Land Grants of New Mexico and Colorado.* Denver, 1949.

DUNBAR, ROBERT G. "Water Conflicts and Controls in Colorado," *Agricultural History*, XXII (1948).

———. "The Origin of the Colorado System of Water-Right Control," *Colorado Magazine*, XXVII (1950).

DUNHAM, HAROLD A. "Coloradoans and the Maxwell Grant," *Colorado Magazine*, XXXII (1955).

ELLIS, ELMER. "Colorado's First Fight for Statehood," *Colorado Magazine*, VIII (1931).

FISHER, JOHN S. *A Builder of the West: The Life of General William Jackson Palmer.* Caldwell, Idaho, 1932.

GREEN, MRS. A. M. *Sixteen Years in the Great American Desert* [Union Colony]. Titusville, Pa., 1887.

HAFEN, LEROY R. *The Overland Mail, 1849–1869.* Cleveland, 1926.

HOMSHER, LOLA (ed.). *South Pass 1868: James Chisholm's Journal of The Wyoming Gold Rush.* Lincoln, Nebr. ,1960.

KELEHER, WILLIAM A. *The Maxwell Land Grant, A New Mexico Item.* Santa Fe, 1942.

PABOR, WILLIAM F. *First Annual Report of the Union Colony of Colorado.* . . . New York, 1871.

SETTLE, MARY LUND and RAYMOND W. *Empire on Wheels* [the story of Russell, Majors, and Waddell]. Stanford, Calif., 1949.

WELLS, MERLE. "Clinton De Witt Smith, Secretary of Idaho Territory," *Oregon Historical Quarterly*, 1951.

———. "The Creation of Idaho Territory," *ibid.*

WHITE, LAURA M. CWA Pamphlet 367, docs. 1–35. Colorado State Historical Society. Contains material on the Georgia Colony, including Brice Patterson's "History of the Georgia Colony of Colorado."

WROTEN, WILLIAM A. JR. *The Railroad Tie Industry of the Central Rocky Mountain Region, 1867–1900.* Unpublished doctoral dissertation, University of Colorado, 1956.

ZEFERS, DANA. *From Ditch to Doctrine: The Origins of the Colorado Doctrine of Water Rights.* Unpublished M.A. thesis, University of Colorado, 1959.

SILVER AND ITS EFFECTS (Chapters 16 and 17)

Background material for these two chapters was found in the place histories, Indian tales, and mining accounts cited earlier, plus Robert Athearn's fine *Rebel of the Rockies.* Detail on Leadville came from the files of the *Chronicle* and the *Democrat,* from an unsigned series in *Frank Leslie's Illustrated Weekly Newspaper,* April 12–July 5, 1879, from Ernest Ingersoll's running account in *Scribner's Monthly,* May through October, 1879, and from two excellent modern studies, Don L. and Jean Harvey Griswold, *The Carbonate Camp Called Leadville* (Denver, 1951), and Eugene F. Irey's unpublished doctoral dissertation, *A Social History of Leadville, Colorado, During the Boom Days, 1877–1881* (University of Minnesota, 1951).

In addition:

ATHEARN, ROBERT. *Westward the Briton.* New York, 1953.

BARTLETT, ROBERT F. "Aspen: The Mining Community, 1879–1893," *Brand Book* of the Denver Westerners (1950).

BEAL, MERRILL D. *I Will Fight No More Forever* [The Nez Percé Retreat]. Seattle, Wash., 1963.

BRADLEY, GLEN D. *The Story of the Santa Fe.* Boston, 1920.

BROWN, ROBERT L. *An Empire of Silver: A History of the San Juan Silver Rush* [Southwestern Colorado]. Caldwell, Idaho, 1965.

CAFKY, MORRIS. *The Colorado Midland.* Denver, 1965.

DARLY, REV. GEORGE M. *Pioneering in the San Juans.* Chicago, 1899.

DAVIS, CARLYLE C. *Olden Times in Colorado* [mostly Leadville]. Los Angeles, Calif., 1916.

EMMONS, SAMUEL F. *The Geology and Mining Industry of Leadville, Colorado.* Washington, 1886.

GANDY, LEWIS C. *The Tabors, A Footnote of Western History.* New York, 1934.

GIBBONS, REV. J. J. *Notes of a Missionary Priest in the Rocky Mountains.* New York, 1898.

HAGIE, C. E. "Gunnison in the Early Days," *Colorado Magazine,* VIII (1931).

HALE, JESSE D. "The First Successful Smelter in Colorado," *Colorado Magazine,* XIII (1936).

HILL, NATHANIEL P. "Letters," a series in *Colorado Magazine,* October, 1956–July, 1957.

INGERSOLL, ERNEST. *Knocking Round the Rockies.* New York, 1883.

———. *The Crest of the Continent.* New York, 1889.

INGHAM, G. T. *Digging Gold Among the Rockies.* Philadelphia, 1880.

JACKSON, W. TURRENTINE. "The Infamous Emma Mine," *Utah Historical Quarterly,* October, 1955.

MARSHALL, JAMES. *Santa Fe: The Railroad That Built an Empire.* New York, 1945.

ORMES, ROBERT M. *Railroads and the Rockies.* Denver, 1963.

PARKHILL, FORBES, "The Meeker Massacre and Thornburgh Battle," *Brand Book* of the Denver Westerners (1945).

POOR, M. C. *Denver, South Park and Pacific.* Denver, 1949.

POPHAM, DONALD. "The Early Activities of the Guggenheims in Colorado," *Colorado Magazine,* XXVII (1950).

RICKARD, T. A. "Across the San Juan Mountains," *Engineering and Mining Journal,* New York, 1903.

SANDOZ, MARIE. *The Battle of the Little Bighorn.* Philadelphia, 1966.

SMITH, DUANE A. *The Silver Camp Called Caribou.* Unpublished M.A. thesis, University of Colorado, 1961.

TURMOIL IN THE BIG BONANZAS (Chapter 18 through first part of 21)

There is no adequate full-length profile of Idaho's Coeur d'Alene mining district, of Butte, Montana, or even of Leadville, Colorado, after the first years of its boom. Cripple Creek, Colorado, fares somewhat better, thanks to Marshall Sprague's *Money Mountain: The Story of Cripple Creek Gold* (Boston, 1953) and Frank Waters' *Midas of the Rockies: The Story of Stratton and Cripple Creek* (reprint edition, Denver, 1959). Likewise, there is no adequate over-all view of the Rockies' industrial warfare, although Stewart H. Holbrook made a start in *The Rocky Mountain Revolution* (New York, 1956).

Contemporary accounts of the labor uproars are violently partisan. Exceptions are two "official" presentations: *Senate Documents 24 and 25 relating to Coeur d'Alene Mining Troubles,* 56th Congress, 1st Session (Washington, 1899), and the U.S. Bureau of Labor's *Report on Labor Disturbances in Colorado from 1880 to 1904* (Washington, 1904). Two admirable later studies include David Grover's *Debaters and Dynamiters, The Story of the Haywood Trial* (Corvallis, Ore., 1964), which is based on court records, and George Graham Sugg's thorough *Colorado Conservatives versus Organized Labor: A Study of the James Hamilton Peabody Administration, 1903–05* (unpublished doctoral dissertation, University of Colorado, 1964).

Additional data came from the files of the Ouray, Colorado, *Solid Muldoon,* a mining camp newspaper as off-beat as its name, from the "place histories" and mining accounts cited earlier, and the following:

ANDERSON, BRYCE W. "The Bomb at the Governor's Gate" [Steunenberg's Assassination], *American West,* II (1965).

BEAL, MERRILL D. *Intermountain Railroads, Standard and Narrow Gauge* [Chiefly in Idaho and Montana]. Caldwell, Idaho, 1962.

CONNOLLY, CHRISTOPHER P. *The Devil Learns to Vote* [Montana politics in the Clark-Daly-Heinze era]. New York, 1938.

DEBOURG, ROGER. *A History of Theater in Butte, Montana, 1890–1910.* Unpublished M.A. thesis, Montana State University, 1963.

FULLER, LEON W. "Governor Waite and His Silver Panacea," *Colorado Magazine,* X (1933).

GLASSCOCK, CARL B. *The War of the Copper Kings.* Indianapolis, 1935.

GREENOUGH, W. EARL. *First 100 Years of the Coeur d'Alene Mining Region.* Mullan, Idaho, 1947.

HEDGES, JAMES B. *Henry Villard and the Railways of the Northwest.* New Haven, 1930.

HIGH, JAMES. "William Andrews Clark, Westerner: an Interpretive Vignette," *Arizona and the West,* II (1960).

JENSEN, VERNON H. *Heritage of Conflict: Labor Relations in the Non-Ferrous Metals Industry up to 1930.* Ithaca, N.Y., 1950.

JORALEMON, IRA B. *Romantic Copper, Its Lure and Lore.* New York, 1934.

KISSANE, LEEDICE. "Steve Adams, the Speechless Witness," *Idaho Yesterdays,* IV (1960).

KIZER, BENJAMIN. "May Arkwright Hutton," *Pacific Northwest Quarterly,* April, 1966.

LANGDON, EMMA F. *The Cripple Creek Strike of 1904* [An "official" statement by the Western Federation of Miners]. Denver, 1904.

LEE, MABEL BARBEE. *Cripple Creek Days.* Garden City, N.Y., 1958.

LIVERMORE, ROBERT. Unpublished *Autobiography* of a mining engineer who was in Telluride, Colorado, during the strife there. Western History Research Center, University of Wyoming.

MARCOSSON, ISAAC F. *Anaconda.* New York, 1957.

MCNELIS, SARAH. *The Life of F. Augustus Heinze.* Unpublished M.A. thesis, Montana State University, 1947.

MCPHEE, WILLIAM. "Vignettes of Park City," *Utah Historical Quarterly,* April, 1960.

ORCHARD, HARRY. *Confessions and Autobiography of Harry Orchard.* New York, 1907.

PARSONS, ARTHUR B. *The Porphyry Coppers.* New York, 1933.

PRATT, GRACE R. "The Great-Hearted Huttons of the Coeur d'Alenes," *Montana* magazine.

RASTALL, BENJAMIN. *Labor History of the Cripple Creek District: A Study in Industrial Evolution.* Madison, Wisc., 1908.

RICKARD, T. A. "The Utah Copper Enterprise," *Mining and Scientific Press,* CXVII (1918).

SALES, RENO H. *Underground Warfare at Butte.* Butte, Mont., 1964.

SCHEINBERG, STEPHEN. "Theodore Roosevelt's 'Undesirable Citizens,' " *Idaho Yesterdays,* IV (1960).

SIRINGO, CHARLES A. *A Cowboy Detective.* Chicago, 1912.

SMALLEY, E. V. "The Coeur d'Alene Stampede," *Century Illustrated Monthly,* October, 1884.

SMITH, ROBERT W. *The Coeur d'Alene Mining War of 1892.* Corvallis, Ore., 1961.

STOLL, WILLIAM T. *Silver Strike* [The Coeur d'Alenes by a contemporary]. Boston, 1932.

TOOLE, ROSS K. "The Anaconda Copper Mining Company," *Pacific Northwest Quarterly,* XLI (1950).

———. "The Genesis of the Clark-Daly Feud," *Montana* magazine, I (1951).

———. "When Big Money Came to Butte," *Pacific Northwest Quarterly,* XLIV (1953).

WARDNER, JIM. *Jim Wardner of Wardner, Idaho.* New York, 1900.
WATKINS, T. H. "Requiem for the Federation," *American West.* III (1966).
Works Progress Administration. *Copper Camp.* New York, 1943.

LIVESTOCK, WATER, TIMBER, RECREATION (Chapter 21 and Epilogue)

American attitudes toward and myths about land and the often shortsighted legislation that resulted are superbly delineated in three very different books: Roy N. Robbins, *Our Landed Heritage* (Princeton, N.J., 1942), Henry Nash Smith, *Virgin Land, The American West as Symbol and Myth* (Cambridge, Mass., 1950), and Wallace Stegner, *Beyond the Hundredth Meridian: John Wesley Powell and the Second Opening of the West* (Boston, 1954). To these should be added John Ise's duo, *The United States Forest Policy* (New Haven, 1920) and *Our National Park Policy* (Baltimore, 1961). An indication that the government knew what was happening to the mountain forests as early as the 1880's but was able to do little about it is clearly indicated by the *Reports* of the commissioner of agriculture, especially that of 1883 (Washington, 1884). Mimeographed histories of the different National Forests, which can be found in the district forest offices concerned, also are helpful to an understanding of the problems.

Water: in addition to the irrigation pamphlets mentioned in the bibliography for Chapters 15 and 16, the Western History Department of Denver's Public Library has preserved considerable ephemera relating to the National Irrigation Congresses launched by William Smythe in 1891. The Conservation Department in the same library is a gold mine for delvers in that field.

Livestock problems have been resoundingly covered. Fullest study of the so-called Johnson County war of Wyoming is Helena Huntington Smith's somewhat polemical *The War on Powder River* (New York, 1966). One important affray that has not yet been fully exploited is the killing of three sheepmen near Tensleep, Wyoming, in 1909. My brief summary is based on the court records of the Fourth Judicial District in and for the County of Big Horn, Wyoming, *State of Wyoming vs. Herbert Brink.* A typescript is available in the Western History Research Center, University of Wyoming, Laramie. A skimming of *Living Wilderness* magazine will indicate the scope of the problems relating to the Wilderness Preservation System. Thanks are due Elizabeth Hannum Smith for permission to quote from the speech she made in Missoula, April 28, 1966, to the Montana Statewide Recreation Planning Conference; and also to *Colorado Magazine* for permission to use in the latter part of the "Epilogue" three or four paragraphs of material from their files.

For the rest, see:

BOLE, ARNOLD, *et al. The Forestry Products Industry of Montana.* Missoula, 1963.
BEHAN, R. W. "The Lincoln Back Country Controversy." Mimeographed pamphlet, University of Montana, School of Forestry, Missoula, Mont., n.d.
CLAWSON, MARTIN. "Issues of Public Policy in Outdoor Recreation," in *New Horizons for Resources Research.* Boulder, Colo., 1962.
COLE, DONALD B. "Transmountain Water Diversion in Colorado," *Colorado Magazine,* XXV (1948).

DUNBAR, ROBERT G. "The Search for a Stable Water Right in Montana," *Agricultural History,* XXVIII (1954).

FORTIER, SAMUEL. *Irrigation in Montana.* U.S. Department of Agriculture, Bulletin 172. Washington, 1906.

FRINK, MAURICE. *Cow Country Cavalcade.* Denver, 1957.

GARD, WAYNE. *Frontier Justice.* Norman, Okla., 1949.

A Hundred Years of Irrigation in Colorado. (A collection of papers celebrating the centennial of Colorado's first irrigating ditch.) Fort Collins, Colo., 1952.

JAMES, GEORGE WHARTON. *Reclaiming the Arid West.* New York, 1918.

JENKS, CAMERON. *The Development of Government Forest Control in the United States.* Baltimore, 1928.

LACHAPELLE, E. R. "Recent Progress in North American Avalanche Forecasting and Control," *Journal of Glaciology,* III.

————. "Report," January, 1964, on avalance control at Alta, Utah.

McLAIRD, JAMES DAVID. *George T. Beck: Western Entrepreneur.* Unpublished M.A. thesis, University of Wyoming, 1966.

"Men, Sheep and 100 Years," *National Wool Grower,* January, 1965.

MERRIAM, LAURENCE C. JR. *A Land Use Study of the Bob Marshall Wilderness Area of Montana.* Missoula, 1963.

OSGOOD, E. S. *The Day of the Cattleman.* Minneapolis, 1929.

Outdoor Recreation in the National Forests. Agriculture Information Bulletin 301. Washington, 1965.

PEFFER, LOUISE. *The Closing of the Public Domain.* Stanford, Calif., 1951.

PINCHOT, GIFFORD. *Breaking New Ground.* New York, 1947.

RICHARDSON, ELMO. *The Politics of Conservation.* Berkeley, Calif., 1962.

ROLLINS, GEORGE W. *The Struggle of the Cattleman, Sheepman and Settler for the Control of the Lands of Wyoming, 1867–1910.* Unpublished doctoral dissertation, University of Utah, 1951.

RUSSELL, DON. *The Lives and Legends of Buffalo Bill.* Norman, Okla., 1960.

SELL, HENRY B., and VICTOR WEYBRIGHT. *Buffalo Bill and the Wild West.* New York, 1955.

Snow Avalanches. U.S. Department of Agriculture, Handbook 194. Washington, January, 1961.

SPENCER, BETTY G. *The Big Blowup* [Idaho forest fires]. Caldwell, Idaho, 1956.

STEINEL, ALVIN H. *History of Agriculture in Colorado.* Fort Collins, Colo., 1926.

Water Resources of Montana and Their Use. Montana Agricultural Experiment Station, Special Report 8. Bozeman, 1941.

WENTWORTH, EDWARD N. *America's Sheep Trails.* Ames, Iowa, 1948.

————. "Sheep Wars of the Nineties in Northwest Colorado," *Brand Book* of the Denver Westerners, II (1946).

The Western Range. Senate Document 199, 74th Congress, 2nd Session. Washington, 1936.

ZON, RAPHAEL. *Forests and Water in the Light of Scientific Investigation.* Senate Document 469, 62nd Congress, 2nd Session. Washington, 1927.

INDEX

Abnaki Indians, 59
Absaroka Mountains, 66, 338
Accidents, 92
Acoma, 19, 26, 30
Adams, Charles, 256
Adams, Steve, 322*n.*
Adams-Onís treaty, 74, 83
Agriculture (*see* Farmers and farming)
Alamosa, 252, 263, 265
Alaska, 34–35, 40
Albuquerque, 30, 337
Alcanfor, 21
Alcohol (*see* Drinking)
Alder Gulch, Montana, 163*n.*, 172–174,
    183–185, 188, 202
Alexander, Colonel Edmund, 124
Alice mine, 249
Allemand, Joe, 344–345
Allen, Henry, 139–141, 145
Alma, Colorado, 250
Alta, Utah, 357, 360
Altitude, 8, 14
Alvarado, Hernando de, 19–21
Amalgamated Copper Company, 326–
    329
Ambush, 92–93, 111
American Federation of Labor, 322
American Fork, 168–171, 175
American Fur Company, 63, 88–89
American Revolution, 38
Ames, Colorado, 5–6
Anaconda, Montana, 327
Anaconda mine, 276, 281, 284–286, 326,
    328*n.*
Anderson, Rezin, 167
Angus, Red, 334
Anian, Strait of, 24–26
Anza, Juan Bautista de, 35, 37–38
Apaches, 28, 31, 37–39, 50, 96, 112,
    118–119, 212
Apex law, 250, 325, 328–329
Arapahoe Indians, 72–73, 76, 92, 119,
    132, 153, 198, 212, 253–254
Arikara Indians, 66, 77, 81, 92
Arizona, 20, 25, 27, 37
Arkansas, 31

Arkansas River, 10, 12, 37, 39, 50–54,
    75–76, 96, 102, 129–130, 152, 258,
    264, 355
Armijo, Manuel, 96, 227
Arrowsmith, Aaron, 41
Arthur, Chester A., 267
Artists, 295, 358
Ashley, William, 77, 82, 84–87, 89
Aspen, Colorado, 272–273, 357
Assiniboine River, 32
Astor, John Jacob, 63, 69–71
Astoria, 69–70, 78
Atchison, Topeka, & Santa Fe, 229, 236,
    251–252, 262–263, 265, 268, 273
Athabasca Pass, 70
Athabasca River, 70
Atkinson, Fort, 78, 80, 82
Atrocities, 82, 256
Auctions and auctioneers, 190
Ault, John, 171–172
Auraria, Colorado, 133–134, 137, 146,
    153
Australia mine, 250
Automation, 353
Automobiles, 10, 356, 360
Avalanches, 9, 360–361

Baboon Gulch, 160
Baca, Marcelino, 118
Baggs, Charles S., 199
Baird, James, 72
Baker's Park, 250–251
Balls and dances, 300, 306
Bancroft, Hubert Howe, 161
Banff Park, 59
Banker, Isaac Alexander, 216
Banks, 180, 311, 349
Bannack City, 171–172, 174, 176, 178,
    181–184, 192–193, 197–199, 201,
    209
Bannock Indians, 67, 92, 112, 117–118,
    126–127, 161–162, 166, 211, 274
Barclay, Alexander, 95–96
Baring Brothers, 324
Barney, Libeus, 180
Bartolomé, 16–18

Baxter, Mr., 247
Bear, 76, 92
Bear Lake, 90
Bear River City, 217
Bear River Mountains, 124
Beaubien-Miranda grant, 227
Beaver, 3, 46, 48, 55, 59, 66, 74–75, 79,
    82–83, 87–89, 91–92
Beaver Dick, 164
Beaverhead channel, 44
Beaverhead River, 79, 167
Beaverhead Valley, 98, 166
Beck, Ezekiel, 130, 133
Beck, George Washington Thornton,
    338–339
Beck, John, 129–130
Becknell, William, 77
Beef, 180, 221, 331
Bell, Captain John, 75
Bell, General Sherman, 319–320
Bell, William, 202, 233, 252, 271
Bennett, Horace, 294–295
Bent, Charles, 96
Benton, Fort, 168–169, 179, 214
Benton, Thomas Hart, 107
Bent's Fort, 96
Berthoud, Edward, 218
Berthoud Pass, 218
Big Belt Mountains, 43
Big Hole Valley, 47
Big Horn Basin, 13, 67, 339, 344
Big Horn Mountains, 12, 33, 59, 67, 69,
    176, 213, 280
Big Horn River, 12, 66, 77
Bigelow, A. S., 325
Billings, Frederick, 274, 278
Bimetallism, 193
Bingham Canyon, 163, 297, 352–353
Bishop, 19–21
Bismarck, North Dakota, 253
Bissonette, Joe, 74
Bitterroot Mountains, 157
Bitterroot Valley, 46–47, 98, 255
Black Bear mine, 361
Black Canyon, 11, 111
Black Hawk, 199
Black Hawk, Colorado, 244–245
Black Hills, 33, 253–254, 275
Blackfeet, the, 44, 48, 58, 60–61, 64–65,
    67–69, 72, 76–78, 80–81, 85, 92–93,
    98–99, 166, 182, 214
Blackmore, William, 228–229, 233, 235–
    236, 252
Black's Fork, 94–95, 124, 126
Blake, William, quoted, 14
Blanca Peak, 118
Bland-Allison Act, 287
Blizzards, 13, 84, 88, 124, 130, 141, 152,
    280, 331–332

Blue, Mr., 137
Blue River, 151, 153
Bob Marshall Wilderness, 363
Boise, Fort, 162
Boise, Idaho, 321
Boise Basin, 161–162
Boise City, 207–208
Bonanzas, 140, 156–173
Bonner, E. L., 279, 284–285
Borah, William E., 316, 321, 333
Boreas Pass, 151, 270–271
Boston and Colorado Smelting Company,
    243, 246, 249
Boston group, 326–328
Boston & Montana Consolidated Copper
    & Silver Mining Company, 280, 304,
    324–326
Boswell, N. K., 282
Boulder, Colorado, 135, 137n., 195
Bourdon, Michel, 69, 80
Bourgomont, Etienne de, 31
Bowers, Frank, 313–314
Bowles, Samuel, 224, 250
Box houses, 300
Boxing, 190
Boyd, David, 237, 335–336
Bozeman, John M., 175–177, 214
Bozeman, Montana, 193
Bozeman Pass, 47, 66, 176, 214
Bozeman Trail, 178–179, 213, 215
Braba, 19
Brannan, Charles, 360
Brayer, Herbert O., 241n.
Breckenridge, Colorado, 151
Breed, A. D., 245–247
Bribery, 327
Bridal Veil Falls, 6
Bridger, Fort, 94, 102, 109–110, 115–116,
    124, 127n., 177, 217
Bridger, Jim, 89, 92, 95, 109, 115–117,
    121, 124, 177, 218
Bridger Pass, 109–110
Brigham Young Express and Carrying
    Company, 59, 122–123
Brink, Herbert, 345
British (see English)
Bross, Mount, 249–250
Bross, William, 250
Broughton, Lieutenant William, 40
Brown, Abner, 195
Brown, James S., 117, 127n.
Browne, J. Ross, 186
Bryan, Electra, 182–183, 202
Buchanan, James, 121–123, 126
Buche, Baptiste, 69
Buena Vista, Colorado, 269–270
Buffalo, 15, 17, 21, 31, 38, 67
Buffalo hides, 28, 42, 94
Buffum, B. C., 335n.

Bull Hill, 312–314
Bull pens, 310, 316
Bullwhackers, 195
Bunker Hill & Sullivan mine, 292, 310, 315–316
Burchett, B. B., 170, 172
Burr, Aaron, 51
Butte, Montana, 4, 248, 276–287, 300–301, 303–304, 308, 311, 323–325, 328, 352
Butte & Boston Consolidated Mining Company, 280
Byers, William Newton, 136–138, 140–141, 145–146, 148, 153, 187, 199, 229–230, 237

Cabaza de Vaca, 17
Cableways, 7
Cache la Poudre River, 237
Cafferal, Pierre, 344–345
Calderwood, John, 312
Calhoun, Secretary of War, 74
California, 24, 27, 30–36, 94, 97, 101, 106, 112, 123, 130, 134, 142–143, 173, 220–221, 225, 240
   gold discovered in, 104, 109
   Gulf of, 23, 32, 35
California Gulch, 152–153, 253, 258–259, 263
Calumet & Hecla, 279–281, 286
Cameahwait, Chief, 44–46
Cameron, Robert A., 231–232, 234, 237
Camp Bird mine, 262, 296n., 351
Campbell, J. S., 174
Campbell, John, 218
Campbell, Robert, 89
Camping, 361–362
Canada, 13, 32, 34, 324
Canadian Pacific, 324–325
Canadian River, 51
Canadian Rockies, 58
Canal Gulch, 158
Canals, 338–339
Cannons, 26
Canoes, 32, 46–47, 62, 66
Canon City, Colorado, 53, 153, 235, 252, 262, 264
Canon City & San Juan Railway, 252–253, 262, 264
Canten, John, 291
Cantrell, John, 133
Canyon Creek, 291
Canyons, 10, 12, 46, 69, 85, 109, 161, 164–165, 222, 247
Cape Horn, 41, 69, 104
Capital, 321
   labor and, 306–307
Carbonate Hill, 263, 265
Cardenas, García López de, 19, 21–22

Carey, Joseph M., 337
Carey Act, 337–339
Caribou, Colorado, 209
Caribou mine, 245–248
Carleton, General James, 211
Carlton, A. E., 329n.
Carnotite ores, 352
Carrington, Colonel Henry B., 213
Carson, Kit, 119, 212
Carter, George, 299
Carter, Thomas H., 285, 326–327, 342
Cartographers, 23–24, 33, 36, 51
Cascade Mountains, 49
Casey, Pat, 218
Caso Calvo, Marqués de, 49
Casto, Kendall & Company, 148
Cataldo, Father Joseph M., 254
Catholics and Catholicism, 35, 87, 97, 117, 120, 196, 212, 254
Cattle, 7, 18, 25, 36, 96, 122, 127, 150, 161, 166–167, 175, 180–181, 184–185, 228, 232–233, 329–333, 342, 344
   (See also Beef)
Cattlemen (see Ranchers)
Caven, J. B., 183
Cavendish, Thomas, 24
Central City, Colorado, 4, 145, 187, 242–243, 301–302, 358
Central Overland California & Pikes Peak Express Company, 218
Central Pacific Railroad, 215n., 216, 222, 272
Cerro Summit, 11
Chaffee, Jerome, 228, 246, 266–267
Chama River, 26, 28, 36
Chambers, Samuel, 72
Champlain, Jean Baptiste, 72–73
Chapman, Arthur, quoted, 14
Chapuis, Jean, 34
Charbonneau, Toussaint, 42, 46, 73n.
Charlot, Chief, 255
Chemical fumes, 304
Cherokee Indians, 129–131, 133
Cherry Creek, 125, 129, 135, 141, 146, 212, 225
Cheyenne, Wyoming, 215–217, 220–221
Cheyennes, the, 76, 130–131, 176, 191, 212–213, 253
Cheyne, James, 316
Chicago Creek, 140
Chihuahua, 49–50, 74
Chihuahua Indians, 24
Chinese miners, 209
Chinooks, 13
Chisholm, Robert, 247
Chivington, John M., 155, 212–213
Chouteau, Auguste P., 73–74, 77–78, 87
Chouteau, Pierre, Jr., 93

Christianity, 18–20, 25, 27
  (*See also* Churches; Missionaries)
Chrysolite mine, 266–268, 308
Churches, 153, 196, 217
Cíbola, 16, 18–19, 23
Cicúique, 15, 18
Cincinnati, 75
Citizens Alliances, 319–320
Civil War, 155, 208–212, 218
Claims, 140, 171, 183, 209, 259, 261, 277,
    288–290, 294, 297, 323, 342, 348
  jumping of, 144, 172
  size of, 143–144, 146–147, 152, 259,
    329–330
Clamorgan, Jacques, 39, 72
Clancy, William, 325–326, 328
Clark, J. Max, 237
Clark, Rufus, 149
Clark, Lieutenant William, 41–43, 45–47,
    52, 55, 59, 65, 67, 89, 176n.
Clark, William Andrews, 248–249, 276–
    277, 280, 284–285, 326–327
Clark Fork, 63
Clark Fork River, 63–64, 164
Clay, John, 334
Clear Creek, 129, 139, 141–142, 145–146,
    153, 244, 293
Clearwater River, 157–159
Cleveland, Grover, 283, 341
Cleveland, Jack, 181–182
Cleveland, Mount, 18
Climate, 20, 355
Clyman, James, 82, 92
Cochetopa National Forest, 346
Cochetopa Pass, 111, 124
Cody, Buffalo Bill, 13, 338–339
Cody, Lulu, 338–339
Cody, Wyoming, 67–68, 339
Coeur d'Alene, Idaho, 287, 289, 307, 309,
    311, 316, 321, 352–353
Coeur d'Alene Lake, 168–169
Coeur d'Alene Mountains, 288
Coeur d'Alene River, 289–293
Cog railroad, 294–295
Colfax, New Mexico, 226
Colfax, Schuyler, 226, 249
Collbran, Colorado, 333
Collins, Arthur, 317–318
Collins, Fort, 237
Colorado, 1, 3–5, 7–10, 12–14, 26, 31, 33,
    38, 50, 53, 72–73, 87, 94–96, 109,
    118n., 119, 139–155, 173, 178, 185–
    206, 209, 212–213, 218–220, 224–
    225, 229–230, 239–246, 255–256,
    268–269, 282, 287n., 293, 299–301,
    311–312, 317–318, 330, 335–336,
    341–342, 346, 354, 356–357

Colorado Canal, Irrigation & Land Com-
    pany, 238–239
Colorado Central Railroad, 221
Colorado City, 153
Colorado Doctrine, 240
Colorado Midland Railroad, 272
Colorado River, 13, 23, 26, 36, 355
Colorado Rockies, 72, 88, 96, 107
Colorado & Southern Railroad, 351
Colorado Springs, 74, 131, 235, 272, 293,
    313–314
Colorado Springs Company, 234
Colter, John, 65, 68, 176n.
Columbia, Lake, 61
Columbia Fur Company, 78, 88
Columbia River, 40–42, 58, 60, 62–64,
    69–71, 158
Colville, Washington, 120
Comancheros, 32–33
Comanches, the, 31, 33–34, 37–39, 58,
    76, 89n., 92
Communications, 17, 41, 162, 201
Comstock Lode, 219
Concentrators, 261
Conejos, the, 54–55
Confederacy, the, 128, 155
Confederate armies, 208, 212
Confederate Gulch, 173
Connah, Fort, 97
Connor, Patrick Edward, 162–163, 211
Conservation and conservationists, 281,
    341–342, 363
Consolidated Ditch Company, 150
Continental Divide, 10–12, 19, 23, 38, 40,
    45–46, 59–61, 63, 69, 79, 107, 111,
    124, 137n., 145, 216, 218, 270–272,
    354
Cooke, Jay, 248, 258
Cooper, J. T., 292
Copper, 3, 243–244, 249, 276–287, 297–
    298, 324, 352–353
Corcoran, Paul, 316
Cornet Falls, 6
Coronado, Francisco Vásquez de, 14, 16,
    18–23, 25
Costilla Estate, 228, 235–236
Cotton, 17, 20, 25
Courtin, Charles, 65–67
Cover, Thomas, 214
Cowboys, 2, 14, 167, 331, 333–334, 345
Crawford, Henry, 181–183
Creuzefeldt, Frederick, 111
Crimes of passion, 199
Criminal codes, 143n., 147
Cripple Creek, Colorado, 3, 53, 287,
    293–298, 301–302, 312, 318, 358
Crow Indians, 67–68, 72, 80, 82, 84, 88,
    176
Cuerno Verde, Chief, 37–38

Cumbres Pass, 271
Cumming, Alfred, 122–123, 128
Cummings, Alexander, 219
Custer, General George Armstrong, 253

Dale, Matthew, 189, 197, 202
Daly, Marcus, 248–249, 276–281, 284–286, 308, 326–327
Dance halls, 189–190
Daniels, James, 210–211
Darrow, Clarence, 321
David Crockett, Fort, 94
Davis, Diamondfield Jack, 332–333
Davis, Jefferson, 110
Davitt, Michael, 324–325
Dawson, Lewis, 76
Day, David, 303, 306
DeCoursey, M. L., 302
Deep Springs school, 6
Deer, 47, 54, 60, 62
Deer Lodge, 181, 185
Deer Lodge Valley, 164, 166–167, 169
Defrees & Company, 148
d'Eglise, Jacques, 39, 49–50
De la Harpe, Bénard, 31
Delaware Indians, 111
Delta, Colorado, 95
DeMar, Joseph, 296–298
Democrats, 209–211, 214, 217, 284–285, 326
Dempsey, Robert, 166, 168
DeMun, Jules, 73–74, 78
Denver, 10, 133, 135–137, 149, 153–155, 193, 212–213, 218–220, 225, 229, 265, 299, 311–313, 339, 351, 355–356
Denver, James W., 135
Denver Pacific, 221, 230–231
Denver & Rio Grande, 229, 233–236, 251–253, 262–265, 268–273, 301, 350–351, 354, 356–357
Denver, South Park, & Pacific, 262, 268–271
Depressions, 74–75, 77, 134–135, 191, 331, 341, 351
De Smet, Pierre Jean, 97–98
Desert Land Act of 1877, 329
Deserts, 13, 37, 85, 111, 352
Dickson, Joseph, 65–66
Dillingham, D. H., 183
Dillon, Sidney, 274
Dinosaur National Monument, 85
Discovery claims, 289
Division points, 215–216
Dixon, Montana, 65
Dodge, Captain Francis S., 256
Dogs, 20–21, 62, 76, 188
Dolores River, 12, 36

Dominguez, Fray Francisco Atanasio, 36
Doyle, J. B., 195
Doyle, Joseph, 95–96, 135
Dragoons, 96
Drake, Francis, 24
Drinking, 70, 85, 90–91, 96, 185
Drips, Andrew, 88
Drought, 38, 122, 280, 331
Drouillard, George, 43–45, 65, 67–68
Du Tisné, Claude, 31
DuBois, Wyoming, 69
Dude ranches, 357
Durango, Colorado, 301, 350, 357–358
Durocher, Laurent, 49–50
Dyer, Elias, 205
Dyer, John L., 196–197, 205

Earthquakes, 9
East, the, 59, 90, 227, 329–330, 340
Easter, John, 131
Echo Canyon, 124
Eddy, R. A., 279, 284–285
Edgerton, Sidney, 201–203, 209–210
Education, 196n., 354
   (See also Schools)
El Moro, Colorado, 252, 262–263
El Paso, New Mexico, 26, 29
El Paso lode, 294, 296
Elbert, Mount, 243
Electricity, 4–6, 277
Elizabethtown, 228
Elk City, 159–161, 178–179
Emge, Joe, 344–345
Emigrant trains, 97, 99
Emigration Canyon, 102
Emma mine, 247–248
Engages, 57–58, 60, 65, 79, 88
Engineering, 20, 112
England, 24, 27, 34, 38, 40, 97
English, the, 34, 48, 73, 78, 82–83, 85, 89, 296, 324
Erosion, 8, 350
Escalante, Fray Silvestre Vélez de, 35
Espéjo, Antonio de, 25, 27
Esteban, 16–17
Evans, John, 155, 212, 220, 269
Evans, Mount, 151
Evolution lode, 288–289, 293
Explorers, 3, 6, 224

Fall Leaf, 131
"Fandango Dollars," 312
Farlin, William, 249
Farmers and farming, 3, 20, 26, 38, 99, 182, 204, 221, 224, 230, 232, 255, 283, 335, 342
Farnham, Thomas, 95
Farrell, Seth, 157
Fauntleroy, Colonel Thomas, 119

Ferryboats, 115, 121
Fetterman, Captain W. J., 213
Feuds, 204, 208, 219
Feuilli, Luis, 34
Ficklin, B. F., 127
Fidler, Peter, 41
Finlay, François, 167
Finlay, Jacques Raphael, 59, 63
Fire departments, 302–303, 305, 313
Fire prevention, 358
Fires, 302–303, 305, 355
　(*See also* Forest fires)
Fish and fishing, 11, 47, 60, 188, 275, 357, 361–362
Fisk, Captain James, 171
Fitzpatrick, Thomas, 82, 89, 98
Flathead Indians, 46, 48, 58, 60, 62, 64–71, 80, 97–98, 255
Flathead Lake, 88
Flathead Post, 79, 82
Floods, 355
Florence, Idaho, 160–161, 163–164, 169, 174
Floyd, John B., 122
Fontenelle, Lucien, 88
Ford, A. C., 199
Forest fires, 188, 255, 340, 345–346, 358–359
Forest Lieu Act of 1897, 342
Forest rangers, 346, 358–359
Forest Reserves, 341–342, 346
　(*See also* National Forests)
Forest Service, 344–345, 353, 359–361, 363
Forests, 8, 187–188, 216, 281–284, 329, 340–344
　(*See also* Lumber; Timber; Wood)
Fortier, Samuel, 336
40th parallel, 137*n.*, 154
Fortin, Casé, 68
Forts, 89, 94–97, 124
Fountain City, 136, 153
Fountain Colony, 234
Fountain Creek, 54
Fourth of July celebrations, 1–3, 305
Fowler, Jacob, 75–76, 91
Frael, Henry, 89
France, 3, 27, 31, 41
　(*See also* French)
Franciscan fathers, 27–30
Franck, Long John, 199–200
Fraser, Simon, 63*n.*, 64
Fraternal organizations, 194, 200
Free Timber Act, 283
Freeman, 79–81, 84–85
Freight companies, 178
Frémont, John Charles, 100, 107–108, 111–112, 122
Fremont Pass, 271

French, the, 31–34, 49–50, 281, 286
Freyer, George, 266
Frodsham, Mr., 304–305
Front Range, 53, 72, 74, 84, 102
Fuller, Oliver, 111–112
Fur traders and fur trade, 12, 32, 34, 42, 56–58, 61, 69, 74, 89–90
Furniss, Norman F., 122, 127*n.*
Furs, 41, 45–48, 58–59, 62–66, 68–69, 73, 77–78, 80, 83–84, 90, 93–94
　(*See also* Trappers)

Gallegher brothers, 262
Gamblers and gambling, 135, 150, 189–190, 300, 302
Gardner, Johnson, 83–84
Garfield, James, 255
Garland, Fort, 118*n.*, 132, 134
Garland City, 252, 262
Gas Creek, 204–205
Gem mine, 309–310
Gemmell, Robert, 297–298
General Land Revision bill, 341
Genoa, Nevada, 123
Georgetown, Colorado, 244, 260, 312
Georgia, 129, 133, 140, 146, 225–226
Georgia Colony, 225
German Colonizing Society, 225–226
Gervais, Jean Baptiste, 89
Gervais, Joseph, 49
Gibbs, Elijah, 204–205
Gila River, 20
Gila Valley, 37
Gila Wilderness Area, 362
Gillett, Mr., 289
Gilpin, William, 154–155, 224, 227–228, 231, 235–236, 242, 252
Gilson, H. C., 208
Glacier National Park, 8, 69, 70*n.*
Glenn, Hugh, 75–76
Glenrock, Wyoming, 176
Gobacks, 138–139, 145–146, 148
Goetz, Dutch Jake, 292
Goetzmann, William, 65*n.*
Gold, 3–4, 21–22, 24–27, 123, 125, 138, 141, 151, 160, 162–165, 169–173, 175, 209, 217–219, 242, 244, 258–259, 276, 286–289, 293, 295, 312, 315, 351
　discovery of, 14, 50, 104, 109, 132–134, 140, 145, 156, 228
　free, 186
　panning of, 148
　placer, 143, 146, 150, 173, 176, 291
Gold King mine, 4–5, 296
Gold rushes, 6, 50, 104, 112, 129–138, 200
Golden, Colorado, 139, 153, 203, 220
Golden, Tom, 139–140

Goldrick, Owen J., 195
Goodale, Tim, 124
Goodnight, Charles, 221
Gould, Jay, 268–269, 274–275
Grand Canyon, 19, 21, 35–36, 55
Grand Junction, Colorado, 124
Granite, Colorado, 205
Grannis, John P., 294
Grant, "Baron," 247
Grant, John, 167–168, 185
Grant, Richard, 167–168
Grant, Ulysses S., 238, 246
Gray, Robert, 40
Grazing, 227, 230, 342–344, 346, 364
Great Falls, 47
Great Lakes, 57, 63, 261, 280, 282, 343
Great Salt Lake, 36–37, 81, 100, 102
Greeley, Colorado, 230, 232–233, 237–238
Greeley, Horace, 146–148, 150, 198, 224, 231
Green, Mrs. A. M., 233
Green River, 12, 36, 81–82, 84, 94, 98, 115
Green River, Utah, 271
Green River Valley, 13, 87, 90, 114, 332
Greenhorn Mountain, 38–39, 118
Gregory, John H., 141–142, 145–146
Gregory Gulch, 141, 144–145, 147–148, 151, 187–188, 218–219, 243
Gros Ventres Indians, 90, 92
Grubstakes, 292, 294
Guadalupe, Colorado, 119
Guadalupe Hidalgo, treaty of, 97, 227
Guggenheims, the, 268–269, 297, 311
Guidebooks, 136–137, 175
Gunnison, Colorado, 269–270, 299
Gunnison, Lieutenant John, 109, 111
Gunnison River, 10–11, 111, 269
Guns, 28, 32, 44–45, 48
Guzmán, Chief, 17

Hagerman, James J., 295
Hagerman, John J., 272–273
Haggin, James Ben Ali, 248, 276–277, 281, 286
Hall, Fort, 89, 109
Hall, Frank, 191, 193, 219–220, 308
Halleck, Fort, 162
Hamlin, Jacob, 127n.
Hammond, A. B., 279, 284–285
Hammond, John Hays, 292, 297
Hamp, Sidford, 241n.
Hancock, Forest, 65–66
Hanging, 198–199, 202–204, 211, 304, 322, 333
Hanna, Mark, 285n., 328
Hannum, Elizabeth, 362
Harney, Edward, 326, 328

Harriman, E. H., 275
Harrington, Mr., 204
Harrison, Benjamin, 341
Harrison, Charles, 199n.
Harrison, Edwin, 262–263
Hartsel, Sam, 149, 180
Hauser, S. T., 175n., 201
Háwikuh, 16–18
Hayden, Ferdinand Vandeveer, 228, 240, 293
Haywood, Big Bill, 317, 321–322
Head, Lafayette, 119
Health, 189
  (See also Sanitation; Sickness)
Healy, John J., 158–159, 164–165
Hearst, George, 248, 276–277
Hearst, Phoebe, 339
Heinze, Arthur, 324, 328
Heinze, Frederick Augustus, 323–329
Helena, Montana, 172, 174, 204, 211, 302, 327, 358
Helmer, Charles, 344–345
Henry, Alexander, 69–70
Henry, Andrew, 68, 77, 82, 84
Henry's Fork, 68–69
Hercules mine, 315, 317
Hereford, Robert, 166–167
Heyburn, Senator, 345
Hilderman, Gus, 199
Hill, Joe, 322
Hill, Nathaniel Peter, 154, 191, 199, 242–244, 246, 249–250, 267
Hoback, John, 68–69
Hollister, Ovando, 187
Holmes, James, 131–132, 136n.
Holmes, Julia Archibald, 131–132, 136n.
Homestake mine, 276
Homestead Act of 1862, 142, 144, 281
Homesteads and homesteaders, 231, 234, 283–284, 329–331, 333, 342
Hood, Mount, 40, 42
Hook, George, 266
Hoosier Pass, 151
Horses, 15, 21, 28, 31–32, 43–46, 48, 58, 60, 62, 73, 76, 85, 92, 125, 180
Horsethief Trail, 365–366
Horsley, Albert, 321
Hosmer, H. L., 203–204
Hospitals, 194–195
Hot springs, 140, 166, 301–302
Hot Sulphur Springs, 256, 356
Hotels, 188, 301
Hough, the Rev. A. M., 196
Howard, Colonel O. O., 254–255
Howbert, Irving, 234
Howse, Joseph, 63–64, 70n.
Hudson's Bay Company, 41, 59, 70n., 71, 79, 82–85, 88–89, 97
Huerfano Creek, 73, 225–226, 252

Huff, a cowboy, 9
Humboldt, Alexander von, 51, 54–55
Hungate family, 190
Hunt, Alexander Cameron, 191, 193, 198, 212, 234, 250, 252
Hunt, Ellen Kellogg, 191–193
Hunt, Wilson Price, 69, 79
Hunters and hunting, 3, 15, 65, 78, 88, 275, 338, 356–357
Hutton, Levi, 315–317

Idaho, 4, 12–14, 67–69, 79, 82, 85, 98, 109, 112, 117, 156, 165, 178, 187, 200–201, 203, 207–209, 254, 274–277, 288–290, 310, 316–317, 330–333, 335, 340, 345, 352–353, 357, 363
Idaho City, 162
Idaho Rockies, 160
Idaho Springs, 140, 319–320
Iliff, John, 180, 221
Illinois, 31–33, 76, 99
Immell, Michael, 77, 81
Imogene Pass, 317, 352
Indian agents, 112, 121, 157
Indian raids, 28, 118, 255
Indian runners, 15, 18
Indian Territory (see Oklahoma)
Indian Wars, 92, 96–97, 109, 114–128, 168, 207, 211–214, 219
Indians, 1, 11, 15–22, 24–34, 37–39, 42, 108, 114–115, 127, 154, 194, 253–254
   and fur trade, 57–71, 88–89, 92–93
   and prospectors, 161–162, 172, 176, 178, 190
   and settlers, 111–113, 253
   (See also Reservations; names of tribes)
Industrial Workers of the World, 322
Inflation, 287, 312
Iowa, 100, 105
Iron Hill, 261, 263, 265
Iron Mining Company, 262
Iroquois Indians, 59, 78, 80, 93, 97
Irrigation, 3, 7, 20, 26, 105, 119, 224, 227, 229–230, 232, 237–239, 330, 335n., 336–338
Irrigation Congresses, 237–238, 337–338
Irving, Washington, quoted, 90
Ives, George, 199–200

Jackling, Daniel C., 297–298
Jackson, David, 85–86
Jackson, Donald, 52
Jackson, George A., 139–142, 145
Jackson, William Henry, 240–241
Jackson Hole, 358
Jacobs, John, 166, 175, 177
James, Edwin, 74–75

James, Thomas, 67–68, 75–77
Janise, Antoine, 136
Jaramillo, Juan de, 19
Jasper National Park, 70
Jefferson, state of, 146, 153
Jefferson, Thomas, 41, 51
Jefferson River, 44, 47, 67
Jefferson Territory, 154
Jennings, Montana, 62
Jesuits, 120, 254–255, 290
Johnson, Andrew, 219
Johnson, Harry, 361
Johnson, Lyndon B., 364
Johnston, Colonel Albert S., 123–126, 128
Jones, Robert, 77, 81
Joseph Chief, 254
Josephy, Alvin M., Jr., 65n.
Jupes, the, 38
Juries and jury trials, 200, 202, 204–205, 210, 218

Kane, Thomas L., 126, 128
Kansas, 31, 39, 50, 85, 122–123, 134, 137, 145–146, 154
Kansas Pacific, 219–221, 225, 228–230
Kaskaskia, Illinois, 49, 65
Kearny, General Stephen, 107
Kelley's Bar, 152
Kellogg, Colorado, 316
Kellogg, Noah, 292
Kern, Benjamin and Dick, 108, 111
Kern, Edward, 108
Ketcham, Idaho, 356
Kimball, Heber, 101
Kinna, John, 135
Kiowa, Fort, 182
Kiowas, 50, 76
Kirkpatrick, James, 176–177
Kirkpatrick, Robert, 176–177, 180, 190, 202–203
Kirkpatrick family, 176–177
Kivas, 16, 30
Knights of Labor, 308
Knowles, Hiram, 325
Kohrs, Carston Conrad, 181–185, 188
Kootenae House, 60, 62–63
Kootenai River, 62
Kottkey, Mrs., 345
Kroeber, Theodora, quoted, 1
Kutenai Indians, 58–61

La Glorieta Pass, 15, 21–22, 212
La Veta Pass, 252
Labor, 321
   capital and, 306–309
   of gold mining, 149
   non-union, 309–310, 315–316, 318, 320
   (See also Unions)
Lacépède, Count Bernard de, 41–42

Lacroix, Dionosio, 49–50
Land grants, 118, 227–229, 235–236, 284, 350
Landslides, 9, 339
Langford, Nathaniel P., 182n., 183, 185, 201, 240
Laramie, Fort, 101, 140, 214
Laramie City, 216, 218, 282
Laramie Plains, 110, 216
Larimer, General William, 135, 137
Laroque, François, 59
Last Chance Gulch, 172–173
Law, 105, 197, 201, 208, 217, 240, 304
    apex, 260, 325, 328–329
    land, 106, 259, 323, 329–330, 340
    martial, 236
    mining, 144
    unwritten, 323
    (See also Criminal codes)
Lawrence, D. H., 12
Lawton, Thomas, 326n.
Lazair, Jules, 344–345
Le Grand Coquin, Chief, 117
Lead, 3, 252, 291, 293, 352
Leadville, Colorado, 4, 53, 153, 253, 261, 263, 265–272, 300, 302, 304–305, 307–308, 311
LeClair, Michaud, 165
Leclerc, 78, 80–81
Lee, Abraham, 152
Lee, Edward, 210n.
Lee, Mabel Barber, 302–303
Legislatures, 208–211, 215, 217–218, 220, 336
Leiter, Levi, 261
LeLand, Baptiste, 49–50, 52
Lemhi Pass, 44, 117
Lemhi River, 46, 80, 117, 165, 192
Leopold, Aldo, 362
Leroux, Antoine, 108
Lewis, Captain Meriweather, 41–49, 52, 55, 59–60, 65–66
Lewiston, 158, 178, 201, 207–208
Lexington mine, 249
Libby, Montana, 62–63
Liberal League, 288–290
Liberty Bell mine, 360
Light, Fred, 344
Lincoln, Abraham, 154
Lincoln Back Country, 363–364
Lincoln Land Company, 339
Lisa, Manuel, 65–66, 68, 72–73, 75
Literary associations, 194, 217
Little, Frank, 322
Little Pittsburgh mine, 266–268
Lolo Pass, 47
Lolo Trail, 158, 255
London mine, 250
Long, Major Stephen, 74–75
Lookout Mountain, 340

Lott, Mortimer, 171
Louisiana, 31, 34, 39–41, 49, 51
Loveland, W. A. H., 220–221
Loving, Oliver, 180
Lumber, 216, 232, 279
    (See also Timber)
Lynching, 202, 217, 236, 304
Lyon, Caleb, 207–208
Lyon, Fort, 212–213
Lytle, George, 245

McDonald, Finan, 60, 62–63, 69–70, 80
McDonald, John, 59–60
McDonald, a miner, 232
McDonald, Scott, 291
Mackenzie, Alexander, 41–42, 58
McKenzie, Donald, 78–79
McKinley, William, 342
McKnight, John, 76–77
McKnight, Robert, 72, 76–77
McMains, Oscar P., 236
McMillan, James, 63, 92
MacNeill, Charles, 297
McRae, T. C., 341
Magruder, Lloyd, 178–179
Maguire, John, 301
Mallet, Peter and Paul, 33–34, 51
Mandan, Fort, 42–43
Mandan Indians, 32–33, 39, 42
Mandan villages, 49, 59, 61, 68
Manitou Springs, 235
Maps, 23–24, 36–38, 41, 51, 54, 67
Marcy, Captain Randolph B., 124–126
Marias Pass, 80
Marshall, John, 104
Martin, William, 245
Massachusetts, Fort, 118–119, 125
Massacres, 81, 88, 99, 119, 190, 213
Masterson, Bat, 236
Matchless mine, 266–267
Maxwell, Lucien Bonaparte, 227–228
Maxwell Land Grant Company, 228–229, 235–236
Mead, Elwood, 340
Meagher, Thomas Francis, 210–211, 214
Mears, Otto, 270
Medical services, 307, 309
Medicine men, 16, 28
Meeker, Nathan, 224–225, 229–232, 255–257
Meeks, Jake, 166–167
Melgares, Facundo, 50–51, 53, 55
Mellen, Mary, 233, 235
Mellen, William Proctor, 233
Menard, Pierre, 65
Mengarini, Father, 98–99
Mercury, 24, 129
Meredith, Emily, 191–193, 197
Meredith, Frederick, 191–193
Metoyer, Jeannot, 49

Mexicans, 87–88, 96, 132
Mexico, 23–24, 27–28, 97
Mexico City, 27–28, 33–34
Meyers, Augustus, 261–265
Middaugh, W. H., 198
Middleton, Robert, 131–132, 135, 153
Miera y Pachero, Bernardo, 36–37, 51
Militia, 114, 155, 308, 313, 320–321, 334
Miller, James Knox Polk, 162, 194, 214
Mine Owners' Association, 309
Mineral springs, 229, 234–235, 356
Miners, 2, 106, 120, 149, 155, 160–161,
   193, 197, 200, 202, 209, 342
   (See also Prospectors)
Mines and mining, 140, 159, 349–350,
   352–353
   labor of, 149
   lode, 3, 155, 173, 186, 259
   mass production in, 261
   placer, 3, 129, 143, 146, 150, 173, 209,
   228, 259
   silver, 245–249, 259, 266
Mining camps, 1, 6–7, 174, 185
   life in, 186–206
Mining Company Nederland, 246
Mining districts, 143, 145, 240
Minnetarees, the, 42–45
Miranda, Guadalupe, 227
Misery, Fort, 94–95
Missionaries, 35, 37, 97–99, 114, 116–
   118, 127, 157, 196, 254–255
Missions, 35, 97–98, 117, 120, 196
Missoula, Montana, 79, 98, 167
Missouri, 73–74, 77–78, 115, 134, 252
Missouri Fur Company, 65–66, 68, 73,
   77, 88
Missouri Pacific, 273n.
Missouri River, 12, 32–33, 35, 42–43, 49,
   60–61, 65–66, 68, 74, 78, 80, 88–89,
   98
Mitchell, William, 182
Mitchill, Samuel, 48
Moffat, David Halliday, 266–267, 354
Moffat Tunnel, 354–355
Molybdenum, 271n., 352
Monida Pass, 166, 276
Montana, 4, 8–9, 12–14, 62–63, 65, 70,
   79, 88, 92, 98, 126, 164, 166, 172–
   173, 175, 178–181, 185, 187, 194,
   199, 201, 203, 208–211, 213–214,
   240, 253, 255, 276–277, 280, 284–
   285, 287, 290, 326–327, 332, 336,
   343, 352, 356–357, 363
Montana Central, 286
Montana Improvement Company, 279,
   281, 284
Montana Ore Purchasing Company, 324
Montana Union, 278, 286
Moore, Augustus, 182

Moose mine, 248
Moqui Indians, 18, 20, 25, 30, 35–36,
   38
Mora, New Mexico, 96, 118
Moran, Thomas, 240
Morley, James, 169–172, 197
Morley, Julius, 169–172
Morley, W. R., 264
Mormon Trail, 109
Mormons, 99–106, 114–128, 162–163,
   166–167, 178, 221–223, 274–275
Morrison, William, 49–50, 52, 65
Morton, Sergeant William, 125
Mosquito Pass, 258, 268
Mosquito Range, 249–250, 262
Mountain House, 160
Moyer, Charles, 317, 320–322
Muir, John, 362
Mules, 7, 25, 108, 125, 179–180
Mullan, Lieutenant John, 111, 168–169
Mullan Pass, 111, 168–169
Mullan Road, 165, 168
"Multiple Use-Sustained Yield" bill, 361,
   363
Munson, Lyman, 210
Murat, Count Henri, 136
Murder, 197–200, 210, 236, 256–257,
   318, 321, 345–346
Murray, Idaho, 289, 291
Muskets, 31, 92, 214
Myers, Julius, 294–295

National Forests, 345–346, 355–356, 359
   (See also Forest Reserves)
National Land Company, 230
National Parks, 357n., 358, 361, 363
   (See also names of parks, as Yellow-
   stone)
National Wilderness Preservation System,
   364
National Wool Growers Association, 342,
   344
Natural resources, 142, 144, 239, 281,
   323, 350, 364
Navajos, 28, 38, 109, 112, 212
Nebraska, 31, 102, 134, 136, 137n., 145
Negroes, 18, 25, 43, 219, 316
Nettleton, E. S., 234
Nevada, 123, 332
Nevada City, 197, 199
New Mexico, 3, 8, 12, 14–15, 20, 23–25,
   27–35, 37, 51, 72–74, 76, 78, 87,
   96–97, 108–110, 112–113, 118–119,
   132, 136n., 145, 154–155, 196n., 211,
   228, 253, 264, 268, 355–356, 362
Newlands Act, 339
Nez Percé, Fort, 79
Nex Percé Indians, 45–49, 58, 60, 156–
   159, 161, 207–208, 254–255

Nez Percé Trail, 178, 181
North Dakota, 32, 42, 49, 59, 61, 253
North Park, 74, 84, 87
North Platte River, 12, 89, 102, 112
North West Company, 41, 57–59, 63–65, 70, 79
Northern Pacific, 253, 274, 278–279, 284, 290, 309, 343
Northwest, the, 35, 40, 97
Nunn, L. L., 4, 352
Nunn, Paul, 4–6

Oakes, D. C., 135
O'Connor, Patrick, 81
Ogden, Peter Skene, 81–83, 85
Ogden, Utah, 109–110, 222–223
Ogilvie, George, 163
O'Keeffe, Sergeant John Timothy, 241
Oklahoma, 31, 75, 129–130
Ollokot, Chief, 254
Olympia, Washington, 200–201
Omaha, 101, 136, 148
Oñate, Juan de, 25–27
Oquirrh Mountains, 163
Orator, the, 64
Orchard, Harry, 321
Oregon, 40, 49, 83, 88, 94, 97, 99, 112, 178, 274, 332
Oregon Short Line, 274–276
Oregon Trail, 79, 94–95, 97, 102, 166, 217
Orem, John C. (Con), 190
Oro City, 152, 258
Oro Fino Creek, 158–159
O'Rourke, Phil, 292
Otermín, Antonio de, 29–30
Ouray, Chief, 250, 256
Ouray, Colorado, 10, 303–304, 306, 320, 358
Outlaws, 181, 200, 236
Overland Trail, 125, 127, 177–178
Owen, John, 99, 111, 120, 127
Owen, William, 241n.
Oxen, 98, 124, 149, 166, 176, 179–180. 184, 192

Pabor, William E., 234, 237
Pacific Fur Company, 70
Pack horses, 33, 57, 79, 88
Pack trains, 89, 96, 160, 169
Pahvant Indians, 111
Painter, Charles F., 320
Paiutes, the, 162
Palladino, Father, 99
Palmer, William Jackson, 220, 225–226, 228–229, 231, 233–235, 248, 251–253, 258, 262–265, 269–272

Panic of 1873, 236, 248, 251, 253, 258, 329
Park City, Utah, 248, 302
Parkman, Francis, 96
Parks, Mr., 247
Parrish, Thomas, 295
Patterson, Joseph Decatur, 225–226
Pawnee Indians, 31, 50, 53, 78
Peabody, James Hamilton, 318
Pearce Richard, 244, 246, 250
Peck, O. O., 292
Pecos Indians, 15, 19
Pecos units, 13, 21
Pend d'Oreille Indians, 62, 98
Pend d'Oreille Lake, 63–64
Pennsylvania mine, 324, 326
Penrose, Boise, 296
Penrose, Spencer, 296–297
People's courts, 198–199, 202
Peralta, Pedro de, 27
Peterson, Joseph, 338
Pettibone, George, 322
Phil Kearny, Fort, 213
Philibert, Joseph, 73
Piegan Indians, 48, 57–61, 69–71
Pierce, Ed, 2
Pierce, Elias Davidson, 156–157
Pierce City, 158–159
Pierre's Hole, 90–91, 98
Pike, Lieutenant Zebulon, 50–55, 74–75
Pikes Peak, 4, 38, 52–53, 74, 131–132, 134, 241, 294
Pilcher, Joshua, 77, 88
Pinchot, Gifford, 344, 346
Pinheads, 5–6
Pizanthia, Joe, 203
Platte River, 31, 33, 53, 88, 110, 129
Plummer, Henry, 181–183, 200, 202–203
Pocatello, Idaho, 275
Police, 302, 305, 313
Politicians, 145, 153, 200–201, 207, 228
Polk, James K., 107
Polygamy, 121–122, 275
Pony Express, 153
Popé, 28–30
Populists, 311
Posses, 198, 202, 212, 265
Potts, John, 65, 68
Potts, Joshua and Martha, 225–226
Pourtales, Count Louis Otto de, 295
Powell, John Wesley, 329–330
Pratte, Bernard and Sylvester, 87
Present Help lode, 250
Price, Eliphalet, 241
Price, Mrs., 256
Prices, 286–287
Prichard, Andrew J., 288–293
Prospect Gulch, 288–289

Prospectors and prospecting 3, 6, 27, 133, 140–142, 150–151, 157, 159–163, 170–172, 174–175, 244, 248–249, 262, 266, 269, 291, 293–295, 300, 342, 352
(*See also* Miners)
Prostitutes and prostitution, 121, 300, 302, 333, 349
Protective League, 319–320
Protestants, 97, 157, 196
Provo, Utah, 81, 126, 128
Provost, Etienne, 78, 80–81, 83–85, 88
Prudhomme, Gabriel, 98
Pueblo, Colorado, 38–39, 73, 96, 102, 107, 118, 136, 195, 235, 265
Pueblo Indians, 15–22, 24, 28, 30–32, 96, 355
Puebloes, 19–21, 26, 30, 80–81
Pullman, George, 4
Purcell, James, 49–50

Quartz, 143, 149, 165, 288, 291, 295
Quivira, 21–23, 26

Radicals and radicalism, 286–287, 315, 322
Raiders, 323, 328
Railroads, 3–4, 106, 109–111, 168, 215–223, 225–236, 251–252, 258–270, 278–279, 296–298, 309, 311–312, 314, 324, 335, 339, 350
narrow-gauge, 5, 7, 10, 233, 251, 262, 301, 357
Rainy Lake House, 62
Ralston Creek, 130, 133
Ranchers and ranches, 3, 95, 118, 126, 150, 180–181, 184–185, 221, 293, 323, 329–335, 338–339, 343, 346, 350, 353, 359
Rankin, Joe, 256
Rarus mine, 324–325, 328
Raton Pass, 37, 251–252, 262–264
Real estate promoters, 133, 135, 196
Recreation, 356–357, 361–362
(*See also* Sports)
Red Mountain, 349n., 350, 353
Red River, 51–54, 75
Reed, Simeon, 292
Reed, Verner, 296
Reeves, Charlie, 181–182
Refractory minerals, 186–187, 191
Regulators, the, 334
Remington, Frederic, 358
Rendezvous, 90, 94
Republicans, 122, 154, 201, 207–211, 217, 239, 266, 284–285, 315, 318, 326–327
Reservations, 120, 161, 250, 257
Reservoirs, 6, 11, 302, 337, 340, 355

Reynolds, James and John, 212
Rezner, Jacob, 68–69
Richardson, Albert D., 146–148
Rio Grande, the, 19–20, 22–23, 26, 54, 77, 107–108, 145
Rio Grande Southern, 5, 350–351
Rio Grande Valley, 15, 20, 263
Rio Grande Western, 271–273
Rische, August, 266
Robert E. Lee mine, 217
Robertson, John, 91, 93, 95
Robidoux, Antoine, 87, 95
Robinson, Edward, 68–69
Robinson, John Hamilton, 52–54
Rockefeller, William 326n.
Rockies, the, central, 55–56, 107, 110–111, 145, 218, 225, 235
exploitation of, 86
geography of, 9–13, 38
northern, 33, 58, 79–80, 88, 110, 120, 156, 203
southern, 38, 52, 78, 87, 89, 94, 119, 225, 229, 354
western, 58
Rocky Mountain Fur Company, 89
Rocky Mountain House, 57–59, 69–70
Rocky Mountain National Park, 36
Rocky Mountain News, 136, 148, 153, 204, 238, 282–283
Rogers, Henry, 285n., 326n., 327
Rollins Pass, 355
Romney, Mrs., 304
Roosevelt, Franklin D., 351
Roosevelt, Theodore, 339, 343–344
Ross, Alexander, 82
Routt, John, 205, 265
Royal Gorge, 10, 53–54, 153, 235, 252, 262, 264–265, 273
Russell, Charles M., 358
Russell, Levi, 130, 134
Russell, Majors & Waddell, 126
Russell, Oliver, 130, 134
Russell, Osborne, 92–93
Russell, William Green, 130, 133–134, 140, 145–146, 150, 188, 226
Russians, the, 34, 40
Rustlers and rustling, 333–334
Ruxton, George, 94

Sacajawea, 42–43, 46–47, 73n.
Sage, Rufus, 95
St. Ignatius Mission, 194
St. Louis, 39, 68, 178
St. Louis Smelting and Refining Company, 261–262
St. Mary's Catholic mission, 97–98
St. Vrain, Ceran, 87, 97, 119
Salcedo, Nemesio, 49
Saleesh House, 64–65, 70

Salisbury, Nate, 339
Salmon River, 46, 155, 159, 164–165, 169, 181
Salmon River Mission, 117, 127
Saloons, 189, 197, 300
Salt Lake City, 104, 106, 109, 115–117, 124, 126–127, 163, 221–222, 337, 354–355
San Francisco, 37, 104
San Francisco Bay, 35, 56
San Juan Mountains, 1, 4, 10–11, 26, 36, 54, 77, 107, 250, 253, 264, 311
San Luis Valley, 13, 38, 54, 74, 107, 111, 118–119, 124, 132, 212, 252
Sanders, Jim, 139
Sanders, Colonel Wilbur F., 199–201, 209, 211
Sangre de Cristo Grant, 227–229, 235, 242
Sangre de Cristo Mountains, 3, 8, 12, 15, 20, 30, 54, 74, 107, 118, 227
Sanitation, 303–304
Sante Fe, 27, 29–31, 34–35, 37, 39, 50, 52, 54–55, 72–73, 76–77, 96–97, 101, 109, 119, 155, 250, 264
Santa Fe Railroad, 236, 252, 262–265, 269
Santa Fe Trail, 96, 102, 153, 178
Sawatch Range, 270
Sawtooth Range, 13
Scabs, 310, 313, 316–317
Scalping, 96, 119, 127, 191
Scenery, 12–14, 19, 36, 131, 229, 240, 272, 355
Schenck, Robert, 247–248
Schools, 195, 305
    (See also Education)
Schurz, Carl, 282
Secretan, Hyacinthe, 281
Settlers, 207–223
    Indians and, 111–113
    (See also Homsteads; Stampedes)
Seven Cities of Cibola, 14, 16n.
Seymore, Almeda, 291
Shannon, Tom, 344
Shear, John, 199
Sheep, 12, 18, 119, 184, 330–333, 342, 244, 245
Sheepmen, 323, 331–333, 344–347, 350
Sheriffs, 181, 183, 198, 203, 205–206, 305
Sherman Silver Purchasing Act, 287, 309, 312
Shoshonis, 31, 44–46, 48–49, 58, 66, 76, 81, 89, 92, 112, 115–117, 126–127, 161–162, 166, 254
Sickness, 38, 91–92, 160, 168, 189, 191, 225, 304, 307
Silliman, Benjamin, 247

Silver, 3, 24–25, 27, 122, 141, 175, 242–251, 253, 259, 261, 266–267, 273, 276–277, 291, 293, 309, 312, 315, 351–353
    coinage of, 286–287
    price of, 280, 286, 311
Silverton, Colorado, 10, 271, 306, 358
Simmons, Z. G., 295
Simpson, George, 94, 96, 125–126, 134
Simpson, Lieutenant James H., 108–110
Sinclair, Bartlett, 316
Sioux, 49, 176, 212–214, 253–254
Siringo, Charles, 309–310
Skiers and skiing, 2, 13, 150, 197, 248, 275, 356–358, 360–361
Slade, Edgar, 203
Slaves and slavery, 17, 25, 28, 43, 122, 155
Smelters and smelting, 243–245, 249, 262–263, 269, 276, 280, 286, 324
Smith, DeWitt, 208
Smith, E. W., 331
Smith Jackson & Sublette, 87–89
Smith, Jedediah, 82, 85–86, 89, 92
Smith, Joseph, 100, 103
Smith, Robert, 327
Smith, Soapy, 313
Smith, Thomas L., 92
Smuggler mine, 273
Smuggler-Union mine, 317
Snake River, 12, 68–69, 157
Social life, 2, 186–206, 300–306
Socialists, 317, 321
South, the, 112, 154
South Dakota, 33, 82, 253, 276
South Park, 49–50, 131–132, 150–151, 153, 180, 212
South Pass, 82, 122, 124–125
South Platte River, 49, 53, 84, 130, 132, 238
Spain, 3, 18, 25, 27, 34, 38–40, 49, 51, 74n.
Spaniards, 3, 11, 15, 17–18, 21–30, 32, 34–35, 39, 41, 49–50, 72, 76
Spanish-Americans, 118, 154, 196n.
Sparks, William Andrew Jackson, 283–284
Speculators, 142, 227, 281, 283
Sports, 190, 305, 355–356
    (See also kind of sport, as Skiing)
Squatters, 142, 228, 236
Stagecoaches, 110, 153
Stamp mills, 3, 6, 186, 218, 245, 276, 350
Stampedes and stampeders, 143, 161, 165, 171, 175, 206–207, 217, 228, 259, 269, 290
Standard Oil, 326–329
Stanley, Bob, 172

Stanley, George, 5
Stansbury, Captain Howard, 109–111
Stanton, Fred M., 238
Steamboats, 168–169, 178–179
Steunenberg, Frank, 316–317, 321, 333, 343
Stevens, Isaac I., 110–111, 120, 157, 168
Stevens, William H., 258, 261
Stevenson, James, 241n.
Stewart, William M., 247
Stillman, James, 326n.
Stinking Water, the, 166n., 167
Stockton, Commodore, 107
Stony Mountains, 41–42
Stratton, Winfield Scott, 266, 294, 296
Strikes, 309–310, 315, 317–319
Strong, William B., 263
Stuart, Granville, 127, 165, 167, 169–170, 172, 175, 181, 188, 193
Stuart, James, 165, 167, 169–170, 172, 175, 181
Stuart, Robert, 69, 82
Stuart, Thomas, 165–166, 170, 175
"Stumpage" tax, 282
Sublette, Milton, 89, 91
Sublette, William, 82, 85–86, 89
Sullivan, Con, 292
Sun Valley, 13, 275, 356, 358
Superior, Lake, 57, 63, 279, 281, 287
Supply, Fort, 116–117
Swansea, Wales, 243–244, 247, 280
Swift, Lieutenant, 74
Sylvanite, 294

Tabor, Augusta, 152, 262, 267
Tabor, Baby Doe, 267
Tabor, Horace A. W., 153, 258, 262–263, 266–268, 301, 308
Tamman, H. H., 339
Taos, 20, 29, 32, 34, 72–73, 80–81, 87–88, 96–97, 108, 125, 132
Tarryall, 151–152
Tarsney, Thomas T., 313–314
Taxes, property, 194, 196n.
  "stumpage," 282
Taylor Grazing Act, 344, 350
Teller, Senator, 342
Telluride, Colorado, 1, 3–5, 9, 11, 317–321, 348–353, 360–361
Telluride Association, 6
Tellurium, 294
Tennessee Pass, 272–273
Terien, Andrés, 49–50
Tetons, the, 8, 13, 90, 240
Tevis, Lloyd, 248, 276–277
Texas, 31–32, 34, 37
Theatrical productions, 2, 193–194, 300–301
Thiebalt, Nicholas, 199–200

Thomas, Henry, 169–171
Thompson, David, 57–65, 69–70, 92
Thompson Falls, Montana, 64–65, 290
Thoreau, Henry, 364
Thornburgh, Major Thomas T., 256
Three Forks country, 67–68, 76
Tierney, Luke, 131
Tiger lode, 291
Timber, 279, 282–283, 341–343, 353, 364
  (See also Forests; Wood)
Timber and Stone Act, 283–284
Tiquex, 19–22
Title to land, 143n., 144, 259, 323
Toby, 46
Tolby, F. J., 236
Toole, Joseph K., 328
Tourists, 234–235, 241, 275, 349n., 357–358, 360–361, 365–366
Town councils, 194–195
Traders and trading, 33–34, 39–40, 44, 72, 76–77, 85, 89–90, 95–96, 156–157, 166–168
  (See also Fur traders)
Trading posts, 75, 88
Trappers and trapping, 59, 66, 68, 72–93, 107, 115–116, 127, 166
Trinchera Estate, 228, 235
Trinidad, Colorado, 202, 263
Trujillo, Teofilio, 331
Tunnels, 272, 354
Turk, The, 21–22
Tutt, Charles, 297
Tuttle, Bishop Daniel, 196–197

Uinta, Fort, 95
Uinta Mountains, 36, 84, 94–95
Ulibarri, Juan de, 31
Umpquas, the, 89
Uncompahgre, Fort, 95
Uncompahgre National Forest, 359
Uncompahgre Peak, 8
Uncompahgre River, 11, 348
Uncompahgre Valley, 11, 36, 269
Union, Fort, 88, 118, 125, 225
Union Army, 210
Union Colony, 231
Union Pacific, 110, 215–216, 218–223, 231, 247, 269, 271–272, 274, 309, 356
Unions, 3, 308–311, 314–318, 321
United States, 3, 39–40, 49–50, 83
United States Army, 43, 49, 51, 55, 120, 122, 178, 310
  Corps of Topographical Engineers, 106–107
United States Bureau of Reclamation, 339
United States Cavalry, 123–124, 130, 254